CW00969103

CITIZENS & CANNIBALS

ALSO BY ELI SAGAN

Cannibalism: Human Aggression and Cultural Form

The Lust to Annihilate: A Psychoanalytic Study of
Violence in Ancient Greek Society

At the Dawn of Tyranny: The Origins of Individualism,
Political Oppression, and the State

Freud, Women, and Morality: The Psychology
of Good and Evil

The Honey and the Hemlock: Democracy and
Paranoia in Ancient Athens and Modern America

CITIZENS & CANNIBALS

The French Revolution, the Struggle for Modernity, and the Origins of Ideological Terror

ELI SAGAN

ROWMAN & LITTLEFIELD PUBLISHERS, INC.

Lanham • Boulder • New York • Oxford

ROWMAN & LITTLEFIELD PUBLISHERS, INC.

Published in the United States of America
by Rowman & Littlefield Publishers, Inc.
4720 Boston Way, Lanham, Maryland 20706

12 Hid's Copse Road
Cumnor Hill, Oxford OX2 9JJ, England

Distributed by National Book Network

British Library Cataloguing in Publication Information Available

Library of Congress Cataloging-in-Publication Data
Sagan, Eli.
    Citizens and cannibals : the French Revolution, the struggle for modernity, and the
origins of ideological terror / Eli Sagan.
        p.   cm.
    Includes bibliographical references and index.
    ISBN 0-7425-0831-5 (alk. paper)
    1. France—History—Revolution, 1789–1799—Influence.   2. Civilization, Modern.   3.
Democracy—France.   4. Liberalism—France.   I. Title.

    DC148 .S28   2001
    944.04—dc21   2001019600

Printed in the United States of America

♾ ™ The paper used in this publication meets the minimum requirements of American National
Standard for Information Sciences—Permanence of Paper for Printed Library Materials, ANSI/NISO
Z39.48-1992.

This Book Is Dedicated to the Wonderful
People Who Have Married My Children

For Andy, for Steve, for Alisa, for Richard,
and in Loving Memory of Robert

CONTENTS

ACKNOWLEDGMENTS

Isser Woloch met with me on a regular basis. He listened, agreed with some propositions, disagreed with others, and always urged me to go ahead.

Daniel Bell has a unique capacity: he can disagree with 90 percent of what one says and still leave one with a sense of encouragement and empowerment.

Burton Raffel has graciously gone over, and corrected where necessary, my translations from the French.

Michael Kennedy kindly sent me a typescript of his extraordinarily important third volume of the Jacobin clubs during the Terror, so that I could use it before its publication.

Several eighteenth-century French historians have made available to me their work, both published and unpublished, that I might have missed along the way: David Bell, Seymour Drescher, Lynn Hunt, Sarah Maza, Darren McMahon, Sophia Rosenfeld, and Timothy Tackett.

Stanley Elkins, Lee Halprin, Edmund Leites, and Steve Thomas responded to specific chapters in a most helpful manner.

Doctors Leon Balter, Rebecca Dulit, and Otto Kernberg were enormously helpful in my research on the borderline condition.

Steve Fraser is the kind of friend one needs when the going gets tough.

Mary Carpenter of Rowman & Littlefield has been a most sympathetic and helpful editor.

Lynn Friendly and Melanie Pimont: wonderful typists, who made this book possible, despite my no-computer, hand-writing *ancien régime* technology.

I cannot imagine writing anything without Bob Bellah at my side. He has, as usual, read every page of this manuscript, correcting mistakes, broadening the argument, demanding an intense intellectual rigor.

Frimi Sagan can listen to a text being read with the sharpest ear and sharpest mind of anyone I have ever known.

I

INTRODUCTION

THE INTENT OF THE BOOK

The aim of this discussion of the French Revolution is to use the history of that Revolutionary period as a prism through which to view, and attempt to comprehend, the Modern world. That world—the social and political stage of Modernity—is one of the most paradoxical, contradictory, ambiguous, and ambivalent forms of society the human community has ever invented. Great promise, accomplishment, anxiety, and disaster follow one another, confound each other, commingle with each other in such a manner that even the most brilliant of human observers have done little more than describe the phenomenon, rendering us very little real comprehension. "We live in curious times and astonishing contrasts," wrote Voltaire with great prescience, "reason on the one hand, the most absurd fanaticism on the other . . . a civil war in every soul."[1] It is the argument of this work that that internal civil war first burst upon the scene, with extraordinary power, during the French Revolutionary period. And one need go no further than the front page of today's newspaper to recognize that, in certain parts of the world, the strife continues—seemingly relentlessly. Something in the human psyche seems incapable of pushing forward into a world of freedom and democracy without, at the same time, constructing great forces of repression and reaction. Nietzsche wrote what could be an epitaph for the Revolution: "Whoever pushes rationality forward also restores new strength to the opposite power, mysticism, and folly of all kinds."[2] "Folly" being a euphemism, in the case of the Revolution, for the unnecessary annihilation of multitudes of human beings.

The paradoxical nature of the Modern world is such that in times of heightened crisis—and the Revolution was certainly such a time—glorious triumphs and catastrophic failures follow one another with dazzling and dismaying speed. Glorious triumphs: Constitutionalism, the Rights of Man, the Sovereignty of the People. Catastrophic failures: the total lack of success in the attempt to achieve democratic stability, the Terror, the millions sacrificed to the paranoid fantasies of Napoleon, whose fantasies were shared by almost all of France. All these worldviews and events are integral parts of the history of the Revolution.

Merely to describe this great paradox is one thing. To go beyond simple description requires the insight that somewhere, somehow, there is a deep, irrational connection between these two seemingly opposite sets of *mentalités*. Was the Terror, as well as the Rights of Man, the result of the Enlightenment? Or was it a question of pushing the Enlightenment too far or too fast? Or not far enough? What role do anxiety and paranoid panic play in the efflorescence of liberty and equality? No simplistic or dogmatic answers to these kinds of questions will be attempted in this work; the assumption is, nevertheless, that it is of profound importance to ask and elaborate such questions.

The history of the Revolution is the narrative of a nation journeying from an Early Modern to a fully Modern stage of society. During the seventeenth and eighteenth centuries, first England, then America and France, undertook this passage. In England, it required the execution of a king, a civil war, dictatorship, and the deposition and replacement of another king before political and social stability were restored. America had the easiest time of all. In France that journey was replete with so many misadventures that, for almost a hundred years, it was a question of whether it would ever be accomplished. The study of this almost cataclysmic struggle, which ultimately ended in success, is not only profoundly important in its own right, but comprehending it may also shed light on other even more catastrophic passages to Modernity: Weimar to Nazi Germany; Csarist to Soviet Russia; agrarian to Communist China. One is immediately struck by the fact that, in these cases, as well as in the circumstance of the Revolution, Ideological Terror played a crucial role. Ideological Terror and the failure to accomplish a successful (i.e., democratic) passage to Modernity go hand in hand. That is one important subject of this work.

The theoretical ground-base that I employ is a form of social evolutionary theory. Though I have my own views on what exactly a useful evolutionary theory should consist of, I place myself as a recipient of the long sociological tradition, in this regard, of Marx, Weber, Parsons, Bellah, and Habermas.[3] Crucial to this theory is the concept that society moves and develops through stages. Not that change and development is lacking within a stage; early Capitalism and late Capitalism are not the same thing, though they are both Capitalism. But the movement from one stage to another requires a quantum leap in energy, a revolution in the political, social, or cultural order, the creation of a radically new paradigm in the system of values.

In the social and political world, rarely has that kind of revolutionary change been accomplished without an acceleration of violence. Let it be understood that, in itself, no claim is being made here that such movement from one stage to another necessarily implies *progress*. Taking the theory of stages in its most limited sense, moral regress is theoretically as possible as moral progress. The question of moral progress or regress is a separate question, and requires a separate discussion, from the one of development through stages. One can maintain the view that society evolves through discrete stages and still affirm that the overall development is morally regressive, or cyclical, or entirely up and down and, therefore, morally random.

I do intend to discuss and elaborate on the theory of social evolution but not until the latter part of the book. Before doing that, I want to look at what the history of the Revolution can teach us. As this discussion progresses, I ask the reader's indulgence to bear with me and make two tentative assumptions: that there are stages in the development of society and that Modernity is such a stage. The one, in fact, that we inhabit today.

The Early Modern stage is a separate and distinct stage from Modernity. A certain confusion may result from the use of the word "Modern" in the description of both stages; I have chosen, however, to make use of the terminology that others have developed and used rather than create neologisms of my own. The evolution from Early Modern to Modernity was as revolutionary a step as the development from Feudalism to Early Modern had been.

The Early Modern stage, which is not my subject, begins in the sixteenth century with the rise of Protestantism and continues, in England and France, through the seventeenth and eighteenth centuries.[4] It was deeply concerned with the creation of centralized and bureaucratized states; in France, the development of a powerful authoritarian monarch was crucial. It made great use of the worldview that assumed human beings were consciously and rationally capable of changing and ordering the social and political world. The economic world as well: mercantilism and physiocratic theory. Richelieu and Louis XIV. And in the realm of thought: Locke, Hume, Montesquieu. The Enlightenment was one of the great achievements of the Early Modern stage.

The perception of these progressive phenomena has prompted many observers to perceive that the *ancien régime* was not as *ancien* as is many times assumed. Toqueville's assertion that the Revolution was not nearly as revolutionary as some imagine—that the centralizing tendencies and accomplishments of the *ancien régime* were continued by Revolutionary governments and brought to a climax by Napoleon[5]—this insight has been used by many to underline the *continuity* of social development, despite the Revolution. This, however, is no world-shaking insight. "Nothing can come of nothing."[6] That every new evolutionary stage develops out of the previous stage; that every new stage is prepared by the previous stage and, possible, even made "inevitable" by it—all this is a given of social evolutionary theory. No new stage develops ex nihilo but is a radical transformation of the values and institutions of the previous stage. Only utopian thought imagines there is such a thing as "totally new."

The perception of stages, and the development through new stages, has prompted several evolutionary theorists to ask what is the energy (if it is, indeed, one) that is driving the process. And "driving" seems to be the correct word: human beings have been driven to create Modernity, almost despite themselves, and certainly despite the anxiety and panic such creation engenders. Hegel, as is well known, gave a metaphysical answer to the question of what is that energy. Marx, and Engels, rendered a so-called materialist explanation, which is, ultimately, a psychological interpretation: Greed, the desire for more and more goods, says Engels, is the engine of history.[7] Here again, I think that a more productive examination of this question can be set in motion *after* the enormous energy of the Revolution has been looked at. What was it, after all, that was driving the Revolution?

The great advantage of this evolutionary mode of thought is that it allows us to ask questions that hardly anyone addresses. One great causal question that has infused Revolutionary studies is: What gave rise to the Revolution? Specifically, was the Enlightenment a significant cause?[8] Evolutionary perceptions can push the question even further: What caused the Enlightenment? What generated in human beings the desires for liberty, reason, liberalism, and freedom? How was it that people discovered they had rights? The answers to these questions, when they are discerned, may help us to see that the Revolution itself was a part of a much grander, much larger movement of history. Tocqueville observed that there was an inexorable movement in society toward equality and democracy. Whether one welcomed it or not, democracy suffused the agenda of the future: even the rejection of democracy would necessitate a new, never-before-seen form of tyranny.[9] Tocqueville could not tell us *why* democracy had become an imperative of human history. No question, nevertheless, can be of greater importance.

One theoretical first principle of this book is that the Revolution—and all its glorious and catastrophic consequences—cannot be understood without placing central emphasis on the fateful drive to move into the Modern world. It was frighteningly unknown territory. It is no wonder that many Frenchmen looked to England, and slightly to America, for some sort of guide to this uncharted territory. By 1800, only three nations had undertaken this journey of discovery. By the twenty-first century, almost every nation in the world—if not *every* nation—is succeeding gloriously or failing catastrophically (or has succeeded or failed catastrophically) in the same endeavor. Denmark and Bosnia; Sweden and Rwanda; democratic England and Nazi Germany; the Netherlands and Stalinist Russia—the struggle for Modernity has set the boundaries and the moral and political agenda for every nation on the planet.

And the outcome has always been in grave doubt because the psychological risks have been enormous. What this mode of analysis postulates is that the steps required to establish a Modern society significantly increase the level of anxiety, in many cases raising it to the plane of almost pure panic. It is remarkable how many present-day historians of the Revolution, who ordinarily are not sympathetic to psychological analysis of society, seem to be forced to use the word "paranoid" when describing incidents such as the September Massacres, the Great Fear of Brigands, or the psychological purging and cleansing properties of the guillotine. Paranoid panic pervades the history of the Revolution; the syndrome of "enemies without, traitors within" is a fundamental *mentalité* of the whole period; the guillotine was invented to eliminate psychological problems, in a very short order.

The great failure of the Enlightenment, or at least the great inadequacy in people's understanding of its message, was the omission of an analysis of how difficult the prodigious passage to rationality and freedom was going to be. The collapse of the glorious enlightened Revolution into Terror shocked almost every sensitive observer at the time (but not Burke)—and even today we cannot claim to understand it; we remain as baffled as Tocqueville before this "*virus* of a new and unknown kind."[10] No fatuous claim is being made here that this present work will reveal the true nature of that virus. The more modest claim is being made, however, that ideological Terror will never be understood until we comprehend fully both the acceleration of paranoid panic as the drive toward Modernity hurtles forward and the psychological defenses raised against that abject fear. It was Engels, that great "materialist," who observed with such clarity: "We take the reign of Terror to mean the rule of people who inspire terror. On the contrary, it is the rule of people who themselves are terror-stricken."[11] We will not be able to understand the Terror until we understand what was terrifying the terrorists.

In summary, it is the argument of this work that the French Revolutionary Terror is incomprehensible without a theory of social evolution that describes development in stages of society and that exhaustively delineates the present stage of Modernity. The ruling hypothesis is, essentially, that the Terror resulted from the failure to achieve a Stable Democratic Society, which is a fundamental attribute of Modernity. That perception immediately raises imperative questions: Why did France, in its first significant attempt, fail to erect a stable democracy? Why was Terror seized upon as a response to that failure? Can productive results of such inquiry teach us something of significance about the great Ideological Terrors of the twentieth century?

✣   ✣   ✣

One of the most difficult tasks I have set myself in this work is to define the "legitimate" Modern stage of society. It is a question, at first, of listing the fundamental attributes that all Modern democratic societies share: for example, Denmark, Italy, Australia. Individual differences will exist, of course, but the quest is to discover those attributes that every Modern democratic society cannot live without. Marxism was the first powerful theory of social evolution, and it made things easy for the theorist: Capitalism defines the Modern stage. All other attributes are secondary manifestations of the basic Capitalist order. One may accept the fact that Capitalism is a fundamental attribute of democratic Modernity, but it is a paltry theory that stops there. The theoretical structure that will be elaborated in this work, in contradistinction to this kind of simplistic analysis, discovers nine basic attributes of democratic Modernity.

The importance of this kind of theoretical exercise for French Revolutionary history is the fact, I believe, that the history of that period could be written by taking each one of these nine essential attributes *separately* as a goal of social development at that time and delineating how certain positions were achieved with great success: Liberalism, Bourgeois Life, Rationalization; while the attempt to achieve others failed catastrophically: Civilian Control of Military Power, Democratic Citizenship; and in regard to still others, a pervasive ambivalence prevailed: Secularism, Individualism. I am incapable of writing that history and will not be making the attempt. An extensive commentary on the Revolution and the components of Modernity, nevertheless, does seem within range.

That exposition proceeds under the assumption that Modernity must not be examined either as one indissoluble piece or as individual components, but rather as *both*. All democratic Modern societies resemble each other in their totality (that comes by definition in a theory of social stages), but each society is uniquely itself. And this individuality results from the fact that the particular components of Modernity have a critical autonomy, one from the other. Two different Modern societies may treat Individualism and Secularism in different manners, even though the theoretical assumption delineated in this work asserts that *all* democratic Modern societies are Individualistic and Secular. French society during the period of Revolutionary history dealt prodigiously with every basic attribute of Modernity described here. That was exactly what that history was.

In this introductory chapter, let me give merely an expanded list of the nine basic elements of Modern democratic society that I perceive—a crucial part of the theoretical foundation of this undertaking.

I. *Democratic Citizenship is of the essence.* The sovereignty of the people is essential. Universal education is immediately placed on the democratic agenda, both for the instrumental purpose of creating an informed citizenry and as a result of the morally transforming values of equality that enter society as soon as Democratic Citizenship becomes an ideal. The problematic within Democratic Citizenship immediately presents itself in every society embarking on this enterprise: How many people are *the people*? Does the sovereignty of the people mean everybody? The development from a limited to a radical (i.e., every male adult) democracy, a situation that ultimately includes women, is one of the great glorious triumphs of Modernity.

Democratic Citizenship cannot prevail without the creation of citizens; those who, in Aristotle's penetrating definition, are capable both of ruling and being ruled.[12] It also requires, in addition, the existence of an attitude within political life of the acceptance of the concept of a loyal opposition: that those who oppose one politically have the right and obligation to do so, that is, are not traitors deserving of elimination. In France, during the time of the Revolution, not only the Jacobin terrorists, but almost all persons in politics, failed in that endeavor. The incapacity to develop the concept of loyal democratic opposition was the great failure of Revolutionary history.

2. *Liberalism, though very closely related to Democratic Citizenship, as a worldview, has a definite autonomous existence.* The degree of Liberalism and the degree of Democratic Citizenship are not necessarily identical in any particular society. For instance, the notion of Rights wherein all men are considered equal—an attribute of the liberal agenda—can be announced with great fervency and almost total unanimity, and yet, at the same time, the franchise be restricted only to property owners. That, of course, was exactly what happened during the course of the Revolution, an anomaly that radical critics pointed out and one that the Jacobin dictatorship proposed to eliminate. This kind of discrepancy can arise because the impulse toward Liberalism and the impulse toward Democratic Citizenship ultimately come from different places, though they share a very close kinship.

The liberal agenda, in the Modern world, beyond the question of Rights also includes: an end to slavery; elimination of torture as a judicial procedure; equality of all persons before the law; careers open to talent, that is, downgrading the importance of birth in the occupations exercised by elites; no civil discrimination against persons because of their religious beliefs (Protestants and Jews, most particularly, in France); freedom of the press; the autonomy of the law and judicial procedures from domination by the state; and the superiority of the law to all interests of personal power. Very quickly it becomes apparent that French society, during the Revolutionary period, was enormously successful in instituting the liberal agenda (though there were, of course, some denials of it), and yet there was almost total failure to achieve stable Democratic citizenship.

3. *Secularism is closely related to Liberalism.* All democratic Modern societies are secular. Most have no state-supported religion; and even in a case such as England, which exhibits such a phenomenon, there is supposed to be no discrimination against people because of religious belief. Freedom of religious conscience is a given. No particular religious faith serves the function as a significant part of the "glue" that holds society together. Any reading of Revolutionary history makes it immediately apparent that, at all stages, the leaders of the Revolution, from the National Assembly through the Directory, went to excess in their drive to establish a secular society. Unnecessary opposition to the Revolutionary movement and counterrevolutionary activity (the Vendée) were the results. Something, however, within their commitment to Modernity was impelling those in Revolutionary power to seek to destroy the dominion of the Catholic Church at all costs.

4. *Nationalism.* Crucial to an understanding of any society is the illumination of the forms of social cohesion: What are the forces that make it *one* society? What is the nature of the shared psycho-social identity of its members? Nationalism is a sine qua non of any society existing in the Modern world, whether it has fully embraced, or severely compromised with, Modernity in other areas. It is almost a biological necessity: without a certain social cohesiveness, without fixed boundaries and an army ready to defend those boundaries, no political entity can continue to exist. The world of international affairs is anarchic; Nationalism is the only defense against possible annihilation.

From the viewpoint of social evolution, it is powerfully revealing to observe how the Nation replaces the king and the church as the provider of security, authority, and legitimacy. Even before the meeting of the Estates General in 1789, the Nation was becoming the rallying point for those intent on the liberal and democratic agendas. After the first great revolutionary act, the transformation of the Estates General into the National Assembly, it was openly stated that *lèse nation* had replaced *lèse majesté* as the foremost sin against society.

The overthrow of the king and the church produced a quantum leap in anxiety and paranoid panic. The only defense against shipwreck and drowning was to cling passionately and fervently to the nation. Nationalism, since it serves all the functions of sacredness, and yet is not a religion, becomes one of the first great manifestations of the secular sacred. The creation of a secular sacred is the unique accomplishment of Modernity and is essential to its existence. The commitment to Nationalism during the Revolutionary period was almost unanimous among all factions; it was one thing virtually everyone could agree upon. There were a few serious manifestations of regionalism (the Vendeé, Lyons at the time of the Jacobin coup), but these were primarily negative responses to excesses of the Revolution. In the nineteenth century, there were no meaningful challenges to the idea of France as one nation.

One momentous problematic within the nationalist persuasion is imperialism and the domination of other nations. The declaration of war on Europe was a significantly tragic, self-destructive act of the Revolution. Here again, almost everybody, from the king to the Jacobins, gave their support to the enterprise. There seems to be some irrational conflict within emerging democratic societies that drives them to imperialist adventure. The French—and Napoleon—carried the attempt to resolve a deep ambivalence to an horrendous extreme.

5. *Individualism.* Daniel Bell has succinctly delineated the role of Individualism in the Modern stage of social evolution. "In the social structure of ascriptive

[pre-Modern] societies—tribe, clan, caste, slave, feudal and bureaucratic despotisms—the 'individual' is wholly a socially determined being, his precise place in the hierarchical order, his social and legal standing, the precedence in the allocation of benefices and abodes, stipulated by his assigned place. He is an individual in the mere biological sense, but he is not a person; he is, one might say, a *persona*, a mask or role or status into which he fits his person. *The breakdown of that kind of ascription and the rise of individual mobility is the primal act of modernity.*"[13]

It becomes immediately apparent that that crucial transformation in values has a significant place in the rise of Capitalism and capitalists to a predominate place in society, and, equally important, to the ascending role of the bourgeois lifestyle. All through the eighteenth century in France people who most accurately may be characterized as "bourgeois" were becoming more numerous and more powerful. Individualism, then, is not only a result of the Revolution but one of its principle *causes*. The thrust toward Modernity began in the *ancien régime*. One way to understand the Revolution is to see it not only as a radical transformation, but also as a fulfillment of certain powerful social developments. The recognition of the role of Individualism is a productive mechanism for comprehending this double causality.

6. *Rationalizing and Consciously Ordering the World.* One *mentalité* that had great significance in the Early Modern stage of society and then comes to be an explosive force in the Modern world is the conception that the world—nature, society, human beings, the economy—can be made more rational and more orderly. Disorder, inconsistencies, disarray, untidiness, clutter, mess—all this is to be done away with. The bureaucratic mind and the institutions it creates become supreme. One standard of weights and measures, one code of law, one language, one system of education, one mode of taxation, one standard of factory inspection, one speed limit must exist for the entire nation. Centralization in the capital city of all significant decisions becomes essential. Here again, though the Revolution did hasten the process, it was in actuality merely another stage in the Early Modern and Modern imperative to Rationalize the World.

7. *Capitalism/Capitalist Society.* The Revolution took place, it is generally agreed today, long before France became a Capitalist Society.[14] It is important to differentiate capitalists and Capitalism, on the one hand, from a Capitalist Society. There were capitalists and significant Capitalism in the ancient Greek world and in the late Middle Ages (Florence, the cities of the German Hansa). Only in city-states, and not in large national polities, were capitalists the most important and most powerful economic class, exercising primary political power. In the

nineteenth and twentieth centuries, however, all Modern societies were moving toward becoming Capitalist Societies, wherein financiers, industrialists, and merchants exercised political hegemony. The complete impulse toward Modernity makes Capitalist Society not only possible but inevitable: industrialization, economic *growth*, rampant individualism, urbanization, the reign of money (that is, capital), the dependence of the majority of people on wages earned from working for other people.

Capitalists, as opposed to bourgeois people, played a negligible role in Revolutionary history. It is even a matter of dispute among historians today whether the central events of the Revolution itself (1789–1799) promoted the interests of Capitalism or not. We will never understand the rise of Capitalism, however, until we comprehend that there can be no Capitalism until there is a capitalist *mentalité*. Human beings are not born capitalist; human society takes thousands of years to become capitalist. The capitalist *Weltanschauung* has to be invented, promoted, and become supreme before Capitalism can exercise dominion over the world. People have to be convinced that the market can hold society together before they will abandon or displace kings and aristocrats. It is true that many of the *mentalités* that the revolutionary period promoted made the world of Capitalism more and more possible. The rise of Capitalist Society, nonetheless, is not the "engine" of the Modern world. Modernity is its own engine.

8. *Bourgeois Life.* The word "bourgeois," as used in this work, is one of the hardest to define accurately. That task, however, is of the essence because it is not an exaggeration to say that the bourgeois ethos made the Revolution, in all its phases: in '89; when the King was overthrown in '92; during the Jacobin dictatorship; and through the Terror. Thermidor, the stage of the Directory, and the Napoleonic dictatorship—all these responses were made as well by bourgeois people, acting on their own perception of the bourgeois ethos. Condorcet, Barère, Saint-Just, Robespierre, Sièyes, Danton, Napoleon—all were bourgeois in their *Weltanschauung*, no matter who or what their parents and their pretensions were. As William Sewell has courageously asserted, the French Revolution was a bourgeois revolution, even though not a capitalist one.[15] Lawyers, for instance, played an enormously important role in *ancien régime* developments leading to the Revolution[16] and represented over 40 percent of the delegates of the Third Estate at the meeting of the Estates General in '89. To what social class do such lawyers belong, if any? Capitalists they are not; aristocrats, equally not so; poor, they had struggled all their lives not to be. They are the true class in the middle. Bourgeois, precisely.

Bourgeois is a lifestyle: a middling, conservative one. It is comprehended most clearly in contrasting it with an aristocratic lifestyle. In its ideal form, it rejects extremes of dress and expenditure; Benjamin Franklin is one of its greatest spokesmen: under no condition should one spend what one doesn't have; sexual excess and experimentation are anathema; the bourgeois patriarchal family is supreme. It is powerfully committed to success, to meritocracy, to careers open to talent. It creates a world of non-noble competent elites. Though noncapitalist (as yet), property values are sacred, and the violent poor are perceived as a threat to social stability and those sacred values.

What was crucial for the Revolution was the fact that eighteenth-century France had created so many powerful bourgeois people, who would not be denied. This development, once again, was part of the inexorable advance toward Modernity. And we live today in that same, but ever changing Bourgeois world.

9. *Civilian Control of Military Power.* The existence of democratic society is dependent, among other things, on the capacity of the civilian power structure to dominate and control the military. Every society advancing into Modernity has strong tendencies toward instability and anarchy. And there is an inevitable inclination of the generals to fill the power void, seizing political control of the nation. Many societies utterly fail in this attempt at civilian control and fall victim to military regimes, of greater or lesser despotism. Thus, the tremendous importance of the militia for emerging democratic societies: a citizen armed force.

The question of who controls the fire power runs all through the history of the Revolution. The Estates General could resist the king and begin the Revolution, but it had no military power. The fall of the Bastille secured the Revolution, but that action gave enormous political power to the people-in-the-streets of Paris. It was they who paralyzed the king by bringing him to Paris from Versailles in October '89 and it was they who finally toppled him in August of '92, when the national legislative body could do no more than sanction that action after the fact.

The fear that the power vacuum left by the weakness of the monarchy could result in military despotism was openly stated, especially during the debate on the declaration of war in the spring of '92. After Thermidor, the Jacobin dictatorship having been overthrown, the Directory failing utterly to establish political stability, the resort to generals become more and more inevitable. Napoleon, of course, was the beneficiary of that process. It seems that no conservative dictator can attain power without first achieving control of the military. Democracy and powerful generals cannot coexist.

✻   ✻   ✻

When a nation sets itself the task of establishing a fully modern society, I descry only six possible outcomes for this project. There may, of course, be various combinations of these six basic modes, but as fundamental forms, as ideal types, there seem to be no more than six. Stable Democratic Society. Anarchy. Gangsterism and/or Military Despotism. Ideological Terror. Conservative Dictatorship. Religious Fundamentalism. In listing these and discussing them at this point in the book, I want to avail myself of Aristotle's terminology in his description of types of society, specifically his distinction between legitimate forms and perverse forms or "aberrant counterparts." In government by the one, monarchy is the legitimate form and tyranny the perverse one; in government by the few, aristocracy is the legitimate mode and oligarchy the perversion.[17]

When a nation undertakes a journey to the Modern world, there is only one form of legitimate and stable outcome: Democratic Society. Since it represents a major concern of this work, there is no need to elaborate on it at this moment. One point, however, is essential: the failure to attain a stable Democratic Society inevitably results in the establishment of one of the perverse forms, or some combination, or alternation, of two or several of these. Only Democratic Society can provide a Modern society with stable forms of social cohesion. It is true that some of these perverse modes may continue to exist for many years—the forty or so years of Leninist-Stalinist Ideological Terror, for instance—but such a society is symptomatic of a pathological compromise with Modernity. It expresses and seeks to institutionalize certain aspects of Modernity: rationalization, industrialization, secularism; while, at the same time, severely repressing other attributes: liberalism, individualism, democratic citizenship. All perverse forms manifest a profound ambivalence about Modernity. Democratic Society lives without any extreme ambivalence, though it exhibits its own acute contradictions.

Of the five possible perverse outcomes, three did not manifest themselves significantly during the Revolutionary period: Anarchy, Gangsterism and/or Military Despotism, and Religious Fundamentalism. There were moments of anarchy during the Revolution—the September Massacres, the Great Fear, and the White Terror, being the most notable—but there definitely was no prolonged period of Anarchy. Whether of a terrorist or more conservative nature, authority held. In the twentieth century, periods of Anarchy have characterized several nations that are limping toward, or fleeing from, Modernity.

Anarchy, however, cannot endure for long, and Gangsterism and Military Despotism (which would include Warlordism) are definite cures for Anarchy. Here again, this was not a significant phenomenon of the Revolution. Possibly some historians may describe the Chouans as a kind of Warlordism, but I cannot accurately speak to that. Even if so, it was not a fundamental problematic of the Revolution. One significant thing about Gangsterism/Military Despotism/ Warlordism is they lack legitimacy. The taint of usurper never leaves the authority of the paramount boss. He can never make himself, try as he may, into a legitimate monarch. In this century, Batista of Cuba and Papa Doc of Haiti were representative examples of the Military Despotism mode of perverse compromise with Modernity. These dictatorships had no moral or ideological basis. The main question they answered was: Who owns the country?

Religious Fundamentalism on the state level seems to be only a twentieth-century phenomenon. In the nineteenth century, certain religious fundamentalist groups arose and/or survived, but only by opting out of the larger society. They created for themselves small enclaves in which their anti-Modern fundamentalism could be exercised. They made no attempt to take over the state. The Amish in America are one of many examples. In the present century, however, Religious Fundamentalism on a state level, as a mode of denying and repressing Modernity, has taken on a greater and greater significance. In almost every case, anti-Modernism, opposition to democracy, and antifeminism are integral parts of this perversion.

The two last nonlegitimate detours to, or compromises with, Modernity were of critical importance for Revolutionary history: Ideological Terror and Conservative Dictatorship. The discussion of each of these, most especially the former, constitutes an essential part of this book. Just a word here, nevertheless, about Conservative Dictatorship. I, naturally, have Napoleon in mind, but there were two previous short-lived attempts at Conservative Dictatorship before his successful go at it. The Jacobin dictatorship, established by the coup of May 31– June 2, 1793, before it transformed itself into the Terror; and the governments of the Thermidorians and the Directory, where democratic elections were systematically set aside when they went against the ruling power—these were ambivalent endeavors to establish such an authoritarian and conservative government. It is probably more accurate to describe the early Jacobin/Thermidorian/Directory regimes as conservative oligarchies, since no man assumed a dictatorial role. This extension of the category to include oligarchy changes the basic analytic theoretical approach insignificantly, though it renders the descriptive analysis more precisely.

"Conservative" carries a double meaning. Such a reign attempts both to conserve certain attributes of the old regime that it feels are being threatened with extinction, but it also desires to conserve and secure particular revolutionary advances toward Modernity. Napoleon, for example, restored a nonadversarial relationship between the state and the Catholic Church, on the one hand, and pushed with great energy the rationalizing, centralizing tendencies of the Revolution, on the other hand. "Conservative" in this sense also means nonradical, not radically transforming society, not using Terror as an end in itself or even as a fundamental attribute of the regime.

It may seem contradictory, at first, to call the pre-Terror Jacobin dictatorship "conservative." The facts are, however, that it maintained property as sacred; was keenly opposed to any imposition of an "Agrarian law"—that is, a redistribution of property for the benefit of the poor; and took the first steps toward the political repression of the sans-culottes movement, which ultimately resulted in the movement's political impotence.

Conservative Dictatorship, then, represents a profoundly important compromise with Modernity and has retained its significance into the twentieth century. The fascist dictatorships of Mussolini and Franco, in contrast to the Ideological Terror of German fascism, are meaningful examples. Denying democratic citizenship, nonetheless, makes them a perversion of the Modern project. Conservative Dictatorships use Terror as a means to an end. Remaining in power is the ultimate end. If closing down opposition newspapers will suffice, the Terror stops there. If the dictatorial power is still threatened, beatings, torturing, and assassinations are resorted to. But all of these remain means, not ends. For those in power, torture is of instrumental use, not an end in itself. What is going on in the psyche of the torturer, of course, is another question, but conservative dictators, like Napoleon and Franco, are not terrorists. They make use of what I wish to call "rational terror." Means/ends rationale, that is.

In the regimes of Ideological Terror, in contrast, Terror becomes an end in itself. It cannot control its cannibal appetite. Having consumed its "enemies," it sets upon its recent friends. It becomes, in the famous phrase, like Saturn, a devourer of its own children. Ideological Terror subsumes a powerful self-destructive dimension in its *mentalité* and its actions. It ultimately participates in its own doom. Nazi Germany, in 1943, fighting for its life on the Russian front, dreadfully short of railroad rolling stock, nevertheless used precious engines and cars to transport Jews from Greece and other occupied countries in order to exterminate them in central Europe. The war effort was compromised, but the annihilation of the Jews had become as important as winning the war. Such is the suicidal imperative in Ideological Terror. Nothing in the Revolution was of the same moral or dramatic order, but we will look intently at Robespierre and Saint-Just relentlessly precipitating their own extinction. Ideological Terror is a profoundly *irrational* terror.

The great advantage of this six-part analysis of the possible outcomes of the perilous journey to Modernity is that it is equally valuable for trying to comprehend twentieth-century phenomena. Post-Gorbachev Russia, for example. What are its possibilities? We have all been hoping for Democratic Citizenship and holding our breath. But signs of possible Anarchy, and the breaking down into smaller and smaller units, are everywhere. Each week in our newspapers we are informed of the literal threat of Gangsterism, and we know that Military Despotism may someday provide an antidote to disorder. Conservative Dictatorship remains a definite possibility. We would not have been shocked to learn that Yeltsin had closed down opposition newspapers, outlawed certain political aggregations, and put in motion a coup, the purpose of which was to set himself up as the Louis Napoleon of post-Communist Russia. Ideological Terror (from the Right) and Religious Fundamentalism do not appear to be real possibilities, though there are small pockets of people who would prefer these resolutions.

The theoretical point being emphasized here is that there do not seem to be any possible outcomes beyond these six prospects, with the assumed caveat that various combinations and permutations of these six elements will create particular social configurations. This theoretical stance, it is hoped, will help illuminate certain aspects of Revolutionary history and bring us closer to understanding why certain events occurred, why particular resolutions resulted.

*   *   *

There are four parts to the structure of this book. The first two will elaborate on the dialectical relationship between Modernity and revolutionary history. In Part I, I intend to amplify extensively on the nine attributes of Modernity outlined above. Part II will examine the "legitimate" and "perverted" outcomes of the thrust toward Modernity that are relevant for revolutionary history.

I will address in Part III the great contradictions and paradoxes of modernization. Anxiety, panic, and paranoid defense mechanisms will be examined in great detail. Hopefully, this analysis will bring us a step closer to understanding the politics of the impossible and its enforcer: Ideological Terror. And specifically, an attempt will be made to understand the almost incredible story of how Robespierre, unquestionably a moral genius, ended his life as a cannibalistic terrorist.

The final section, the most conjectural, will focus on the theory of social evolution and Modernity as a specific stage in that evolutionary process. Why the inexorable thrust toward Modernity, at least in some countries? That kind of question will immediately bring us to the most hypothetical of all: that of the engine of history. What power, or powers, drive the historical process? It is presumed that those speculations will be worth the journey, even if no definitive answers emerge. At the least, it is hoped that such theoretical investigation will make more intelligible the concept that evolutionary theory can be enormously helpful in understanding of a particular historical era and thus of human history in general.

PART I

THE GREAT STRUGGLE FOR MODERNITY

2

THE TRIUMPH OF LIBERALISM

VALUES, MORES, *MENTALITÉS*

The great questions for sociological theory or for any analytical historical writing are those of cause. Why did certain things occur? What caused the French Revolution to take place? Why did it degenerate into Terror and Conservative Dictatorship? What enabled Lenin to overthrow the Kerensky regime? Why did Italy and Spain become fascist societies and France did not? The string of such questions is endless.

Few, if any, clear, profound, and unarguable answers have ever been given to these momentous questions. Not that people haven't tried. And the most brilliant moments of sociological and historical thought transpire when the theorist or historian of uncommon ability comes tantalizingly close to a profound understanding of the cause of change. The most exhilarating occasions in the writings of Tocqueville—who may be considered both a sociologist and an analytic historian, and certainly of uncommon brilliance—occur when his analytic genius seems to cut like a knife through the question of causality.

Despite the pitifully few real successes, the quest goes on relentlessly. The human desire to know "Why?" has enormous power. The feeling persists that, if we keep on asking "Why?" and answering it to the best of our capacities, we will move closer and closer to the truth. How much exactly we have succeeded in attaining even an approximate valid truth is seriously debatable. Regardless, the mission itself is admirable.

I have observed that the specific answers given to particular questions of cause fall into four clear and distinct categories: External Circumstances, Interests, Institutions, and Values-Mores-*Mentalités.* External Circumstances are the most obviously perceived. The circumstance that huge quantities of oil lie beneath the Arabian peninsula has profoundly changed the history of that part of the world. The lands of Western European Catholicism were invaded by Germanic tribes, whereas the peoples of Eastern Orthodox Christianity were conquered by Asiatic peoples. Certain crucial differences in Germanic and Asiatic cultures had profound effects on the future history of those areas. In the nineteenth century, the United States had available to it, within its own borders, significant quantities of coal and iron, necessary elements for a take off of industrial capitalism. The examples are plentiful and usually obvious. What is common to all causal explanations that I designate "External Circumstances" is that the generating factor lies outside the structures and values of the society itself. It is true that something within the nature of Western European society tempered its resistance to the conquest by Germanic peoples and generated a particular response to that conquest, but the fact that the conquerors were Germanic rather than Asiatic was the result of circumstance, something external to social structure. The other three categories of causal explanation, on the contrary, have reference to the situation *within* the particular society.

The place of Interests in the social theory has been a large one and much more debatable than the role of External Circumstances. Theories and explanations based upon Interests assume that almost all human beings desire to have as much political, social, and economic power as possible in order to assure the existence of themselves and those dear to them and to allow them as much of the benefits of life's pleasures as possible. These powers, however, are most times limited and, therefore, a person or a class of people can increase its own powers only at the cost of others. Social life becomes, in great part, a violent or nonviolent struggle for power: a more or less civilized Darwinian world. The most thorough sociological theory of the primacy of Interests is classical Marxism. Changes in technology (from the watermill to the steam engine) result in the creation of a bourgeois-capitalist class. The interests of this class push it to assume hegemony within society; this necessitates the overthrow of the current hegemonic class: the aristocracy. The aristocracy attempts to preserve its domination of society but is vanquished by the rising bourgeoisie. The interests of this latter class are now to stay in the position of dominating society, but its rule is threatened by an increasingly powerful proletariat whose interests call for an overthrow of the bourgeois-capitalist class. This is the class struggle and history. We have no need to go beyond conflicting class interests in order to understand the history of the world.

Liberalism, also, has erected a theoretical structure based primarily on Interests: Utilitarianism and Contract Theory. For both of these, society is composed of various groups and various individuals with separate and distinct—and many times conflicting—interests. There is a clear and present danger that such conflicts of interest will cause society to degenerate into an anarchical Hobbesian world: nasty, brutish, and short. It is to *everyone's* interest, however, that this not occur. Ultimately, a stable, rational, peaceful society serves everyone's interest. If people are rational enough to understand this, they will erect a society where citizens agree to disagree without recourse to violence. This essential rationality plus good will plus adequate law accomplishes the task. History, then, becomes the story of these competing, and most times conflicting, Interests.

Whether revelatory of the truth or not, theories of Circumstances and Interests retain a certain simplicity. Two or three basic propositions suffice to give the essence. Such is not true of the theoretical structures of Values-Mores-*Mentalités* and of Institutions. Not only are the theories themselves of a definite complexity, but also the use of either one immediately demands that one consider its relationship to the other. Any theoretical approach that deals only with Values and totally neglects Institutions proves grossly inadequate. And the same for the opposite situation. The great sociological tradition of Tocqueville, Weber, Durkheim, and Parsons lays great emphasis on Values-Mores-*Mentalités*, but within each body of theory Institutions play a greater or lesser role. How much of a role, in fact, becomes a crucial part of the theoretical stance. This question of what weight to give to each theoretical approach was already clearly perceived by Tocqueville in 1853. He writes to Claude-François de Corcelle:

> You say that institutions are only half of my subject. I go farther than you, and I say that they are not even half. You know my ideas well enough to know that I accord institutions only a secondary influence on the destiny of men. Would to God I believed more in the omnipotence of institutions! I would have more hope for our future, because by chance we might, someday, stumble onto the precious piece of paper that would contain the recipe for all wrongs, or on the man who knew the recipe. But, alas, there is no such thing, and I am quite convinced that political societies are not what their laws make them, but what sentiments, beliefs, ideas, habits of the heart, and the spirit of the men who form them, prepare them in advance to be, as well as what nature and education have made them.[1]

What I am designating Values-Mores-*Mentalités* has many different names. In addition to Tocqueville's sentiments, beliefs, ideals, habits of the heart, and the spirit of men, we could also list ideals, worldviews, *Weltanschauungen.* There is, undoubtedly, a book to be written that will differentiate significantly between Values and Mores and *Mentalités* and worldviews, and so forth, and so on, but that is of no consequence here. I use the words, especially the first three, interchangeably to signify those attitudes toward the world, other people, and reality that people use to guide their personal and social lives. And my own personal *Weltanschauung* coincides with Tocqueville's: nothing seems more important for understanding cause in history than comprehending the cause of significant changes in Values.

Institutions, in this view, rest upon a foundation of Values-Mores-*Mentalités.* There is no institution of monarchy without a value system that legitimates monarchy; no democratic society without democratic Mores; no Capitalism and the hegemony of the market without a *Mentalité* that pronounces such institutions legitimate and worthy. Institutions, nevertheless, have an autonomy of their own, and radical changes may arise within institutions that do not originate in the Values that originally created and supported them. The international relations of nation-states are anarchic; to survive, every state requires an army to protect its borders. The institution of the army is legitimated by the Value that certifies the nation as a fundamental necessity of political life. Once the military institution has been established, nevertheless, it has interests and a life of its own. It wants to continue to exist; in many cases it seeks to expand its power. Such institutional interests may come into conflict with other institutional interests, may even bring a political crisis onto society.

In addition to this, changes in Institutions that are integral to the institution itself and independent of any change in Values may shake the value system of society. When the capitalist system and the reign of the market came near to collapse, in 1929–1935, that crisis did not arise from any questioning of the legitimacy of these institutions, but it did drive many people in democratic societies to doubt their continued value. Similarly, when the monarchical nation-state system of seventeenth- and eighteenth-century Europe resulted in even more complex, and, most especially, even more costly wars that necessitated greater and greater taxes—when all this occurred, and the monarch was incapable of merely imposing new taxes on society in an authoritarian manner, a crisis of monarchy occurred. This, as is well known, was one of the causes of the

French Revolution—at least of the Revolution of 1789. In both these examples, changes in Institutions forced a revaluation of Mores.

This distinction between fundamental changes in Institutions and fundamental changes in Values-Mores-*Mentalités* is essential to a theory of revolutionary transformations. It is a particular distinction that few have perceived, and one that even Tocqueville, though he struggled to comprehend the Revolution his whole life, and even though he was keenly aware of the dialectical relationship between Values and Institutions, did not enlighten. *There are no Revolutions in Values. Any historical event that may rightly be termed a "Revolution" effectuates a radical change in Institutions but not in the system of Values.*

"Revolution" is here defined as the production of fundamental or radical changes within society that take place within a very short space of time. The Estates-General defies the king, transforms itself into the National Assembly, whose main task is to produce a written constitution for France. The night of August 4, 1789, the entire remaining Feudal regime in France is swept away. August 10, 1792, the king is deposed, and very shortly thereafter a Republic is proclaimed. Lenin overthrows the Kerensky regime by coup d'état and establishes a Bolshevik dictatorship. Hitler is elected in 1933 and within two years has transformed Germany into a Nazi society. These profound social changes occur "overnight." The changes in Values that made these revolutionary events possible took place, however, over a period of 50, 100, or even 150 years. The acute challenge to the legitimacy of authoritarian monarchy did not begin in June 1789. The extreme discontent with and "cultural despair" concerning Modernity, which made fascism possible and, perhaps, inevitable in some countries, did not arise in 1933.[2]

"La République," Danton tells us in August 1793, "était dans les esprits vingt ans au moins avant sa proclamation" ["The Republic was in the minds and hearts of men for at least twenty years before its proclamation."][3] It would prove relatively easy to push this "twenty years" to fifty or more. Tocqueville, in fact, does just that when he indulges himself in a slightly exaggerated mood: "I cannot believe that God has for several centuries been pushing two or three hundred million men toward equality just to make them wind up under a Tiberian or a Claudian despotism. Verily, that wouldn't be worth the trouble. Why He is drawing us toward democracy, I do not know; but embarked on a vessel that I did not build, I am at least trying to use it to gain the nearest port."[4] And Virginia Woolf's ironic comment that human nature changed "on or about

December 1910"[5] humorously, but powerfully, asserts that such radical changes in *Mentalités* do not occur instantaneously.

Radical and fundamental transformations of Values-Mores-*Mentalités* obviously do occur in history but not with revolutionary speed. The evolution of Western society from a pagan to a Christian one—a process that took several centuries—was such a transformation, but it was not a revolution. Constantine's conversion to Christianity was revolutionary, however, because it radically changed the nature of a crucial institution—the Emperorship—and did so in a matter of a few years. This one example is indicative of all revolutionary change: a gradual evolution in Values over a considerable amount of time prepares the ground for revolutionary alterations in Institutions, which can take place with lightning speed. Hegel, with reference to this very evolutionary development from Paganism to Christianity, not only points to this kind of profound change in Values over time but also asserts that the process itself may even be *unconscious:*

> Great revolutions which strike the eye at a glance must have been preceded by a still and secret revolution in the spirit of the age *(Zeitgeist)*, a revolution not visible to every eye, especially imperceptible to contemporaries, and as hard to discern as to describe in words. It is a lack of acquaintance with this spiritual revolution which makes the resulting changes astonishing.[6]

The argument being made here, of course, is that Hegel's "still and secret revolution" is not really a revolution at all, even though it is a supremely significant social-historical development.

The long, slow, but nevertheless accelerating process by which a radical change was effected in the system of Values that governs society has been convincingly elaborated by the historical work on eighteenth-century France that has been done over the last thirty years. Keith Michael Baker, an eminent historian of that century, has amplified the "emergence of enlightened public opinion as a political force" and quotes the 1782 work of Louis Sébastien Mercier: "In the last thirty years alone, a great and important revolution has occurred in our ideas. Today, public opinion has a preponderant force in Europe that cannot be resisted. Thus in assessing the progress of enlightenment and the change it must bring about, we may hope that it will bring the greatest good to the world and that tyrants of all stripes will tremble before this universal cry that continuously rings out to fill and awaken Europe."[7] And Marx, a brilliant theorist of social evolution, recognized that revolutions, when they did occur, were the result of developments over centuries: "The [English] revolution of 1648 was the victory of the seventeenth century over the sixteenth century, the revolution of 1789 was the victory of the eighteenth century over the seventeenth."[8]

Revolutions—precipitate changes in Institutions—do occur, however, at some point when these changes in Mores have reached a critical mass. But revolutions have a way of not just fitting nicely into a logical schema of quantum leaps after slow evolutionary changes in Values. The great problems of the French Revolution—the Terror and the failure to achieve Democratic Citizenship—cannot be explained by the growing power of enlightenment and liberalism during the eighteenth century. The increasing eighteenth-century demands for democratic reforms, equality, freedom of the press, freedom of religion, and so on, cannot explain the moral catastrophes that the Revolution gave birth to. The evolution of liberal and enlightenment thought in the eighteenth century had a certain powerful logic within it. Most of these ideas survived Robespierre and Napoleon and became part of the permanent value system of French culture.[9] Revolutions, on the contrary, have a way of producing illogicality after illogicality. Revolutions in the Modern world can even create radical transformations in Institutions that violate the logic of evolutionary process of changes in Values that preceded the revolution. The Bolsheviks destroyed the capitalist system and the market and erected a communist economy in their place, not in accord with Marxist evolution theory but in violation of it—as the Mensheviks had argued before Lenin had begun the whole revolutionary process.

Benjamin Constant used this distinction between Mores and Institutions in the attempt to critically appraise the French Revolution. He begins by distinguishing between a legitimate and an illegitimate revolution. Mona Ozouf describes Constant's position: "When 'the harmony between a people's institutions and its ideas is destroyed,' revolutions are inevitable. These legitimate, reasonable revolutions are implicit in the necessary progress of the human spirit." That is to say, when the gradual change in Values (the growth of equality and democratic thinking) creates a situation where Institutions (authoritarian monarchy and feudal privilege) are no longer compatible with the spirit of society, a revolution can correct this incongruous situation by a radical transformation of Institutions. However, it does not necessarily happen that way. Describing Constant's thought, Ozouf continues: "Revolutions run wild and fail to end at the appropriate point; flawed revolutions bring on reactions, arbitrariness succeeding arbitrariness. . . . By learning how to distinguish the good revolutions from the bad, one can stabilize institutions and keep from 'losing hope in liberty.' "[10]

Failed revolutions—and by implication, ideological terror—Constant is saying, push the changes in Institutions beyond the point where they can be sustained by the Mores of society. "The harmony between a people's institutions
and its ideas is destroyed," but this time because institutional arrangements have
outrun the stability of the value system. Madame de Staël, in a pessimistic statement that directly contradicts the optimistic one from Danton given above, gives
her opinion of a specific example of this contradictory situation: "The Republic
was established 50 years before opinion was ready for it . . . free elections would
be incompatible with its maintenance."[11]

One further thing, moreover, we must understand in order to comprehend
Terror: *the ideological terrorist refuses to accept the fact that revolutions in Values are impossible.*
In his commitment to a revolutionary *Weltanschauung* he pretends—to himself as
well as to others—that he can do with Mores what he has just done with Institutions: overthrow and replace with lightning speed. And thus, the birth of the
Politics of the Impossible.[12] Why some revolutions push onward into this area
of illegitimacy and others do not; why ideological terrorists, who always seem to
be around in the Modern world, succeed in gaining control of some revolutions
and not others; why we had reached the point in the twentieth century when
some revolutions were created by the terrorists themselves—are obviously enormously difficult questions of great import. As this book progresses, we will
return to them, not in the hope of finding ultimate answers, but with the more
modest project of amplifying the questions as much as we can.

THE ACCELERATING POWER OF THE LIBERAL
AGENDA DURING THE *ANCIEN RÉGIME*

One of the finest moral achievements—if not *the* finest achievement—of the Revolution was the institutionalization, almost completely and certainly for the most
part, of the liberal agenda. This triumph not only transpired, but was accomplished with remarkable ease, because almost the whole of French culture, almost
all the transformations in the system of Values during the eighteenth century,
were being driven toward that climax with immense power. When it came time
to create revolutionary changes in institutions, this realization of the liberal
agenda was one of the things almost every revolutionary actor could agree with.

A partial listing of that extraordinary program would include: (1) The bold
assertion that all men are equal in rights. (2) The institutionalization of equality

before the law. (3) Freedom of opinion. (4) Freedom of religion and the prohibition of discrimination in social and political matters due to religious preference. (5) A tremendous bolstering of the rights of the accused, including most specifically the establishment of juries and provision for defense counsel. (6) An end to judicial torture and other modes of cruel and unnecessary punishment, including an unsuccessful challenge to the continued existence of capital punishment. (7) A successful attack on the slave trade, but only an ambivalent approach to total emancipation.

This liberal agenda is closely related to that of the liberal political agenda: liberal democracy and democratic citizenship. It is, in many instances, impossible to differentiate them one from the other; the Mores of each realm interpenetrate the other. And certainly the actors at the time made no conscious differentiation between these two realms. Crucial words like "freedom," "liberty," "equality," and "justice" suffuse both these worlds of Values. The 1789 *Declaration of the Rights of Man and of the Citizen* and the preamble to the Constitution of 1791 know nothing of any separation between political rights and the abstract rights of the liberal agenda.

One crucial word that also completely commingles these two separate spheres is the word "Enlightenment." In a typical analysis, Bronislaw Baczko writes:

> In reading the countless brochures published when the Estates General were convoked and even more in studying the minutes of the National Assembly, especially in its early debates, one is struck by the remarkable knowledge of Enlightenment political literature on the part of the new political elites. Their spokesmen and ideologues saw the crisis and defined its issues . . . in terms of values and concepts elaborated by Enlightenment thinkers. It was in the language of the Enlightenment . . . that they elaborated a global interpretation of the crisis, and interpretation that opposed the rule of law to arbitrary rule, liberty to despotism, justice to privilege.[13]

Preferring "liberty to despotism" and "justice to privilege" are certainly basic attributes of *both* social-legal liberalism and liberal democracy. At first glance it would appear that these different sets of Values are only separate aspects of one fundamental *Mentalité:* the Enlightenment.

It is essential, however, to discriminate between the liberalism of rights and democratic citizenship. Social, legal, and religious liberalism were the great triumphs of the Revolution. The failure to institutionalize democratic citizenship its greatest catastrophe. This observation alone indicates that there must be a profound difference between the two no matter how many concepts like "justice" permeate both worlds. To be able to say, theoretically, exactly what that dissimilarity is, is a much more difficult task than that of merely describing it. The essence of democratic citizenship, and how it differs from liberalism as such, must be analyzed. Democratic citizenship will have a chapter of its own. This chapter is about triumph.

In order to keep these two worlds theoretically separate, I will not treat here certain events and ideas which belong primarily to the world of politics: the calling of the Estates General, its transformation into the National Assembly, and so on. The description in this chapter of the triumph of liberalism will rest almost entirely on a delineation of Values-Mores-*Mentalités*. The liberal agenda, as I have been describing it, is deeply embedded in the Values of society and arises from these value imperatives.

The analysis offered here will be overwhelmingly descriptive and only sparingly analytical. An analytical analysis of the rise of liberalism in the eighteenth century and its climax and institutionalization during the Revolution would require a thorough and complex analysis of the origins of the Enlightenment, its development, and its ambivalences. Such an analytic project is beyond the scope of this book and of my personal competence. What can be done is to give some sense of the irresistible tide of liberalism and Enlightenment that was sweeping France forward in the eighteenth century. The current state of French historiography, especially among a younger group of historians dealing with the *ancien régime*, has demonstrated, almost beyond argument, that such was the case.* Only a few typical, compelling examples are necessary to demonstrate the power of this evolution of Values.

"The Revolution did not overturn, it accelerated." Charles Tilly has made this keen observation in regard, primarily, to certain institutional changes: "The construction of a centralized nation-state . . . a kind of economic rationalization and market expansion."[14] The exact same observation, however, can be made about the evolution of Mores: certain developments were occurring during the eighteenth century, but these took a quantum leap, came to a kind of moral climax, under revolutionary auspices. The reform of certain primitive "feudal" modes of judicial torture and unreasonable punishment was already underway before the fall of the Bastille. Pretrial torture, for example, was renounced by a

---

*See the works of David Bell, Jack Censer, Roger Chartier, Dale Van Kley, Ann Sa'adah, and Sara Maza listed in the bibliography.

royal decree in May 1788, but the revolutionary acceleration of reform resulted in the penal code of 1791 that "eliminated altogether such common punishments as banishment, whipping, and branding, while decriminalizing such offences as sorcery and blasphemy."[15] Such an example, which is merely one among literally a myriad, demonstrates the power of liberalism in the thrust toward Modernity.

If it was Tocqueville's God who was the mover of this development, it is ironic that it included a profound de-emphasis on the religious legitimation of Mores:

> Religious titles, all categories included, accounted for one-half of the production of Paris printers at the end of the seventeenth century and still made up one-third of their output in the 1720s, but they accounted for only one-fourth of the book production early in the 1750s and only one-tenth in the 1780s. Since the other general bibliographic categories (law, history, belles-lettres) remained fairly stable throughout the century, it was the arts and sciences whose proportional share doubled between 1720 and 1780, that benefited the most from the decline in books of liturgy and piety.[16]

Similarly, in the 1770s we can already observe a reform wing of the intellectual and scientific elite—led by d'Alembert, Condorcet, and Turgot-at war with a conservative party *(les devots)* in intense competition for control of the French Academy and the Academy of Sciences and, in the latter case, including even a fierce struggle for control of the provincial academies. Here again, the Revolution provided the occasion for a precipitate movement forward: "The Revolution was able to sweep away the barriers to reform projects already fully conceived under the old regime."[17] Condorcet himself became a member of the Legislative Assembly (1791–1792), which succeeded to the National Assembly. He proposed a project on public education to the Assembly on behalf of its Committee on Public Instruction: "This reformed and revitalized system of scientific academies . . . became the very lynchpin of an educational system intended to transform subjects into citizens."[18] The Jacobin dictatorship and the Terror put an end to any hopes of adopting this educational approach, but the continuity in the evolution of Values remained: "Only after the Terror, when the Thermidorians recovered the Enlightenment discourse of the social . . . did the Convention turn to [Condorcet's report and] its combination of individualism, liberalism, and scientific elitism as the basis for the educational legislation of the Year III."[19]

Of enormous significance for world history is the fact that, in regard to certain Values-Mores-*Mentalités*, a revolution can, and does, do more than bring them to a moral climax. With those that have a permanent validity and legitimacy for the future, revolutionary energy can set these Values in stone upon a rock foundation. They become permanently inscribed in the minds and souls of humankind. There is no going back to the time when they did not exist or were not permanently potent. Every future society must take account of their existence: either by expressing them and giving them life, or by repressing them in the hope that they will remain silent and impotent, or by working out some sort of compromise between expression and repression by exercising a bit of both approaches. This establishment of permanence was precisely what the Revolution did for the liberal view of what it meant to be human: freedom and equality were no longer dispensable for that definition. R.R. Palmer, the sage historian of Democratic Revolutions, says that the *Declaration of the Rights of Man and of the Citizen*, "by laying down the principles of the modern state, remains the chief single document of the Revolution of the Western World."[20] That is to say, it permanently transformed the world.

It was Hegel, however, who so powerfully elaborated the point of permanence being made here. Joachim Ritter elucidates what Hegel conceived of as the true meaning of the Revolution, beyond the contingencies of Jacobin dictatorship, Terror and the Emperor Napoleon:

> *Every present and future legal and political order must presuppose and proceed from the Revolution's universal principle of freedom.* Against this, all reservations concerning its formalism and abstractness lose their force. After the polis entered into history in the ancient world and therewith, human being as the principle of justice *(Recht)* (albeit in restriction to the citizen and in exclusion of the slave), all political and legal forms which did not correspond to it had to become inessential for political theory. Plato and Aristotle therefore grounded political philosophy upon the polis alone. Where justice has become the justice of man, then justice which is not justice of man can only be called "justice" in a homonymous sense. The same holds for the French Revolution. After it made freedom for all, as men, the principle of right *(Recht)*, all institutions and positive laws which contradict it lose by the process of historical necessity, every legitimate claim to validity. . . . It is no longer possible to retreat from this principle. Right—now in principle the right of man—has attained the universality of the species; this cannot be restricted without leading to a contradiction with the human being of man and thereby with the new-won universal principle of law.[21]

Since it is not intended here to look even cursorily at the history of the *ancien régime*, the few examples of the power of liberal Values are given in this chapter solely to be exemplary of that vast movement. Its tremendous power had been emphasized by Tocqueville, who knew, in François Furet's comment, "that the revolution took place before the Revolution."[22] Tocqueville, however, in his analysis of the *ancien régime* that he completed, concentrates almost entirely on the centralization of the State and the debilitation of the aristocracy. At times he does emphasize the great surge of liberal Mores, as in the case where he describes pre-Revolutionary opposition of the parlements to the absolutism of the king: "This does not prove that a great revolution was near," Furet goes on to say, "but that a great revolution had already taken place."[23] Certainly, in the Values-Mores-*Mentalités* of the society, that was unquestionably the case.

THE NATURE OF LIBERALISM

First, I will not attempt to differentiate between the concepts of "Enlightenment" and "liberalism." There is, undoubtedly, some value in an extended discussion of what that differentiation might involve, but it is not necessary to the present purposes. Essentially, I will use the two concepts interchangeably. One may correctly regard the Enlightenment as the French (with some extensions) version of the great Western drive toward liberal Values-Mores-*Mentalités*.

What is most important to the argument being made here is that French Revolutionary culture was almost completely committed to the *permanent* perpetuation of liberal Mores. None of the morally negative historic events of the Revolution itself could destroy, in the long run, French commitment to these Values. In the future, many complex compromises would be worked out between these Values and more repressive ones, but liberalism, as such, never died. Hegel was correct that every future state had to take cognizance of its reality, even if that recognition took the form of deliberate repression or compromise.

The liberal *Mentalité* may be characterized as suffused with a commitment to rational humanism. Humanism was not new. Christian humanism, most particularly associated with the thought of Erasmus (1466?–1536), was a crucial development in the evolution of Values during the Early Modern stage of society, and remained important in some areas of Catholic culture down through the eighteenth century. With rational humanism, however, Divinity was no longer the ultimate legitimator of Values. Human reason and natural law sufficed to legitimate the system of Values. Tocqueville comments on the writers of the eighteenth century: "Though their ways diverged in the course of these researches, their starting point was the same in all cases; and this was the belief that what was wanted was to replace the complex of traditional customs governing the social order of the day by simple, elementary rules deriving from the exercise *of human reason and natural laws*."[24] Enlightenment thinkers were not yet faced with the great nineteenth-century dilemma that, if God is dead, the moral center will no longer hold: an ambiguity most powerfully put by Ivan Karamazov's cry of despair that, if there is no God, anything is possible. Liberalism, rational humanism, was committed to the proposition that the moral center and the forms of social cohesion could be provided by means other than religious ones. Natural laws, which included, most important, universal human rights, would provide the answer. Whether these views were utopian or not, whether they were tragic manifestations of the sin of pride, as certain critics of the Enlightenment contended, such questions would not be fully answered in Western society for a hundred years.

Three basic propositions sustained Enlightenment thought: That human life and liberty are sacred. That human beings are ends in themselves, and not a means, not a tool, to be used by others. That natural laws and natural rights are universal: applicable to all people, not just to some people.

As for sacredness, the preamble to the *Declaration of the Rights of Man and of the Citizen* begins: "The Representatives of the French people, constituted as the National Assembly . . . have resolved to set forth, in a solemn declaration, the natural, inalienable, and sacred rights of man."[25] This sacredness, it is important to note, is no longer an absolute religious sacred but is already on the way toward that remarkable creation of Modernity: the secular sacred. This secular sacred will be discussed at length when we address the question of secular society. Here, however, it may be helpful to cite one example. Under the absolute monarchy, the worst crime one could commit was *lèse majesté*: a violation of the sacredness of the king. Almost immediately after the establishment of the National Assembly in June 1789, it was recognized that the nation was beginning to replace the king as the primary force of social cohesion, that which held society together. Quickly the concept of *lèse nation* arose to indicate the sacredness of the nation, but this sacredness was much more secular, much less fundamentally religious than the sacredness of the king had been. And the "sacred rights of man" were sacred in this partly religious, partly secular manner. The creation of a viable secular sacred proved not to be as simple as many had imagined, and the struggle around this endeavor led to one of the fundamental ambivalences in Modernity.

That human beings are prohibited by natural law and the principle of universal rights from using other human beings as a means was most eloquently set forth in the night session of August 4, 1789, that swept away the remains of the feudal regime, by an unknown Breton deputy, Leguen de Kerangal, a linen-draper living in small town:

> Let us be just, gentlemen; let them bring to us here those title-deeds which are an outrage, not only to our sense of shame, but to our very humanity. Let them bring us those title-deeds which humiliate the human races by demanding that men should be harnessed to the plough like beasts of burden. Let them bring us the title-deeds which oblige men to spend the night beating ponds to prevent the frogs from disturbing the sleep of their pleasure-loving lords. Which of us, gentlemen, in this enlightened century, would not make expiatory pyre of these infamous parchments and set fire to it in order to sacrifice them upon the altar of the fatherland.[26]

As to the third basic proposition of Enlightenment thought, the universality of rights, proclaimed in hundreds of ways and occasions, it was destined to become problematic, because the new society that replaced the *ancien régime* immediately developed its own new structures of hierarchy and continued the perpetuation of certain hierarchical conditions inherited from the past. People with moral vision, like Robespierre, were quick to observe that equality would prove a most difficult project. From the discourse *"Sur la constitution"* of May 1793:

> Tant de marchands stupides, tant de bourgeois egoists conservent encore pour les artisant ce dédain insolent que les nobles prodiguaient aux bourgeois et aux marchands eux-même.[27] [So many ignorant merchants, so many egoistic bourgeois still retain the insolent disdain for the artisans themselves that the nobles lavished on the bourgeois and the merchants.]

A profoundly important movement in society toward equality does not necessarily result in the total elimination of hierarchy and dominion.

THE NEARLY UNANIMOUS ACCEPTANCE
OF CERTAIN LIBERAL VALUES

The most remarkable fact about the liberal agenda is how solidly it was accepted in the minds of the elite members of society. And not merely the members of

the Third Estate, but also, most particularly, the Nobles and, to a lesser degree
but still significantly progressive, the members of the Clergy. When elections
were conducted to select representatives to the Estates General in 1789, the
members of every election district, in each of the three Estates, prepared a com-
pilation of grievances, a *cahier de doléances*, wherein the electors expressed their
hopes for changes in French society: grievances *and* remedies. Sixty thousand of
these have survived, providing us with a remarkable look into the spirits of men
who composed French society. Tocqueville described the *cahiers* as "le testament
de l'ancienne société française, l'expression suprême de ses désires, la manfesta-
tion authentique de ses volontés,"[28] and he devoted himself to the study of them,
most especially the *cahiers* of the nobility.

"The most striking feature of the *cahiers* of the nobility," Tocqueville writes,
"is the perfect harmony which exists between these noblemen and their age.
They are imbued with its spirit and speak its language. They speak of 'the
inalienable rights of man,' 'principles inherent to the social compact.' "[29] The
demand is made from these nobles for an explicit declaration of rights that
should include guarantees of liberty and safety for all men. Serfdom should be
abolished in those areas where it still remains; the slave trade, and even slavery
itself, should be abrogated. All men should be free to travel and reside wherever
they wish, without fearing arrest. Some of the noble *cahiers*, especially those of
Paris, demanded the destruction of the Bastille. All forms of corporal punishment of prisoners, including torture, should be done away with; and the conditions of a prisoner awaiting trial should be ameliorated.[30]

Twentieth-century historiography is able to supply an accurate statistical analysis of noble *cahiers*, all of which confirms Tocqueville's more general observations. Guy Chaussinand-Nogaret writes:

> 82% of the *cahiers* demanded the abolition of the commissions and evocations
> which removed cases from ordinary justice, 69% wanted abolition of *lettres de cachet*,
> 44% the limitation of imprisonment without a court appearance to a maximum
> of 24 hours. . . . Sixty per cent of the *cahiers* demanded that liberty should be
> declared "inviolable and sacred" for all citizens without exception. . . . everyone
> should have the right to think and publish whatever they wanted. . . . The most
> detailed *cahiers* set out a plan for the new legislation. They stipulated safeguards
> for the accused persons; trial by jury, right to counsel, reasoned verdicts, the
> abolition of torture and ignominious interrogation, criminal prosecution in public,
> restriction of the death penalty, improvement of the prisons.[31]

All this, from the noble *cahiers*. Those of the Third Estate were, as we would assume, even more unanimous in their liberalism. But what is so noteworthy is the remarkable agreement that there seemed to be among the three orders. William Doyle comments that the only significant area of disagreement was on the question of the franchise for voting. Beyond this, a vast majority agreed that authoritarian monarchy had seen its day, that the king must rule under the provisions of a written constitution, wherein taxes required the consent of the governed. There was no disagreement that, in the future, rights must be guaranteed by the supremacy of law. Some members of the clergy opposed full liberty of religion, of thinking, and of public expression, but the overwhelming sentiment supported these liberal notions. "Behind the arguments over voting," Doyle concludes, "there lay a broad reformist, liberal consensus which transcended all three orders."[32]

The groundwork having been prepared so magnificently, it is no wonder that the institutionalization of the liberal agenda was one of the great triumphs of the Revolution.

THE PARADOXES AND CONTRADICTIONS OF EQUALITY

There was, however, a menacing fault line in this solid rock fundament, and the threatening earthquake erupted and broke the back of the liberal Revolution in the two years from August 1792 to July 1794. *Equality*, on which there was no consensus, proved to be the great problematic. What exactly did "equality" mean? How was it to be institutionalized in the legal, political, economic, and gender realms of society?

The great, awesome drive toward equality and its pervasive institutionalization in law was the most important contribution to the moral history of the world that the eighteenth century—and its revolutionary climax—bequeathed to us. For both Hegel and Tocqueville, it was the very essence of the brave new world that God or history had thrust upon us. "The gradual progress of equality," Tocqueville wrote in 1833, "is something fated. The main features of this progress are the following: it is universal and permanent; it is daily passing beyond human control, and every event and every man helps it along."[33]

For Hegel, the French Revolution was a "world-historical turning point," "an epoch in the world's history," which meant that it represented a fundamental and radical movement in the evolution of moral progress. It was such because it stood for an *equality of freedom*. Political and legal freedom in the ancient world had been limited to certain classes of people and excluded others: slaves and the politically disenfranchised. The Revolution, however, had made the premises of freedom universal: all men were equal in freedom. Man becomes the subject of the political order "in virtue of his manhood alone, not because he is a Jew, Catholic, Protestant, German, Italian, etc."[34]

The end of the eighteenth century and the whole of the nineteenth was to demonstrate, however, that this "world-historical turning point" was exactly just that: a turning point and no more. It pointed in the direction of a reality that was to prove extraordinarily difficult to achieve. The great ambiguity within the concepts of freedom and equality was that they were far from monolithic. Just as the ancient world could give freedom to some and not others, just so the Modern world could give equality to some and not others or, more accurately, could deliver equality in certain realms of society and not others. The old saw about how all men are created equal, but some are created more equal than others, underlines the fact that Modern society, and the liberal ethic that defines its value system, have no intention of going all the way down the road of equality. And the Revolution was one crucial time when the question "How far?" was posed with enormous energy and urgency and, ultimately, answered with tremendous violence.

The concept of equality concerns itself with four basic realms within society: (1) Equality before the law, in the courts, and in prisons. (2) Equality of political rights, which historically breaks down into two phases: a limited democracy and a full, radical democracy (the latter including poor people). (3) Equality of material existence and of economic goods and power. (4) Equality between men and women. Though the *Weltanschauung* of equality permeates all these four areas, the history of equality in each obviously has varied enormously.

The world history of equality—and of liberal democratic thought—begins in the ancient world, though it is only from Athens that we have really full data. Equality before the law comes first; starting with Solon in 595–594 B.C., poor people had the same rights in connection with criminal matters as did the elite and were fully eligible to sit on juries. Unlike even the *ancien régime*, there were juries deciding all criminal cases in Athens. The second stage, that of political equality, begins with the democratic reforms of Cleisthenes in 508 B.C., resulting in the creation of a limited democracy, wherein property restrictions on political participation excluded the lowest classes from real political power. Around the middle of the fifth century, Ephialtes and Pericles led the successful struggle to institute a full, radical democracy that lasted, with certain interruptions, for 350 years. Despite this extraordinary achievement, however, one thing was missing: universality. All Athenians were certainly equal, but the notion that *all men*—even all nonslave men—were created equal was never put forward and would have been considered alien, even in Athens. Ancient democracy was kinship-born: it could not transcend, even in thought, the boundary of the individual *polis*.[35]

After the long hiatus of the medieval world, Early Modernity and Modernity began the same, almost identical, odyssey again. This time, there is England, Switzerland, Belgium, the Netherlands, America—and France.[36] Followed, eventually, by many others. Including the nineteenth century, which brought us the first modern radical democracy, the stages in this evolution replicate those of Athens: equality before the law, limited democracy, radical democracy. Modernity and liberalism, however, add three crucial elements that were missing in the *polis:* the universality of all men, in terms of rights; the demand for an equalization of economic opportunity and power; the concept that equality for all *men* is not sufficient, that women, too, are people.

Modern societies—and France is a perfect example—had a relatively easy time with three of these elements of equality: before the law, limited democracy, and the ideal of the universality of rights. Modern societies—and France— almost tore themselves apart in connection with the other elements of equality: radical democracy, economic equality (whatever that might mean), and gender equality. And one indication that post-Modernity remains purely a theoretical exercise and bears almost no relation to social reality is the fact that, in regard to these three areas, we still live completely immersed in the contradictions of Modernity: the rich still overwhelmingly dominate democratic politics; the poor still suffer economic hardship and have begun again, in the last twenty years, living on the streets; the struggle over gender equality resembles a continuous warfare: win some battles, lose some combats. In all truth, we cannot blame the Revolution for not solving problems we ourselves cannot reconcile, but possibly, fewer people had to die.

It is interesting to note, in regard to this evolutionary scheme of stages or realms, that Mona Ozouf states that Tocqueville distinguishes three stages in the advance toward equality: legal status, political rights, and conditions of material existence.[37] In my view, such an evolutionary schema can provide a significant tool for illuminating the paradoxes of the Revolution. As to the first stage, within the Revolutionary movement, from the most conservative to the most radical views, there was nearly unanimous agreement of equality of legal status.

This unanimity starts to come apart with regard to the second stage of equality of political rights. When we consider the three constitutions written and adopted between 1789 and Napoleon, and add to them the suffrage requirements legislated in 1792 for the elections to the National Convention after the deposition of the king, and also consider the proposed but never adopted constitutional provisions of early 1793—in all this, we find wide differences on fundamental political questions: who can vote, who can serve, whether the poor have equal rights with the rich. Only the constitution of 1793, adopted but never actually put into practice, written after the coup d'état of May–June that created the Jacobin dictatorship—only this could be considered as establishing a radical democracy, wherein there was full male equality of political rights. The majority of the men who made the first Revolution in 1789 had no intention that the poor should have an equal say in the politics of the nation. The Jacobin dictatorship, of course, had no actual intention that *le peuple* should rule, just as the Stalinists in the 1930s, with their glorious liberal, egalitarian constitution, did not expect that the sovereignty of the people would become a reality. Both Jacobins and Bolsheviks assumed that the masses would, at best, assume a role like the queen of England: reign, but not rule. Dictators would rule in the name of the people.

The Jacobin dictators and soon-to-be terrorists, of course, made brilliant use of *le peuple* in their drive for absolute political power. The people's energy and power arose from the desire for equality and the sense that the new world entitled them to it: direct-action political power and economic equality, or at least some kind of guaranteed minimum of existence. It was they who brought the king back to Paris in October 1789 as a semicaptive, deposed him in August 1792, and provided the revolutionary shock troops that produced the Jacobin coup of May–June 1793. The people assumed they were equal in political and economic rights. They were soon to learn differently.

In regard to Tocqueville's third stage, that of the conditions of material existence—the question of economic equality—since the rights of property were considered sacred and ideas of socialism nonexistent except within an infinitesimally small radical fringe, the only question that could be raised was: What can be done to ameliorate the condition of the economically disadvantaged? The sacrosanct nature of property had been certified by the original *Declaration of the Rights of Man and Citizen* of 1798. "Article 17. Property being an inviolable and sacred right, no one can be deprived of it, unless legally established public necessity obviously demands it, and upon condition of a just and prior indemnity."[38]

And this article of faith was never challenged by Revolutionary leaders, not even radical Jacobins such as Marat, Danton, Robespierre, and Saint-Just.

The liberal *Weltanschauung*, however, demanded the equality of all men, and it was not easy to exempt the realm of material existence. What resulted was the liberal-bourgeois-capitalist compromise formation wherein great differences in wealth and the existence of an economic elite were allowed, and the moral thrust of liberalism concerned itself with the prevention of severe economic distress for the poor. The power within society and the course of the immediate future, however, lay with the interests of the bourgeois-capitalist classes, and not with the more radical economic levelers. It took Western society 150 years before its moral values, in regard to economic equality, caught up with the most advanced thinkers of the Revolution. It is remarkable how these latter raised certain proposals that would not become a permanent part of Modernity until the creation of the welfare state in this century. Three remedies for economic inequality were put forth during the revolutionary years: (1) The declaration that the right to subsist was a fundamental human right, and that it was the obligation of the state to see that it becomes and remains a reality. (2) The recommendation that taxes should be progressive: that the rich should pay a larger percentage of their income. (3) The proposal that discrepancies of income be kept to a minimum necessary for economic productivity.

It was the moral genius of Robespierre that recognized almost immediately that, lacking concerted action to keep it from occurring, a tyranny of wealth would quickly replace the overthrown tyranny of aristocracy, and that those at the bottom of society would have gained nothing by the Revolution. Already in April 1791, he announced: "Est-ce pour retomber sous le joug de l'aristocratie des riches, qu'il [le peuple] a brisé avec vous le joug de l'aristocratie féodale?"[39] ["Is it in order to fall again under the yoke of the aristocracy of riches, that the people have broken with you the yoke of feudal aristocracy?"] He, therefore, proposed in April 1793 that in the declaration of rights to be attached to the new constitution a provision should be included insisting that society "provide for the subsistence of all its members either by procuring them work or by furnishing the means of existence to those who are not in condition to work." And the declaration as finally adopted declared that "public assistance is a sacred debt."[40] In America, it took Franklin Roosevelt to give some substantial reality to this Revolutionary dream of equality. It is pathetic that in the movement in the last twenty years, in both England and America, to "downsize" the welfare state, if not almost completely dismantle it, the one cry that people of compassion have raised is that we should not destroy the "safety net" that keeps people from falling into abject poverty. They could easily quote from the 1793 declaration of rights about the sacredness of public assistance.

Taking note of similar historical irony, whereas in the United States it required the twentieth century and a constitutional amendment to legitimate a tax on incomes, Robespierre had given voice to such a necessity in 1793:

> Moreover, you are talking of taxation to establish the incontestable principle that it can only emanate from the will of the people or of their representatives, but you are forgetting to declare the basis of this taxation progressive. Now, in the matter of public contributions, it is a principle plainly deriving from the nature of things and from eternal justice that those who impose on citizens an obligation to contribute to public expenditure should adjust it progressively, according to the extent of men's fortunes, that is to say, according to the advantages they reap from society.[41]

The proposition that economic inequality and economic injustice be seriously ameliorated by narrowing the economic space between the richest and the poorest was, and remains, the utopian dream of righteous philosophers. Gabriel Bonnet de Malby, an enlightenment thinker, had insisted that, in order "To banish mendicancy and excessive opulence from the state," there should be a serious reduction in the inequality of wealth. Similarly, Rousseau had insisted: "My purpose is not to destroy private property but to confine it within narrow limits."[42] But this manner of thinking goes all the way back to Plato, who had declared in the *Laws* that "It is impossible for someone to be both unusually good and unusually rich" and had proposed in that same work that poverty be prevented by giving each citizen a basic allotment of land from which he can never be severed and that great riches be prevented by limiting the total wealth of any citizen to four times the value of the basic allotment. Anything above this would be subject to confiscation.[43] The most recent history of capitalist society would seem to indicate that there is no solution to the problem of severe economic inequality within contemporary society. Society will have to transcend Modernity, apparently, before that particular moral problem will be seriously addressed.

What we see happening at the moral frontier during the French Revolution is the exact circumstance that occurred with regard to the Levellers and Diggers during the English Revolution of the seventeenth century: as soon as notions of universal rights and equality are raised with energy and urgency, the question of economic rights and the perennial problem of what-shall-we-do-about-the-poor? imposes itself upon the liberal agenda. The great problematic for Modern society is that liberalism, as such and within itself, had—and has—no intention of resolving that ambiguity. As great a moral achievement as the realization of Modernity may be, it is important to recognize that Modernity has its own moral limits. The Levelers, the Diggers, the people-in-the-streets of Paris, Robespierre, Saint-Just were all pushing at that frontier. They were all doomed to fail, in this regard. Modernity and liberalism have not legitimate claim to represent that chimera "the end of history."

The kind of psychological splitting that is necessary in order to stop the march toward equality at certain points is clearly demonstrated by what has become a cliché of moral critique: the slave-owner Jefferson composing—and truly believing in—the greatest hymn to universal rights ever written. Samuel Johnson, who died before the Revolution but who already perceived the equivocation in liberalism, was unmerciful in underlining this moral ambiguity: "How is it that we hear the loudest *yelps* for liberty among the drivers of negroes?"[44]

Ambiguity and contradiction pile on top of contradiction and ambiguity: it was the future cannibalistic terrorist Robespierre who saw most sharply what society should, but would not, do. At the very minimum, Robespierre argued a year before the Terror, society has the obligation to assure the continued existence of every member of the commonwealth: "Food that is necessary for man's existence is as sacred as life itself. Everything that is indispensable for its preservation is the common property of society as a whole. It is only the surplus that is private property and can be safely left to individual commercial enterprise."[45]

His political analysis goes even deeper than this moral imperative: Great inequalities of wealth, Robespierre insists, will lead to the political tyranny of the rich over the rest of society. In a speech of April 1791, decrying the establishment of a standard of substantial wealth required to serve as a national representative: "Les lois, l'autorité publique, n'est-elle pas établie pour protéger la faiblesse contre l'injustice et l'oppression? C'est donc blesser tous les principes sociaux, que de la placer tout entière entre les mains des riches. . . . quelle est la source de cette extrême inégalité des fortunes qui rassemble toutes les richesses en un petit nombre de mains? Ne sont-ce pas les mauvaises lois, les mauvais gouvernements, enfin tous les vices des sociétés corrumpues?"[46] ["The laws, the public authority, have they not been established to protect the weak against injustice and oppression? It is then to injure all the principles of society to place it entirely in the hands of the rich. . . . What is the source of the extreme inequality of fortunes which gather all wealth in a small number of hands? Is it not bad laws, bad governments, and finally, all the vices of corrupt societies?"] If these decrees are allowed to exist, he asks, what will be the declaration of rights? "Une vaine formula." And what will the nation be? "Esclave." And the constitution? "Une véritable aristocratie. Car l'aristocratie est l'état où un portion des citoyens est souveraine et le reste sujets. Et quelle aristocratie! La plus insupportables de toutes; celle des Riches."[47] ["A true aristocracy. For aristocracy is the condition where some citizens are sovereign and the rest are subjects. And what an aristocracy! The most unbearable of all: that of the Rich."]

And with an amazing prescience of what the bourgeois-capitalist world would bring to the United States in the nineteenth century, Robespierre in an exaggerated manner imagines the future as already existent: "Who would want to exchange the sublime destiny of the French people for the constitution of the United States of America which, *fondée sur l'aristocratie des richesses,* already descends towards monarchical despotism?"[48] A true democracy, we are being told, is impossible when wealth rules. An exaggeration, for sure, but one that points to a fundamental moral paradox of Modernity.

The solution? The Welfare State, premature by 140 years. In May of 1794, the Jacobin dictatorship, author of the Terror, decreed a system of social security, "bienfaisance nationale," that took as its starting point, but far exceeded, the clause in the Declaration of Rights of 1793 relating to public assistance. These measures, which never became a reality, sought to provide relief in cases of serious economic distress and made provision for medical benefits, old-age pensions, and special grants for large families. It was an extraordinary prevision of what the finest in Liberalism might someday institutionalize within society.[49]

The final result that reflected all these contradictions and paradoxes within liberalism in regard to a definition of "equality" was, in all advanced democratic societies in the nineteenth and twentieth centuries, not just in France, an Age of Ambivalence[50] wherein almost all the great political battles ultimately reduced themselves to the question of what it meant to be "equal." In the three basic areas of equality, Modernity—exactly as Revolutionary France—had no problem at all with equality for all men before the law; equality for women before the law remained, however, deeply problematic. Modernity, again like Revolutionary France, was profoundly ambivalent about extending the rights of a limited democracy to all citizens: creating a radical democracy for all men, and eventually for all women. Only the twentieth century saw a final resolution of these two problematics of equality. And in regard to the third realm, equality of material existence—or at least a reasonable compromise with that ideal—no satisfactory resolution has ever been reached. In the United States at this moment, the most strident political differences center exactly on the question of how much equality in regard to material existence shall exist—that is, how much poverty is to be tolerated, how much of a fully human life are all people entitled to?

The opponents of the full extension of equality knew exactly that what had to be attacked was the conception of universal rights. Once all men had rights, they argued, the demand for economic equality would be imminent. The Thermidorians who took power after the fall of Robespierre and the Terror knew precisely what had to be done. In the making of the Constitution of the Year III, August 1795:

> If they thought fit to formulate a Declaration of Rights, they were careful to eliminate from it the essential article: "Men are born free and remain free and equal in rights." To those who proposed restoring it, Mailhe and Languinais replied on August 13 that it was ambiguous and therefore dangerous: men were no doubt equal in rights, but not in ability or in property either; in adopting this article, the Constituent Assembly had not realized that it was banning in advance the property qualification for suffrage. "Civil equality," Boissy said, "is all a reasonable man can demand." The following definition was therefore adopted: "Equality consists in the fact that the law is the same for all." This was indeed what the Constituent Assembly had meant to say; thus defined, equality became a sort of attribute of liberty which it confined itself to insuring for everybody. The State had no other function but to guarantee that liberty by maintaining order, which in practice amounted to allowing one group of citizens to subjugate the rest by means of their ability and above all by means of their wealth. . . . The article [in the Declaration of Rights of 1793] to the effect that "the aim of society is the common happiness" aroused Lanjuinais' sarcasm; and when the right to work was brought up, Thibault exclaimed: "They will come and ask you for bread again!"[51]

The profoundly ambivalent moral, political agenda for the next two hundred years or so was now firmly in place.

3

THE TRIUMPH OF LIBERALISM

INSTITUTIONS

From the *Declaration of the Rights of Man and of the Citizen*, August 1789: "The Representatives of the French people, constituted as the National Assembly, considering that ignorance, disregard, or contempt for the rights of man are the sole causes of public misfortunes and the corruption of governments, have resolved to set forth, in a solemn declaration, the natural, inalienable, and sacred rights of man, so that the constant presence of this declaration may ceaselessly remind all members of the social body of their rights and duties. . . .

"Article 1. Men are born and remain free and equal in rights. Social distinctions can be based only on public utility.

"Article 2. The aim of every political association is the preservation of the natural and imprescriptible rights of man. These rights are liberty, property, security, and resistance to oppression."[1]

As deeply as these words may move our hearts and souls, as powerful as these thoughts have been in the history of the world, there remains a deep rational ambiguity and contradiction within the whole discussion and pronouncement of rights: Nothing that is said about rights can even begin to be proved or established by reason. That rights exist; that they are sacred; what in particular they are; that people have them; that all men possess them equally—all this must be taken on faith; there is no way to establish rationally these propositions. Should I assert that there are no such things as rights or that if they do exist, they are not sacred, no real rational argument is possible since both the assertion of rights and its denial are not arrived at by reasoning. The sacred existence of rights is "believed in" in the same manner that most people believed in God in those pre-Enlightenment days when people had such faith, and in the same manner that people today believe in the existence of God and His power.

It is ironic that the Enlightenment, the "Age of Reason," which placed so much value on rationality, could change society only by substituting one new faith for an old one. This is not to assert, therefore, that there was no moral progress. The sovereignty of rights was a formidable moral advance, but reason was not the cause. Enlightenment thinkers unconsciously recognized the problem of where legitimacy for these new values of rights was to come from if Divinity could no longer serve. "Nature" was brought in to resolve the dilemma: rights are "natural"; it is essential to preserve the "natural and imprescriptible rights." The legitimating power of Nature, however, was no more rationally satisfying than Jefferson's "self-evident." Critics of the Enlightenment and the moral progress it was bringing observed these contradictions of rationality. Joseph de Maistre, a believing Catholic of conservative, even reactionary, politics knew that substituting Nature for God was, in definite ways, a trick of reason. Mocking the Encyclopedists' pervasive reliance on Nature for legitimacy, de Maistre inquired: "Who on earth is this woman?"[2]

That human rights exist, are sacred, and belong equally to all people are first principles, which differ radically from de Maistre's first principle that human morality is given by God. No rational thought can reconcile the difference in these two faiths, and faiths they are. One accepts the reality of rights in the same manner as one accepts the reality of God: on faith alone. All of which, of course, does not answer the question of why the great new faith of rights was generated and expanded to the point where it, like the previous faith (Christianity), transformed the world.

One possible contradiction in the proclamation of rights was foreseen and disposed of by liberal thinkers at the time. The liberal world was a bourgeois world, and it recognized immediately that the proclaiming of equality in rights by no means meant that men were to be equal in everything. The Abbé Sieyès, a potent maker of the first Revolution of 1789, explained a month before the adoption of the *Declaration of Rights:* "There exist, it is true, some great inequalities of means among men. Nature makes some strong and some weak; she bestows on some an intelligence that she refuses to others. It follows that there will be between them an inequality of work, inequality of profit, inequality of the availability of life's pleasures, but it does not follow that one can have inequality of rights."[3]

And as far as rational proof of articles of faith is concerned, obviously it was much easier to demonstrate that Nature "departit aux uns une intelligence qu'elle refus aux autres," than that this same Nature bestowed an equality of rights on all men. What Sieyès is emphasizing was destined to become a fundamental, seemingly unalterable, Value of liberal-bourgeois society: Elitism plus universality of rights, without one excluding the other.

The potency of the concept of universal rights and its capacity to fundamentally alter institutions is demonstrated by the continuity of that energy through all phases of the late pre-Revolution and the Revolution itself. The *Weltanschauung* of the latter part of the old regime, the *Declaration* of 1789, the liberal constitution of 1791, the post-Thermidor constitution of 1795—at every stage this universality was reiterated, with the stated implication that institutions within society must be altered to conform to this ideal. Tocqueville, in his discussion of the old regime, emphasizes the belief in equality "and its corollary, the abolition of all privileges of class, caste, and profession." And he goes on to say that these ideas and those of equality before the law were the "most fundamental, durable, and authentic characteristics" of the Revolution.[4] Similarly, the bishop Talleyrand in an address to the nation, February 1790, summarized the work of the National Constituent Assembly, insisting that it had destroyed and then reconstructed everything. Feudalism, the system of privileges, the absolute monarchy, were no more. The sovereignty of the nation and equal rights before the law reigned in their stead. All of this resulted, Talleyrand asserted, from institutionalizing the Values inherent in the *Rights of Man*.[5]

The first constitution adopted after the Revolution was that of 1791. In its preamble, equality of rights is assumed, and it addresses itself to the transformations in institutions that will make a reality of that ideal:

The National Assembly, wishing to establish the French constitution on the principles that it has recognized and declared irrevocable abolishes the institutions that have done injury to liberty and to the equality of rights.

Nobility no longer exists, nor peerage, nor hereditary distinction of orders, nor feudal regime, nor patrimonial courts, nor titles, denominations or prerogatives deriving therefrom, nor any order of chivalry, nor any of the corporations or decorations for which proofs of nobility used to be required or which presupposed distinctions of birth, nor any other superiority than that of public officers in the exercise of their functions.

Property in office and its inheritance no longer exist.

No privilege or exceptions to the common law for all Frenchmen any longer exists for any part of the nation or for any individual.[6]

The Constitution of 1795, written after the overthrow of Robespierre and the Terror, when the fear of a Revolution-going-too-far was in every bourgeois heart—even this Constitution did not turn its back on all previous assertions of the universality of rights, though it naturally assumed that elites would rule the new society. The Constitution, Furet and Richet assert, was a definite improvement on the two previous constitutions and became the basis of the whole of nineteenth-century constitutional law in France.[7]

No matter how many compromises with full equality in the future were written into law or erected within society, bourgeois-liberal culture never really rejected the ideal of equality of rights. That challenge would occur only with twentieth-century fascism and the temporary overthrow of liberal Modernity. A certain commitment to a certain kind of equality had become, in Western society, an almost ineradicable aspect of the human psyche. No finer example exists of the power of culture to transform psychic reality.

There is no new great idea or ideal that is incapable of being transmuted into a perversion. If society is capable of being transformed as the result of new ideals and a new faith; if institutions that have served society, for good or ill, can be overturned with lightning speed by the force of ideas—if all this is possible, then maybe anything is possible. As long as society is capable, in Talleyrand's conception, of being destroyed and reconstructed, then why not reconstruct it as perfect? And thus is born utopian ideology: the perversion of wisdom; the curse of Modernity. If a new faith can be established by vote in a national assembly, why not make it a morally perfect faith? "Which of us would care to descend from the height of the eternal principles we have proclaimed," announced Robespierre in the fall of 1792, after the overthrow of the king and before the institution of the Terror, "to the actual government of Berne, Venice, or Holland? . . . It is not enough, therefore, to have overturned the throne: our concern is to erect upon its remains *holy equality* and the imprescriptible Rights of Man."[8]

Ideological terror results from forcing the notion that there is *no limit* to the changes in institutions that a new faith can bring about. Tocqueville, Hegel, Marx—each in his own way—pointed toward this moral exaggeration as the origin of Terror. I will return to that observation later. Here it remains to catalogue the ways the Values subsumed under the *Rights of Man* effectuated a revolution in French institutions.

EQUALITY BEFORE THE LAW

"Article 6. The law is expression of the general will. . . . It must be the same for all, whether it protects or punishes. All citizens, being equal in its eyes, are equally admissible to all public dignities, positions, and employments, according to their ability, and on the basis of no other distinction than that of their virtues and talents."[9]

The *Declaration of the Rights of Man and of the Citizen,* adopted by the National Assembly in the latter part of August 1789, was preceded by the session of the night of August 4, which destroyed the "feudal regime" in France and by the decrees adopted on August 11, which solidified into law all the modernizing sentiments and actions of that fateful night. A profound difference in the circumstances of the French and the American Revolutions—a fact noted by many in France at the time—was that the French Revolution had to overthrow, destroy, and replace with some other form of authority an entrenched class of nobles. The Americans were blessed in having inherited no such problem. Aristocracy, and the privileges its members enjoyed, was an *institutional* arrangement that had to be transcended if Modernity was to be achieved. During its heyday, aristocracy and aristocratic privilege were supported by a system of Mores that almost completely certified such an arrangement as legitimate and of value for society. By the time of the Revolution those aristocratic Values were almost completely eroded. A revolutionary explosion, a fundamental and radical change in Institutions took place, literally, overnight. And within a week, such revolutionary changes were matters of law. That night "marks the moment when a judicial and social order, forged over centuries, composed of a hierarchy of separate orders, corps, and communities, and defined by privileges, somehow *evaporated,* leaving in its place a social world conceived in a new way as a collection of free and equal individuals subject to the universal authority of law."[10]

Even though the decrees passed on August 11 are dramatically prefaced by the statement: "The National Assembly entirely destroys the feudal regime,"[11] it was not feudalism, as we understand the term, that was demolished but the seigneurial regime. Feudalism was a societal system wherein there were multiple centers of power, each governed by a legitimate petty or grand tyrant who enjoyed noble status. Kings, with greater or lesser power, also existed, and the relationship of the monarch to these localized centers of power was very complex and ambiguous, as was that of greater and lesser lords to each other. Whether feudal France should be described as one society or several hundred is an open sociological question. It was the Early Modern stage of society that swept away the feudal regime and put centralized monarchy and the ideal of one nation in its place. Many remnants of the local power and privilege of the lord remained, however, and it was these that were finally abolished the night of August 4. These remnants and survivals of feudal days were acknowledged as violating the ideal of equal rights for all men, and modern usage has, more accurately, described them as a seigneurial, rather than a feudal, system, since it was the rights and privileges of the local seigneur that were done away with.

In that eight-day period:

ABOLISHED WITHOUT COMPENSATION: (1) All remnants of personal servitude; all traces of the old serfdom. (2) Any form of seigneurial courts or justice. (3) All rights reserved to nobles for hunting, for fishing in certain areas, for the raising of pigeons and maintenance of dovecotes. (4) All compulsory uses of the lord's mill or well. (5) All private toll houses. (6) All rights to lay claim to common woods. (7) All unequal or nonrational charges on land or labor that existed under the old regime, such as inequitable demands of corvee labor. (8) All "feudal" privileges such as the *droit d'indire*, wherein quit-rents were doubled during the year a lord's daughter was married.

DONE AWAY WITH: (1) All special privileges granted by the king to cities, provinces, or ecclesiastical benefices. (2) Fees for justice in the courts. (3) All privileges and allowances in regard to the payment of taxes. (4) Any sale of offices.

PROCLAIMED: All citizens, regardless of birth, are to be admitted to all church, civil, and military employments.

It was a remarkable achievement, accomplished in the atmosphere of almost religious revival and conversion. In the future, moreover, rather than regretting what had been done under the influence of enthusiasm, and going back on it, the Revolution pushed increasingly forward. The division into three Orders of Nobility, Clergy, and Third Estate was abolished in November 1798. In March 1790, primogeniture was abolished. In June of that year all titles were abrogated. And of extraordinary importance, Parlements, which were courts of justice privileged to nobility and monied elites, were disestablished in September of 1790, as was every privilege in regard to judicial procedures. In the future, all citizens would enter the system of justice "sans distinctions . . . en la même forme at devant les mêmes juges dans les mêmes cas."[12]

The swelling tide of demand for legal reform that was evident, but mostly ineffectual, in the old regime was institutionalized during the Revolution with astonishing speed. Chrétien de Lamoignon was appointed head of the judiciary in 1788. His attempts at reform of the system met the predictable resistance from the magistrates, since they would have resulted in the most thorough reform of government in the century. In a few months, however, the Brienne-Lamoignon ministry fell and the reforming spirit was suspended. The moral, modernizing impulse within the culture did not disappear, however: "Little did any minister or magistrate at the time imagine how drastic an overhaul of the judicial system would be accomplished a mere three years later when the Constituent Assembly voted into effect a new code of criminal justice that would have been any eighteenth-century reformer's dream."[13]

The crucial thing for the future of France was that, despite the many ambivalences, compromises, and regressions in the years ahead, the power of Modernity was not to be denied. There was no going back to the old regime. Isser Woloch's book on *The New Regime* demonstrates with unarguable conviction how lasting were many of the reforms institutionalized by the Revolution.[14] "The decrees of August 4 to August 11," writes Furet, "number among the founding texts of modern France. They destroyed aristocratic society from top to bottom, along with its structure of dependencies and privileges. For this structure they substituted the modern, autonomous individual, free to do what ever was not prohibited by law."[15]

All of this, it must be noted, before there were any Jacobins or sans-culottes or *enragés* or Terror or guillotine or the people-in-the-streets of Paris changing the direction of the Revolution at crucial times. That kind of political violence was obviously unnecessary for this first great enlightenment-liberal Revolution.

ENHANCING THE RIGHTS OF THE ACCUSED

"Article 7. No man may be accused, arrested, or detained except in cases determined by the law and according to the forms it has prescribed. Those who solicit, expedite, execute, or effect the execution of arbitrary orders must be punished."

"Article 9. Every man is presumed innocent until he has been found guilty; if it is considered indispensable to arrest him, any severity not necessary to secure his person must be strictly repressed by law."[16]

With regard to this crucial item of the liberal agenda, we find the same trajectory as has been described for others in this movement of radical reform:

old regime attempts at reform that are mostly unsuccessful but are indicative of
the accelerating movement for a radical change in Values; followed, after the
Revolution, by an almost unimaginable radical change in institutions; concluded,
after all the revolutionary vicissitudes, by a permanent institutionalization of
most of these Values within French culture.

The establishment of the rights of the accused as part of universal sacred
rights followed exactly that progression. Tocqueville's analysis of the *cahiers* of
the nobility, as has already been cited, provides support that the old regime had
clearly pointed the way toward judicial reform. State prisons and other nonlegal
places of detention should be abolished, the *cahiers* announced, and the conditions
under which prisoners are kept should be greatly ameliorated.[17] For thirty years
before the Revolution the movement for criminal-law reform was accelerating.
Between 1760 and 1789, no less than 108 books on criminal law were submitted for censor approval, the number growing as each year passed.[18] And Robespierre, who began political life as a great son of the Enlightenment and
understood its message as deeply as anyone ever had, could announce in December 1789 that "It were better that a hundred guilty men be pardoned, than
that a single innocent person should be punished."[19] Most everything that was
happening within French culture was indicative of the fact that the demand for
a modern view of criminal justice was not to be denied.

Almost immediately, the Revolution saw to it. Within a few months of its
founding the National Assembly created a committee on reform of the criminal
law. Already by October 1789 the committee had established that, whereas in
the past the accused was assumed to be guilty, exactly the opposite view would
now prevail. Exact limits were set within which arrests were to be made and
citizens tried. In 1790 the two most far-reaching reforms were instituted. In the
old regime prisoners were tried by judges; there were no trials by jury. Trials
were not conducted in public. Henceforth, public trials were necessary and juries
of twelve citizens taken from a list of two hundred would decide the guilt or
innocence of the accused. The defendant now had the right to counsel, which
had been specifically denied by ordinance in 1670, under the rationalization that
the presence of lawyers would make it harder to arrive at the truth. And finally,
in the penal code of September 1791, it was decreed that punishment of the
convicted should be proportionate to the crime committed. All forms of torture,
which had been used primarily to obtain confessions or evidence against a defendant, were abolished.[20]

It was an extraordinary achievement, as morally significant as anything human beings had ever done, and would have created a shocked sense of disbelief in the reformers of the 1770s and 1780s if they had been told that, within ten or fifteen years, such a program would become a reality. For Robespierre, our beacon of light, it did not go far enough. The question arose as to whether the vote of guilty in the juries should be unanimous or only by a majority of seven:

> The Committee proposed majority verdicts: Robespierre, not that he had any knowledge of, or respect for English procedure, but because he had been impressed by a case quoted in his *Eloge de Dupaty*, in which the vote of one judge had prevented a serious miscarriage of justice, preferred the Anglo-American requirement of unanimity. A minority, he said, remembering Rousseau, may be right or wrong, but unanimity is a sacrament of the general will. . . . If it were only to save one innocent life in a century, such a rule would still be worth having. But he did not persuade the House.[21]

To repeat the line of thought being developed here, what is so significant for the ultimate triumph of Modernity is the continuity of these reforming institutions. In the "New Regime" that followed the extreme vicissitudes of the Revolution, trial by jury, the right to defense counsel, public trial—despite certain abberations in certain exceptional cases—these institutional reforms endured.[22]

CRUEL AND UNUSUAL PUNISHMENT—THE DEATH PENALTY

The penal code of 1791 outlawed all forms of torture, specifically including the pillory and red-hot irons. Here again, the old regime had made significant steps toward reform. In 1789, the *question préparatoire*—pretrial torture to obtain a confession—and in 1788, the routinely administered torture of a convicted criminal in order to elicit from him the names of his accomplices (the *question préable*) were abrogated.[23]

Descriptively, that narrative follows the general lines of the institutionalization of the liberal-enlightenment agenda. Of much greater ambiguity and lack of unanimity is the question of the legitimacy of capital punishment. Here again, on the moral frontier of the Revolution, questions were raised that have resisted a final resolution down to this moment. And the introduction of the question of capital punishment immediately brings us to the thought and profound moral perception of Robespierre and his transmigration from moral genius of enlightenment thought to paranoid terrorist. His descent into hysterical killing and the descent of the Revolution into cannibalistic Terror are parallel narratives. Rightly understood, they may each shed light on the other.

What is remarkable in the story of the descent of Robespierre is that he *became* a terrorist. Unlike Marat, for instance, whom one feels was born to terrorism and required no deterioration, but only power, to find himself in that place. And "moral genius" is no exaggeration. He had a profound, compassionate concern for the disadvantaged in society: the poor, the unjustly accused, the unnecessarily and exaggeratedly punished guilty. His intellectual brilliance allowed him to perceive what in the future would be the great moral ambiguities and problematics within liberal society: that the poor would continue to suffer; that a tyranny of money would replace the tyranny of birth; that immersion in warfare would bring the political despotism of generals; that capital punishment was a form of human sacrifice that even liberal-enlightenment society was terrified to abandon and that would corrupt its moral nature.

In what follows, I intend to quote from Robespierre at length, not out of some stylistic indolence, but because it is important to observe that he was a great rhetorician. That capacity, moreover, in the early years never degenerated into pure rhetoric, as was the case with most revolutionary speeches. With Robespierre, except at the very end when he succumbed to hysterical paranoid raving, the rhetoric was in the service of the moral faculty, giving evidence and making use of a passionate depth of feeling. His descent into terrorism, in fact, can be clearly traced by means of an analysis of the speeches. Gradually, but persistently, the moral rhetoric grows less and less important and the hysterical paranoia larger and larger. In the early years, in the argument over the death penalty, he was at his finest.

Robespierre's first significant struggle against cruel and unnecessary punishment took place in the summer of 1790. The Assembly was debating the question of exactly what kind of punishment could be inflicted on the guilty. The majority of the delegates favored a two-tiered structure with a greater and lesser severity, the more severe reserved for that which officers in the army could inflict on soldiers. This last, which was designated *peines de discipline*, was distinguished from *peines afflictives*, which could be imposed only by a *conseil de justice*. Robespierre argued vehemently against the preservation of *peines de discipline*, even though it was a mode of punishment completely acceptable at the time in England as well as France. He lost the argument. The final decree allowed both forms to continue and compromised to the extent that the death penalty could be imposed only by a *conseil de justice*. Robespierre was vindicated not long afterward. The severity of the punishments caused mutinies in the ranks; the decree permitting them was rescinded two months after its adoption.[24]

The great speech on capital punishment was delivered on May 30, 1791. "I have come to beg the legislators to efface from our penal code the bloody laws that sanction judicial murder, laws which are repugnant to the Frenchman's way of life and to their new constitution."[25] He continues:

> Je veux leur prouver: 1° que le peine de mort est esentiellment injust; 2° qu'elle n'est pas la plus réprimante des peines, et qu'elle multiplie les crimes beaucoup plus qu'elle ne les prévint.[26]

> [I wish to prove to them: first, that the penalty of death is fundamentally unjust; second, that it is not the most restraining of penalties, and that it multiplies crimes more than it prevents them.]

> Ainsi, aux yeux de la vérité et de la justice, ces scenes de mort qu'elle ordonne avec tant d'appareil ne sont autre chose que lâches assassinats, que des crimes solennels, commis, no par des individus mais par des nations entières, avec des formes légales.[27]

> [Thus, in the eyes of truth and of justice, these scenes of death that society orders with so much ceremony are nothing else but cowardly assassinations, nothing but solemn crimes, committed, not by some individuals but by entire nations, with due legal formalities.]

Not only does capital punishment fail to prevent future crimes; not only does it perpetuate injustice; but most important of all, its persistence degrades and corrupts the commonwealth. In the two hundred years since this speech, no more profound arguments have been raised in favor of abrogating this unconscious example of primitive revenge.

> Partout, où elles offensent l'humanité par un excès de rigueur, c'est une preuve que la dignité de l'homme n'y est pas connue, que celle du citoyen n'exist pas; c'est une preuve que le législature n'est qu'un maître qui commande á des esclaves, et qui les châtie impitoyablement suivant sa fantasie. Je conclus à ce que la peine de mort soit abrogée.[28]

> (Above all, where they offend humanity by an excess of rigor, it is proof that human dignity is there unknown, that the dignity of the citizen does not exist; it is proof that the legislature is only a master commanding its slaves, punishing

them pitilessly according to its own whim. I conclude that the penalty of death must be abolished.)

When one considers what Robespierre will become capable of in 1793–1794, it is almost unbelievably tragically ironic that, even when the 1791 debate came down to preserving the death penalty in only one circumstance—when "a party leader was declared a rebel by decree of the Legislative Body"—he remained adamant in his opposition. He proceeded to quote all kinds of examples from Greece, Rome, Russia, even Japan to demonstrate that capital punishment was ineffective and degrading.[29]

The slope, most deplorably, however, was downward. The first breach, which would eventually produce a flood, came with the question of executing the king after his deposition in August 1792. In January of '93, after Louis's guilt had been voted, the motion to have him guillotined was passed by a very small margin. Robespierre, however, had already in early December '92 made his position clear:

> For my part, I detest the death penalty that your law prescribes so freely; in the assembly that you still call "Constituent" I moved for its abolition; and it was not my fault if that assembly regarded the first principles of reason as moral and political heresies. But now you propose to set aside the death penalty in the case of the one man whose death could justify it. I agree, the death penalty is, in general, a crime; and that, for the very reason that it can be justified only where it is politic. But where you have a dethroned king at the heart of a revolution which is entirely held together by just laws—a king whose very name brings the scourge of civil war upon a distracted nation; in such an event neither imprisonment nor exile can prevent his presence affecting the public welfare; and if justice, in his case, admits this cruel exception to the ordinary law, it is simply the punishment of his crimes. Such is the fated conclusion which, however much I regret it, I cannot avoid. Because *la patrie* must live, Louis must die.[30]

One can hardly imagine a more passionate, a more profound, justification for human sacrifice than this last sentence: throughout history, all human sacrifice was instituted in order to sustain the living.

Once it was agreed that the health of the commonwealth required the death of its enemies, it was only a short distance to this article of faith pronounced by Robespierre as the Terror accelerated: "To good citizens revolutionary government owes the full protection of the State; to the enemies of the people it owes only death."[31] And far be it from a great moralist to deny people what they are owed.

Who can fathom this prodigious catastrophe? Both in its personal and its social dimensions? Something deep in the nature of the life demanded by enlightenment-liberal-modern values proves unbearable, and panic-anxiety creates and sustains the killing-defense.

FREEDOM OF OPINION AND OF RELIGIOUS BELIEF

At the end of December 1788, almost five months before the meeting of the Estates General, a remarkable document was published that indicated, in no uncertain terms, how far the revolution before the revolution had gone in France. It was composed neither by some member or leader of the reform wing of the clergy or aristocracy nor by some third-estate firebrand, a future Jacobin, but by the most important and most well-known minister in the king's council: Jacques Necker, the minister of finances. It was entitled, innocently enough, *Rapport fait au roi dans son conseil par le ministre de ses finances* and was the result of a fierce controversy that was raging within the group of the king's advisers as to how to respond to the threatening political upheaval created by the calling of the Estates General, a protolegislative body that had not met since 1614.

The question that the king and his council had to decide in December was whether or not the number of representatives to the third estate was to be doubled from the traditional number of 250, thereby giving them 500 members, which number would equal the combined total of 250 clergy and 250 nobles. Eventually, before the elections were held, the numbers were raised to 300 and 600. The king's council did not pronounce on the question of whether the three estates should be combined into one legislative body and votes taken by head—which measure would give tremendous power to a doubled third estate—but everyone in France knew that this question could come up once the Estates General met.

The final decision of the council, *Résultat du conseil d'etat du roi*, decreed on December 17, was a compromise between the reforming and the reactionary factions of the king's advisers. The number of third-estate delegates was doubled to 600; no mention, however, was made of voting by head. The discussion had been intense and predictions of future chaos dire. On December 12, five princes of the blood had memorialized the king, with a remarkable prescience generated out of fear:

> The unhappy progress of this effervescence is such that opinions, which a little while ago would have appeared the most reprehensible, appear today just and reasonable. What today makes respectable people indignant will in a little while perhaps be accepted as regular and legitimate. Who can say where this temerity will end? The rights of the throne have been called in question; the rights of the privileged orders are subjects of popular debate; soon the rights of property will be attacked; the inequality of fortunes will be presented as an object of reform; already the proposition has been made to abolish feudal rights on the ground that these rights are oppressive and barbarous.[32]

Necker, of course, was of the opposite view and of the opposite camp. When the *Résultat du conseil* was published, for reasons unknown, it lacked the customary preamble with which such reports traditionally began. In place of such a preamble Necker attached to the *Résultat du conseil* a revised version of a memorial that he had presented to the king as a basis for discussion in the conferences of the ministers. He entitled it *Rapport fait au roi dans son conseil par le ministre de ses finances.* It could have been written by Sieyè or Mirabeau or Talleyrand or any of those radicals who were to make the first Revolution of '89.

"You have frequently said, Sire, to the ministers who are honored with your confidence, that you propose to limit your prerogatives: (1) By restoring to the nation the right to consent to all taxes; (2) By consenting to periodical meetings of the Estates General; (3) By acknowledging that the Estates General alone have the right to appropriate the public moneys; (4) By submitting to the Estates General the question of restricting the use of *lettres de chachet;* (5) *By submitting to the Estates General the question of granting or restricting the liberty of the press* [italics added]; (6) By establishing provincial assemblies subordinate to the Estates General."

The esteemed historian of the Revolution, Aulard, has commented that such a program, " 'was not a simple reform; it was a revolution. . . . It was indeed the parliamentary regime that Necker was making Louis XVI accept.' "[33] One cannot help but wonder whether, if more of the Enlightenment had been internalized by Louis, there might have been no Bastille (the attack against which was triggered by Louis's dismissal of Necker), no guillotine, no Terror.

Returning specifically to the subjects of this section, freedom of opinion and of religion, once again we observe the inexorable continuity of liberal-enlightenment Values. It has already been observed that 60 percent of the noble *cahiers* demanded freedom of opinion. The *Declaration of Rights* of August was insistent: "Article 11. The free expression of thought and opinions is one of the most precious rights of man: thus every citizen may freely speak, write, and print, subject to accountability for abuse of this freedom in the cases determined by law."[34] And the preamble to the 1791 Constitution guarantees: "Liberty to every man to speak, write, print, and publish his opinions without having his writings subject to any censorship or inspection before their publication, and to worship as he pleases."[35]

The demand for freedom of public opinion was concomitant with the rise of public opinion itself, a primarily eighteenth-century phenomenon. In 1770 three times as many books were published as were in 1701. The number of news-papers, in this same period, went from three to several hundred. A myriad of pamphlets appeared after 1750.[36] It was a veritable explosion of attempts of future citizens to communicate with each other. Keith Baker has documented in great detail this "invention" of public opinion as a political act.[37] And David Bell has demonstrated how "even a nobleman imprisoned by royal order sought release not by asking for the help of a powerful patron, but by launching an appeal in print. . . . the 'politics of privilege' was now losing ground to the 'politics of opinion.' "[38] It is obvious that the system of Values in France in 1789 was radically different from what it had been in 1700. The *Declaration of the Rights of Man* of August '89 was the climax of a social evolution that had developed for a century—or even more.

It is of interest to ask ourselves the speculative question: What were the causes of this "revolution before the revolution?" Without an attempt to answer, nonetheless, one observation is worth making. If we would ask the exact question of America in the eighteenth century, we would immediately come up with entirely different explanations than those one might offer for France. Why was the primary document of the American Revolution a declaration of universal rights of all men "endowed by their creator?" Why was the new constitution unadoptable until amended to include an elaborate specification of rights? First, we might say, it was a Protestant country and Calvinist in one crucial area. There is a complex and intimate relationship between the rise of modern democracy and Calvinism (which most pointedly includes Puritanism): England, Geneva, the Netherlands, America.[39] Second, one would point out the obvious connection with England, which had moved significantly in the direction of modern democracy. And then there was all that experience with democracy on the individual colony level, including state constitutions. So obvious does the answer appear, at first glance, that one feels no particular necessity to ask why the Americans were so interested in rights at the time of their revolution.

None of this was true of France: no Protestantism, no English connection, no democracy on the local level or individual constitutions. "The Enlightenment" is the quick and easy answer, but why did the Enlightenment arise in a Catholic, monarchical country permeated with "feudal" survivals and suffused with aristo-cratic values? We know today that the old Marxist explanation of the rise of capitalism and the bourgeoisie is a theoretical fantasy. Having set aside that simplistic and erroneous explanation, we remain left with the great question of the origins of this revolution before the revolution. In the last twenty-five years the historians of the *ancien régime* have added tremendously to our knowledge of the eighteenth century. That work has been almost exclusively descriptive, not analytical: answering the question "What?" The fundamental analytical question "Why?" remains.

✳   ✳   ✳

The claim of Modernity is that no individual should be denied the full benefits of citizenship because of his religious orientation. Premodern France was replete with religious discrimination. Only Catholics could enjoy a full participation in society. Protestants, with a few exceptions, and a much smaller number of Jews, could become only second-class members of the commonwealth. The Revolu-tion put an end to this premodern paranoid definition of citizen. Here, once more, the first attempts were made in the years immediately preceding the Revo-lution, leading to the 1789 *Declaration of Rights* announcement of full equality. The great reforming ministry of Brienne-Lamoignon of 1787, which enjoyed only a short life, had granted limited civil status to Protestants,[40] and Article 10 of the *Declaration* stated that "No one must be disturbed because of his opinions, even in religious matters."[41]

When it came time for the National Assembly to enact legislation to institu-tionalize this full equality, Protestants presented no problem, but on the Jewish question there was no unanimity. During 1790 and 1791 the debate continued on the question of full rights for *all* Jews. Robespierre, as we have come to expect, in these early years was passionate on the subject of equality. "How can you blame the Jews," he proclaimed in '91, "for all the persecutions they have suffered in certain countries? These are, on the contrary, national crimes that we must expiate by restoring them their imprescriptible rights of man of which no human authority can deprive them. . . . Let us give them back their happiness, their country and their virtue by restoring their dignity as men and citizens."[42]

The problem with the Jews was that there were two kinds of Jews in France. Those of the south and the west lived in long-assimilated Sephardic Jewish communities. Many of them were descendants of Spanish Jews who had left Spain centuries before, fleeing persecution. Many were successful in commerce, enjoying the benefits of enlightenment culture. In a word, a modern people. In Alsace, however, resided the majority of French Jews who were of Ashkenazi background and had immigrated from eastern regions. These Jews remained unassimilated: they did not look like, think like, or talk like Frenchmen. It was easy to argue that they did not belong in modern France. In the debate in the Assembly, the representatives from Alsace adamantly argued against granting full citizen rights, most especially the franchise, to this alien people. At first, the Assembly voted a remarkable split: for the elections of 1790 and 1791, the Sephardic Jews were enfranchised and the Jews of Alsace excluded from voting. Before it was dissolved in 1791, however, the enlightened principles of Modernity won out and full citizen rights were granted to all Jews, even those "gypsie Jews" of Alsace.[43]

The main opposition to the granting of full freedom of religion resided, naturally enough, within the Catholic Church. The Church's opposition, though not strong enough to prevent the enfranchisement of Protestants and Jews, added strength to the formidable impulse to disestablish the Church and completely secularize society. To extend tolerance to Protestants and Jews, to create a secular society, required breaking a powerful attachment to the Church. When people feel the need to abolish a potent attachment and are yet ambivalent about the prospect, since all attachments are precious and painful to give up—when all this is true, one thing that happens is that the separation may be accomplished in an exaggerated way with a quantum leap of aggression. A little bit of separation, a little bit of violent withdrawal, doesn't seem to work. The result is an exaggerated, overreaching, violent separation that many times severely injures both parties more than seems necessary. Exactly that happened to the Revolution in its relationship to the Church. Turning on the Church with exaggerated violence was one of the greatest mistakes that the revolutionaries made. We will look at that in greater detail when it comes time to discuss secularization of society. Here the point being made is that it is important to understand that the institutionalization of the liberal-enlightenment agenda, in particular freedom of religious belief, as rational and as moral as that action seems to be, may be fraught with deep conflict, anxiety, and defensive violence.

SLAVERY AND THE SLAVE TRADE

Once we understand that there was a powerful and compelling moral thrust in the evolution toward Modernity, we will not be surprised to discover that two of the things that came under attack by revolutionaries were slavery and the slave trade. This observation has great theoretical significance. What, after all, did slavery in the colonies have to do with the sovereignty of the people, the attack on absolute monarchy and aristocracy, freedom of the press and of religion, or the question of getting enough food for the people of Paris? Essentially, it had nothing to do with all the great problems of the Revolution. And yet, it became part of revolutionary concern and legislative action. It did so because the moral impulse in the modern project insisted that it was time to establish a new view of what it meant to be human. No human being should be subject to that particular form of degradation. Practically speaking, there was no slavery within European France, but in the colonies of the West Indies, there were a tremendous number of plantation slaves. The men who made the French Revolutions of '89, '92, and '93 ultimately abolished that involuntary servitude, and it was only the Napoleonic reaction that reinstituted slavery in the colonies.

The abolitionist movement demonstrates, like so much else, that the intellectual and moral ferment in the few years before the Revolution had explosive force. True, the *Weltanschauung* of the Enlightenment had begun the attack on slavery and the slave trade years before. Montesquieu, Rousseau, Diderot, and Voltaire all eloquently questioned and denounced the legitimacy of one or both of these institutions. It was, however, on the eve of the Revolution that abolition took on the character of a movement. In November 1787, Jacques Pierre Brissot—destined to become one of the great political leaders of the Revolution and the nominal head of the Girondin faction in the Convention—was in London and contacted the newly established English committee committed to abolishing the slave trade, which had been formed by Wilberfore, Granville Sharp, and others. It was decided that Brissot should form an identical society in France, and on his return to Paris, along with a group that included Condorcet, Lafayette, and Mirabeau, the *Societé des Amis des Noirs* was established. After the Revolution of '89, certain members of the Society who had their political differences with Brissot and his allies withdrew from the Society, but its power was enhanced by the new membership of delegates to the Constituent and Legislative Assemblies, some of whom were destined to play crucial roles in revolutionary history: Pétion, Buzot, Grégoire, Vergniaud, Gaudet, and Gensonné. Whatever lists of members of the original society that we possess indicate that they were mostly recruited from "high French society."[44]

The *Société* was conservative in its aims. It endeavored to put an end to the slave trade and, in the Constituent and Legislative Assemblies, strove to establish and protect the political rights of free people of color in the West Indies against the attack by white colonists. The complete abolition of slavery it did not imagine except as something for the future. Brissot and his Girondist allies were a powerful force in the Legislative Assembly (October 1791–September 1792), and when a Girondist ministry was installed in the spring of '92, one of its first acts was to proclaim the equality of political rights for all free men of color in the colonies. The slave trade, however, was not abrogated.[45]

It was only the third and most radical of the Revolutions (the Jacobin of June '93 to July '94) that was passionate enough on this issue to risk the abolition of slavery itself. That kind of moral rage, of which the Girondins were incapable, was of an essential nature for Robespierre. Already in 1791, he had declared: " 'Let the colonies perish,' rather than slavery continue. Slaves were not property. 'Ask this merchant of human flesh what is property. He will tell you, pointing to this long coffin that he calls a ship, in which are locked and chained men who appear to be alive, "Here is my property. I bought them at so much a head." ' "[46]

In France, unlike in America, people with John Brown's passion and rage were not just outlaws to be executed but, for a brief moment, were in control of the state. They could send their former friends and allies to the guillotine seemingly without the slightest remorse, and yet on the fourth of February 1794, slavery was abolished without compensation in France and all its colonies. "It was the first time that such a measure was taken by a slave-owning society."[47] By the time this world-transforming decree was approved, those who had begun the antislavery movement found themselves in a strange world: Lafayette had abandoned the Revolution and gone over to the enemy; Brissot and Vergniaud had been guillotined; and Condorcet, having fled Paris to avoid execution, was to die in prison within two months. Of such a nature was the moral splitting the Revolution was capable of in the midst of its Terror.

The proclamation of the end of slavery was greeted by tremendous applause in the Convention. Paris responded to the occasion with a great public procession to Notre Dame. The people carried on their shoulders numerous citizens of color—in triumph.[48] The end of the Jacobin dictatorship brought the end of the Terror, but ultimately it brought back slavery to the colonies. In May 1802, a law of Napoleon not only reestablished slavery in the colonies but reaffirmed second-class citizenship of free men of color in these territories.[49] The tragic irony in revolutionary history continued to play itself out.

4

ONE REVOLUTION OR THREE?

On May 4, 1789, the Estates General convened at Versailles. The number of deputies to the Third Estate numbered 600: twice the traditional number and equal to those of the Clergy and Nobility combined. No official decree had permitted the three Estates to meet and vote as one body, which act would have given the Third Estate enormous power and radically moved the Estates General in the direction of becoming a national assembly of all the French people. From the very beginning, the Third Estate was almost unanimous in its desire that such a revolutionary act should be accomplished. Hopefully, with the consent and blessing of the king. Reluctantly, but persistently, even without his approval. The king would not give in. The Third Estate forced him to do so. That was the first great act of the French Revolution.

From May 4 to June 17 the Third Estate was unsuccessful in its efforts to get the other two Estates to join it in one assembly. Regardless, it pushed on, insisting that it would not constitute itself as merely one of three equal legislative bodies. On June 17 it designated itself the National Assembly, implying that it spoke for all of France, and thereby asserting the ultimate sovereignty of the people as the legitimate political power in the nation.

On June 20, the Third Estate returned to its usual place of assembly to find the doors locked, obviously at the orders of the king or his ministers. Finding a neighboring tennis court unoccupied, the deputies assembled there and passed the following resolution *with only one dissenting vote:*

"The National Assembly, considering that since it has been called to decide the constitution of the realm, to achieve the regeneration of public order, and to maintain the true principles of the monarchy, nothing can prevent it from continuing its deliberations in whatever place it may be forced to establish itself, and that wherever indeed its members are assembled, there is the National Assembly;

"Resolves that all the members of this assembly shall immediately take a solemn oath never to separate, and to reassemble whenever the circumstances demand, until the constitution of the realm has been established and secured on solid foundations; and that, the said oath having been taken, all its members, each individually, shall confirm by their signatures this unshakeable resolution."

The report of the events of that day announces: "The declaration having been read, the president asks, on his own behalf and on that of the secretaries, to take the oath first, which they immediately do; the assembly then takes the same oath between the hands of the president."[1]

Who were these determined and courageous revolutionaries? The elite of French bourgeois, non-noble society. Among the deputies, there were no peasants and no artisans. Merchants, manufacturers, above all lawyers and officeholders of all kinds made this 1789 revolution.[2] Though it is true that the Third Estate's revolution was ultimately made secure against the military force of the king when the people of Paris overthrew the Bastille in July, this revolution was made entirely without them.

Was this the First French Revolution or was it only the first significant stage in The French Revolution? And why might it be important to make such a distinction?

On October 6, 1789 the people of Paris, mostly women, forced the king to leave his palace at Versailles and take up permanent residence in the Tuilleries Palace at Paris, with his family. He lived there for almost three years as a semi-prisoner. The National Assembly not only did not protest this action, it made no attempt to bring the king back, and moved its own scene of deliberations to Paris as well. After more than three years of a failed attempt to establish a stable constitutional monarchy, many Frenchmen, possibly most Frenchmen, and certainly a majority of those still politically active, had had enough of the king. No legal action to end the monarchy was taken, however, until after the day of August 10, 1792. On that occasion, the people-in-the-streets of Paris invaded the Tuilleries, captured the king, and made him prisoner. All of which had absolutely no legal sanction. The people in the rest of France were not consulted. That same day the rump of the national Legislative Assembly agreed to call a National Convention to write a new constitution for France and to decide the fate of the king. On

September 22 the new Convention declared the monarchy ended and France a Republic.

Was all this just another logical extension of THE French Revolution, or should it be more accurately described as a SECOND Revolution? Did the same kind of people—the same class of people—as those who took the Tennis Court Oath in June 1789 accomplish this overthrow of the monarchy? If one seeks for the "origins" of the French Revolution, or the "causes" of the Revolution, would one come up with the same answers for June 1789 and August 1792?

> The Convention elected in September 1792 could never succeed in compre-
> hending the true nature of democratic citizenship. The two primary factions—
> Girondins, led by Brissot and others, and the Jacobins, the dominate person being
> Robespierre—were at each other's throats from the start. No democratic resolu-
> tion of differences, no developed concept of a loyal opposition, seemed possible.
> The Jacobins had the people-in-the-streets of Paris as their allies. The Girondins
> had no equivalent power. "At the Jacobins on 26 May [1793] Robespierre 'invited
> the people' to rise up against the Convention's 'corrupt deputies' and declared
> himself in insurrection against them."[3] Seven days later the Paris Commune and
> people from the Parisian political Sections surrounded the Convention with five
> thousand national guardsmen and forced it to expel twenty-nine "perfidious"
> Girondin deputies.[4] This *coup d'état* put an end to democratic government and
> paved the way for the Jacobin dictatorship and, eventually, the great Terror.

To ask the, by now, obvious question: Were the historical and sociological causes of these last events the same as produced the *Declaration of the Rights of Man* in 1789? Is our theoretical task that of explaining the occurrence of one revolution or three different ones?

✻   ✻   ✻

The observation that has led me to ask with such urgency the question: One Revolution or three? is that we do something with French revolutionary history that we never, or almost never, do with Russian revolutionary history. We write books entitled *The Oxford History of the French Revolution*[5] and publish *A Critical Dictionary of the French Revolution.*[6] In such works we expect to find discussion of historical events and ideas all the way from the late *ancien régime* to the fall of Robespierre on the 9th of Thermidor, and we feel no contradiction in the fact that both the *Declaration of the Rights of Man* and guillotine cannibalism are parts of the history of THE Revolution. With Russian history, on the contrary, if we were to pick up a book titled *The Oxford History of the Russian Revolution*, we would be slightly jolted and would immediately ask: 1905 or February/March 1917 or October/November 1917? Democrats or Bolsheviks? Kerensky or Lenin? Nobody calls the successes of Kerensky and Lenin THE Russian Revolution. Why, then, do we do it with France when the Jacobin dictatorship and Terror are as far from the Tennis Court Oath as Lenin's coup d'état and revolution are from the overthrow of the Tsar?

For intellectuals there is something enormously seductive—and, therefore, destructive—in the dream of revolution. Even Hegel, considered by some ultimately a Prussian reactionary, could not resist this vision. We are told that every year of his life he celebrated the anniversary of the Fall of the Bastille,[7] symbol for him of the world-historical importance of the Revolution. But why, we may ask, did he choose that event rather than the Tennis Court Oath or the writing and adoption of the *Declaration of Rights?* Is there something about overthrow, something about the use of violence, something in the mythical notion of total rebirth that feeds this dream of THE revolution? Nadezhda Mandelstam, wife of the great Stalinist-era poet Osip Mandelstam, has written of the seductive power of this revolutionary vision: "My brother Evgeni Yankovlevich used to say that the decisive part in the subjugation of the intelligentsia was played not by terror and bribery (though God knows, there was enough of both), but by the word 'Revolution,' which none of them could bear to give up. It is a word to which whole nations succumbed, and its force was such that one wonders why our rulers still needed prisons and capital punishment."[8]

Liberal, democratic people who have no sympathy for Jacobin terrorism, who have no desire, unlike some other most respectable historians of revolutionary history, to excuse the Terror as a "necessity" to save France, still use the words "the French Revolution" to describe their work. I myself have been caught in that dilemma in regard to the subtitle of this book. At first it was "The French Revolution and the Struggle for Modernity," under which banner I have given several speeches, and everyone assumed we understood what I meant by that title. Writing this chapter, I became discontent with that subtitle and felt it should be changed to "The French revolutions," but that immediately brought the contraindication that people would assume I also meant 1830, 1848, and 1871, especially when the phrase "struggle for Modernity" followed. Clarification could come by elaborating: "The French Revolutions, 1789–1794, and the Struggle for Modernity." But immediately it became apparent that, in becoming theoretically more accurate, some kind of communicative energy with the potential reader was lost. "THE French Revolution" speaks much more directly to people's interest and emotions than "The French Revolutions, 1789–1794" because nobody dreams of revolutions but only of THE REVOLUTION. Evgeni Yankovlevich and his companions would not have been seduced and subjugated by fine theoretical distinctions surrounding the idea of Revolution. Maybe we all entertain, in the Kafkaesque part of our minds, more sympathy with Jacobin terrorism than we would like to admit. Maybe the dream of Revolution, of all-consuming rebirth, has such power because overthrow and killing have an essential share in it.

And, perhaps, that may be the reason why we do with French revolutionary history what we do not do with the Russian: treat it as one continuous narrative. The slaughters of Stalinism are too fresh in our minds. The destruction of humanity decreed and executed by Marxist ideological terror is still ever present today in some part of the world. Jacobins? The guillotine? The fact that "Les dieux ont soif,"* that the Gods are thirsty and are demanding human blood? That's a long way in the past. That's history. We can still play with that terrible dream in our minds without being forced to act out anything.

Significantly, the argument against THE Revolution has been made by many reflective people over the years. Louis Blanc (1811–1882) "argued that the first Revolution belonged to Voltaire and the bourgeoisie; the second to Rousseau and the people."[10] In the middle of this century, Raymond Aron, a brave warrior in the struggle against Marxist ideology, "challenged historians to forsake the 'fatality' implicit in positivism and study 'retrospective probability.' Such a method implies the necessity of escaping from the single homogenous 'revolution' which hypnotised contemporaries. . . . There were many revolutions within the one Revolution, each with its own 'causes,' and there were also 'causes' which explain why all these interlocked."[11] And the English historian Alfred Cobban, writing in the late 1960s, optimistically reports: "There is now general agreement that the picture of the French Revolution as a bloc with one inspiration, though used in the propaganda both of supporters and opponents of 'the Revolution,' is invalid. The historic reality is a series of revolutions, very different in their aims and therefore in any theoretical affiliations they may have had."[12]

Ironically, however, historians—many of whom would probably agree with Aron and Cobban—continue to write books whose titles imply, somewhere, there is still a metanarrative of *the* Revolution: *Penser la Révolution Française* (1978),

---

*A cry of anguish from Camille Desmoulins after the execution of Lavoisier, France's greatest scientist.[9] The expression was used as the title of a book by Anatole France late in the nineteenth century.

Origins of the French Revolution (1980), *Inventing the French Revolution* (1990), *Rewriting the French Revolution* (1991).[13]

No matter how the French may have thought or talked in revolutionary times, they certainly acted as if there was more than one revolution. Various groups and individuals chose to leave the revolutionary tide at various times, indicating that they felt it was no longer *their* revolution. Certain nobles, including the king's brothers, left right at the start: they were opposed to any revolution. Many more, however, were willing to live with the first revolution but not with the second or third. The *monarchiens* left at one point; people like Lafayette and Dumouriez and Constant left at another; the cities of Lyon and Marseille revolted against the Convention at the time of the Jacobin *coup* in May–June '93; the most important civil war spawned by the revolutions, that in the Vendée, did not begin until March '93, almost four years after the Tennis Court Oath. And those like Danton, executed in April '94 and the Girondin deputies who were guillotined after the establishment of the Jacobin dictatorship—all were exterminated out of the path of the third revolution. The radical Jacobins could, obviously, live with Brissot and Danton during the first two revolutions. *Their* revolution, however, demanded unanimity. All of those who left or were executed would have been surprised to be told, we may assume, that what happened was the result of what they did in June–July, 1789.

To repeat what Aron has said, each revolution had its own causes. To look for one set of causes for THE French Revolution is a chimerical pursuit. In essence, if we search for the reasons "Why?" of the Tennis Court Oath, the fall of the Bastille, and the *Rights of Man* will we find the same causes as those for the Jacobin dictatorship and the Terror? And yet our language, reflecting something very complex in our unconscious, pushes us to continue to speculate on THE French Revolution, as if it were a monolithic phenomenon.

What the two previous chapters on the triumph of Liberalism are intended to establish is that there is essentially no great mystery about the cause of the first revolution. There are things to explain and discuss, of course: What would have happened if the king were willing to be an "English King?"; what were the implications of the fact that the legislative body sat in Versailles and then in Paris with no military or other force at its command, or as its ally, except the people-in-the-streets of Paris? The third revolution, however, and its descent into cannibalistic terror *is* a great mystery, and no one has yet come even close to explaining it to us. Tocqueville's "virus of a new and unknown kind"[14] [i.e., ideological terror] did not truly arrive until June '93, though there were hints of its coming during the previous years. It seems more accurate to describe its birth, not as the result of the triumph of Liberalism but of its failure. All the great work that has been done on the *ancien régime* in the last thirty years, referred to in the previous chapters, has made it more and more clear how "inevitable" the first revolution was. It has done practically nothing to explain the Terror, and that has not been its intention. All the profound analysis of the creation of "public space" and the invention of public opinion cannot explain why it became "necessary" to execute Brissot and Danton.

THE FIRST REVOLUTION

After careful consideration of the great thrust of Liberalism during the eighteenth century, the crucial historical-sociological question would seem to be not why the first revolution occurred, but why it could not hold. Why, in essence, was not a stable democratic polity—however limited in suffrage—the outcome of this great tide of Enlightenment thought and revolutionary action? Why did it take France almost a hundred years—some have argued even longer—to achieve a stable, modern democratic society?

That the essential preparation of the work of the first revolution was fulfilled before '89 was emphasized by Chateaubriand when he announced, paradoxically, that the revolution was accomplished before it occurred.[15] And thoughtful English observers, naturally judging by their own experience and expectations of stability, felt that, after the fall of the Bastille, it was all over. "Thus, my Lord," the Duke of Dorset wrote in his dispatch to London on July 16, 1789, "the greatest revolution that we know anything of has been effected with the loss of very few lives: from this moment we may consider France as a free country, the King as a very limited Monarch, and the Nobility as reduced to a level with the rest of the Nation."[16] And Arthur Young, a most perspicacious observer, resident in Paris when the king finally capitulated on June 27, '89, and ordered the clergy and nobility to join the Third Estate in one united National Assembly, wrote: "The whole business now seems over and the revolution complete."[17] Only those passionately opposed to what had happened, such as reactionary nobles at the king's court or a critical observer like Burke, could have imagined the catastrophes to come. But they lacked any conviction that a stable democratic society, based on the sovereignty of the people, was possible, and they would have predicted disaster no matter what the actual circumstances.

There was one significant wrinkle, however, and Young was aware of it: he felt the court would not "sit to have their hands tied behind them,"[18] and he was correct. The king moved up troops, threatening the National Assembly with forceful dissolution. The rising in Paris that ended with the fall of Bastille saved the Third Estate. The people-in-the-streets of Paris, who had not made the liberal-bourgeois revolution, were thusly endowed with inordinate power and, undoubtedly, with feelings of omnipotence. It was they who provided the shock troops for the second and third revolutions. Why, we may still ask, did the liberal-bourgeois elite members of society let the revolution get out of their hands? And what would the outcome have been if the king had not threatened the National Assembly, had been contented to become a constitutional monarch, had formed an alliance with the liberal-enlightenment world to keep the non-elite masses down—as the Directory and Napoleon were subsequently to do after all three revolutions were over? One may only speculate on such a question.

What must be remarked upon is the great coalition that coalesced, first, to inaugurate the first revolution and, second, to legislate so much of the journey into Modernity. The Third Estate, with its one dissenting voice at the Tennis Court, was joined by most of the lower, and several of the higher, clergy and strengthened by an important group of liberal nobles, such as Lafayette, the Duke of Orleans, Mirabeau, Condorcet. Such a powerful coalition should have been more than a match for a vacillating king and for *le peuple*. And yet, by the time the Convention convened in September 1792, after the second revolution, only two great political powers remained in the centralized polity: Girondins and Jacobins, each determined to triumph over the other and assume, in one form or another, sole power. Having had practically no experience in citizenship, neither faction was capable of understanding that a citizen, as Aristotle has said, was capable of both ruling and *being ruled*.

One important consideration in understanding the hesitancy and ambivalence of the bourgeois-liberal elite was the fear that the Revolution would to too far: that it would be pushed beyond the bourgeois-liberal society that the elite imagined and desired. In the summer of 1791, Antoine Barnave cautioned the French: "This revolutionary movement has destroyed all that it set out to destroy, and has brought us to the point where it is necessary to halt . . . one more step towards equality must abolish private property."[19] One productive mode in the attempt to understand the course of the French revolutions is to elaborate on the comparisons with England and America. What was unique to France? Do those exceptionalisms explain the failure of democracy and the Terror? In the comparison with America, many people have pointed out that the Americans were extraordinarily fortunate in not having an entrenched, ancient, "feudal" aristocracy to overthrow. It was equally significant that America did not have to deal extensively with a radicalized and politically active class of people who did not consider themselves bourgeois and did not aspire to its lifestyle and ideals.

Whether *le peuple*, the sans-culottes, the people-in-the-streets of Paris are to be considered a proletariat, a proto-proletariat, or a group of political actors whose class affiliations ran all the way from under-class to masters who employed several journeymen—all this was irrelevant to the bourgeois elite at the time. They had not read their Marx. What they knew is that *le peuple*, or the sans-culottes, had saved the Revolution at the Bastille, had forcibly brought the king from Versaille to Paris in October '89, and had overthrown the monarchy in August '92 and that *enragés*, Hébert and Roux, were agitating the people toward a very different kind of revolution than had yet occurred. In essence, the bourgeois elite had not succeeded in creating a state, in Max Weber's terms, that maintained a monopoly of legitimate force in society. The people-in-the-streets represented a powerful center of force independent of the national legislature, which force the elite legitimized when it moved the National Assembly to Paris *following* the people's transporting the king and proclaimed a Republic *following* the people's deposition of the monarch.

It is no wonder that enlightenment-bourgeois people became alarmed. In America none of this existed. The elite made the revolution and remained in complete control, at least until the age of Jackson, when even that "secondary revolution" was accomplished without great violence. In France, the makers of the first revolution did not have the space and the leisure to create the kind of compromised modern society that would endure, since there was pressure from below and from the left to expand continually revolutionary action.

It took France more than eighty years to resolve its profound ambivalence about monarchy. Between 1789 and 1871 it experimented with more than half a dozen different forms of it before finally abandoning the need, though some have argued that it was not until de Gaulle declined to attempt to make himself the Louis Napoleon of the twentieth century that the French ceased, in biblical terms, to go awhoring after strange gods.

The ideal of the first revolution, held almost unanimously by the revolution's makers, was some form of constitutional monarchy-English style, wherein sovereignty was divided between the king and an assembly elected by restricted male suffrage. "In the idealised Constitution proposed by a number of *cahiers*, everything depended on a harmonious relationship between king and country."[20] The one Third Estate deputy to the Estates General who dissented from the Tennis

Court Oath did so because he felt it challenged the king's authority. Bailly, chairing that auspicious meeting, "tried to reassure him by saying that everyone recognized that all future legislation and the constitution itself would require the royal assent. It seemed obvious enough at that time."[21]

Those courageous deputies who risked imprisonment, or even worse, to make the first revolution, had no intention of extending social and political anxiety by demanding that the Nation live without the psychological reassurance of monarchy. Even Robespierre, two years after Bastille, saw no necessity to go beyond a constitutional monarchy [July 1791]:

> The word republic does not mean any particular form of government. It is applicable to every form of government under which men can enjoy freedom and a fatherland. One may be as free under a king as under a senate. What is the French constitution at the actual moment? It is a republic with a monarch. It is neither a monarchy nor a republic: it is both.[22]

Again, what made it necessary, eighteen months later, that Louis had to die that France might live? The constitutional monarchy established by the Constitution of 1791 was a most reasonable compromise of the various conflicting forces in the society. What was it that prevented reasonable men from maintaining reasonableness?

The task of answering these questions may be assisted by drawing attention to the two great "mistakes" that the authors of the first revolution made. Many times intelligent people make "mistakes" not from an inadequacy of intellectual comprehension but from some internal conflict that pushes them toward irrational action. The first great mistake was the Civil Constitution of the Clergy, compounded by the requisite Oath that all churchmen had to take. The second, the declaration of war against the European powers and the eventual extension of the war into Belgium and the Netherlands, aggressive acts that made it inevitable that England and all its military and naval might would declare war on France. In the struggle for survival, two things the fragile revolution did not need were a first-class war against half of Europe or a disastrous civil war over matters concerning the relationship of the state to the church. And yet, the leaders of the monarchical republic brought both these catastrophes on themselves. It is ironic that a primary excuse made by twentieth-century historians for the dictatorship of the Committee of Public Safety is that it saved France during the terrible trials of external and civil wars. And yet, neither of these wars was "inevitable" or "necessary." It is of great significance that these two tactical errors were committed, not only by the Jacobins and the radical fringe of the first revolution but, most important, by the bourgeois-liberal elite itself.

Later in this work I will discuss in detail these two catastrophic blunders. Here it is important to suggest that their origins may be looked for in the paranoid dimension of French political culture at the time. In a previous work[23] I have argued that the establishment of a stable democratic society is fundamentally dependent on a culture's overcoming the paranoid position. Also, that the paranoid position is fraught with the possibility of self-destructive behavior. In that book it was argued that the Athenian invasion of Sicily near the end of the Peloponnesian War, when Athens was already overextended and on the defensive, was a suicidal act—and that some keen observers in Athens, including Euripides, understood this. Eventually, there is no question that it contributed significantly to Athens' defeat in the war. A most recent similar suicidal decision—one that, fortunately, ended in a benefit for humankind—was Hitler's resolution to invade Russia before England was conquered and at a time when Stalin was making no move to contest the domination of Europe with Germany.

Similarly, it seems reasonable to suggest that the wars declared on the Catholic Church and on Europe certainly had near-suicidal consequences and may have had similar intents. I am advancing the concept that the failure to achieve a stable democratic polity, the subject of the following chapter, was also deeply related to, and a consequence of, the failure to go beyond the paranoid position. It was not just the radical Jacobins and the Terrorists who exhibited and acted out deep paranoid impulses. The liberal-bourgeois-enlightenment creators of the first revolution also could not free themselves from these impulses in the political culture. The failure of the first revolution is directly related to that fact.

The collapse of the first revolution and the demand for the second resulted from the failure of the political culture to establish and maintain a constitutional monarchy wherein the king had any real political power. That these two revolutions were separate and distinct phenomena is underlined by the fact that many of the makers of the first revolution were transformed from supporters to opponents of the Revolution as it became more and more apparent that a constitutional monarchy, along essentially English lines, was not going to be institutionalized. Those who would have been satisfied with this political resolution were either in the minority of those active in national politics or were too busy fighting each other to create a united political force that was capable of saving the king and the Revolution. The radical liberals who prevailed ultimately had no use for the king. "We should have today," wrote Necker in 1795, after Thermidor, "the English government, and an improved version of the English government, if the king, the nobility and the Third Estate, who each desired it at one time or another, could all have wanted it at the same time."[24] Whether such a coalition, even if in existence, would have been able to prevail over radical Jacobins and the people of Paris is still a speculation. And the question remains: Why could not the king, the nobility, and the moderate elements in the Third Estate perceive, and act on, their own best interests?

Almost from the beginning, in the latter half of August 1789, the National Assembly was already clearly divided by issues, conflict over which would eventually produce the second revolution. Specifically, whether there should be one house in the legislative body (the more liberal position) or an additional upper house, obviously to be filled by the ultra-elites (the conservative view); also, whether the king would have an absolute veto over legislation (the conservative position) or merely a suspensive veto that would require two or three successive passages of the same legislation in successive years in order to become law without the king's approval.

In August, the conservatives formed themselves into a protopolitical party. A committee of fifteen constituted the leadership and included some of the foremost makers of the first revolution: Malouet, Mounier, the comte de Lally-Tollendal, and the bishop of Langres, enjoying, also, the support of Lafayette. These *monarchiens*, as they were designated, met in August with the leaders of the more liberal faction: Duport, Lameth, and Barnave in the house of Lafayette in the attempt to work out a compromise that the Assembly would accept. The *monarchiens* seemed to have a majority in the Assembly, from August 17 to September 28 winning every fortnightly election for the presidency in the Assembly. That made them arrogant, and they consequently rejected a remarkably compromising offer by the liberals to accept an upper house, provided it had no veto over legislation, and to agree to an absolute royal veto provided the king could not dissolve the Assembly.

The negotiations were broken off on August 29. The following evening at the Palais Royal, the center of radical activity in Paris, a raucous meeting occurred that proposed marching to Versailles to bring the king back to Paris, obviously as a semiprisoner. More sober heads restrained the firebrands from taking such action.

In the face of this popular hostility the *monarchiens* drew towards the aristocratic Right and after a meeting with some of the leading royalists urged the king to withdraw further from Paris—advice which Louis rejected. The constitutional debate within the Assembly therefore opened somewhat ominously, with the Third Estate divided, the radicals looking to popular forces in Paris to intimidate the Assembly and the *monarchiens* turning towards an aristocracy whose intentions they had good reason to suspect.[25]

The path toward the second revolution was now clearly laid out. In October, the women of Paris accomplished the first stage of that revolution when they translated the king and his family to Paris. The National Assembly could not resist this patently extralegal action and moved the scene of its deliberations to the capital city. No longer would those factions that had every intent of keeping the monarchy alive be able to negotiate the future of France without listening to the voice of the people of Paris. Left-leaning historians who sympathize with the most radical elements of the revolutions refer to the kind of activity like the women's march to Versailles as "direct democracy." One wonders who, within that "democratic" action, had elected the people-in-the-streets to speak for the whole of France.

The conservatives, many of whom were leaders of the first revolution, such as J.J. Mounier, who had sponsored the Tennis Court Oath and the *Declaration of Rights,* got the message and left France. By 1792 a whole group of conservative, not reactionary, émigrés were in touch with each other, outside the French borders, with the obvious hope of returning to a less radical revolutionary France. The group included, in addition to Mounier, Mallet du Pan, P.V. Malouet, and the former archbishops of Aix, Toulouse and Bourdeaux, who belonged to the "more liberal émigré clergy."[26] They certainly must have felt, and could easily have said, what many émigrés have felt in similar circumstances: "I did not leave the Revolution; the Revolution left me." They conceived that their primary obstacle to the restoration of a rational constitutional monarchy was the extreme right, whose failure to undertake any reasonable compromise had forced France to the radical left. "Their trouble was," R.R. Palmer writes, "that, however, intelligent, they had no following."[27] Once a reasonable compromise between conservative and liberal believers in a constitutional monarchy English style became impossible, it was inevitable that the forces even further to the left would attempt the second revolution.

By the time the National Constituent Assembly had completed its work and had given France its first constitution, in September 1791, the first revolution had completed its task. The *ancien régime* had been dismantled. "[The Assembly] had laid down the principles of a new order and established structures whose outlines were to endure down to our own day."[28] And yet, despite this great achievement, it had also prepared the way for future reaction and successive revolutions:

> The seeds of these later extremes were already sown, and the Constituent Assembly was responsible for them, too. By forcing the clergy to choose between Church and State, it had split the country and given counter-revolutionaries a higher cause than self interest. . . . As to the nobles who had done so much to launch the Revolution, most had by now opted out, hiding themselves in royal obscurity or slipping across the Rhine to join the princes. None of this promised well for the Feuillant [constitutional monarchists] dream of post-revolutionary life. The British ambassador's prediction of April 1791 was truer than ever in October: "The present constitution has no friends and cannot last."[29]

The left, which proved remarkably powerful, and which included, at the beginning, not only radical Jacobins and Robespierrists, but also Dantonists, and Girondins, responded to this volatile situation by pushing more and more extreme measures: radical punishment of émigré nobles, severe penalties against the clergy who refused to take the Civil Oath, and total war against Austria that would ultimately require the drafting of troops in the countryside. Not only did the enlightenment nobles feel betrayed by the revolution, but also the peasantry of western France, who had originally supported the Revolution as much as peasants in other parts of the country, by March of '93, after the second antimonarchical revolution, had had enough of left-leaning Jacobins, attacks on the church, and the drafting of their young men as soldiers, and raised the banner of civil war.[30] That war in the Vendée was to cost the revolutionary government an enormous amount of effort and resources. Undeterred, the left pushed on and accomplished the third revolution with the *coup* of May–June '93. The left—that is, radical democrats—proved more potent politically than any other faction in France.

All of this, though probably accurate enough, is purely descriptive. From the theoretical point of view, it raises many powerful questions. Why was the bourgeois-liberal left—and that is an accurate description of radical Jacobins—politically so potent and psychologically so extreme as, ultimately, to invent the Terror? Why were the king and the liberal nobles so incapable of compromise and leadership? Something more than Enlightenment was going on in eighteenth-century France. The enlightenment made the first revolution "inevitable." That unknown "something more" made it untenable, and, somehow, seemed to make the second and third revolutions "inevitable" as well.

THE SECOND REVOLUTION

The second revolution was played out in two acts. The first act, the forceful removal of the king from Versailles to Paris in October '89, took place within the temporal boundaries of the first revolution, and produced the first serious defections from that revolution by those who had originally heralded it. Less than four months after the Tennis Court Oath, the king was not only translated to Paris against his will, but the whole episode was infused with degradation and "mob violence." An unruly group of Parisian citizens, overwhelmingly women, invaded the palace at Versailles; there was no military power available sufficient to repel this invasion; several of the king's bodyguards were killed; the king and queen, to save their lives, decided to be transported to Paris; a triumphal procession marched to the capital, the royal family in its carriage, the heads of the murdered bodyguards mounted on pikes providing the banners.

Any deputy favoring a constitutional monarchy, at this point, would begin to have very serious doubts whether any kind of monarchy was still possible in France. Mounier was presiding at the Assembly in Versailles when the women from Paris invaded it before they proceeded to the royal palace; the raw power of the people-in-the-streets could not help but make a deep impression on him. He attempted to organize a mass defection from the Assembly, which failed. Although over 301 deputies asked for their passports, only 26 actually resigned from the Assembly.[31] Mounier himself withdrew to the provinces and eventually to Switzerland. The chance of establishing a stable, democratic constitutional monarchy were growing slimmer and slimmer.

For almost three years afterward a charade was played out in regard to the monarchy. Nothing demonstrates with greater power the fierce ambivalence with which France regarded the monarchical situation than the strange circumstance in which Louis was placed. He was, clearly, "a hostage, a prisoner of Paris, in the guise of a constitutional monarch."[32] And yet, when he took ill in March '91, the Jacobin societies all over France held public prayers and solemn masses, and on his recovery, more than two hundred clubs held celebratory ceremonies.[33] Just as if he were a real king. And even the radical-liberals did not abandon the pretence until 1792 that a constitutional monarchy, with the king more than just a ritual figurehead, was possible. Even though Louis had attempted to flee the country, and was captured in Varennes, in June of '91, and forcibly returned to Paris, even so, Michael Kennedy, our foremost historian of Jacobinism, asserts that: "Not until 1792 can Jacobinism be associated unequivocally with republicanism."[34] And Robespierre himself maintained the position all through the spring of '92 that the constitution, which provided for a king with some reasonable political power, must be supported. Only in July did he come out for direct action against the monarchy.[35]

Anticlerical sentiment—or, more accurately, hostility to the power of the Catholic Church and its subservience to Rome—and antimonarchical sentiment were intimately entwined during this revolutionary period. The most radical elements, including the most vigorous street demonstrators, were passionately opposed to both institutions. The bourgeois-liberals who controlled the National Assembly established a truly revolutionary control over the Church. First, confiscating all Church property; then, making the clergy employees of the state; and finally, passing laws that determined the structure and personnel of the Church hierarchy. The king exhibited strong sympathy with those members of the clergy who were resisting state control. A clash was inevitable. The radicals won out. The king was swept away. The second and third revolutions brought harsher and harsher treatment of noncomplying priests and bishops and more and more violent antireligious activity.

The Civil Construction of the Clergy was decreed in July 1790. It provided for clergy salaries to be paid by the state and elections of priests and even bishops by popular franchise. There was a very strong reaction, both positive and negative, to these measures within the Church, but there was no significant civil violence protesting these radically new arrangements. But as the opposition began to grow, the Assembly decided to take the offensive. In November '90 the deputies declared that all clerics were to be dismissed if they did not accept the new institutions. As proof of this acceptance they were required to swear an oath "to be faithful to the nation, the king and the law, and to uphold with all their power the constitution declared by the National Assembly and accepted by the king."[36]

The refusal to take the Oath became the rallying point for all those, clergy and citizens alike, who were passionately opposed to the anti-Church direction of the Revolution. In January 1791 one-third of the clerical members of the Assembly dramatically took the Oath. Two-thirds did not. The country was now completely divided on this issue (about 54 percent of the parish clergy took the Oath), and it was within this violent clash of feelings and opinions that Louis attempted to assert some independence, refusing to remain a passive prisoner in the Tuilleries. Street insurgents asserted their own extralegal power against refractories (those Clergy who refused the Oath). On April 18, 1790, the Paris police closed the chapels of four convents that were used by nonjuring priests, because they were expending too much effort in keeping rioters from closing them down violently.[37] Three days later Louis attempted to leave his palace and drive to Saint-Cloud to receive Easter communion from refractory priests. Somehow the Paris radicals learned of the attempt, and his carriage was turned back after proceeding only a little distance.

In June, the king attempted to flee the country, getting only as far as Varennes. Still the majority of the Assembly maintained its contradictory stance toward the two issues of monarchy and church. Louis was not deposed, despite his flight, but in November the Assembly decreed severe measures against nonjuring clergy. On December 19 Louis vetoed this measure, which act was "a turning point in the Revolution," for the Jacobin clubs outside of Paris, and obviously for liberal-radical public opinion in the nation. "The veto had a more decisive impact on opinion than the flight to Varennes. To use a phrase that was popular with the clubs, 'the veil was torn.' The 'Restorer of Liberty' had become 'Monsieur Veto.' Everywhere his supporters were put on the defensive."[38] The path toward August '92 was clearly marked out.

One of the most significant, if not the most significant, phenomenon leading to the end of the monarchy concerned the conflict within the Jacobin clubs after the flight to Varennes. That history has been well-documented but not really explained. The power struggle within the Jacobin community and its final resolution on the side of the radicals had enormous significance for ultimately putting an end to the first revolution. Without the power of the Jacobin Club in Paris—using the people-in-the-streets as its military arm—it is reasonable to say there would have been no second revolution (overthrowing the king), and, certainly, no third one. And yet, in July and August 1791, after the king's failed flight to freedom, there was every indication that the Club's power was seriously fading and might never recover.

After Varennes, there was a serious divide between the liberal and radical elements of the Jacobin Club in Paris. The massacre on July 17 of Parisians at the Champs de Mars, who were peacefully demonstrating in favor of a deposition of the king, was followed by repressive measures, and arrests, of several radicals in Paris. Two days before the Champs de Mars bloodbath a crowd of several thousand people had invaded the Jacobin Club, demanding that the society draw up a petition calling for the replacement of Louis "by all constitutional means." The following day, the moderates in the Club, who had already ceased to come to meetings, formally resigned and joined with Lafayette (who was destined to become the villain of the Champs de Mars affair), and others, to form a new society at the Feuillant convent; hence the appellation *feuillants.* Bouche, who was the president of the Jacobins, and twenty-five out of the thirty members of the correspondence committee of the society, defected to the *feuillants.* Whereas previously the society had had almost 2,400 members, on the evening of the Massacre only an infinitely small number appeared in the hall. "Mass resignations took place." At Lyon, the society went over to the *feuillants.* Other provincial clubs did the same. It began to look like the power of Jacobinism was broken.[39]

And yet, within less than two months, exactly the opposite took place. The clubs were prospering and the radical wing was triumphant:

> By September 30, when the National Assembly terminated its labors, the Jacobin network had risen Phoenix-like, from the ashes. In quantitative terms, it was sadly weakened by the closures and defections of July–August. On the other hand, virtually all the major societies had returned to the field and non-affiliates had begun to clamor once more for certification. A new period of growth had commenced. More importantly, the ordeal by fire left radicals and democrats firmly in control.[40]

Why this new life for radicalism, that is, antimonarchism? It must be emphasized, first, that the typical adherent of a Jacobin Society was not a member of the lower- or under-class, was not a sans-culottes, and was not unemployed or living on the margins of society. Though certainly not a capitalist, since there was so little capitalism as yet in France, he was without question a bourgeois, leading a bourgeois life, exhibiting bourgeois values in his lifestyle, committed to stability and comfort.[41] Why would such a group in society opt for a radical alternative when the perfectly respectable liberal-constitutional monarchy position of Lafayette and the *feuillants* seemed a viable alternative? Michael Kennedy, the most thorough chronicler of these events, offers this explanation: "The trickle back to the Jacobins became a cascade by September. . . . The great trump cards of the Jacobins in the schism were Robespierre and Pétion."[42] This explanation, even if true, does not go half far enough. Why should radical demo-crats and republicans be trump cards for bourgeois citizens rather than anath-ema? It would not be surprising should we read that the provincial societies were disenchanted by the raucous radicalism of Robespierre and Pétion. But they were not. There was something within the political culture of the first and second rank of the bourgeois elite that had an affinity for political radicalism and de-sired the end of monarchy. That "something" made Jacobinism, and in particular the Paris Club, the most powerful political force in France. Given all this, the second revolution became eminently possible; a certain amount of efficient organization would make it "inevitable." Did that "something," whatever it may have been, also make these bourgeois radicals tolerant of terror, at least at its beginning, to the point of only turning away from it when the eating machine posed a threat to their own persons? Would the Terror have been possible if Tocqueville's "virus of a new and unknown kind" had not infected the bourgeois life of France?

In 1792 the sentiment against the king, and, most significantly, the tendency of radical elements to resort to violent extralegal political action, accelerated. As example, "From February to April, national guardsmen from Marseille, acting on orders of the [Jacobin] club and municipal government, brutally eliminated counterrevolutionary elements at Aix, Arles, and Avignon. Henceforth, the Marseillais were the virtual masters of Provence."[43] By July, the Club in Paris became increasingly supportive of the deposition of the king by insurrection. The Paris sections—the centers of radical politics in the city—"began to peti-tion openly for the king's immediate deposition. . . . Similar calls were now coming in from major provincial towns."[44] Considering the willingness of radical elements to resort to direct action—that is, political violence—and taking into account the lack of police or military power on the part of those committed to orderly political process, it is no big wonder that by August the king was a total prisoner of Paris, and the second revolution was an accomplished fact.

It is of interest to note that, even though the country as a whole, and the Jacobin network in particular, had been reluctant to take the final step of over-throwing the king, when it finally occurred as the result of crowd action on August 10, the act itself was greeted with great enthusiasm. Kennedy states that, though it was not until 1792 that Jacobinism can, "be associated unequivocally with republicanism,"[45] to the day of August 10, "the response of the clubs was overwhelmingly favorable. Almost all adhered promptly to the decree of suspension, and many were positively euphoric . . . the day of August 10 had 'saved France,' 'put the seal on our liberty,' 'completed the victory over tyranny.' "[46]

Beyond the Jacobin clubs, in the whole of France, among those who remained politically active, there was almost unanimity in support of this second revolution. When the primary assemblies met in September to elect delegates to the new National Convention, only eleven in the nation desired the retention of the monarch.[47] One may wonder why, when the country appeared so united in its wish for republican government, was subsequent duly elected government incapable of stability. As with the first revolution, the identical question must be raised about the second: Why was it that it could not hold?

THE THIRD REVOLUTION

Without the benefit of any Gallup poll, it seems reasonable to suggest that the first revolution had the support of the vast majority of the Nation. The second revolution is much harder to judge, but a positive response somewhere between 40 percent and 60 percent seems a conservative guess. The third revolution, without question, was a minority affair. And, as it proceeded, the percentage of citizens supporting its development grew smaller and smaller. A minority revolution, if it is to remain in power even for several months, ultimately requires terror as an instrument of preservation. An infinitely small minority revolution will require an infinitely high degree of terror.

The third revolution had absolutely no moral or social dimension or meaning. True, the shock troops that accomplished the actual overthrow were the sans-culottes of Paris, but they were being used by the Jacobins in order to establish the dictatorship; and within a year, sans-culottes' independent political action was almost entirely repressed by Jacobin dictatorial power.

If one's definition of a revolution includes some radical change in the values or the class power structure in society, then this third act of revolutionary history should be more accurately described as a coup rather than a revolution. In the course of history we have had circumstances where different factions of the aristocracy fought each other for ultimate power: the War of the Roses in England, as example. There was nothing revolutionary in that activity; neither the value system, nor the class structure, was affected by the outcome. Similarly, if Trotsky had succeeded in the early 1930s in overthrowing Stalin's dictatorship, assuming that dictatorial role himself, the history of Soviet Russia might very well have turned out differently, but such action by Trotsky in no way would have been a revolution but merely a factional conflict within the Bolshevik Revolution. In the same manner, if two factions of radical democrats, Girondins and Jacobins, who shared so many political values, with the leaders of both parties coming essentially from the same social class of society—if both parties resorted to violence to settle their struggle for power, it may be equally inappropriate to give to the outcome of that pathetic and tragic conflict the very name of "revolution."

This third "revolution" of May–June '93 aimed neither at the overthrow of the king, nor at the replacement of aristocrats by citizens, nor even at the elimination of constitutional *monarchiens* or *feuillants*. All these had already left the scene—and France. The primary purpose of this coup was to eliminate the Girondins as a political force and leave the Mountain and the Jacobin Club of Paris unopposed. On June 2, the Paris Commune and the sections surrounded the Convention with five thousand armed national guards and forced the expulsion and arrest of twenty-nine "perfidious" Girondin deputies.[48] These deputies had been duly elected by their constituents in the provinces to represent their views and interests. Another example of that chimera "direct democracy." A good number of these twenty-nine ended up under the blade of the guillotine. Politics, after the second revolution, became a loser-lose-all game.

There was nothing spontaneous in this May 31–June 2 coup. Five thousand national guard troops did not just coincidentally appear together at the Convention Hall on June 2.[49] The insurrection was the result of an alliance between the Jacobin Club and the political radicals in Paris. On May 26, at the Club, Robespierre gave the clarion call for the rising, pulling out all the cliché paranoid stops:

> When the people is oppressed, when it has no recourse left but itself, he would be a coward indeed who should not call upon it to rise. It is when all laws are violated, it is when despotism is at its height, it is when good faith and decency are being trampled under foot, that the people ought to rise in insurrection. That moment has arrived.[50]

Knowing to whom the absolute political power would pass after the elimination of the Girondins, the Jacobins that evening declared the Club to be in a state of insurrection against the corrupt deputies.[51]

Paris, however, was not France. And the Girondin factions in other large cities were not reluctant to take their own "direct" action against Jacobin militants. The Girondin deputies to the National Convention have been described by many historians as "weak," "vacillating," "indecisive." Some have even postulated that Jacobinism triumphed in Paris because of these inadequacies in the Girondin faction. That remains an open question, but what is of great interest is that the anti-Jacobins in other large cities—Lyon, Bordeaux, and Marseille—demonstrated as much insurrectional militancy as the Jacobins of Paris and their allies in the Sections.

Lyon had overthrown Jacobin rule on May 29, a few days before the completion of the Paris coup. After hearing the news from the capital, Marseille and Bordeaux did the same. "The *conseil général de la commune de Lyon* issued a manifesto denouncing the local Jacobins as 'anarchists,' and encouraging their betrayal to a newly constituted Police Committee."[52] Girondins from Paris fled the capital and scattered throughout France, narrating the story of how the coup had destroyed revolutionary democracy. Their message fell on remarkably fertile ground. "Within two weeks more than sixty departments were in rebellion" against the "cleansed" Convention.[53] To the civil war that had erupted in the Vendée in March was now added this so-called federalist civil war. The fact that the Jacobin dictatorship managed to triumph in both these intranational insurrections at the same time that it was fighting an international war is a great tribute to its energy, its courage, and its capacity for organization. That it somehow demonstrates a moral superiority or even excuses the Terror—as some modern-day Jacobins have argued—is a much more doubtful proposition, especially when we consider that its authoritarian inflexibility made any kind of democratic compromise impossible, creating a situation where a war-to-the-death was inevitable. In both the Vendée and in Lyon, the dictatorship triumphed and proceeded to extract a vengeance that bordered on the genocidal.

The development of political life after the May–June coup clearly indicates that this "third revolution" was no revolution at all. Those who held the dictatorial power had absolutely no real intention of extending political power to the sans-culottes. True, many concessions were made to the crowd in Paris, such as the institution of the *maximum*-price ceilings on the most important items needed for basic living—and the creation of a revolutionary army, but these were passed primarily to quiet the radicals in the street and keep the crowd from doing to the Jacobins what it had done to the Girondins.

The Jacobin dictatorship represented no class interests and had no intention of transferring power from the bourgeois elite to lower classes. Albert Soboul, who had profound sympathy with the sans-culottes, of whose history he was the great historian, writes:

> The consequences of all this for Sanscullote democracy was serious. The Sanculottes clung above all to their electoral power, which symbolised the sovereignty of the people. This they now lost. Thus in Paris, the Revolutionary Committees of the Sections had at first been elected by the general assemblies. In the autumn [1793] they came under the censorship of the General Council of the Municipality; in the winter, under the control of the Committee of General Security. By the spring of the year II their members were purely and simply nominees of the Committee of Public Safety. The General Council of the Paris municipality went the same way. After . . . the execution of Hébert and Chaumette, the Committee of Public Safety deposed a good many of its members and nominated replacements without consulting the Sections. . . . In Floréal and Prairial [1794], under pressure from the government and the Jacobin Club, the "Sociétés Sectionnaires," which were the basic units of the popular movement, were dissolved; the reason most generally given was, that the Jacobins must be the sole centre of public opinion. In fact, the popular organizations and Sansculotte democracy appeared to be incompatible with the revolutionary government and Jacobin dictatorship. . . . Thus the spring of the year II saw in political matters the irrevocable divorce between the popular movement and the revolutionary government.[54]

Thus, ironically, THE French Revolution assumes world-historical meaning, in Hegel's terms, not only because of its permanent realization of equality and rights but also because it so eerily prefigures the twentieth-century history of ideological terror: revolutions made in the name of the people that amazingly quickly become dictatorships perfectly willing and capable of oppressing the people, along with everyone else. And terror remains essential to this journey.

The history of the Jacobin dictatorship itself is that of becoming narrower and narrower. After the destruction of the Girondins, it was exercised by an alliance between the left delegates in the Convention, known as the Mountain, and the Jacobin Club, with Robespierre being a central figure in both camps. The dictatorial power then passed more and more into the hands of the Committee of Public Safety, consisting of deputies of the Convention. "In the past the Jacobins had been the forum where the Montagnards argued out the policies that they would support in the Convention. By the summer of 1794 all the life had gone out of the club, where ordinary members scarcely dared to risk any initiative. Members of the Committee of Public Safety introduced resolutions which the club duly endorsed and referred back to the Committee!"[55]

The final step in this constriction of dictatorial power occurred when the triumvirate of Robespierre, Saint-Just, and Couthon for a short while took most power into its own hands. That made the overthrow of the dictatorship relatively easy. Other members of the Committee of Public Safety joined with anti-Robespierrist radicals, and moderates, and the whole fragile structure crumbled in two days. The execution of the three and a handful of their close allies was enough to put a Thermidorian end to the dictatorship, the Terror, and "THE Revolution."

Having discarded the concept of THE Revolution, having abandoned the project of looking for *one* set of causes for its failures, we seem to be left with two revolutions and a coup. Each of these three events would seem to have a separate set of explanations both for successes and for ultimate failure. Such a demarcation certainly makes our theoretical task more difficult but, hopefully, in the long run, more fruitful.

5

THE PROMISE OF DEMOCRATIC CITIZENSHIP

Many different theses have been offered as to what may be the essential nature of democratic citizenship. Daniel Bell, for instance, has stated that "Democracy is a socio-political system in which legitimacy lies in the consent of the governed."[1] For our present purposes, this translates easily into the conception that the people as a whole are sovereign. There are, however, several other equally "essential" attributes of democratic citizenship. I do not intend to attempt here an exhaustive analysis of how many there may be, and what particular form they may take. My purpose is to elaborate on the remarkable circumstance that French society, during the Revolutionary period, managed to incorporate into its system of values most—if not nearly all—the essential attributes of democratic citizenship but totally failed in one particular, crucially important instance: going beyond the paranoid view that those in political opposition were traitors to the polity and, consequently, creating a conception of a *loyal* opposition. This failure resulted in the impossibility of a viable democratic polity, made terror an alluring prospect, and ultimately required conservative dictatorship to stabilize society.

By the time the Convention convened in September 1792, after the king had been overthrown and a Republic established, there was almost unanimous agreement among those within the polity on certain basic principles. There were, of course, many Frenchmen who were outside the polity: émigrés, nobles, and priests who did not accept the Revolution, counterrevolutionaries of various kinds. As would be expected, there were also a great number of passive opponents of the Revolution, who took no public antirevolutionary action and did not flee the country. Among those who were active in republican politics—the people who voted, the members of political clubs, the delegates to the Convention: Girondins, Montagnards, moderates of the Plain—all these, almost unanimously accepted certain basic democratic political values: That the people are sovereign and reign supreme in the polity. That no monarch is necessary for a political system that establishes the rule of law and constitutionalism as the ultimate political authority. That every adult male enjoys certain basic political rights (although their exact content would be, and had been, disputed). That a certain ideal of equality pervades all political life. That universal education is an imperative of democratic society.

It was a remarkable vision for the world at that time. Excepting England and America, no other country came even close to this modern conception of what a society might be. It immediately became apparent, however, in the very first months of the Convention when Girondins and Montagnards started viciously castigating and lacerating each other, that Frenchmen had no comprehension of the nature of a loyal democratic opposition, no understanding that democratic society was possible only if one was able to grant good faith to one's political opponent. If all political opponents were traitors, no democracy was possible. And so it proved to be the case, not only during the period of the Jacobin Terror, but for almost a hundred years of French history.

The lesson that the French in the Revolutionary period could not—would not—learn had been preached by Aristotle 2,000 years before and, more recently, taken up by Machiavelli. A citizen, Aristotle says, is a person capable of both ruling and being ruled. "The fact remains that the good citizen must possess the knowledge and the capacity requisite for ruling as well as for being ruled, and the excellence of a citizen may be defined as consisting in 'a knowledge of rule over free men from both points of view' [i.e., that of the ruler as well as that of the ruled]."[2] Echoed by Machiavelli when he stated that it was incumbent on the citizen "neither arrogantly to dominate nor humbly to serve."[3] It was a discourse that neither Jacobin, nor Girondin, nor Thermidorian, nor the political leaders of the time of the Directory were prepared to understand. They felt powerfully the desire to rule—but not over free men.

It was the siren song of what Sorel has called "the terrible postulate of unanimity"[4]—ambivalently implicit in Rousseau's conception of the General Will—that made the French incapable of understanding this view of citizenship.

This "rotten fruit of Rousseauism," as Mona Ozouf has designated it,[5] did not dominate French political culture because people had made the mistake of reading Rousseau instead of Aristotle. It would have remained supreme even if that great French philosopher had died in his cradle. The brilliance of Rousseau, in this instance, was to give accurate voice to a *mentalité* that was pervasive in the culture. Sociologically, the view that all the virtuous people in the polity will hold, more or less, the same political opinions was pre-Modern. Psychologically, it reflects a basic attitude of the paranoid position. And a society overwhelmingly committed to this latter *Weltanschauung* is incapable of democratic citizenship. In political life, French Revolutionary values reflected an ancient, pre-Aristotle view of Athenian society found in Herodotus and most succinctly put by Thucydides (III, 45), when he has a speaker use the phrase "freedom, or the rule over others."[6] One wonders how much more advanced was the French conception of freedom at the time. Freedom to rule? Yes. Freedom to rule and *be ruled?* Impossible.

It is helpful and necessary at this point to look at the historical data that would support these broad assertions. A slightly fanciful imaginative exercise may prove illuminating. Imagine that we are standing in Versailles in September 1789, after the Estates General had transformed itself into the National Assembly, after the Third Estate had defied the king at the Tennis Court, after the people-in-the-streets of Paris had provided the military power to secure the Third Estate's Revolution, after the Assembly had set itself the task of writing a new constitution for France, after "feudalism" had been abolished during the night of August 4, and after the Assembly had promulgated the *Declaration of the Rights of Man and of the Citizen.* Also imagine, for the fanciful nature of this exercise, that we possess all the sociological and psychological knowledge available to us today, and all the historical knowledge that has been accumulated over the past years, which indicates how profoundly the *ancien régime* was driving toward a conception of democratic citizenship. And yet, deny us knowledge of what the ten years after 1789 would bring. Could anyone, under these circumstances, proceeding from a rational analysis, envision the various coups of the Directory, the guillotine, and the Terror? It is true that for people like Burke and, even more especially, those who maintained an extreme hatred toward every aspect of the Revolution, the very worst horrors were to be expected. For almost everyone else, in these circumstances, such a bleak future would have been unimaginable.

The world's greatest survivor, the bishop Tallyrand, succinctly expressed that essential opitimism. François Furet writes:

The Constituent Assembly, having "destroyed everything" to begin with, soon came to feel that it had subsequently "reconstructed everything." Tallyrand used these very words in his address to the nation of February 11, 1790, in which he summarized and celebrated the accomplishments of that legislative body. Under the heading of things destroyed were the absolute monarchy, the Estates General, the system of orders and privileges, and feudalism. Among the things reconstructed were the sovereignty of the nation, embodied in the Assembly; citizenship; a new division of the kingdom; the basis of a just system of representation; and equality before the law. Having contrasted the new "edifice" point by point with the old, the bishop of Auton cited the fundamental principle on which the whole structure was based, namely, the Rights of man: "Ignored and insulted for centuries, the Rights of Man have been reestablished for all mankind."[7]

Something went wrong. Something that should have happened—inevitably?—did not happen. The Terror was not responsible for that failure. The Terror resulted from the nonfulfillment of the promise. What did not occur was the firm establishment of a *Weltanschauung* of democratic citizenship that included the conception of a loyal opposition. This last statement is a descriptive analysis only. An analytical analysis would drive deeper: Why was democratic citizenship impossible for society at that time? A question that Hegel, Tocqueville, Marx, and Quinet all addressed without quite coming to a satisfactory answer. I will set it aside for now and return to it in a complex manner later, but only after much has been said about the course of the Revolutions' attempt to gain the Modern world. It is a question, however, that pervades this entire discourse. It is a question, furthermore, that takes on a tragic poignancy when set beside the great humanistic accomplishments of these very same Revolutions. It was Tocqueville, possessing the most extraordinary capacity to exercise what Keats called "negative capability," who underlined, with such feeling, this enormous ambiguity: "I do not know of another event in history that contributed more to the well-being of succeeding generations or more entirely demoralized the generation that brought it about."[8] What, we may ask, was the cause of this demoralization?

The French nation pushed itself, screaming and kicking, into the Modern world, before it was fully ready to enter it. It was the first nation to attempt this perilous journey prematurely. It was not to be the last. The history of the attempt on Modernity was to witness an enormous number of catastrophes, as well as many eventual successes, that followed intense periods of demoralization. Triumph and Terror have defined the passage to Modernity.

THE TRIUMPH OF THE CONCEPTION OF DEMOCRATIC CITIZENSHIP UNDER THE OLD REGIME

La Republique était dans les esprits vingt ans au moins avant sa proclamation.
—Danton, August 13, 1793[9]

The first French Revolution—June 1789 to August 1792—was accomplished with an almost unbelievable minimum of violence and annihilation of persons. Unlike the Bolshevik Revolution of November 1917, and the Jacobin coup of 1793, it was accomplished by an obvious majority of the elites in society. There was no terror during the first Revolution simply because it was not a minority affair. When the National Assembly began its deliberations in June 1789, there was a remarkable agreement among most of the members of all three Estates as to what fundamental changes were necessary in French social and political life. Of primary importance, the writing of a "democratic" constitution for France. Today, there exists almost unanimous accord among historians of the *ancien régime* in regard to this basic proposition.

We are concerned here with sovereignty, with constitutionalism, with politics. Not with liberalism and the assertion of rights. It was the moral collapse of revolutionary *political* life that brought on the catastrophes of the period. And yet, the culture of the old regime seemed to be pushing with as much energy toward democratic citizenship as it was toward Liberal mores. Though society was ruled by a monarch with claims to near absolutism, there was a growing sentiment within the culture toward political equality and democracy. As with the institutionalization of Liberal values, it would be correct to assert that the first Revolution did not invent any new conceptions of equality and democratic citizenship but merely grounded those values in a democratic constitution, which was legitimated by the sovereignty of the nation, even though the question of exactly who constituted "the nation" remained undecided.

Whereas with the triumph of liberalism, the key word was "Rights," in the case of the struggle for Democratic Citizenship, the powerful words were "Sovereignty," "Nation," and "Constitution." Absolute power had to be wrested from the monarch, Sovereignty had to be invested in the Nation, and the whole process institutionalized in a written Constitution—if democratic citizenship was to become a reality. In the quarter of a century before the first Revolution, there was a growing powerful wave of the critique of the absolute power of the king. Already in 1764, the Parlement of Rennes had the audacity to announce

to the monarch: "It is the consent of the nation, which your parlement represents, that completes the law."[10] J.K. Wright has succinctly summed up this
portentious development:

> The various strands of our argument . . . all point to the period between 1771
> and 1786 as the decisive juncture for the consolidation of this "republican" con-
> sensus. . . . The fifteen years immediately preceding the Revolution . . . was the
> period of the final de-legitimization of the Bourbon monarchy [when] a significant
> current of public opinion began to converge on the formulae of "national sover-
> eignty," "the general will," and the "separation of powers" as an alternative pro-
> gram to that of absolutism.[11]

The culmination of this revolutionary development came to pass with the adoption of Article 3 of the *Rights of Man:* "The source of all sovereignty resides in
the nation. No body, no individual can possess authority that does not derive
from it."[12]

And in the twelve months preceding the convening of the Estates General in
May '89, there was a virtual explosion of what can only be called democratic
sentiment. It began as a confrontation between the Court and the various parlements in France, including the most significant one in Paris. Since the members
of these august bodies represented the high elite of French society, this protest
cannot be described simply as "bourgeois" or "democratic." It was, more accurately, a struggle between the king and what was left of "aristocratic" power. But
almost immediately the "people" of France—specifically, the elite of the Third
Estate—jumped into the struggle and completely transformed the political ecology in which the conflict was being played out. It was the Parlement of Paris
that called for a meeting of the Estates General, an event that had not occurred
since 1614. It obviously did not imagine that it was calling for its own demise.

Throughout the eighteenth century, there were several significant challenges
to the absolute authority of the king from the parlements of France, which were
courts, not legislative bodies. All such challenges were issued under the stated or
unstated assumption that there was, somewhere, a constitution in France that
the king had to respect and could not transgress. These controversies came to a
climax in 1771, when the king, at the direction of his first minister Maupeou,
exiled the Paris parlement from the capital city and attempted to reform totally
the parliamentary system, which action would have enhanced the king's absolute
authority. This attempt failed; the parlement was recalled in 1774, and the possi-

ble challenge to absolutism by appeal to "constitutional" forms remained. There was nothing, however, of a potential "bourgeois revolution" in all these controversies. Nobles and the highest monied elites composed the parlements.

In the year or so before the meeting of the Estates General, however, the cry for constitutionalism reached a crescendo that made a true revolution possible. An attempt in 1788 on the part of the court to institute another Maupeou-like reform resulted, as William Doyle writes, in "[An] atmosphere that produced the most extreme constitutional statement of the century from the parlement of Paris on 3 May 1788. Throughout the century in their remonstrances they had invoked 'fundamental laws' of the kingdom which no king had the right to transgress. Now for the first time they presumed to list them. . . . Maxims scarcely spoken of until 1787, such as that taxation must have the free consent of the Estates-General meeting regularly, and that all arbitrary arrests and imprisonments were illegal."[13] We recall that the Estates General was a *legislative* body that had not met since 1614.

The resistance by the Paris parlement provoked an unforeseen tidal wave of pamphlet literature coming both from the courts themselves and from the general public. "The time had come for the Estates-General to pronounce, not just on new taxes, but on the whole range of reforms which, however desirable, could only be made legitimate by its consent. The social contract had been broken, the general will defied. It was time to give France a new constitution. Such themes occurred again and again in the pamphlet literature."[14] And finally, once it was apparent that Necker would do nothing about the severe financial crisis until the Estates-General met, it became clear that "Having run out of money, the old monarchy and its servants had also run out of ideas. Here, in the last weeks of August 1788, the Ancien Régime, as a political system collapsed."[15] This, in the realm of politics, was the revolution before the revolution.

The two and one-half years before the first Revolution witnessed the appearance of a crucial phenomenon for the existence of democratic politics: beyond public opinion and intense pamphleteering, political clubs began to exist in significant number in Paris in the spring and summer of 1787. Brienne, the king's minister, had feared their political power, and they were forbidden to meet in August. With his fall from office, this prohibition lapsed and, by November, official sanction was given to their existence. One of the most significant clubs was that which met at the Duports, called the Societé des Trente. "In its ranks were magistrates, priests, courtiers, bankers, academicians, lawyers, and journalists . . . a complete cross-section of the metropolitan social and intellectual élite [nobles and *haut bourgeois*]."[16]

The central political question became that of whether the number of deputies in the Third Estate was to be doubled or not. The Societé des Trente took the lead in demanding such a reform. No longer, it was argued, could the bourgeoisie, "with all its wealth, talent, and experience," be excluded from an equal voice in the polity and in national budgetary decisions. "The 'forms of 1614' must therefore be opposed with all available means, while as a first step the number of third estate deputies should be doubled."[17] This "conspiracy of gentlemen," as Mirabeau designated it, opened the gates to a veritable flood of pamphlets and petitions. By December 1788, when the decision about the numbering of the Third Estate was finally made, over 800 petitions favoring such action had been received in the capital. There was no longer any question what the politically vocal and active part of the nation desired.[18]

What must be remarked upon is how prepared the delegates to the Third Estate were to take the necessary revolutionary steps, when they appeared in Versailles, how clear they were as to their task, and how close to unanimity was their condition. On June 17, 1789, on the motion of the abbé Sieyès, the deputies to the Third Estate, by a vote of 491 to 90, declared:

> The assembly, deliberating after the verification of powers, recognizes that this assembly is already composed of representatives sent directly by at least ninety-six percent of the nation.
> . . . The assembly therefore declares that the collective work of national restoration can and must be commenced without delay by the deputies present, and they must pursue it without interruption and without obstacle.
> The title of *National Assembly* is the only appropriate one for the assembly in the present circumstances, whether because its members are the only legitimately and publicly known and verified representatives, or because they are sent directly by the near totality of the nation, or finally because, since representation is one and indivisible, no deputy, no matter from what order or class he is chosen, has the right to exercise his functions apart from the present assembly.[19]

The primary task, it was almost unanimously agreed, was to write a Constitution for France, one in which, obviously, the king was no longer absolute. The report of the *Comité préparatoire* of July 9, in effect, declared the monarchy of the old regime illegitimate: "When the manner of government does not derive from the clearly expressed will of the people, there is no constitution; there is only a *de facto* government, which varies according to circumstances."[20]

What they thoroughly understood was the necessity of replacing an absolutist regime: the replacement of monarchy with monarchical republicanism; the replacement of the sovereignty of the king with the sovereignty of the Nation, that is, with the sovereignty of the Third Estate and those members of the other two Estates who were willing to join them. What this revolution before the revolution did not understand was the way a modern democracy was to work. There was, actually, no real discussion of the problem, absolutely no equivalent, for instance, of Madison's discourse on the great problematic of "factions" in Federalist #10. Montesquieu, it is true, had emphasized the importance of the separation of powers, but this was still an argument about structure, not about process. It was in the realm of process that the great failure occurred in the immediate future: finding no other way to treat defeated political opponents except with exile or execution.

The two conceptions that were in the air, thanks to Rousseau: that of the General Will and that there was something somehow illegitimate about representative democracy, that only direct democracy could truly express the people's will—these two beliefs were premodern, kinship, tribal views of the polity that, if taken literally and actually put into practice, would make a modern democratic citizenship impossible. That direct democracy was legitimate, and representative democracy illegitimate, was a cruel fantasy of ancient Athens or Sparta. How ten million citizens were to gather together in the *ecclesia* no one bothered to explain. That all this, combined with the conception that the creation of a political party was iniquitous "factionalism," destroyed the possibility of a nonparanoid democratic polity, will be discussed at length a little later on. For now, let us return to those democratic ideas and ideals that were thoroughly comprehended.

Political equality was one. The attack on the aristocracy and aristocratic privilege was undertaken under the banner of "equality." When Sieyès declared that, in regard to the terms "the nation" and "the people": "These two terms must be synonymous,"[21] the first principle being enunciated was that any socially constructed inequality was illegitimate. It has already been noted that the notion of equality played a crucial role in the writing of the *Declaration of Rights*. "Liberty as protection against authority appears in ten of the Declaration's seventeen articles (2, 4, 5, 7–11, 16, 17), liberty defined as participation in four articles (3, 6, 14, 15), and equality also in four (1, 6, 13, 14). These three principles fitted together more easily than one might think, and together they formed the package democracy."[22] True, the question of *actual* suffrage—how many could possess the franchise—was never fully resolved. The franchise for the election of delegates to the Estates General, however, was the widest of any that had existed anywhere in the world up to that point, and the Jacobin constitution of 1793 "was the work of the most determined partisans of universal suffrage."[23] That constitution never was put into effect. With all the conflict and ambivalence about universal suffrage, nevertheless, an ideal of equality remained powerful within the culture, and any institutionalization of inequality had to be rationalized. Even the Thermidorians, after the overthrow of Robespierre and the Jacobin dictatorship, faced the problem of "how to reconcile the principle of popular sovereignty and institutional stability."[24]

It must be remarked, at this point, that unresolved conflicts over the question of the universality of suffrage are not necessarily an indication of the nonexistence of a democratic polity. All developing democratic societies (Athens, England, America, France) begin as limited democracies. The great democratic society of 1789 that we celebrate in America—even putting aside the question of women's suffrage—was far from a radical democracy. The great question for revolutionary France is why the *various factions of the elites* could not democratically deal with each other even after the political power of the lower classes had been severely repressed. In America, for instance, Hamilton and Jefferson could compete for power, sometimes with great acrimony, without recourse to banishment or guillotine.* Marxist historians, such as Mathiez, would have us believe that the essential political question and failure revolved around the problem of upper versus lower classes. All this is important, but a further question remains the one we are asking: Why did the upper classes need an authoritarian leader in order to resolve the conflicts within their own house? Napoleon was necessary, not only to keep the sans-culottes impotent (and they had actually ceased to be a political factor by 1795), but also to keep moderates and Jacobins—both of whom were bourgeois elites—from murdering each other.

The reconciliation of institutional stability and popular sovereignty, moreover, is *the* question for democratic citizenship. Many who have opposed such citizenship, as a matter of principle, have argued that universal sovereignty and stability *cannot* be reconciled, and, therefore, radical democracy can lead only to anarchy or dictatorship. We know today that such a miraculous reconciliation

---

*It is the case that American society, in the years 1789–1800, came very close to *not* making the transition to a stable, nonparanoid democratic society, even though it is hard to imagine such a failure leading to a collapse into ideological terror. In Chapter 7, this proposition is discussed at length.

is, indeed, possible. In this regard, however, French revolutionary history from September '92 onward is the story of a complete inability to go beyond the paranoid position and create a stable democratic citizenship. The great question remains: Why was that true?

One most positive result of the revolutionary impulse toward democratic practice was the efflorescence of local democracy on the commune level. Tocqueville has made us all acquainted with how important local democracy—the town meeting—was for the prosperity of American democracy on all levels of government. Revolutionary energy in France, most particularly manifest within the four to five thousand Jacobin clubs that existed at some point during this period, produced that very same local democratic spirit. Crane Brinton tells us:

> Each little town was a new Athens, at least as far as political opportunities go. In the earlier records of the clubs there is an unmistakable delight in the game of politics, in posturing before the public, in going through the ordinary rites of collective action—not an ignominious nor a puerile delight, though it seems so at first sight, for it was a part of a genuine and as yet almost unembittered freshness of emotion real enough.[25]

And yet, this Athenian spirit was not strong enough to save France.

Of enormous significance for a revolutionary transformation of values in the direction of equality and democracy—a crucial element of the revolution before the revolution—was the "insurrection of the curés" that had arisen in some parts of France several years before the meeting of the Estates General. Its main thrust was to give the lower clergy more say and more power in church affairs. It pitted the curés against the magnates of the church. In the province of Dauphiné the curés had begun to act independently of their bishop and had even formed an association that began an intense critique of Church structures and policies. In three dioceses of Dauphiné—Gap, Grenoble, and Vienne—the lower clergy had won the right to meet in conferences that elected deputies to the diocesan tax boards. These actions had all the qualities of peaceful, but forceful, rebellion. At first, all the grounds of discontent centered on theological issues and ecclesiastical institutions. But with the national crisis that began in 1787 and ended with the assembly of the Estates General, a remarkable politicization of these efforts resulted. "The longstanding clash between upper and lower clergy developed into an overt social conflict between the largely noble absentee tithe owners, including the bishops, and the commoner parish priests. The curés increasingly identified their struggle with the cause of the Third Estate."[26] What was it that entered into the spirit of these parish priests—the lowest rung of the hierarchical ladder—and caused them to imagine they were entitled to some kind of equality?

For two years, 1787 to 1789, they were doing what every liberated person in France was doing: meeting together, talking, agitating, and writing pamphlets in support of their position. Miraculously, the curés got what they had been clamoring for: Necker's regulations for elections to the First Estate provided them with extraordinary power. Curés could vote individually, whereas chapters could send only one voter for ten canons, and monasteries only one for each community. It proved to be as significant an act as that which doubled the representatives to the Third Estate. "By a stroke of the pen, Necker had set up a clerical democracy alongside the lay democracy."[27]

The rhetoric during the election campaign took on the revolutionary flavor that we associate with the Revolution in general. A 1789 pamphlet *Les curés du Dauphiné à leurs confrères les recteurs de Bretagne* declared:

> The interest of the people is inseparable from that of the curés. If the people rise up from their oppression, the curés will escape the degradation into which they have been thrust and so long held down by the upper clergy. . . . In fighting for themselves, the people are also fighting for the curés.[28]

During the election campaign of '89, the Bishop of Gap made the mistake of writing a letter that quickly became public knowledge, in which he lamented that it was "a travesty to see an unenlightened curé, with neither birth nor talent competing on a ballot with prelates." The response to this antidemocratic tirade was immediate and vociferous. The curé Dominique Chaix wrote to his friend: "In a free and monarchical state, despotism invariably arises from time to time, and [of late] the aristocracies of the nobility and of the clergy have exercised their tyranny against their respective subordinates. May the Supreme Judge of empires break at last the yoke of oppression!"[29]

What is of great consequence is that we can confidently assume that Chaix did not arrive at this revolutionary position by reading Voltaire and Rousseau. A keen sense of equality and justice—combined with Old Testament rhetoric—gave him the courage and the power to write as he did. It was, then, not only the *moyen* and *haut bourgeoisie* and the sans-culottes of Paris that dreamed of revolution, but also the lowliest parish curé in an obscure village. The word "Enlightenment" truly refers only to the intellectual tip of a cultural movement that extended all the way down into French society. It is this miracle of cultural and moral transformation that cries out for explanation.

The results of the election of deputies to the Estates General were astounding:

whereas in 1614 curés made up only 10 percent of the clerical delegation, in 1789 two-thirds of the deputies of the First Estate in Versailles came from the parish clergy.[30] The bishops of Metz, Evreaux, Dax, Aire, and Coutances failed of election despite their stated desire to become deputies. Several other bishops were only elected after intense electioneering, some of it of the political-boss variety, and in many cases it took several ballots eventually to choose the bishop.[31] Nothing could give greater indication that a modern democratic society was on the agenda. And in Versailles itself, after the Third Estate had sent invitation to the other two to join it in one national assembly, the very first delegates to break ranks and come over to the Third were some of these same parish clergy. It is profoundly ironic that revolutionary France, once in power, proceeded to institute exaggerated and unnecessary antireligious and anticlerical policies that, ultimately, made enemies of a great many of its very first friends.

ROBESPIERRE: RADICAL DEMOCRAT

Nothing demonstrates with greater poignancy the tragic contradictions in French revolutionary history than the fact that the one man who understood the nature of democratic citizenship probably better than any other important revolutionary actor was the very man who eventually became the prime executioner of whatever democracy had been established. Robespierre was not just a power-intoxicated politician using ideology as a means to domination; he possessed a deep and profound understanding of the qualities without which a modern, radical democracy cannot survive.

I use the word "radical" in connection with democracy in contradistinction to a "limited" democracy. Essentially, "radical" means universal adult male suffrage. In the modern world, once universal male suffrage is a reality, female suffrage becomes an important part of the moral agenda of society and, barring social regression, becomes a reality. In ancient Athens, female suffrage never became an issue, although the development from a limited to a radical democracy was one of the great moral triumphs of that culture. Limited democracies erect barriers of status or wealth as boundaries of political participation. The elimination of those impediments to the full partaking in political action is a fundamental narrative of political life in, for instance, nineteenth-century England and America. In France, we are not surprised to find, the demand for universal male suffrage was there almost from the beginning of the first revolution, and Robespierre was a foremost advocate and exegetest of this position.

Radical democracy, similarly to a radical conception of rights, means *all men*. From a speech of April 1791, when the large majority of revolutionary political elites actively supported some sort of limitation of the franchise that was based upon wealth: "All men born and domiciled in France are members of the body politic termed the French nation; that is to say, they are French citizens. They are so by the nature of things and by the first principle of the law of nations. The rights attaching to this title do not depend on the fortune each man possesses, nor on the amount of tax for which he is assessed, because it is not taxes that make us citizens."[32] Principles, by themselves, were not sufficient, however. If poor people were to be able to participate in political life, there must be payment for public service; otherwise it becomes the sole prerogative of the elite. Even before the Estates General met at Versailles, Robespierre had begun to advocate such policy.[33]

He also keenly perceived that the corruption of state power was a constant threat to democratic action. He went out, as a great public hero, from the Constituent Assembly that had given France its first constitution. Fearing for the fragility of the new democracy, in his last speech to that assembly, Robespierre warned against any police supervision of public meetings and insisted that politicians be subject to severe critique by popular societies.[34] Alfred Cobban has summed up the remarkable vision of this extraordinary man, as he stood before his catastrophic degeneration:

> Universal franchise, equality of rights regardless of race or religion, payment for public service to enable rich and poor alike to hold office, publicity for legislative debates, a national system of education, the use of taxation to smooth out economic inequalities, recognition of the economic responsibilities of society to the individual, the right of national autonomy, religious liberty, local self-government—such were some of the principles for which he stood, and which are now taken for granted in democratic societies.[35]

"Taken for granted," we might add, only after more than one hundred years of intense, and sometimes violent, struggle even in the "most advanced" democratic societies.

The great problematic with Robespierre begins when the call for virtue and democracy starts to become exaggerated, when too great a demand is put on society, when virtue dictates the politics of the impossible. In the years from 1792 to his fall in July 1794, he lived on the thin edge between morality and domination. As late as February '94, after the establishment of the Jacobin dictatorship, when he was the single most powerful man in France, he could still understand—at times—that restrained virtue was the essence of democratic life. "It is only under a democracy that the state is the fatherland of all individuals who compose it and can count as many active defenders of its cause as its citizens. There lies the source of the superiority of free peoples above all others. . . . One could say, in a sense, that in order to love justice and equality the people have no need of a great degree of virtue; it suffices if they love themselves."[36] Not that it is an easy matter to get people to love themselves, but this "utilitarian" view of democracy—that it is, ultimately, in everyone's best interest—is necessary to prevent virtue itself from becoming murderous.

When the utopian scales were lifted off his eyes, Robespierre could accurately observe things about the dangers in democratic society that no one before Tocqueville, and possibly not even he, could perceive. We have been struck, in the early 1990s in America, by how many people have decided that the politicians governing the country are crooks and scoundrels. As if, somehow, those in office were imposed upon us by some foreign power. The people do not seem to reflect on why it is that the people keep choosing scoundrels and crooks. Concerned observers worry that, should this populist, anti-Washington outcry grow in effectiveness, a man will arise who will vow to put an end to all this corruption, and the democracy will be held in the balance. Remarkably enough, Robespierre descried exactly this danger two hundred years ago: "Democracy perishes by two kinds of excess: either the aristocracy of those who govern, or else popular scorn for the authorities whom the people themselves have established, scorn which makes each clique, each individual take unto himself the public power and bring the people through excessive disorders, to annihilation or to the power of one man."[37]

It was an extraordinary capacity for analysis and insight, but brilliant though Robespierre may have been, his genius operated within, and was the product of, a society that had established democracy—and possibly radical democracy—as an imperative. It was Tocqueville and Robespierre who most clearly perceived that, in the future, democracy could be denied only with inordinate repression. One had learned this from having been born into, and the other from studying in great detail, the *ancien régime*. Within this latter, supposedly corrupt society was born the dream of democracy.

UNIVERSAL EDUCATION

One thing that almost all sections of French elite society—except for the most unenlightened segments—seemed to agree upon was the need to improve the quality of education of the young. For the most progressive elements, universal education became inevitably intertwined with radical democracy. Even more conservative citizens, who resisted the push toward full democracy, acted as if Modernity and the reform of education were each a condition of the other. One powerful demonstration of how insistent was the drive toward the Modern world within eighteenth-century culture was the widespread approval of the reformation of the system of education.

Tocqueville, in his explication of how even *ancien régime* nobles were filled with the spirit of their age, refers to the *cahiers* of the nobility: "In their eyes, as in those of everyone else, public education seems the grand panacea, and its director must be the State. One *cahier* says that 'the Estates-General will give their attention to forming the national character by modifying the education of children.' "[38]

Once the revolutionary process had significantly progressed, universal public education became a central concern for those of radical and Jacobin persuasion. Not waiting for the central government, many local sections initiated their own system of instruction. In March of '93, for instance, the patriotic society of the Luxembourg section in Paris announced its own plan for the instruction of children: boys and girls, between the ages of six and twelve, were to be taught twice a week. Improvement of personal character and the first attributes of citizenship were to be elucidated: good manners, respect for parents, natural pity, and concern for the aged; understanding of a government based on freedom and equality, comprehension of the sovereignty of the people, the human degradation in tyrannical government, and the celebration of the joys of a republic.[39]

Not surprisingly, education of the young became a passionate concern of Robespierre. Louis Michel Le Pelletier, born a high-status noble of a substantial fortune, developed into a Jacobin and a radical democrat. President for a time of the National Constituent Assembly, delegate to the Convention, member and sometime president of the Jacobin Club, he was assassinated in January '93 because of his views and became one of the three great martyrs of the third revolution, along with Marat and Chalier. A little before his death he had prepared a *Plan d'education publique et nationale:* an all-encompassing, almost totalitarian, prescription for universal education. Le Pelletier had stated that education was to be "the revolution of the poor."[40] Some months after his death, Robespierre took up the *Plan* as advocate and, in a long and important speech, presented it in paraphrase to the Convention on July 13, 1793.

After paying passionate tribute to Le Pelletier's memory, Robespierre begins: "The National Convention owes three monuments to history: the Constitution, the code of civil laws, public education. . . . I have dared to conceive a truly vast conception; and considering at what point the human specie is degraded by the vice of our ancient social system, I have convinced myself of the necessity to perform an entire regeneration and, if I may express myself thusly, to create a new people. To create men; to propagate humane knowledge; such are the two parts of the problem that we have to solve."[41]

The steps advocated by Le Pelletier and approved by Robespierre, however, went far beyond anything that has even been instituted by any democratic society. Not only the education of the young, but the very formation of their personality and character, becomes the obligation of the State. When Robespierre decreed that: "It is no longer a question of forming gentlemen . . . but rather citizens," and also that: "The nation alone has the right to raise children,"[42] it was as if he were echoing the ancient voice of Plato, who indicated that the only way to establish his new utopian Republic was to take everyone over ten years of age and ship them out of the city, leaving the young to be completely molded by the new State.[43]

The plan itself, which was, of course, never instituted, was to take all boys and girls at the age of five years to be raised up in common by the State, at the expense of the Republic, and "all under the holy law of equality will receive *mêmes vêtements, même nourriture, même instruction, mêmes soins.*" The costs would be raised by a progressive tax that would fall almost entirely on the rich. The boys would stay until the age of twelve; the girls until eleven. "At five years, the fatherland will receive the infant from the hands of nature; at twelve years, it will return him back to society."[44]

Already, at the very beginning, one great ambiguity in Modernity makes its presence known. In the utopian wish to create a new man, *un nouvel homme*, the totalitarian mode becomes an enormous temptation for people with a particular mindset.

The drive toward universal education, nevertheless, was not the prerogative of radical Jacobinism alone. It was an imperative of Modernity, and Thermidor by no means put an end to this impulse toward the Modern world. Four months after the end of the Terror the Convention decreed a liberal-bourgeois version of the Le Pelletier-Robespierre project. A primary school was to be established in every commune of over a thousand inhabitants; the teachers were to be employees of the State; in addition to reading, writing, and arithmetic, the students were to be taught the Declaration of the Rights of man, the Constitution, and the history of "free peoples." Social virtue was to be taught by taking students to hospitals and workshops and arranging for them to help the elderly. No religious instruction was decreed.[45] No matter what the conscious intentions of the makers of this plan were, once it became effective, it could not help but result in strengthening the impulses toward universal democracy.

And yet, the struggle for Modernity, in many varied societies, has produced almost every possible manner of compromise between true Modernity and the preservation of old forms of social cohesion. It is striking to observe that Prussia, at the very time of the French revolutions, embarked on a modernizing program with regard to education that, seemingly, had nothing to do with democratizing or secularizing drives but resulted purely from the desire for an efficient, rational—that is, "Modern"—society.[46] One can wholeheartedly embrace the rationalizing, orderly aspects of Modernity and yet reject the impulses toward democracy and a secular society. Napoleon, indeed, did not need to learn this lesson from the Prussians. The history of the world for the past two hundred years has been the narrative of each nation attempting to create a stable society, some by picking and choosing which particular aspects of Modernity they wish to reject. Sometimes these compromises work remarkably well, as in post–World War II Japan; and sometimes these attempts produce catastrophes: Nazi Germany, Bosnia, Cambodia, and so on. Revolutionary France was one of the first societies—if not the first—that attempted to make these decisions in an atmosphere of near hysteria.

Even paying close regard to all these reservations and ambivalences, there is no question that eighteenth-century France and the first two revolutions gave enormous promise of the success of democratic society, based upon democratic citizenship. That promise was betrayed. They could not do it. No one has yet adequately explained to us why that journey proved so treacherous. Such explanation may not yet be available to us. It may be helpful, nevertheless, to keep harrowing that question.

6

THE BETRAYAL OF THE PROMISE
OF DEMOCRACY

By the middle of September 1792, the great republican and democratic future of France seemed assured. The king had been overthrown and a republic proclaimed. Democratic elections had taken place for deputies to a National Convention whose mandate was to write a new republican constitution for France. When the Convention assembled in Paris on September 21, there was only a small handful of royalist, aristocratic, or counterrevolutionary delegates, and they maintained a complete silence. There was almost total unanimity on the necessity of writing a constitution based on the sovereignty of the people and of there being no need for monarchy of any kind. Within nine months, all this had collapsed, and France was on the way to dictatorship, civil war, and terror. No aristocratic or monarchical party was responsible for this tragic outcome. Those *outwardly* committed to democracy did it to themselves. It was an almost unprecedented act of self-destruction. The failure of the Revolution cannot be laid at the door of royalist, aristocratic, traitorist, counterrevolutionary forces. Girondins and Jacobins (the Mountain) in the attempt to murder each other ended up annihilating France.

September 4, 1792. The bodies of those massacred in the prisons by the people-in-the-streets of Paris had barely cooled before Robespierre began a possibly murderous attack on the Girondin faction. "No one has dared to name the traitors. Well then, for the salvation of the people, I shall name them. I denounce the liberticide Brissot, the Gironde faction . . . I denounce them for having sold France to Brunswick [the Prussian general who commanded the allied forces in the war against France] and for having received the price of their treason in advance."[1] Responding to this accusation, the Vigilance Committee of the Commune of Paris, which took police action independently of any national law enforcement agency, issued warrants for the arrest of Roland, Brissot, and other prominent Girondins. Had the warrants been executed and these future delegates to the Convention been imprisoned in Paris, when the smell of human sacrifice remained strong in the nostrils of *le peuple*, there is no telling what might have become of these "traitors." And Robespierre could not have been ignorant of this possible outcome. The situation was saved—and the deputies as well—by that great accommodater Danton, who had no fundamental taste for human blood; he secured the withdrawal of the warrants.[2]

September 25, 1792. Four days after the Convention convened, three days after the Republic was proclaimed with no significant opposition, the Gironde began its vicious attack—or its counterattack, depending on whose point of view one takes. Though they themselves had not condemned the September massacres at the time, the Gironde made constant reference to them as the responsibility of the anarchical elements of Paris, approved of by the likes of Robespierre and Marat.[3] In the September 25th debate, Lasource, deputy for the department of the Tarn and a former leader in the Legislative Assembly (1791–1792), led the attack but was ably supported by other leaders of the Gironde faction: Brissot, Vergniaud, Boilleau, Barbaroux, and Rebequi. They implied that the emergency powers still exercised by the Paris Commune were to become an instrument toward the establishment of a dictatorship over all France. Robespierre was especially singled out. And Marat, whose reputation for political violence was known to everyone, came under particular attack. All the Montagnards were subjected to guilt by association with Marat,[4] who was indeed a leader and sometime president of the Jacobin Club in Paris, and who was to become a holy martyr for the Jacobins after his assassination the next July.

Lasource was not content to charge only the two most prominent Montagnards but put the whole of the Paris deputation under indictment, including not only Marat and Robespierre, but also Danton, Collot-d'Herbois, and Billaud-Varenne. The accusation of dictatorship was made directly, with no ambiguity. There is a party, he charged, "qui veut dépopulariser la Convention, qui veut la dominer et la perdre, qui veut régner sous un autre nom, en réunissant tout le pouvoir national entre les mains de quelque individus."[5] ["that wants to depopularize the Convention, that wants to dominate and destroy it, that wants to rule without saying that's what they're after, gathering all the powers of the nation in the hands of a few individuals."] There was no reason to actually mention names, since Lasource was only giving voice to current rumors that the dictatorship of Robespierre, or a dictatorial triumvirate of Danton, Marat, and Robespierre, was being plotted.

The attack failed. Marat responded that he, indeed, had felt, at one time, that the Revolution required a dictatorship or a triumvirate but that Danton and Robespierre disapproved of either course. The Convention was ready to forgive Marat an excess of feeling, and the Gironde did not take up the assault on the dictatorial plans of Robespierre for another month.[6]

Was Robespierre conspiring for a dictatorship? There was a profound pathology in the political culture of the Revolution at this point. If Robespierre was planning—and we do not, and may never, know the answer to this query—a dictatorship in order to save the Revolution from the likes of democrats Brissot and Roland, and not from reactionary counterrevolutionaries—if such was the case, it certainly establishes the point of pathology. That Robespierre would become capable of such a démarche in '93 and '94, that we know with certainty. For the fall of '92, the answer is not forthcoming. But if Robespierre was, indeed, not planning a dictatorship, then the accusations by the Gironde could only have as their intent the indictment, arrest, and eventual execution of an innocent duly elected deputy to the Convention. What kind of democracy, then, was this that, from the very beginning, established such an environment? Imagine Jefferson and Hamilton behaving in a similar manner, and it would not be difficult to envision a hundred years of American history before a stable democratic society could become a reality. Whether Robespierre was guilty of dreaming of dictatorship or not, either way, something was sick in the body politic.

Other Convention delegates, who were not infected by the virus, found the situation incomprehensible. "In the convention newly elected provincial deputies looked on incredulously as those who had battled side by side against despotism and aristocracy now ripped one another apart. In their eyes this was an unnatural confrontation."[7] A delegate from the provinces, Dechézeaux, wrote home a letter expressing his disbelief: "I cannot comprehend how the men, who have battled together despotism and the aristocracy and who appear equally to fear their power and their return, find themselves all of a sudden opposed the ones to the others. I blame the stubbornness, the pride and self-love [*l'amour propre*] of [the Girondins], but I cannot approve the means employed by [the Montagnards]."[8]

Would that it were only a question of self-love and incorrect means. Such were capable of correction. The pathology, however, ran much deeper than this.

October 1792. Our understanding of the intensity and the irrationality of this fratricide that ruined the possibility of French democracy is heightened when we recall that both factions, Montagnards and Girondins, including many of the leaders of the Gironde, were members in good standing of the Jacobin Club in Paris when the Convention began its work in September. Several of the Girondin leaders, such as Brissot and Vergniaud, had been there almost from the beginning. And the future Girondins did not secede from the Club and join the Feuillants after the king's flight to Varennes in 1791. At the time of the overthrow of the king in August '92, the Jacobins included Danton, Robespierre, Marat *and* Brissot, Vergniaud, and many other important members of the Gironde. What quickly tore the Convention apart can only be described as a political civil war between Jacobins and former Jacobins. And here, again, the provincial societies could not comprehend such behavior.

> After the opening of the Convention, the party strife became endemic. . . . The next few weeks were fateful ones for the Paris club. The Girondins, along with most of the other deputies [to the Convention], ceased to attend. In retrospect it is clear that this was a mistake. They should have fought for control of the society. By gathering separately and in secret, they exposed themselves to charges of conspiracy. One of the Jacobins, on October 5, likened them to ungrateful children "tearing at the bosom" of their "tender mother." Their names were gradually stricken from the rolls. The first to go was Brissot on October 10. The flight of the Girondins from the nest allowed it to be taken over by a tiny brood of militants. . . . The schism caused anguish in the [provincial] clubs.[9]

At the end of October, Robespierre responded, at the same primitive level of discourse, to the accusations being hurled at him. The surest way to prove his innocence was to indict the members of the Gironde as traitors. In a speech at the Jacobins, he declared that revolutionary history was repeating itself: the Girondins were the new Feuillants, abandoning all principles in the quest for power. "Take away the word 'republic' and I see no change. . . . [The Girondins were] more criminal in their tactics than all the factions that had preceded them." And they had no reluctance to restore the monarchy, he asserted, if it served their obviously treacherous purposes.[10] The problem with this primitive level of political discourse is that it raises in every hearer's mind the question: What is the appropriate punishment for such traitors and criminals? Within a year, the inexorable answer was forthcoming.

On October 29, in the Convention itself, the Gironde fired off its greatest artillery attack in the attempt to indict Robespierre. It failed again in this effort, but the whole experience could not help but convince Robespierre and many other radical Jacobins that the stakes had risen to the ultimate level: from now on, no stable compromise was possible; it was going to be either them or us.

Almost from the beginning of the Convention, some of the leaders of the Gironde had been calling for detachments of troops from the provinces to come to Paris with the express purpose of protecting the Convention from a possible attack by the people-in-the-streets, which attack would obviously be in the interests of the most radical wing of the Convention: the Mountain. In October, the first of such militia arrived, and their presence may have inspired the Gironde to make its heavy attack on Robespierre.[11] Roland delivered the first salvo. He denounced "those who incite to murder . . . they don't want to hear anyone but Robespierre and pretend that he alone can save the nation."[12] Robespierre arose to the tribune to defend himself, but an old opponent of his, Guadet, was in the chair and made things difficult for him. Many interruptions almost prevented him from finally making some remarks on the scandal of personal intrigue, when Louvet erupted, "I demand a hearing to accuse Robespierre." "And so do we," joined in Rebecqui and Barbaroux. Danton suggested that Robespierre should defend himself against personal attacks in the courts. "If I take your advice," Maximilien replied, "will the Convention pay the costs of the trial?"

"If every member of the House were so touchy," Buzot began his own indictment, but Robespierre rushed again to the tribune. "He is trying to intimidate this House by speeches," declared Rebecqui, "as he has succeeded in intimidating the Jacobins." Guadet overruled Robespierre's claim to reply to Buzot,[13] and now it was time for Louvet's long prepared and lengthily delivered *Robespierride*, a full denunciation of his career since the first break between the Gironde and the radical Jacobins.[14]

Robespierre's party, Louvet insisted, had been responsible for the September massacres and for the exclusion of voters in Paris sympathetic to the Gironde. He had made himself the leader of the Paris Commune, which would become his instrument toward a dictatorship. Bringing false claims against Brissot and his friends was a step toward the establishment of a personal dictatorship. "The authority of the Assembly was insulted and set aside by an insolent demagogue, who came to the bar of the House to dictate its acts, and returned again to the Commission of Twenty-One to threaten it with a call to arms."[15]

Louvet's speech did not destroy Robespierre's credit and power within the Convention. He was given a week to reply to these charges. When he did so, his defense was accepted by the Assembly, and the Girondins had to wait for another more fruitful opportunity to eliminate Robespierre. He, of course, managed to get them first.

Looked at intently, this is frightening data. Robespierre's indictment and conviction would mean the guillotine for him and undoubtedly for others who would be carried down with him as co-conspirators. This political game was not a question—as it is in a stable competitive democracy—of who gets what, when, and how but a more sinister question of who lives and who dies. We cannot help but be dismayed and threatened by the fact that the two great *democratic* factions, the makers of the second revolution, were capable of no more than this suicidal fratricide. It is, somehow, more comforting to give the whole experience a "more rational" dimension: it was, let us say, a battle for power, or a "class struggle." Either of these makes more sense to us; contending for power, we have been led to believe, is a rational pursuit. Relying on such phrases, we are not required to see the severed heads. Mona Ozouf has perceptively seen how "rational" explanations of this catastrophe defend against the anxiety of having to admit how profoundly irrational and self-destructive such behavior was:

> No matter which of these accounts is chosen, one senses that the point is to suppress the scandal of fratricidal struggle by ascribing its origins not to the revolution itself, nor to the struggle it touched off, but to the development of a preexisting structure. If the elimination of the Gironde by the Mountain was the necessary culmination of a conflict between classes or ideas, a clash between two segments of the bourgeoisie distinguished by their incomes or their theories, then the human waste of the French Revolution seems less terrifying and the lessons of conflict seem more clear.[16]

If it was not, then, a conflict of classes or an ordinary contending for power, what was it that made this fratricidal struggle so murderous? The answer to this question might shed light on several of the great problems of these profoundly ambiguous revolutions.

"WE ARE ALL REPUBLICANS—WE ARE ALL FEDERALISTS."

Thus Jefferson, in his 1801 inaugural address, gives powerful voice to the non-paranoid, nonmurderous *mentalité* necessary for an enduring democratic society. On the most important things, he states, we are basically in agreement: "Every difference of opinion is not a difference in principle. We have called by different names brethren of the same principle."[17]

What must be remarked upon is how much Jacobins and Girondins were in almost total agreement on the basic questions facing French society, which fact underlines the almost total irrationality of their murderous competition. The one disagreement that historians have emphasized is that of alliance with different classes of society: the Jacobins with lower classes, the Girondins with the middle and upper bourgeoisie. Depending on whether one is sympathetic to their cause or critical, one may say of the Jacobins either that they were truly compassionate about the suffering of the poor or that they were merely using the people of Paris as a powerful weapon to break the Girondin resistance. Similarly, with the Girondins: critically, that they had no real concern with the catastrophes of poverty; or understandingly, that they clearly perceived that social and political stability required, as Aristotle had elaborated,[18] the support of the middle ranks of society: a bourgeois republic, led by the likes of a Condorcet and not by a Marat.

But, here again, even assuming that there was a firm disagreement about the political future of different classes—as there was, for instance, in America during the Great Depression and the coming of the New Deal—that still does not answer why it was that the disagreement became so homicidal. Especially, when in so many other respects, they were "brethren of the same principle." On the Republic, for instance, for neither party was there any inclination or temptation to bring back the monarchy, no matter how many times the Girondins were accused of such scheming, and no matter how many times Robespierre stood charged with planning a dictatorship.

On the question of the sanctity of property, there was also complete agreement. Danton, who was neither a Girondin nor a close political companion of Robespierre, but still clearly on the left, arose the day after the Assembly convened to reassure those who feared that "Some ardent friends of liberty were able to harm the social order" by threatening property. "Let us abjure here all exaggeration; let us declare that all property territorial, individual and industrial will be eternally defended." And from the Convention itself: *"Il se'élève des applaud-issements unanimes."*[19] At no time did the concept that property was theft become part of Jacobin thought or rhetoric. Jacqueline Chaumié writes: "If one compares the report of Vergniaud on the constitution with the discourse of Robespierre on the right of property on April 24, 1793, one is struck by their similarity. An equal respect for property; an equal will to prevent the formation of large fortunes, in particular by the use of a progressive tax."[20]

The one area where there seemed to be a clear difference in emphasis is an attitude on the part of the Girondins that may be called "elitist." They had no patience with "the wanderer, the idler, the bohemian." On the other hand, however, they were passionately committed to the concept that gifted beings and even workers be permitted "to accede to culture and to responsibilities, despite the modesty of their fortune and of their birth." This view Chaumié ascribes most particularly to Vergniaud, Masuyer, and Vernier and goes on to comment that Madame Roland, "of all distinctions admitted only those coming from virtue and talent."[21] And before we jump to the conclusion that, in regard to the question of "elitism," the Jacobin view was morally superior to that of the Gironde, we must ask ourselves whether Robespierre and Saint-Just were really prepared to be ruled by a moderately capable group of sans-culottes. The fact remains, as has been said, that it was the Jacobin Terror that put an end to sans-culotte "democracy."

Mona Ozouf has summed up this particular agreement between the two great parties; an admittedly arguable point of view, but one certainly worth considering. "Economic and social views thus did not single out a Girondin group except for the period of a few weeks (the month of May) that separated the Mountain's unenthusiastic embrace of the sans-culotterie from the Gironde's exclusion."[22]

Both factions were in almost complete accord on the necessity of universal and *free* public education as a condition of democratic culture.[23] Girondin "elitism" did not go so far as to exclude anyone from the opportunity of public instruction. "If all men are equal in rights," wrote the Girondin Masuyer, "instruction must be public and common to all. . . . it is necessary that it be free because the poor have nothing with which to pay. If, then, you create, a mode of instruction in which the costs are beyond the reach of the poor, the poor cease to be equal in rights with the rich, and thus you vitiate the first law of equality . . . the fundamental base of all the social order . . . a base without which your Republic is not able to exist."[24] The Jacobins had no monopoly on an understanding of what a modern radical democratic society would require and on the wish to implement it.

Concerning the crucial issues of the abolition of slavery and of war with Europe, one can discover no significant difference between the warring factions. Mention has already been made of the lead taken in the antislavery movement by Brissot and his political ally Sonthonax. Here again, compassion for human misery cannot be designated primarily a Jacobin attribute. War with Europe will be discussed later in some detail. Here it is necessary only to emphasize that there was absolutely no difference between the parties. Robespierre, it is true, had the great vision to oppose the declaration of war on Austria in 1792, before the Republic was established, but he carried almost no fellow-Jacobins with him. When war was declared on England and Holland in February '93 the vote in the Convention was unanimous, and when the question of a declaration against Spain came up a month later, it was accepted by the Convention without discussion.[25]

Never, it seems, had two implacable enemies agreed on so many fundamental issues. Even their class backgrounds were almost identical. Mathiez, the historian most committed to the concept that the basis of the Gironde-Mountain clash was a class struggle, writes that "Most of the Montagnards, indeed, were like the Girondins, of middle-class origin. The class policy which they inaugurated had not sprung directly from the people." A truly remarkable statement when one considers that Mathiez had written, a moment before, that "The conflict between the Girondins and the Mountain was a deep-rooted one, almost amounting to a class conflict. . . . The Mountain . . . represented the humbler classes, those who were suffering from the crisis caused by the war, who had overthrown the monarchy and risen to political power through insurrection." And, immediately before the first quote, he stated that "The rivalry between the Gironde and the Mountain . . . had become, since August 10, more than a political rivalry. The class struggle was already taking shape."[26]

What Mathiez is asserting is that a large, significant, politically powerful group of the bourgeoisie (the Jacobin/Montagnard) was acting in a deliberate way to bring a class lower than itself to political power—certainly a unique experience in the history of the world and totally at variance with traditional Marxist theory. What phenomenon, if it could be true, could be more worthy of examination and explanation; but no explanation is forthcoming from this historian. This fascinating circumstance is left hanging in the air. Fantasy theories have no need for reality testing.

THE PEOPLE-IN-THE-STREETS OF PARIS

The people-in-the-streets of Paris were a powerful political factor, one that was absent in other early democratic or antimonarchical revolutions: England, Holland, America. Whether it is accurate to designate them "sans-culottes," "proletariat," or *"menu peuple,"* two things are clear: they were definitely not bourgeois, nor were they law-abiding. Direct action, riot, violence—all these were considered legitimate modes of action. And, up to September '92, they had won three great battles of the Revolution: the Bastille, which saved the first revolution; the October days of '89, which set the scene for the second revolution; and the final overthrow of the king in August '92. It is no wonder that the most bourgeois party, the Gironde, having no equal military force, was legitimately fearful that the Convention itself could become the next object of violent overthrow. This was no paranoid anxiety. Such fears were real, as subsequent history was to show.

And it did not take great political perspicacity to perceive that the Mountain-Jacobin alliance was perfectly willing to use the people of Paris as a final weapon in its struggle with the Gironde. Some crucial factors were the September Massacres in the prisons and the reactions of the factions to them. At first, neither Jacobins nor Girondins publicly denounced that slaughter, even though most tried to distance themselves from the actual events. Each side seemed, somehow, afraid to criticize revolutionary violence, since it had brought the Republic into existence. By November, however, two different and opposite myths of the Massacres had evolved, each one giving a different interpretation of the past, each one pointing toward a different mode of political conduct in the future. "In the Jacobin Club a more doctrinaire attitude was increasingly adopted, and responsibility for the September Massacres, now acclaimed as the result of revolutionary zeal, was openly accepted and even made a cardinal point of Jacobin faith." "Without those days," said Collot d'Herbois, a future terrorist, "the Revolution would never have been achieved."[27] The Girondins, on the opposite hand, began using the term *"Septembriseur"* to indicate any person capable of terrorist action, and more and more hurled that accusation at the Montagnard faction. Such a primitive level of competitive political discourse could only lead to a destruction of democracy.

Even before its final overthrow in May–June '93, the Gironde had enough indication that political violence would be the arbiter of their competition with the Mountain. In the evening of March 9, '93, a crowd marched into the Jacobin

Club and insisted that a purge of the Convention, including ministers and leading Girondin deputies, be set in motion. That night, unruly bands destroyed the
presses and vandalized the print shops of the leading Girondin journals. Forty-
three deputies to the Convention, fearing even greater violence, stayed in their
Convention seats the whole night determined, if necessary, to die honorably for
the sake of their beliefs. The insurrection fizzled, however, because neither the
Paris Commune nor the Jacobin Club joined in the action. The violence was the
product of only the most radical elements in Paris, those known as *enragés*.[28] For
the moment, the political streets returned to quiet. It was, however, a foreboding
indication of what was possible and of how fragile was the infant democracy.
Obviously, when the Jacobin-Mountain alliance would decide to join forces with
this illegitimate street power, the outcome would be much different.

One failed tactic that the Gironde employed to counter the insurrectionary
force of Paris was to call upon armed volunteers from the provinces to come to
Paris in order to preserve the integrity of the Convention. At first, success in this
venture seemed assured. By the middle of November, 16,000 men were in the
capital, mounting guard over the Convention, marching through the streets recit-
ing a ditty, the refrain of which concerned itself with Marat's and Danton's and
Robespierre's heads. At the same time, a mob marched to the Palais Royal,
demanding "Death to Marat and Robespierre."[29] And in December, a fresh
contingent of troops from Finistère arrived, the occasion being celebrated with
a speech indicating their intent was to crush anarchy in Paris.[30] Remarkably,
however, these troops were won over by Marat's diplomatic perspicacity—he
visited their barracks, invited some of them to dinner—and by Robespierre's
calls for calm. The Jacobins had the common touch in a way that the Girondins
completely lacked. "Ultimately those who remained in Paris came under Jacobin
influence, and remained to strengthen the forces at the disposal of the Mountain."[31] When it came to playing populist politics, the Gironde was no match
for the Jacobins.

One further defensive tactic that was bruited about was the same that had
been suggested to the king in the summer of '89: move the central legislative
body out of Paris and, thereby, neutralize the power of the Paris streets. A
month before the '93 *coup* against the Girondins, Tom Paine, who was one of
several foreign deputies to the Convention, wrote to Danton: "I see but one
effectual way to prevent a rupture . . . to fix the residence of the Convention, and
future assemblies, at a distance from Paris."[32] Such wisdom could not prevail.

THE INSTABILITY OF THE REPUBLICAN CITY-STATE

"The republican [i.e., nonmonarchical] city-state was fundamentally an unstable form of society. Athens in ancient Greece and Venice in Italy were exceptions to the otherwise valid observation that the republican city-state was vulnerable to dissolution. . . . The psychological power of monarchy derives, ultimately, from a particular view of paternal potency. Once the king—the father—is removed, the locus of psychological-political power becomes indeterminate. Freud was wrong in the fable he told in *Totem and Taboo* wherein the brothers in prehistoric times, after killing and eating the father, shared out the women and lived together in equality. . . . That fable was a metaphorical description of the revolutionary birth of a democratic state. The history of the republican city-state demonstrates that once the father is removed and the possibilities of equality become real, the brothers begin to war with each other, either seeking sibling equality or determined to become the new father and the new tyrant. There is no longer a father with the power to command the sons to stop slaughtering each other. Unless a stable democratic state eventually prevails or the monarchy is reborn, the fraternal killing never seems to stop. Since almost all republican city-states were incapable of democratic resolution of their conflicts, monarchy proved to be the *telos* of the *polis.*"[33]

The preceding quotation comes from a recent work of mine, from a chapter on the unendurability of the nonmonarchical state in premodern times. The data used as a basis for the theoretical conclusions in that chapter came from the ancient Greek *poleis,* from the history of republican Rome 133–27 B.C., and from the experience of Italian city-states c. 1000 to c. 1350. When writing it, I had done no work on the French Revolutions, and in no way did I have the history of France from 1789–1799 in mind. When re-reading that chapter in the course of writing this book, I was astounded to discover how similar were the political problems, and their failure of resolution, of these premodern city-states and postmonarchical France.

Three fundamental attributes characterized these premodern states and also France after the deposition of the king: (1) The competition for political power became almost unbelievably murderous. And this murderous competition truly had no moral or ideological basis, though a certain amount of pretense existed that such was the case. In the late Roman Republic and in Italian city-states of the late medieval times, the primary lethal political activity took place between different factions of the nobility. In France, Jacobin and Girondin elements of the newly empowered bourgeoisie were intent on annihilating each other. (2) In both the premodern and the French circumstances, one of the competing factions would make alliance with lower classes, promising to alleviate their impoverished condition, only to betray and dispose of them once victory over the other faction was achieved. (3) Fratricidal anarchy was only overcome with the reinstatement of some form of monarchy and its subsequent tyranny.

It is not appropriate to rehearse here the variety of data used in that chapter from the three premodern circumstances. It would be helpful, nevertheless, to look at the hundred-year period when the Roman aristocracy committed suicide and destroyed the Republic, for no rational reason that anyone at the time—nor any historian since—could or can as yet discover. Three circumstances lend weight to this particular presentation: (1) At the time of Marius and Sulla, the decade of the 80s B.C., the reign of political terror and annihilation of political enemies was so incredibly murderous that it forces one to wonder what insight it might provide into the French Terror. (2) The history of that fratricidal civil war was present in the mind of French revolutionary actors, who sometimes used the analogy with Marius and Sulla to accuse their opponents. (3) Though one party in the Roman civil wars was called "Optimates" and the other "Populares," which would imply a fundamental difference of class alliance, such attributions were a political fiction. "The political life of the Roman Republic," writes Ronald Syme, a historian of the collapse of Rome, "was stamped and swayed, not by parties and programmes of a modern and parliamentary character, not by the ostensible opposition between Senate and People, *Optimates* and *Populares*, *nobiles* and *novi homines*, but by the strife for power, wealth, and glory. The contestants were the *nobiles* among themselves."[34]

The political revenge inflicted on defeated opponents had an almost genocidal fury. Theodor Mommsen describes the scene after Marius took Rome in 87 B.C. "He then entered, and with him the reign of terror. It was determined not to select individual victims, but to have all the notable men of the Optimate party put to death and to confiscate their property. The gates were closed; for five days and five nights the slaughter continued without interruption; even afterwards the execution of individuals who had escaped or been overlooked was of daily occurrence, and for months the bloody persecution went on throughout Italy. . . . he forbade the burial of the dead bodies: he gave orders . . . that the heads of the senators slain should be fixed to the top rostra of the Forum.[35]

Five years later it was Sulla's turn to play headhunter—literally, not metaphorically. "In the proscriptions of Sulla Italy endured the consummation of her sufferings. The execution of the captured Marian leaders and the butchery of the Samnite prisoners were followed by continual murders in the city. . . . At length one of [Sulla's] own partisans questioned him in the Senate as to his intentions. His response was the issue of a series of proscription lists, by which he outlawed all who had in any public or private capacity aided the cause of his opponents. . . . Rewards were offered to those who murdered or betrayed any of these outlaws."[36]

The suicidal fratricide of the Roman Republic and the murderous politics following the overthrow of the monarchy in France, are not, obviously, precisely analogous. It is true that, in both cases, we observe a homicidal competitive politics between factions of the same ruling class, a struggle that had no authentic moral or ideological content. The Romans, however, had lived for 500 years without a king before the nobles began to wantonly annihilate each other, whereas the French fratricide began immediately after the king's overthrow. One fact, however, is striking. The Roman Civil War between nobles began almost immediately after the failed experiment in social and economic equality associated with the activities of Tiberius and Gaius Gracchus (beginning in 133 B.C.), both of whom were assassinated by the reactionary nobility because of their efforts to bring a minimum economic security, necessary for a dignified life, to even the lowest of Roman citizens. We know, also, that the great questions of social and economic equality were immediately raised with great force by the Revolution of 1789. Maybe the granting of full equality to all human beings— the terrible renunciation of one's hierarchical superiority, no matter how "civilized" that hegemony appears to be—maybe this renunciation is as frightening as the abandonment of the security of the monarch. It is possible that the profound ambivalence about equality, and the frenzy caused by the failure to resolve the issue one way or another, set the Roman nobility on the path of annihilating each other. And, possibly, this may help us understand that awesome experience of the French Terror, which no one, as yet, has adequately explained to us.

The general history of the instability of the Republican city-state (Greece, Rome, Italy) does present other striking similarities to the French Revolutionary experience. The Jacobin use of the street power of the sans-culottes to triumph over the Gironde, and the subsequent destruction of sans-culotte political power by these same Jacobins, had myriad analogies in ancient Greece, Rome, and late medieval Italy. There is no need to repeat here the extensive data to support this observation that is contained within my chapter, but a few summary statements may be in order. "The history of the Republican city-states repeatedly tells the pitiful tale of the *demos:* Like so many attractive yet powerless heroines of nineteenth-century novels, it refused to take power into its own hands but deposited its potential and its faith in the keeping of one man, or a small group of men, who quickly progressed from savior to betrayer. . . . 'Now when a people goes so far as to commit the error of giving power to one man,' writes Machiavelli [*The Discourses,* Book I, Chapter 40], 'so that he may defeat those whom they hate, and if this man be shrewd, it will always end in his becoming their tyrant. For with the support of the people he will be enabled to destroy the nobility, and after these are crushed he will not fail in turn to crush the people; and by the time that they become sensible of their enslavement, they will have no one to look to for succor.' "[37] It was a vision of Robespierre and Saint-Just and an unheeded and unknown message to the Kronstadt sailors.

Historically, the empowered faction that uses the people does give it some semblance of relief at the beginning, just as the Jacobins/Montagnards did establish price controls on many necessities and provided enough food for Paris. In the end, the sans-culottes got what the *demos* in ancient Greece, the Populares in Rome, and the lower classes in Italian city-states received: two parts relief and eight parts betrayal.

The last striking parallel between 1789–1799 France and premodern city-states is how the political anarchy unleashed by fratricidal politics leads, inevitably, to the reestablishment of the monarchical form, many times under a significant variation of the original kingship, as the only way to keep the radical forces down and establish some form of political stability. The rise of Napoleon to almost absolute power is not our subject, but it must be said that that narrative is not unique in history. Napoleon stands at the end of a long line of postmonarchical monarchs: Pisistratus, tyrant of Athens; Philip of Macedon; Pompey the Great; Augustus Caesar; all the greater and lesser *signorie* of the Italian Republics, most notably the Medici in Florence; Oliver Cromwell. Once the establishment of a stable, modern democratic society proves impossible, one form or another of Napoleon becomes inevitable.

The crucial word is "modern." It seems, from looking at all this history, that a stable democratic citizenship in the premodern world was almost impossible. Ancient Athens, alone, seems to be the only significant exception. *Modernity was a necessary condition in order to achieve this state in more than exceptional cases.* Without their using the vocabulary of "premodern" or "Modernity," it is clear that Madison and Hamilton, in their discussion of the new American constitution, were keenly aware of the tremendous failures of democracy and stability in previous republican states. Their argument specifically asserts that the new constitution should be adopted because it will guarantee that what has happened in the past will not take place in America: "A Firm Union will be of the utmost moment," writes Hamilton, "to the peace and liberty of the States as a barrier against domestic faction and insurrection. It is impossible to read the history of the petty Republics of Greece and Italy, without feeling sensations of horror and disgust at the distractions with which they were continually agitated, and at the rapid succession of revolution, by which they were kept in a state of perpetual vibration, between the extremes of tyranny and anarchy. If they exhibit occasional calms, these only serve as short-lived contrasts to the furious storms that are to succeed."[38]

The struggle for a stable democratic society is the battle for Modernity. The struggle for Modernity is the great endeavor for democracy. So long as society remains primarily in a premodern stage, no truly democratic society is possible.

THE PRIMITIVE LEVEL OF POLITICAL DISCOURSE

On September 25, 1792, four days after the Convention commenced sitting, the Gironde began its attack on Marat, when Boileau read out to the Assembly an article by Marat in which he called for a new insurrection and the establishment of a dictatorship. Shouts of "Marat to the Abbaye" rang out, and a decree of indictment was almost voted when the accused calmly announced that he had, indeed, written that article in a moment of indignation but had subsequently changed his views and now gave his wholehearted allegiance to the Convention: his *"nouvelle marche."* Turmoil and confusion ensued, whereupon Marat took out a pistol and, pointing at is forehead, announced: "I am bound to state that if my indictment had been decreed, I should have blown out my brains at the foot of the tribune. So this is the result of three years spent in dungeons, and the tortures I have endured to save the country! This is the result of my vigils, my toil, my poverty, my sufferings, and the dangers to which I have been exposed! Very well! I will remain among you and brave your fury!"[39]

This was no scene from a tragedy on a Roman theme composed by Corneille or a Romantic drama by Schiller—this was the fourth day of the sitting of the highest legislative body in France, which had been convened to write a new constitution and determine the political future of the Nation. This was, nevertheless, merely an exaggerated experience of what marked the entire level of

BETRAYAL OF THE PROMISE OF DEMOCRACY

political discourse of the revolutionary years. The most accurate description is supplied by the word "hysterical." So much of the level of political declamation at the time was of an hysterical nature that it makes one wonder how democratic process was possible in such a heated environment.

And Marat was, of course, one of the worst offenders. Of the most influential newspaper he published and edited, Ozouf writes: "This rhetoric without argument, breathless and full of vengeful injunctions ('arrest,' 'inspect,' 'impale,' 'flay,' and so on) makes the *Ami du peuple* resemble a frantic monologue."[40] He could play the primitive theme of the necessity of human sacrifice to save the Revolution with great passion and persuasion. "Put to the sword all the prisoners of the Abbey," he announced on August 19, '92, and, when the September Massacres subsequently took place, he signed the circular of September 3, encouraging the provinces to imitate the actions of Paris.[41] He was periodically calling for the decapitation of a certain number of heads, the number accelerating as the Revolution progressed: first it was the heads of the émigré Capets, then "600 well-chosen heads," and finally "200,000" heads. "Shed drops of blood"—punish "a few individuals"—in order to save the lives of so many more.[42] Such has always been the primitive logic of the sacrificial mode. Marat had a direct line to that savage part of the mind.

He was one of the most radical of radical Jacobins, but it is important to emphasize that, unlike the *enragés*, Roux and Leclerc, unlike the nonbourgeois radical Hébert, Marat was within the mainstream of Jacobin politics. He was, at times, the president of the Paris Club. When he was assassinated, he was elevated to the ranks of the three great Martyrs of the Revolution. He was revered at the Jacobin Club. And yet, he was a born terrorist. Varying the old cliché about greatness, one may say that some were born terrorists (Marat, Roux); some achieved terrorism (Robespierre, Saint-Just); and some had terrorism thrust upon them (Barère, Danton). A born terrorist, mightily effective with the rhetoric of bloodletting and sacrifice, would yet remain and succeed within the ranks of the bourgeois revolutionary world.

There was something within the political culture of the time that made this possible. As has been observed by many, one helpful mode in understanding the French Revolutionary experience is to compare and contrast it with the English and American experience, with the latter, of course, being much closer in time to the French Revolution. We scarcely find this primitive level of political discourse among the leaders of the American Revolution. And Marat did not start it. In July 1789, the conquerors of the Bastille had "hacked the governor of the

Bastille to pieces and massacred the city's chief magistrate, Flesselles, who had delayed the issue of arms. Their heads were paraded through the streets on pikes."[43] Understandably, no outcry against this primitive violence was expressed in the National Assembly, since the Revolution had been saved by the very people who took such action. Eight days later, however, Bertier de Sauvigny and his father-in-law Foulon were lynched and decapitated by a Paris mob because they were suspected of wishing to starve the city as a counterrevolutionary act. This savagery was condemned in the Assembly in a speech by Lally-Tolendal. Antoine Barnave rose to answer Lally-Tolendal's criticism. Barnave was no radical. He was destined to be imprisoned after the overthrow of the king because he was implicated by a document found in the monarch's cabinet. He was guillotined in Paris in November 1793. In defense of the mob action in the streets, Barnave in 1789 gave voice to an epigrammatic remark that received great currency during revolutionary times: "le sang qui vient de se répandre était-il donc si pur?"[44] ["The blood which has just been shed, was it then so pure?"] If we attempt to imagine Franklin or Jefferson or Madison giving voice to such cold hysteria, we begin to perceive what a different world endured in Paris.

And that hysterical mode of both rhetoric and action accelerated and infected the highest level of political action as the Gironde and the Jacobins continued their life-and-death struggle. More important, the Girondin leaders, though considered more conservative, were no less committed to a struggle to the death. In March '93, Danton met with some of their leaders in the attempt to work out a political truce. He was violently rebuffed by Guadet: "War and may one side perish!"[45] Similarly, as the coup against the Girondin leaders grew more imminent, on May 25, 1793, a delegation from the Paris Commune entered the Convention, only to be rebuffed by the Girondin Isnard, who had no hesitancy in quoting from a sinister proclamation made many months before by the Prussian Duke of Brunswick who was threatening to destroy Paris: "I tell you in the name of the whole of France that if these perpetually recurring insurrections ever lead to harm to the parliament chosen by the nation, Paris will be annihilated, *and men will search the banks of the Seine for traces of the city.*"[46] Thus does impotence pathetically express itself in fantasies of omnipotence.

From the Jacobin/Montagnard quarter we have no surprise in hearing the expression of the paranoid all-or-nothing political *mentalité.* As only one example among many, Saint-Just explained, on March 13, 1794, that "what constitutes a Republic is the total destruction of all that is opposed to it."[47] The word "total" is crucial to this paranoid *Weltanschauung:* we will create a totally new man, totally reform society, totally eliminate all enemies of justice. To imagine that one can do anything, socially or politically, "totally" is a fantasy: a fantasy erected as a defense against paranoid anxiety. The fantasy of totality pervaded the revolutionary discourse, especially during the Jacobin months.

And when the great leaders or the people are blazing the trail, it is no surprise that the people themselves are capable of giving perfect voice to the paranoid solution to all social problems: blood and human sacrifice will make the world whole again:

> *Petition of the William Tell Section to the Convention, 12 November 1793.*

REPRESENTATIVES OF THE PEOPLE

You have just given a terrifying example, made to astonish the universe and strike fear into the most guilty.

The William Tell Section congratulates you. It will congratulate you still more if you maintain fear and terror as the great order of the day, that fear and terror which are the two most powerful levers of revolutionaries.

Blood is necessary to punish so many liberticidal and nationicidal crimes; still more is necessary to prevent those that would follow.

It is from this moment only that the soul of Pelletier, Marat, Chalier and so many other glorious martyrs of liberty begin to find appeasement.

Representatives, the death of a handful of conspirators cannot sever all the threads of the most execrable plot ever conceived in the human heart; a hecatomb of traitors is necessary to bring healing to all the wounds of the fatherland, butchered by unnatural children.

The aristocracy has not renounced its twilight schemes. Its favorite nourishment is murder and carnage. The fall of twenty-one heads [the Girondin leaders], that of the indecent Marie-Antoinette and of the beastly inhabitants of the infernal palace, has only kindled its fury, and perhaps at this very moment it is planning to overthrow the firmest column of liberty.

There are still more enemies, no less dangerous.

There are the foul public pillagers. Legislators, spare none of these vampires of the *patrie*. Scrutinize the scandalous fortunes that ceaselessly insult the public misery and close the tombs only when our infernal enemies, the most perfidious of all, are swallowed up within them.

Representatives, the days of mercy are past. Let the avenging blade fall upon every guilty head, let no criminal be spared. A great people expects great measures from you.

Never forget the sublime words of the prophet, Marat: *Sacrifice 200,000 heads, and you will save 1,000,000.*[48]

A veritable textbook case of the giving voice to paranoid anxiety and the defensive measures erected to assuage it: blood, and more blood.

Over and over again, the central problem was to go beyond the point where those who disagreed with one on political matters were designated unqualified traitors. The paranoid position, which decidedly fails to transcend this view, suffused the political culture of the revolutionary period. On December 6, 1792, Marat attacked Roland and his "royalist faction," insisting that the vote on the fate of Louis be by open and personal declaration "so that the traitors in this assembly shall be known."[49] As the movement to expel the Griondin delegates accelerated, the rhetoric of traitor and betrayer became more commonplace. On April 5, 1793, the Paris Jacobin Club memorialized its affiliates: "Friends! We are betrayed. . . . The center of counterrevolution is in the government in the Convention. . . . Rise up! . . . All popular societies must flood the Convention with petitions manifesting a formal wish for the immediate recall of all its unfaithful members who have betrayed their duty in not wanting the death of the king, and especially those who have led astray a great number of their colleagues. Such deputies are traitors, royalists, or fools."[50] This, we understand, not from some radical-fringe newspaper, but from the very center of political power in the nation. And Robespierre, having previously been reluctant to attack duly elected deputies to the Convention, finally saw his way to a just accusation of the traitors, on April 10, '93: "His speech was more than mere recrimination. It was an accusation of complicity by 'Brissot, Guadet, Vergniaud, Gensonné, and other hypocritical agents of the same coalition' in a criminal and treasonable conspiracy. The members of the faction were 'a profoundly corrupt coalition,' participators in a plot against the Republic, 'links in a chain connecting all the hostile chancelleries of Europe.' "[51]

The *mentalité* that ultimately prevailed in this fratricidal struggle and that poisoned the political environment of France for more than a hundred years has been succinctly summed up by David Jordan: "It is one of the melancholy facts of revolution that there is no provision for a loyal opposition; there is only victory or death."[52] But not only in revolutionary circumstances. *All* societies moving from a premodern to a modern polity, which means a basis in democratic citizenship, must make the transition to a world of loyal opposition. Failing this, other concomitant failures are inevitable.

A scene observed in New York City in the early 1970s, when the agitation against the war in Vietnam was at its height: A group of construction workers, at their lunch hour, was disgruntedly watching a band of mostly young demonstrators marching and chanting against the war. The temptation to go out and break a few heads of these cowards and traitors was almost overwhelming, but sound judgment prevailed, in part, because at a crucial moment one of the workers gave voice to a political commonplace: "After all," he said, "they are entitled to their opinion."[53] After we express relief and admiration at this peaceful resolution, we are still left with the prodigious theoretical question: What measures are necessary, what revolutions, not in politics or institutions, but in values and mores, are required in order that a political culture reach a point where even "possible traitors" are entitled to their opinion? The answer to that question is the key to understanding all the tragic failures of the French Revolutions.

7

THE MIRAGE OF DEMOCRATIC CITIZENSHIP

The politics of France, from the forceful expulsion of the Girondin deputies in May–June 1793 until the ascension of Napoleon in November 1799, was a government, almost exclusively, by coup d'état. There was not one peaceful (i.e., civil) transfer of power during this whole period of supposed government by "the people." The Jacobins and Robespierre came to power in the coup of '93 and were removed from power by the Thermidor coup in '94. The Thermidorian government retained its political power only by defending itself against three attempted coups: two by sans-culottes (Germinal: April 1795 and Prairal: May 1795) and one by a royalist faction (Vendémiaire: October 1795). The government of the Directory, which succeeded the Thermidorians, had to defend itself successfully against the intended coup of Babeuf in February 1797 and, even more important, only maintained its political hegemony by two in-power coups that negated the results of legitimately conducted elections (the coups of Fructidor: September 1797 and Floréal: May 1798). It is a vast understatement to assert that it was an environment enormously inimicable to democratic citizenship. Reading this pathetic history, one is far from being shocked to discover that conservative dictatorship was finally resorted to in the search for some form of social stability.

An accurate narrative of this period of repression-of-anarchy-by-coup-d'état is not difficult to come by and has been elaborated by several insightful historians. There is no need to try to tell it again here. It may be helpful, however, especially for the reader unfamiliar with this dolorous period, to give some of the flavor of a post-Terrorist, but yet profoundly unstable, time.

The Terror, as such, was gone, but ordinary tyranny was an accessible political weapon, and the defenders of whatever temporary status quo existed did not hesitate to take down the innocent along with the guilty. As in all periods of intense political oppression, justice was of very little consideration. In April 1795, after the failed sans-culottes coup of Germinal, reprisals against members of the political opposition progressed in the usual manner: arrested were Hentz, Lecointre, Granet, Maignet, Levasseur of Sarthe, and Crassous. "Most of them," Mathiez writes, "had taken no part whatever in the demonstration. They were not even charged with having used imprudent language on that day. They were the leaders of the opposition, and that was enough. On the 12th Germinal the Dantonist Garnier of Aube, in moving the arrest of all members of the old governing Committees in a body, frankly admitted this: 'When it is a question of getting rid of tyranny, we ought not to stand upon formalities. Did we observe any on the 9th Thermidor?' "[1]

Arrests, deportations, and executions—the usual arsenal of tyrannical hegemony—were resorted to in "defense of the Republic." After Prairal, the very last sans-culotte uprising, a military commission was set up by the Convention. "They pronounced a number of death-sentences," Mathiez tells us, "for reasons which were often trifling. The most distinguished victims were the ex-deputies Romme, Dequesnoy, Du Roy, Bourbotte, Soubrany, and Goujon, who were condemned to death 'for having conspired against the Republic . . . tried to bring about the dissolution of the National Convention and the assassination of its members, attempted by every means to organize revolt and civil war and revive all the excesses and horrors of the tyranny which preceded Thermidor.' "[2]

It is one thing for a legitimate government to defend itself, even with an excess of "justice," against attempted coups. It is an even more damaging—probably fatal—experience for democracy to institute a coup to nullify a legitimately conducted election, which had been authorized and administered by that very government. In the present-day world, where every country on the earth is engaged in the struggle for, or resistance to, Modernity, every couple of months or so our daily newspapers report an election somewhere nullified by one sort of coup or another. We have grown used to the experience. It always means, nevertheless, that democratic citizenship is profoundly problematic in that political culture.

The attempted insurrection of Prairal (May 1795) was the last serious sans-culotte uprising. After that, the lower classes in France represented no threat to the hegemony of the various bourgeois factions. These latter, however, perpetuated the crisis mentality that allowed almost any means, legal or not, in the conceived interests of stability and order. The resolution of political conflict by means of democratic citizenship, where various factions form themselves into parties, grant to each other the position of nontraitorist loyal opposition and are capable of peaceful transfers of power after elections adverse to the ruling faction—all this was impossible for French political culture at the time. Instead, the government of the Directory (November 1795 to November 1799) insisted on conducting elections and then disallowing their results when they proved hostile to the governing faction.

From the early fall of 1792, when deputies to the National Convention were elected, until October 1795, there were no national elections in France. Having lived through the establishment of the first Republic, the Jacobin dictatorship, the Terror, the fall of Robespierre, and the conservative reaction of the Thermi-dorians—throughout all this the deputies to the National Convention retained the supreme political power in the nation. Most of them had been elected in 1792. With the exclusion, of course, of radical Jacobins, Girondins who had not been reinstated, those killed by the Terror, and others who had ceased to sit for various other reasons. In everyone's mind, it was still the National Convention that wrote the Constitution of the Year III in August–September 1795, and instituted it in October–November of that year.

In the interest of political stability and slowing down the pace of political change, the new Constitution was accompanied by the infamous "two-thirds law," which dictated that only 250 out of 750 members of the new legislatures would be elected in the first election in October 1795; all of which would allow two-thirds of the sitting delegates to remain in the assembly. A hue and cry was raised against this maneuver, as perpetuating even longer the power of the members of a Convention that had overstayed its welcome. The deputies of the assembly acquired the opprobrious epithet: the "perpetuals." And yet, this seeming antidemocratic demarch made great sense. Elections were scheduled for October 1795; for March–April 1797; and for March 1798. Within two and one-half years, all the seats in the legislature would have been up for election. And had not France already suffered enough from extreme political impatience, which can be understood as an essential part of the hysterical nature of French political culture at the time? The attempts to create a *nouvel homme* in one generation, to establish a republic of virtue overnight, to completely overhaul the mores of society with lightning speed—had not all this ended in catastrophe?

The opponents of the Thermidorian powers, however, were indignant and adamant. They could not wait thirty months to seize power. The most vigorous and violent opposition was royalist, determined to reinstate some form of monarchy. On the 5th of October, 1795, before the first elections were held, they rose up in Paris in an attempted coup against the Convention and, most particularly, in opposition to the two-thirds law: the uprising of Vendémiaire. The constituted power succeeded in forcibly putting down the insurrection; quiet returned; no particular disruptions accompanied the elections two weeks later. On the second of November, the Directory—the new constitutional government—was established. Of the five Directors, who composed the executive power of the new government, all of them were *Conventionnels*—that is, former elected delegates to the Convention.

The nation, however, was fatally divided politically. On the right, antirepublicans and promonarchians, running the gamut from conservative to radically reactionary inclinations. On the left, a nonradical, but nevertheless intensely liberal faction that would come to be designated neo-Jacobin. In the center, this Convention turned Directory: bourgeois republicans, trying to keep power and hold the country together. It was not necessarily a prescription for disaster, but, once again, there was no mechanism of democratic citizenship, based upon political parties peacefully competing for power. Lacking this, coup d'états, insurrections, and eventual dictatorship were inevitable.

FRUCTIDOR: SEPTEMBER 1797

The second election under the new constitution, March–April 1787, was a disaster for the Directory. Two hundred thirty-four members of the Convention had to retire. They were, however, subject to re-election if the voters so chose. Only 11 were returned. Of those newly elected, 228 were without any previous political experience; 182 were announced royalists. A more profound vote of no-confidence in the existing government cannot be imagined. Reubell, one of the five Directors, immediately proposed that the election be annulled. His colleagues disagreed and wished to wait and see what would occur before taking action. The prognosis was bleak, however. The Council of Five Hundred (the lower of the two new legislative bodies) elected Jean-Charles Pichegru president, who was a known royalist sympathizer and avowed enemy of the Directory. In July, the Directors had troops moved up within striking distance of the capital. By early September, the existing executive felt strong enough to strike. On the night of September 3–4, troops were ordered to seize all the strong points in Paris and surround the legislative chambers. Arrests were commenced.[3]

The next morning the Directory covered the walls of the city with a proclamation justifying the coup as a defense against a planned Anglo-royalist conspiracy. Anyone who desired to restore the monarchy or revive the Jacobin Constitution of 1793 was to be shot without trial. Terror had obviously become an automatic response in French political culture. The elections in forty-nine departments were annulled. Normandy, Brittany, the region of Paris, and the North were left without any parliamentary representation. Fifty-three deputies were ordered deported to Guiana, called the "dry guillotine" because so many died there without the help of the steel blade. Two members of the Directory, who had opposed the repressive measures of the three ruling members, were also arrested and ordered to Guiana. Four days later, a new law was passed, which gave the police complete control of the press and listed by name forty-two journals, the editors of which were scheduled for deportation.[4] Robespierre and Saint-Just could not have done the job more efficiently.

FLORÉAL: MAY 1798

So volatile was the political situation in Directory France that in the very next election, held only twelve months after royalist victories in the election of March–April 1797, the results of which produced the coup of Fructidor—so volatile that the elections of March 1798 created an equal threat to the hegemony of the Directory, but this time from the neo-Jacobin left. The standing government had anticipated serious electoral opposition and had resorted to various questionable measures even before elections were held. "Inspectors" were sent into various provinces, ostensibly to examine the condition of the roads but actually to rally the supporters of the existing government. The existing Counsels, before the retirement of those destined to leave, were made the judges of the electoral process in any disputed department. And there were many of the latter, in part because the existing political machine had given instructions to its supporters that, if in the electoral assemblies they should find themselves in the minority, they should secede from the assembly, reassemble, and elect their own deputies. The existing Counsels, the instrument of the Directory, would then judge between the two "disputed slates."[5]

Despite all these Mayor Daley maneuvers, the final results were a catastrophe for the Directory. There was a slight hesitation in the Counsels about how far the repression of the results should go. Courage, however, prevailed when arguments were raised, such as: "The guillotine is ready, do you want to mount it?" [Asked because the new opposition party was Jacobin.] "Will it be necessary that our brave defenders [i.e., the army] intervene again?"[6] Torn between the supposed alternatives of a new Jacobin Terror or the dictatorship of the army, a moderate coup appeared to be the wisest course. Whether this was an accurate perception of the political options remains, of course, a matter of discussion.

The law of 22 Floréal (May 11) purged 127 deputies even before they had taken their seats. In eight departments, the election results were completely annulled; in only 47 out of 96 were the outcomes untouched. "Eighty-six identifiable Jacobin winners were 'Floréalized,' along with a number of newly chosen local officials."[7]

A most important question, of course, is whether this Jacobin opposition represented, if allowed to live, the beginnings of a constitutional opposition: the emergence of a true democratic party system—or whether the Jacobins, come to power through elections, would then "Floréalize" their opponents. There is nothing inherently contradictory in using a democratic election to come to power and then illegally destroying all democratic opposition. We recall that Adolph Hitler did not seize political power in a coup d'état. So, one cannot know for sure how neo were these neo-Jacobins. Isser Woloch, our foremost historian of this movement, is optimistic in retrospect:

> With due allowance for an element of capriciousness and inconsistency, the Directory made good on its threat of 9 Germinal. Eighty-six Jacobins or candidates sponsored by the Jacobins, duly elected by a majority of their department electors, were barred from the Legislature. More important is the fact that the Jacobins of at least twenty departments saw the fruits of their efforts wiped out almost completely. The painstaking work of building up a constitutional party of opposition was arbitrarily canceled out and stigmatized as subversive. It was not simply the individual candidates who were the object of this arbitrary purge, but the nascent party formations themselves.[8]

One thing, nevertheless, seems certain: if the neo-Jacobins were capable of democratic citizenship, they appeared to be the only such sizable group in all of France.

UNANIMITY, FACTIONALISM, AND POLITICAL PARTIES

The alternative domination of one faction over another, sharpened by the spirit of revenge natural to party dissension, which in different ages and countries has perpetuated the most horrid enormities, is itself a frightful despotism. But this leads at length to a more formal and permanent despotism. The disorders and miseries which result gradually incline the minds of men to seek security and repose in the absolute power of an individual, and sooner or later the chief of some prevailing faction, more able or more fortunate than his competitors, turns this disposition to the purposes of his own elevation on the ruins of public liberty.[9]

The speaker of these cautionary words had previously sounded similar admonitions: "Let me now . . . warn you in the most solemn manner against the baleful effects of the spirit of party generally. . . . [All governments share some of this spirit] but in those of the popular form it is seen in its greatest rankness and is truly their worst enemy."[10]

A *philosophe* immersed in the Rousseauist tradition of the necessity of the General Will? A French politician trapped in the crippling notion of French revolutionary political culture that factions, and therefore political parties, are evil? A political prophet foreseeing the rise of Napoleon to power? Far from any of these possibilities, it is the voice of the first president of the United States delivering his famous Farewell Address, sharing with his countrymen all the accumulated wisdom of his political years.

The similarity in the anxiety over the formation of political parties between early republican America and France from 1789 to 1799 is absolutely striking. It seems that all societies in the eighteenth century that were attempting to move from an early modern to a fully modern society—in part by creating a polity based on democratic citizenship—each one faced the problem of overcoming a fundamental hostility to politics based upon political parties, though these latter are essential for a modern democratic society. In the almost exact same ten-year period, America succeeded in overcoming this ambivalence and created a party system. Revolutionary France was totally incapable of doing so. And, thus, the profoundly different nineteenth-century histories of these two societies.

In the early part of the fateful decade of the 1790s, most Americans shared Washington's anxiety. "There was still in 1792," Elkins and McKettrick tell us, "the widest range of inhibitions against out-and-out party activity, and it was this—rather than any slowness to 'discover' organizational techniques—that accounts for the curious ambiguity in political behavior everywhere during that year. One area in which this could be seen was the process of nominating candidates for office. Such a process is logically one that requires some form of group action prior to the election—and when issues and sentiments that introduce divisions in a community have made their appearance, such action, by the element of informality in it, verges unavoidably upon partisanship. Yet the imperatives of getting done what has to be done, on the one hand, and those of coming to terms with the negative values of factionalism . . . outside legally sanctioned boundaries, on the other, can produce a truly divided mentality—a conscience that no longer fully knows itself. So it was in 1792."[11]

At that date, even good Republicans, who were to take the lead eventually in breaking this taboo, could only express horror at the prospect: "Hugh Henry Brackenridge could publish . . . a sturdy tirade against tickets, state meetings, and committees of correspondence—all instruments of faction, which invaded 'the right of the citizens at large to think, judge and act for themselves.' "[12] By the time of the Sedition Act of 1798, however, Republican activists were beginning to see the necessity of permanent parties that would compete with each other and refrain from accusing their competitors of disloyalty and traitorous activity. Being the potential victims of this Sedition Act, Republican statesmen began to understand that "the very concept of seditious libel was flatly incompatible with party politics"[13] and, therefore, incompatible with the future of democratic citizenship. The crossroads had been reached: it would be either parties and democracy or some perversion of the latter.

French political culture in the eighteenth century could never overcome this ambivalence, could never break this taboo. "The terrible postulate of unanimity"[14] held dominion over political life. And it was the misfortune of French political culture that one of the saints of the Revolution, the great Rousseau himself, had certified this metaphysical mode. There existed, somehow and somewhere, the "General Will" of the nation. This Will was definitely not plebiscitary; it could not be discovered by counting the votes of various factions on particular issues. It was not identical to the majority will at the moment. And it had a virtuous dimension. The General Will represented what the people, in its enlightened sovereignty, would will if it were determined to pursue the good of the commonwealth in all matters. If, then, people could only perceive what it is, there would be a unanimous, or certainly a near-unanimous, agreement on what course of action to take. All factions, therefore, could only be a hindrance to the perception of the General Will and the following of its dictates. "It is important therefore," Rousseau writes, "in order to state the general will that there exist no partial associations within the state." Families, guilds, associations, religious groups—all these would speak only of their own interest and obscure the perception of the General Will. Political transparency required the suppression of particular interests.[15]

There was only one great problem: How are we to know the General Will? Who is, with certitude, to speak for it? How can we choose between two different prophets each of whom claims to represent the General Will? Since Rousseau, and the enlightened elites of French culture, must have known, at least in their preconscious minds, that there were no adequate answers to these questions, there was something profoundly fraudulent in this whole discussion. Hannah Arendt clearly perceives that the conception of the General Will grew, not out of a rational perception of the political world, but from an irrational need to maintain some sort of authoritarian presence in political life. "Rousseau's notion of a General Will, inspiring and directing the nation as though it were no longer composed of a multitude but actually formed one person, became axiomatic for all factions and parties of the French Revolution, because it was indeed the theoretical substitute for the sovereign will of the absolute monarch."[16]

And Rousseau himself, faced with the question of exactly how this metaphysical being of the General Will was to be formulated, could only assert an intellectual and mythical version of a transformed monarch: "To discover the best rules of society appropriate to the Nations, it would take a superior intelligence, who sees all human passions and who does not experience any of them, who would have no connection with our nature and who would know it to the core, whose happiness would be independent of us and yet who would be willing to take care of ours."[17] When grown-up men insist on believing in a fantasy, it is indication that some deep childish need has not been transformed or overcome. French political culture of the late eighteenth century could not create viable political parties, which would function successfully in a stable democratic citizenship, because it could not renounce the wish for some authoritarian force that would "take care of us." The notion of the General Will—the "terrible postulate of unanimity"—was the pathetic response of a culture failing to go beyond the necessity of an authoritarian power.

The very fraudulent nature of the rhetoric of the General Will is clearly demonstrated by the fact that those who yapped most about the necessity of implementing the General Will and eliminating all factions were the very ones who created, maintained, and brought to power the one really potent faction in early revolutionary history: the dictatorial regime created by the Jacobin-Montagnard-sans-culotte coalition. That the Jacobin network, with its headquarters in Paris, was an organized faction, bordering on a political party; that the sans-culottes of Paris were a sometimes organized, sometimes not, faction—of these assertions there can be no doubt. This fraudulent rhetoric in regard to faction is intimately related to another corrupt rhetoric: that which claimed that representative democracy was a contaminated form of politics, that only "direct democracy" could assert the true will of the people. How "direct democracy" was to operate in a country of over twenty million people, no one succeeded in figuring out. The "direct democracy" of the people-in-the-streets of Paris—when they overthrew the king, for instance—had nothing at all to do with democracy. "Direct democracy" meant merely the dictatorship of the people of Paris over the rest of the nation.

This sinister 1984 mode of "doublespeak," wherein the interests of the people are piously invoked in order to oppress the people—so important for twentieth-century ideological terror—was invented in France 1789–1794. We are not surprised to hear Saint-Just, one-third of the dictatorial triumvirate that was overthrown at Thermidor, sanctimoniously moralizing against the evil of concentrated political power: "Every party is therefore criminal, because it makes for the isolation of the people and the popular societies, and for the independence of the government. Any faction is therefore criminal, because it neutralizes the power of public virtue. . . . The solidity of our Republic is in the very nature of things. The sovereignty of the people requires that it should be one. . . . it is opposed to factions. Every faction is therefore an attempt on sovereignty."[18] Every faction, obviously, except his faction.

And Robespierre, we are not shocked to learn, once he had begun that treacherous journey to dictatorial power and Terror, could still brilliantly defend the concept of a virtuous people coming to political decisions without any acrimonious debate or resort to coalitions. An English type of opposition party would be proof of despotism, according to him, because "there is no opposition to patriotism." To allow that "men equally devoted to the public good could be divided," as was suggested to Robespierre by Léonard Bourdon, provoked Maximilien to announce that his own faction was only a *temporary* expedient: "There should be no Mountain where a pure people reigns."[19] The purpose of the factional power of the Mountain, then, is to create a virtuous people, whose existence will then make the Mountain unnecessary. We can observe a direct line from this mode of thought to that of the necessity of the Dictatorship of the Proletariat, which will rule *temporarily* until the new society and the new men are in place, and the State has withered away. Fraudulent and sinister, without question.

Here, again, Mona Ozouf has masterfully exposed the hypocritical core in this manner of thinking:

> But in order to counteract the newly forged unity of the enemies of the Revolution, [the Jacobins] created the fiction of a united people wholly at one with its government. This mythical unity, the rotten fruit of Rousseauism, vital to the Jacobin regime, proved fatal to liberty as independence. The allegedly unified voice of the people and the government disguised the fact that power was in fact exercised, controlled, even seized by a governing "people" quite different from the governed one. Under this regime individuals were more radically powerless than under any other, because the constraints that bound them were supposed to emanate from themselves.[20]

And this "rotten fruit of Rousseauism" was a powerful instrument of intimidation. The mythical postulate of unanimity could be used to oppress people on a day-to-day basis. One pejorative definition of "ideology," as opposed to the morally neutral concept of worldview or *Weltanschauung*, that I find useful is the concept that ideology always proves to be an instrument of domination, whereas a worldview may or may not be put to such use. A *Weltanschauung* may even insist that domination itself is an evil that has to be exposed. In the world of the sans-culottes, the insistence on unanimity, that everyone should think and act alike, served the annihilation of freedom. Albert Soboul, most sympathetic to the sans-culotte movement, nevertheless tells us: "In the hands of the sans-culottes, unity became a political weapon, a guarantee and means of victory; they wanted complete union between political organizations, and even more so, between the various social classes bent on the ruin of the aristocracy. Correspondence and fraternization were the means of achieving unity; the brotherly kiss was its symbol; the oath gave it a religious value."[21] And woe to heretics of this religion. The Bondy section of Paris launched an attack on the uninvolved on April 10, 1793: *Last Appeal to the Uninvolved*. We note the threat in the notion "last appeal." Anyone missing three successive sessions of the section's assembly would be decreed a bad citizen. Names of the uninvolved would be passed on to the sectional committee, which would deny them certificates of civism, the absence of which could keep a person from earning his living. Such refusniks were to be considered inferior citizens, and ultimately "suspects," which made them liable for arrest and detention.[22] All of this condemnation, not from actively opposing the Revolution, but merely from wanting to live a private life. Ideological terror most always puts an end to the option of a private life.

It was not only Jacobins and radical sans-culottes who were violently opposed to the formation of parties. It is not surprising to discover that Washington's anxieties about factions and parties were shared by most everyone at this crucial crossroad to Modernity. Condorcet, as far from a terrorist as one can imagine, announced on February 23, 1793: "Constitutions based on a balance of powers presuppose or cause the existence of two parties, and one of the first needs of the French Revolution is to avoid party altogether."[23] And Louvet, the Girondin prosecutor of Robespierre, began a pamphlet attacking the incorruptible with a sentence in English: "In politics there exist onless [sic] two parties in France, the first composed of philosophers, the second of robbers and murderers."[24] So much for loyal opposition!

The Girondins themselves were one of the first people attacked for behaving like a faction: attending planning sessions before the Assembly met, assigning members a particular task, attempting to dictate a premeditated plan for the legislature. This, in the *mentalité* or the political culture of the time, was considered a violation of the role a representative of the people was supposed to take: independence of any organized group, following only his own conscience.[25]

It proved to be an enormously difficult task to overcome the conception that political parties, that is, a pluralistic political culture, was legitimate. Moderate republicans, Girondins, Jacobins, Thermidorians—hardly anyone could go beyond this premodern vision of society. Bronislaw Baczko writes of the Thermidorian period: "The Constitution of the Year III remained the prisoner of the revolutionary mythology of the unified nation and of political life as the expression of that unity. The Thermidorian Convention did not accept political pluralism, not even as a necessary evil. It therefore did not seek to invent mechanisms by which such pluralism could function. When public opinion, which of course changed from election to election got too far out of step with the government in power, the only remedy was a coup d'état."[26]

At the end of the nineteenth and the beginning of the twentieth centuries, protofascist thought—stepped in antimodernism—decried the corrupt, nonheroic nature of petit bourgeois parliamentary politics. This attitude had been prefigured already in the 1790s in France. La Ravellière-Lepeaux, a member of the Directory, announced that "It was better to die with honor defending the republic and its established government than to perish or even to live in the muck of parties and the playthings of factions."[27] It is almost as if we can anachronistically imagine Napoleon announcing: "You want unanimity, I'll give you unanimity—and all the heroism you desire."

Factions manifest their illegitimacy when they lead to tyranny and violence. In the famous #10 of the *Federalist Papers*, Madison addresses the questions of factions in a democratic society: how they pose the greatest threat to the democracy, and yet how democratic institutions will prevent the tyranny of any one faction. This analysis is remarkably mirrored in a brilliant discussion by Sieyès in his 1789 pamphlet "What Is the Third Estate?" Sieyès begins with delineating three types of interest in man: (1) "in respect to which all citizens are alike"— their common interest; (2) "the interest whereby an individual allies himself to a few others"—corporate interest; and (3) "the interest whereby everyone stands apart, thinking of himself alone."

The first and third are of no danger to society: the common interest obviously not, and the personal interest is too singular and too powerless to present any problem. It is the corporate interest that poses the greatest threat: "This type of interest leads to conspiracy and collusion; through it antisocial schemes are plotted; through it the most formidable enemies of the People mobilise themselves." Sieyès' solution against this threat differs radically from Madison's. Madison cannot imagine outlawing factions, even though their existence and exercise may be problematic. Sieyès insists "that the social order inflexibly requires that no citizen must be allowed to organize themselves in *guilds*."[28] The only solution for a modern, stable, democratic society, a pluralist politics—however untidy and problematic—is denied. And the more conservative elements in American political society similarly saw the greatest danger of tyranny coming from organized factions. "You are afraid of the one," John Adams wrote Jefferson in 1787, "I, of the few."[29]

In France, the fear of faction and the dream of unanimity led to the native assumption that this problem for democratic society could be solved simply by outlawing all factions. This view was augmented by the intense desire to destroy all remnants of "feudalism"—guilds and corporations had to be eliminated in a free society. Isaac René Le Chapelier, a radical revolutionary and author of the law of June 1791 that is known by his name, which law pronounced all guilds and corporations illegitimate—Le Chapelier had previously underlined the dread of faction: "If these societies are able to have some influence, if a man's reputation is at their disposal, if, formed into corporations, they have from one end of the country to the other branches and agents of their powers, *the societies will be the only free men.*" For identical reasons, he rejected all political factions (i.e., parties) because they would strive for a monopoly of power, and the struggle between several of them would result in anarchy.[30]

Tocqueville, however, in his brilliant manner, observed that overcoming the potential tyranny of factions could be accomplished, not by legislation outlawing factions, but only with a profound change in the spirit of society:

> So the exercise of the right of association becomes dangerous when great parties see no possibility of becoming the majority. In a country like the United States, where differences of view are only matters of nuance, the right of association can remain, so to speak, without limits.
>
> It is our inexperience of liberty in action which still leads us to regard freedom of association as no more than a right to make war on the government. The first idea which comes into a party's mind, as into that of an individual, when it gains some strength is that of violence; the thought of persuasion only comes later, for it is born of experience.
>
> . . . Furthermore, we have such a passionate taste for war that there is no enterprise so reckless or dangerous to the state, but it is thought glorious to die for it with arms in one's hands.[31]

If it is a question, then, of overcoming a readiness to resort to violence, of sublimating sufficiently the passionate taste for war, in order to achieve democratic stability, we can understand why it took the French so long, why democratic citizenship could not be achieved in one or two or three generations.

JACOBINS AS THE ONLY "LEGITIMATE" PARTY

If we return to Sieyès' penetrating analysis of the tripartite division of interests in society; and if we eliminate, by law or force if necessary, the corporate or factional interest, as the transitional modernists would have us do; we are then left with only the individual and the common interest. At this crucial point of transition to Modernity, optimistic democrats like Washington imagined that, after refusing the corporate interest, individuals would be free to exercise autonomy and virtue in political judgment: that the intelligent exercise of individual interest would lead to democratic citizenship. It did not quite work out that way.

On the other hand, there were those who rejected the corporate/factional interest and feared that the pursuit of individual interest would lead to corruption, and not to virtue. Virtue, and the Republic of Virtue, were to be discovered only within interests in common. The imperative toward unanimity was considered legitimate because the General Will would, somehow, prove to be virtuous. But how are we—poor nonvirtuous individuals as we are—to know what the virtuous General Will *is*? A prophet is necessary—a spokesman for the General Will. It does not necessarily have to be an individual; it could be an assemblage of people: the sans-culottes, *le peuple*, the Nation—it could even be the network of Jacobin clubs. And thus was born the first manifestation of what Talmon has called "Totalitarian Democracy."[32]

And if the phrase "Totalitarian Democracy" has a deliberate paradoxical resonance, it calls to mind the existence and the strategy of the Jacobin clubs, especially at the time of the Terror, which demonstrated the very same profound paradox. Corporations, factions, political parties were, in the announced rhetoric, anathema. Virtue resided, nonetheless, in the one most powerful faction of all: the Jacobins. It was not an intellectual confusion. It was a manifestation of a formidable and sinister psychological compromise: the pursuit of totality within society under the banner of equality and liberty. Unfortunately for humankind, such a sinister syndrome had not only a short terroristic presence in France, but also was to enjoy, in the last century, a great efflorescence in many parts of the globe.

The ominous compromise, with sinister intent, has been most perceptively elaborated by Bronislaw Baczko, who describes Jacobinism as "both the expression and the perversion of the political arena as unified."[33] The word "perversion" is critical. Both Washington and Jacobinism could agree on the mortal threat represented by the corporate interest, but Washington would not then go out and organize one of the most powerful *popular factional* instruments in world history up to that time. Baczko elaborates:

> In 1791 the Jacobins, thanks to their ideology and organization, were already asserting themselves as the political force best suited to making the most effective use, in the struggle for power, of a *unitary conception of the political arena*. Against Le Chapelier and the liberal conservatives the Jacobins defended freedom of speech, the right of association and of forming a national network of affiliated societies.

They claimed this right for "good patriots" alone, for those who united the Nation and not for those who divided it. This right would be, all things considered, *their exclusive right* only, insofar as they brought together precisely all "pure" patriots. Political and moral "purity", this key concept of Jacobinism, was a criterion that excluded any idea of pluralism. In fact, "pure patriotism" did not acknowledge diversity but only an extreme purism; it condemned *a priori* the existence of *different patriotisms.* "Pure patriotism" implied a *multiplicity of patriots* but not of patriotisms.[34]

One great reason for Jacobin success was the ambivalence—or incompetence—of its opposition. Brinton remarks that the opposition was "divided, timid, inept," whereas it is clear that the Jacobins were united, daring, and competent. The opposition's ineptness, Brinton asserts, "need not be accepted off-hand as a sign of superior morality."[35] A typical situation developed in Poitiers, where rivals of the Jacobins attempted to establish their own club. The radicals then resorted to street violence: stones thrown at windows, headquarters trashed, and the altercations blamed on the victims. The local authorities, in sympathy with the Jacobins, then closed down the rival club as a public nuisance.[36] Anyone who has ever been involved, in present times, with a liberal-left organization or a labor union, where left-wing elements are intent on a takeover, will immediately recognize two fundamental dispositions: the soft liberals lacking courage to stand up to illegality or violence; the left radicals lacking the spirit of pluralist democracy.

Remarkably, this failure to go beyond the premodern position of the fear of faction proved a major handicap for political culture even through the period of the Directory. These latter Thermidorians refused to organize a party committed to their aims or even to set in place a patronage system that would preserve their political power. Individual members tried, but the Directory government as a whole continued to live in the fantasy of the Roman Republic, where no faction should disturb the "communion of citizens."[37] Napoleon, however, gave no evidence of being "divided, timid, and inept."

FACTIONALISM AND THE STRUGGLE FOR MODERNITY

The commitment to the opinion that factions (and, therefore, political parties) were illegitimate kept the political culture from maturing and transforming itself into a modern political culture. The conception that unanimity was a necessity for the political arena was a *premodern, traditional mentalité.* Nothing demonstrates with greater power the struggle for Modernity than this failed effort, in France, to go beyond premodern society. The contrast with America is startling and revealing. In the years from the writing of the Constitution in 1787 to the election of Jefferson in 1800, American political culture legitimated political parties, entered the modern world, and made a stable democratic polity a possibility. France could find no stable way out of its political dilemma except conservative dictatorship. The one true path being rejected, some form of perversion in the Aristotelian sense was inevitable.

Once again, Bronislaw Baczko is our most profound interpreter of this phenomenon and deserves to be cited at length:

> The Revolution invented a democracy which, by an apparent paradox, joined together individualism and a true cult of unanimity, representative government and the refusal to allow any interest other than the "general interest" to be represented, the recognition of the freedom of opinion and the mistrust of divisions in public opinion, the desire for a transparent life and the obsessive search for "plots"; in short, *a democracy which in politics mixed modernity and archaism.* [italics added] . . . They never succeeded, at any stage of the revolution, in agreeing to disagree, in recognizing that conflicts in a society are at the origin of its working and not a vice to be eradicated. This is a particularly striking example of the mixture of the traditional and the modern in the political concepts, institutions and workings of the Revolution, which marked all its experience with its seal. As a result, *exclusion* swiftly became the regulatory mechanism of the political game; the adversary was excluded in the very name of the fundamental unity of the Nation, of the People, or of the Republic. This principle is, moreover, appropriate to the functioning and preservation of traditional communities, where unity and solidarity tend to be confused with unanimity. The persistent obsessions of the revolutionary imagination, particularly the plot and the hidden enemy, could only nourish, through hatred and suspicion, the idea-image of *healthy exclusion.*[38]

A crucial form of social cohesion—that which holds society together—in "traditional communities" is kinship. One is reminded of certain kinship societies (that is, prestate social orders) that have developed a form of a council of elders to make certain social decisions, where matters are never settled by vote: the discussion goes on and on, sometimes for days, until the conclusion is agreed to unanimously. The modern world is the least kinship world of any ever seen.

Going beyond kinship forms of social cohesion is by no means the least of the problems that the journey to Modernity faces. Leaving the kinship world behind always crucially raises the level of anxiety within society. If there is little or no capacity to withstand that anxiety, modern democracy is doomed. *Das Volk* will then, inevitably, reassert its prerogatives. And the return of repressed kinship values in the modern world always includes an alliance with an authoritarian leader and a portentous acceleration of violence.

In the latter part of his penetrating book, Baczko sums up his basic insight: "It was a matter, in a word, of a *democracy at a quite rudimentary stage of its historical development.* . . . The Thermidoreans were unable to consider or imagine the political arena *as necessarily divided into opposing tendencies, therefore as necessarily contradictory and causing conflict.* . . . [It was a] situation of a *modern political arena created in a largely traditional culture and mental environment.*"[39]

Revolutionary France was not unique in having to face up to this prodigious problem. All societies advancing toward Modernity must contend with it. The stage of Modernity develops out of Early Modernity, which itself is a mixture of traditional and modern institutions and mores. That is, of kinship and non-kinship forms of social cohesion. Modernity—and a stable democratic society—is possible only by transcending that "inherited conglomerate."[40] In America, the crucial turning point occurred when the Federalist faction and party, now in control of the federal government, passed the Sedition Act of 1798, in good part in order to prevent the press of the Republican faction and party from passing judgment on those in office. Seditious libel is the destruction of modern political parties. Elkins and McKitrick elaborate: "Parties, in any modern sense, cannot function at all under such a principle, and parties by now—though nobody could yet admit it without some discomfort—were there. . . . Whether [the Federalists] knew it or not—perhaps nobody entirely knew it—they were striking out furiously at parties in general, in a desperate effort to turn back the clock."

"Turn the clock back," because, Elkins and McKitrick speculate, one may read the narrative of the writing of the constitution in 1787, with its elaborate checks and balances, as having as one of its primary purposes the prevention of the establishment of political parties. The result may be interpreted, as it was by Richard Hofstader, as a "constitution against parties." "The Federalists," they conclude, "in their role as founding statesmen had done their utmost to leave as little room in the structure of government for the growth and activity of parties as possible."[41]

The crucial point, of course, is that in this case, the story ends happily: Parties were legitimated; political disagreements were allowed without the accusations of seditious libel or traitorous intent; democracy became a real possibility.

A deeper analysis of why this transition to loyal opposition proved to be so problematic and so difficult for human beings—to the point where we are moderately amazed that any society succeeded in this endeavor—a deeper analysis makes us confront the paranoid position. Going beyond the paranoid position is essential for the establishment of a modern democratic polity. It is the *Weltanschauung* of the paranoid position that is responsible for "the terrible postulate of unanimity," that sees all opposition as perfidious. Even further, the paranoid position demands an ultimate authority for an individual's identity and beliefs *outside* the individual herself or himself. Hence, the tremendous importance of the Church, the king, and the kinship system. This underlines the great power in Arendt's analysis quoted previously: the General Will becomes the new monarch after the legitimacy of king and Church are overthrown, since the General Will represents the kinship system reborn with inordinate power. Democracy, on the other hand, requires the ultimate authority of an individual's political identity and beliefs to reside *inside* the self. We do not need to go all the way back to France in the 1790s to recognize the enormous difficulty of that psychological development. Almost every day our newspapers are full of reports from different parts of the globe and of political cultures tragically failing in that very enterprise. We live daily with the great burden that Modernity has laid upon us.

ANTIDEMOCRATIC THOUGHT AND ACTION

There are those, Aristotle tells us, whose "minds are filled with a passion for inequality."[42] It is a question of numbers. How many, within a society, conform to Aristotle's characterization? If there are enough to significantly affect the spirit of society, then democracy becomes problematic. Tocqueville suggests rather strongly that such a *mentalité* within French culture destroyed the possibility of a democratic polity, at least up until the time of his writing:

> To be accurate, it must be said that the human intellect which some of these philosophers adored was simply their own. They showed, in fact, an uncommon want of faith in the wisdom of the masses. I could mention several who despised the public almost as heartily as they despised the Deity. . . . They were as far from

real and respectful submission to the will of the majority as from submission to
the will of God. Nearly all subsequent revolutionaries have borne the same character. Very different from this is the respect shown by Englishmen and Americans
for the sentiments of the majority of their fellow citizens. Their intellect is proud
and self-reliant, but never insolent; and it has led to liberty, while ours has done
little but invent new forms of servitude.[43]

A basic mistrust of democratic equality, a fundamental anxiety that truly
institutionalizing the sovereignty of the people would destabilize society—these
views pervaded French political culture. Antidemocratic thought originated
from both *the left* and *the right*. There was a sincere egalitarian and democratic
Weltanschauung among a small minority in the center, but it was insufficient to
overcome this grave mistrust.

Even moderate liberals could not abide the idea that all people were to be
included in the polity. "This centralization alone will assure liberty," Benjamin
Constant assures us: "Two nations share the soil of France: the nation of free
men, and the mob of slaves. If you accord these last the least part of the administration of the Republic, the Republic will be, to that extent, debased and degraded."[44] And Boissy d'Anglas, deputy to the Convention, a moderate member
of the plain, declared in 1795 after Thermidor that reasonable men could only
expect civil, but not political, equality. The best government will be ruled only
by those who have a share in the property of the nation; only rarely does one
find political sagacity among those who are without a proprietary interest. "A
country governed by property-owners belongs to the social order, one governed
by those without property is in a state of nature."[45]

These latter arguments were, by no means, unique to France. Every modernizing nation that was progressing from a limited to a full democracy raised up
such arguments, in almost the exact manner. Mistrust of the lower classes
is endemic in bourgeois culture. What was remarkable about end-of-the-
eighteenth-century France was that it produced an antidemocratic *left*: a dreadful
portent of the twentieth century, a crucially significant contradiction and perversion in the rise of Modernity.

The antidemocratic tyranny of the Jacobin dictatorship and the Terror needs
no documentation here. What needs to be emphasized, however, is the nonterrorist antidemocratic actions that preceded the dictatorship. The left wing of the
Revolutions had no reluctance to suspend democratic citizenship once it was
convinced that the opposition was counterrevolutionary. And such conviction

was readily available in almost any circumstance. The Jacobin club of Rodez "decided to 'survey with the greatest care all the printing-presses in town,' in order to prevent the clericalists from printing pamphlets—and this early in 1791."[46] In the very small town of Eymoutiers in November 1791, the Jacobin candidate for mayor suffered defeat in the election, 58 to 39. The club refused to accept this verdict and appealed to the departmental *directoire* at Limoges, who was a Jacobin sympathizer. He immediately dismissed the elected mayor and appointed three Jacobins to run the town temporarily. A special governmental commission, however, reversed this decision and restored the duly elected mayor. After the overthrow of the king in August 1792, the Jacobins of Eymoutiers became more emboldened; they appealed again to their brothers in Limoges. An armed force of patriots from Limoges and St. Leonard marched on Eymoutiers, relieved the mayor of his office once again and replaced him with a committee of five Jacobins.[47] All this, of course, before Terror became the "order of the day." And, naturally, we are not surprised to learn that the Paris Commune had no respect for democratic process when it was necessary to save the Revolution. The day after the overthrow of the king, the Commune took steps to assure that no royalist sentiment could be voiced at the next elections. It suppressed all royalist newspapers, confiscated their presses, and distributed them among "patriot" papers. The Legislative Assembly raised no objection to this violent and illegal procedure. The people, obviously, had no right to vote for monarchy even if they wanted to.[48]

What we see happening in the political culture of the time is that no matter what the liberal values of rights may say, *political* rights are not universal, *do not belong to all men.* Political rights can be suspended whenever the nation is declared to be in danger, either from counterrevolutionaries or from lower-class anarchists: two permanently available excuses. All this, combined with the situation where the various factions of the bourgeois elite insisted on annihilating each other, marked the death of democratic citizenship.

8

THE BOURGEOIS LIFE AND CAPITALISM

In the realm of social theory, one unfortunate legacy of classical Marxism still holds dominion over much, if not most, social thought: the almost complete conflation of capitalism and the bourgeoisie. The rise of capitalism creates the hegemony of the bourgeoisie, which then proceeds to live the bourgeois life, which is completely compatible with its capitalist class dominion. And it is not only the small band of surviving Marxist theorists who assume this historical sequence. Why, I am constantly asked, do you assert that capitalism and the bourgeois *Weltanschauung* are two different fundamental aspects of Modernity, when they are actually two facets of the same social phenomenon?

History, however, and most particularly the history of France in the eighteenth century with its climax in the period of Revolutions, establishes that the rise of the bourgeois *Weltanschauung* and lifestyle, and, subsequently, the ascent of bourgeois elites to political power, precedes the predominance of capitalism within society. There was, it is now generally agreed, some capitalist activity in eighteenth-century France but not a great deal. There were a number of capitalists, but no capitalism as such.

Without going into an extended discussion, it is important for the theoretical argument of this chapter to make certain distinctions like the one indicated in the previous sentence. We must distinguish between capitalist activity, capitalists, capitalism, and capitalist society.

Capitalist activity is what capitalists do. There can be, within the economic system, a great deal of capitalist activity and a great many capitalists without the existence of capitalism. The economic sphere of society may be described as capitalism only when the economic system consists *primarily* of capitalist activity, in distinction from noncapitalist forms of economic activity. There were, for instance, much capitalist activity and many capitalists in ancient Athens: manufacturers employing 80 to 100 slaves or workers in one factory; bankers accumulating large fortunes. No one, however, would describe Athens as a manifestation of capitalism. The same was true of eighteenth-century France: a good number of capitalists but not capitalism.

Capitalism may also be distinguished from capitalist society. This last exists only when capitalists as a class are of equal *political* power with any other class in society—or, naturally, of superior power to any other class. The United States, for instance, at its founding, was not a capitalist society even though there was a significant amount of capitalist activity. By 1900, however, the capitalist class was the most powerful one within society and, therefore, it had truly become a capitalist society. When did that happen? And what were the means by which it was accomplished? These are very important theoretical questions, though not our subject now.

One further distinction. There were premodern capitalist societies where capitalists ruled the polity: the city-states of the German Hansa; Renaissance Florence and Venice. No premodern capitalist society existed, however, in the large nation states such as England, France, or Spain. The existence of premodern capitalist societies seems to have been a city-state phenomenon. Only Modernity has produced capitalist societies in large nation states. A theoretical explanation of why this has been so is, at present, beyond my capacity. One element, however, seems significant: premodern capitalism was primarily commercial, whereas modern capitalism was fundamentally industrial.

In *ancien régime* France there were capitalists and capitalist activity, but definitely no capitalism and no capitalist society, either of a premodern or Modern variety. It is the argument of this chapter that, even though such was the case, a bourgeoisie and a bourgeois *Weltanschauung* were alive, prospering, and expanding.

Despite this nonexistence of capitalism, people who can only best be described as "bourgeois" began to dominate, first, the intellectual culture and then the political culture of the society. *The three French Revolutions of the end of the century (or, the two Revolutions and a coup), 1789–1793, were made by bourgeois actors.* The Third

Estate was primarily a bourgeois, not a capitalist, space. Even those present-day intellectuals who have a competent working knowledge of general French history are hard put to name, offhand, even one capitalist who was an important actor in that revolutionary history. Bourgeois people—lawyers, physicians, landlords, professors, journalists, administrators, intellectuals of all kinds—there were thousands: Robespierre, Saint-Just, Danton, Brissot, Vergniaud, Barère, Marat, R.R. Palmer's "twelve who ruled [eight of whom were lawyers],"[1] and so forth and so on. We are reminded, as just one instance, that over 40 percent of the delegates to the Third Estate were lawyers. Were such barristers capitalists? Certainly not, and certainly not aristocrats. To what social class, then, can they be assigned? To the bourgeoisie, precisely.

These two chapters will argue an even more radical position: that behind the ascent of the bourgeois worldview and lifestyle lies the rise of individualism: that one of the greatest motivating factors in the thrust toward Modernity is the psychological drive toward individuation and individual autonomy. Weber's argument concerning the *Protestant Ethic*[2] can be read as a description of the birth and advance of individualism that becomes embedded in a Protestant religion that asserts that the individual needs no intermediary between himself/herself and God. Every individual is his/her own priest. No such religious reformation is possible without first postulating an autonomous person: a view that is not central to premodern Catholic thought.

This individualism, it will be argued further, is a prodigious gift and, simultaneously, an immense catastrophe for humankind. The greatest happiness—and the greatest despair—that Modernity brings us results, in good part, from the fact that the evolution of society has been pushing all of us in the direction of becoming autonomous individuals. Those who succeed find themselves living in a society more free, more democratic, more egalitarian than any society ever seen since the breakdown of the kinship system and the beginnings of the State. Those who fail bring us religious fundamentalism, fascism, ideological terror, and genocide. Of the various aspects of Modernity, we may mention industrialization, urbanization, rationalization, a secular society, but the most difficult psychological task is to move from traditional forms of social cohesion (kinship, kingship, authoritarian religion) to a society of individuals who have to learn how to stand alone and still stay connected to others in the commonwealth. Lengthy is the list of those societies, in the twentieth century, who have succeeded in this task and, equally, those who have floundered or met with disaster.

The paradoxes and contradictions of individualism are apparent—and deeply problematic—even in those societies that are capable of achieving a democratic citizenship. The egoistic, intensely competitive, ultimately destructive aspects of moral advance, individualism that democratic capitalism and the bourgeois *Weltanschauung* celebrate and generously reward creates the foremost moral problematic within successful Modern societies. Such individualism is the perversion of true individualism: a morally autonomous, and yet responsible, individual. To go beyond Modernity, to create a nurturing society, requires transcending the morally suffocating boundaries of bourgeois individualism. On no other issue is our present society more ambivalent. We are immersed in a moral malaise, unhappy with where we are but incapable of transcending our present contradictions. We have arrived at the point, as Livy described the late degenerate Roman Republic, "when we can endure neither our vices nor their cure."[3] And this unfettered, unfeeling, rampaging individualism is our greatest vice, the cause of our deepest alienation from society.

Yet without the birth and development of individualism, there would be no liberal society, no democratic citizenship, no rights of man and of the citizen, no emancipation of repressed minorities, no end to slavery, no true gender equality. Immediately that the French Revolutions began, the struggle with this great paradox commenced: How can one let individualism flourish and still serve and save *la patrie?*

First, it is necessary to examine the proposition that the Revolutions at the end of the century were made primarily by people who can only accurately be described as "bourgeois." Then, we are forced to confront the question of the role of individualism within the bourgeois value system. And, finally, the great ambiguity of individualism will be looked at in order to understand, possibly, the very origins of the Modern world and the great paradoxes and contradictions it has brought us.

THE FLOWERING OF BOURGEOIS CULTURE

There was a vibrant, healthy, expanding, exuberant bourgeois culture in eighteenth-century France. Lawyers, small- to medium-sized merchants, public functionaries, medical men, scientists, journalists, book publishers and book sellers, masters employing five or six journeymen, *rentiers*, playwrights, a reading public eager for the latest work of fiction or social discourse, individual artisans with no employees, school teachers, estate managers, civil engineers. Colin Jones estimates that the size of the bourgeoisie grew from 700,000 or 800,000 in 1700 to possibly 2.3 million in 1789, almost 10 percent of the nation.[4] A veritable "'bourgeoisification' of the Old Regime society."[5] A class of people that would flood the 4,000 to 5,000 Jacobin societies and make them the most potent pre-Thermidor political force in the country. So overwhelming is the data to support this proposition that the problem is not to collect and present examples but to condense and organize the material in a convincing, but not overextended, manner.

"Je ne suis pas de la caste nobiliaire," wrote Bertrand Barère, a lawyer from the southwest of France, a crucial actor in the radical revolutionary drama, member of the great Committee of Public Safety, "je m'honore d'être né dans la classe du peuple: un homme de loi et la fille d'un propiétaire agriculteur me donnèrent le jour."[6] ["I am not of the noble classes; I pride myself on having been born into the ranks of the people: a man of the law and the daughter of a land-owning farmer brought me into the world."]

It is much easier to define "bourgeois" by what it is not than by what it is. A bourgeois is not a noble and is not poor. He belongs exactly to that class in the middle, leads a middle-class life, and generally shares middle-class values. Those who fit this description made the 1789–1799 revolutionary history. The bourgeois class, however—just like any class—does not present a monolithic rigid appearance. "The first thing to catch our notice," Tocqueville writes of this middle class in the Old Regime, "is the immense number of separate elements of which it was composed."[7] Andre Siegfried has proposed dividing this non-noble, nonpoor class into four or five categories: *grande, haute, moyenne, petite,* and (possibly) *très petite.*[8] Obviously, the life lived by a *haute* bourgeois and that of a *petite* bourgeois differed radically—just as today the upper-middle class enjoys a different life experience from the lower-middle class—and yet, what is true of all levels is that those in them are not noble or poor. And competition for status, it seems, was and is a constant concern in this middle-class world. Tocqueville goes on to describe a typical urban circumstance: "At last an order has been passed that the holy water is to be given to the judges of the presidial court before being given to members of the town corporation. The parlement had been unable to come to a decision, so the king took the matter up in Council and has decided it himself. It was high time, too, as the whole town was in ferment."[9] A vibrant, ambitious, exuberant, but also, in many ways, a pathetically narrow-minded world.

The point has been made before, but is worth repeating, that of the Montagnards and Girondins it can be said, with truth, that both factions came from the bourgeoisie. Albert Soboul asserts that the Montagnards generally inclined toward the *moyenne* and *petite* bourgeoisie, whereas the Girondins were closer to traders and manufacturers, toward the *haute* bourgeoisie, but he is careful to add: "Ils ne différaient pas tellement, par l'origine de classe."[10] "They did not differ so much in their class origins." Gary Kates confirms Soboul's description of the Girondin leaders, describing the outstanding members of the Confédération des Amis de la Vérité (an early organization of what would soon become the Girondin movement): "Most were lawyers, physicians, priests, landlords, professors, journalists, or administrators," but others were definitely not *haute* bourgeois: "An unusually large number were also aspiring intellectuals who wrote plays, essays, and books on topics other than current events."[11] One way or another, all such were intent on living the bourgeois life, with greater or lesser success.

There may even be a very complex relationship between the *recent* bourgeoisification of certain individuals and the capacity for revolutionary action. "It is extraordinary," Gordon Woods writes of America, "to realize what a high proportion of the revolutionary leaders were first generation gentlemen. . . . many were the first in their families to attend college, to acquire a liberal arts education, and to display the marks of an enlightened eighteenth-century gentleman. Samuel Adams, John Adams, Thomas Jefferson, James Otis, John Jay, James Madison, David Ramsay, Benjamin Rush, James Wilson, John Marshall—the list goes on and on, down even to the second and third ranks of revolutionary leadership."[12] It would be of great interest to pursue the question of what relationship there may have existed, in France, between first-generation bourgeois *arrivistes* and revolutionary leadership.

Lawyers

In France, above all, to an almost incredible degree, the bourgeois leaders of the revolutions were lawyers. Two-thirds of the great Committee of Public Safety. Forty-six percent of the delegates to the Third Estate in 1789,[13] whereas all the liberal professions outside the law and civil service produced less than 5 percent of the deputies.[14] Things had even reached the point where, as in our present society, "lawyers" had become a possible pejorative term, one that had rhetorical power. Napoleon in 1796, already predicting a great future for himself, spiced his rhetoric with a swipe at lawyers: "What I have done up to now is still nothing. I am only at the beginning of my career. Do you think I have triumphed in Italy only to make the reputations of the lawyers of the Directory, the Carnots, and the Barrasses? And do you suppose it was in order to establish a republic? What an idea!"[15]

This political hegemony of lawyers was not surprising. David Bell has chronicled the struggle of lawyers for liberal values that goes back almost a hundred years before the Revolution, in a book entitled, appropriately enough, *Lawyers and Citizens*.[16] In 1698, the magistrate and future chancelor Henri-François d'Aguesseau delivered an oration, which presented a remarkable "modern" worldview, giving voice to views that were taken up and reiterated by the members of the bar throughout the eighteenth century. The subject of the orator was "the independence of the barrister":

> These distinctions which are based only on the hazard of birth, those great names with which most men flatter themselves, and which dazzle even the wise, are no help in a profession where virtue is the source of all nobility and where men are reputed not for what their fathers did, but for what they do themselves. In entering this famous body, they abandon the rank which prejudice attributed to them in the order of nature and truth.

Certainly radical talk in a traditional, aristocratic society. d'Aguesseau then finishes by calling on his audience to carry out their duties to their "fellow citizens." Bell concludes that since d'Aguesseau was not calling for open political action, what he really had in mind was a form of "depoliticized republicanism."[17]

In a critical dispute between the Crown and the barristers in October 1730–December 1731, d'Aguesseau was a leader of the conservative forces, but the majority of the lawyers was willing to dispute the absolute authority of the monarchy: "the Parisian Order of Barristers, five hundred men of predominately moderate means, predominately bourgeois origins, and little obvious political influence." " 'All laws are contracts between those who govern and those who are governed,' " announced a legal brief, signed by forty Parisian barristers and condemned by the royal council. Ultimately, the crown pulled back, and the lawyers celebrated a " 'triumph.' "[18] Already, sixty years before the declaration of the National Assembly, the audacious bourgeois voice of radical reform or possible revolution was abroad in the land.

This capacity for formidable opposition came to a climax in the crucial "Maupeou Revolution" of 1771–1774, which Bell considers, "the greatest political upheaval in France since the Fronde [which] foreshadowed the much greater Revolution to come."[19] Without the obstinacy and energy of the barristers, that crisis would never have come about. Lawyers, from several different levels of the bourgeoisie, were quickly becoming the vanguard of revolution.

No other professional or bourgeois group had an influence on the course of the revolutions equivalant to that of lawyers. Taken all together, however, these other sturdy members of the bourgeoisie were a powerful political and cultural force. I do not have the capacity to elaborate on the existence of these other professional groups (nonaristocratic, not poor), and it is not necessary to do so here. It may be helpful, however, to take a quick glance at the importance of professionals in general, functionaries, journalists, doctors, and teachers.

Of the representatives to the Third Estate in 1789, outside of lawyers and civil servants, only thirty-one deputies came from the liberal professions. After the occurrence of the second revolution, the influence of this latter group increased substantially. "The Convention [1792] had a very solid medical contingent, plus a respectable number from the armed services and the world of letters. As a cross-section of the French intelligentsia, it was an improvement on the [delegation to the] Third Estate; if its social composition was very much the same, its professional outlook was very much broader."[20]

Government Functionaries

Of the old regime in the years preceding the Revolution, J.M. Thompson writes: "The old aristocratic families had long ago lost any direct part or power in the government of the country. Duties of local magistracy or administration which were still performed by their counterparts in England had been transferred to lawyers and officials of middle-class origin."[21] And R.R. Palmer concludes that: "A revolution, to be successful, was bound to be 'bourgeois.'"[22] A Modern society—even an early Modern society—is too complex bureaucratically to be left in the hands of a nonmodern aristocracy. Some aristocracies were capable of a degree of efficient modernization—the Prussian and the English, each in its own unique way—and that capacity or incapacity directly affects what role the bourgeoisie will take in the process of modernization: that is, rationalization and centralization. The French aristocracy, for whatever reason, obviously left the door wide open for the bourgeoisie to attain bureaucratic power.

Journalists

"Journalists," Jack Censer asserts, "shared some important characteristics in their backgrounds. All were well-educated and most were members of some liberal profession. . . . None had wealth or position that was seriously jeopardized by the liquidation of the Old Regime."[23]

Doctors

The eighteenth century witnessed the increasing professionalization of artisinal surgeons, who had previously enjoyed a status inferior to university-trained physicians. They succeeded in raising their prestige, wealth, and status in part by requiring a liberal education as necessary for a surgical career. The physicians also succeeded, as the century advanced, in raising their professional prestige. The Royal Society of Medicine, established in 1776, "stood as the scourge of the medical 'charlatinism,' and argued that social utility and public health required the enforcement of a monopoly of medical services by trained physicians. Even before 1789, medical eulogists were portraying the dedicated physician as a bastion of citizenship, a cross between an altruistic notable and a secular saint devoted to his ailing flock."[24] In essence, a hero of the bourgeois life. We are not surprised to learn of the substantial participation of doctors in the political space of the revolutions.[25]

Schoolteachers

"Schoolteachers," writes Colin Jones, "—very largely within the aegis of the church—were a group amongst which this civic ideology made a particular mark. The pedagogy of the last decades of the Old Regime was thoroughly infused with civic values. Schoolteachers included some of the most eloquent and persuasive members of the revolutionary assemblies: Lanjuinais, Fouché, Billaud-Verenne, Daunou, François de Neufchâteau, Manuel, and Lakanal are a representative crop."[26]

Educated, enlightened, ambitious, capable—but not of nobility born. It is hard to imagine a more accurate short definition of what it meant to be "bourgeois" in the years directly preceding the Revolution.

THE SANS-CULOTTES

Twentieth-century historiography has revealed to us the fact that even the leaders of the sans-culottes, the revolutionary people-in-the-streets of Paris, cannot accurately be considered working class or proletarians but were bourgeois, middle-class citizens. Albert Soboul, our guide to this class analysis, writes in no uncertain terms: "During all the important days from July 1789 to Prairial, year III, one must conclude that the revolutionary vanguard of the Parisian sans-culottes was made up not of the working proletariat, but of a coalition of small employers and journeymen who worked and lived with them. . . . On the whole, the attitudes of the working class were strongly influenced by the attitudes of lower middle-class artisans, and, like the latter, they *shared bourgeois ideology.* During the Revolution, the workers were unable, either in thought or action, to form an independent group."[27] "It was the lower middle-class craftsman who fashioned the mentality of the worker."[28] All sans-culottes except the most radical who followed the *enragés,* therefore, shared a bourgeois *Weltanschauung.*

Equally remarkable with these revelations is the analysis of the class membership of the *Comité central revolutionnaire,* which directed the insurrection of May–June 1793 that removed the Girondins from power and brought the beginnings of the Montagnard-Jacobin dictatorship. Its membership was primarily middle-class or bourgeois, and even of a bourgeois rank a step or two above the bourgeois leaders of the sans-culottes. There were, Morris Slavin tells us, remarkably few master craftsmen, artisans, journeymen, workers, or petty shopkeepers among its membership. Three members may accurately be termed "sans-culotte"; two were ex-nobles; and two were involved in commerce. However, six were connected with the law; five with the liberal professions; and six were public functionaries.[29] In the late spring of '93, therefore, the most radical elements in Paris, the makers of the third revolution (or the first coup d'état), whose rhetoric reflected almost total agreement with sans-culottes aspirations—the leadership of such a group was primarily composed of actors solidly in the middle ranks of the bourgeoisie.

PUBLIC OPINION AND THE PUBLIC SPHERE

Among the most important results of historical work of the last twenty-five years on the *ancien régime* has been the revelation of the profound importance of public opinion in prerevolutionary society (most especially Keith Michael Baker: *Inventing the French Revolution*[30]) and the efflorescence of the "public sphere" as a manifestation of bourgeois, liberal, modernist values (Jürgen Habermas: *The Structural Transformation of the Public Sphere: An Inquiry into a Category of Bourgeois Society*[31]). If we ask the questions who were the people, for the most part, who constituted that public whose opinion grew in importance, and who created and acted within this new public sphere?—there seems to be no more accurate answer than "the bourgeoisie, naturally." When we read that barristers began printing legal briefs, which were immune from censorship, addressed to the general public, in quantities of 10,000,[32] it seems clear that most of the readers were not enlightened, liberal, literate aristocrats. "The expanding reading 'public' of the eighteenth century," as David Bell asserts, "was not a public of merchants and industrialists [since true capitalism was still in its infancy, or at least, its childhood], of outsiders to the sphere of government. It was a public of officeholders, financiers, idle *rentiers*, nobles, and, of course, lawyers."[33] A true eighteenth-century mix of enlightened aristocrats and bourgeois: the very mix, with the bourgeoisie in the majority, that made the first revolution.

One powerful manifestation of the importance of this expanding public opinion was the fact that, in the past, if a nobleman was imprisoned—improperly, in his mind—by a royal order, he sought release by seeking aid from a powerful patron. Now he could seek the same end by "launching an appeal in print. In other words, broadly speaking, the 'politics of privilege' was now losing ground to a 'politics of public opinion.'"[34] Bell elaborates on the important consequences of the successful challenges to the Crown by lawyers in the 1730–31 Affair of the Barristers:

> These dramatic admissions underline the real significance of the affair of the barristers. For one of the first times in French history *a group largely composed of commoners*, without powerful noble patrons and without violence, caused the monarchy to lose face in a political confrontation. Their success vividly demonstrated the growing importance of their two chief sources of influence—the ability to form an autonomous association capable of independent action within the structure of French institutions, and especially their ability to appeal to the new nebulous force of public opinion. . . . Voltaire . . . gave what amounted . . . to the highest praise: "simple citizens triumphed . . . having no arms but reason."[35]

It is amusing to discover that, in the days way before the cultural domination of the television, as soon as "mass culture" began to assert itself, the narcissism of the performers and the hunger for sensationalism on the part of audiences had already produced a derogation of cultural life: "Instead of effacing themselves, barristers made spectacles of themselves, justified the practice in a flood of writings, and were rewarded for doing so by attention in the press and a host of cases. This was not merely the triumph of Ciceronianism, but Ciceronianism gone wild."[36]

Habermas's notion of the "public sphere" is similar to, and grows out of, the concept of "civil society": a public space, not dominated by the state or the state apparatus, wherein a dialogue can develop among morally autonomous individuals. Such dialogue can, and does, subject the received values of the society to critique and, therefore, in fortunate circumstances, leads to a transformation of the mores of society. In that circumstance, certain public "performances" were played out " 'before' the people."[37]

In the decade before the first revolution, voluntary societies and clubs developed into powerful instruments of potential social change. Almost entirely this was a bourgeois phenomenon. Gary Kates asserts:

> In an age when periodicals were manifold and expensive, societies served as reading clubs, allowing their members easy access to the news of the day. More important, clubs provided ways for thinking men to develop personal connections and political constituencies; indeed, *virtually every politician*, journalist, and intellectual of any importance belonged to some club during this period.[38]

URBANIZATION

In his essential work on the civil war that developed in the Vendée, Charles Tilly has placed enormous emphasis on the importance of urbanization in determining where a particular area found itself on the prorevolution/antirevolution divide. "The segments of western France's society which supported the Revolution were those which urbanization had enveloped; the segments in which opposition appeared were those which urbanization had touched but little. . . . The interest conflicts arose at the junctions of rural and urban life."[39]

Tilly recognizes that the old theoretical formulation that capitalism had promoted economic development and that political institutions lagged behind such development—therefore making revolution possible, if not inevitable—was no longer valid. The "cultural lag," in his view, was that between urbanization and political institutions, with this growth of city-life being primarily dependent upon "trade and state centralization."[40] If we ask ourselves: What class was it that primarily was living this urban life?, we recognize that only one class provides an accurate answer.

QUI EST-CE QUE LE TIERS ÉTAT?

This is to vary Sieyès' portentious pamphlet "What Is the Third Estate?" to ask: "Who is?" "In all these ways," writes William Doyle, "the bourgeois of the 1780s were coming to think of themselves as an integral part of the political nation. It was a notion that would not have occurred to their grandparents, who had merely been silent onlookers of a game strictly for nobles. But the generation of 1789 naturally assumed that, in the new order that the Estates-General was bound to usher in, bourgeois would have an important part to play, and a significant say in what was to be done."[41]

Every calculation of the composition of the delegates of the Third Estate in 1789, in regard to the occupations of the deputies, overwhelmingly demonstrates the bourgeois nature of the makers of the first revolution. There were no peasants and no artisans.[42] The great number of lawyers has already been cited several times. Although they all did not practice law, nearly two-thirds of the deputies had some legal training. Out of 600, 127 were bailiwick magistrates. Over 40 percent held administrative offices that had been purchased. Businessmen and landlords accounted for 20 percent of the delegates. And, in regard to the importance of urbanization, nearly three-quarters came from towns of over 2,000 in population at a time when only 20 percent of the nation lived in such cities.[43]

When the Estates General transformed itself into the National Assembly— the first truly revolutionary act—the noble and clerical deputies to the Estates General, naturally, made up almost half of the National Assembly delegates. When, however, the National Assembly dissolved in 1791 and new elections were held for the Legislative Assembly, under the new constitution: "Gone were the clerics and nobles who had made up half the deputies elected in 1789; only a handful of either stood for election in 1791 or were returned. All the 745 new deputies were comfortably off, having been elected while the silver-mark requirement [for a deputy] was still in force; but very few owed their enrichment to trade or industry. Mostly they were men of property, and above all lawyers."[44]

All that is being elaborated here seems obvious; it could not have been otherwise. Who else could possibly have formed the politically active Third Estate if not the bourgeoisie? If there had been no potent bourgeois life, there would have been no revolutionary Third Estate; there would have been no Revolution. All this has been apparent to most historians for almost a hundred years. But what has not been perceived was that the existence of this bourgeoisie owed only very little to the rise of capitalist enterprise. *It was not a capitalist-bourgeois class; it was a bourgeois class with a modicum of capitalists.* And all this raises some great theoretical questions in regard to the history of the West and of Modernity.

THE BOURGEOIS WELTANSCHAUUNG

Just as no society can exist without a system of shared values, which system of values (mores, *mentalités*, etc.) exercises a crucial function of holding society together—just so, no class within society can exist, as a class, without its own particular order of shared values that holds the class together and also sets it off as distinct from the society as a whole. There is, in the Modern world, a bourgeois system of values that all bourgeois share, to a greater or lesser degree. This worldview may differ from country to country, may and does change over time, but, considered from the point of view of an ideal type, the bourgeois *Weltanschauung* has had a tremendous influence on the rise and existence of Modernity. Eighteenth-century France witnessed the continuous growth, and ultimate empowerment, of this bourgeois worldview.

This ascent to power obviously involved a challenge to the aristocratic value system that had held dominion over society. This latter was most vulnerable on the point of ability: the capacity to rule and administer. The bourgeois protest against aristocratic domination of political and social power took place under the banner of *"la carrière ouvert aux talents"* [the career open to talents]. "Those distinctions which are based only on the hazard of birth," announced the magistrate and future Chancellor Henri-François d'Aguesseau, in his oration given to the barristers as early as 1698, "those great names with which most men flatter themselves, and which dazzle even the wise, are no help in a profession where virtue is the source of all nobility, and where men are reputed not for what their fathers did, but for what they do themselves. In entering this famous body, they abandon the rank which prejudice attributed to them in the world, to resume the rank that reason has given them in the order of nature and truth." Words that were quoted, over and over again, during the century that followed.[45]

It was natural that, after revolutionary history began, the ideals of liberty and equality should be equated with professional opportunity and advancement for all. An obscure orator traveling in the south of France announced, at some time after the fall of the Bastille: "O holy liberty, o holy equality, who makest it possible for me to boldly say: I am but a poor peasant, I am but a simple workman, and my son may become a magistrate, a legislator, a ship master, a general."[46] And most famous of all the critiques of aristocratic pretensions was Beaumarchais' Figaro: "Nobility, fortune, rank, position! How proud they make a man feel! What have you done to deserve such advantage? Put yourself in the trouble of being born—nothing more!"[47]

The obvious result of a successful institutionalization of careers open to talent was social mobility on a scale previously unheard of in the world.[48] Such fluidity of social status accelerates as the bourgeoisification of society grows, to the point where it characterizes our present world. That so many people are living a life so different from that of their parents is one important cause of the anomie and anxiety of the Modern world. In eighteenth-century France, even for those who remained in the professional or commercial social strata, individual options were available. Alison Patrick, in an analysis of the professions of the deputies to the Convention, elected in 1792, states that: "There was a good deal of freedom in the choice of occupation." A surgeon's son might become a lawyer; a son destined for the army or the church become a doctor instead; merchants' sons became professionals, establishing close family links between different strata of the bourgeoisie.[49] This was no longer a "traditional" society but clearly a transitional one on the way to Modernity.

A work ethic was an essential aspect of the bourgeois *Weltanschauung*. The Abbé Sièyes writes in his *Essai sur les privilèges:* "What is a *bourgeois* next to a privileged person? The latter always has his eyes on the noble time *past*. . . . The bourgeois, by contrast, his eyes always fixed on the ignoble *present*. . . . [He] is, instead of having been; he endures hard work, and even worse the shame of employing his entire intelligence and all his strength for our present service, and lives from work which is essential for us all."[50] The unsettling fact is that 90 or 95 percent of these hard-working bourgeois were Catholic. We are encountering a *Catholic work ethic*. It should make us reconsider our sociological inheritance from Weber. Maybe the work ethic and the thrust toward capitalism are not merely manifestations of a Protestant *mentalité*. Possibly Protestantism itself is a result—not a cause—of a much more overriding movement: the great impulse toward Modernity. Perhaps a Protestant work ethic and a Catholic work ethic, a Protestant bourgeoisie and a Catholic bourgeoisie, are two distinct and separate aspects of one great historical movement: the bourgeoisification of the world.

Though it is generally agreed today that France was not a capitalist country in the eighteenth century, it is true, nevertheless, that commerce and trade were changing the face of society—and its mores. The last three-quarters of the century had witnessed a remarkable growth in commercial activity and of a "consumer society." A substantial number of people, and no longer just a narrow elite, enjoyed "an expanding taste for a whole range of consumer goods: clocks, books, coffee, sugar, chocolate, furniture, cutlery, glassware, textiles, and minor luxuries of all kinds."[51]

Up to about 1760, the state had strictly enforced the rules of *dérogance,* whereby any noble intent on pursuing a career in commerce lost his noble status. A complete turnabout occurred at this time: the king ennobled merchants in recognition of their service to the country. Letters of nobility given to two brothers doing business in Rouen in 1756 stated: "Commerce has always been regarded as one of the sources the most sure and the most productive of the force and power of states. . . . We remark that most of the families who devote themselves to commerce only envisage it as a means to pass on to some employment decorated with titles and prerogatives, which appear to them to represent a more honorable state. . . . [Such an attitude is] a prejudice so harmful to the progress of commerce. It is important to make known to the nation that it can find in commerce what is honorable as well as what is useful."[52]

This intimate connection between the rise of the bourgeoisie and commerce and capitalism is, of course, a standard part of historical analysis of the early Modern and Modern world. The point being made in this chapter is not to deny the fact but to see that connection as only one of many factors that finally produced the dominance of bourgeois life.

CATHOLIC "PURITANISM"

If one may be permitted a speculation that projects discussion way beyond the boundaries of this work—a speculation that may, if valid, indicate a productive future area of research—then it may not be inappropriate to ask if the value system of the bourgeoisie in the eighteenth century did not differ radically from that of those engaged in trade and commerce in Europe during the fourteenth and fifteenth centuries. Those centuries witnessed many non-noble individuals occupied with trade, commerce, money-lending, and banking. They were neither noble nor poor: the class in the middle. Some, like Jacques Coeur in France, were extraordinarily wealthy. There were, in addition, middle-class people of all ranks of wealth. Were all these folk—*petite* to *grande*—bourgeois? And if one chooses to so designate them, the speculation offered here is that the system of values of such bourgeois-middle-class people was profoundly different from that of the eighteenth century. The great Fugger banking family was started by Johannes Fugger, the son of a weaver, who became a textile merchant and left a small fortune at his death in 1409. His son Jakob expanded his business and, at his death, was one of the wealthiest men in Europe. Did such people, on their ascent to the highest level of financial power, share a *Modern* bourgeois *Weltanschauung?* It may very well be that they did not. What is being proposed here is that it takes more than commerce and banking to create a Modern bourgeois worldview and that the latter is necessary for, and antecedent to, the rise of capitalism. In Asia, for instance, the Chinese were great traders and bankers for centuries, and yet no capitalism arose. The great industrial and capitalist "take off" in England has been explained by the existence of sufficient surplus wealth created by commercial ventures. And yet Spain had, from its American adventures, more surplus gold than the whole of Europe combined, and it lagged far behind the great movement toward capitalism. Could it be that Weber was entirely correct and that the spirit of capitalism precedes, rather than follows, industrialization? That the steam engine is as much a result of an ethos as its cause?

After the Protestant Reformation *and* the Catholic reform movement *and* the efflorescence of Christian humanism, the world had changed immensely. Most important, the way of being bourgeois had been transformed. The crucial concept here is "Puritan," used in a metaphorical sense to describe a view of the world. The hypothesis is that one would not be tempted to describe pre-Reformation bourgeois life, in any country, as "Puritan," and yet eighteenth-century bourgeois *mentalités,* in a Catholic country like France, profoundly echoed that Protestant experience.*

---

*I discovered, too late to be used in this chapter, a marvelous book by George Huppert: *Les bourgeois gentilhommes: an essay on the definition of elites in Renaissance France.* University of Chicago Press, 1977. Huppert describes the creation in France, c. 1550–1600, of a vibrant *grande* and *haute* bourgeois lifestyle and *Weltanschauung* by a class of people who made it a deliberate point not to ape the aristocracy but to create a unique bourgeois world committed to culture, the promotion of secular education, and a firm work ethic. It remained, overwhelmingly, a Catholic culture, when Jansenism was not yet an important religious phenomenon. The reading of the book very intensely raises certain fundamental questions:

This "Puritan" sensibility is most easily perceived in the conduct of the Jacobin clubs. "Against the more normal vices," writes Brinton, "the Jacobins were always firm." Drunkenness was sinful, gambling disapproved of; prostitution an anathema.[53] "There was a puritanical streak in Jacobinism," Kennedy asserts. No off-color humor was allowed; swearing was taboo; speakers cried out against avarice, dishonesty, and prostitution; gambling houses were to be closed; even billiard halls were "regarded as dens of iniquity."[54] Paris, under the domination of the Robespierrists, was not on the way to becoming a new Geneva. However, prostitution was surpressed; pornographic pictures outlawed; and soldiers were forbidden to bathe nude in the Seine, where they would be visible to all. "The element of Puritanism in the Revolution," claims Palmer, "was very strong."[55]

So much for the repression of vice. The virtuous life was defined in exactly the manner that we might expect from a Modern bourgeoisie. It is of great significance that, at least in the ideal, the family became one essential center of virtue. Soboul quotes a well-known pamphlet at the time of the Revolution, wherein a dialogue is presented between a citizen from Philadelphia and a French republican. The latter announces: "To be a good citizen, one must be a good son, a good husband and a good father; one must unite in a single word every private and public virtue . . . only then will you have a true definition of the word patriotism."[56] This bringing together of private and public virtue—and, therefore, private and public vice—was a significant aspect of the *Weltanschauung* of the radical bourgeoisie, whose leader and foremost spokesman was designated "the incorruptible"—an adjective applicable to both Maximilien's public and private lives. Palmer elaborates: "The Robespierrists set a high value on frugality, not alone because material goods were scarce; on discipline, not alone because France was in a state of confusion; on chastity, not alone because promiscuous sex habits might take the patriot's mind off his civic duty. They believed that these virtues were good and adequate ends in themselves. They identified them with a particular structure of society, the democratic Republic."[57]

Of great significance was the fact that part of the nobility itself was being won over to this modern lifestyle and worldview. On a daily basis, society was becoming more orderly and less violent. "To be sure, France cannot be said to have become bourgeois in the sense that 'modes of production' were radically altered in a material way. But a large segment of its land-owning population,

---

The relationship of a "Protestant" *Weltanschauung* to a reform Catholic one; the bourgeois versus the noble life; the development from an early Modern to a truly Modern culture.

including nobles, came to accept the basic cultural assumptions of bourgeois life, such as individualism, a sense of measured order, and the desireability of thrift."[58]

In summary, the ideals of the Jacobin world celebrated a solid modern bourgeois life: liberalism in the world of politics and conservative, patriarchal, family virtues in the private sphere. Brinton offers these conclusions:

> Our mythical "average" Jacobin would have accepted as a statement of his aims something like this: An independent nation-state, a republican form of government, universal manhood suffrage, separation of church and state; equal civil rights for all, and the abolition of hereditary distinctions and social privileges; a competitive industrial and agricultural society, with private ownership of property, but without great fortunes and dire poverty; a virtuous hard-working society, without luxuries and without vices, where the individual freely conforms to standards of middle-class decency.[59]

Can one fail to think of Tocqueville's America: a profoundly "Protestant" world?

The total intermingling of private and public virtue, of family and community control, resonates with the one great contradiction of Puritan life: the inquisitorial power of the church exercised in Geneva, the Netherlands, and America. The Jacobin clubs never rose to this kind of tyranny, but they did feel it was the job of the community to correct personal behavior. Brinton asserts that, "Examples crowd upon the investigator." And he provides one amiable example wherein a club called in the parties to a dispute in a situation where a rich father had denied his daughter's wishes to marry a poor, but virtuous lover. The society resolved the situation.[60] Such activity, however, contains a great ambiguity in it. The destruction of private life is a totalitarian exercise, no matter under what banner of virtue it is conducted. The great Terror of '93–'94 garnered much of its energy from the worldview that there was only one truth, and that the community had the right and obligation to impose it on its members. When private life is subjected to the same scrutiny as political action, an increase in tyranny is inevitable.

Antoine Pierre Joseph Marie Barnave was a significant actor in the first revolution, became a Feuillant after Varennes, and was guillotined in Paris under the Terror of An II. His immediate family background and history were typical of many of the rising bourgeoisie in eighteenth-century France: the money made in commerce and manufacturing was used to purchase the lowest noble status, even though the worldview retained many significant bourgeois attributes and attitudes. His father made his fortune in commerce and the throwing of silk, moved to Grenoble, exercised for a long while the office of prosecutor, and finally bought an appointment as *avocat consistorial,* which conferred on him a noble status.[61] His son Antoine, however, was capable of arguing brilliantly the superiority of the bourgeois view of reality over that of the nobility. "In general," he writes in his notebooks, "the merchant is opposite of the warrior: the one wants to acquire by industry, the other by conquest; the one makes power a means to wealth, the other, wealth a means to power; the one is disposed to save what comes from his work, the other to squander what comes from his valor; the one sacrifices only to his interests under the appearance of probity; the other, in the midst of brigandage and violence, is at least capable of some candor. The one is much occupied in not being disturbed, the other works ceaselessly to disturb others. The one is the prototype of what in our modern states is called bourgeois; the other is the prototype of nobility."[62]

A powerful differentiation that is pushed even further by Joseph Schumpeter's celebration of capitalism as the first society in which a man can prove he is a man without killing someone.[63] It is worth considering that, just as Tocqueville argued that a stable democracy was not possible in France until a certain commitment to violence was abjured,[64] just so capitalism may be possible only when the society as a whole renounces the noble-warrior mentality. A commercial, trading, and banking elite that is continuously forsaking capitalist enterprise for the life of a noble—as Pirenne argues was true in Europe in the late Middle Ages, creating a situation wherein capitalist enterprise had to be continuously and periodically reborn with new families of entrepreneurs[65]—such an elite may be incapable of launching the kind of capitalist "take-off" that England inaugurated in the eighteenth century.

If it is true that centuries of trading, commerce, money-lending, and complex banking are incapable in themselves of being transformed into a true capitalism—that is, an economic system wherein capitalist activity predominates over all noncapitalist enterprise—and if that transformation depends upon a revolutionary sublimation of violence into capitalist competition, then the enormous importance of the *Modern* bourgeois *Weltanschauung* becomes apparent. The great historical questions, then, become: Why was England one of the first, if not the first, to produce a Modern bourgeois worldview? Why was France so ambivalent about that venture? Why did Germany—the home in the thirteenth, fourteenth, and fifteenth centuries of enormous trading and commercial activity—arrive on the true capitalist scene significantly later? How much does the understanding of the commitment to violence, and the possibilities of its sublimation, help us to arrive at the answers to these questions? How much of the excessive repression exercised by early Puritanism was truly aimed, not at sexuality, but at violence and aggression? Repression that could only become transformative and sublimative when Puritanism gave way to Liberalism.

François Furet, in a brilliant theoretical stroke, has written that in Europe in the eighteenth century, there were essentially three types of aristocracy or nobility: An English aristocracy that was willing to share in the march toward Modernity and maintain a great deal of its power by not opposing the gradual move toward democracy, a Polish know-nothing aristocracy that sought to preserve a medieval culture forever, and a Prussian aristocracy that attempted to institutionalize certain aspects of Modernity but only at its instigation and under its direction. France, Furet insists, had significant elements of all three types of aristocracy. Neither the king nor the nobility, however, Furet argues, took the kind of political and social initiative that would make one or another of these three possible options viable for France.[66]

What we need today is a historical analysis of the bourgeoisie along similar lines. It is no longer productive to talk about *the* bourgeoisie in global terms, as if there was only *one* European bourgeoisie that was the same in all countries and unchanged over a 500-year period: a theoretical tradition that extends all the way from Marx to Habermas. Edward Cheyney has underlined the fact that the 50 years from 1250 to 1302 saw the beginning of regular participation of representatives of the cities (in addition to the nobility and the clergy) in the national assemblies called by the king in Castile and Leon in 1250, in Catalonia in 1285, in the German diet in 1255, the parliament of England in 1265, and the first appearance of the Third Estate in France in 1302. No coincidence, Cheyney argues: the efflorescence of commerce had created a well-to-do middle class (a "bourgeoisie?") with financial power that had to be accommodated within the political sphere.[67] Did all these different middle classes share the same *Weltanschauung,* and was there no development and transformation of the bourgeois system of values from 1250 to 1750? It is doubtful that such could be the case. Why then should we assume that, in the eighteenth century, the English bourgeoisie was the equivalent of the Dutch or the German? And what sort of bourgeoisie was the French?

One thing seems clear: the French bourgeoisie was plunging precipitously into Modernity. That is why the first French Revolution proved such an extraordinary example for the whole of the Western world. Why it failed so miserably for such a long time to achieve that Modern goal is, of course, the great question. One essential element in finding the answer to that query will be a profound understanding of exactly what kind of bourgeoisie was the French bourgeoisie.

Possibly the great trouble for France, and its bourgeoisie, was not that the king and the aristocracy resisted for so long its rise to power, or that, once empowered, it was threatened with overthrow by a violent sans-culotte protoproletariat. Perhaps, the great trouble for the French bourgeoisie and its drive for power lay precisely within that bourgeoisie itself. It failed, most especially, in its Jacobin manifestation, to fulfill and go beyond Puritanism (i.e., to reject the repressiveness of virtue) and achieve the liberal position.

OF PURITANISM AND LIBERALISM

Michael Walzer, in his book on Puritanism, *The Revolution of the Saints,*[68] postulates that Puritanism, most especially of the most inflexibile, rigid variety—as practiced, for instance, in Calvin's Geneva—was, in the large historical perspective, a transitional phenomenon. The future belonged not to Calvin but to Locke, not to Puritanism but to liberalism. Walzer begins with the observation that Puritanism, in its most repressive mode, became most powerful during the period when society was moving beyond the necessity of authoritarian kingship. Why, then, he asks, should it institute a cultural mode that, in many ways, was more intrusive, more authoritarian—especially in the invasion of private life—than any monarchy had ever been? This is precisely, he goes on to argue, the nature of this kind of transitional historical phenomenon: one authoritarianism can only be surmounted by putting another—but profoundly different—authoritarianism in its place, which manages, somehow, to overcome and move beyond the basic need for an absolute authority.

When we ask the crucial question: What kind of bourgeoisie was the French bourgeoisie in the eighteenth century? we do find a rather complex mix of puritan and liberal values. And here, I use the word "liberal" not in regard to politics, law, rights, and so on, but as a description of a certain lifestyle that, in the Modern world, became essential to the bourgeois value system. At its best, that lifestyle has been characterized by a faith in comfort, culture, and commitment.[69] This complex mix of puritan and liberal values is most visible in the sharp critiques offered by both Rousseau and Diderot, in the 1750s, of the current sad state of the theater: a public space wherein the bourgeoisie occupied a significant place.

In 1757, Diderot presented his new play *Entretiens sur le Fils Naturel* and published as well an exegesis on the play. "Diderot believed that the theatre could become an agent of moral education if the repertoire were rewritten. . . . the attempt to recast . . . the theatre into a form of lay preaching. Diderot argued for a new type of drama, which he called the *genre sérieux*. . . . The essence [of which] was its didactic conveying of a moral lesson that would impress upon the spectators 'the love of virtue and the horror of vice.' "[70] His exegesis makes perfectly clear the bourgeois nature of this new virtuous theater:

> *Dorval:* So you would wish to put on the stage the man of letters, the philoso-
> pher, the tradesman, the judge, the lawyer, the politician, the citizen,
> the magistrate, the financier, the great nobleman, the steward.
>
> *Moi:* Add to that every sort of relationship, the father, the husband, the
> sister, the brothers. . . . Just think that every day new conditions are
> taking shape. Think that nothing is more unknown to us than those
> conditions, and that nothing ought to interest us more. We each have
> our own station in society, but we have truck with men of every other
> estate.[71]

Rousseau, who inclined much more to the puritan *mentalité*, enjoyed the aggressive dimension in the attack on vice. His *Lettre à M. d'Alembert Sur le Théâtre* was an excoriating attack. The theater taught corruption and vice, instead of virtue. Actors and actresses, in their private lives, enjoyed a degenerate existence. The theater weakened the moral fiber of society. What was needed, he argued, was not a reformed theater but new republican ceremonies that would educate the people toward the virtuous life.[72] As in so much else, Rousseau was already anticipating the complex system of rites and festivals that the Revolution—especially the Jacobin dictatorship, the most puritan experiment of the times, though of a perverse nature—would attempt to institutionalize.

What is remarkable is how quickly Diderot's prescription for reform, for the creation of a "bourgeois" drama,[73] became a reality. Almost immediately, a whole series of profoundly mediocre plays included family terms in their titles: *"époux, épouse, fils, mère, père,"* while another whole group used occupations and social status positions: manufacturer, men of letters, the vinegar maker, *Le Bon Seigneur*, the three farmers.[74] Here was no repression of the imaginative experience of the theater, as the Puritans had insisted upon, but the very use of its magical powers to advance the liberal-bourgeois *Weltanschauung*. Not surprisingly, we are told with great frequency that these bourgeois values are more virtuous than those of a selfish and corrupt aristocracy. "In his treatise *Du Théâtre*, published in 1773, Louis-Sebastien Mercier exhorted the playwright to consort with the *honnête bourgeois*: 'There you will see mores that are frank, gentle, open, diverse; there you will see the picture of daily life as Richardson and Fielding observed it; there you will see those worms of the morning [grandees], polished crooks, appear to deceive the good man and seduce his daughter.' "[75]

Looking beyond the naiveté, the sentimentality, and the propagandist intention of these commitments, what is most important to observe—once again—is how alive, thriving, and growing was the bourgeois culture in France 30 years or so before the revolution, and 50 or 75 years or more before France could be described as a "capitalist society." The creation of a bourgeois culture enjoys an autonomous existence of its own, independent of, though certainly related to, the rise of capitalist institutions.

A crucial concept for the Modern world, and one that sharply differentiates the liberal-bourgeois lifestyle from the puritan, is a commitment to the pursuit and enjoyment of comfort. Weber's potent insight that Puritanism was a harbinger of the modern world with its emphasis on worldly asceticism, which denied the world-rejection asceticism of the Middle Ages, can help us understand that the fully Modern position renounces all asceticism, of this or another world.[76] Whether or not we regard that commitment to comfort, and the renunciation of asceticism, as a virtue, it is crucially important to see that is an essential of the Modern worldview and that the bourgeoisie was, and is, its champion. And these desires for comfort are not restricted to a "capitalist" worldview: the Soviet Union might be alive and thriving today if it had been able to deliver to its citizens, in large enough quantity, the bourgeois goods: comfortable couches and color TVs.

Here, as in so much else, it was Tocqueville who so clearly perceived the crucial role of comfort. He praises American middle-class society for its capacity to adopt a sane, moderate view of the necessity of a sufficiency of creature comforts:

> The passion for physical comfort is essentially a middle-class affair; it grows and spreads with that class and becomes predominant with it. Thence it works upward into the higher ranks of society and thence spreads downward to the people.
>
> In America I never met a citizen too poor to cast a glance of hope and envy toward the pleasures of the rich or whose imagination did not snatch in anticipation good things that fate obstinately refused him.
>
> On the other hand, I never found among the wealthy Americans that lofty disdain for physical comfort which can sometimes be seen among even the most opulent and dissolute aristocrats.[77]

But the love of physical pleasures never leads democratic peoples to excesses. Among them love of comfort appears as a tenacious, exclusive, and universal passion, but always a restrained one.[78]

This passion for comfort, however, produces one of the great problematics in bourgeois-liberal society: a continuing, contemporary contradiction. It is an aspect of the current *Weltanschauung* most vulnerable to perversion. An exaggerated comfort for some—and who is to define what "reasonable" comfort is?—and equality for all are in violent contradiction with each other. Comfort, and in its perverse manifestation, the greed for goods, turns out to be not only a universal, reasonable human desire but also a defense against anxiety. Consumption becomes a powerful way to defend against the anxieties of Modernity. It becomes, then, almost impossible to lessen its effects as long as the anomie of Modernity holds dominion over most people's lives. Following the usual course of perversion, comfort and consumption are converted from a means to the greater end of a happy life, to ends in themselves. Being such, moderation becomes almost impossible to achieve.

Tocqueville saw the passion for moderate comfort and the passion for freedom united in the great middle-class democratic society in America. By the time he wrote the volume on the *Old Regime,* however, he began to see that these two passions were not necessarily joined together. Physical comfort can be desired for its own sake, and freedom regarded merely as a means to that end. We see, today, in the lands of the former Soviet Union and the former Soviet Empire, a great confusion as to whether the new divinity—the market—is to be worshiped for the freedom, or the plethora of goods, it is supposed to bring. They would do well to recognize the profound truth in Tocqueville's injunction: "Those who prize freedom only for the material benefits it offers have never kept it long."[79]

TO EXTIRPATE THE ARISTOCRACY AND CREATE THE BOURGEOIS REPUBLIC

A "class" may be defined, in part, as a particular group of people, similarly situated economically, who, as an assemblage, stand in a distinct relationship to political power. This latter may be negative: a class may be defined by the political impotence of the group. An essential aspect of revolutionary history is the narrative of the bourgeoisie becoming a class and assuming the primary political power in the nation. To accomplish this, obviously, it was required to eliminate and replace the current ruling class. "Though there can be no certainty about the future," Tocqueville comments, "[certain] facts are plain to see in the light of past experience. First, that all our contemporaries are driven on by a force we may hope to regulate or curb, but cannot overcome, and it is a force impelling them, sometimes gently, sometimes at headlong speed, to the destruction of the aristocracy."[80]

The growing Enlightenment commitment to ability, knowledge, and moral worth—to a rationalization of social and political experience—made the aristocracy vulnerable and opened doors to bourgeois political power. If the right to rule was dependent on capacity, understanding, and virtue, then who better than the bourgeoisie should enjoy this right? Even the monarchical-aristocratic establishment was infected with this Modern inclination. As early as the 1760s letters of nobility given and/or sold to bourgeois folk declared that "nobility 'takes its *origin* from the union of virtue and knowledge.' "[81] To become knowledgeable and "virtuous"—whatever that might mean—was the way of upward mobility. And in its most propagandistic stance, the bourgeoisie claimed almost a monopoly of these attributes. Its intent was to create not only a republic but a bourgeois republic. "They wished for a republic only on the condition that they themselves would govern it, according to the ideas and in the interests of the educated middle class to which they belonged. . . . By the term republic," Lamartine continues, "they understood rule by men of intelligence, virtue, property and qualities which henceforth were the privilege of their class."[82]

What is so striking is how willing, how quickly, this bourgeoisie was to assume political power. Not only was this apparent on the national level of the transformation of the Third Estate into a National Assembly, but also local elections on a city-basis immediately after 1789 revealed the impulse to power within the bourgeois ethos. In Troyes, for instance, the local elections of early 1790 overthrew the rule of nobles and royal officials and substituted a coalition of artisans and merchants of the moderate sort, even some members of the *petite* bourgeoisie. Of the new officers, only 13 percent of them were office-holders in the Old Regime.[83] This pattern was repeated over and over again in the years after the first revolution. Between 1789 and 1792, "every administrative council for every government unit, from department down to commune, had to be elected, and so did departmental *procureurs,* town clerks and tax gatherers, judicial officials, the clergy, and the commanders of the National Guard."[84] It was a veritable explosion of Tocqueville's local democracy and had its definite impact on the central state. A significant number of deputies elected to the national legislatures in 1791 and 1792 had begun their political life on the local and departmental level.[85]

All these political gains were achieved, obviously, at the expense of the aristocracy. And here we can observe a significant *mentalité* that revolutionary history reveals. The French bourgeoisie had little, if any, ambivalence about overthrowing the power of the aristocracy and replacing it by itself and any of the nobility who were willing to go along with the New Regime. This explains why the institutionalization of the liberal agenda and the "destruction of feudalism" proceeded with lightning speed. The bourgeoisie had no conflict about eliminating any class that stood between it and the king. All attempts, for instance, to institutionalize a bicameral legislature wherein the upper house would resemble the British House of Lords, were beaten back. About the monarch, however, there was a profound ambivalence. It was never clearly decided what kind of government should replace the Old Regime kingship: a constitutional monarchy with a strong king? With a weak king? A republic? And the final revolutionary decision was made, not by, but for, the bourgeoisie by the people-in-the-streets in August 1792. The bourgeoisie assented, with hardly a murmur, but it took almost a hundred years before it renounced its longings for an authoritarian ruler; and for many, it took longer than that. The bourgeoisie was ready to replace the aristocracy with itself. The king was a more complicated and conflicted story. To live without that imperious presence turned out to be much more difficult than liberal optimism allowed.

THE TRI-PARTITE BOURGEOISIE

Using an analysis of ideal-types, the French bourgeoisie during revolutionary times falls into three distinct categories. First, there was the truly liberal bourgeois, willing to take a chance on the consequences of full democracy: a Jefferson-Madison-Tom Paine view of the world. Second, there were those frightened of the political left and of the poor, full of anxiety that property would be abolished along with privilege. And third, there were the radicals and the terrorists, most of whom were themselves bourgeois. It is a most difficult task, and certainly beyond this author's capacity, to determine how large each category was, especially since there were obviously enormous shifts from one stance to another as the years progressed. It seems certain, for instance, that the group of the property-conscious and property-anxious grew each year as the Terror and the guillotine did their work.

The Jacobin clubs up until Thermidor, and in the time of the revival of Jacobism, 1797 forward, were home to both the truly democratic and the radical-terrorist bourgeois. Illustrative of the democratic view was the Jacobin affiliate in Bordeaux, which numbered between 1,500 and 2,000 at its height in 1790–1791. Its members included "many wealthy businessmen, successful lawyers, and intellectuals," and "it dominated the delegates of the Gironde to the Legislative Assembly and Convention." It almost monopolized local political offices. And its citizens represented the very finest of bourgeois virtues: "Its members were not mean-spirited. They gave unstintingly of their time and money to patriotic and benevolent causes."[86]

That kind of solid, democratic citizen became important again during the Jacobin revival, especially outside Paris. In the Eure, for instance, J. Touquet was the editor of the *Bulletin de l'Eure*, which began publication in December 1796 and was suppressed by the Directory in April of '98. The publication was the voice of Jacobinism in the Eure. Touquet, a passionate believer in democracy, felt that there was no longer any threat to it from the hereditary nobility. The new danger, however, came from a new aristocracy—"celle des riches"—who were not royalists, who were committed to a republic, but who, nevertheless, cared primarily for their economic position and status. They "support the republic so that they can maintain their wealth, while democrats support the republic because they wish to be free."[87] No radical, certainly no terrorist, Touquet and his Jacobin comrades represented a solid democratic-citizen point of view that, unfortunately, had no immediate future.

The most significant segment of the bourgeoisie—most significant since the future (or at least the next two hundred years) did belong to it—was the second category of bourgeois ideology: liberal but determined to maintain the sanctity of property and determinedly antiradical. The Terror had provided more than enough evidence of the danger of not adding a substantial dose of conservatism to revolutionary liberalism. From a certain moral point of view, they were an unattractive lot, but it does not follow that their anxieties were exaggerated or mistaken: concern and worry that *both* property and liberalism were threatened by ideological terror.

The sanctity of property, the necessity of possessing it in order to be a full citizen, and the social necessity of inequality were crucial shibboleths of the modern bourgeois *Weltanschauung* and have remained essential to it down to the present day. True to its position on the threshold of the fully modern world, revolutionary times brought forth clear and determined support for these values. Benjamin Constant, of course. A speech he gave in 1798 was widely publicized by the *Moniteur*, the published voice of the Directory. "All interests are grouped around property. The slightest blow against it will resound in all parts of the empire; whoever dispossess the rich menaces the poor; whoever proscribes opulence, conspires against modest fortune."[88] Supply-side economics in America was merely one of the latest manifestations of this enduring principle that the amelioration of the poor depends primarily on the economic liberty of the rich.

Property qualifications for either voting or office, then, became the simple and effective way of holding democracy in check, of keeping it a limited, and not a full, democracy. Those without a certain amount of property were not, therefore, complete citizens. From 1789 to 1848, the French bourgeoisie wrote, or lived under, nine constitutions: 1791, 1793, 1795, 1799, 1802, 1804, 1814, 1815, and 1830. Only the Montagnard constitution of 1793 (never instituted) and the first Napoleonic constitution of 1799 (soon corrected in 1802 and 1804) did not require some minimum of property for suffrage or office-holding, with the latter usually requiring more substantial wealth.[89] Even if it was to be some version of a republic, it was clear who owned that polity.

That the health of the commonwealth demanded some substantial inequality was an assumed great principle. From Necker, the great friend of the Third Estate, we hear: "It will be said, imprudently, that if distinctions of property are an obstacle to the establishment of a political morality, we should strive to destroy them. . . . One may dream of a state where things would be otherwise, and where equality reigned among men, but would one imagine that these primitive relations can be restored at a time when the disparity of means has considerably increased, and when all the superiority of state and power is consolidated by the immutable force of disciplined armies?"[90] Almost eighty years later, the state was determined that this lesson be learned by all. A first-year civics textbook, c. 1870, is summarized by Eugen Weber:

Society: (1) French society is ruled by just laws, because it is a democratic society. (2) All the French are equal in their rights; but there are inequalities between us that stem from nature or from wealth. (3) These inequalities cannot disappear. (4) Man works to become rich; if he lacked this hope, work would cease and France would decline. It is therefore necessary that each of us should be able to keep the money he has earned.[91]

This continuing bourgeois anxiety about, at its worst, the elimination of property or even, at its least, a substantial economic leveling—all this had profound implications for the nineteenth- and twentieth-century history of the struggle for democracy. Bourgeois liberals were in a quandary: if they supported a revolution against monarchy and aristocracy, they were opening the Pandora's box of mobocracy or socialist revolt. Especially in Germany, these moderate liberals became severely compromised and frightened about doing what the French bourgeoisie had done in 1789.[92] The final catastrophic act occurred in the twentieth century when many bourgeois, who in other circumstances would have been liberal democrats, threw their support to fascist regimes as the only possible bulwark against the communization of the world.

JACOBINISM: BOURGEOIS IDEOLOGICAL TERROR

The third category of bourgeois citizens is made up of those who composed the radical wing of Jacobinism. They were most powerful in Paris but found many supporters in the 4,000 to 5,000 clubs throughout the nation.

That Jacobin ideological terror was created and maintained by bourgeois citizens seems to us, at first, a sociological contradiction. And yet, such was undoubtedly the case. Even the radicalism of the sans-culottes, of the people-in-the-streets of Paris, was fed and nurtured by members of the *petite* and *moyenne* bourgeoisie. Soboul elaborates on how the ideology of many workers was formed by the small master-craftsmen, whom they worked for and lived with: "The small workshop *compagnon* inevitably derived many of his ideas from his employer . . . [and] had basically the same attitude to the great problems of the day."[93] To us, a very strange bourgeoisie that conforms not at all to a simplistic Marxist class analysis, which many of us non-Marxists still carry, to some extent, in our baggage.

One of our foremost authorities on Jacobin clubs, Michael Kennedy, has absolutely no reluctance to pronounce on the bourgeois nature of Jacobinism: "One could spend a quarter-century scrutinizing membership rolls, studying tax records, and compiling charts and graphs, and still conclude that the Jacobins were basically middle class."[94] His own typical data demonstrate that, of 35 citizens of Clermont-Ferrand who petitioned the Paris club requesting affiliation in early 1790, 5 were *négociants*, 4 lived off invested capital (*bourgeois*), 4 were members of the clergy, 2 medical men, and "nearly all of the remainder some type of lawyer or judicial official."[95] And his final conclusion is that, whereas Brinton had announced a figure of 66 percent for middle-class membership for 1789–1792, he himself comes up with a result of 71 percent for 1789–1791.[96]

Not only bourgeois, which itself presents a wide discrepancy of income and wealth, but further data seem to indicate that many members of the clubs came from the higher echelons, though not the highest, of the bourgeoisie. Brinton's figures indicate that club members paid a significantly larger amount of taxes than the average citizen (1789–1795)[97] and that Jacobin purchases of national-ized church property (*biens nationaux*) were significantly larger than those of non-members.[98] And those bourgeois in a higher than *moyenne* status had obviously already begun to play the game of using their financial and political position to bring pressure on legislators to aid their economic interests. Bourgeois lobbying was apparently a fact of life: "The minutes of the agriculture and commerce committee of the National Assembly, in 1791, are laden with references to the clubs."[99]

All Jacobins, of course, were not terrorists who represented the radical fringe of the Jacobin movement; however, the data we have definitely indicate that a significant number of the members of the clubs shared the political views of Robespierre and Saint-Just. After Thermidor occurred a counterrevolutionary White Terror that, legally and illegally, annihilated many former terrorist activ-ists. In some cases, lists of those proscribed were prepared, and it is from these lists that we can retrieve significant data on the occupations, and therefore class status, of the most radical Jacobins. Brinton's particular figures indicate that, of 637 terrorists, 61 percent were middle class; of another selection of 456 pro-scribed citizens, the average terrorist paid a tax almost twice as much as the typical townsman.[100] Another calculation indicates that in Toulouse, of the 293 known terrorists, 90 were merchants or liberal professionals, 133 were artisans, but the majority of these were masters and small employers.[101]

Again, what we are faced with, a phenomenon that cries out for explanation, is bourgeois ideological terrorism. No simplistic class explanation is helpful. Brinton addresses this great paradox:

From hundreds of these brief *cursus vitae* of revolutionary leaders, the impression clearly arises that they fitted their old environment, that to an observer in 1788 or 1789 they would appear essentially normal in thought and action. In 1794, most of them talked nonsense and some of them acted on it. In 1794, then, they are to be distinguished from the normal respectable *bourgeois*. Yet as their social origins are essentially the same as those of the normal respectable *bourgeois,* one may perhaps be pardoned for doubting if the explanation of their conduct in 1794 lies in the social origins.[102]

A strange virus, as Tocqueville tells us, was eating at the souls of some men at the end of the eighteenth century, and it was not just a few crazies like Marat or Roux or just a handful of murderous ideologues like Robespierre and Saint-Just. It had infected a significant number of that rising, progressive class that was destined to bring us to Modernity. If we were capable of understanding this paradox, we might be closer to comprehending all the other catastrophes that this latest stage of social evolution has brought us as well.

Michael Kennedy's third volume on the Jacobin clubs during the Terror and immediately after Thermidor was not published until the year 2000. He, however, most kindly, made the unpublished manuscript available to me. An analysis of Kennedy's data is given in Chapter 21. Here, it may be appropriate to anticipate one remarkable conclusion: Paris was not the problem; many members of the provincial clubs were as murderous terrorists—a significant number, even more murderous—as their Parisian brothers. A murderous, terrorist bourgeoisie? Such was a French phenomenon in 1794.

For the future revolutionary history of Europe (both bourgeois and "proletarian" revolutions), the particularity of the French situation was that it seemed to be the first, and the last, time that a significant segment of the bourgeois class themselves pushed revolutionary activity to a radical extreme. Only in France, Hobsbawm writes, was, "one section of the liberal middle class . . . prepared to remain revolutionary up to and indeed beyond the brink of anti-bourgeois revolution."[103] What is obviously striking is that no economic analysis, no class analysis, can explain why this was so, and Hobsbawm, who would ordinarily be sympathetic to such analysis, does not offer one. The French bourgeoisie at the end of the eighteenth century, in some crucial regards, remains a mystery: occupying a mysterious place wherein ideological terror can hold dominion.

CAPITALISTS?

To many careful analysts of the Revolution, it seemed obvious that the data revealed that businessmen played a minor role in revolutionary history. Cobban sympathetically cites Lefebvre and Marcel Reinhard to the effect that "men of business played no leading part in the revolution."[104] And Patrick, our foremost authority on the class make-up of the Convention, states that "of the 694 *conventionnels* (among our 730) with known vocations, fewer than 1 in 5 had been engaged in agriculture, commerce, or industry."[105] She also points out that Jaurès, coming from a Marxist background, found it difficult to understand why businessmen were so underrepresented in revolutionary activity.[106]

What was significant for the future of capitalism, however, was the fact that the values of these noncapitalist bourgeois included, with very few exceptions, a commitment to laissez-faire economics and individualism.[107] Before the Revolution, Higonnet speculates, many bourgeois had an inclination to find a full capitalist economy an unattractive prospect, and yet their commitment to certain values helped open the way to that future: "There is not doubt that the respectable *grand-bourgeois* gentlemen of the 1780s would have been appalled to realize that high capitalism would soon emerge from the enthusiastic demolition of rural traditionalism and their defense of economic individualism. But this only means that capitalism differs from the bourgeois structures of thought and action that are its necessary and organic preconditions."[108]

That high capitalist future, however, was still a long way off. Looking at French "protocapitalism" from the American point of view is illuminating. We discover that the French capitalists before capitalism were not very adequate at their trade. Commercial activity with France had a significant political reverberation in American politics in the 1790s. In the intense rivalry between the Jefferson-Madison faction and that of Hamilton and his associates a sharp disagreement, based on ideological considerations, arose about whether primary trade relations should be developed with England or France. Hamilton, the economic modernist, favored England regardless of the fact that England had been the enemy. The Jeffersonians strongly inclined toward France, because the latter had aided the revolution against the English but also because England, and its mode of trade, represented a cunning and corrupt Modern economic practice. The problem for the economic conservatives was that French capitalism was not up to the task. Elkins and McKitrick tell us:

Neither the state of French manufacturing, the mentality of the French bourgeoisie, nor the condition of the French economy as a whole could provide the least basis for theorizing that France was America's "natural" trading partner, or even that France might become, in the foreseeable future, a major commercial power. For one thing, the French had a very limited experience with the American market, almost all of it bad. The increased numbers of French cargoes coming into American ports immediately after the Revolution represented, for the most part, a disaster to their owners, who had very little knowledge of the people they hoped would buy them. Made up ineptly and with considerable guesswork, they consisted of products that were either badly packed, inappropriate to the season, unsuited to the tastes of the public, or else inferior to similar goods furnished cheaper and better by the British. Unable or unwilling to extend credit, requiring quick payment, in constant fear of being cheated, and having few established connections, the owners—or rather the ship captains or supercargoes they often used as their agents—in case after case were constrained to dispose of these lots hastily and at a loss in order to get rid of them.[109]

In addition to their incapacity, no serious attempt was made to correct the situation. The port cities of France consistently refused to grant concessions to American trade, since they felt such actions would disrupt their situation in the French internal market.[110]

We may accept the Yankee skeptical judgment: France was no Modern capitalist society. It takes something more than a flourishing bourgeoisie to make a Modern capitalist society. It is hard to say exactly what that "something" is, but one thing seems clear: it had not yet appeared in a healthy, expanding manner in France, even by the end of the eighteenth century. Strange to say, the French bourgeoisie was, as yet, unfitted for its "historical task."

What we are left with, finally, in this discussion of the middle class, is a French bourgeoisie flourishing and expanding, ready to take political power and doing so—and yet, there was only a minimum of Modern capitalist spirit or enterprise. And, in addition, we are presented with the remarkable circumstance of a bourgeoisie, a significant percentage of its members willing to exercise an ideological terror of a left-wing variety. Our received sociological wisdom is incapable of answering the theoretical questions thrown up by these apparently total contradictions. Perhaps, a beginning can be made if we go beyond received theoretical orthodoxy and confront the great paradoxes of Modernity.

9

THE TERRIFYING PARADOX OF INDIVIDUALISM

'Tis all in pieces, all coherence gone;
All just supply, and all Relation:
Prince, Subject, Father, Sonne, are things forgot,
For every man, alone thinkes he hath got
To be a Phoenix, and that there can bee
None of that kinde, of which he is, but hee.
—John Donne[1]

Several brilliant observers of the human condition, from Donne in the seventeenth century to Erich Fromm and Marshall Berman in the twentieth, have perceived the same essential phenomenon: that nothing is more exhilarating and more terrifying; nothing offers human beings greater promise and greater anxiety; nothing gives as much freedom and creates, at the same time, the passionate desire to run from freedom back to a new/old tyranny—nothing in the world does this as much as the imperative to become a morally autonomous individual. Modernity, as has been said here over and over again, creates an extraordinary number of contradictions and paradoxes. All of these are of enormous human importance, but the greatest paradox and contradiction of all is the exhilaration and terror of having to stand, seemingly, almost alone. The French Revolutions, 1789–1793, became a complex, tragic playing out of this paradoxical nature of human moral evolution. After the September massacres in the prisons in 1792, Pierre Louis Manuel, in a speech at the Paris Jacobin Club, reflecting on the sight of the dead, perceiving (perhaps unconsciously) the human sacrificial nature of the deed, uttered a great cry of despair: a question that heralded the Modern world: "Is it better to dream of liberty than to possess it?"[2]

It was Erich Fromm, in this century, who made us acutely sensible to the idea that freedom itself is a frightening prospect. "Our aim will be to show that the structure of modern society affects a man in two ways simultaneously: he becomes more independent, self-reliant, and critical [i.e., morally autonomous], and he becomes more isolated, alone, and afraid. The understanding of the whole problem of freedom depends on the very ability to see both sides of the process and not to lose track of one side while following the other."[3] One of the greatest problematics for human happiness and human progress is the fact that people— full to the brim with anxiety—do not stay passive within that psychic fibrillation. They take measures to ease the pain; they defend against that anxiety. One method is to remove the torment by making Modernity and its anxiety-freedom, go away. Another mode is to assuage the agony by the destruction of others less fortunate or powerless.

Fascism was a grandiose attempt to turn the clock back on Modernity. The protofascist theorists during the first part of the twentieth century understood full well that the problem with Modernity was that it destroyed the kinship connections that had sustained people for millennia. For them the liberal, Modern world was one void of connection with other folk. "Liberalism is the expression of a society that is no longer a community," wrote Arthur Moeller van den Brock. "Every man who no longer feels a part of the community is somehow a liberal man."[4] He argued that liberalism had destroyed the true freedom of the Middle Ages, substituted a parliamentarianism that was a sham of liberty, and that the only solution was to go back, somehow, to that previous time.[5] In this reactionary project, the first thing that had to be exterminated was democratic individualism. The first thing to be resurrected was a potent recommitment to the power of *Das Volk*. No longer would Modern man be required to stand isolated and alone, locked in "the solitude of his own heart." [Tocqueville, see below.]

The second powerful mode of dealing with the terror of liberty is to unleash previously repressed aggressive impulses. All fascist regimes were committed to a culture of violence. All ideological terrorists end up annihilating many more people than is necessary to make an omelette.* It is worthwhile to repeat the statement of Engels given at the very beginning of this work: "We take the reign of Terror to mean the rule of people who inspire terror. On the contrary, it is the rule of the people who themselves are terror-stricken. Terror implies mostly useless cruelties by frightened people in order to reassure themselves."[6] In the third part of this book, when the attempt is made to understand ideological terror, I will perforce return to this question. Here, the comment may be in order that it may not be far from the mark to assert that what was frightening Robespierre and others was precisely the individualism that was an imperative of Modernity. After the Festival of the Supreme Being in June of 1794, Carol Blum writes that Robespierre declared, "the *mass* of the people was always pristine; to the extent that a person distinguished himself from the mass, either as an individual or as a part of a group, he was corrupt."[7] And the political radical Anarcharsis Cloots proclaimed it directly in the fall of 1793: "France, you will be happy when you are finally cured of individuals."[8] Thus, we see how Rousseau's General Will, antimodernist in its essence, became the new tyrant.

One further method of dealing with the anxiety of freedom is to undertake a massive repression of the anxiety, accomplished by turning inward. "Egoism," as opposed to "individualism" is the name Tocqueville gives to this maneuver. The great problematic, he argues, is that in democratic societies individualism ultimately merges with egoism. In America, the danger was palpable. "Egoism is a passionate and exaggerated love of self which leads a man to think of all things in terms of himself and to prefer himself to all. . . . Thus, not only does democracy make men forget their ancestors, but also clouds their view of their descendants and isolates them from their contemporaries. Each man is forever thrown back on himself alone, and there is danger that he may be shut up in the solitude of his own heart."[9] A deservably famous quotation. What has been missing in its interpretation, however, is the understanding that this egoism that perverts individualism is a defensive strategy. If morally autonomous individualism, and the freedom that is intimately associated with it, were not so frightening, then these various debased defenses would be unnecessary. It makes one understand how difficult of attainment the Modern project is.

In recent years, one of the most insightful analyses of paradoxical Modernity

---

*Though no longer heard today, at one time the expression "You can't make an omelette without breaking eggs" was used to excuse the "excesses" of revolutionary violence, most particularly of the Stalinist variety. From the psychological point of view, it is fascinating that the metaphor for annihilation refers to something one eats. The cannibalistic aspect of terrorism is not negligible.

has been that of Marshall Berman. He understands that modernist art has, as one of its subjects, the basic paradoxical nature of the Modern experience: "All forms of modernist art and thought have a dual character: they are at once expressions of and protests against the process of modernization."[10] Berman further comprehends that the one authentic way to deal with the increased anxiety of freedom is not to defend against it but to learn to live with it. That process is precisely one of the subjects of modernist art:

> To be modern . . . is to experience personal and social life as a maelstrom, to find one's world and oneself in perpetual disintegration and renewal, trouble and anguish, ambiguity and contradiction: to be part of a universe in which all that is solid melts into air. To be a modern*ist* is to make oneself somehow at home in the maelstrom, to make its rhythms one's own, to move within its currents in search of the forms of reality, of beauty, of freedom, of justice, that its fervid and perilous flow allows.[11]

The modernist project can only be completed if one abandons the need for certainty. One thing that all regressions from, and refusals of, Modernity promise (fascism, ideological terror, religious fundamentalism) is that we no longer have to live with moral ambiguity: the truth is known; we will follow it and impose it on all those who do not understand.

THREE TYPES OF INDIVIDUALS

In order to define accurately what we mean by Modern individualism, it is essential to differentiate it from other types of individualism that history offers us. Three types of "great individuals," three types of individualism, have been of importance for human history. Two of them premodern: Predators and Civilizing Pirates. The third, the morally autonomous individual, is the gift of the Modern world.

Predators are those individuals of extraordinary power and daring who have been able to conquer and dominate whole areas of the world, but who do so only in the interest of the profit it gives them. They create no nations, build no great temples, care not for any kind of cultural advance. Exploitation of the conquered is their primary—and, in many cases, their only—aim. When they die, or withdraw, or are pushed back, they leave only a cultural desert behind. Genghis Khan, Tamerlane, the Barbary Pirates, Cortes, those in this century who have subjected Amazonian native peoples to genocide. In many instances, some begin as Predators, evolve to some degree, into Civilizing Pirates. They end up caring something for political or intellectual culture. Certain peoples begin as Predators but evolve into civilizers as they settle down in the conquered lands: Vikings, Visigoths. The line is hard to draw, but the difference of psychological ideal-types seems accurate, and important to emphasize.

Civilizing Pirates made much of world history up to the Modern era. They were a complicated lot. They were perfectly willing to use all the piratical methods of the Predators in their passage to conquest: killing, torturing, pillage, rapine—no tactic seemed beneath them. Once in power, however, once masters of the conquered land, some strange imperative to build or improve culture became evident. In many cases, these Civilizing Pirates considered themselves culturally superior to the conquered "barbarians" in the first place. To impose their own culture was regarded, by them, itself as cultural progress. The list of such individuals is lengthy. When I was young, and first learning history, many of these Pirates were considered heroes: Alexander, Julius Caesar, William the Conqueror, the Emperor Napoleon, Cecil Rhodes. One great value of the intense critique of Western Civilization of the last thirty years is that it has forced us to redefine what it means to be a hero.

One great blessing for Western Europe—crucial to the ultimate invention of Modernity in that area of the world—was the fact that the peoples who conquered it after the Roman Empire fell, though beginning as Predators, became Civilizing Pirates with lightning speed: Franks, Anglo-Saxons, Normans. Christianity, and the conversion of these pagan peoples, played an essential role in this cultural transformation. Europe might never have become Europe without this most extraordinary fortunate circumstance.

The morally autonomous individual, and the *Weltanschauung* that directs that *large numbers* of people within society should become such, is the gift of the Modern world. Such individuals take a critical stance toward the values of society. They accept most of them, not because they are given and must be accepted, but because they find them acceptable; consent is given. Other values are subjected to challenge. Moral transformation is essential to this autonomous stance. A critical disposition in regard to values is the means to that end.

It may be correctly argued that there were some morally autonomous individuals in premodern societies. Plato, for instance, certainly fits that description. But Plato's whole political philosophy is based on the assumption that only an extremely small number of people are capable of that moral position. He, and his few philosopher kings, at the most. The modern *Weltanschauung*, first visible among Protestant makers of the Reformation, is that a significant number of people are capable of—and obliged to attain—that lofty state.

Starting in the twelfth century, western Europe began to produce a very small number of moral geniuses who were the harbingers of the culture yet to come centuries later. First there was Abelard (1079–1142), then Thomas Aquinas (1225?–1274?), and William of Ockham (1285?–1349?). There were a few others of lesser note, as well as followers of each of these. It was not until the Renaissance, as had been said many times, that the ideal of this kind of individual characterized a cultural movement. Burckhardt's oft-quoted phrase that it was a time of "discovery of the world and of man," if analyzed deeply, reveals that what was discovered within man—among other things—was the capacity for moral autonomy. The history of the Renaissance itself, however, presents the picture of an extraordinary number of Predators and Civilizing Pirates. Machiavelli's work, praised by many as the beginning of the Modern world, is not about how a large number of people can become morally autonomous individuals but a prescription for how a few individuals can become rational, sane, nonselfdestructive Civilizing Pirates. The ethos of the ancient world plus Machiavellian rationality, by themselves, could not make Modernity. Without the necessary addition of a reformed Christianity, the Renaissance *Weltanschauung* would have produced merely an updated version of the Roman Republic—and its catastrophes. The political history of Italy during the period is illustrative.

This simply put, and oft-repeated, historical narrative is being recounted to make one important theoretical point. Just as the emphasis on the observation that there was a thriving bourgeois culture *before* the maturity of capitalism leads us to wonder whether the bourgeois life *precedes* capitalist development—equally so, the similar observation that the construction of a morally autonomous individualism preceded bourgeois culture raises the significant theoretical question: Is morally autonomous individualism a necessary condition for the rise of a Modern bourgeois society? And, therefore, for Modernity itself? My theoretical inclination is to answer "yes" to both these questions. The bald theoretical proposition stands thusly: The primary "engine of Modernity" is the deep, powerful, psychological drive toward separation, individuation, autonomy, and a morally transforming individualism. This is the fundamental attribute that makes Modernity—and all its basic characteristics, such as capitalism, democratic citizenship, and secularism—possible.

We recall that Weber, after having established the intimate relationship between Protestantism and the rise of capitalism, spent a good part of his life studying non-Western civilizations, in part, to seek the answer as to why they never gave birth to a capitalist ethos. That great question remains unanswered. It is being suggested here that the key factor that must be considered is not the existence of cities, or the Roman law, or crucial aspects of philosophy, or the ambivalence about usury—the truly fundamental element that was either present or lacking was the thrust toward morally autonomous individualism. The many, complex twentieth-century compromises with Modernity that several societies have engineered are illustrative. Fascism, Soviet Communism, and religious fund-amentalist societies, for instance, have incorporated several aspects of Modernity into their systems of values and have sharply rejected others. The argument over whether fascism was antimodern or not has been forced to pay attention to the fact that fascism, though profoundly reactionary about many aspects of Moder-nity, had no problem with industrialization, urbanization, secularization, and rationalization. Precisely "Reactionary Modernism."[12] One thing, however, no fascist compromise allowed (and no Soviet or religious fundamentalist compro-mise either): Individualism, most especially morally autonomous individualism, was and is severely repressed. And equally, those aspects of Modernity that flow from it: liberalism and democratic citizenship.

And the great irony in Modernity—in many instances, a tragic irony—is that this fundamental energy drives us to a place where it's almost impossible to stand. All kinds of forms of defense, of compromise, of perversion respond to an almost unbearable isolation. So-called radical individualism—the most egoistic variety of this attribute—has been under theoretical and moral attack in recent years.[13] To its existence has been ascribed much of the evils in late twentieth-century society. One cannot understand its prevalence, however, without seeing that it represents a perversion of morally autonomous individualism. A perversion erected as a de-fense against the anomie, anxiety, alienation, and isolation of the Modern world.

Here again, French revolutionary times represent a remarkable prefiguration of the paradoxes of Modernity. The ambivalence about individualism was never resolved.

INDIVIDUALISM AND REVOLUTION

On the 14th of June, 1791, the National Assembly passed the Le Chapelier Law, named for the deputy who introduced it. Its intent was to destroy all corporations within French society. The stated reason for doing so was to strengthen the individual and the general interests. It was another attempt to suppress the power of "factions." The preamble to the law read:

> There are no longer corporations in the State; there is no longer anything but the particular interest of each individual, and the general interest. It is permitted to no one to inspire an intermediary interest in citizens, to separate them from the public interest by a spirit of corporation.[14]

That this decree was, in some way, going against a normal human inclination may be implied from the prototoalitarian language of its commandment: "It is permitted to no one . . ." When a society is intent on changing a fundamental value, and such attempt is inauthentic, premature, or impossible of accomplishment, resort may be had to repressive virtue: prototoalitarian discourse and imperative. Individualism was being decreed by the State.

Abolished, along with all the "feudal" corporations of the Old Regime, were trade guilds and any organization of workers or apprentices. Not many years ago, the general interpretation of the Le Chapelier law was that it was a manifestation of the bourgeois desire to preserve the rights of property against any challenge from the lower classes. William Sewell has helped us see that the true intent was to move society forward by abolishing all corporate-feudal ties. Into Modernity, we might say. "The Assembly's purpose in passing it was not to protect the rights of property against the claims of labor but to protect the Revolution against the counterrevolutionary 'spirit of corporation.'"[15]

These corporations worked exactly as a corporation does: a group of people join together in an institution that acts as if it were one person. They served an essential role in the Old Regime state. Some were responsible for paying special fees to the king or for assessing and collecting taxes paid by their members. Militia service, up to the seventeenth century, was organized corporately. Electoral units, including the election to the Estates General in 1789, were founded on the same principle. "In short," Sewell asserts, "corporations were seen—not only by their own members but by the governing authorities and by the society at large—as constituent units of the kingdom, as indissoluble parts of the constitution of the realm."[16]

On the necessity of abolishing corporations, opinion was almost unanimous along all political factions of revolutionary leaders: all the way from Marat, Robespierre, Saint-Just, and Danton to Sieyès, Mirabeau, Brissot, and Condorcet.[17] The impulse toward the destruction of the corporate social order and the autonomy of the individual was overwhelming. It was not the lure of capitalism that was driving the process but something deep within the psyche and the culture. Psycho-social identity was no longer to be defined by attachment to others of the same class or status but by what one was uniquely oneself. A utopian dream, destined for failure. And when the final draft of the first French constitution was issued in 1791, it specifically abolished "irrevocably the institutions that have injured liberty and the equality of rights." Specifically mentioned for infamy and annihilation—as we would expect—were "nobility, peerage, all hereditary distinctions, orders of chivalry, the sale and inheritance of public office, and religious vows." Along with these obviously "feudal" monarchical elements, corporations were specifically included as "contrary to natural rights."[18]

Individualism by decree was a very complex matter. The notion that one could eliminate "intermediary interests" and leave only "the particular interest of each individual, and the general interest" was a fantasy and, as has been discussed, destructive of the creation of the institutions necessary for democratic citizenship—political parties. And yet, something very significant was going on. If we think in terms of degree and not of absolutes, then it is clear that individualism was being magnified and that corporate interests were diminishing. Once a radical individualism was imagined as standing alone, with nothing between her/himself and the State—much as Protestantism insisted that nothing substantial should stand between an individual and God—once that process was accelerating, the real question was not if it would reach an exaggerated, absolute end, but: How far are we going with this?

Tocqueville, once again, saw the complexity in this great historical process, the continuity with the past, and enjoyed enough of Keats's "negative capability" to understand that there had never been a corporatism without some dimension of individualism, and that, by implication, there would never be an individualism completely divorced from corporate impulses and needs:

> That word "individualism," which we have coined for our own requirements, was unknown to our ancestors, for the good reason that in their days every individual necessarily belonged to a group and no one could regard himself as an isolated unit. Nevertheless, each of the thousands of small groups of which the French nation was then composed took thought for itself alone; in fact, there was, so to speak, a group individualism which prepared men's minds for the thorough-paced individualism with which nowadays we are familiar.[19]

PROTESTANTISM AND OPTIMISM

A crucial element within the attribute of individualism is an optimism about human nature. Human beings have no need of intermediaries between themselves and the State, or between themselves and God—intermediaries whose job it is to promote and assure correct action—because they will, if left to their own devices, if they are granted freedom, choose the moral way. This moral optimism underlies all liberal thought: the crucial difference between Locke and Hobbes is that Locke believes human beings can be trusted with freedom, and Hobbes does not. In the sixteenth century, with the Protestant Reformation, the northern Renaissance, and Christian humanism, this optimism became a fundamental element of the European *Weltanschauung*, though the culture as a whole was severely divided on the issue. For Rabelais, for instance, the perfect society exists in the Abbey of Thélème where everyone is enjoined simply to do as they wish. Life "was directed not by laws, statutes or rules, but by their own devices and free-will." Durkheim, in his work on educational thought, declares: "At the root of this entire theory is the fundamental postulate of the whole Rabelaisian philosophy, that nature is good, completely and without reservation or restriction."[20] A utopian exaggeration, certainly, and one that, undeniably, Rabelais would not offer as a dogmatic statement, but a view that contained, within its essence, an idea of human nature that was destined to change the world.

This optimism was essential for the creation of Modernity, and yet, like many other aspects of Modernity, it was vulnerable to perversion. That aspect of ideological terror that is dedicated to the project of creating a New Man in one generation is an exaggeration of liberal optimism to the point of perversity. By setting a task that cannot be done, under the banner of morality and moral progress, it assures disappointment, the acute sense of betrayal, and revenge to assuage the pain of treachery. Such may be the journey by which great moralists become executioners.

The roles of Protestantism, and any sincere Catholic reform of the Church, in the nonperverse advancement of morally autonomous individualism were crucial ones. In the work of Edgar Quinet, as analyzed by François Furet, a close connection is made between the historical failure of France to accept the Protestant Reformation, and the failure of the French Revolution to achieve democratic citizenship.[21] He contrasts the historical situation in England, United States, and Holland where "the political revolution crystallized pre-existing religious beliefs and institutions, with France at the end of the eighteenth century, which remained a Catholic monarchy. On the one side, there is a religious terrain antecedent to, and appropriate to, political transformation; on the other, a new spirit which had to be invented against religion."[22] The French, who had refused the Reformation in the sixteenth century and had severely repressed it in the seventeenth, "had no system of beliefs with which to conceive of modern liberty. They had, at their disposition, only a system of ideas, formed by "philosophy.' "[23]

Quinet felt strongly that philosophy alone—abstract ideas—could not accomplish the task. No modern liberty was possible without religion, but it must be a reformed religion. "The tragedy of the French Revolution was that it conceived the emancipation of modern man without offering him any religious foundation."[24] This Modern, reformed Protestant religion had for Quinet, in its essence, a new kind of individualism, what I have been calling here "morally autonomous individualism." For him, "Christianity had never ceased to be betrayed by the Roman Church, and periodically rediscovered by some heretics faithful to the word of Jesus: the Reformation had expressed exactly that spirit in establishing the face to face circumstances of the individual with God, and giving back to Christ alone all that the Church of the Middle Ages had improperly appropriated. The Christianity of Quinet . . . is founded precisely on that which Buchez detested so forcefully: modern individualism . . . individual conscience and its inalienable character."[25]

These powerful ruminations of Quinet can become the starting point for an even more extended discussion of the stages in the evolution of morally autonomous individualism, a discussion made necessary by the observation that Protestantism did not start the process, and by the questions: Is democratic liberty and citizenship possible without a foundation in religion? Is the secular sacred necessary and/or sufficient for the modern democratic project?

Looking back only as far as the high Middle Ages, I perceive three stages in this crucial evolution: (1) Reform Catholicism. (2) Protestantism. (3) A modern secular sacred, which holds citizenship as sacred but not religious.

Reform Catholicism begins way before the Renaissance; certain unique individuals are, unquestionably, the first representatives of the evolution toward autonomous individualism, with its great emphasis on moral autonomy: Abelard, Aquinas, Ockham. Unlike Wycliffe and Hus, they are not early manifestations of Protestantism. No radical break with the authority and power of the Church is contemplated or advocated. This impulse toward Christian Humanism comes to a grand fulfillment with Erasmus† and More (sixteenth century), but there is a way that, even in its highest development, it does not lead to Modern liberty. It was the failure to go beyond this humanism that provoked Quinet to argue that the French Revolution was doomed to fail without the existence of a large dose of Protestant ethos in the society. "He sees and he knows," writes Furet, "by the European example, that the problem *par excellence* of modern society is to unite the individualist principle of Protestant origin, with the Catholic idea of the community of people. It is by the character of a necessary synthesis between the spirit of these two Christian traditions that constitute Europe, that he poses the classic question of a rapport between the modern individual, absolute master of himself, and society which can be conceived as coming from that liberty."[27]

Protestantism, and its conception of autonomous individualism or, at the very least, a Catholicism informed and reformed by a Protestant ethos, we may conclude, is necessary for the creation of democratic citizenship. It has been observed by many that the first democratic societies—even if only limited democracies—were of Protestant origin and also Calvinist: England, Holland, America, Geneva.

However, for good or for evil, the drive for moral autonomy does not stop there. Modernity—or whatever it is that is driving toward it—does not stay content with early Calvinist Protestantism and Reform Catholicism. The fully Modern world rejects Quinet's argument that there must be a religious foundation of modern liberty. The drive toward autonomous individualism carries modern society *beyond* religion. And here the construction of the secular sacred becomes crucial. Those cultures that succeed in that project find themselves living in free societies, with all the contradictions and failures to which we are sensitive. Those societies that fail in this endeavor turn on individual autonomy with an unimaginable fury: they annihilate freedom along with multitudes of their own people. It is no wonder that many thoughtful, good people, keenly aware of the destructive anxiety of Modernity, lament the fact that human beings have attempted to construct a free society without a religious foundation. They feel that the secular sacred cannot fully replace the religious sacred. Many of the great paradoxes and contradictions—and the great pain—of Modernity arise from the endeavor to renounce the religiously sacred fundament of society.

Here, once again, French Revolutionary history, most especially in its terrorist phase, prefigured the worst experiences of the twentieth century. Furious at reli-

---

†Erasmus used the metaphor of awakening to describe the quantum leap in the importance of individual autonomy: "The world is coming to its senses as if waking out of a deep sleep."[26]

gion, it plunged headlong into a secular world. Its festivals of Liberty, Reason, and of the Supreme Being were artificial creations that spoke not to people's souls. The new sacred, which was supposed to replace the ancient religion, was ersatz and hollow. A fundamental form of social cohesion had been destroyed, and nothing equivalent was put in its place. Robespierre's terror lasted for only about a year. Bolshevik terror endured for more than half a century.

INDIVIDUALISM AND CAPITALISM

The repression of individualism in traditional (premodern) society resulted in the creation of a kind of Pandora's box. The lid could not be raised without all sorts of evils and corruptions flying forth. It was not possible, it seems, to release the impulses toward moral autonomy without, at the same time, allowing new Predators and Pirates to roam the landscape. Pirenne describes one of the first manifestations of wild capitalism in the sixteenth century:

> The spirit which is now manifested in the world of business, *is that same spirit of freedom which animates the intellectual world.* In a society in process of formation, the individual, enfranchised, gives the rein to his boldness. He despises tradition, gives himself up with unrestrained delight to his virtuosity. There are to be no more limits on speculation, no more fetters on commerce, no more meddling of authority in relations between employer and employed. The most skillful wins. Competition, up to this time held in check, runs riot. In a few years enormous fortunes are built up, others swallowed up in resounding bankruptcies. The Antwerp exchange is a pandemonium where bankers, deep-sea sailors, stock-jobbers, dealers in futures, millionaire merchants jostle each other—and sharpers and adventurers to whom all means of money-getting, even assassination, are acceptable.[28]

Remarkable how the description, even to assassination, resonates with contemporary Russian capitalism, where it is still a question—repression having been abolished—whether a civil society or a predators' and pirates' paradise will prevail.

So intricately entwined were the various aspects of individuation that it became impossible to differentiate them. In late eighteenth-century France, the Enlightenment of the *philosophes* and the challenge to all restrictions on commerce of the physiocrats were joined together in one portentous worldview. Ann-Robert-Jacques Turgot—friend, colleague, sometime patron of the great *philosophe* Condorcet, a contributor of several articles to Diderot's *Encyclopédie*—was appointed controller general of France by Louis XVI in 1774. He proceeded to attempt to institute a series of economic reforms that, anachronistically, would gladden the hearts of present-day libertarians. The grain trade was to be free of all restrictions; the *corvée* (compulsory labor service) was abolished; all trade corporations were to be suppressed. The attempt was unsuccessful; resistance from various quarters was enormous; Turgot was dismissed by the king in 1776.

Though this institutionalization of radical economic laissez-faire failed, the ideas behind it are of great importance in elaborating the growing power of individualism in the *ancien régime*. The purpose of the edict, Turgot announced, was to provide for " 'commerce and industry the entire liberty and the full competition which they ought to enjoy.' "[29] The prologue to the edict gave detailed reasons for the abolishment of all trade corporations: they had restricted the practice of the trade only to members; they had excluded products made outside the confines of the city; they had prevented technological progress by suppressing new techniques of working; entrepreneurs were not free to hire whichever workers they wanted. The results of all those practices had been higher prices for consumers, unemployment for capable artisans, and technological stagnation. "Not only were all rights, privileges, and statutes of corporations abolished, but persons exercising the same trade were henceforth forbidden to congregate or associate for any purpose."[30]

It is inaccurate to attribute this kind of action only to some form of rational-interest pursuit on the part of capitalists or a rising bourgeoisie determined to dominate society. The impulse toward separation and individuation had—and has—a powerful irrational component, resonating with partly ancient needs within the psyche, that has nothing to do with making a profit and the bottom line. The drive toward individualism has an autonomy, independent of rational real-world considerations. Capitalism has been so enormously successful in dominating almost the entire Modern world, in good part, because it is seen as an indispensable element of the culture of individualism. Every attempt, in the past, to modify the state of capitalism, whether through labor laws or the creation of the welfare state, has been met with the intense objection that such actions violate individual autonomy. And it is incorrect to analyze this as *only* a capitalist rationalization and defense. The myth of radical individualism—that a person within society could truly stand alone, needing no support from other citizens—such myth was not born of capitalism. It took its origins in the defensive mechanisms of the psyche determined to solve the conflicts over separation anxiety. True, capitalism seized upon this myth and used it potently for its own purposes. In order to institute capitalism with a human face, however, it has been, and remains, necessary to address the great anxiety—and the defenses against it—that autonomous individualism brings.

To sum up, if individuation is merely a passenger on the capitalist express, we would not be witness to the great contradictions and paradoxes of individualism: represented in their negative aspect by alienation, anxiety, ambiguity, and anomie. Nothing in the nature of capitalism, as such, brings these disorientations. The mania for individuation, however, has catastrophic possibilities. If we return to Engels's great question of what was terrifying the terrorists, it makes no sense to answer "capitalism." Capitalism hardly existed. Individuation, on the other hand, had begun to extend itself beyond the limits of the cultural and psychological support system. Fromm's fear of freedom was already a clear and present danger. Further insight into this paradox may be gained by looking at the relationship between the breakdown of the kinship system and human sacrifice.

HUMAN SACRIFICE AND THE BREAKDOWN OF THE KINSHIP SYSTEM

In order to comprehend the tensions and anxieties created by both early and late Modernity, it is essential to examine the fact that all social development, since early Modernity, was moving in the direction of a breakdown of the kinship system and a significant lessening of the importance of a face-to-face community. More and more, people began living in a world where those around them were not kin, were in many cases unknown, and could certainly not be counted upon to pick one up should one fail and fall. In great part, cities created that world. This frightening urban world of isolation and alienation is portrayed nowhere with greater power than in the work of Dostoevsky. One walks alone during the summer months, on the Nevsky Prospect: 5,000 people pass one by; none of them are known; one calls no one's name. There is a significant way in which it is appropriate to cry out: "Human beings were not meant to live like that!" And yet, Modernity—and its essence in individualism—has made that world *the* world.

The separation from the kin and the kinship system is a development that has been going on for 10,000 years of human history, starting when the first early states became a reality, as a transformation of kinship-system societies. There were times, however, when there was a particular acceleration of this moving-away-from-the-kin process. The twelfth century in Europe, for instance, when an unusually large amount of people moved from rural areas to the cities, was such a time. The postwar period in America, when millions of people moved out of ethnic city neighborhoods to mixed-ethnic suburbs, was another. At that time, church attendance skyrocketed to its highest level in American history. An obvious attempt on people's part to preserve certain connections with old ties while continuing to live in the stranger-anxiety suburban world, where "all kinds of people" provided one's social environment.

Early and late Modernity have been times when this leaving-the-kin phenomenon has reached an almost unacceptable intensity. "Social mobility" it's called when we want to perceive only its surface effects. Under the surface, this giving-up of the kinship ties of psychological security produces an extraordinary amount of distress. No understanding of anomie and alienation is possible without taking this phenomenon into account. Every reactionary response to Modernity—religious fundamentalism, fascism, as examples—cries out against the destruction of *Das Volk* and attempts to restore kinship cohesion in one form or another. And always, individualism is the enemy that has to be annihilated.

This process of individuation, and its concomitant anxieties, was already operating, in the view of Lawrence Stone, in early seventeenth-century England, and this early modern experience was, in his analysis, a significant cause of English revolutionary upheavals. It is profitable to cite him at length.

> At all levels, therefore, there was a sense of insecurity. In the upper ranks of society high social mobility generated jealousy, envy and despair among the failures, and status anxiety among the successful. In the lower ranks extraordinary geographic mobility and periodic catastrophes due to epidemic disease, combined *to shatter the traditional ties to family, kin, and neighbours, and to wrench men away from their familiar associations and surroundings.*
>
> At the very same time the ideological props of their universe were falling away. Competing religious ideologies shattered the unquestioning and habit-forming faith of the past. . . . the decline of craft guilds freed labour from both rules and companionship; the bonds of kinship were loosened under pressure from new religious and political associations, and from new ideals of love and freedom within the nuclear family. The upsetting of the hierarchy of status as a result of rapid social mobility was thus just one of many factors which generated unease, anxiety, anomie. Social mobility, personal insecurity, geographic migration, and ideological chaos were all part of the life experience of early seventeenth-century Englishmen. They were deeply unsettling.[31]

The role of the cities in breaking down kinship forms of social cohesion was crucial. Tom Paine gives us evidence from a contemporary about how the anonymity of the city was impoverishing people's lives:

> Cases are continually occurring in a metropolis different from those which occur in the country, and for which a different, or rather an additional mode of relief is necessary. In the country, even in large towns, people have a knowledge of each other, and distress never rises to that extreme height it sometimes does in a metropolis. There is no such thing in the country as persons, in the literal sense of the word, starved to death or dying with cold from want of a lodging. Yet such cases, and others equally miserable, happen in London.[32]

Why, then, would people seek out the city and leave the warm, comforting, stifling kinship system behind? The easy, readily available answer is the economic one: there was no work in the countryside. This may be a necessary, but hardly sufficient, explanation of cause. Work, or no work, without a culture of individualism—with its myth that a person could, or even should, stand alone—the great urban migration would have been impossible.

Human beings, however, are not content merely to live with heightened anxiety. Two fundamental modes of reacting to this social and psychic fibrillation are possible. One is to construct a new symbolic form that can replace the kinship system and do its work of comfort and security: democratic citizenship with its foundation in *nationalism.* That is the subject of our next chapter. The second mode is to lash out aggressively, committing acts of destruction, usually against those within society who are not quite full members of society (Jews, Gypsies, poor people); that is the way of human sacrifice. The understanding of it becomes crucial to the comprehension of ideological terror and guillotine cannibalism, and I will treat it in much greater detail in Part III of this work, after paying some mind to it in what follows.

In a previous work, *At the Dawn of Tyranny,*[33] I have looked at the very first societies—early states—that emerged out of kinship-system societies. Up until, maybe, 10,000 to 8,000 B.C. all societies on the face of the earth were kinship system–based, held together by kinship forms of social cohesion. The first human societies that were not so centered were early states, ruled by tyrannical kingships. Two crucial cultural phenomena all these early states shared: the kinship system had been transformed to a great extent and political forms of social cohesion (loyalty to the king, a national judicial system, a complex taxing machinery) put in its place. And second, human sacrifice was the characteristic form of ritualized aggression, in states such as ancient Buganda and Hawaii, carrying away 4,000 or 5,000 people yearly. Observing this confluence of forms, I postulated that human sacrifice was the defensive response to the intense anxiety generated by the serious decline of the kinship system. The argument was long, the data huge, and obviously cannot be repeated here. Not only does the analysis still seem accurate to me but, remarkably, capable of giving insight into certain irrational phenomena during revolutionary times. Patric Higonnet brings together extraordinary anxiety and the persecution (i.e., sacrifice) of nobles at the end of the eighteenth century in a striking passage:

> Bourgeois detested nobles not only because nobles were a marginal and traditional category, as were Jews, but because their own situation in the new class structure, which they did not fully understand, created within them an unprecedented anxiety that was real but which they could not fully articulate. The persecution of Jews in the 1930s and of nobles in the 1790s came at moments when the fears and hatreds that characterized social life at the time were apprehended but not understood. . . . In France, a more organic and traditional society would not have generated the bitterness which nobles elicited in 1789–99, while a more mechanistic one would have produced new categories (like the celebrated *classes dangereuses*) which would have channelled bourgeois fears and anxieties.[34] [That is, victims were necessary; lacking any reasonable alternative, the nobles were the logical selection.]

Of all this, much more later on. One final thought, however, about the role of capitalism in this greatest paradox of Modernity. Capitalism represents a perfect compromise formation of the extreme conflict and contradiction that has been elaborated here: intense individualism engenders intense anxiety that creates the necessity of the human-sacrifice defense, which then requires the existence of victims. For those in the elite, for those destined to be successful, capitalism gives full rein to all forms of individualism. At the same time, the system works in such a manner that we are never short of sacrificial victims. Late capitalism, within late Modernity, has been profoundly ambivalent about moving on to a victimless capitalism. One may describe the social policies of the Scandinavian countries in the last fifty years as precisely the project of creating such a victimless capitalism. Lyndon Johnson's "Great Society" was a vision of exactly that same resolution. The United States, however, suffered a failure of nerve and refused that moral transformation. The politics of the country, since 1980, has been ambivalently circling around and around the question of whether victims are essential to Modern society. The great question: "What shall we do about the poor?" holds dominion over half our political life. Neither shame nor guilt nor even self-interest is strong enough to force a moral resolution of the problem. The victims live among us. There must be some powerful irrational psychological need dictating this moral catastrophe. What, we may ask, is so terrifying the governors of society that so many of them are willing, despite the fact that such action will result in hundreds of thousands of unnecessary deaths, to annihilate the Welfare State—that marvelous re-creation of kinship morality—and are still, unlike Macbeth, able to sleep at night?

10

SECULAR SOCIETY, NATIONALISM, AND THE SECULAR SACRED

All human societies are held together by three essentially different, though inter-penetrating, social constructs. FORCE: The capacity of those who are empowered (either an individual, a group of individuals, or the community as a whole) to make recalcitrant members obey certain customs, rules, or laws; and, in the latter two categories, to make those rules and laws in an arbitrary, authoritarian manner; that is, without the consent of the governed. INTERESTS: The perception by an overwhelming majority of the society that it is to its own best interest to keep society stable and predictable; this assumes a basic trust in society's functioning. SHARED VALUES: These values not only legitimate social forms, but in almost all cases give particular meaning to life, render courage to face sickness and death, define who one's enemies are, prescribe what is worth dying for, and regulate sexuality and marriage.

Taken together, I designate these three constructs "the forms of social cohesion." Nothing is more important for society. The universal is that all societies require such forms. Historical narrative reveals that the particular nature of the forms of social cohesion changes profoundly over time. One productive way of thinking about the great movement from premodern to Modern society is to elaborate on the necessary changes in the forms of social cohesion essential for that transition.

All consensual forms of social cohesion (therefore, excluding force), those symbolic forms that significantly hold society together, are *sacred*. In kinship societies, the kinship forms of cohesion are sacred; in ancient Greece, the *polis* itself was sacred; in all monarchies, the emperor, the king, or duke is sacred; in democratic societies, the sovereignty of the people and the constitution of the land are sacred. Durkheim, in the seminal work *The Elementary Forms of Religious Life*,[1] makes two essential distinctions that are many times confused with each other. The sacred is differentiated from the profane, the religious from the secular. Anything that is religious obviously cannot be profane and must be sacred. But everything that is sacred is not necessarily religious. There is a *religious sacred* and a *secular sacred*. In Durkheim's book on *Moral Education*,[2] this distinction between the religious sacred and the secular sacred is crucial for the prescription for a moral, modern education. Durkheim argues that a modern educational system must eliminate the religious dimension in pedagogy, but in doing so, it must keep the sacred quality. If we are to continue to teach morality—which, he argues, is an imperative—the sacred quality of a moral worldview must be maintained. Such moral instruction, then, becomes a manifestation of the secular sacred. It will be argued here that the secular sacred becomes an important form of social cohesion only in Modernity and is absolutely necessary for construction of that stage of society.

Borrowing from Durkheim, once again, in his designation of elementary forms, it may be asserted that kinship represents the elementary form of the shared-values conditions of social cohesion. All developed forms of voluntary social cohesion (i.e., excluding force) are transformed forms of kinship, whether they be sacred monarchy, citizenship in the *polis,* or modern democratic sovereignty. The developed forms are both kinship and nonkinship simultaneously. Social evolution is directly conditioned by the capacity to create new developed forms of kinship to replace those no longer viable. Crises may occur within society when old forms of social cohesion are destroyed and newly adequate forms are not yet sufficiently developed. The former Soviet Union today presents such a spectacle, and the outcome is still seriously in doubt. France from 1789 to the mid 1870s can be understood, in good part, as suffering from that particular form of agitated and unresolved transition. Raymond Aron has argued precisely that: "The fact is . . . that the *Ancien Régime* collapsed at one blow, almost without resistance, and that it took France nearly a century to find another régime acceptable to the majority of the nation."[3] It was an extended crisis of legitimate forms of social cohesion.

In the traditional, premodern, and early Modern world all societies exhibited two essential forms of such cohesiveness: authoritarian monarchy and authoritarian religion. A successful passage to a truly modern society, therefore, inevitably involved the overthrow and abolition of these two forms of absolutism. Abolition, however, was not sufficient. Some new forms of social cohesion had to be created, to be put in place of the old forms. New forms that would do what the preceding forms had done: hold society together, and yet be transformative enough to provide for liberty, freedom, democratic citizenship, religious tolerance: a stable Modern society. To overthrow, and not replace, was to invite chaos. The political chaos in many parts of the world that fills the front pages of our newspapers today in many, if not most, instances results from the destruction of traditional, kinship or authoritarian, forms of social cohesion and the failure to erect new, viable Modern forms in their place. And once again, the failures of the French Revolutions can be described in exactly that manner.

The successful passage to Modernity, then, involves two crucial steps: the replacement of authoritarian religion—whether Roman Catholicism, Greek Orthodoxy, or Islam—by a secular society, in which the society as a whole becomes sacred: the sacredness of religion is not lost but transformed into the community of citizens. And second, the sacredness and omnipotence of the monarch is replaced by the sovereignty of the people and the constitution of the Nation.

The great symbolic form, essential to any modern society, powerfully representative of the secular sacred is nationalism. In the Nation old forms of kinship cohesion are reborn and reaffirmed. The Nation is sacred. Loyalty to it is an expression of sacred activity. Disloyalty to the Nation is the highest crime, punishable by death. Nationalism tells us who are our enemies, who our friends, and for whom we are obliged, if necessary, to die: namely, the Nation. One cannot exaggerate the enormous importance of nationalism in the creation of Modern society. Such a perception also helps explain how tremendous is the difficulty in trying to go beyond nationalism to some universal species concern, how powerfully disruptive to the peace of society is it when the omnipotence and omniscience of the Nation are attacked, as in the successful challenge to the legitimacy of the war in Vietnam.

One way of understanding the history of French Revolutionary times is to trace the complex, ambiguous, paradoxical journey from authoritarian religion to a secular sacred society, from authoritarian kinship to the sacredness of the people—and to observe how nationalism was called upon in the attempt to resolve conflicts and establish the new society. This chapter intends, in brief, to discuss that history.

THE VIOLENT OVERTHROW OF AUTHORITARIAN RELIGION

What is missing in Quinet's analysis of the failure of the Revolution, and the relationship of this failure to the previous miscarriage of a religious revolution (Protestantism), is the perception that in the intense, and sometimes violent, antireligious and anticlerical activity of the Revolutions, France was finally making its own version of the Protestant Reformation: doing what Germany, Switzerland, Holland, and England had done two centuries before. This seemingly irrational intensity and violence exhibited in regard to the Roman church during the years 1789 to 1799 can be better understood if it is recalled that in no other country was the Protestant Revolution made without numerous examples of excesses of aggression: torturings and burnings at the stake, violent destruction of works of art, forcible closings of monasteries and convents, expulsion of thousands of people from their native country. Not to mention the wars of religion in France, the English Civil War, and the most horrible of all wars: the thirty years of annihilation of central Europe. In case one is inclined to comment, as one must be, that the French Revolutionaries should have been more reasonable and rational in their overthrow of the authoritarian Roman church, the history of the Protestant Reformation could make one more diffident in one's judgment. No one overthrows a cultural form that has held society together for almost 1,500 years in a gentle, rational manner.

There is no need here to outline in great detail the Reformation-like overthrow of the established Catholic religion, which process did not conclude—since we are now in the eighteenth, and not the sixteenth, century—in Protestantism but in a society in great part secular, and one on its way to being a fully secular society. The data for such narrative are easily available, and the history itself has been expertly recounted by, among others, John McManners, Timothy Tackett, Michael Kennedy, and most recently Susan Desan.[4] One phase only is worth elaborating here in some detail: the post-Thermidor history of the antireligious attack. Many informed, general readers, especially those whose interest in "the Revolution" ends with the overthrow of Robespierre, are unaware of the fact that the destruction of Catholic power and hierarchy continued, unabated, under the Directory and came to a halt only with Napoleon. It was not merely radical Jacobins who were committed to the destruction of hierarchical religion: almost the whole of the bourgeoisie was committed to that position.

I. *The Growing Pre-Revolution Critique and Attack.* From Voltaire to lesser lights, the critique of intellectual and moral absurdities of the established religion is part of what is generally designated "the Enlightenment." The adverse judgment centered around the notion that religion, as practiced, was in opposition to reason and freedom. "The class for which he preserved the greatest bile," Baker writes of Condorcet, "was, of course, the priesthood: the primal intellectual class, whose original sin it had been to betray human reason for corporate advantage."[5] And even the more conservative Tocqueville remarked, years after the Revolution, that: "In France I had seen the spirits of religion and of freedom almost always marching in opposition directions. In America I found them intimately linked together in a joint reign over the same land."[6]

There was, however, another source besides Enlightenment thought for this radical antireligious sentiment, one that extended way back to the pre-Reformation, late-medieval exasperation with the corruption of the Church. It is a question whether this profound disenchantment and sense of betrayal might have been as important, even more important, as an explanation of the almost uncontrollable intensity of the attack on the established religion. Pre- and post-Reformation times were full of the retelling of stories, some comical, some despairing, depicting the clergy and those in monasteries and nunneries as whoremongers, sybarites, and money-grubbers. In France, a few months after the fall of the Bastille, a previously forbidden drama, Chénier's *Charles IX*, was performed, wherein, "everyone could go to see a cardinal blessing the daggers for the massacre of St. Bartholomew. By mid-July 1790 the anti-clerical theatre had graduated from the sinister to the lewd—the *Souper des Nonnes* [the *Supper of the Nuns*], *Les Fourberies Monacles* [*The Deceitful Monks*] and *La Journée du Vatican*, complete with the Pope dancing a fandango with the Duchess of Polignac."[7] This subjection of the clerics to comic, pornographic attack is similar to the existence of the vast number of underground depictions of the king, and most especially the queen, that pervaded prerevolutionary culture. The sacredness of both the clergy and the monarchy was being undermined; their moral legitimacy was under a fatal attack.

Also similar to social developments in late-medieval times was the tendency of the rising, newly enriched bourgeoisie to assert its exceptional status by declaring itself superior to the beliefs in "superstition" of the lower classes. "This 'monsieur' who left his village long ago to seek his fortune and who, after making it . . . has come back to show himself in his new plumage . . . has read . . . and heard what the right people think . . . the intelligent people. So now he comes to enlighten his fellow villagers: 'What, you do this! You believe that! What simpletons you are!' "[8] And the pastor of Gap noted: "Those who have made money have a marked aversion for the ministers of the Church."[9] So many different currents were driving the French elite, but not necessarily the mass of French men and women, toward the overthrow of religion.

2. *The Nationalization of Church Property.* One of the first significant acts of the National Assembly was the nationalization on November 2, 1789, and subsequent sale, of church lands. The Assembly, it must be remembered, still contained most of the noble and clerical deputies elected to the Estates General, even though over thirty of them resigned after the October days. This did not prevent this amazing anticlerical move from becoming a reality.

Looked at only from the point of view of French history, such acts as the appropriation of church property and the subsequent persecution of the clergy who refused to go along with revolutionary radical anticlericism seem startling and almost incomprehensible. From the perspective of the whole modernizing history of Europe, however—with clear emphasis on the Protestant Reformation—one may regard it simply as France catching up, two hundred years later, to advances made in the rest of Northern Europe. In the sixteenth century, appropriation of Church property had been accomplished in Denmark, Sweden, Bohemia, much of Germany, and, most familiar to us, in the England of Henry VIII. Such nationalization had nothing whatever to do with the rise of democracy and the challenge to authoritarian monarchy: in almost all cases, the monarchs were the instruments of such confiscations. The suggestion is being made here that French radical anticlericalism may have been as much a part of Reformation history as of revolutionary history.

And the motives for such actions, in both the sixteenth and the eighteenth centuries, were profoundly mixed. As with Henry VIII, for example, it is almost impossible to disentangle the objective of severely needed ready cash from a deep anticlericalism that could turn the revered Church into an object of plunder. Both circumstances were of great importance.

3. *The Civil Constitution of the Clergy.* Decreed on July 12, 1790, this awesome measure attempted to establish a liberal, state-supported Catholic church for all of France: salaries for curés and bishops, who were now to be elected by their parishioners, were to be paid by the government: the number of dioceses was to

conform to the new political departments in the country. Such a compromise might have worked if it were not challenged by those on the right and the left. The reluctance to go along—and active sabotage of the arrangement—on the part of the clerics and their congregants was met, at the national and local level, by an even more radical hounding of the clerks that led very quickly to an almost mortal struggle between the traditionalists and the radical modernizers.

4. *The Oath to the Civil Constitution, November, 1790.* The oath, now required of all clerics, in itself was harmless enough: it pledged loyalty to the nation, the law, the king, and the future constitution to be determined by the National Assembly and accepted by the king. Its immediate effect, however, was to add indignity to defeat. It created enormous resistance and enormous counterattack against that resistance. Many observers consider it and the declaration of war on Europe as the two most formidable mistakes of the revolutionary government. Many citizens who were ready to live with nationalization and the Civil Constitution were converted into enemies of the Revolution by this debasing insistence. "From the month of January 1791," Kennedy writes, "a state of quasi-religious warfare existed in the French provinces. In Provence, Languedoc, and Alsace violent confrontations took place between partisans of the new Church and the old. For the first time, sizable elements of the lower clergy turned against the Revolution."[10] And McManners emphasizes the consequences of such overzealousness: "If there was a point at which the Revolution 'went wrong,' it was when the Constituent Assembly imposed the oath. . . . This marked the end of national unity, and the beginning of civil war. *For the first time popular forces were made available to the opponents of the Revolution.*"[11]

As many times happens in such circumstances, the conflict, the refusal of the defeated to yield, only made the fanatical "antifanaticism" forces more violent. After the overthrow of the king in August 1792, the soon-to-expire Legislative Assembly passed a decree that compelled all non-oath-taking clerics, except the sick and those over sixty, to leave France within a fortnight or face deportation to Guiana.[12]

Once the Jacobin dictatorship had been instituted, it was now open warfare against religion on the part of many Jacobins, despite the fact that Robespierre himself was opposed to any repression or violent destruction of religious practice. In June 1794, Vernery, a representative of the Convention to the provinces, wrote from the Allier: "Before my arrival in this department Roman Catholic worship was carried on openly in nearly every commune. Apostles of Truth and Reason were sent out: they talked to the people with prudence and wisdom, and before I left not a single church remained open. Fanaticism expired without a groan."[13] We may doubt whether this triumph of Reason was accomplished with the consent of the governed.

The psychological violence, the repression, the almost total disregard of some citizens' wishes—all this is deeply reminiscent of the violent history of the Reformation. But no Protestant religion was available to put in place of Catholicism. Only a civil religion of Truth, Reason, Liberty, and the Supreme Being was being offered as an alternative. That secular sacred, however, was too philosophical, too abstract, too intellectual: it did not resonate in people's souls. It provided no solution and had no future.

5. *Civil War in the Vendée.* The greatest internal manifestation of antirevolutionary sentiment and activity occurred in the area of the Vendée, coming to a climax with the civil war in 1793. Charles Tilly has demonstrated, beyond argument, that the antireligious policies of the central revolutionary government was the prime cause of this counterrevolutionary movement. As early as 1791, he asserts, "it was correct to speak of an 'ecclesiastical party' opposed to the supporters of the Revolution."[14] "In short, the religious issue immediately became political and split the entire population."[15] Once the Oath had been decreed, the clergy in the entire country became divided between those who took the oath and the "refractories" who refused. The percentage of those in each category in any particular district was a clear indication of pro- and antirevolutionary sentiment: "On the whole, the more common the rejections of the Oath, the more intensive the counterrevolutionary activity."[16] In conclusion, Tilly asserts that the extreme hostility to organized religion on the part of the national government had converted those in the Vendée from supporters to enemies of the Revolution: "The 'attitude of the people of southern Anjou toward the Revolution' changed deeply from the time of the Estates General to the time of the war of the Vendée."[17]

Once that war had begun, persecution of nonjuring priests accelerated. The decree of April 1793 proclaimed that all clerics who had not yet taken the oath should immediately be transported to Guiana. After the coup against the Girondins, the Montagnard Convention passed the law of October 1793: priests holding communication with the enemies of the *patrie* were to be put to death within twenty-four hours of being found guilty; priests who returned to France could be executed if two witnesses "agreed that they were under sentence of transportation." Even those who had taken the Oath could be transported after having been denounced by six citizens, brought to trial, and found guilty.[18]

There was a tremendous hatred and rage against the established church on the part of a significant number of citizens in this new republic founded on liberty and fraternity. Of enormous significance was the fact that this description does not fit only radical Jacobin terrorists. The clergy remained a prime scapegoat of the Revolution as long as it lasted. Thermidor and the fall of Robespierre did not lessen the severity of antireligious violence.

6. *The Continued Persecution of the Clerks under the Directory.* In my own experience, it came as a surprise, when studying revolutionary history, that Thermidor made no difference in the oppression of the Church. Tocqueville, however, as in so much else, perceived the circumstance directly, although he was unable to answer the question of why this persecution was so intense.

> The causes of the violent hatred against priesthood and religion should be sought with much care. It is the most vivid and also the most persistent of the revolutionary passions. The suppression of the priests came last but their persecution lasted beyond that of all the others: so far as the priests are concerned, the Terror continues under the Directory. The hatred against them is more violent and more persistent even than the hatred against the émigrés, against the very Frenchmen who were fighting France with arms.[19]

On February 3, 1797, after Napoleon had achieved certain remarkable successes in Italy, the Directory sent a letter to Bonaparte stating that " 'the Roman' religion would always be the 'irreconcilable enemy of the Republic' and that it was therefore desirable 'to destroy the center of the Roman Church,' in other words 'the papal government.' "[20] Napoleon ignored the letter and made his own peace arrangements. He clearly did not suffer from any antireligious fanaticism and proved most flexible on that issue. Free from any ideological imperatives, he was always at liberty to pursue power unencumbered by this particular fanaticism.

Seven months later, the Directory instituted the coup of Fructidor against an aristocratic threat to its government. Intense persecution of the clergy followed. Priests, even those who had sworn the original oath, in order to conduct services had to swear an even more intense one of "hatred of royalty." The Directory started to deport clerics simply by its own administrative order. This anti-Catholic hatred had immediate terroristic consequences in the recently conquered departments of Belgium. Almost 1,000 priests were arrested. These arrests, combined with those in France, resulted in almost 250 clerics transported to Cayenne, where the majority died of fever. In France itself, 2,000 priests were imprisoned. There were very few actual executions, but the message was clear: the priesthood was the enemy of the state and the republic.[21]

In this second intense dechristianization campaign of 1797–1799, the Directory at least had the wisdom of trying to put the new revolutionary religion in the place of Catholicism. The revolutionary calendar, which repressed Sunday observance by celebrating a secular sabbath every ten days, was imposed with greater intensity. Revolutionary festivals were emphasized more and more. Churches were forcibly closed.[22] In some areas, this second round of persecution hit even harder than the Jacobin repression. "This . . . campaign," Susan Desan writes, "struck the clergy of the Yonne harder than the first: many priests were deported or imprisoned. Eighty-four from the Yonne were condemned to deportation during the years VI and VII (1797–1799), and half of those were in fact deported."[23]

When we find the conservative, even reactionary, members of the Directory, many of whom were perfectly ready to jump on the Bonaparte bandwagon, occupying the same "antifanaticism" ideological position as the Jacobins under the Terror, we have come to a very complex theoretical place. The causes of that seeming contradiction should be sought, as Tocqueville mentions, with much care. I am not able even to offer some plausible possibilities. Two things, however, suggest themselves. First, the answers will not come by considering the narrow history of the Revolution itself. The much broader narrative of the journey from traditional to Modern society must be considered. As has been suggested, Modernity is only possible by escaping from, and transforming, authoritarian religion. The whole religious history of Europe, from the Reformation forward, including this intense antireligious experience in France, is wracked with violence, killing, and the unnecessary annihilation of human beings. Maybe there was no other way that this particular task could be accomplished. And second, it may again be underscored that the treacherous road to Modernity is strewn with human sacrifice. For a short while, the priests of France fulfilled that seemingly inevitable necessity.

MODERN SECULAR SOCIETY

The cultural transformation that distinguishes Modernity from early Modern society has been, on the political level, the secularization of morality and the forms of social cohesion. "This is the cultural shift," Charles Taylor writes, "which we have to understand. Secularization doesn't just arise because people get a lot more educated, and science progresses. This has some effect, but it isn't decisive. What matters is that masses of people can sense moral sources of a quite different kind, ones that don't necessarily suppose a God."[24] Two stages in this historical process may be distinguished. First, people are ready to grant others the right to belong to the primary community even if they have a different conception of God (Protestants and Catholics). Second, God drops out of the definition of loyalty to the Nation altogether.

The number of corpses on the battlefields of Europe in the sixteenth and seventeenth centuries, and the number of executions and banishments, testify to how enormously difficult was the achievement of the position that we take for granted today, except when it is a question of prayer in the schools, the teaching of evolution, or abortion. That secularization of religious belief also had profound effects on the growth of democracy. Marx commented that: "The modern state secularized the religious spirit by transposing the Christian idea of equality to the political level."[25]

Certain elite elements in eighteenth-century France were pushing very hard toward exactly this secularization of moral, and therefore social, forms of cohesion. Necker, a moderate liberal, was opposed to this development: "For some time, now, we have been constantly hearing about the need for composing a catechism of morality, in which no use would be made of religious principles— antiquated incentives which it is time to set aside."[26] Others, however, understood its necessity for the evolution of society. "A catechism of morality is today the first requirement of the nation. . . . The wise await it, the religious fanatics fear it, the government made it necessary" (Rivarol). "It is said, and that is the fashionable sentiment nowadays, that, independently of all religion, there is a certain love of justice which nature inspires in us, and which suffices at least to form an upright character" (Caraccioli).[27]

The Nation remained ambivalent, conflicted, and severely divided. Even though impulses toward reform of the Church and religious tolerance were very powerful at the eve of the Revolution, a true resolution of the conflicts over secularization took a hundred years in France. The Brienne-Lamoignon ministry, in 1787, had already granted a restricted civil status to Protestants.[28] The *cahiers* of both the nobility and the Third Estate were almost unanimous in urging freedom of religious beliefs.[29] That attitude was institutionalized by the Declaration of Rights. Article 10: "No one may be disturbed for his opinions, even in religion, provided that their manifestation does not trouble public order as established by law."[30]

This great movement of religious toleration was part of the transition from a Puritan to a Liberal mentality. As important for the evolution of the modern world as was the Protestant Reformation and Puritanism, religious tolerance was not one of its attributes. It was necessary to go beyond primitive Protestantism to get to Article 10, or the stated separation of Church and State in America. It is interesting that the great Incorruptible, Puritan that he was, could not yet take those necessary steps. He was ready to tolerate any religion but not the absence of religion. Atheism was anathema to him. In a speech of November 1793, Robespierre bewailed the fact that anticlericalism had, in some men, turned into atheism. A private person may think what he likes, but the polity demands belief: "For a public man or the legislator to adopt such a system of thought would be utter insanity. The National Convention detests atheism. . . . it is a representative body charged with the duty of securing respect for the character as well as the rights of the French people. It was not without significance that it published the Declaration of Rights in the presence of the Supreme Being. It will be said, perhaps, that I am a narrow-minded man, a prejudiced person, a fanatic. . . . The French people pins its faith, not on its priests, nor on any superstition, or any ceremony, but on worship as such—that is to say, upon the conception of an incomprehensible Power, which is at once a source of confidence to the virtuous and of terror to the criminal."[31] We note that the Convention has a fundamental responsibility to form the character of the French people. We observe the capacity to transform the sacred to the very border of the secular, but not the ability to pass over that border. Society was unimaginable for Robespierre without the aid of this "incomprehensible Power." As late as the beginning of the twentieth century, the issue was still not completely resolved, and Durkheim felt the necessity of arguing passionately for the creation of a secular sacred morality, that could make people morally responsible without the necessary assistance of that unknowable Power.[32]

The significant fact was that, although there were tremendous potential swings from left to right in the revolutionary years 1789–1799, there was a steady, consistent development toward a secular society, which was halted, and only partly reversed, by Napoleon and the Concordat with the Church in 1801. After the king was overthrown in 1792, the attack on clerical influence was extended by the establishment of secular control over marriage, divorce, and remarriage. The State, and not the church, was now responsible for recording births and deaths, and civil marriage was now an option for everyone.[33] The first constitution after Thermidor, that of the Year III, provided that: "No one can be prevented from exercising, comformably to the laws, the religion of his choice. No one can be forced to contribute to the expenses of a religion. The Republic pays no stipends."[34] The separation of church and State was almost complete. Even under the Napoleonic reaction when, for instance, regressive measures in regard to divorce were instituted and the church more or less re-established under the strict control of the State, freedom of religious belief and practice remained in force. We may, ironically, parody Tocqueville's statement about democracy and inquire why it was that God was impelling 300 million people for 200 years toward a secular society? Clearly, it was not God, but it was something. A full reflection on what that "something" might be has to await Part IV of this work and the full discussion of social evolution.

FROM THE OMNIPOTENT KING TO
THE OMNIPOTENT NATION

The attribute of omnipotence to kingship was accomplished, in good part, through the symbol of divinity: the king was not God (that would be blasphemy, and we are not talking about ancient Egypt), but the king was *a* god. He participated in divinity; God spoke through him; his presence and his power were, somehow, divine; to challenge him was unlike any confrontation with a mere mortal man. Such a symbolic form of semi-divine kingship must have served deep, powerful psychological needs. Having overcome and left behind such urgencies, it is difficult for us to imagine how necessary kingship was in people's lives—and, therefore, how profoundly difficult it was to give it up, most especially when that transformation required overthrowing. In the seventeenth century, Richelieu, who was creating this shadow of divinity in the interests, among other things, of establishing the absolute state, unashamedly praised his master, Louis XIII: " 'It is because of God's will and on his authority that kings reign. . . . Kings are the most glorious instruments of divine providence in the government of the world. The ancients who were not flatterers called you *corporeal and living* gods, and God himself has taught men the same language and desires that you be called Gods.' "[35] In the eighteenth century, when that divine status was being challenged, Louis XV, in 1766, reaffirmed the ancient religion:

It is in my person alone that sovereign power resides. . . . It is from me alone that my courts derive their authority; and the plenitude of this authority, which they exercise only in my name, remains always in me. . . . It is to me alone that legislative power belongs, without any dependence and without any division. . . . The whole public order emanates from me, and the rights and interests of the nation . . . are necessarily joined with mine and rest only in my hands.[36]

Faced with such sacred power, one can begin to understand why, in order to establish the sovereignty of the people, it was necessary to execute the king.

Lest we respond to these assertions as merely cynical affirmations that had only a calculating political intent, something that no sophisticated person could believe in, it may be helpful to recall our last overthrow of a "king"—the Watergate impeachment process. It was extraordinary to observe, at the time, how many politically intelligent people could not believe, up until almost the last moment, "that the President could do such a thing." And those representatives whose job it was to render the final decision almost trembled, acting as if they were walking on sacred, terrifying ground. If the office of the president, in the twentieth century, can still carry that kind of charismatic charge, we should not underestimate the divine power of kings in the eighteenth.

Michael Walzer cites an argument that asserted that the divine right of kings, "kept alive the organic concept of the state. . . . God was actually incarnate as he never would be again once sovereignty had been vested in impersonal and abstract powers."[37] If our only reaction to this kind of statement is: "And a good thing, too," we lose the capacity to understand how difficult, how problematic it was for people at the end of the eighteenth century to give up that organic conception, that divine protection. If there are no kings, will rule be possible? Will anarchy inevitably result? Even in America, that most fortunate land, at the end of the eighteenth century these were portentous, disquieting questions. Gordon Wood describes those fears:

Would people respect rulers who were not God or their fathers or their masters, who had no visible sacredness or awesomeness, who had no inherent patriarchal authority? . . . Were people to yield to rulers "not on account of their persons considered exclusively on the authority they are clothed with, but [only on account] of those laws which in the exercise of this authority are made by them conformably to the laws of nature and equity?" . . . Were kings really "the servants and not the proprietors of the people," as Jefferson asserted in 1774? . . . did this mean that rulers were not to be great men, "perhaps not even gentlemen?" Were rulers really "of the same species . . . and by nature equal with those they ruled?"[38]

If Americans, who had never even had a true king, could exhibit such anxiety, we may imagine what was going on in the psyches of French men and women at the time.

Toward such an omnipotent ruler, one consents to be ruled. The key word in Wood's description is "patriarchal." "The King's subjects felt towards him," writes Tocqueville, "both the natural love of children for their father and the awe properly due to God alone. Their compliance with his orders, even the most arbitrary, was a matter far less of compulsion than of affection, so that even when the royal yoke pressed on them most heavily, they felt they still could call their souls their own. To their thinking, constraint was the most evil factor of obedience; to ours, it is the least."[39] To create a Modern society, one has to want to grow up and become an adult, whose sense of power and agency are attributes of the self and not pathetic borrowed reflections of the potency of some father-king. "There was a time under the old monarchy when the French experienced a sort of joy in surrendering themselves irrevocably to the arbitrary will of their monarch and said with pride: 'We live under the most powerful king in the world.'"[40] Like a latency-stage child who proudly announces: "My father can . . ."

The fact that people assent to the king's omnipotence—and, therefore, his capacity to command—creates a hole in certain theoretical distinctions that have currency today. For many, democracy is described as that society where political power is derived from the consent of the governed: citizens, not subjects. But, if the subjects of a divine king also consent to his omnipotence and governance, that distinction no longer holds in the same manner. Aristotle distinguished between a legitimate and a perverse form of rule by the one: monarchy the legitimate form; tyranny the perversion. Rule by a tyrant is not legitimate, but kingship is. Legitimacy is conveyed through the consent of the governed: they assent to the monarch's political power. A king is not a tyrant who imposes his will on the polity regardless of the wishes of its members. A king becomes a tyrant when he goes beyond the legitimate boundaries of monarchy, when he totally disregards the desires of his subjects.

Something is missing, therefore, in the simple definition of democracy in terms of consent of the governed. I have no facile answer to the question of what that definition should be. Possibly, we may again resort to Aristotle, when he includes democracy in his category of rule by the many, even though he regarded democracy as the perverse form of this kind of polity. Perhaps democracy is more accurately defined as the situation where citizens consent to be ruled by other citizens. This imposes on us, however, the urgent necessity to define "citizen." Not an easy task, and one that I cannot undertake. This maneuver, nonetheless, does move us beyond the simple notion of consent.

So powerful was the belief in the monarch's omnipotence, in his passion for justice, in his concern and love for his people that we have many remarkable instances where peasants rioting against the local established authority believed that they were doing so at the behest and command of the king himself. In Naples, in Sicily, and above all, in Russia, at various historical times, the belief was abroad that the sovereign had commanded the rioting. In Russia in 1908 the rumor in the countryside was that a general from Petersburg had come from the Tsar with a manifesto written "in letters of gold" commanding the peasants to seize the corn they needed to survive.[41] And on an earlier occasion, while making the sign of the cross, rioting peasants called out to the troops sent to repress the violence: "Don't fire on us. . . . you are shooting Alexander Nikoleye-vitch, you are shedding the blood of the Tsar."[42]

Intense anxiety and near panic ensue, therefore, when this protecting, comforting omnipotence is removed. Death of the monarch—interregnum—is one thing. Overthrow of a king doubles the anxiety: not only is security gone, but the oedipal act of revolutionary dethronement brings unconscious fears of retribution from the deposed father/king. One reason that the king must die that la patrie must live is that people must prove to themselves that they can act, even when impelled not to do so by an anxiety attack. It proves that they are not afraid to stand alone, to be their own source of omnipotent protection. Whether this revolutionary act of beheading succeeds or not, depends upon what other sources of psychic and political maturity are abroad in the culture. Despite all the background of eighteenth-century Enlightenment and liberalism, it still took France several generations before it could live without some kind of monarch, even if only the "farce"[43] of Louis Napoleon.

Two intense circumstances of paranoid panic during revolutionary times were intimately related to the overthrow, or portended overthrow, of the king. Killing, most especially in its human sacrifice form, is one unfortunate mode of defense that humans resort to when faced with this kind of intense anxiety. The September Massacres in the prisons in Paris occurred within a month of the overthrow of the king. The situation was overdetermined: not only was the king's protection no longer there, but France was faced by an invasion by foreign forces that threatened to overthrow the revolution. Human sacrifice was the time-honored ritual in such situations of intense anxiety,[44] and the killings in the prison resonated powerfully with that sacrificial mode.

Riots in the countryside are even more illuminating. Georges Lefebvre is our fundamental historian of the Great Fear of 1789—*La Grande Peur.* He observes that this paranoid panic began before the meeting of the Estates General, but after the fall of the Bastille, on July 14, there was a quantum leap in the number and intensity of the disturbances. We may observe that, during the whole of 1789, due to the calling of the Estates General, the preparation of the *cahiers de doléance,* and the general antimonarchical agitation, there was already a deep feeling in the country that the king was losing his omnipotent capacity for protection and security. Then, when the first violent challenge to the king's authority (the Bastille) was successful, there was no holding back the paranoid acting-out in the countryside. Lefebvre concedes that he cannot determine the true cause of this acceleration of fantasy and violence: "After 14 July, when riots of every sort were on the increase it was natural that, on the eve of the harvest, feeling of anxiety should run high and panics occur and multiply more freely than before. But the disproportion is such that *it would be rewarding to find some additional explanation* which would apply to the second fortnight in July."[45]

He himself provides the direction to follow. In 1848, Paris ended monarchical rule and proclaimed the Second Republic. Already in April there was an outbreak of fear in Champagne. Intense street fighting began in Paris in June: "There was desperate anxiety everywhere. At the beginning of July, a panic swept through Calvados, Manche and Orne, right up to Seine-Inférieure. . . . It was 1789 all over again."[46] A fantasized foreign invasion was a crucial aspect of these disturbances. An almost identical experience, Lefebvre tells us, occurred in England in the seventeenth century: "It was exactly the same in England when James II was deposed and everyone thought that hordes of wild fanatical Irish would invade the country to set him on the throne again: panic broke out everywhere during 'the Irish night.' "[47] *Le roi est mort; vive le panique!*

A legitimate monarch, one who reigns with the consent of a large percentage of the people, represents a fundamental form of social cohesion in traditional society. His omnipotence and his justice hold society together. From the appearance of the first early states, with certain exceptions such as the republican states of ancient Greece and Rome, early Modern Italy, the Netherlands, and Switzerland, until the Modern world, omnipotent kingship was *the* primary form of social cohesion. Size made no difference: what held feudal society together, on the crucial local level, was the count or duke who held the local omnipotent power. It is no wonder that panic that anticipates the collapse of society should follow the fall of such near-gods. Society can only be held together if something as powerful, as protecting, as comforting as the king can be put in his place. In the Modern world, the complex symbolic form of the Nation—direct product of the sovereignty of the people*—enabled that great transformation to take place. The Nation and *le pueple* who constitute it become the heirs of the king's sacredness. However, unlike divine kingship, that nationalism is not religious. It may feel *like* a religion, but it is not one. The secular sacred becomes a fundamental instrument of social cohesion. In many places, it did not work nearly as well as the intellectual vanguard of the society had anticipated.

The moral transformation that made the first French Revolution consisted, essentially, in the assertion of three basic propositions, and the immediate institutionalization of these radical values: (1) That the Nation was superior to the king. (2) That, therefore, political sovereignty resided in the Nation and the people who constitute it. (3) That political democracy—and its concomitant form, citizenship—was an inevitable accompaniment of the process of according sovereignty to the Nation.

As with everything of importance that happened in 1789, this radical transformation was prefigured in the fifty or so years before the climactic events. The Marquis d'Argenson, who wrote several notable works of political theory, announced in 1753: "The nation is above kings just as the universal church is above the pope."[48] The abbé de Véri, in his memoirs, describes the situation on the eve of the Revolution: "The trivial expressions of my youth: *to serve the king, to serve* le patrie . . . are no longer in the mouth of the French. . . . One scarcely declares to say: to serve the king; one substitutes the words: *to serve the State.* . . . Today hardly anyone dares to say in the circles of Paris: 'I serve the King.' . . . 'I serve the State.' . . . that is the expression that is most common."[49] And, here again, we find in England, which led the way to democratic citizenship, a voice as early as 1556: John Poynet, formerly Bishop of Winchester, asserted, "Men ought to give more respect to their country than to their prince, to the commonwealth than to any one person. For the country and the commonwealth is a degree above the king."[50]

One must pay close attention to the metaphor of height, of higher and lower. Faced with an authoritarian monarch or an autocratic priesthood, moral transformation becomes possible by imagining the potentiality of moral appeal to a

---

*For a complex challenge to this theoretical statement, see the Appendix in this chapter.

presence superior to visible authority. The Protestant conception that an individual could relate directly to God, without the need of priestly intermediaries, plays a crucial role in the rise of democratic citizenship. There must be, nevertheless, something to appeal to. Politically, there must be something to put in the place of the sovereignty of the monarch. Modernity and democratic citizenship were impossible without the Nation.

The transformative ground having been so well prepared, the Third Estate, meeting in Versailles, took the action that "was, from the juridical perspective, the crucial event of the Revolution of 1789. It transferred sovereignty from the king to the nation and placed a National Assembly of the people's representatives at the head of the state."[51] Declaration of the Third Estate, 17 June 1789:

> The motion of M. the abbé Sieyès is passed by majority of 491 votes to 90. The assembly consequently adopts the following declaration:
>
> "The title of *National Assembly* is the only appropriate one for the assembly in the present circumstances, whether because its members are the only legitimately and publicly known and verified representatives, or because they are sent directly by the near totality of the nation [that is, the Third Estate], or finally because . . . no deputy . . . has the right to exercise his functions apart from the present assembly."[52]

The Declaration of the Rights of Man and Citizen, adopted in August, after the success of the first revolution, said it succinctly: "3. The principle of all sovereignty rests essentially in the nation."[53]

The intricate relationship between the rise of democracy and the sovereignty of the Nation has been elaborated by Leah Greenfield: "The location of sovereignty within the people and the recognition of the fundamental equality among its various strata, which constitute the essence of the modern national ideal, are at the same time the basic tents of democracy. Democracy was born with a sense of nationality. The two are inherently linked, and neither can be fully understood apart from this connection. Nationalism was the form in which democracy appeared in the world, contained in the idea of the nation as a butterfly in a cocoon."[54] The reason *why* this was so was that the sovereignty and all-powerfulness of the Nation enabled people to live without the omnipotence of a king.

For France, as for any modernity-emerging society, even after the principle had been set forth that the Nation was sovereign, the question still remained: who or what constituted the Nation? Sieyès' powerfully influential pamphlet

"Ou'est-ce que le Tiers État?," written on the eve of the Revolution, had dog-matically declared that the Third Estate was the Nation; the delegates to the Third Estate agreed, in 1789, and therefore concluded that the estate, by itself, could constitute the National Assembly. This conclusion and action had been anticipated already in 1755. The *Catéchisme du citoyen*: "The Third Estate, finding itself composed of the greatest part of the members of society, forms, properly speaking, the society itself; and the two other orders must only be considered as particular associations, whose interests are, by the very constitution of the civil State, really subordinate to that of this numerous Order."[55]

And all of this attribution of sovereignty to the Nation is not merely a ques-tion of interests and rational politics. The love of the Nation in modern socie-ties—patriotism—is *sacred*; it is a fundamental form of social cohesion; whatever holds society together in a consensual way is a configuration of the sacred. Tocqueville describes the traditional, sentimental order of patriotism: "Those who feel it love their country as one loves one's father's house." These senti-ments, however, are capable of expanding into a different realm: "This same patriotism is often also exalted by religious zeal, and then it works wonders. It is itself a sort of religion; it does not reason, but believes, feels, and acts."[56] A "sort" of a religion, but not, critically considered, truly a religion, because there is no deity, no metaphysical being or entity which legitimizes its power: a perfect manifestation of the secular sacred. After the fall of the king, Jacqueline Chaumié writes, for the revolutionaries: "The love of *la patrie* is one of the essential motors of their action. The patriotism of the men of the Revolution, Girondins and Montagnards, has a religious character and implies a veritable ethic. The sacred love of the *la patrie* has taken, for them, most of the place of divine love."[57]

There is no new, progressive social or cultural form that is not vulnerable to perversion. And the sovereignty of the Nation and love for *la patrie* was extraordi-narily subject to such vulnerability. In a perverse form, the exaggerated love of the Nation could become an instrument in the re-establishment of absolutism. The Nation will become a tyrant, and not a sovereign, unless it recognizes some-thing higher and superior to itself: a commitment to justice and universal human rights. Robespierre announced that he was not only the spokesman of *le peuple* but *peuple* himself. And since the Nation and the people were now sovereign, he was coming dangerously close to Louis XIV's infamous announcement: "L'état, c'est moi." "I am not the courtesan, nor the moderator, nor the tribune, nor the defender of the people. . . . *Je suis peuple moi-même!*"[58] A very dangerous sacred.

The nation, since it is now the inheritor of the king's omnipotence, is in a

perfect position to do two things kings were required to do: demand total obedience and make war in which citizens are required to die. It is a question of how
transformed, how sublimated is that omnipotence as it passes from monarch to
le peuple. A fundamental problem for the French Revolutions, a crucial reason for
their ultimate failure, was that the need for omnipotence did not suffer a greater
metamorphosis, did not undergo a sufficient sublimation. The king was dead,
but the longing for primitive omnipotent power remained overwhelming; nobody understood that better than Napoleon. Democratic citizenship was the
inevitable sacrifice to the omnipotent Nation.

I have already discussed, at length, the failure to establish a political party
system required for a democratic polity. That discussion underlined the paranoid
incapacity to conceive of a loyal opposition. At this moment, it is important to
emphasize the results of the failure to sublimate the need for omnipotent power,
because without such transformation, omnipotence is merely *transferred* from
monarch to the republican state. "The Revolutionaries," Sydenham writes, "inherited the absolutist belief that the State must be directed towards a single
ultimate good by the single will which alone could comprehend that ideal. . . .
Thus to differ from the opinion of the majority, once it had been established by
freely-expressed individual opinions, was to commit the crime of *lèse-nation,* as
heinous an offense as *lèse-majesté* had been in the days of the monarchy. To all
these conceptions the idea of party as a desirable form of political association is
entirely alien."[59]

The great problematic in the movement from monarchical to republican
omnipotence is the increasing anxiety that the Nation will not prove as capable
of exercising overwhelming power as was the king. We are acquainted with the
kind of intense unrest that periods of interregnum produce, but that panic can
be assuaged with the establishment of a new sovereign. But what if there is no
king to put in the place of the dead king? Can the Nation really maintain the
Power? One way to answer that question positively and end that disquiet is to
go to war, with the use of citizen (i.e., republican) armies. Victory proves the
potency of the Nation.

Aggressive warfare—not defensive—proved to be the most catastrophic, most
self-destructive mode of social action in the whole of revolutionary history,
1789–1815. My most superficial memory of courses on Modern European history left me with the incorrect notion that the reactionary powers in Europe,
frightened of revolutionary France, had instituted a war in order to destroy the
Revolutionary aspirations at their source. That was my recollection, because such

a course of action would have made sense, would have been an expression of
rationality. That Revolutionary France, with all its economic problems, with all
its difficulties of public finance and food supply, should decide, almost unanimously, to declare war on much of Europe—that seemed incredible because it
was so irrationally self-destructive. And Robespierre, not yet descended to the
paranoid depths, was almost alone in seeing what the catastrophic consequences
for France would be. If, however, that was the only way to assuage the panic-
anxiety about the disappearance of kingly omnipotence, by demonstrating the
potency of the Nation, then such action remains comprehensible, though no less
pitiful. And the Emperor Napoleon, who is not our subject here, once started
on a career of European conquest, could not stop killing and conquering any
more than the radical Jacobins could stop the appetite of the cannibalistic guillotine.

In the speeches at the Assembly that preceded the declaration of war, an
exaggerated nationalism, a childish illusionary commitment to feelings of omnipotence are palpable. The leaders of this push to war-madness were the deputies
around Brissot, a group that eventually would become the Girondins. Almost all
the factions in the Assembly, nevertheless, shared this paranoid thrust to strike
at "them" before they strike at us. T.C.W. Blanning illuminates:

> Thus Austrophobia was, of course, only the reverse side of a far more positive
> force: nationalism. Every Brissotin speaker stressed the need for the reassertion of
> French greatness. In the words of Larivière, the French were "the most loyal, the
> most open, the most generous, the most sympathetic and the most human people
> in the universe"—and it was high time the universe was reminded of the fact.
> There was much harping on the special virtues, as numerous as they were virtuous,
> which went to make up "la grande nation" and no apologies were offered for
> asserting them: "If vanity demeans and degrades a private individual, among whole
> peoples there is a national vanity which makes them great, which elevates them.
> (*Applause.*)" The very best way to express this superior form of vanity, to reassert
> those special virtues, was to go to war against the power which had been responsi-
> ble for past humiliations. War against Austria, Gensonné claimed, would raise
> France "to the height of her destiny."

Crucial to this aggressive stance was the assertion that France was defending
itself against intrusion, was preserving its own independent space:

> Behind the rather comic claims of French greatness lay a much more important
> principle: national sovereignty. One speaker after another, and not just the Brissot-

ins, stressed that the affairs of France could only be conducted by Frenchmen. On that fundamental principle there could be no compromise, no negotiation. Hence the decree of 14 January 1792 which established the ultimate crime of *lèse nation*. . . . Every time a speaker proclaimed his absolute rejection of outside interference, he was rewarded by a storm of vocal approval from all sides of the chamber. To the sound of "repeated applause," the Fayettist minister of war, Narbonne, for example, proclaimed on 11 January 1792: "everything is possible for us, except enduring the shame of a treaty which would allow foreigners to meddle with our political debates."

Blanning also emphasizes the culture of omnipotence that dominated the debates, pointing out "the extraordinary optimism which suffused the war-party's speeches. Time and again, the same argument was heard: war involved no risks because a quick and easy victory was certain."

And now that sovereignty had passed from the monarch to the people, omnipotent *citizen* armies were available to the Nation. In December 1791, Brissot brought the Assembly to its feet: "If we want to remain free, we should ask, as the Spartans did, *where* are our enemies, not how many are there of them (*Applause*); for now every French citizen is a soldier, and a willing soldier at that! (*Applause*) And where is the power on earth, where is Genghis Khan, where is Tamerlaine, even with clouds of slaves in his train, who could hope to master six million free soldiers?"[60]

We are listening, be it remembered, to the finest of the liberal bourgeois elite: not radical Jacobins or *enragés*; not compromising *monarchiens*, who would not go all the way to a democratic republic. Sincere, democratic, liberal, republican aspirations were no proof against panic-anxiety about abolishing the king's omnipotence. If we would understand some of the prodigious contradictions in democratic liberalism—if we would comprehend, for instance, nineteenth-century England, moving inevitably toward a full male democracy at home, gradually downgrading the monarchy from all-powerful to constitutional, while compulsively expanding its domination of "inferior peoples" abroad—it would be of value to contemplate these war-mongering Brissotins.

One usual explanation of such imperialist imperatives is "capitalism." If we look at the ancient Greek world, however, we find the exact same sequence of events—radical democracy followed by the construction of *demos*-ruled imperialist empires—in circumstances where there was no capitalism. Athens in the fifth century B.C. is the prime and most well-known example, one that inspired Jacqueline de Romilly, the great expositor of Thucydides, to write that "moderate imperialism is the policy of moderate democracy and extreme imperialism the policy of extreme democracy."[61] And then there was Syracuse on the island of Sicily. First, the *demos* overthrew the tyrants and established a democratic *polis*. Then came imperialist domination that made her "the greatest state in Sicily. . . . Her wealth enabled her to double her force of cavalry, maintain a fleet of 100 triremes, and build up financial reserves. Her aim was to win the whole of Sicily. Her methods resembled those of Athens, whose ambitions had already made themselves felt in the West."[62]

This is not to say that tyrants and monarchs did not set out to create empires, but their motivation may not have been the same as the newly empowered *demos*, wondering if power could hold when there was no longer a king. And when a tyrant's paranoid ambition should combine with the capacities of a "people's army," there was no telling where ambition might end: even in a catastrophic retreat from Moscow. It was a horrendously pitiful demonstration of the limit of what reason could do for people when irrational anxiety held dominion over culture.

NATIONALISM, THE SECULAR SACRED, AND MODERNITY

The most persuasive, the most eloquent discussion of the existence—and the importance—of the secular sacred occurs in Durkheim's book on *Moral Education*. A system of morality, a moral imperative, a moral education—all these, he argues, are always sacred. They may be, however, either religious or not. There exists both a religious sacred and a secular sacred. In a traditional society, and in France throughout the nineteenth century, moral education in the schools was pursued almost completely under a religious sanction. The present task, he argues, is to teach morality, to emphasize a moral imperative, but not within a religious context. The sacredness of the task is to be preserved, but the religious sanction must be transformed into a secular sanction. The institution of the secular sacred consists, essentially, in that metamorphosis.

Durkheim discusses the secular sacred, in this instance, only within the context of morality and education. He does not address the question of what other dimensions of social life may give rise to such a form. Nationalism, it is argued here, in the Modern world, is a prime manifestation of the secular sacred. The sacredness of the Nation, ultimately, does not emanate from God or any metaphysical entity. Nationalism is not a religion, though its sacredness has often confused observers into calling it a religion. The love of one's country, the moral imperatives it imposes on us, the protection and security it offers, its profound importance as a form of social cohesion—all this certifies to its sacred character, and it needs no deity to legitimize it. All of this represents a unique and fundamental attribute of Modernity.

To return to Durkheim and to savor the eloquence of his discourse:

> If, in rationalizing morality in moral education, one confines himself to withdraw from moral discipline everything that is religious without replacing it, one almost inevitably runs the danger of withdrawing at the same time all the elements that are properly moral. Under the name of rational morality, we would be left only with an impoverished and colorless morality. To ward off this danger, therefore, it is imperative not to be satisfied with a superficial separation. We must seek, in the very heart of religious conceptions, those moral realities that are, as it were, lost and dissimulated in it. We must disengage them, find out what they consist of, determine their proper nature, and express them in rational language. In a word, we must discover the rational substitutes for those religious notions that for a long time have served as the vehicle for the most essential ideas.

✻   ✻   ✻   ✻   ✻

> The domain of morality is as if surrounded by a mysterious barrier which keeps violators at arm's length; just as the religious domain is protected from the reach of the profane. *It is a sacred domain.* All the things it comprises are as if invested with a particular dignity that raises them above our empirical individuality, and that confers upon them *a sort of transcendent reality.* Don't we say, casually, that the human person is sacred, that we must hold it in reverence? As long as religion and morals are intimately united, this sacred character can be explained without difficulty, since, in that case, morality as well as religion is conceived as an attribute and emanation of divinity, the source of all that is sacred. Everything coming from it participates in its transcendence and finds itself by that very fact implicated in other things. But if we methodically reject the notion of the sacred without systematically replacing it by another, the quasi-religious character of morality is without foundation....
>
> ... If the eminent dignity attributed to moral rules has, up to the present time, only been expressed in the form of religious conceptions, it does not follow that it cannot be otherwise expressed; consequently, one must be careful that this dignity does not sink with the ideas conventionally associated with it....

Here is a first body of eminently complex and positive problems that compel our attention when we undertake to secularize moral education. It is not enough to cut out; we must replace. We must discover those moral forces that men, down to the present time, have conceived of only under the form of religious allegories. We must disengage them from their symbols . . . and find a way to make the child feel their reality without recourse to any mythological intermediary.[63]

Everything said here about a moral imperative may be repeated, with only minor changes, about nationalism and the Nation. Two parallel developments into Modernity may be descried: From an omnipotent God commanding morality to an omnipotent secular sacred moral imperative. From an omnipotent king holding society together to an omnipotent Nation serving the same function. Both of these developments were part of the prerevolution Enlightenment project. Hardly anyone, however, announced how difficult—how frightening—these two passages to Modernity would be. Terror and a long continuing necessity of some kind of authoritarianism were the fruits of failure.

Montesquieu had, early on, announced the arrival of a secular morality. In his *Avertissement* to *L'Esprit des lois,* he declared: "What I call virtue is love of one's country, that is, love of equality. It is not a moral or a Christian virtue, but a political one; and it is as much the mainspring of republican government as honor is the mainspring of monarchies."[64] We notice that there is still not yet the capacity to distinguish between a religious and a secular sacred, that what is moral is still, somehow, connected with what is religious. That failure to differentiate continued and was manifest by the use of the word "catechism" to designate a new non-Christian system of morality. Whereas, in 1758 Helvétius had called for the invention of a system of nonreligious morality, "like an experimented physics," a few years later d'Alembert had declared that the capacity to persuade the poor to be virtuous had not yet been revealed: "If I had discovered a satisfactory solution to this question, I'd have long ago written my catechism of morality."[65]

The psychological task was to transfer to mere mortals the prerogatives that had belonged to God alone, to capture His omnipotence and lodge it within human beings, to declare that moral imperatives arise only from human necessity, and that, once so lodged, these imperatives could be as efficacious as divine sanctions had been. Dostoevksy's Ivan Karamazov spoke for much of the nineteenth century when he declared that such a transformation could not be accomplished, that, if there were no God, everything was possible (debauch, murder, rapine). Despite its great difficulties, dangers, anxieties, however, precisely this Promethean-Faustian demarche was on the Enlightenment-Revolutionary agenda.

Starobinski comments on Rousseau's *Héloïse,* one of the most popular novels of prerevolutionary times:

> Wolmar does not believe in God but sees himself as the analogue of God, a being who lives in meditative satisfaction, in possession of himself and all he surveys. . . . Is it not surprising that an atheist should wish to be so like God? Nothing here is incompatible with the (avowed or implicit) tendencies of "Enlightenment philosophy." As has often been observed, the philosopher's major ideas are for the most part secularized religious concepts. In the words of Yvon Belavel, it is as if the philosophy of the eighteenth century "transferred to the world the infinite attributes of God and permitted transferring to man God's moral attributes."[66]

Was this new secular faith, this non-Christian catechism, this Modern belief system—and the cult of the Nation—were these various forms merely a new religion? Or were they *qualitatively* something else? The debate on this question continues down to the moment. Tocqueville was ambivalent in his response and analysis: he did not wish to see the demise of religion, and yet he vaguely understood that this new secularity was not exactly a religion: "When religion was expelled from their souls, the effect was not to create a vacuum or a state of apathy; it was promptly, if but momentarily, replaced by *a host of new loyalties and secular ideals* that not only filled the void but . . . fired the popular imagination."

In the very next paragraph, however, these new transformative forms are declared a new religion: "The men who made the Revolution . . . had a fanatical faith in their vocation—that of transforming the social system, root and branch, and regenerating the whole human race. Of this passionate idealism was born *what was in fact a new religion,* giving rise to some of those vast changes in human conduct that religion has produced in other ages."[67] And, in addition, when he had been writing years before of America, the most secular of all societies, he gave equal power in people's social lives to religion *and* nationalism: "Look where you will you will never find true power among men except in the free concurrence of their wills. Now, patriotism and religion are the only things in the world which will make the whole body of citizens go persistently forward toward the same goal."[68]

This possible intellectual confusion, in both Tocqueville and others, is easily accounted for by two circumstances: since the new secular creeds maintained the continuity in sacredness, they required and gave rise to rituals, which had a close affinity to traditional religious ritual observance. And secondly, some people began to treat the cult of the Nation, the love of the *patrie*, as if they were, indeed, religious manifestations; as if Nationalism was, precisely, a new religion. Just as today we are keenly aware of religious fundamentalism, there has been, since the birth of the Nation, a fundamentalist Nationalism, a fanatical patriotism. Both of these manifestations pose basic problematics for Modernity, most especially for democratic citizenship, although that is not our subject here.

In regard to the new rituals of the Nation and of the Revolution, they absorbed much revolutionary energy. The scripture came from Rousseau, who had keenly foreseen the need for transformative ceremonials if society was to accomplish a significant moral advance. "I want to speak of national festivals. Bring men together, you will make them better. Man is the greatest object existing in nature and the most magnificent spectacle is that of a great people assembled."[69] His direct descendent and prophet was Robespierre, who did attempt to make the Revolution into a religion. His festival of the Supreme Being, conducted less than two months before his fall, was a pathetic attempt to achieve that goal, a performance that attempted to exalt Robespierre as much as the new deity and much too closely bordered on kitsch.

Jacqueline Chaumié has argued that one crucial distinction between the Girondins and the Jacobins was that the former were coldly intellectual, not comprehending what the Jacobins apprehended: "They understood the needs of the popular soul to fill the void created by the suppression of the Catholic practice."[70] These cults of the Revolution and of the Nation have been documented in great detail and included cults of reason, the cult of the Supreme Being, devotions to patriotic saints and holy martyrs of Liberty, altars to the fatherland, celebration of National Federation and national brotherhood, and the planting and preservation of Liberty Trees, at the base of which patriots declared their intention to be buried and the life of which was to be fertilized by the blood of kings.[71]

That these sacred rites were intended to replace Catholic ritual was palpable. Altars were erected, before which oaths to the fatherland were taken, and patriotic orations given. In many cases, the new secular ceremonial was combined with traditional religious practice: first, the citizens went to mass at church and then proceeded, often accompanied by the parish priest, to the altar of the fatherland for revolutionary observances. Sometimes, mass was celebrated on the very altar of the fatherland, as happened in Paris when the Bishop Talleyrand served the offices on the altar in the Champs de Mars.[72]

In many cases, the Liberty Tree was planted in the exact open-air place where the cross had stood, with the ceremony of tree planting being concluded with a ritual destruction of the pedestal of the destroyed cross.[73] The Tree itself could be protected by railings or stone walks or thorn hedges, which created an enclosed space, often referred to as "sacred," and into which only magistrates were allowed to penetrate, making the obvious connection between the new civil, secular authorities and ancient high priests.[74] Deeply reminiscent of the near-hysteria concerning flag burning in our country during the 1960s and 1970s—although on a much more primitive scale—was the incident at the commune of Bédouin, which was declared in a state of counterrevolution, with sixty-three of its citizens condemned to death, and the order given to set the commune on fire. The cause of such annihilation: the digging up and destruction of the Liberty Tree.[75] Such response indicates not the establishment of a secular sacred but a perversion of that form: a religious fundamentalism of nationalism, which is intended to replace and destroy all traditional religion. Such perverse forms cannot last long, although they many times bring much human destruction and, in a very short time, the whole edifice of revolutionary rituals collapsed in ruin.

One permanent result of the institution of the cult of the Nation was the establishment of the French language as *the* language for the whole of France, by means of a serious attack on the various non-French languages that were current in many sections of the country (Provence, Languedoc, Brittany, Alsace, etc.). This endeavor, associated with the deputies Bertrand Barère and Henri Grégoire, became a particular project of the Jacobins in 1794. Barère announced: "The language of a free people must be one and the same for all."[76] The ideology of the sacredness of the Nation and the campaign for one universal language for the whole country powerfully converged together, creating eventually the total dominion of the French language.

THE FAILURE OF THE ENTHRONEMENT OF THE NATION

The complex psychological maneuver whereby society is no longer held together by the two arms of traditional omnipotence and religion—religion itself and the divine kingship—but now coheres through the *secular* sacred symbol of the Nation, proved to be enormously difficult. Two opposite dangers threatened this passage: first, that Nationalism would be offered as a *new* religion, eliminating the necessity for a secular form; second, that the secular dimension of the new form would prove inadequate to nurture people's souls, and they would, biblically, "go awhoring after strange gods" or revive reverence for the familiar gods of monarchy. Both these failures resulted from an incapacity to go beyond a primitive conception of omnipotence and made the French journey from Revolution to Modernity a treacherous one.

The emotion-laden word that symbolized the sacredness of the Nation was *patrie*. *Patrie* evoked love, devotion, sacrifice, communion, fullness of soul. There was no *patrie* under the traditional monarchy. The Chevalier de Jaucourt wrote the article *"Patrie"* for the *Encyclopédie*. A person only interested in geography, he wrote, "might define the *patrie* as a place of one's birth, but a philosopher would recognize that it expresses the significance we attach to the concepts of *'family, society, free state,* in which we are members, and of which the laws assure us our liberties and our happiness. There is no *patrie* under despotism.' "[77]

In conclusion, I return to Edgar Quinet's illuminating critique of revolutionary culture. Recalling Furet's summation: "The drama of the French Revolution is to have conceived of modern emancipation of humanity without offering it a basis of religious support."[78] Quinet himself saw, during the Second Republic, in 1850, the same unresolved conflict continuing. The Revolution could offer only the total emancipation from religion. The counterrevolution's solution was an inflexible return to traditional orthodoxy. Neither démarche could succeed. "Il est évident que La France ne peut se promettre aucun dévelopment normal, ni dans un sens, ni dans un autre, mais une série de changements où le hasard, l'imprévu, la contradiction tiendront longtemps encore la place de la logique et de l'esprit de suite."[79] ["It is evident that France is not able to promise itself any normal development, neither in one sense, nor in another, but only a series of changes where chance, the unforeseen, and contradiction will occupy for a long time the place of logic and the sense of order."]

The crucial words are "normal development" and "logic and the sense of order." What logic? That, obviously, of political and social evolution. For Quinet normal developmental runs: (1) Traditional Catholic religion. (2) Protestant Reformation (Early Modernity). (3) A stable Modern democratic society based on some religious foundation. What he is saying, in essence, is that the Revolution attempted *to skip a stage in social evolution* by going from traditional orthodox religion to Modernity, without having experienced the Reformation state.

What is missing in Quinet's analysis of the need for a Modern religion is an understanding of the possibility and the power of the secular sacred. By 1789 it was too late to make any sort of Protestant Reformation in France: in too many regards, Early Modernity had already given way to a Modern culture. It was too late to create a Modern religion that would engender a fundamental form of social cohesion. What finally succeeded, at the end of the nineteenth and the beginning of the twentieth centuries, in the creation of a stable, Modern, democratic society was not Quinet's new Modern religion but Durkheim's secular sacred, wherein a nonreligious but yet sacred nationalism was an essential element in that transformation.

It is not that Modern nationalism has not brought its own catastrophes: World War I came close to bringing the very collapse of Modern societies. And the next moral advance for society—to go beyond Modernity—is enormously hindered by the stranglehold that nationalism still maintains over Modern culture. But that is a whole complex story in itself.

APPENDIX TO CHAPTER 10

Steve Thomas has vigorously objected to the linkage of nationalism and democracy made in the previous argument. Rightly so. He has convinced me that, in writing specifically about France, I have inaccurately made generalizations to all nationalisms: an erroneous maneuver. One cannot think and theorize about nationalism, in the singular: nationalisms is the true situation. Democratic nationalism is only one variety of the species.

Responding to the contention that the progress of nationalism in France went from the sovereignty of the people to democratic citizenship, Thomas writes: "This process was not repeated elsewhere in Central Eastern Europe, yet nationalism flourished nonetheless." He responds to the contention that the Nation is the direct product of the sovereignty of the people: "Not necessarily. The birth pangs of nationalism in the Austrian Empire, at least in Hungary and Bohemia, were a reaction to the centralisation of the state during the reign of Joseph II, 1880–1890, and made no claim to the sovereignty of the people."[80] This last relates directly to observations made recently by other scholars of nationalism that the fall of empires brings about an efflorescence of nationalisms of many different varieties, with democratic, or civic, nationalism occurring only in a minority of cases: the Indian subcontinent, southeast Asia, Africa. Once the imperialist powers withdrew or were pushed out, there was no predicting what particular course nationalism would take.

Liah Greenfeld has elaborated on the crucial distinction between "civic" and "ethnic" nationalism, which has become a generally accepted discrimination for many scholars. It is only civic nationalism that is intimately linked with democracy (the sovereignty of the people). "Nationalism," she writes, "may be distinguished according to criteria of membership in the national collectivity, which may be either 'civic,' that is, identical with citizenship, or 'ethnic.' In the former case, nationality is at least in principle open and voluntaristic; it can and sometimes must be acquired. In the latter, it is believed to be inherent—one can neither acquire it if one does not have it, nor change it if one does; it has nothing to do with individual will, but constitutes a genetic characteristic."[81] In the beginning, she argues, nationalism and democratic citizenship were intimately linked:

> Nationalism was the form in which democracy appeared in the world, contained in the idea of the nation as a butterfly in a cocoon. Originally, nationalism developed *as* democracy; where the conditions of such original development persisted, the identity between the two was maintained. But as nationalism spread in different conditions and the emphasis in the idea of the nation moved from the sovereign character of the uniqueness of the people, the original equivalence between it and democratic principles was lost.[82]

This civic/ethnic dichotomy has been further elaborated in a manner that raises some very large and intense historical questions. Civic nationalism is designated "Western" (i.e., western Europe and the nations owing their political culture to England: America, Canada, Australia, etc.). This "Western"/"Eastern" divide was elaborated by Hans Kohn in 1955 (*Nationalism: Its Meaning and History*) in a manner that easily was transposed into the civic/ethnic divide. Anthony D. Smith elaborates on Kohn: "He distinguishes a 'Western,' rational and associational version of nationalism from an 'Eastern' organic and mystical version."[83] And, for Smith, certain equivalences are clear: "We can term this non-Western model an 'ethnic' conception of the nation."[84] It becomes crucial, then, always to distinguish what particular kind of nationalism one is talking about.

Even with all these crucial distinctions and elaborations that establish the importance of the concept of nationalism*s*, certain generalizations concerning the relationship of omnipotence, nationalism, and democratic citizenship—as developed in this chapter—based on the data from French revolutionary history, still seem very much worth consideration. First, there is, in *all cases*, an intimate relationship between the omnipotence of the king/emperor/imperial power and the omnipotence of the Nation. All nationalisms claim supreme power for the Nation. Here there may be a significant dichotomy between civic and ethnic nationalism. With civic nationalism the sense of omnipotence not only passes from king to Nation, but in that process, it is also *transformed* and sublimated. It no longer has the same primitive dominion. This abatement of primitive omnipotence allows society to go beyond the paranoid position, making democratic citizenship possible. With ethnic nationalism the sense of omnipotence is merely *transferred* from king/emperor/imperial power to the Nation. The degree of transformation or sublimation is slight. Essentially, the need for primitive omnipotence is not abandoned. There is no limit to explosive violence that may be unleashed. One way of reading the French Revolution/Terror/Napoleon catastrophe is to underline the failure to sublimate the need for omnipotence even when there was a definite passage from king to Nation. Despite all the Enlightenment culture; despite all the rights of man and citizen; despite all the free elections based on wide sovereignty—despite all this, the need for radical omnipotence was never surmounted. And all the corpses could not satiate it.

The great paradox and contradiction was that France was not aiming at ethnic, but at civic, nationalism. "In Britain, France and America," Anthony Smith tells of Hans Kohn, "he argued, a rational concept of the nation emerged, one that viewed it as an association of human beings living in a common territory under the same government and laws."[85] Ideological terror can result when a powerful rational concept meets an equally powerful irrational resistance to psychological and social progress.

A second generalization that still seems to hold true is that even though you can have Nations without democratic citizenship, the reverse situation does not hold. There can be no democratic citizenship without the Nation, without nationalism of the civic form. Modern democratic citizenship is impossible without a successful passage to a sovereignty-of-the-people nationalism and the genesis of the secular sacred that makes such a form possible. And that is why I consider this cultural form an essential attribute of Modernity. The French revolutionary experience is powerfully illustrative: no secular sacred, no civic nationalism = no democratic citizenship = explosive violence, either directed internally (the guillotine) or externally (the intended subjugation of all Europe). Today, there is a theory abroad that there is something of the nature of a democratic polity that makes international peace possible, that there has been no major war between democratic societies.[86] The evolution and transformation of the need for omnipotence might possibly tell us a great deal as to why this has been so.

II

TO RATIONALIZE SOCIETY— TO ORDER THE WORLD

Modernity is the inchoate Promethean aspiration, now made flesh, of men to transform nature and transform themselves: to make man the master of change and the redesigner of the world to conscious plan and purpose. [Daniel Bell][1]

As though in the course of the French Revolution the lawfully irresistible movement of the heavenly bodies had descended upon the earth and the affairs of men, bestowing upon them a "necessity" and regularity which had seemed beyond the "melancholy haphazardness" (Kant), the "sad mixture of violence and meaninglessness" (Goethe) which up to then had seemed to be the outstanding quality of history and the course of the world. [Hannah Arendt][2]

This is a short chapter. This book is about ambivalence, ambiguity, contradiction, anxiety, moving forward and backward simultaneously: the paradoxes of Modernity. The one fundamental aspect of Modernity that exhibited almost no ambivalence, ambiguity, or contradiction was the inexorable drive to rationalize all aspects of the social order. For various reasons, through the last thousand years, that enterprise might proceed at a greater or lesser pace—or even seemed stalled for shorter or longer periods—but the path and the telos were never lost sight of. This is true, at least for Western Europe from the twelfth century onward.

With such an ancient history, this impulse cannot be considered an invention of Modernity. The Norman conquerors of Britain were intent on creating a rationalized, centralized state with a complex and efficient bureaucracy. Until the truly modern period, in matters that concerned the polity, monarchs intent on centralized state power were the primary instruments of rationalization. All state-building required it: at the beginning of the sixteenth century and the dominion of the three great kings, Charles V, Francis I, Henry VIII, and during the exuberant reign of Louis XIV. In the course of the fourteenth and fifteenth centuries, the bankers of Italy and Germany were intently rationalizing the business of finance. Tocqueville's insight that in promoting centralization and rationalization, the Revolution was only continuing the work of the *ancien régime* was true but historically shortsighted.

What Modernity did was to install the commitment to a rational order in all social areas as a fundamental and urgent value of society. There was a quantum leap in the amount of energy expended in the project; the Revolution eagerly took its place in that enterprise.

Tocqueville had a deep intuitive sense of social evolution that was many times expressed by the questions he asked, but could not answer. Such as the case with the developmental thrust toward rationalization. Speaking of the eighteenth century: "Their starting point was the same in all cases; and this was the belief that what was wanted was to replace the complex of traditional customs governing the social order of the day by simple, elementary rules deriving from the exercise of human reason and natural laws. . . . How was it that at this particular point of time it could root itself so firmly in the mind of writers of the day? Why, instead of remaining in the past the purely intellectual concept of a few advanced thinkers, did it find welcome among the masses and acquire the driving force of a political passion to such effect that general and abstract theories of the nature of human society not only became daily topics of conversation among the leisure class but fired the imagination of women and peasants?"[3]

Possibly the inclusion of peasants is an exaggeration of Tocqueville's, but the question remains powerful: How was it that at this particular point of time? I am incapable of anything except possibly a first-step answer to that question, but one thing does seem certain to me: without a conception of Modernity as a stage in social evolution, no full answers will be forthcoming. For Tocqueville, hard evidence for his description came from examination of the *cahiers*, not from the Third Estate, where one would expect a commitment to change in the direction of rationalization, but from the nobility itself, the class that had the most to lose from modernization. "They seek a uniform administration, uniform laws, etc. as ardently as the Third Estate. They call for all kinds of reform, and those radical enough."[4]

The evidence of this accelerating rationalization in the early Modern state that preceded the Revolution is overwhelming. François Furet writes:

> By the eighteenth century the French monarchy was no longer the unreliable instrument for mobilizing national resources . . . it had inherited the advances made by Louis XIV. . . . Encouraged by the spirit of the time, the monarchy was able to devote more money and attention to the great tasks of modernity, such as urban planning, public health, agriculture and commercial improvements, the unification of the market, and education. By now the *intendant* was well entrenched in the provinces. . . . Deeply engaged in an immense administrative effort of fact-finding and reform, he . . . rationalised his activities with the help of the first social statistics in French history. He stripped the clergy and the nobility of almost all their functions of local leadership at least in secular matters. Even elementary education, that old preserve of the Church, came increasingly under his control. . . . Far from being reactionary or beholden to selfish interests, the monarchical State of the eighteenth century was thus one of the major agents of change and general progress—a permanent builder of "enlightened" reform.[5]

And once the Revolution was in power, although profound differences among different political elites manifested themselves, almost everyone was in agreement on the desirability of modern rationalization: "Including the king, the Old Regime courts, the liberal nobles, the constitutional monarchists of 1790, the Girondins, the Jacobins, and the Directorials."[6] It was a manifestation of what was to become, in the twentieth century, a world project of modernization. "The great French Revolution," Charles Tilly writes, "anticipated the powerful 'modernizing' and 'nationalizing' revolutions of such countries as Egypt, Japan, or Argentina."[7]

The sustained impulse toward rationalization can be understood as standing behind several social reforms already dealt with, such as the abolition of all forms of corporations and the almost tyrannical insistence on the absolute supremacy of the French language. Equally so was the arithmetical division of the country into eighty-three new provinces and the fact that the reform of religious institutions took the provinces as its basis and disregarded old divisions for dioceses. Tocqueville comments that nothing shocked Europe more than the fact that the Constituent Assembly partitioned the country as if it were virgin land in the New World and not an ancient kingdom with years of local history behind it. He quotes Burke, who was nothing if not ambivalent about modernization, to the effect: " 'It is the first time that we have seen men hack their native land to pieces in so barbarous a manner.' "[8]

Once the juggernaut of imposed order was in operation within the culture, all areas were subject to its power of reform: law, education, taxes, and finances. And, once again, this revolutionary mode was not the invention of *the* Revolution. Typical of the "feudal" disarray under the traditional society was the situation in the city of Ste. Menehould, where a population of 3,000 people was served by nine different law courts. The revolutionary reform replaced all these with one panel of four judges.[9] But the radical modernization of the legal system, instituted by the Constituent Assembly in 1791, had already been anticipated by the failed attempts of the Lamoignon ministry three years earlier.[10] This same ministry began the project of legal reform by abolishing judicial torture, initiated the process of religious tolerance by giving a limited civil status for Protestants, and even undertook studies for reforming the educational system, which had traditionally been dominated by the Church.[11]

The most significantly chaotic situation in the Old Regime existed in the area of taxation and state finances. It is not an exaggeration to say that the Revolution occurred, in good part, because the Regime found itself incapable of a reform in regard to state finance that would take the French state into the Modern world. Attempts were made, but they all led to failure. The monarch possessed no central treasury where an annual budget could be prepared or audited. Most of the taxes were collected by independent financiers, who many times did the state as much harm as good. A central state bank could have corrected much of this situation, but it was never instituted. Attempts were made, from 1770 onward, to consolidate public finances into one central department. The efforts of Terray, Turgot, and Necker in this direction came to very little. When Calonne became minister of finances, he backwatered on many of those attempted reforms.[12] By 1786, however, Calonne had come to the realization that only a full and thorough radical reform of political and financial institutions could save the day. He beseeched the king: "I shall easily show that it is impossible to tax further, ruinous to be always borrowing and not enough to confine ourselves to economical reforms and that, with matters as they are, ordinary ways being unable to lead us to our goal, the only effective remedy, the only course left to take, the only means of managing finally to put the finances truly in order, must consist in revivifying the entire State by recasting all that is vicious in its constitution."[13]

What he then presented to the king was a prescription for reform, to some degree, of the whole of French society. Entitled *Summary of a Plan for the Improvement of the Finances,* it made no appeal to Enlightenment moral notions of equality for all men or inherent rights or the expansion of sovereignty in the direction of the people. It concerned itself strictly with *raison d'État:* efficiency, order, organization that will lead to power.

> The disparity, the disaccord, the incoherence of the different parts of the body of the monarchy is the principle of the constitutional vices which enervate its strength and hamper all its organization; . . . one cannot destroy any one of them without attacking them all in the principle which has produced them and which perpetuates them; . . . it alone influences everything; . . . it harms everything, . . . it is opposed to all good; . . . a kingdom made up of lands with estates, lands without [*pays d'élections*], lands with provincial assemblies [*administrations provinciales*], lands of mixed administration, a kingdom whose provinces are foreign to one another, where multifarious internal barriers separate and divide the subjects of the same sovereign, where certain areas are totally freed from burdens of which others bear the full weight, where the richest class contributes least, where privileges destroy all balance, where it is impossible to have either a constant rule or a common will, is necessarily a very imperfect kingdom, brimming with abuses, and one that it is impossible to govern well; . . . in effect the result is that general administration is excessively complicated, public contributions unequally spread, trade hindered by countless restrictions, circulation obstructed in all its branches, agriculture crushed by overwhelming burdens, the state's finances impoverished by excessive causes of recovery. . . . Finally, I shall prove that so many abuses, so visible to all eyes, and so justly censured, have only till now resisted a public opinion which condemns them, because nobody has attempted to extirpate their germ, and to dry up the source of all obstacles by establishing a more uniform order.[14]

Calonne was no radical, certainly no revolutionary, but his intelligence was offended by the abuses of orderliness that pervaded French society. In this one regard, he was as fierce a modernist as anyone.

THE STANDARDIZATION OF MEN

One very complex relationship that I would like to touch upon, even though incapable of explaining, is the relationship of science, reason, and the equality of all men to this insistent drive toward order and standardization. The rise of science in the early Modern world clearly had a powerful influence on the drive toward social order. If Nature's laws were more and more being revealed as consistent and orderly and capable of being comprehended by people; if gravity operated in the exact same way in every part of France and, indeed, in every part of the world; if there are universal laws governing the physical universe—then would it not be reasonable that the social world conform to an equal regime of orderliness? Was there not a *natural* social world that was the social equivalent of the physical world of Nature?

People began to speculate that, just as science had revealed the secrets and regularity of gravity, magnetism, electricity, and energy—correspondingly, the laws of morality should be capable of human divination. John Witherspoon, president of Princeton University in America, a typical child of the Enlightenment, contemplated the time "when men, treating moral philosophy as Newton and his successors have done natural, may arrive at greater precision."[15]

And should the standardization that we find in Nature, which should be enforced on society, did it also apply to human beings? Were all men—at least as far as rights and moral worth—alike in the same way that all molecules of oxygen were alike? Was inequality between men an abuse, in the same manner that internal tariff and tax differentials were abusive and debilitating to society? Tocqueville does, at one point, bring these two possibly discrepant realms together: "We find that the chief permanent achievement of the French Revolution was the suppression of those political institutions, commonly described as feudal, which for many centuries had held unquestioned sway in most European countries. The Revolution set out to replace them with a new social and political order, at once simple and *more uniform, based on the concept of the equality of all men.*"[16]

Was it possible, nevertheless, to pursue uniformity in areas of *raison d'État* without basing them on the equality of all men? In the twentieth century, with its various roads to Modernity, such attempts would certainly be made. The French Revolution, however, was for so many people, for such a long time, *the* revolution precisely because it did not separate those two realms: equality for all men never left the political agenda, no matter what regressions manifested themselves.

CAPITALISM AND THE DESTRUCTION OF THE NOBILITY

The time is now ripe for our sociology to rethink the problem of the origins of capitalism. We owe an enormous amount to Weber,[17] who demonstrated that it was not only that the rise of capitalism was producing crucial changes in values and in culture but, equally so, that the evolution of culture and values was preparing the ground for a capitalist take-off. That left the question, nevertheless, of what was causing this significant transformation of culture. To answer "Protestantism" only pushes the question in a critical direction. What, then, we may inquire further, was the cause of the rise of Protestantism? Maybe there was a larger wave of cultural and social evolution, beginning in the West in the twelfth century, that ultimately resulted in Protestantism, capitalism, the rise of science, political democracy—Modernity. Maybe Abelard's *Sic et Non* was as essential to the ultimate rise of capitalism as Calvin's *Institutes*.

My only hope here is to clarify the question as sharply as possible by underlining the powerful thrust toward rationality, science, order: Daniel Bell's "aspiration to make man the master of change and the redesigner of the world to conscious plan and purpose." Such aspiration pre-dates the Reformation, pre-dates what I have been calling here "early Modernity." That rationality, science, and orderliness are conducive to the rise of capitalism is almost self-evident. Why, nevertheless, did different nations of Western Europe embrace these imperatives with different degrees of conviction? Why England and not Italy? Why France and not Spain? One thing that ultimately helped save France, despite all the conflicts and ambivalences, was an almost unambivalent embrace of these particular attitudes toward Modernity: clearly palpable during the *ancien régime* and significantly intensified by revolutionary and post-revolutionary activity. Whatever else France could not do in the struggle for Modernity, this she could, and did, accomplish.

On the 9th of Thermidor of the Year VI—July 27, 1798—a celebratory procession took place in Paris, the purpose of which was to give honor to Liberty. Professors and students from the newly reorganized Museum of Natural History marched before carriages loaded with exotic plants and minerals, followed by a bear from Bern, lions from Africa, camels from Egypt. The phenomenal art plunder from Italy came next. Titian, Raphael, the Apollo Belvidere, and the four great bronze horses that had traveled from Corinth to Byzantium to Venice and now to Paris. They had been brought, so it was said, that they could now " 'rest at last upon free soil.' "[18] Very soon thereafter, on the Champs de Mars, was installed Europe's very first industrial exposition, on the main purpose of which was to display and to judge products submitted by 110 French manufacturers and *artistes*. François de Neufchateau, the Minister of the Interior, opened the exposition with the kind of speech that was destined to become a cliché of celebratory nationalist capitalism. In Palmer's summary: "Our French manufacturers will abundantly demonstrate the superiority of a free people in matters economic; genius and ingenuity are now liberated from gilds and monopolies and from ancient regulations and routines; the day foreseen in the *Encyclopédie*, the day of systematic and public sponsorship of the practical arts, has at last arrived."[19] Four years after the fall of Robespierre, under the "reactionary" leadership of the Directory.

Charles Tilly has undertaken to elaborate on the fundamental attributes of Modernity, though he would not use this latter term. He does avail himself of a "collective term," a catch-all phrase: "urbanization." Four aspects of this new world fall under this urbanization rubric. *Differentiation:* "the subdivision of existing social positions into more specialized ones." *Standardization:* "the development of uniform procedures, vocabularies, norms, and forms of organization." *Change in the quality of social relations:* the substitution of legal-rational modes for emotive, or kinship, ways of social intercourse. *Concentration of population:* "mainly the growth of cities."[20]

Not to argue for or against Tilly's theoretical reflections by speculating on whether they are too encompassing, or not encompassing enough, only one particular point is being made here. Every one of these attributes, every particular development of social values and forms in the direction of "urbanization" is significantly productive of the development of capitalism. It cannot, in fact, mature without, at least, all four of Tilly's elaborated attributes. There can be no capitalism without a capitalist ethic—what Weber calls "the spirit of capitalism"—and that ethic takes much of its power and energy from the drive to rationalize and order the world.

One aspect of this modernizing drive differentiated France from the whole of Western Europe; one action taken by the Constituent Assembly was truly revolutionary and cannot find its ancestry in the *ancien régime*: the almost compete destruction of the power of the aristocracy except where it preserved economic wealth, the complete overthrow of the aristocracy from its position as a privileged class enjoying the highest status within society. True, aristocratic privilege—so called "feudal" survivals—was under attack in the years preceding the Revolution, but there was absolutely no indication of the radical attack on aristocracy itself that would be successfully undertaken once the Assembly set itself the goal of writing a new constitution for France.

In his Foreword to *The Old Régime*, Tocqueville begins by making the point that many have taken up: that there was more continuity and less radical break between the *ancien régime* and revolutionary institutions: "I am convinced that though they had no inkling of this, [the revolutionaries] took over from the old régime not only most of its customs, convictions, and modes of thought, but even those very ideas which prompted our revolutionaries to destroy it; that, in fact, though nothing was farther from their intentions, they used the debris of the old order for building up the new."[21] And yet, only a very few pages later, he deplores what he sees as a different, but certain, developmental imperative that had no ancestry in the Old Regime: "Though there can be no certainty about the future, three facts are plain to see in the light of past experience. First, that all our contemporaries are driven on by a force that we may hope to regulate or curb, but cannot overcome, and it is a force impelling them, sometimes, gently, sometimes at headlong speed, to the destruction of the aristocracy."[22]

That impulse toward total destruction first manifested itself with great force in the decrees of the National Assembly of June 1790. And, in this regard, at no point does Tocqueville even attempt to find a continuity of attitude and position with the old regime. This new attack was truly revolutionary. During a night session of June 19, "the Assembly voted to suppress the hereditary nobility and all the symbolic accoutrements pertaining to the Old Regime caste structure."[23] So radical an action alienated a significant number of the noble deputies from the Revolution. In the following year or so, one-fifth of these deputies left the Assembly and joined counterrevolutionary armies in neighboring countries that were committed to the overthrow of the Revolution. Many other noble deputies simply went home.[24] This attack on noble privilege and the Civil Constitution of the Clergy were the two most radical actions the Assembly took; they permanently changed the face of French society.

When the Constitution—France's first—was finally completed in 1791, like all constitutions, it required a Preamble. Reading its text carefully, we can observed that inequality of rights is not only abolished for its violation of "Enlightenment" ideals, but also because there is something disorderly in such discrepancies: the abolition of privilege helps order the world.

> The National Assembly, wishing to establish the French constitution on the principles that it has recognized and declared, irrevocably abolishes the institutions that have done injury to liberty and to the equality of rights.
>
> Nobility no longer exists, nor peerage, nor hereditary distinction of orders, nor feudal regime, nor patrimonial courts, nor titles, denominations or prerogatives deriving therefrom, nor any order of chivalry, nor any of the corporations or

decorations for which proofs of nobility used to be required or which presupposed distinctions of birth, nor any other superiority than that of public officers in the exercise of their functions.

Property in office and its inheritance no longer exist.

No privilege or exception to the common law for all Frenchman any longer exists for any part of the nation or for any individual.[25]

Not surprisingly, the one group in France of whom it cannot be said that it favored the move toward rationalization and order in most areas was the nobility, especially in regard to its own privileges. With the probable exception of the high clergy, it had the most to lose from such modernizing impulses. And it was perfectly conscious of what might be in the offing, before all that revolutionary activity began. In the section where Tocqueville comments on the *cahiers de doléances* of the nobility, he underlines the point that, in regard to many areas, they exhibited an intense spirit of reform, equal at times to that of the Third Estate. However, he goes on: "It is chiefly, or, rather, it is only when they come to deal with distinctions of rank and class divisions that the nobles turn their backs on the prevailing spirit of reform. They make important concessions, but, on the whole, they adhere to the spirit of the old régime. They feel they are fighting for life. Their *cahiers* thus demand energetically that the nobility and the clergy be maintained as distinct orders. . . . All the *cahiers*, in short, demand that the nobility be maintained in all its honors. Some think it would be well for men of rank to wear a distinctive badge."[26] Not all French aristocrats felt that way, however. Two remarkable things about French society at the end of the eighteenth century: first, that so many aristocrats were willing to go a significant part of the way toward the destruction of aristocratic privilege (one recalls, most especially, the exhilarating night of August 4, 1789, which put an "end to feudalism" with the cooperation of many nobles); and second, that so many of the bourgeoisie were eager to engage the aristocracy in a battle to the death. Neither of these things was true even in most of Western Europe (Spain, Italy, Germany) at the time. One is more and more driven to the theoretical conclusion that the Revolution itself, and the course it took, will never be truly understood without a series of comparative studies that will tell us why some nations could take these radical steps toward Modernity and some could not.

That all this was potently conducive for the growth of capitalism seems obvious and has been stated many times by others. The movement toward the elimination of aristocratic power opened the way for the bourgeoisie to become the most powerful class within society. It was not, however, to be the likes of Robespierre, Saint-Just, and the Jacobins—the *moyen* bourgeoisie—who would, in the long run, assume that role, no matter what, in their fantasies, they might have imagined. Capitalism and the growth of capital create a new social and political elite and small-town and medium-size-town lawyers, like Robespierre, are not the leaders of that new elite. Second, the rationalization, centralization, orderliness of society are the perfect soil in which modern capitalism can flourish. Tocqueville did not foresee modern capitalist society, but he did understand the significance of the destruction of the aristocracy for social evolution: "Indeed, I would go so far as to say that whenever a nation destroys its aristocracy, it almost automatically tends toward a centralization of power; a greater effort is then needed to hold it back than to encourage it to move in this direction. All the authorities existing within it are affected by this instinctive urge to coalesce, and much skill is needed to keep them separate. Thus the democratic revolution, though it did away with so many institutions of the past, was led inevitably to consolidate this one; centralization fitted in so well with the program of the new social order that the common error of believing it to have been a creation of the Revolution is easily accounted for."[27] In one of the great ironies of history and social evolution, it was to be industrial capitalism, and not democracy, that was to become the heir and beneficiary of that particular development.

WHY FRANCE? WHY WESTERN EUROPE?

This concluding section is devoted mostly to raising questions. It is profitable to look once again at Furet's analysis of the three ideal-types of nobility in France after the death of Louis XIV.[28] First, "a 'Polish style' nobility . . . hostile to the State, nostalgically attached to its ancient local prerogatives, and ready to reconquer an idealised past." Second, "a 'Prussian style' nobility that wished . . . to use the modernisation of the State for its own ends, to monopolise all public offices, and especially military grades, and to make service its new *raison d'être.*" And third, "an 'English style' nobility that favoured a parliamentary aristocracy in keeping with the new era."

The failure of any one of these three divisions of the elite to thoroughly dominate the development of society; the failure of the king to build a consensus around one position and one elite—all this, Furet argues, was a leading cause of the political and financial impotence that led to the Revolution. These three different elite positions were taken in regard to "the modernisation of the State"[29]—what I have been calling here "rationalization and ordering the world." It is an easy matter, moreover, to document at what point each of these elites abandoned the Revolution: the "Polish" in opposition from the start; the "Prussian" after the "end of feudalism" in August 1789 and the removal of the king to Paris in October; the "English," with Lafayette as its most famous representative, once all reasonable hope of a constitutional monarchy was lost.

Assuming Furet's analysis to be mostly correct, then a significant cause of the Revolution cannot be comprehended without understanding why none of these three attitudes toward modernization prevailed in the eighteenth century with either the nobility or the king: why France was trapped with no clear view, no effective consensus, of the future by those in power. Why, then, did the "Polish aristocracy" prevail in Poland and not in France? Why the dominance of the "Prussian nobility" in Prussia and Germany and not in France? And the same inquiry about "English style" aristocracy.

To use Tocqueville's vocabulary, some "instinctive urge" was pushing "all the authorities" toward centralization and rationalization—in France. From whence comes this "instinctive urge?" And why did it manifest itself so differently in the different nations of Europe? Not to even mention China, India, the Islamic world. We are back to Weber's great unanswered question: Why capitalism— that world historical event—arose in only one part of the world? I would, moreover, add "Modernity" to that inquiry. Even within Europe—the Western World—the discrepant attitudes toward modernization were remarkable: compare even ambivalent France in the eighteenth and nineteenth centuries to Russia, for instance, where Tolstoy's Levin exhausted and exasperated himself trying to "modernize" the mode of peasant agriculture.

To many readers, undoubtedly, all this pushing the questions of origins back several centuries may seem fatuous and fruitless. And yet, is it any more fatuous than the attempt to "interpret the French revolution,"[30] reveal the "origins of the French Revolution,"[31] or "rewrite the French Revolution,"[32] without, for instance, explaining why modernization was such an important part of the French eighteenth-century political and cultural agenda? Not to argue that important historical work on *causes* has been neglected. The last forty years has produced an extraordinary profitable harvest of historical insights about revolutionary history, the result, to a significant degree, of the demise of the Marxist hegemony over revolutionary historiography. At the moment, however, even though exemplary work continues to be done, we seem stalled. Various schools of explanation exist, but none seems to give a satisfactory answer as to why the Revolution happened, took the course it did, and experienced the catastrophic moment of the Terror. All I am suggesting, at this point, is that it may prove of great value to change perspectives. Instead of regarding modernization as an aspect of pre- and revolutionary history, it may prove deeply explanatory if we regard the Revolution as an aspect—indeed, a most significant aspect—of modernization and, consequently, of Modernity. The great history of Modernity has yet to be written. It is sure to illuminate the questions that remain of revolutionary history.

A NOTE ON THE TRANSITION
FROM PART I TO PART II

At this point in the work, the previously announced logic would call for a chapter on the last of the proposed fundamental aspects of a Stable Democratic Society, or Modernity: that is, Civilian Control of the Military. That particular social and political form, however, is so intimately related to the subject of Part II: the possible outcomes of the struggle for Modernity—most especially, the threat of Anarchy, Gangsterism, and Conservative Dictatorship—that is seems wise to postpone the discussion of Civilian Control until Part II, which follows.

PART II

THE POSSIBLE OUTCOMES OF THE
STRUGGLE FOR MODERNITY:
STABLE DEMOCRATIC SOCIETY, CONSERVATIVE
DICTATORSHIP, RELIGIOUS FUNDAMENTALISM,
ANARCHY, IDEOLOGICAL TERROR, GANGSTERISM

12

ANARCHY AND THE
FEAR OF ANARCHY

AN INTRODUCTION TO PART II

This chapter is being written during the week in 1997 when Mobutu of Zaire abandoned his capital to the successful rebels who had overthrown him. Mobutu was a monstrous political entity who milked and impoverished his country for over thirty years, becoming in the process one of the richest men in the world, with a fortune estimated in the billions. All this was accomplished by the exercise of a tyrannical dictatorship that methodically put down any opposition. He and his regime were a perfect representation of what I call Gangsterism or Warlordism, as one of the six possible outcomes after a nation begins the struggle for Modernity: one of the five possible perverse outcomes.

As yet, apparently, it is unknown what kind of polity the rebels, now empowered, intend for Zaire. The usefulness of the theoretical approach being elaborated here is that it underlines the point that the possibilities are not unlimited. It is highly unlikely that the victorious rebels will invent a political entity not included in this theoretical six. Anarchy may result if the rebel leaders fail to create some sort of unified power. The renewal of Gangsterism is possible if the new leaders merely put themselves in the place of Mobutu as the collectors of spoils. Islamic fundamentalism seems not to be a possibility in that part of the world, though we have numerous examples, in the present century, of this particular form of compromise with Modernity. Ideological Terror, at this late date, could only be of some Marxist variety. At the moment it seems doubtful even though, for years, the American CIA supported Mobutu through anxiety about that alternative. Conservative Dictatorship seems eminently possible and, perhaps, the best-to-be-hoped-for outcome. If the rebel leaders have the vision of rebuilding the country, and if they conceive—rightly or wrongly—that only they are truly capable of this endeavor, such a dictatorship is eminently possible. Barring the establishment currently of a Stable Democratic Society, which seems most unlikely, such a dictatorship could offer a development that would eventually lead to a democratic society (cf. Spain).

Africa in this century, most especially since the end of the second World War, has presented the picture of a whole continent struggling for Modernity. Success has been various, compromises abundant, and perverse polities only too frequent. I am far from being a historian of modern Africa, but the theoretical position being offered here would suggest that—since the struggle for Modernity is the overriding theme of political and social development—every African polity, at every historical point in this last half century, presents the aspect of one of the six possible outcomes delineated here or some amalgamation of two or three of them. A complex discussion of this, of course, lies beyond the capabilities of this writer.

For revolutionary France, however, there is here obviously much more to discuss. Of the six, two, Gangsterism and Religious Fundamentalism, were not real possibilities. Stable Democratic Society has been the essential, much elaborated topic of Part I. Ideological Terror deserves a whole section of its own, and Part III will be devoted to it. That leaves Anarchy and Conservative Dictatorship, both of which are intimately related to the need for Civilian Control of the Military, which has been postulated as one essential attribute of authentic Modernity. Such discussion defines the boundaries of Part II.

THE FEAR OF THE LOWER CLASSES

We live in strange times. In those nations that have achieved Modernity, for the first time in two hundred years, there is no perceived threat to the political hegemony of the bourgeois elite from the lower classes. Communism is gone. Revolutionary socialism no longer exists: certainly, the British Labor Party and "socialist" Sweden present no challenge to the established power. And in

America, where socialism never presented a serious threat to capitalism, even the labor movement is practically moribund. Many commentators, even some who have read no Freud, have observed that the Cold War being ended, there is no longer a severe external threat, all of which poses a problem of what to do about the seemingly necessary expression of social aggression. Almost no one, however, has examined what it means that Modern democracies no longer face any *internal* threat. It was almost exactly two hundred years from the fall of the Bastille to the Velvet Revolution. During all that time, Marx's "spectre haunting Europe"[1] had, with greater or lesser intensity, disturbed the sleep of the ruling elites. No more. With the impotence of the Communist Parties in France and Italy; with Mitterand's "socialism" and the British Labor Party's program reminding one more of FDR than Engels or even Leon Blum, though serious political struggles still exist within Modern democratic society, there has ceased to be any *class* opposition. No fear exists that the deprived classes in society will rise up and overthrow. Benjamin Constant would be amazed.

There was no widespread anarchy during French Revolutionary times. There was, regardless, a pervasive fear of anarchy, which arose from three sources. First, the panic over the elimination of monarchical omnipotence that has been elaborated previously. Second, a substantial number of lawless acts were committed: in the countryside even before the meeting of the Estates General, and then accelerating after Bastille; and also, the people-in-the-streets of Paris taking the Revolution in their own hands and sticking the heads of their opponents on the ends of pikes. Three times they moved the Revolution "forward" without the previous permission of the nationally elected deputies: moving the king to Paris, overthrowing and deposing him, and generating the coup against the Gironde. The one act that took on the greatest symbolic significance of societal chaos was the September Massacres, which gave rise to the condemnatory epithet *"septembriseur,"* the very picture of a murderous anarchist, a *"buveur de sang"*[2]—a drinker of blood.

All of this, when combined with other factors, resulted in the third cause of the fear of anarchy: the belief that lower classes presented a threat to the new bourgeois order. Even the Jacobin dictatorship, it must be remembered, found it necessary to repress the political power of the sans-culottes. There was no organized socialist or communist movement during revolutionary times: no coherent theory of proletarian uprising, even among the *enragés* or the Babeufists. That did not safeguard the political elites from the intense anxiety that those near the bottom of society, if they could not take and exercise power, could certainly spread anarchy.

It was remarkable how widespread and pervasive was this alarm about lower-class anger and violence. The question of the legitimacy of economic inequality was immediately raised. The legitimacy of "property"—which really was a symbol of unequal economic advantage—for some reason had to be defended and reiterated. Once political equality had become an ideal, a telos of social development, the question of economic disparity took on a certain urgency. And the French Revolution had raised the banner of political equality with an intensity that no other nation exhibited up to that time or for some time thereafter. "Equality of [political] power," wrote Lord Acton, "readily suggests equality of property."[3] That suggestion does not have to be taken up, but it is significant how much discussion it gave rise to in revolutionary times: an important part of the nineteenth-century moral agenda was already in place. Tocqueville was keenly aware of how one kind of equality gives possibility and urgency to another. Speaking of the February 1848 revolution, but applicable to the first rumblings during the great Revolution, he commented:

> At first the people hoped to help themselves by changing the political institutions, but after each change they found that their lot was not bettered, or that it had not improved fast enough to keep pace with their headlong desires. Inevitably they were bound to discover sooner or later that what held them back in their place was not the constitution of the government, but the unalterable laws that constitute society itself; and it was natural for them to ask whether they did not have the power and the right to change these too, as they had changed the others. And to speak specifically about property, which is, so to speak, the foundation of our social order, when all the privileges that cover and conceal the privilege of property had been abolished and property remained as the main obstacle to equality among men and seemed to be the only sign thereof, was it not inevitable, I do not say that it should be abolished in its turn, but that at least the idea of abolishing it should strike minds that had no part in its enjoyment?[4]

Nobody quite knew, of course, what it might mean to "abolish property" until the first half of the nineteenth century produced socialist and communist theory (Saint-Simon, Marx). During the first Revolution, this radical discussion revolved around the question of complete economic equality in contradistinction to the elimination of great disparities of wealth, or "leveling." The concept that private property could be totally eliminated was already alive in the eighteenth century, causing Rousseau to advocate the more reasonable principle of leveling: "My purpose is not to destroy private property but to confine it within narrow limits."[5] Such degree of equalizing was, for sensitive and compassionate reformers, both a moral and social necessity: "I can hardly believe," Robespierre announced in April '93, "it took a revolution to teach the world that extreme disparities of wealth lie at the root of many ills and crimes."[6]

Robespierre's answer to the problem was remarkably reasonable and not radical but proved to be enormously difficult to institute in the bourgeois society to which Modernity gave birth. "What is the first object of society?" he asked in December '92. "It is to maintain the imprescriptible rights of man. What is the first of these rights? That of existence. The first social law is then that which guarantees to all the members of society the means to exist; all the others are subordinate to this."[7] It is clear that "the means to exist" did not signify existence at an impoverished, animal level. It meant, for Robespierre and for those who cared about it, an existence that included the capacity for citizenship.

What person who believed passionately in the Rights of Man and celebrated their establishment into law—as the majority of French elites did at the time—could possibly disagree with Robespierre's right to exist? And yet, this tragic moral splitting is of the very essence of stable democratic society: the one legitimate outcome of the struggle for Modernity. Two hundred years after Robespierre's plea, one of the richest capitalist countries in the world, after fifty years of incredible economic prosperity, is still continually debating what is the *minimum* "safety net" to be allowed to the poor.

And that moral splitting: celebration of universal rights and of equality and yet disregard, or even contempt, for the poor, must inevitably produce anxiety (even though deeply unconscious) that these very poor will rise up, demand their rights, and seize the property of the well-off. Before looking at the data that would support the contention that such fear was pervasive at the time, it is of interest to note that Robespierre himself was still enough of a bourgeois—or a realist, as the case may be—to oppose a complete leveling of economic circumstance. At the time certain radicals raised the cry of total confiscation and redistribution of the land, which went under the slogan of the *loi agraire* (the "agrarian law"), harkening back to ancient Rome and the attempts of the Gracchi to correct the great disparity of land ownership and land poverty among Roman citizens. In his April '93 speech, Robespierre unequivocally declared: "You must know that the agrarian law of which there has been so much talk, is a bogey created by rogues to frighten fools. . . . We are not less conscious that the realization of an equality of possession is a visionary's dream."[8] His own vision, nonetheless, was that human rights were superior to property rights and he, thus, subsequently proposed a declaration "to the effect that property was not a natural and imprescriptible right but a social institution guaranteed by law."[9]

In all the research that has been done for this book, I have been unable to discover who were the large number of people demanding the *loi agraire* to the point where they terrified both the conservative and the radical bourgeoisie. It leads one to suspect that, possibly, the fear of the *loi agraire* was as positively founded as was the fear of brigands that led to *le grand peur*.* Whether realistic, or significantly paranoid, intense anxiety there was, leading the Convention on March 18, 1793 (before the expulsion of the Gironde or the establishment of the Terror) to decree: "the punishment of death against whomever will propose *une loi agraire* or any other proposal subversive of territorial, commercial, and industrial property."[11] Three years later, after Thermidor but before the arrest of Babeuf for his "communist conspiracy," in April 1796, the condemnation to death was even more elaborate in a new decree: "They are culpable of a crime against the interior security of the Republic and against the individual security of its citizens and will be punished by the penalty of death, in conformity to article 612 of the Code of criminal offences and punishments, all those who by their discourse or by their published writings, either distributed or publicly posted, advocate the dissolution of the natural representation . . . or the pillage or the redistribution of particular properties under the name of the agrarian laws or in any other manner."[12] Neither the American nor the English revolutions had to deal with panic about the revenge of the lower classes to the intense degree as did the French. It is no wonder that the bourgeois elites should have longed for a conservative dictatorship that would allay that anxiety.

The *loi agraire* was one aspect of what can only be described as "class-conflict rhetoric"—that asserts that the upper classes are the enemies of the poorer— beginning as early as 1790 with Robespierre, who had no reluctance to set the moral struggle in *class* terms and coming to a climax under the Terror and the repression of the revolts against the central government in 1793–1794. Nothing brought the extreme radicals (*enragés*, etc.) and the merely radical bourgeoisie (Robespierre, Saint-Just, etc.) so close together as this rhetoric of class struggle.

---

*Mathiez, in his attempt to establish the concept that "the agrarian law which alarmed the Girondins was neither a myth nor a phantom"—namely, that it was a real threat—can only cite a few obscure writers who made such demand. His point would have carried much more weight if he could have made reference to some of the most famous activists on the extreme left: Hébert, Roux, Leclerc, or Marat, but such evidence was not, and is not, available.[10]

From the extreme left, we are not surprised to hear the most violent class antagonism. The early days of September 1793 saw the beginnings of a popular insurrection in Paris, led in good part by Hébert, which marched on the Assembly demanding certain radical economic and political measures. Chaumette, a leader of the Paris Commune and a charismatic figure for the sans-culottes, at one moment got up on a table in front of the crowd besieging the Convention: "I too have been poor and so I know what poverty means! We have here an open war on the rich against the poor; they want to crush us. Well, we must forestall them, we must crush them ourselves, we have the power in our hands."[13] That night one of the Paris sections (that of the Sans-culottes) declared itself in insurrection, not against the Convention nor the State but against the rich.[14]

Joseph Fouché, in an age of brilliant chameleons and survivors, was possibly—with the exception of Talleyrand—the most magnificent survivor of all. Ultimately, he played a significant part in the coup of Napoleon and served the dictator as minister of police and minister of the interior. He began his career, however, close to the Gironde and subsequently allied himself with the views of the Hébertists.[15] Sent on a mission to the Nièvre and Allier in September '93, his rhetoric and actions took on a class-warfare aspect and he "ordered that 'unfortunate citizens be clothed, fed and housed at the expense of the excess of the rich' because 'the wealth in the hands of individuals is only a deposit which the nation has a right to dispose of.' Other deputies such as André Dumont on a mission in the Somme and Oise and Joseph Le Bon in the Pas-de-Calais and the Nord expressed almost identical beliefs."[16]

What is so surprising about the French Revolution—and also, so confusing and requiring a very complex explanation—is that this same kind of class-warfare rhetoric was retailed, not only in the midst of the protoproletariat by those seeking the in-the-streets leadership of the sans-culottes (Chaumette, above), but by the *moyen* bourgeoisie itself, even in the heart of the national legislature. If Robespierre had been a lone radical voice, we would need only a psychological explanation, but when a man destined to become the virtual dictator of the revolutionary nation, rides to power, in part, on a wave of class-conflict exhortation, then a very complex social psychology is imperative if we would understand the condition of the culture. *Item.* [Published Speech of December 1790.] "It is the people who are good, patient, generous; our revolution bears witness to this, as is shown both by the crimes of its enemies and its own innumerable heroic deeds in the recent past, which came naturally to it. The rich and powerful thirst after honours, wealth and sensual enjoyment. The interest and desire of the people is that of nature itself, of humanity; it is the general interest. The interest and desire of the rich and powerful is that of ambition, pride, greed and the wildest fantasies of passions that are fatal to the happiness of society as a whole. The abuses that have ravaged society were always their doing. These men have always been the scourge of the people. Who made our glorious revolution? Was it the rich? Was it the people? *Only the people could will it and achieve it. For the same reason the people alone can maintain it.*"[17] *Item.* [Speech published in April 1791.] "The abuses are the work and the domaine of the rich, they are the scourge of the people: the interest of the people is the general interest, that of the rich is the particular interest; and you wish to render the people nothing and the rich all-powerful!"[18] *Item.* [Speech of January 2, 1792.] "A revolution . . . begins with the nobles, the clergy, the wealthy, whom the people supports when its interests coincide with theirs in resistance to the dominant power, that of the monarchy. . . . The people appeared on the scene only later. Those who gave the first impulses have long since repented, or at least wished to stop the revolution when they saw that the people might recover its sovereignty. But it was they who started it."[19] A brilliant "Marxist" class analysis, long before Marx.

One did not have to be a reactionary bourgeois, intent on reversing the Revolution and restoring the *ancien régime,* to be frightened when such a man was waxing toward the highest power in alliance with, and with the support of, the people-in-the-streets of Paris. Anybody with any foresight might tremble at the future prospect. Jérôme Pétion, who had been a delegate of the Third Estate and had been elected to the Convention in 1792 and designated its first President, was in the camp of the Gironde and, as the struggle between the Gironde and the future Jacobin dictatorship was coming to a climax, in April 1793, addressed a *Letter to the Parisians*: a wake-up call to the bourgeoisie to recognize the class-warfare nature of the current situation:

> Your property is threatened, yet you close your eyes to this danger. War is being stirred up between the haves and the have nots, yet you do nothing to avert it. A few schemers, a handful of factious persons, are laying down the law to you and dragging you into violent and ill-advised measures; yet you have not the courage to resist; you dare not appear in your sections to combat them. You see all rich and peaceable persons leaving Paris, you see Paris being reduced to impotence; yet you remain calm. . . . Parisians, shake off your lethargy at last, and send these poisonous insects back into their holes.[20]

Mathiez comments that a year before this, Pétion had urged the rich and poor members of the Third Estate to unite against their common enemy. "But in

Petion's eyes the enemy was not longer aristocracy, but anarchy."[21] The formula that was to dominate the anxiety syndrome in bourgeois culture for almost the next two hundred years was now firmly in place: *Political power to the lower classes = anarchy.*

And the class-warfare tonality was more than rhetoric. As the political culture hurled its way toward Terror, and after the establishment of the Terror itself, more and more to be "revolutionary" meant to attack the rich in defense of the poor. The provinces led the way, since they did not have a sitting central government to inhibit them, as did the Parisian sans-culottes. Typical experiences were those of the radicals from Marseille, beginning as early as 1792, who were not content to operate only within their own city but actually invaded neighboring communes in order to extract reparations from "bourgeois-aristocrats," or levy indemnities on the rich. At Salon, in early 1793, months before the establishment of the Jacobin dictatorship in Paris, a terror against the bourgeois elite was imposed with all the necessary violence. Forced loans extracted, domiciles pillaged, imprisonments imposed, and one priest and three recalcitrant bourgeois executed. Once the conservative elements had reasserted their control, a trial was held of these *"commissaires"* from Marseille, wherein testimony asserted they had "preached unceasingly against the rich and the bourgeoisie." One was quoted as saying that one of these invaders had declared: "We must destroy them; we must not leave one of these bourgeoisie alive."[22]

Hundreds, if not thousands, of incidents of a class-warfare nature occurred in Paris in the terror years of 1793–1794. Each of the forty-eight Paris sections had the capacity to order the arrest of "counterrevolutionary" persons. One can imagine what kind of abuse this resulted in, and so much of it had an anti-rich, antibourgeois resonance. Two typical incidents: September 18, 1793, the *comité revolutionnaire* of the Mutius-Scaevola section "ordered the arrest of the chief secretary of the Paris police, Duval, on two charges: showing contempt for the assemblies of the Section, and for enjoying a private income of 2,000 *livres* a year."[23] In the early winter of '94, Pierre Bequerel was incarcerated after a police raid in the Palais-Royal for "having said he was living off his private income."[24] All this cannot quite accurately be described as "anarchy," but it certainly was an in-between state, where hundreds of local agencies were taking "the law" into their own hands.

In the spring of '93, as a result of the death struggle between the Gironde and the Jacobins, certain communes of France revolted against the central government and installed anti-Jacobin, probourgeois governments: the so-called Federalist revolt. In time, all of these were repressed, and the power of the

National Convention reasserted. In certain cases, most particularly that of Lyon, the aftermath of the triumph of the Convention took on almost massacre proportions. The victims were overwhelmingly to be the better-off citizens. Lyon was not only to be reincorporated into the revolutionary government, but it was also to be punished for its crime of rebellion. Collot d'Herbois was chosen representative of the Committee of Public Safety designated to carry out this retribution. Houses were to be destroyed. The Committee had indicated that only houses of the rich should suffer this penalty, but Collot was a "fanatic," and, "the cause for which [he] labored was the struggle against the bourgeoisie."[25] His intended destruction of edifices was to go much beyond the instructions from Paris: "He prepared to smash the city with mines and artillery fire."[26]

As an aid in the work of destructive retribution, Collot and Fouché created a Temporary Commission to carry out this "justice," which drew up an "Instruction to the Constitutional Authorities." This document had a remarkable nineteenth-century class-warfare ring to it: "According to the Instruction the Revolution was especially made for the 'immense class of the poor.' The authors found 'a shocking disproportion' between toil and income. They assailed the bourgeoisie; and they cried to the working class somewhat in the manner of Marx: 'you have been oppressed; you must crush your oppressors!' "[27] The proof was in the eating: by April 1794, almost 2,000 executions had taken place, according to Palmer's figures, more than 10 percent of all the executions under the Terror in the whole of France. Of the total of all executions in the country, 28 percent were from the middle and upper class. In Lyon, the figure was 63 percent.[28]

There was a history in France of peasant rebellions against the rich and the manor houses going back, at least, to the fourteenth century. In a way, the peasant riots during revolutionary times were nothing that new. What is remarkable about the incidents being described here is that the class-warfare was taking place within the cities, with the protoproletariat as its soldiers, and the bourgeoisie as the *stated* object of attack. This was the birth of a conflict that was destined to become a major problematic for Modernity, despite its great moral achievements in so many other areas.

As the Terror accelerated, as the Jacobin dictatorship felt, more and more, that it needed the enthusiastic, unambivalent support of the sans-culottes against its many enemies, its opposition to the spirit of the *loi agraire* weakened, and the redistribution of income was advanced to the political agenda. It is a most important question, and difficult to answer, as to what was the true motivation of the terrorists in this circumstance. Was it merely, or primarily, a play for political support from the lower classes? Or/and did they feel real pity and compassion for the poor and suffering? Or/and were they so into killing and annihilation that, having eliminated the aristocracy and most of their democratic allies, their appetite could only be assuaged by the destruction of the upper bourgeoisie? Or was it an act of suicidal self-destruction, wherein they brought upon their heads the powerful enmity of a class of people who, up until then, had been anxiously content to support the Revolution and the Terror? Most probably it was a very complex mixture of all four motives: the very mixture that makes an ideological terrorist.

In any event, on February 26, '94, Saint-Just delivered an extraordinary speech to the Convention, with the obvious support of Robespierre and the inner circle of the dictatorship.[29] No republic could survive, he postulated, unless it created institutions that would redeem the morals of the citizens, translating them into naturally virtuous beings. "A State in which such institutions are lacking is but an illusory republic. And since everybody interprets liberty as meaning the independence of his passions and his avarice, the spirit of conquest and selfishness is established between one citizen and another, and the individual idea of his own liberty formed by every man according to his interests leads to the slavery of all." [One may remark, parenthetically, that all the philosophical and moral criticisms of liberalism and radical individualism of the following two hundred years have added very little to this essential critique.]

Then came the ideological terrorist solution to this human problem. Until the institutions had been created that would expunge selfish individualism from the hearts of men, the Terror must be continued. For any thinking person, that meant there was no end in sight. A beginning may be made, however, Saint-Just insisted, by destroying the selfish among us and distributing their property to the poor. "Wealth is in the hands of a fairly large number of enemies of the Revolution; the people, the workers are placed by their necessities in dependence upon their enemies. Do you imagine that an empire can exist if the structure of society favours those who are opposed to the very form of its government? Those who make revolutions by halves are only digging their own graves. The Revolution is leading us to recognize the principle that he who has shown himself the enemy of his country cannot own property in it. . . . The property of the patriots is sacred, but the property of conspirators exists for the needy. The needy are the powers of the earth. They have the right to speak with authority to the governments which neglect them."

A decree was immediately passed that called for confiscation of the property of all people considered enemies of the Republic. Five days later, every commune was ordered to prepare a list of the needy, and vigilante committees instructed to prepare a list of everyone imprisoned since May 1789 for political reasons, all for the purpose of transferring property from the latter to the former. It was, as Mathiez comments, "a fresh revolution."[30] "Neither the Hébertists nor the Enragés," he concludes, "had ever dreamed of such a radical measure, such a vast transference of property from one political class to another."[31]

There was no other country on the face of the earth at that time—not even the emerging democracies of America, England, Holland, and Geneva—where this kind of class-warfare rhetoric existed except in very small pockets of the society. There was no other antimonarchical democratic revolution that was made or pushed along by this kind of anti-rich, antiproperty ideology. There was no other society in which the *bourgeois* leaders of the revolution assumed they would strengthen their political position by this kind of pandering to the economic egalitarian fantasies of the poor. To understand the course of the *French* revolution, we must go beyond the great impact of progressive Enlightenment, which affected all the emerging democratic societies, and look at what was unique to France: a protoproletariat that had the courage to use its powers of numbers to change the world and a radical, ideological section of the bourgeoisie that was prepared to ally itself with this "anarchic" power. There is absolutely no surprise that the propertied classes should become panic-stricken and look for any means to restore "order."

Not only was there class-conflict between "rich" and "poor," but, also, the history of the provincial Jacobin clubs reveals a serious political struggle between the upper and lower bourgeoisie. Here, again, one cannot imagine that kind of split in any other country in the eighteenth century, except for France. In the city of Lyon, for instance, during the period of the Constituent Assembly (1789–1791), there were two clubs that Kennedy describes as "moderate, elitist": the Society of Friends of the Revolution and the Society of Friends of the Constitution. The latter was the official Jacobin affiliate. The famous Girondist Roland and François-Xavier Lanthenas were not satisfied, however, because both societies "excluded the poor," and they proceeded to establish a new club in September 1790: Popular Society of Friends of the Constitution, wherein the dues were set very low. By 1791 it had 3,000 members.[32] Neither Roland nor Lanthenas can be even closely described as members of the *petite* bourgeoisie;

neither became a terrorist; and yet, both were willing to ally themselves with and use politically those in the lower ranges of society.

As the Revolution progressed, this breach widened, and evidence grows of class rhetoric, and even violence, directed at the *haut* bourgeoisie by bourgeois of a lower condition. We even get "class-consciousness" against the bourgeoisie, as in this pronouncement from the club in Avignon in a circular to its affiliates: "Born in that class called the *haut tiers,* they fought against aristocracy not to procure general equality, but to insure their own supremacy. They were supportive of their constitution before August 10 [the overthrow of the king] because it favored the rich."[33] An analysis that could warm an unreconstructed Marxist's heart.

The greatest efflorescence of lower bourgeois political power occurred in Marseille. In the winter of 1792–93, four hundred members of the Jacobin club were purged. Many, many more enrollments of "sans-culottes," subsequent to this, increased the power of the club. "The radicals who directed the Marseille club in 1792–93," Kennedy writes, "were quintessential lesser men of the moyenne bourgeoisie."[34] Their prime political targets were those in the upper ranks of this same class category. The Marseille club became the center of political activity, and a commanding power, for the whole region. "In almost every town, so it seems, there were rival 'bourgeois' and 'popular' societies. . . . Marseille meddled regularly in these disputes [between the clubs], taking the side of the 'popular' faction. Indeed, its 'commissaires' waged a kind of class war against the bourgeoisie of rural Provence."[35]

Illegal violence was not excluded. Commissars from Marseille, accompanied by a contingent of national guardsmen, marched into one commune to break up a meeting of "bourgeois-aristocrats." Others forcibly entered another city, deposed the "bourgeois-aristocrats" from office, and formed a popular club. All violence during the Revolution had a tendency to accelerate; the Marseillais were no exception to this inclination. Not being content to intervene in the politics of certain communes, they began extracting reparations from the *haut* bourgeois citizens, forcing them to pay what was, in reality, a kind of protection money.[36] The implication of not paying, clearly, was that even worse penalties would be imposed.

Who were these "quintessential lesser men of the moyenne bourgeoisie"? What was it that made them decide that the sans-culottes were their natural political allies and the *haut tiers* their enemies? Can one imagine the *moyenne* bourgeoisie of England or America in the eighteenth century—or in any century—

taking a similar position and not allying themselves with the upper bourgeoisie and fearing the protoproletariat? What was it in French political culture that made this happen? Just as there is a theory of "American exceptionalism" [no king; no aristocracy; unlimited territory] that made the road to democracy and Modernity so easy in this blessed land, just so, maybe there was also a "French exceptionalism" [people-in-the-streets, sans-culottes, and a *moyenne* bourgeoisie expressing political agency by allying themselves with lower classes] that produced the exactly opposite effect: a violent, treacherous struggle for democracy and Modernity. Looking down the road from revolutionary times, it can be observed that there was nothing in the rest of the nineteenth-century modern capitalist world that came close to the Paris Commune of 1871. And if we begin to understand all this, might it make more comprehensible Robespierre and Saint-Just—who came from these same *moyenne* ranks—and the great Terror that was their creation?

What is certain is that the fear of the lower classes, of "leveling," of the disappearance of the sanctity of property became a permanent aspect of French culture—permanent, or at least alive for 175 years. It is remarkable how early these anxieties expressed themselves, obviously because something special was perceived within the culture. It is of value to repeat here a reference given much earlier in this work. In December 1788, before all the action began, the five princes of the blood memorialized Louis on the danger of compromising with the Third Estate, with an almost unbelievable prescience:

> The unhappy progress of this effervescence is such that opinions, which a little while ago would have appeared the most reprehensible, appear today just and reasonable. What today makes respectable people indignant will in a little while perhaps be accepted as regular and legitimate. Who can say where this temerity will end? The rights of the throne have been called into question; the rights of the privileged orders are subjects of popular debate; soon the rights of property will be attacked; the inequality of fortunes will be presented as an object of reform; already the proposition has been made to abolish feudal rights on the ground that these rights are oppressive and barbarous.[37]

Once so much of this had become a reality, the king overthrown and the Republic proclaimed, those who represented the elite of the bourgeoisie felt impelled to sound the identical alarm. In a speech to the Paris Jacobins, in October '92, Brissot, a chief of the Gironde, anathematized the "levellers":

The disorganizers are those who want to level everything: property, the amenities of life, the price of food, the diverse services rendered to society. . . . who want to level also the talents, the knowledge, the virtues because they possess nothing of all these![38]

The continuity of this mindset, wherein those who, on the one hand, were passionately committed to political democracy and, on the other hand, became almost panicky at the prospect of economic equality, was sustained by the great Tocqueville himself. On the eve of the 1848 revolution, October '47, Tocqueville and some of his parliamentary colleagues decided to publish a manifesto, written by Tocqueville, in anticipation of the next legislative session and commissioned Tocqueville to compose it. The very economic equality that he had pronounced such a political and social virtue in America became for him, in France, "the old democratic disease of the times":

Soon the political struggle will be between the Haves and the Have-nots; property will be the great battlefield; and the main political questions will turn on the more or less profound modifications of the rights of property owners that are to be made. Then we shall again see great public agitations and great political parties.

Why is everybody not struck by the signs that are the harbingers of this future? Do you think it is by chance, or by some passing caprice of the human spirit, that on every side we see strange doctrines appearing, which have different names, but which all deny the right of property, or at least, tend to limit, diminish or weaken the exercise of that right? Who can fail to recognize in this last symptom the old democratic disease of the times, whose crisis is perhaps approaching.[39]

Once the Chamber of Deputies was in session, the great chronicler of democracy delivered to it a speech on January 29, 1848 that elaborated the very basic doctrine of fear of anarchy; that is, revolt of the lower classes:

It is said there is no danger because there is no riot, and because there is no visible disorder on the surface of society, we are far from revolution.

Gentlemen, allow me to say that I think you are mistaken. True, there is no actual disorder, but disorder has penetrated far into men's minds. See what is happening among the working classes who are, I realize, quiet now. It is true that they are not now tormented by what may properly be called political passions to the extent they once were; but do you not see that their passions have changed from political to social? Do you not see that opinions and ideas are gradually spreading among them that tend not simply to the overthrow of such-and-such

laws, such-and-such a minister, or even such-and-such a government, but rather
to the overthrow of society, breaking down the basis on which it now rests? Do
you not hear what is being said every day among them? Do you not hear them
constantly repeating that all the people above them are incapable and unworthy
to rule them? That the division of property in the world up to now is unjust?
That property rests on the bases of inequity? And do you not realize that when
such opinions take root and spread, sinking deeply into the masses, they must
sooner or later (I do not know when, I do not know how) bring in their train the
most terrifying of revolutions?[40]

People faced with intense anxiety do not remain passive; they do something.
They defend against that anxiety. Some defenses are productive, even morally
progressive. Others are destructive, either of others or of the self. Still others are
complex compromises between productive and destructive forms, such as, in this
case of anxiety about lower-class anarchy, resort to conservative dictatorship,
which was so important in France in the hundred years or so after 1789. Before
looking at this latter mode, I want to touch on other reactions to the perceived
threat of class anarchy.

MECHANISMS FOR DEALING WITH
THE THREAT OF ANARCHY

1. *The Ritual Reiteration of the Sanctity of Property and the Continual Threat to Its Existence.*
A belief in the sanctity of property became a shibboleth of the nonradical political culture in revolutionary times, and the public announcement of one's belief
became a testimony of support for the position that the Revolution had gone
far enough and that what was now required was a stabilized society. So incessant
was the necessity to reiterate that position that we may conclude there was a
pervasive anxiety that property would be overthrown along with "feudalism"
and monarchy. It would be an interesting experiment in comparative history to
determine whether, in England and America, this same ritual repetition of the
sacred-property mantra was the case or not. If not, it would add credence to the
idea that there was something special in French class-conflict anxiety.

Antoine Joseph Barnave, an unambivalent maker of the first revolution, remained a convinced monarchist and, after the king's flight to Varennes in June
1791, defended both the king and monarchy as a defense against the anarchic
destruction of property. "Are we going to end the Revolution or are we going

to begin anew? . . . For those who may wish to go further, what other 'night of August 4,' can there be but laws against property?"[41] "One step more would be a deadly and reprehensible act, one step more in the direction of liberty would be the destruction of royalty, one in the direction of equality, would be the destruction of property."[42] Obviously, for Bernave, the Revolution had to stop in order not to traduce these sacred grounds.

The first meeting of the Convention, after the dethronement of the king, took place on September 20, 1792. The very next day, Danton delivered his speech certifying the sanctity of property. The convention responded with a resolution declaring that both property and personal security "were placed under the safeguard of the nation."[43] As the struggle between the Mountain and the Gironde became more and more perilous, the Girondist Vergniaud, in a reply to Robespierre on April 10, '93, saw fit to emphasize his belief in the perpetuation of property, and thereby, cast suspicion that "the incorruptible" was not firmly in that bourgeois camp.[44] The implication being that the Gironde stood for the stabilization of society, and Robespierre and the Jacobins for more and more revolution.

In France, it seems, as soon as there was a challenge to authoritarian or monarchical government, the specter of class overthrow took on new life and the sanctity of property was raised high as the banner of defense. In the winter of 1798, a few months before the coup d'état of Floréal, which was directed against the growing power of the phoenix-like Jacobins, Benjamin Constant gave a speech, subsequently widely publicized, that Isser Woloch asserts became "for historians a classic exposition of the Directory's anti-Jacobinism," wherein Constant reiterated the property-doctrine with no apparent imaginative gift: "All interests are grouped around property. The slightest blow against it will resound in all parts of the empire; whoever disposes of the rich menaces the poor; whoever proscribes opulence, conspires against modest fortune."[45] Tocqueville's Manifesto of 1847, previously quoted, reflected equally dangerous times. The rumblings of coming revolution could not be denied: the July Monarchy, another French version of Conservative Dictatorship, was in deep trouble. This time, Tocqueville feared, it would be a total, not partial, revolution:

> The time is coming when the country will again be divided between two great parties. The French Revolution, which abolished all privileges and destroyed all exclusive rights, did leave one, that of property. Property holders must not delude themselves about the strength of their position, or suppose that, because it has so

far nowhere been surmounted, the right to property is an insurmountable barrier; for our age is not like any other. When the right to property was merely the basis of many other rights, it would be easily defended, or rather, it was not attacked: it was like the encircling wall of a society whose other rights were the advanced defence posts; the shots did not reach it; there was not even a serious intention to reach it. But now that the right to property is the last remnant of a destroyed aristocratic world, and it alone still stands, an isolated privilege in a levelled society; when it no longer has the cover of other more doubtful and more hated rights, it is in great danger; it alone now has to face the direct and incessant impact of democratic opinions.[46]

Of course, Tocqueville is speaking of the immediate pre-1848 revolutionary period, but the hypothesis being explicated here is that the same anxiety, though possibly to a lesser degree of intensity, was active and important from 1789 onward. In writing of Barnave and his failure to create a potent political consensus behind a conservative-liberal monarchical position, François Furet lists certain specific political failures (for instance, the inability to gain the confidence of the king and queen), but he concludes: "The central reason for his failure was that France in that summer [of '91] was still the France of 1789: the propertied class was not yet mobilized by the threat from below."[47] The energy behind their eventual mobilization was, naturally, the essential anxiety about property and lower-class anarchy. Once the threat was clearly perceived, the solution in the form of Conservative Dictatorship, the period of which extended from 1799 to 1871, became both "necessary" and appropriate. The great nineteenth-century question, in both France and England, was how to allow political liberty for the lower classes and yet assure the sanctity of property. The very existence of democratic society demanded a solution to that assumed dilemma.

2. *Universal Education as an Answer to Class Anarchy.* Three separate and distinct impulses were propelling Modern culture toward free, universal education. First, the rationalizing force that assumed the more efficient, the more educated the society was, on the whole, the more powerful it would be. Second, the radical democratic view that conceived of education as one of the essential human rights—an egalitarian thrust. And third, the rational defensive view that recognized that if political democracy was going to become a "necessity," then education could keep the lower classes from acting like barbarians: education could convert most people into seekers of the bourgeois life. All three of these combined to make free, universal education a prime item on the modern agenda, so

that even those societies that produced complex compromises with Modernity retained very little ambivalence about instituting universal education, at the least, up to a certain age for boys.

The motives impelling any individual, or group of individuals, to support the spread of education might combine two, or even three, of the incentives given previously. The Jacobin view joined the radical egalitarian with the commitment to efficiency and social power. The Girondin position—and the Gironde was as committed to universal education as its radical rivals—grew out of a concern for human rights and a fear of lower-class barbarism and anarchy.

As to the first consideration, that of promoting knowledge and overcoming ignorance, it is significant that at the same time that French society was moving in the direction of strengthening the educational system, exactly the same process was underway in Prussia, hardly a leader in democratic or Enlightenment culture. Starting in the 1790s, there was a serious and powerful movement, most especially against rural "ignorance and superstition," that concentrated on state intervention to improve the quality of teachers, "a cause notably advanced during Humboldt's brief ministry after 1806. State penetration thus converged around the status and pay of the schoolmaster for whom Prussian reformers had even greater aspirations than their French counterparts."[48] A wonderful demonstration of the autonomous nature of the separate aspects of Modernity. The roads to Modernity were several and various; rationalization and social power could be pursued for their own sakes without bothering—for the moment, at least— with the disorganizing effects of democratic rights.

That universal, free education was concomitant with democratic equality, and necessary to it, was the logic of the Jacobin view. The most complete Jacobin plan for education was that constructed by Lepeletier that Robespierre presented to the Convention on July 13, 1793. Reflecting Lepletier's view, he declared education to be "the revolution of the poor."[49] A republic required republicans, which, in turn, required education: "It is no longer a question of forming gentlemen . . . but rather citizens."[50] The plan, on the whole, had a remarkable Platonic *Republic* quality to it: the basic values that an individual would carry through life would be inculcated by the fatherland: "At five years, *la patrie* will receive the infant from the hands of nature; at twelve years, it will render it to society."[51] The plan itself provided for free, universal education during those seven years (six for girls).

Some of the Paris sections dominated by sans-culottes did not wait for the national government to act. In March 1793, for instance, the patriotic society of the Luxembourg section decided that it would teach boys and girls, between age six and twelve, to read and to comprehend what it meant to be remarkably moral citizens. The idealism and the optimism expressed are both stirring and saddening: the task for society was to prove much more difficult than the writing of preambles:

> Education will be based on explaining to children their duties and obligations toward their country and their parents, to inculcate the manners and attitudes which they must aim for in order to be useful members of society; we will nurture their natural goodness, teach them pity, respect for the aged. . . . We shall show them by suitable examples the purpose of every society, and the various forms of government which might be adopted; above all, we shall teach them about government based on freedom and equality. We shall explain to them natural laws, political laws and civil laws. To this will be added the definition of sovereignty, of the will of the people, of freedom, of equality, of the Republic; and we shall tell them about the horrors attached to all tyrannical government and about the happiness which naturally emanates from republican government.[52]

To a great extent, the Girondins were as committed to the idea of universal, *free* education as the Mountain. Unlike the radical democrats, however, they made a point of judging harshly those who, having been given the opportunity to make something of their own lives, refused that possibility and lived on the margins of society. Wanderers, idlers, and bohemians were stigmatized in their rhetoric.[53] The stated ideal, nevertheless, was that universal education would provide every citizen the chance of developing his/her capacities and talents to the limit. Knowing that there was also a cautious element in the Girondin psychology, it is a reasonable assumption that they also regarded education as civilizing the democratic process, as providing a barrier to social anarchy. The Girondin Masuyer presented a remarkable memorandum on national education:

> If all men are equal in rights, it is necessary that education be public and available to all. . . . For that, it is necessary that it be free because the poor do not have the means to pay for it. If then we create a mode of instruction that is beyond the capacity of the poor, the poor cease to be equal in rights with the rich, and thus we vitiate the first law of equality, of that Holy Equality, the fundamental basis of all social order, the foundation on which we ought to erect the French constitution and without which our Republic cannot exist.[54]

Even after Thermidor, a serious attempt was continued to create a modern, universal system of education. The Lackland Law of November '94 committed the national government to provide every commune of a thousand or more citizens with a primary school, and a schoolmaster and schoolmistress paid by the central authority. The curriculum was to include: "reading, writing, arithmetic, the Declaration of the Rights of Man, the Constitution, republican morality, the principles of the French language, elements of geography, the history of 'free peoples,' and notions about natural phenomena."[55]

The first great attempt to create a new democratic world, however, proved to be a chimera. As the Thermidorian period advanced, the will weakened and the cost regarded as prohibitive. The law of October 1795 "explicitly renounced the dream of educating an entire people. . . . Neither the State, nor the communes were constrained to organize elementary schools and their creation was thus left to the good will of local authorities. . . . The great hope of regeneration of the nation was shattered."[56]

That faith and optimism, nevertheless, did not die. The Revolution bequeathed to the future not only certain laws, institutions, and mores but also certain ideals and promises: the twin dreams of universal education and universal democracy, inevitably tied to each other, lived on long enough to be transformed, during the century that followed, from dreams to reality—just as the revolutionary visionaries had imagined.

3. *The First Intimations of the Welfare State.* By "welfare state" I mean a conception that goes beyond charity, beyond dependence upon the compassion of the rich, to the idea that the community as a whole—through its most powerful instrument, the State—has an obligation to provide at least a minimum of material existence for all its citizens. That the poor cease to be invisible in the arena of national politics. It is to the great credit of the Jacobin radicals, the very people who instituted and conducted the Terror, that they raised this issue, in precisely this manner, with such urgency. That people such as Bertrand Barère and Saint-Just were capable both of real compassion for human suffering caused by economic want and yet were perfectly efficient in cannibalizing their political opponents is one of the great personal and political mysteries and ambiguities. In precisely this mode, it was the very first time history revealed such a contradiction. Lenin, Mao, Castro, and several others have guaranteed that it was not to be the last.

As in the similar case of free, universal education, one might endorse a program of support for the poor either out of true compassion or from the utilitarian, rational calculation that a minimum standard of living was a powerful defense against anarchic, lower-class uprising. Or from both considerations. We do know, with certainty, that during the Great Depression in America, when the welfare state in its modern form was born in this country, many found it an acceptable alternative to anxiety about what the twelve million unemployed might do.

Here, as in so much else, the Enlightenment, and even the *ancien régime*, was moving in this direction. Unlike certain simplistic conceptions of what was the essence of Enlightenment thought, that thought was not only about the sovereignty of reason. Rousseau, in fact, had argued that pity and compassion, and not rationality, were the fountains of morality.[57] And Leo Gershoy writes that "The age of reason converged upon the age of sentiment. It moved toward that mood of repentance which expressed itself, as Condorcet phrased it with noble naiveté, in 'compassion for all the ills that afflict the human race.' "[58] Even in the real world of action, Tocqueville claims that the developments from 1740 to 1780 demonstrated "a real concern for the hardships of the poor," which sentiment was very difficult to find in the years before 1740. Louis XVI, he argues, took a personal interest in increasing the expenditures on "charity workshops" in rural areas, and these sums showed a significant rise in the years preceding the Revolution.[59]

The dismantling of the church by the Revolution had left a serious void in the functions it had traditionally served, including that of dispensing charitable care to the poor. The sans-culottes sections in the larger cities and even the bourgeois Jacobin clubs in the provinces were sensitive to this lack and, for a very short while, made attempts to cure it. During the radical revolutionary years 1793–1794, in Paris: "Each section's general assembly elected a welfare committee ranging in size from sixteen to twenty-four members. In traditional fashion each committee divided its section into wards of one or several streets. Two commissioners were assigned to each and did most of their work out on those streets, identifying the needy, distributing aid after the committee's approval. . . . The frequency and duration of committee meetings increased steadily. One year after their election, the welfare commissioners were among the most overworked officials in the city, despite their unpaid status."[60]

As for the Jacobin clubs, even before the Jacobin dictatorship, Kennedy informs us that they took pride in being "guardians of the poor and the oppressed." Any needy person brought to their attention was immediately the recipient of a collection on his/her behalf. A much-discussed topic of debate was: "How can poverty be abolished?" All of which produced a quantity of programs for public workshops and charitable institutions. The Versailles club, in late 1791, took the radical step of proposing a *national* welfare system.[61]

The concept of a national system was a revolutionary moral advance because it moved the discourse from charity to a human right, from pity and compassion on the part of the giver to dignity and entitlement on the part of the receiver. The radical Jacobin leaders were the first politically empowered people to proclaim that, of all human rights, the right to exist was the primary one. In a speech to the Convention in April '93, Robespierre proposed some additional articles for the Rights of Man, which he felt were lacking:

> Art. 11—Society is obliged to provide subsistence for all its members, either in procuring for them work, or in assuring the means to exist in the case of those unable to work.
> Art. 12—The assistance necessary for the indigent is a debt of the rich towards the poor; it is the obligation of the law to determine the manner in which that debt is to be acquitted.[62]

As far as rhetoric was concerned, the Convention ultimately responded by declaring that "Le soin de pourvoir à la subsistence du pauvre est une dette nationale."[63] [The burden of providing for the subsistence of the poor is a national debt.]

The moral advance represented by the rhetoric, and the adoption of resolutions by the Jacobin Convention, was profound. It anticipated the welfare state of Modern society by more than one hundred years. Whether such programs could actually be put into operation, even if Thermidor had not come and the Jacobin dictatorship remained in power—all this was highly doubtful. The society lacked the financial resources and the bureaucratic efficiency for such an endeavor. The moral climax of the intent—that the care of the disadvantaged was the concern of the *State*—came in May 1794. A nationwide system of social security (*bienfaisance nationale*) was decreed. "In a democracy," Barère announced to the Convention with great pride, "everything should tend to raise each citizen above his primary needs, by work if he is able-bodied, by education if he is a child, by aid if he is disabled or aged."[64] It was decreed that every district prepare a register of indigent aged, disabled workers, widows, and needy mothers of numerous children. Not only financial aid but also free medical care and medical supplies were to be provided by the government. (Parenthetically, one cannot avoid the irony of the fact that so much of present-day American politics turns on the questions of welfare mothers and Medicaid.) Even old-age pensions were proclaimed.[65]

In all reality, it was visionary. But what a remarkable vision! And the radical Jacobins are no more to blame for the failure of this dream than is Lyndon Johnson that his declared War on Poverty was ended by a society that lacked the moral courage for that war and declared an ignoble retreat. After the fall of the dictatorship, even the dream and the rhetoric were gone. "Of all this," Soboul writes, "nothing was to survive Thermidor, except the realization that a great hope had not been fulfilled."[66]

✻   ✻   ✻

No amount of institutional change, by itself, no matter how great, will guarantee success. The establishment of a radical democracy—wherein every adult male participates in the full sovereignty (at least in theory) of voting and holding office—is replete with enormous risk. Two almost unimaginable things are required for success: the *demos* must become mature enough for responsible democratic citizenship and the entrenched elites must, somehow, decide to take the risk that radical democracy entails; and these latter are always inclined to exaggerate that hazard. To paraphrase Aristophanes' half-ironic, half–deadly serious comment, they have to allow garlic-smelling, charcoal burners their say in the decisions of the polity. Both developments take enormous time. The nineteenth-century history of those societies that entered the twentieth century as radical democracies was precisely the struggle to attain those two objectives. And, for many societies struggling today for Modernity, this double-problematic for radical democracy is the fundamental question.

One great, unexplored question is: What is the social-psychological process by which the elites of society—both aristocratic and bourgeois—become convinced that this moral risk is worth taking? Conservative thinkers (i.e., Hobbes and Burke) were convinced that there was no sense in chancing such a development because it could not succeed. One opted for monarchy, the other for limited democracy, as the only mode to preserve social stability. The fear of lower-class anarchy underlay those conclusions. The liberal optimists (Locke, Rousseau, Madison) believed that the risk could be taken because "the people"—whoever they might be—could be trusted not to traduce democratic citizenship. It was only a naïve liberalism, however, that imagined that the two hazards had been eliminated. And when that noble experiment gave indication of collapsing, ideological terror and conservative dictatorship remained impatiently in the wings. For lower classes, ideological terror because it promised economic equality. For elites, conservative dictatorship because it delivered social stability. It may almost be considered miraculous that some societies ultimately rejected both these perverse alternatives and successfully traversed this treacherous ground.

13

RIOT, GANGSTERISM, CONSERVATIVE DICTATORSHIP

Early September 1792. The king had been deposed and was in prison. Enemy armies needed only one more battle victory to march on Paris. Thousands of Parisian citizens were leaving for the front to defend their city, their families, and *la patrie.* In order to aid these recruits and to prevent an enemy victory, the people of Paris massacred some 1,500 people being held prisoner in the city jails.

A motion was approved in the Faubourg Poissonnière that all political suspects and priests in prison should be executed before the volunteers left for the front. The Luxembourg, Louvre, and Fontaine-Montmoreney sections approved the proposal. The next day a group of priests who had refused to take the Oath, on their way to prison, were massacred by their guards. Those latter were joined by a group of typical sans-culottes (artisans, shopkeepers). The augmented group marched to the prison at the Carmelites and brutally murdered a large group of imprisoned priests. Such reckless "justice" was a little too much for the vigilance committee of the Commune, which directed, that evening, that all the prisoners at the Abbaye were to be tried before execution. Stanislas Maillard was appointed chief of the tribunal to judge the prisoners. In each case, he gave extraordinary efficient justice; consulting the prison record, discussing briefly with his assistant judges, he quickly pronounced sentence. The pile of bodies grew larger and larger. Pétion, who visited one of the prisons the next day, reported on the prideful manner of those sage judges: "They boasted to me of their justice, their care in distinguishing the innocent from the guilty, and the services which they had rendered."[1]

The massacres spread, during the next two days, to the prisons at La Force, the Conciergerie, the Tour Saint-Bernard, the Châtelet, Saint-Firmin, Saltpê-trière, and the Bicêtre. All sense of political vengeance was lost in the feeding-frenzy: common-law prisoners, women, and children were slaughtered with equal enthusiasm. Many corpses were severely mutilated. True, some restraint was exercised: they did not go so far, in their vengeance, as to eat their victims.

What may be even more remarkable is the reaction of some of the "respect-able" members of society to this lawlessness. Mathiez quotes, as a typical atti-tude, the wife of Julien of Drôme, who he describes as an "excellent bourgeoise, a disciple of Jean-Jacques." She wrote to her husband the very evening of Sep-tember 2: "The people has arisen, the people, terrible in its rage, is avenging the crimes of three years of the basest treachery! The martial fury which has seized all the people of Paris is prodigious." All this, it must be remembered, after the final victory over the *ancient régime* had been won: the king was deposed, the proclamation of the Republic imminent, elections were being conducted to a Convention that was to write a new Constitution for France. The double anxiety occasioned by the possibility of being conquered by foreign troops when no omnipotent king could protect us, produced the most savage aggression-as-defense behavior.

All of this, true, is not yet anarchy. Enough murderous riot, however, can provoke as much fear of anarchy as anarchy itself. There was also something primatively murderous in French culture at the time: a certain repressed and fragilely controlled rage remained just below the surface. In March of '93, as the coup against the Gironde was building, a delegation from this same Poissonnière came to the bar of the Convention, "and demanded the heads of Vergniaud, Gensonné and Gaudet."[2] So far, the only political culture that seemed to have evolved was one in which the losers, if they did not flee or were not sent into exile, could not count on continuing to remain among the living.

THE CENTRE CANNOT HOLD

> Things fall apart; the centre cannot hold;
> Mere anarchy is loosed upon the world,
> The blood-dimmed tide is loosed, and everywhere
> The ceremony of innocence is drowned;
> The best lack all conviction, while the worst
> Are full of passionate intensity.[3]

If, as has been postulated, it is true that shared values represent a great part of what holds society together, then it must follow that intense disagreements about fundamental values pose a clear and present danger to social stability. There is a limit to what even the most stable and open-minded society can tolerate in regard to lack of consensus concerning fundamental values. Such failure of the center to hold is certainly exhibited in revolutionary times. However, even the normal evolutionary development of social norms can produce a similar lack of social coherence. Unusual moral progress (democracy) or moral regress (fascism), coming from a significant part of society but one that does not represent a large majority, can create this situation of intense social discord and raise the spectre of anarchy. Most recently in America, in regard to the war in Vietnam and, with less intensity but still with an acceleration of violence and lawlessness, the question of the morality or immorality of abortion. These struggles are most intense when the division in society is close to equal: 55 percent in favor of the war, 45 percent against; 57 percent supporting choice, 43 percent pro-life. Modernity, since it pushes forward, many times unheedingly, toward moral progress (radical democracy, equality for women, the end of racism, sexual freedom for all adults, a secular society) is a great progenitor of the anxiety of societal disorder. Even after the almost hundred-year period of revolutions was over in France, it was Modernity that caused Durkheim to observe, in his work on *Moral Education*:

> For we are living precisely in one of those critical, revolutionary periods when authority is usually weakened through the loss of traditional discipline—a time that may easily give rise to a spirit of anarchy. This is the source of the anarchic aspirations that, whether consciously or not, are emerging today, not only in the particular sects bearing the name, but in the very different doctrines that, although opposed on other points, join in a common aversion to anything smacking of regulation.[4]

The great question raised by the rise of democracy, the overthrow of monarchy, and the sovereignty of the people was whether this new revolutionary culture could achieve the same kind of stability as had been exhibited by traditional, monarchical, religious society. Hegel, a great admirer of the *first* French Revolution, nevertheless, at the end of the *Philosophy of History*, understood the fundamental problematic it had raised. " 'Thus agitation and unrest are perpetuated.' The problem of political stabilization remains the 'nucleus . . . with which history is now occupied, and whose solution it has to work out in the future.' "[5]

It takes a great act of imagination for those of us who live in a stable democratic society, where any threat of anarchy arising from political chaos or economic catastrophe seems fantastically remote, to realize how recent is our
achievement of a complacent comfort. In the 1930s two major European democracies (Germany, Spain) abandoned recently achieved democratic citizenship,
and even Third-Republic France had an intense struggle to prevent a similar
outcome. One no longer hears the shibboleth of my youth that "External vigilance is the price of liberty." So secure have we become in the belief in the
permanence and *stability* of democracy (certainly, a good in itself) that our politics seems to be flirting with decadence. After the heroic regimes of Reagan,
Bush, and Clinton, the unstated, but powerful, reigning political maxim remains:
"Eternal fund-raising is the price of office."

In its youth, however, democratic society is so vulnerable that its continued
existence can never be taken for granted. Even Tocqueville, the great champion
of American democracy, could ruminate his book on that subject: "One must
not shut one's eyes to the fact that unlimited freedom of association for political
ends is, of all forms of liberty, the last that a nation can sustain. While it may
not actually lead it into anarchy, it does constantly bring it to the verge thereof."[6]
And, certainly, during the early years of the first French Revolution, only a wild-
eyed optimist could imagine that the drive toward democratic society was certain
to bring a stable order. In late 1790, a writer in the *Feuille du Jour*, at Paris,
summarized the current political situation: "A king without a crown, an assembly
whose power is not established, disobedient troops, finances hampered by a lack
of credit, a religious order without religious spirit, a monarchy without order, a
thousand opinions which rage without any concern for the public—such is, in
this moment, our position."[7] A prescription, in a word, for anarchy—or a strong
man committed to restore order. And even R.R. Palmer, no Robespierrist, unequivocally announces that "It can be considered certain that France could not
be governed in 1793 by liberal or democratic constitutional means. To disband
the Convention [and institute a new constitution] could only perpetuate anarchy."[8] In situations of political instability, either a one-man dictatorship or a
group of men assuming a dictatorial role is the most frequent defense against
incipient anarchy.

Social stability requires forms of social cohesion. In regard to the latter, force
and shared values are in inverse relationship to each other. The greater the power
of shared values, the less need there is of force. And the opposite. Once the road
to Modernity has been entered upon, democratic citizenship represents the one

legitimate form of social stability. If the democratic center cannot hold, gangsterism (a nonlegitimate, predatorial strong-man) and conservative dictatorship
(either of one-man or one-party rule) represent the only alternatives to anarchy,
once ideological rule (either of a terrorist or religious nature) is rejected. Stable
democratic society requires its own form of force, but here civilian control of
military power is crucial. That is the subject of the next chapter.

It was the good fortune of revolutionary France—and a cogent sign of the
relative health of its political culture—that, although it terminated in conservative dictatorship, it never seriously considered gangsterism. The gangsters, or
warlords, almost invariably begin as generals. As do many of the conservative
dictators. Long before anyone had heard of Bonaparte, Burke had predicted his
coming, through the perception of what role generals would play in times of
political chaos:

> In the weakness of one kind of authority, and in the fluctuation of all, the officers
> of an army will remain for some time mutinous and full of faction until some
> popular general, who understands the art of conciliating the soldiery, and who
> possesses the true spirit of command, shall draw the eyes of all men upon himself.
> Armies will obey him on his personal account. There is no other way of securing
> military obedience in this state of things. But the moment in which that event
> shall happen, the person who really commands the army is your master—the
> master . . . of your king, the master of your Assembly, the master of your whole
> republic.[9]

Rudé argues that once the Convention had destroyed the military power of
the sans-culottes and the Parisian Sections, in situations of crisis, "the Convention had no other resort but to call in the army. . . . From October 1795 the
military coup d'état already looms on the horizon as the ultimate arbiter of
political disputes."[10]

There was, however, a profound difference between France at the end of the
eighteenth century and other less developed cultures that have attempted the
march on Modernity. In the twentieth century, the aspiration for Modernity has
spread to many societies that have not even achieved an early Modern culture.
In these latter, gangsterism and warlordism have became definite possibilities and
realities. In revolutionary France, however, the dictator had to be revolutionary.
A certain commitment to revolutionary ideals—and, therefore, a certain definite
aura of legitimacy—had to adhere to his position. Not just any general would

do; it had to be a general born of the Revolution. "The armies of Lafayette and Dumouriez," Jordan writes, "continued to fight under the same crude discipline as had the armies . . . in the previous century. Yet these armies resisted the treason of both generals, whose failed coups d'état drove them from France, accompanied only by their staffs. The armies developed a revolutionary perspective that alienated them from their counterrevolutionary officers, and it was only when the army was commanded by a man of the Revolution, Napoleon, that the soldiers followed their leader into rebellion."[11]

Military gangsterism can put down anarchy and restore an oppressive social stability, but it cannot in itself raise the banner of legitimacy, as can the conservative dictator. And it cannot, again unlike the latter, advance society forward toward a stable Modernity. For Tocqueville, very little of what was problematic in the struggle for Modernity was unnoticed. In the book on America, he offers an aside on contemporary Mexico. First, he observes how a written constitution (in this case, copied almost completely from the American) by itself can never produce democratic stability if the spirit of society does not call for it. Even conservative dictatorship, it seems, was not a real possibility. Only gangsterism and anarchy: "At present Mexico is constantly shifting from anarchy to military despotism and back from military despotism to anarchy."[12] Today, the news from many parts of the world chronicles that same deadly cycle.

CONSERVATIVE DICTATORSHIP

An emerging democratic society is like a person with a potentially serious mental illness, who has a breakdown, goes into a hospital, responds positively to intelligent and effective treatment, and returns to the world. Such a person will remain fragile and vulnerable: loss of employment, divorce, the death of a close loved one—this kind of crisis may bring on a relapse and force the subject to flee back to the sanitorium. In this metaphorical sense, the sanitorium to which emerging democratic societies may flee under the pressure of intense crisis is some form of dictatorship. Such societies cannot avoid a basic fragility and vulnerability. Famine, warfare, economic collapse, international crisis, political near-anarchy— all these will result in severe pressure on society to abandon the inefficiency and untidiness of democracy and place most all political power in the hands of one man or a reasonably small group of men. In the twentieth century, one-party systems in emerging Modern societies, such as Japan and Mexico, can provide political stability under the sham of democratic elections for many years.

Such is the possible virtue of this kind of analysis, that it could prove profitable to set down a history of the French Revolutions, from 1793 to 1802, as a series of possible, or actual, dictatorships that were the responses to severe political crisis. The specter of Cromwellianism that was consciously raised against Robespierre and others; the potential dictatorships of those powerful "traitors to the Revolution," like Lafayette and Dumouriez; a Girondin authoritarian alternative to the coming Jacobin rule; the conservative dictatorship of the Jacobins that quickly degenerated into ideological terror; the actual conservative dictatorship of the Directory; and finally, Bonaparte himself. The great Corsican, it must be remembered, did not overthrow a functioning polity, but a nearly nonfunctioning conservative dictatorship of the one-party variety. Needless to say, I will not attempt that extensive narrative. A few comments, however, on each of these potential or actual authoritarian regimes may prove illuminating.

First, it may be observed that four of the greatest commentators on the Revolutions were aware of this impulse toward despotism that political instability gave birth to and the role that generals would play in that regression. We have already heard from Burke; there remain Robespierre, Tocqueville, and Napoleon. Robespierre was passionately against the declaration of war on Europe that was being supported by almost the complete spectrum of political opinion, from the Gironde to the king, in the early part of '92. It was not until he himself was at the center of power, and the war had become a primary concern of the State, that he developed into an ardent supporter of a Republican victory in war. In January of '92, however, he predicted, with great prescience, what would be the result of a military culture arising out of war with Europe:

> What I fear, in a revolution odious to the court, in a revolution made against the court, is the victories of the generals chosen by the court. What ascendency they acquire over the army which has shared their success and which attaches its glory to those of its leaders! What ascendency they acquire over the nation, in which all the ideas have turned towards the warlike exploits and *in which the need still appears to be to make itself some idols!* What influence a general, a victorious army will not exercise in the middle of diverse parties who divide a nation! . . . How, in the middle of the universal enthusiasm, will the Legislative Assembly have any other spirit than that of the victorious general and of the monarch of whom he will have been the organ and the aid? . . . In the midst of civil troubles, *under the empire*

of an all-powerful king, supreme chief of the armies, dispenser of all the most important offices, master of 40 million who are his property, depository of the public
fortune, rallying center of all those malcontented, for the men most powerful and
most rich, for the majority of administrators, judges, public functionaries; in the
midst of a people disarmed, divided, exhausted, fatigued, starving, do you not fear
that a general, that a victorious army surrounded by enthusiasm for that general,
would not tip too easily the balance to the side of the ministerial faction, moderate
and anti-popular, of which he would be the instrument and the chief?[13]

All periods of intense social anxiety and crisis bring an inclination to regress
to more primitive forms of psychological defense. We have, for instance, no
definite proof that the ritual of human sacrifice was practiced in the Roman
Republic. True, the barbarism of the arena may rightly be considered as a form
of human sacrifice, but it was not consciously so designated by the Romans. The
only direct, conscious reference to ritual human sacrifice occurs in the myths
relating the history of the Republic—but only in regard to times of extreme
crisis: famine or imminent defeat in warfare. Faced with an extremity of anxiety,
human beings easily abandon a more advanced psychological position, most especially if it has been recently achieved. The French, in 1792, had just given up
belief in, and reliance on, the omnipotence of the monarch. And many had not
even come that far. The closest thing left to an omnipotent leader would be a
general who has, miraculously, saved *la patrie* and the Revolution when it was
threatened with destruction by foreign powers. It is this irresistible pull toward
the re-creation of omnipotence that Robespierre feared. And he understood the
need for its existence almost better than anyone, although he would resurrect
omnipotence not through victorious generals but by means of the Republic of
Virtue. Generals were more easy to come by. The future belonged not to Robespierre but to Bonaparte and—more lastingly—to Bonapartism.

Tocqueville, once again, saw with great clarity what dangers the intense anxiety of a major war could bring to society. "For a nation to be ready to face a
great war, the citizens must impose great and painful sacrifices on themselves.
To believe that a large number of men will be capable of submitting themselves
to such social exigencies is to have a poor knowledge of humanity. For that
reason all nations that have had to engage in great wars have been led, almost in
spite of themselves, to increase the powers of the government. Those which have
not succeeded in this have been conquered. A long war almost always faces
nations with this sad choice: either defeat will lead them to destruction or victory
will bring them to despotism."[14]

It is of interest that the monarchy supported the declaration of war in 1792 because it recognized that it would profit from either victory or defeat. Defeat would bring the end of the Revolution; victory would bring a celebration of the monarchy. Why those most committed to the Revolution, and eventually to the creation of a Republic—the Girondins and most of the Jacobins—did not understand this and blindly rushed off to vote for war remains a great mystery. Understanding the self-destructive dimension in the paranoid position and the continuing need for omnipotence, after the king had been downgraded to a mere constitutional monarch, may prove to be a key to unraveling this irrational behavior. The king was no longer a hero larger than life; even the liberals and the radicals still needed heroes; war would assure them that only a hero could save them. But they had read the wrong fairy tale. In this story, the new hero-general ends up eating his creators.

The genius of Burke and Robespierre had perceived this conclusion. Girondins were just ordinary men trapped in an impossible transitional historical time, from which there seemed to be no escape. On St. Helena, Napoleon understood clearly what his role had been: "In this gigantic struggle between the present and the past, I am the natural arbiter and mediator."[15] There is a way in which conservative dictatorship is the most effective—through far from the most admirable—compromise possible for a society not yet capable of democratic stability and yet still craving Modernity.

CONSERVATIVE DICTATORSHIPS: POSSIBLE AND ACTUAL

The Example of History: Rome and Cromwell

The Roman past was alive in the minds of many revolutionaries. The appointment of a temporary dictator, in times of extreme crisis, had been a Roman political mode. Several important revolutionary actors, most especially Marat at several times, intimated that such example might be exactly what the Revolution required. In 1792, Michelet writes that Marat, "commending Robespierre highly, said that salvation would be at first a single leader, *un grand Tribune.*" Earlier, in 1791, after the flight of the king to Varennes, someone had said of Robespierre: "If a king is necessary, why not him?" Michelet goes on: "A number of people thought that France would end up by having a Cromwell, a Protector, making the public spirit conformable to that idea."[16] From the early days of the

Convention onward, one of the main accusations leveled at Robespierre was that he was intending to make himself into a Cromwell. All of which indicates that a dictatorial outcome was a real possibility in many people's minds, several years before the coup of Bonaparte.

Revolutionary Generals: Dumouriez and Lafayette

It is a question whether Lafayette had the stomach or even the intelligence to seize political power and make himself into a conservative dictator dedicated to putting an end to the radicalization of the Revolution. What is beyond speculation is that the radical republicans eventually came to the conclusion that exactly such a course was his intention, despite their perception of his essential mediocrity. When he was accused at the Jacobins of Caesarism, Brissot retorted that "Cromwell had character, but Lafayette has none."[17] As early as June 1790, Mirabeau (certainly no extremist), in a letter to the king, predicted possible action: "He is going to have himself made supreme general [and] accept de facto dictatorship." If his ambition was not curbed, he would become "the most absolute, the most redoubtable of dictators."[18] One may regard this as a wild exaggeration of the general's capacity and reach, but, once again, it does confirm that the possibility of a dictatorial outcome was a speculation in many different political circles.

At the end of his revolutionary career, his appointment to a generalship at the front heightened the anxieties of the left as to his intentions. It was not until after the overthrow of the king that Lafayette defected and surrendered himself to the Austrian enemy, in August '92. Already in June, however, he wrote a public letter to the Assembly, from his command at the front, denouncing the Jacobins as the source of all the revolutionary troubles and disasters. "His intervention merely confirmed suspicions widespread since he had been given a command that he was planning a military coup."[19]

Dumouriez had been politically more to the left than Lafayette. Several members of the Gironde, and Danton himself, had been his associates and were, ultimately, embarrassed and compromised by his traitorist defection to the enemy. At first a celebrated victorious general, in March '93 he suffered the near-fatal defeat at Neerwinden. Dumouriez made no attempt to regroup, asked the Austrians for an armistice, and pledged himself to march with them on Paris, where he personally would free the queen and the dauphin and install the boy as Louis XVIII, with himself as the regent.[20] The perfect conservative dictatorial plot. His soldiers, committed to the Revolution, refused to join him; he and a few of his staff defected to the Austrians. Defeated generals are not likely candidates for a military despotism; wildly successful ones are a much different story.

A Girondin Dictatorship?

Morris Slavin has argued that the political mentality of the Gironde would not have excluded a conservative dictatorship, if they thought it necessary—or possible. I venture no opinion on this conclusion. His observations are worth hearing: "Nor were the Girondins such legalists as they claimed: from 23 September 1792 on, Kersaint advocated the gallows for his adversaries; and Pétion on 12 April 1793 boldly declared that the defeated party must perish. The same month the Girondins violated Marat's immunity; they clamored against the September massacres only later, when they saw the political gains that could be made from their opposition. Mme. Roland wrote after Varennes that liberty could not be installed until after 'a sea of blood.' The coup of the Girondins and their allies in Lyons preceded the insurrection of 31 May [at Paris] by two days."[21]

It is important to emphasize that I am talking here of conservative dictatorship, not ideological terror. That the Gironde was incapable of an ideological reign of terror seems a reasonable speculation. That they were capable of resort to a nonterrorist dictatorship in order to circumvent a Jacobin terror (whether accurately, or exaggeratedly, perceived)—that is not beyond the realm of the possible. On the whole, the political culture lent itself as much, if not more, to dictatorship as it did to democracy.

Jacobin Conservative Dictatorship

Unlike many twentieth-century ideological terrors, which came to power carrying a full previously erected political ideology, the Jacobin dictatorship began, as it were, not knowing where it might go—or even where it wanted to go. Preserve the Revolution and win the war were the two things about which it was certain. Exactly what the former intention meant, no two people could quite agree. There was no body of ideology, developed over decades, that had to be instituted. No Dictatorship of the Proletariat to be inaugurated. And, at its beginning, the

Jacobin dictatorship was not yet a terror. "Terror" implies some very specific things: all tyrannies, all authoritarian governments, are not terrors. "Terror" implies a regime in which terror (including, most specifically, the torturing and killing of human beings) has become an end in itself and not just a means to maintaining power. During the most recent Fascist episode in Argentina, there was a debate, among the inner circle of the regime, as to how much pure terror was still required: extensive torture and throwing opponents out of airplanes into the sea. Some argued that the regime was now strong enough so that such measures were unnecessary. The terrorists countered that if they ceased their methods, people would not remain frightened enough not to challenge the dictatorship.[22]

Such an argument was making precisely the distinction between conservative dictatorship and terror that is being attempted here. In the ancient days, when there were still people one knew who retained an ideal of Marxism and communism, one line of reasoning that persisted was that Marx and Lenin were virtuous, but that the communist ideal had been betrayed by Stalin. In essence, that Lenin had been a dictator, but Stalin was a terrorist.

The Jacobin dictatorship began as no more than that. The infamous Committee of Public Safety, which was the instrument, first, of dictatorship and, finally, of the great Terror, was instituted in April '93 by the Convention before the coup against the Girondins, with most of the latter group voting for its establishment. Palmer writes of the pressing need for strong government.

> The month of September [1793] was the turning point in the transition from anarchy to dictatorship. The Levy in Mass, the enlargement of the Revolutionary Tribunal, the Law of Suspects and the General Maximum [price control of a large number of necessities] were means toward controlling the resources of the country in the interests of the Revolution. They would have been useless, however, without a relatively stable body of leaders to integrate and apply them. What the revolutionists needed for their own salvation was, above all else, an authoritarian government. The Committee of Public Safety had begun to supply this need.[23]

The course of modern dictatorship was first set down by these autocratic Jacobins: elections were to be suspended or rigged; centralized authority was to be used to control the country politically. Couthon, a central member of the Committee, delivered to the Convention, in December '93, the kind of morally despicable hypocritical concern for *le peuple* that we have heard, over and over again, in this century from different quarters of the globe: "Under an ordinary government, the people have the right to elect officials. Under an extraordinary government, it is from the central power that all impulses must emanate, it is from the Convention that elections must come. We live in extraordinary circumstances. Those who invoke the rights of the people would render false homage to popular sovereignty. As long as the revolutionary machinery is still running, you would hurt the people by giving them the task of electing public functionaries, for the people might name men who would betray them."[24]

The country was controlled by the Committee of Public Safety operating through the districts and bypassing the departments, which were not necessarily reliable. *Représentants en mission* were sent out by the committee to the provinces, many of whom became small dictators on the local level. In addition, local "purgative elections" were held in the districts, wherein only those citizens sympathetic to the radical revolution were entitled to vote.[25] It is striking that, once the mode of conservative dictatorship has been invented in order to both go forward to, and compromise with, Modernity, how limited the repertory of its means turns out to be—how familiar all this political manipulation is to us.

One of the first essential acts of a dictatorship is to repress the freedom of the press. Fascinating to observe how the thinking of the Jacobin dictatorship and that of Bonaparte were identical on this subject. Chabot at the Jacobin Club, November '93: "I hear you talk of the freedom of the press and till now we have not agreed on that. The freedom of the press was necessary against tyranny and the nation approved this liberty; but that this same nation can instinctively distinguish the true limits of this liberty is proved by its approval of the smashing of the presses of Gorsas and other counterrevolutionary journalists. The freedom of the press is necessary for the support and defense of liberty; those are its limits. . . . this freedom should not degenerate into a license which might destroy it. In the composite government of England or under our former royalist constitution the freedom of the press against the government is necessary to counterbalance despotism, to prevent the governors from oppressing the governed. But under French republican government I maintain that . . . the author . . . who curses democracy should be crushed."[26] We are only too well-acquainted with where this sophistry leads.

Bonaparte, after he took office, did not have to invent any new mode of repression. In 1801, as soon as any opposition to his regime surfaced, all but thirteen newspapers in Paris were suppressed; a little later, four more were closed. He could not tolerate political opposition any more than his Jacobin forebears.

Those who opposed a special tribunals bill were anathematized as "vermin that got under my skin. . . . They need not think that I will let myself be attacked like Louis XVI. I won't stand for it."[27]

There was a gradual transformation, one step at a time, of the Jacobin dictatorship into Jacobin ideological terror. I will elaborate on that, as best I can, in Part III, which follows. Here, while the question of the nontolerance of opposition is under discussion, one aspect of that metamorphosis into terror could be mentioned: the insistence on eliminating every aspect of political opposition, not only from aristocrats and monarchists and counterrevolutionaries, but also from former allies of the left. Palmer concludes the quote given previously about how the Revolution "needed" authoritarian government, with a significant reservation: "but Jacobins, Mountaineers, Hébertists, Dantonists, etc. were not men to be easily governed."[28] Nor the-people-in-the-streets of Paris. Faced with continued opposition from the radical left, a leftward-leaning dictatorship may easily resort to the obvious solution: more and more repression, and end up annihilating, not Louis XVI, but Danton and Hébert. Terror was now in the saddle and rode men.[29]

Couthon, destined to die with Robespierre, announced that absolutely no opposition was to be tolerated, that even the sans-culottes who had made the Jacobin dictatorship would become victims of the Terror, if they did not curb their arrogance: "All societies must be destroyed, even those founded before 10 August. If they survive, there will no longer be a unity of opinion; the aim of one and all will be to unite all good citizens to render the Sociétés des Jacobins deserted if they can; forty-eight societies in Paris present a hideous spectacle of federalism; it is time for them to disappear and for all patriots to be concentrated among the Jacobins."[30] The number of those who might be considered virtuous and pure grew smaller and smaller; the guillotine was very busy taking care of the rest.

The Conservative Dictatorship of the Directory

The government by coups d'état from Thermidor to Brumaire has previously been examined. Another mode of describing the sovereignty of the Directory is that conservative dictatorship was its aim and coups d'état—when necessary—its method. The various coups included the usual dictatorial modes of repression. The coup of Fructidor (September 1797), against a regenerated royalism, placed the press under police control; forty-two publications were immediately suppressed.[31] A decree was published that anyone desiring to restore the monarchy or the Jacobin Constitution of 1793 would be executed without trial. Furet and Richet observe: "With the collapse of parliamentary institutions France had returned to dictatorial government. This time it was the army that seized control—the military glory achieved in the European war had brought its almost inevitable consequences."[32]

It is a significant question whether there was any real possibility, at the time, of a stable democratic society. Palmer and Bonaparte, 150 years apart, both concluded that there was no true prospect of such an outcome. The situation, according to Palmer, was tragic: there was no possible virtuous resolution:

> It seems likely that the chances for a moderate and constitutional settlement in France, in the years after 1795, were virtually nil. . . . The Revolution—or rather the last years of the old Regime of which the Revolution itself was the outcome—had left the country too divided, with too many memories, hopes and fears, hates and attachments, disillusions and expectations, for men to accept each other with mutual trust or political tolerance. Any conceivable regime would have to use force to repress intransigent adversaries. There are times when real choices become very restricted, and consist in little more than a choice of evils, when all that one can really decide, short of becoming wholly unworldly, is which side he prefers to embrace and whose repression he will endure.[33]

In essence, one's freedom consists only in choosing what form of dictatorship one wishes to live under. Bonaparte knew what particular variety he favored: "*Moi!*" In the year before Fructidor, he fulminated: "And do you suppose that it was in order to establish a republic [that I have triumphed in Italy]? What an idea! A republic of thirty million people! With our customs and vices! Is such a thing possible? It is a chimera of which the French have become enamored, but it, too, will pass, like so many other things."[34]

The everpresent danger for conservative dictatorship is that, as its hold over society weakens, it is more and more driven in the direction of terrorist means. The Directory, in its death-pangs, made use of—may even possibly have invented—a method of terror-control that was favored by the Nazi occupiers of Europe during World War II. On July 12, 1799, the "Law of Hostages" was decreed, making the relatives of émigrés and resident nobles, who had been deprived of civil rights, pay the price of civil disorder. In any department de-

clared "disturbed," these hostages were to be arrested. For every patriot murdered, four of them were to be deported, and all of them, as a collectivity, were
responsible for compensating the victims of "royalist" attacks.[35] They did not,
unlike the Nazis, conduct mass executions in the village square or blow up
churches with citizens within. That far into terror they did not go. And, of
course, by that time, the great ideal-type of conservative dictator was just a
moment away.

Bonaparte

Napoleon, of course, is not truly a subject of this work, but he does represent,
in so many fundamental ways, the telos of the ten revolutionary years, and he
did become, once in power, the very example of a nonterrorist conservative
dictator; therefore, it is imperative to give some thought to his advent and regime.

In many ways the answer to the question: Why Napoleon? is more available,
possibly even more obvious, than the answer to the question: Why the first
Revolution? and certainly not as difficult to answer as: Why the Jacobin Terror?
We can do no better than to quote one twentieth- and one nineteenth-century
historian. William Doyle writes:

> [1799] The war of the second coalition was disastrous in its early months. With
> Bonaparte lost in Egypt and a seasoned Russian army under Suvorov active in
> Italy and Switzerland, the Republic underwent a long series of crushing defeats.
> At the same time there was a revival of royalist and rural terrorism in the west of
> the country, while Belgian peasants had revolted against French authority in No-
> vember 1798. It began to look like another 1793 crisis, and it was natural that
> the Jacobinical politics that had saved the Republic then should win renewed
> popularity. The summer of 1799 accordingly witnessed the regime's last great
> leftward swing. Political clubs flourished, conscription was rigorously enforced,
> and there was talk of resurrecting the Terror. New severe steps were taken against
> the relatives of émigrés and a forced loan was decreed against the rich. Such severi-
> ties provoked royalist uprisings in the southwest, but more seriously, they alarmed
> all moderates, who had no wish to return to the bloody and uncertain days of
> 1793. Desperately they looked around for somebody to save them.[36]

And Tocqueville had said much the same thing, although with a little more
intuitive insight into psychological states: "In politics fear is a passion that fre-

quently grows at the expense of all others. Everything is feared when nothing is any longer ardently desired. . . . At this time, though preoccupied with their own petty affairs and dissipated by pleasure, they were worn by political anxieties. An almost unbearable suspense, a terror that seems to us incredible, took possession of every soul. Although the dangers of 1799 were, on the whole, infinitely less than those at the beginning of the Revolution, they inspired terror that was more intense and more general because the nation now had less energy, feebler passions, and more experience. All the evils that had overpowered the people for 10 years had assembled in their fancy to form a picture of the future; after having contributed to the most terrible catastrophes, they now trembled at their own shadows."[37]

In choosing Bonaparte—or, more accurately, in accepting the choice made for them by others—they had chosen wisely. One thing he knew accurately: how to assuage the anxieties of the new and old elites. He told a delegation of bankers and other notables that the government was to be one of "social defence, friendly to order, respectful of all forms of property, and pacific in foreign affairs." Who would not trade a little bit of freedom to criticize the government for such benefits after everything one had lived through? And he was not a terrorist. "Whatever his motives may have been," writes Sydenham, "and however rigorous his rule was to prove, his advent at least offered France the novel experience of a coup d'état which was not accompanied by immediate purges and prompt proscriptions."[38] All dictators are not terrorists. All tyrants are not cannibals.

WHY "CONSERVATIVE?"

The assumption is that most readers are willing to accept the notion of "dictator" all the way from early Jacobin rule until Bonaparte. The qualification "conservative," however, has presented problems for some readers of this work in manuscript. How can one call Napoleon a "conservative," when he was pushing revolutionary reforms in conquered areas (most particularly the Rhineland societies), had established the Code Napoleon, and brought to a climax the rationalizing and centralizing impulses in the culture? The same question, from a different point of view, is raised about the pre-Terror Jacobin rule. What could be conservative about anything Robespierre, Saint-Just, and Barère might do?

I use the designation "conservative" to indicate a person interested in conserving certain values within the culture. A radical dictatorship—and I cannot imagine one that is not ideological—is committed to continuing radical change, most especially in one particular area: the creation of a new man (*un nouvel homme*) in one generation. Neither the early Jacobin dictatorship, nor certainly Napoleon, and most certainly not the Directory were committed to this radical remaking of human nature overnight. Only when the Jacobin regime moved on to the Terror did such a démarche become a fundamental impulse behind the rule.

It may be asked, therefore, what was it that Bonaparte and the early Jacobin rule were conserving? Napoleon is easy. "There was a whole bourgeois side of him," writes Furet, "that was well suited to this role: he believed in the sanctity of property, the idea of marriage and the family, women in the home, order in the streets and careers open to talent [this last an important shibboleth of the first Revolution]. . . . 'We have finished the romance of the Revolution. Now we must begin its history, looking only for what is real and possible in the application of principles and not what is speculative and hypothetical. To pursue a different course today would be to philosophize, not to govern.' "[39]

He retreated on matters having to do with women, the family, and divorce: taking back critical advances that the more radical Revolution had achieved. He put a final end to the revolutionary attack on the church and worked out a conservative compromise between it and the State. "The people must have a religion; this religion must be in the control of the government. . . . Society cannot exist without inequality of fortunes." Only a belief in life after death allows the poor to accept their misery. If traditional religion is abolished, some disruptive form of worship will take its place: "Religion is a sort of inoculation . . . which, by satisfying our love of the marvelous, makes us immune to charlatans and sorcerers."[40] And, most certainly, any progressive thrust toward democracy had to be repressed. One of the fundamental things his dictatorship was conserving was the psychological and political need for authoritarian government, while, at the same time, conserving many revolutionary advances.

The conservative nature of the pre-Terror Jacobin rule is more difficult to establish. What it was attempting to preserve had only been instituted yesterday: the Revolution itself. It was in danger, and all energy was necessary to save it. Two distinct groups of enemies had to be repulsed. Those on the right intent on undoing the Revolution, the usual betrayers: counterrevolutionaries, aristocrats, monarchists, monopolizers, federalists, traitors to *la patrie*. But the danger from the left was equally great: those who would push the Revolution further and further in the direction of equality, direct democracy, destruction of religion. In the first months of Jacobin rule, before the institution of the Terror, consolidation of the Revolution and victory in the war were the two main goals of the dictatorship—hardly a radical program. Robespierre announced that the task was a difficult one because of two kinds of enemies: "ultrarevolutionaries," who did not know how to stop; and "citras" [from the Latin, and opposite to "ultra," the literal meaning being "on the nearer side"], who wanted to turn the Revolutionary clock backward.[41] In order to maintain the support of the people-in-the-streets, the Jacobin Dictatorship decreed certain radical measures: the maximum on prices of food, the Revolutionary Army, and so on. Those decisions were as much tactical as arising out of revolutionary belief. The transcendent moderate metaphor was pronounced by Saint-Just: "The Revolution is frozen."[42] That is to say, let us work to preserve what we have established. The great irony was that, as the regime moved to terror, the Robespierrists themselves became the ultras.

A complex theory of conservative dictatorship could prove fruitful toward an understanding of many circumstances of twentieth-century political history. I cite again the comment made in the previous chapter about the successors of Mobutu of Zaire that, barring the establishment of a stable democratic society, conservative dictatorship might prove the most optimistic outcome of the revolutionary change. For a society undertaking the treacherous journey to Modernity and not yet capable of a democratic resolution, conservative dictatorship represents a very complex compromise. On the one hand, naturally, it denies democracy, freedom of the press, the sovereignty of the people. On the other hand, however, it pushes forward with other aspects of Modernity that, somehow, make an ultimate democratic outcome possible. Most especially if the whole region, in which the particular society exists, is committed to a democratic culture. Conservative dictatorship is compatible with industrialization, urbanization, rationalization, a high level of universal education, and the creation of a bourgeois elite that upholds individualism as a foremost value. The latter circumstance may lead, ultimately, to a "modern" bourgeois elite that challenges both the religious authoritarianism of the culture, if it exists, and the dictatorship.

Twentieth-century Spain is a prime example. When the fascist regime finally fell, a stable democratic society emerged. Even communist Russia may be understood in these terms. It may be overly optimistic to describe the Yeltsin era as a stable democratic society, but the definite possibility is there. The point is that Russia did not develop from Stalin to Yeltsin. It did not progress from ideological terror to democracy. A long period of what can accurately be designated conservative dictatorship intervened: Kruschev, Brezhnev, Andropov, Gorbachev. It was this regime of conservative dictatorship that created the soil in which democratic society might thrive.

Such analysis underlines the importance of not referring to all right-wing European dictatorships as "fascist." One must not categorize Nazi Germany and fascist Spain and Italy by the same designation. It confirms Arendt's thesis that, in twentieth-century Europe, there had been only two totalitarian societies: Germany and the Soviet Union.[43] In terms of the theoretical distinction being undertaken here, they were ideological terrorist regimes. Italy and Spain represented a much more tolerant, much more flexible, much more ambivalent compromise with the march to Modernity. It is significant that genocidal anti-Semitism—that near-cannibalism of the Nazi regime—played absolutely no part in Spanish and Italian fascism. Italian persecution of the Jews resulted primarily from Nazi pressure when the Germans had partly occupied the country. And in Spain: "Spanish falangists took particular pride in the absence of a single anti-Semitic remark in all the writings of Antonio Primo de Rivera [the founder of Spanish fascism], while even such a 'classical' Fascist as Franco's brother-in-law Serrana Soñer declared racism in general a heresy for a good Catholic."[44]

There is a way in which one may read the modern history of Italy and Spain, not as some catastrophic experience of fascism, but as an inevitable compromise with emerging Modernity in a circumstance in which there may have been no better options. This is, naturally, not to excuse fascism or to prefer it to democratic citizenship, but merely to bring a tragic understanding to the most complex of historical circumstances. It might give one pause when judging the pathetic political history of the first seventy-five years of the French nineteenth century. In the twentieth century, monarchy—even of the degraded French variety—was no longer an effective political alternative. Fascism, but not Naziism, may be understood as filling the need for conservative dictatorship.

THE DESTRUCTION OF THE ARISTOCRACY

A crucial question for twentieth-century historiography has been: How did it happen that Italy, after twenty-five years of fascist rule, a shameful subordination to Nazi Germany, and defeat in a world war, emerged as a stable, energetic democratic society? And, equally remarkable, how is it that Germany, after the Nazi experience, emanated into the same exalted political realm? It has been suggested that the answer to this seeming paradox is that fascism and Nazism, among the other things they carried out, destroyed forever the inordinate political power of the aristocracy. That aristocratic power had been a fundamental hindrance to the establishment of a democratic polity.[45] After the war, in both nations, there were still some people of wealth or power who might have been termed "aristocrats," but the whole social scene had changed radically. No one, for instance, any longer used the word "Junker" in describing German society. Effete Italian aristocrats became a stock object of mockery in Fellini movies. Fascism—and capitalism—had finally put an end to the rule of nobles that had persisted for hundreds of years. Democratic society was the great beneficiary of this evolution.

A similar developmental progress, though not of the same intensity or completeness, remarkably enough, was carried out by the Emperor Napoleon. Geoffrey Brunn describes this revolutionary social process in talking mostly about the demise of monarchical omnipotence, but the decline of aristocratic society is also included in this transformation:

> Better than any of the enlightened princes of the eighteenth century, he had been able to reconstruct and energize the state because all of the inherited obstacles of kingly power had been subordinated or swept away in the Revolution. The relics of feudalism, the privileged church and the privileged nobility, the provincial estates, the conflicting codes and tariffs, the guilds, the corporations and the *parlements*, all had been crippled or abolished. Reorganized through the consular reforms, France became the most powerful state in Europe. It was under this form, as Sorel has pointed out, the form of enlightened despotism, that the French Revolution was consolidated.[46]

Joseph de Maistre, with his razor-sharp intellect, perceived, after Napoleon, that the old form of monarchy was dead forever, incapable of being revived. A new form of monarchy had taken its place: "Louis XVIII has not been restored to the throne of his ancestors: he has simply ascended the throne of Bonaparte."[47]

In the ancient Greek world, there was an "Age of Tyrants," which followed the era of aristocratic supremacy. In many cases, this "tyrannical" period was followed by societies that either experimented seriously with democracy or managed to establish stable democratic polities. The most famous and well-known example was the tyranny of the Pisistratidae in Athens, which was followed by the democratic reforms of Cleisthenes. Syracuse and other city-states followed a similar developmental course, though most of them with much less success than Athens.[48] All these cases, however, were wondrous examples of what I am calling here conservative dictatorships giving birth to nondictatorial societies.

A complex and paradoxical political evolution. No more complex or paradoxical than Modernity itself. Conservative dictatorship has played a crucial role in the struggle for Modernity, not only in revolutionary France, but in the whole of human history in the last, remarkable and tragic century.

14

CIVILIAN CONTROL
OF THE MILITARY

The Militia and a Citizen Army

A fundamental problematic for stable democratic societies, most especially for emerging democratic societies, is the establishment of civilian control of the military. Most especially in the twentieth century, more fragile democratic polities fall as a result of a military takeover than from any other cause. In almost all cases, when reading a headline in the daily newspaper: "Coup d'état in . . . ," the first paragraph gives the names of the general or generals who have overthrown the established government. In many cases, even ideologues, such as Fidel Castro, who instigate an ideological revolution take on a distinctly military persona as the revolt progresses.

Militarism and democracy are incompatible. Civilian control of the military establishment prevents militarism and allows democracy to live. "Militarism" implies the dominance of the political culture by generals. Warfare, of course, places unusual power in the hands of the generals. Even a long-established, mature, sophisticated democracy as that in America found itself having to deal critically, during World War and Cold War years, with overbearing generals: Patton and MacArthur. George Marshall and Eisenhower, who warned us of the "military-industrial complex," were of the very essence of generals in a democratic society: they assumed the hegemony of civilian politics. Their great ancestor, and possible role model, was Washington, who took on intense symbolic meaning during French revolutionary times: Was Lafayette destined to become another Washington or another Cromwell? After the second World War, the French had an even more treacherous time with generals than did America. In France only a protodictator general was able to put down the conspiracy and treason of the reactionary generals and, consequently, set the society on a democratic course.

All societies, even the most consensual, are held together, in good part, by force and the threat of force. Military force functions as the defensive arm of the Nation in an anarchic world of international politics. Police power, on the contrary, is the internal, domestic force that preserves order and holds society together. When police power is no longer sufficient and military power is necessary for civil order, democracy is in danger. Further on, the circumstance of the directory, where exactly that occurred, will be looked at. Democracy can not survive in such an atmosphere.

Psychologically, what makes this whole question of control of the military so problematic is the fact that democracy is, essentially, a peaceful mode of civil existence. A certain definite renunciation of civil violence is essential for the life of democratic society: it cannot long survive a political culture that regularly permits the killing of one's political opponents. Even the ordinary day-to-day, in-the-street, violence that was de rigeur, for instance, in Renaissance Italy has to be foregone if democracy is to survive. Generals, however, are in the business of killing people. No matter how abstract tactics, questions of supply, geographical considerations, and so on, may be, they are all merely means to an end. And the end is the extermination of other human beings. Possibly in a good cause, but it inevitably does something to the psyche to be in that line of work, something that does not lend itself easily to regarding all human beings as equals. Generals live in a culture of dominance.

The problem, no matter how difficult, is capable of solution, as history demonstrates. That requires, however, that the good, liberal citizens of the democracy are not fearful of becoming grown-ups. That is, they must overcome the natural liberal reluctance to exercise power. A grown-up in a liberal society is a person afraid neither of morality nor of power. Liberal citizens exhibit an unusual ambivalence about power. Lord Acton's famous remark about all power corrupting should really be modified to read: "All lack of power corrupts." His thesis is concerned with the power of domination; the corrected version is about the power to stand up to the predators and pirates within society. Too many democratic societies have been lost as the result of a failure of nerve on the part of their most important supporters.

Enough has been said about conservative dictatorship, in the preceding chapter, to establish that the tension that exists between militarism and democratic society was fully conscious in people's minds during revolutionary times. The *Declaration of Rights* of 1789 states: "To guarantee the rights of man and the citizen requires a public force; this force is therefore instituted for the benefit of all, and not for the personal advantage of those to whom it is entrusted."[1] Burke elaborated on how, in his opinion, the Revolution was doomed to fail because representative institutions and an effective armed force were incompatible. His argument, in essence, was that the statement in the Declaration was utopian. "The army will not long look to an assembly acting through the organ of false show and palpable imposition. They will not seriously yield to a prisoner [the king]. They will either despise a pageant, or they will pity a captive king. This relation of your army to the crown will, if I am not greatly mistaken, become a serious dilemma in your politics. It is, besides, to be considered whether an assembly like yours, even supposing that it was in possession of another sort of organ through which its orders were to pass, is fit for promoting the obedience and discipline of an army. It is known that armies have hitherto yielded a very precarious and uncertain obedience to any senate or popular authority; and they will least of all yield to an assembly which is only to have a continuance of two years. The officers must totally lose the characteristic disposition of military men if they see with perfect submission and due admiration the dominion of pleaders; especially when they find that they have a new court to pay to an endless succession of those pleaders, whose military policy, and the genius of whose command (if they should have any), must be as uncertain as their duration is transient."[2]

Burke has, with great brilliance, defined the problem that faces all democratic societies. He underestimated the human capacity to transform society to the point where this formidable dilemma could be resolved. Robespierre felt that the answer lay in avoiding unnecessary wars, like the one the Revolution was about to declare on Europe. "During a war, the people forget the issues that most essentially concern their civil and political rights and fix their attention only on external affairs. . . . [They tend to give] all their interest and all their hopes to their generals. . . . [In the Roman Republic] when the people, fed up with the tyranny and the pride of the patricians, reclaimed its right through the voices of its Tribunes, the Senate would declare war."[3] We are still left with the great question of why, when the danger was so palpable, did the good liberal Girondins and Jacobins walk into this trap by declaring war on Europe?

The Revolution, however, did not remain passive in the face of the threat from the generals. It resorted to two forceful institutional measures that gave hope of preserving both democracy and military effectiveness. One, a citizen militia, had been established or strengthened by other European emerging democracies. The other, a citizen army dedicated to democratic military institutions, was the invention of the Revolution. The combination of these two instruments of civilian control almost succeeded, and most probably would have done so, if political collapse had been avoided.

THE MILITIA

> The National Guard was an invention of great import, for it was the army of society, distinct from the army of the state, opinion in arms apart from authority. It was the middle class organized as a force, against the force above and the force below; and it protected liberty against the Crown, and property against the poor. [Lord Acton][4]

The militia, or the National Guard, was the organized armed force of the rising bourgeoisie. It was the military arm of civil society, just as the army was the military arm of the State. A militia is a *voluntary* organization of *citizens,* who in most cases are required to provide their own uniform and arms. This latter requirement automatically excludes the poor, which is exactly what bourgeois society desires. In the typical case, aristocrats never become members, preferring service in the army if they desired a military experience.

The militia played a crucial role in several societies engaged in the struggle for Modernity. In those cases where that endeavor, along with the intention to establish a democratic society, were combined with a war of liberation against foreign domination—as happened in America and Holland—the militia easily developed into an effective military force, playing a significant role in the emancipatory struggle. We all know about Lexington and Concord. In Holland, in the 1780s, the Free Corps represented exactly this kind of bourgeois fighting arm. "They were mainly middle class. . . . it was in these Free Corps that the democratic wing of the Patriots came to have an organized existence. With the first meeting of a National Assembly of Free Corps, held in Utrecht in December 1784, Dutch burghers outside the regent class met and discussed political action for the first time."[5]

During the first French Revolution—what many refer to as "the Bourgeois

Revolution"—the militia, organized officially into the National Guard, was a significant factor in political developments. Some even argue that the first revolution could not have succeeded without the existence of this citizen armed force. We first hear of it, in revolutionary times, during the early period of the Great Fear—and peasant uprisings—in the months preceding the meeting of the Estates General in 1789. Peasant riots, and even anarchic disturbances in the cities in the spring of '89, brought forth an active response from the bourgeoisie to defend order and property. Militia units that had become inactive were reformed: in Caen on April 25, in Orleans April 27, in Beaugency on the 29th. "As harvest time drew nearer, the rural communities demanded the right to bear arms and in Flanders a compulsory guard was mounted on the harvest from June onwards."[6] All of this from voluntary militia units, not from the army.

"In an attempt to protect their property from the 'fourth estate' [the very poor]," aristocrats and bourgeois came together in the interest of preserving order, at a time when, politically, they were intensely antagonistic to each other. In April at Étampes, in Caen, and in Provence, members of the Second and Third Estates either armed jointly, or, in some cases, aristocrats even decided to serve in the militia.[7] Members of the bourgeoisie, organized in the militia, began to render what we would describe as "vigilante justice." In the Mâconnais courts were established in Mâcon, Tournus, and Cluny: brief trials resulted in the execution of twenty-six peasants.[8]

Anarchic disorder continued in the countryside through the summer months. Antoine Barnave urged his political followers in Grenoble: "So what is to be done? two things: hundreds of addresses must go to the National Assembly, and a bourgeois militia must be ready to march. . . . The rich are the most concerned for the general good. The greater part of the Paris militia is drawn from solid bourgeois citizens and for this reason it is as efficient in the maintenance of public order as it is tireless in the struggle against tyranny. We must not lose a single moment in circulating these ideas throughout the province."[9]

Three things about all this must be emphasized. First, that these actions were a manifestation, not of the State and its military power in the army but of civil society. Second, that the militia was an institution of bourgeois life and designated as such. And third, that this bourgeois militia was not invented in 1789. As far as I know, the great comparative history of the bourgeois militia has not yet been written. The earliest reference I have seen, in an admittedly superficial endeavor, is to the Paris militia, in 1588, at the time of Henry III, and the wars of religion.[10] Not only is it important to ask when the bourgeois militia was instituted in France, but also, how did other countries in Europe compare with France at the end of the eighteenth century? Were Spain or the states of Germany and Italy capable at that time of mounting a nonstate, powerful, *bourgeois* fighting force? Once again, this may be to push the history of the Revolutions back, possibly, several hundred years. But, perhaps, there is no better way to comprehend the successes and failures of this revolutionary period.

In July of '89, not only was the first revolution accomplished and made secure in Versailles and Paris, but an equally important revolution was put into effect in the municipalities of the provinces. This revolution against the king and the State was remarkably widespread and successful. Four things characterized the revolt. First, it was instituted and carried through by the Third Estate: the bourgeoisie. Second, it was violent in nature. Third, in almost all cases, the regular troops of the army refused to fire on these bourgeois revolutionaries. And fourth, in place of the regular army, the bourgeoisie created a militia to keep order. Norman Hampson describes these circumstances:

> When the crisis broke many of the towns took action without waiting for the capital. When Rennes heard of Necker's dismissal the *Tiers État* ransacked the arsenal and the troops refused to fire. . . . Arthur Young witnessed the pillage of the Hôtel de Ville at Strasbourg while the garrison looked on. . . . in most cases an insurrection, led by the bourgeoisie, encountered no resistance from the army. Commanders showed little inclination to fight, and if they had done so their troops would have mutinied. The formation of the *milices bourgeoises* maintained order and created a military force whose enthusiasm would have more than made up for its lack of training if confronted by regiments whose sympathies were on its side. In many towns the old municipal oligarchies were swept aside and replaced by committees drawn from electors to the Estates General. . . . Within the space of a few weeks the royal government lost control over the provinces, for in matters of importance the towns henceforth took their orders only from the [National] Assembly.[11]

A militia ready to step into the place of the army prevented the spread of anarchy and made revolution possible.

Robespierre, we are not surprised to discover, was keenly aware of the crucial role the militia had to play and was intent that it should be a militia that was totally committed to the Revolution. In February of '90, Le Chapelier introduced a bill for the restoration of order, which many considered too repressive. Maximilien delivered a speech in opposition to the measure claiming that the policy of repression was excessive: "There was never a revolution which cost so little blood, or so few cruelties. . . . [The remedy lies] in just laws, and the National Guard."[12] In December of that same year, he publicized a plan for the National Guard. All men over eighteen were to serve; the *cavaliers de la maréchausée*, the national police, were to be eliminated; no army officers could serve in the Guard; officers of the Guard were to be elected for a six-month term; and all those who served were to be armed at state expense.[13] The Guard was to become less bourgeois and more democratic. The radical, democratic proposals never attained reality. In Paris itself, the Guard, as instituted, became an instrument not only of bourgeois opposition to the king but also repressive of the people-in-the-streets. In France, the bourgeois militia would face an opposition that it did not have to face in any other country: a potent challenge from the lower classes. It would take more than a powerful militia to make the Revolution hold.

PARIS: THE NATIONAL GUARD VS. *LE PEUPLE*

In July '89, when the first great crisis of the Revolution was resolved with the taking of the Bastille, two very different manifestations of the power, as well as the sovereignty, of the people were underway. On the one hand, the people-in-the-streets were saving the Third Estate, and the Revolution, by presenting an armed force in opposition to the resisting monarch. On the other hand, the bourgeoisie was getting its act together and creating a National Guard that would be its instrument. This latter was an effective extension of the new political institutions. Deputies to the Estate General had been selected by a process involving different tiers of election. The actual deputies were finally chosen by a group of electors. In many places, these electors did not disband after exercising their function and stayed together as an unofficial, but potentially potent, group. In Paris, the 407 Electors of the Third Estate had formed themselves into a political club, which, in early July, was already talking of forming a Parisian militia. "They themselves came in the main from the wealthier strata of the middle class." When the crisis broke with the king's dismissal of Necker, with the streets already in turmoil, the electors made their way, on July 12, to the Hôtel de Ville. By midnight, a quorum had gathered, and the assembled group took revolutionary action. It created a new committee of 24 to rule the municipality, in which the electors held a majority. A militia composed of 200 men from each district was decreed, which number was increased on the 13th to

48,000 militia men, whose primary job was to be to maintain civil order in Paris. "The National Guard, as it was christened on 16th July," Hampson concludes, "was the perfect weapon for the bourgeoisie."[14]

Not only was the order to be maintained by a civilian power without the help of generals, and the concomitant threat of conservative dictatorship, but the army itself could no longer be relied upon to defend the king against the Revolution. During July '89: "Commanders were increasingly reluctant to put men's discipline to the test, and Broglie was too experienced an officer to take risks in such circumstances. He advised the king that he could no longer rely on his army."[15] The first revolution was secure, but the people-in-the-streets were not content to stop at that.

The bourgeoisie in Paris were intent that the National Guard should reflect the power relations within society, as they understood them. The Constitution established by the National Constituent Assembly in September '91 did not provide for universal suffrage. Society was divided between active citizens, who could exercise the vote, and passive citizens, who could not. The dividing line, naturally enough, was erected on the basis of wealth: that is, taxes paid. The decree of September 12–13, 1791, in regard to the National Guard, provided that it be organized into battalions, one for each Parisian district. Only active citizens had the right to serve; the poorer sans-culottes were to be excluded. Once the people-in-the-streets had overthrown the king in August '92, however, it was not possible to maintain that distinction: "everyone could carry arms."[16] The protoproletariat imitated the bourgeoisie and created its own permanent armed forces. "The pike became the symbol of the armed sovereign people and of the new order; it was lauded, it became the *holy pike*, and ended by becoming the symbol of the sans-culottes themselves."[17]

A bourgeois militia, once the Revolution against the king and the *ancien régime* was secure, could be counted on to preserve order and put down any manifestations of social chaos. It provided an important defense against the fear of anarchy. But a militia, or even a less formally organized fighting force, made up of nonbourgeois, even antibourgeois, members of the lower classes or radical members of the middle class—this was an entirely different proposition, and one that the American Revolution, for example, did not have to face. It is one powerful demonstration of "French exceptionalism" that the bourgeoisie knew what its function was in revolutionary times, set out competently to do it, but was not left in peace. Having settled reasonably well with the aristocrats and the king, it was faced with a "people" like no other people in the world at that time.

Charles Ferrières, in his *Mémoires* of the Constituent Assembly, published in 1799, succinctly stated the dilemma the bourgeois revolutionaries found themselves in: "The men of the Constituent Assembly, always suspicious of the King's sincerity, feared that if they checked the people too severely they would deprive themselves of the means of employing them when they should need to set them in motion. Hence this alteration of anarchy and order, of sedition and repression."[18] By the time "the people" were allowed into the National Guard, they had already taken the Bastille, brought the king from Versailles to Paris, and dethroned him. One cannot imagine that they were unaware of their power. "The Parisians . . . knew they had saved the Revolution, and they were proud of it. What they had done once they could, and did, do again. For good or ill, the French Revolution was to be characterized by regular popular intervention."[19]

What developed that had such a modern ring was that the power of the people was co-opted not by those exercising the general interests of the Revolution as such—as had been the case with Bastille—but by a particular radical faction whose aims could, in no way, any longer be described as bourgeois. The Bolshevik cry of "All power to the Soviets" was the twentieth-century echo of this sans-culottes/Jacobin alliance. Robespierre, a brilliant political tactician, knew where the power lay. In October '92, Louvet delivered to the Convention a powerful accusation against Robespierre: one of the opening salvos of the Girondin/Jacobin war to the death. La Croix, who was the president of the Legislative Assembly from August 19 to September 2, directly after the overthrow of Louis, interrupted Louvet in order to support his accusations:

I have demanded the right to speak in order to attest a fact advanced by Louvet. One evening, during my presidency of the Legislative Assembly, I had ceded the chair to Herault, the vice-president. Robespierre, at the head of a delegation of the counsel-general of the Commune came to demand that the National Assembly confirm the dissolution, already accomplished, of that Commune and of the Director of the Department. I had the courage to oppose that proposition, and to make the Assembly pass to the order of the day [that is, not to take up Robespierre's proposal], which was decreed. Descending from the tribune, Robespierre said to me that if the National Assembly does not, of its own volition, do what he demands, one knew well how to make it do such, with the help of the toscin [bells rung to call the people to arms].[20]

Kings, with their armies, were a force. Armies, with their generals, were a force. A bourgeois militia, armed and intent on preserving order, was a force.

French exceptionalism is exemplified by the fact that, at the end of the eighteenth century, only in France could one say that *le peuple*, armed with pikes, was a force equal to kings, armies, generals, and a bourgeois militia. The co-opting of this force by future ideological terrorists is best exemplified by the Jacobin use of the people-in-the-streets to execute the coup of May 31–June 2, '93, which put an end to the opposition by the Gironde. Democracy was dead. A political culture of dictatorship was established.

The tragic irony of the French Revolution was that this seemingly democratic and progressive phenomenon—that the people refused to remain passive and were intent on actively pursuing their interests, as they understood them—was the very thing that made the generals a "necessity." If only the people had left the bourgeoisie and its efficient militia alone; if only the radical democratic leadership had not raised up this Frankenstein, then panic, anarchy, and the fear of anarchy would not have ruled. What Napoleon eventually established by force was very much the society that bourgeois liberals had desired in 1789–1792, except that any hint of real political democracy had to be extirpated. After Thermidor, the ruling bourgeois elite recognized that, among its first priorities, was to withdraw any military power from *le peuple*. Ten days after the fall of Robespierre, the commander-in-chief and the second commander of the Paris National Guard were placed under the tight control of the Conventional Committees of Public Safety and General Security. Over the following year, the National Guard was repeatedly reorganized, becoming less and less autonomous. "Finally on 15 Vendémiaire, year IV [October 1795], the National Guard was placed under the control of the commander-in-chief of the Army of the Interior." Soboul concludes: "It was all over."[21]

The great confrontation between the "bourgeois" National Guard and the people of Paris, one that subsequently took on intense symbolic significance, was the so-called massacre of the Champ de Mars that occurred on July 17, 1791. The king's attempt in June to flee the country, interrupted at Varennes, had split the revolutionary forces. The program of the moderates was to forgive the king, publish the fiction that he had been spirited away and not left of his own volition, and proceed with the establishment of a constitutional monarchy. The radicals reacted to the king's flight by calling for an end of monarchy and the establishment of a republic. In the latter part of June, a petition calling for the end of monarchy was drawn up and circulated. Meanwhile, in the normal course of things, an altar to the Fatherland had been erected on the Champ de Mars to celebrate, on July 14, the second anniversary of the fall of the Bastille. The radical republicans intended to use this altar as the occasion for a mass signing of their petition.

On the 17th of July, perhaps 50,000 people gathered on the field. About 6,000 people put their signatures to the petition. Unfortunately for all, two men were found hiding under the altar, were taken for spies, and were killed by the crowd. The mayor of Paris, hearing the news, declared martial law, and Lafayette, as the Commander of the National Guard, with his troops, "marched to the Champ de Mars flying the red warning flag. They were greeted with a hail of stones and some shots. Thereupon they opened fire on the largely unarmed crowd, shooting them down, as one participant put it, 'like chickens.' Perhaps 50 people were killed and several more wounded. . . . In the weeks that followed . . . another 200 or so known activists in the Parisian popular movement were arrested, although Danton escaped to England, and Desmoulins and Marat went into hiding."[22] Charles Lameth, the president of the Assembly, praised the action. Martial law continued in Paris for almost a month. The Assembly passed a bill making the following actions illegal: "incitement to break the law, provocative cries during riots and attempts to tamper with the loyalty of the National Guard."[23]

The battle line, which would take five or six years to efface, had been drawn. On the one side, the bourgeois militia and its tainted leader Lafayette, dedicated to preserving the monarchy and civil order. On the other, radical republicans, Jacobins, and their shock troops, the people-in-the-streets of Paris, also known as "sans-culottes." So powerful were these latter forces—in France—that, in the future, the bourgeois militia would prove insufficient to preserve bourgeois power. There was, however, an alternative source. It would take a few years, but ultimately, the generals would prevail, and a stable democratic society would be sacrificed on the altar of civic tranquillity.

THE ATTEMPT TO CREATE THE FIRST CITIZEN ARMY

Robespierre, brilliant tactician that he was, went beyond merely fearing the rise of the generals to power and the institution of a military dictatorship. He also conceived of a solution: "A citizen army," Jordan explains, "organized on democratic principles, which would dilute the regular army, especially its officer corps, still littered with the dangerous debris of the *ancien régime*." Democratization of the army would be a continuation of the revolution in the social order: "You have destroyed aristocracy," Maximilien announced, "and the aristocracy still lives at the head of the army; the aristocracy reigns in the army."[24]

In the traditional, monarchical, predemocratic society, almost every officer of the army was an aristocrat; certainly this was true for all officers of high rank. Two institutional solutions to the problem of an aristocratic army were attempted by the Revolutions. First, beginning with the initial Revolution and continuing on with the others, a serious endeavor was made to democratize the regular army. Many of these reforms persisted through Napoleonic times and became permanent aspects of the French society. And second, with the coming of the Jacobin dictatorship, an entirely new "revolutionary army" was created. It had only an ephemeral existence and disappeared even before the Terror itself passed away. Both of these reforms were intended to keep the generals from taking political power. In themselves, without the help of a political culture conformable to a stable, democratic polity, these reforms proved powerless to prevent that eventual military-political resolution.

Democratization of the Army

Reforms in the military establishment reflect the same modernizing mix of rationalization and democratic impulse that characterized the Revolution itself. "Cruel and humiliating punishments were abolished. The officer grades were filled on the basis of merit rather than for reasons for social precedence. The king's dependence on foreign mercenaries was ended. The distinction between the line and the militia was abolished, as well as the practice of pressganging. . . . The provincial attachments of individual regiments were abandoned, and men were called upon to serve France, the nation, the *patrie* . . . as part of the obligation implied by the fact of citizenship."[25]

The new army was to be filled by *volunteers*. These new recruits brought with them a revolutionary concept of citizenship. They represented a very different kind of soldier than those who had fought under the traditional society. These voluntary recruits enjoyed certain privileges that were denied the regular army, including the right to resign at the end of each campaign and go home.[26] Even more remarkable, the National Assembly decreed that they were allowed to elect their own officers. After the failed flight of the king to Varennes in June '91, the Assembly resolved that a volunteer force of 300,000 to 400,000 be created. The provincial Jacobin Clubs were electrified: "These decrees sent the clubs into feverish activity. . . . Overnight, many clubs were transformed into recruitment bureaus."[27]

Such a cadre of citizen-soldiers could prove very difficult to control for the *ancien régime* aristocratic generals, particularly after the institution of the *amalgame*, decreed by the Assembly in February '93: distinctions between volunteers and regular brigades were abolished, the two being merged together to form new units, called demibrigades. All differences in uniform, pay, and discipline were abolished. Junior officers and noncommissioned officers were to be subject to election. "The law . . . though scorned by many contemporaries for its raw idealism, played a vital part in molding the revolutionary armies into an effective and victorious military force."[28]

And in the matter of replacing aristocratic generals as they increasingly retired or went into exile, here the Revolution produced one of its most brilliant successes. The new democratic culture brought forth an almost unbelievably capable group of young, democratic generals, one-third of whom were middle-class,[29] generals who were to make French history for the next twenty years. "It may be doubted," Palmer writes, "whether any other government, in an equal time, has matched their record, for before the end of 1793 they raised to the rank of general (among others) Bonaparte, Journdan, Hoche, Pichegru, Masséna, Moreau, Davout, Lefévre, Perignon, Serrurièr, Augereau and Brune. One of these became an emperor, eight others marshals of his empire; the remaining three (Hoche, Pichegru, Moreau) rose to be distinguished commanders under the Republic. These twelve were all new men. Their average age in 1793 was thirty-three."[30]

The government deserves the credit for opening to talent the career of general, but nothing demonstrates with greater power than this experience how marvelously explosive was French culture at the end of the century. It was, literally, bursting with new ideas, new men, new possibilities for political life. Something, nevertheless, went wrong. Some deep failure of nerve eventually exercised dominion over the culture. The generals, however, were winners either way.

The new army, with its brand-new generals, was like nothing ever seen before. It was a fighting force deliberately politicized by the national governmental authority. The soldiers could vote, form political clubs within the army, join civilian clubs in towns where they were stationed, take part in political demonstrations. In some cases, as is not unexpected by us knowing the twentieth-century history of radical movements, army cells of Hébertists and enragés—the very left wing of the political culture—were formed. In Lille and Cambrai, these radicals from the local garrison imposed their views on the city Jacobin clubs and made of them centers of political extremism. Newspapers, and not just those of a lukewarm variety, were distributed in the millions by the central government to the soldiers. The *Père Duchesne,* the vehicle of Hébert and one of the most outspoken radical voices, for instance, was widely circulated to the army of the north. Even matters of discipline laid emphasis on violations of conduct of *citizens.* Fighting men were to think of themselves as citizens as well as soldiers. "*Propos inciviques* widely defined to include virtually any criticism of the Revolution and its leaders, were not tolerated from soldiers any more than they were in civilian society."[31]

The result of all this education and indoctrination, which went on for years, was that the revolutionary culture stayed alive and healthy within military ranks. The comment has already been cited of how the army was ready to follow a Napoleon, who was a son of the Revolution, but never a Lafayette or Dumouriez. Mathiez emphasized this idea, possibly to the point of exaggeration: "Officers and generals had risen from the ranks and owed everything to the Republic. . . . Their men, formed in the same school, loved them because the officers shared in their own life and exposed themselves to the same dangers, in the same sansculotte spirit of fraternity. . . . The army was the impregnable rock upon which the Republic was based."[32] All of this, of course, did not prevent these very same generals from betraying that Revolution. It was not the first time in history that well-intentioned, moral people of the lower classes had put their faith in perfidious leaders—Greek tyrants and Roman chiefs of the Populares were no strangers to betrayal of their popular supporters. Nor was it to be the last time—the Bolsheviks, and all their ideological progeny, would see to that.

The Creation of a Revolutionary Army

In addition to democratizing the regular army through the volunteers and other means, during the time of the Jacobin dictatorship and the Terror, the attempt was made to create a military force that was the direct expression, and instrument, of the radical revolution. It was not easy to control and quickly presented a possible problem to the centralized government of the Terror. Its life was very short.

On June 2, 1793, in the very middle of the anti-Gironde coup, the Convention decreed the establishment of this "Revolutionary Army." It was intended to operate as much within the nation against hoarders, suspects, and all other varieties of traitors, as against any foreign threat. It, obviously, was supposed to serve the Convention's shock-troop interests wherever they were needed.[33] No immediate steps were taken, but in early September '93, when the people-in-the-streets of Paris marched on the Convention—an action that quickly produced the Maximum of prices on food, the Law of Suspects, and the beginnings of the culture of Terror—the Convention, in the midst of the demonstration, decreed the immediate institution and dispatch of the Revolutionary Army.[34]

The process of creation of Revolutionary Armies quickly spread to the provinces. In the fall of '93 as many as 30,000[35] or 40,000[36] citizens were enrolled in these semivigilante squadrons. Representatives of the Convention on mission to a province quickly established such units or made immediate use of those previously created, in order to police the radical revolutionary policies against hoarding and suspects and the enforcement of the Law of the Maximum.[37]

December of the same year, however, brought what Doyle refers to as the end of "anarchic Terror," wherein representatives on mission had been free to institute practically any radical revolutionary measures they wished, including radical dechristianization, without prior approval of the Convention, through its dictatorial instrument, the Committee of Public Safety. Revolutionary Armies were now "reduced to a single force under close central supervision." It took several months to close down all the provincial armies, but, ultimately, the centralization of the Terror was accomplished. This experiment in radical-democratic military-police force was over.[38]

AND, IN THE END, ONLY THE GENERALS
WERE LEFT STANDING

One method of keeping the generals from taking political power was to maintain a life and death civilian control over the military establishment. And the word "death" is not an exaggeration: between 1791 and 1794 three commanding generals were guillotined for their military failures.[39] It is of interest that one historical precedent we have of such murderous supervision of generals is from ancient Athens, which was in the process of instituting one of the first radical democracies. In that democratic city, several army or naval commanders were executed for what we would regard as only military failure or mistakes, not treason.[40]

Early on in the Revolution, the provincial Jacobin clubs singled out military commanders—a last remaining cadre of aristocratic control and power—as the foremost possible source of counterrevolutionary action. In January '91, the Marseille club petitioned the National Assembly to purge ("to license") officers in the line army, who would be replaced by "patriots." The petition was also circulated to all its affiliated clubs. In April, the Strasburg club announced: "Feudalism has been overthrown, royal courts destroyed, the power of the clergy annihilated, and fanaticism disarmed. Gentlemen! Will you permit military despotism, the most formidable of all, to raise its audacious and menacing head?" From May 20 to June 6, almost fifty societies petitioned the central club at Paris or the National Assembly to "license" the army.[41]

These radical revolutionaries had a clear idea who their internal enemy was. The hegemony of the Jacobins, and then of the Jacobin Terror, created, for a short while, an antimilitary culture possibly never seen before in Europe. Alan Forrest informs us:

> When . . . generals lost battles or committed their troops to hopeless causes, they might find themselves subject to political sanction—to reprimand, dismissal, and even criminal charges. In the Nord, for instance, three commanding officers, Luckner, Custine, and Houchard, were tried and guillotined for their military failures. . . . Incompetent generals could be replaced at the head of the armies by political commissars whose experience of war was based on debate in the Club or the Convention. Dugommier, a Jacobin deputy sent on mission to the army of the eastern Pyrenees, resolved the problem of poor leadership by taking over the command himself and . . . succeeded in reversing French fortunes along the treacherous Spanish frontier. In an age when careers were suddenly thrown open to talent, there was no reason why ambitious men should not excel in both military and political spheres. . . . Saint-Just, one of the most active of the deputies on mission to the armies, was in no doubt that political responsibility was essential to effectiveness of the battalions as fighting units.[42]

Jacobin hegemony, however, as we know, did not last. The new citizen armies, ultimately brought, not more revolution, but the conservative dictatorship of the generals. Civilian control of the military, a necessary condition of a stable democratic society, had failed. Not because the generals were so strong, but because the capacity to create a truly democratic polity was so weak.

At some point during the Terror a violent anti-Robespierre cartoon appeared. Having executed everyone in France but himself and his executioner, Robespierre was now required to eliminate the guillotine and executioner himself. It was not, however, Robespierre who was left alone at the end. The bourgeoisie was not to be exterminated. The bourgeois militia, after some significant help on Bastille day from the sans-culottes, had put an end to the exclusive police power of the king's army. The people-in-the-streets of Paris put an end to the power of the bourgeois militia and brought the Jacobins to rule. The Jacobin Terror then destroyed the military power of the sans-culottes. And when the Thermidorians destroyed the hegemony of the Terror, no other military power was left standing but the republican army—and its generals. All the political factions that could have preserved civilian rule had destroyed each other. As the remaining factions (royalists, neo-Jacobins) continued to plan new coup d'états that failed in their accomplishment, only one real question remained: Which particular general was it to be?

This tragic, or perhaps pathetic, narrative is easy to observe and follow. Many historians have told the tale. Rudé gives us this summary:

> In Thermidor the Convention had been able to depend on the support, or at least the benevolent neutrality, of the bulk of the Parisian Sections—including those in which the *sans-culottes* were still firmly entrenched—to overthrow Robespierre. In Prairial [May 1795, the last *sans-culotte* uprising], in order to overcome the *sans-culottes* and the active Jacobin remnants, it had been able to call upon the armed citizens of the 'respectable' western Sections. In Vendémiaire [October 1795, Royalist uprising repressed by Bonaparte], when faced with a rebellion from this very quarter, having destroyed the Jacobin cadres and silenced the *sans-culottes*, arrested their leaders, and driven them out of the Sectional assemblies and committees, the Convention had no other resort but to call in the army. The precedent, once established, was not easily abandoned; and from October 1795 the military *coup d'état* already looms large on the horizon as the ultimate arbiter of political disputes.[43]

In the ten years from 1789 to 1799, six different forms of polity had been tried. (1) A limited, liberal democracy with a constitutional monarch. (2) A republic under bourgeois hegemony. (3) Radical democracy. (4) A left-wing conservative dictatorship. (5) Ideological terror. (6) A thermidorian Republic determined to bring civil order, at all costs. None of these brought enough political stability to enable the society to endure. What is remarkable is that France was not exhausted by the effort. On the contrary. Enough energy remained to erect a new king-general and set out to conquer the whole of continental Europe. A very complex society and culture, equally admirable and lamentable.

PART III

MODERNITY PSYCHOSIS: THE GREAT TERROR

15

PARANOID PANIC; HUMAN SACRIFICE AS PARANOID REVENGE; SCAPEGOATS

All ideological terrorists—the greatest and the insignificant, the powerful and the impotent—all have been severely paranoid. It has made no difference, in each case, what the moral insights and the moral stance and actions have been. Morality at the beginning has been no proof against acute paranoid perception and activity at the end. In regard to virtue, our list runs all the way from Robespierre, a moral genius, at one end, to Hitler, the devil incarnate, at the other. Even the great Rousseau, a giant of righteousness for Western civilization, ended his life in a critically paranoid state.[1]

However much they may differ in their moral stance, whether they are of the left or of the right; whether they march under the banner of equality for all or extermination for the Jews—all ideological terrorists share this one psychological symptom: an extreme paranoid view of the world. Savanarola, Robespierre, Lenin, Stalin, Hitler, Mao, Pol Pot—and a whole host of others who have never made it into the history books.

An important note about the use of certain crucial words. In general usage, or in the technical vocabulary of psychology, the word "paranoid," as an adjective, is used ambiguously. A person suffering from paranoia is called "paranoid," and his/her actions may also be so designated. It is important, for my purposes, to distinguish sharply between "paranoia" and "paranoid." Paranoia is a psychotic state. To be paranoid, in my usage, is not to be psychotic but to be suffering from several paranoid distortions of reality. A person who is able to keep his job, maintain a bank account, make his mortgage payments on time, and believes that all the stories of alien abduction are true—such a person is not suffering from paranoia but is, in the usage adopted here, clearly paranoid.

A severely paranoid person may pass over to paranoia itself, but, equally possible, he/she may never make that journey. Two illustrative cases from recent American history. James Forrestal was the Secretary of Defense in the late 1940s, one of the great promoters of Cold War anxieties. Some of his attitudes and statements while he held that office may easily be described as "paranoid"— critical exaggerations of what might have been a legitimate fear. But when he was hospitalized for mental collapse and announced that the Russian tanks were coming down Pennsylvania Avenue, he was no longer paranoid but suffering from paranoia. Richard Nixon, with his incredibly exaggerated fear of losing the election to George McGovern, which led to the Watergate break-in; with his construction of "enemies" lists; and so on, manifested many attributes that can accurately be called "paranoid." But when the Watergate crisis came to its frightful climax, many sensitive, thoughtful people in Washington were fearful that the president would go over the line and move on from paranoid behavior to paranoia itself. In the last days before Nixon resigned, Secretary of Defense James Schlesinger apparently informed all U.S. commanders that any orders from the White House concerning troops or weapons had to be approved by him, before being executed.[2]

In order to understand ideological terror, it is not necessary to address an analysis of the psychosis of paranoia. "Paranoid," however, is essential. I shall use it as an adjective to describe behavior and attitudes that are not in the paranoia state but, in certain ways, look in that direction: paranoid attitudes, paranoid acts, paranoid persons. I shall also use the word occasionally as a noun: he was a paranoid. Here again, no reference is being made to a person suffering from paranoia. In addition, I plan to make use of the phrase "the paranoid position" to describe a state in which a person or a society may be when he or it manifests several basic paranoid attitudes to reality. In a previous work, I have argued that predemocratic, premodern, traditional societies, which required authoritarian leadership of society (mostly kingship), occupied the paranoid position: that only by overcoming and moving beyond the paranoid position can democracy become a reality.[3]

That all this is extraordinarily meaningful for French revolutionary history is, I believe, remarkably easy to demonstrate. To make the connection between the paranoid position and ideological terror, is not, however, to really understand the latter. The problem is that we do not understand paranoid behavior itself. The psychological theory of paranoid behavior on the part of nonpsychotic people is, at present, woefully inadequate. What I will be attempting to do, in this Part III, is to construct the very beginnings of a theory of paranoid personal and social behavior—and ideological terror—simultaneously. Hopefully, insight into one area will help illuminate the other. The data from the revolutionary history that can be called upon is enormous.

Significantly, although one theoretical ground base of this work is a psychoanalytically informed sociology, when it comes to problems of paranoid action or even paranoia itself, Freud is almost of no use. He had very little to say that would help us understand paranoid behavior in both individuals and society. Those psychoanalysts who have come after Freud have added remarkably little. We learn much more from Richard Hofstadter's classic essay "The Paranoid Style in American Politics"[4] than from the body of psychoanalytic theory.

We are better off to start with Engels rather than with Freud. The great question implicit in Engel's rumination to Marx is the key to understanding the essence of ideological terror: What was terrifying the terrorists? It is of value to look once again at his reflections:

> Thanks to these perpetual little terrors mounted by the French, one has a much better idea of the Reign of Terror. We imagine it as the reign of those who spread terror, but, quite to the contrary, it was the reign of those who were themselves terrorised. To a large extent the terror was nothing more than useless cruelty, perpetuated by frightened people who were trying to reassure themselves by it. I am convinced that the Reign of Terror *anno* 1793 must be imputed almost exclusively to overwrought bourgeois playing the rôle of patriots, to philistine petits-bourgeois who were messing their pants with fright, and to the dregs of the people, who made the Terror their business.[5]

If Engels's answer to the question of what was terrifying the terrorists has any truth in it, it raises an even more awesome question: What was it in society that, even for a short time, people chose to be ruled by little boys who, out of fright, could not even control their bowels? Robespierre, certainly, cannot be dismissed with such superficial psychological analysis, even one that may have some truth in it, but all this only makes a more complex analysis an imperative.

The importance of Engels's rumination is that it places primary emphasis on *fright* and defense against that fear. I choose to begin this analysis of ideological terror by inquiring about what was it that was frightening people: the terrorists themselves and those who chose to be ruled by—or allowed themselves to be ruled by—terrorists. Two basically different kinds of fear must be differentiated: realistic fear and paranoid panic. Even realistic anxieties may be of great intensity: a child is hospitalized with a death-threatening disease; Hitler occupies Paris; the destruction of the environment threatens the quality, even the existence, of life. Paranoid panic is not realistic and arises from two sources: (1) An exaggeration of a realistic anxiety or concern. (2) Fright about a completely nonreal circumstance. As example of the first, during the first French revolution, there was as legitimate concern that the monarchical forces in Europe *might* invade France in order to destroy the Revolution. To elevate this anxiety to the level of panic, and to defend against that panic by declaring war on Europe, and bringing on all manner of destructive elements for the Revolution—such declaration was no longer realistic but a paranoid act. The fact that paranoid behavior has a significant self-destructive dimension, in regard to which this war declaration is a prime example, will be discussed at length further on. As instance of the second (fictional) mode of paranoid panic, one may recall the great Fear of Brigands in 1789—there were no brigands! Or, the many, many traitorous plots against the Revolution that were constantly being discovered—in the majority of cases, there were no plots!

An analysis of paranoid behavior should operate on two distinct levels: the individual psyche and the larger society. It is obvious that society cannot adopt the paranoid position if individuals are incapable of it, but the relationship between individual paranoid action and the values and institutions of society is a very complex one. As ideal types, paranoid individuals are of two genera. The private paranoid makes no, or very little, attempt to project his/her paranoid views onto society and onto history. Such a person could be deeply involved with problems of body fluids and astrology and alien invasions and yet make no attempt to defend against paranoid panic by changing society and the course of history. It is probable that such a person expends a great deal of time and energy on compulsive-obsessional rituals, that are his/her primary mode of defense. The nightmare that is history does not arise from such people.

Then there is the other ideal type: those who defend against their own personal paranoid panic by projecting onto society and history a complex paranoid myth, wherein the great danger of destruction is defended against, usually by some primitive aggressive acts that society undertakes. The Jews were polluting society; the Jews were a gangrened limb that had to be amputated in order to leave the rest of the body of society healthy; the Jews were a cancer that had to be cut out that society might regain health. Note the assumption: society is suffering from a life-threatening malady; if nothing is done about it, the death of society is certain; only extraordinary radical measures can save the social world. The most horrible aggressive acts are committed under a huge banner of morality: the Jews are exterminated so that society may be cleansed and restored to health; the king must die that *la patrie* may live.

Agreed, the Nazi genocidal case is the most extreme imaginable, but in the twentieth century, it has not stood alone (the Armenians in Turkey, Cambodian madness, Mao's Cultural Revolution, etc.). True, nothing in French history ever went that far, but we will never understand why it was so "necessary" to send Danton to the guillotine if we refuse to believe that nonpsychotic human beings are capable of creating, and acting on, such horrendous parables of destruction. And not only did the very small number of leaders of the Terror create a human sacrifice out of Danton, but *le peuple* cheered them on their way.

Those powerful individuals who have projected their own paranoid myth onto society and history—and have found multitudes who would share that destructive fantasy—have been of enormous importance for the course of social life. In projecting, and acting on, their own personal nightmares, they have truly created a good part of the nightmare that is history. They were neither predators nor civilizing pirates. They were, precisely, pathological people, suffering from Tocqueville's "*virus* of a new and unknown kind." And, as Tocqueville goes on to remark, they are still with us. Modernity Psychosis continues to hold dominion over many parts of the world. It is imperative that we try to understand anxiety, panic, terror if we are ever to understand *the* Terror.

PARANOID PANIC IN REVOLUTIONARY TIMES

I. *The Great Fear.* The fierce paranoid panic of 1789, primarily in the countryside and villages, has been so brilliantly documented by Georges Lefebvre that the only real need here is to cite some passages from his work. His *Le grand peur*[6] is one of the minor masterpieces of historical research and narrative. Lefebvre differentiates between the Fear of Brigands, which began at the end of the winter of 1789, and the Great Fear, primarily occurring in the second fortnight of July (after Bastille), when the panic over brigands was combined with fright of an "aristocratic plot" that would overthrow the Revolution.[7]

The nonexistent brigands would produce the following typical hysterical activity:

> First, the tocsin would sound and then for hours and hours the sound of the bells would hang over the surrounding cantons. Mass hysteria would break out among peasant women: in their imagination, it was already too late—they were raped, then murdered, their children slaughtered, their homes burnt to the ground; weeping and wailing, they fled into the woods and fields, a few provisions and bits of clothing clutched to their bosoms. Sometimes the men followed close behind once they had buried anything of value and set the animals loose in the open country. Most often, though, whether through common decency, genuine bravery or fear of authority, they responded to the appeal of the *syndic*, the curé or the seigneur. Preparations would be made for the defence of the village under the direction of the seigneur himself or some old soldier. Everyone armed himself as best he could; sentries were posted; barricades were thrown up at the entrance to the village or at the bridge; scouting parties were sent out. At nightfall patrols were kept up and everyone stayed on the alert. In the towns, there was a sort of general mobilization: it was like being in a city under siege. Provisions were requisitioned, gun powder and munitions collected, the ramparts repaired and the artillery placed in position.[8]

After the first revolution had been made and secured by the violence of Bastille, a powerful new panic—an "aristocratic plot" to reverse the revolutionary process—burst into existence. "One way or another, fear of brigands and fear of aristocrats always managed to occur simultaneously in the mind of the people."[9] And so: "During the second fortnight in July, there occurred a sudden synthesis between innumerable causes of insecurity and the 'aristocrats' plot' and this was the determining cause of the Great Fear."[10]

All the paranoid stops were pulled out to describe this totally fictional threat, even memories of 1,400 years previous:

> M. le Comte d'Artois [the king's brother] is coming with forty thousand men, all of them brigands he has brought from the kingdom of Sweden and other bands in the north, and they have seized all the convicts from the king's galleys in the parts of France and all the criminals who were in prison and he has made an army out of them; [he] . . . is doing all he can to get together all the runaways and

vagabonds in the kingdom of France just like the Vandals did in 406 and that with this fearsome army he wants to ravage the whole of France and conquer the Third Estate.[11]

As the heated paranoid imagination did its work, all manner of foreign soldiers were menacing the security of France: Hussars were south of Paris; a German army in Limagne; the emperor of Austria was sighted in Forges in the Caux region, in Lyons, and in Caylus in Quercy; English invaders, Spanish troops, Piedmontese; and all manner of exotic threats: Polish troops, Genoese brigands, Croatian troops in the service of the Austrian Emperor, and even Moors.[12] It was a nightmare that terror made into a reality.

2. *September 1792.* All the manifestations of paranoid panic discussed in this section share one enormously important symptomatic ceremony: aggressive acting out as a defense against almost unbearable anxiety. During the Great Fear: plundering and burning of manor houses; the degradation, and occasional murder, of the *seigneur.* Why aggressive action, sometimes of the most primitive kind, should allay anxiety is, at present, an unanswerable question. There is absolutely no question, however, that we observe this phenomenon over and over again during periods of heightened panic. We cannot, in fact, understand Modernity Psychosis and the great Terror, without observing the ever-presence of this destructive psychological maneuver. It is essential not only to try to answer Engels's question, about what was terrifying the terrorists, but also to observe acutely in what primatively aggressive manner they sought to deal with their terror.

One particular mode of aggression-to-allay-anxiety deserves our attention, since it may help us understand why the Revolution eventually cannibalized its own children: a not-very-disguised mode of human sacrifice. Victims are selected—not by any considerate or rational process—and then dispatched, so that *le peuple* can breathe again. Later on, I will look at greater length at human sacrifice as paranoid revenge and we have already observed the psychologically primitive nature of the September Massacres. Here, it may be helpful to quote a solid, conservative historian, who ordinarily is not given to psychological explanations. Faced with the moral anarchy of the massacres, however, D.M.G. Sutherland comments: "All of these elements may have made the massacres worse than they might otherwise have been, but they did not cause them. Panic, self-defence and vengeance were enough."[13]

"Vengeance for what?" we must ask. What made the *septembruseurs*, in the deep irrational part of their minds, imagine that those helpless victims were the cause of their panic? What made them imagine that they would feel better if they revenged themselves on those poor, pitiful prisoners? And why, then, did Robespierre and Saint-Just imagine they were saving the Revolution by sending Danton to the guillotine?

3. *Le pacte de famine.* Throughout the eighteenth century, and most especially in the years preceding the Revolution, a fully paranoid conspiracy theory was abroad in the French culture that sought to explain any shortage of food. Such lack of adequate food supply (*disette*) was not the result of natural causes, such as drought or other productivity failure, but was manufactured by malevolent forces, intent on starving the people. It was an artificial shortage, a *disette factice*, the result of a pernicious *pacte de famine*.

The perpetrators of these malicious conspiracies were, frequently, the highest powers in the land. "In 1789 there is the *pacte de famine*, with the Queen and the Comte d'Artois—it would be hard to find a more ill-assorted pair—in fell alliance to keep the people down through hunger."[14] Some conspiracy theories did not even exempt the king and his ministers from the intention of starving the people.[15]

Attributions of a *pacte de famine* persisted throughout the early years of the Revolution to explain the almost chronic shortage of basic foodstuffs. In the spring of '94, when the Terror turned on and executed *enragés*, such as Hébert, in addition to the usual traitorist activity, the latter was accused of creating disorders so that Paris would starve.[16] The persistence of paranoid, conspiracy thinking is taken as proof, by Baczko, "that although the Revolution certainly invented a new political arena, and, in particular, new political institutions, the *mental environment* remained the largely traditional one of the *ancien régime*."[17] And William Sewell, Jr., goes even further toward the classical theory of the paranoid style by underlining the process of projecting one's own murderous impulses onto one's enemies:

> The rhetoric of subsistence was a crucial constituent of the discourse of terror. Hoarders who starved the people were an inseparable element in the great conspiracy against the Republic. They were links in a great chain of paranoid equivalences that identified scarcity with riches, greed, counter-revolution, treason, aristocracy, British or Austrian agents, priests, tyrants, and a desire to starve the people, and hence an unnatural lust for human blood. The rhetorical marking of hoarders as bloodthirsty and inhuman beasts was a sign of the terrorists' own impatience to shed the blood of their real and imagined enemies.[18]

This mode of thinking very readily produced an intense need for victims and revenge on those bringing the disaster. No matter that the *pacte* was fictitious, the "hoarders" and "monopolisers" had to be discovered, and the human sacrificial rite exercised on real victims.

4. *The Declaration of War.* At the end of January 1792, the French delivered an ultimatum to Austria that it should declare its peaceful intentions toward France and act accordingly. By mid-April, war fever was at a pitch, and a "defensive" war was declared against the Austrian Empire. The psychological culture under which this near-catastrophic move was taken was the time-tested and future-viable paranoid conception that we-have-to-get-them-before-they-get-us. In democratic ancient Athens, exactly this rhetoric created the Athenian expedition to Sicily during the Peloponnesian War. A catastrophic move that was the main contributory to the final Athenian defeat.[19] In autocratic Nazi Germany, the exact same conceptualization sent German troops into Russia before England had been conquered and produced a similar catastrophic, suicidal outcome. The internal politics of terror produced an identical first-strike defense: "*Il faut guillotiner, ou s'attendre à l'être,*" said Barras. ["It is necessary to guillotine or to expect the guillotine oneself."][20]

French culture, at the time, was permeated by a paranoid *Weltanschauung.* Blanning, our foremost authority on the declaration of war, writes: "More than eighteen months before the Terror of Year II actually began, the psychological preconditions were well established. Dangerous as it is to employ psychopathetic categories to explain the past, it is difficult to read accounts of the debates of the autumn and winter of 1791–92 without being struck repeatedly by the symptoms of paranoia evinced by the orators and by the deputies who responded so fervently. The belief in a 'vast conspiracy against the liberty of France and the future of liberty of the human race' (Hérault de Séchelles) was repeated with liturgical regularity."[21]

French energy and the power of the French state, however, kept this war declaration from becoming a total disaster, although the country was constantly on the brink of such an outcome. No rational person could imagine that what the French Revolution needed in the spring of 1792 was food shortages and total war. Only seven deputies in the Legislative Assembly voted against the war declaration, demonstrating how powerful is the paranoid position in turning rational human beings into something else.

The campaign for war was led, remarkably enough, by the Gironde: the leaders of the liberal bourgeoisie. Brissot fired the opening salvo on October 20,

1791. Blanning describes this brilliant, inspiring, paranoid raving: "In a long but consistently eloquent speech . . . he deftly brought together in one combustible package all the most emotive grievances of the revolutionaries. The main theme was the existence of a gigantic international conspiracy designed to restore the old regime. . . . This farrago of truths, half-truths and misinformation was brought to a climax that was to prove a persistent feature of Brissotin oratory." And then comes the fatal either/or of paranoid aggressive rhetoric: to refuse belligerent action is to die a coward: " 'I tell you that you must avenge your glory, or condemn yourselves to eternal dishonour.' " Should the enemy refuse to declare its intentions concerning its arms and the French émigrés, then, " 'you will not have to think twice; and you will not have to think just about defending yourselves, you will have to head off the attack, you yourselves will have to attack. (Applause)' "[22]

Paranoid defensive-offensive action requires grandiosity. Nobody can push us around, for we are the greatest there is. Insard, another important Girondin, announced to the Assembly a month later: " 'The French have become the foremost people of the universe, so their conduct must correspond to their new destiny. As slaves, they were bold and great; are they to be feeble and timid now that they are free? (Applause)' "[23]

Caught in that paranoid frenzy, a truly heroic moment in revolutionary experience, the Tennis Court Oath, is spontaneously resurrected in order to encourage those bent on the path of self-destruction. In mid-January 1792, after Gensonné reported to the Assembly on the inconclusive negotiations with Austria, Gaudet left the presidential chair to deliver a resounding speech against the antirevolutionary European coalition. The official minutes of the meeting describe the ensuing explosive scene:

> So, gentlemen, let us tell all these princes [of the Holy Roman Empire] that the French nation is determined to maintain its constitution in its absolute entirety; we shall all die here. . . . (*Yes! Yes! Enthusiastic applause.*)
>
> At these words, all the members of the Assembly, inspired by the same feeling, rise and shout: *Yes, we swear it!* This surge of enthusiasm communicates itself to everyone present, inflames all hearts. The ministers of justice and of foreign affairs [who happen to be present], the ushers, the citizens, male and female, attending the session, join with the representatives of the people, rise, wave their hats, stretch out their arms to the President's desk and take the same oath. The cries of: *We shall live in freedom or we shall die! The Constitution or death!*, are heard and the chamber resounds with applause.

A motion is passed equating the day's events with the Tennis Court Oath and providing for the printing and distribution to the nation of the minutes of the session.[24] The usual pathetic heroism cannot be dispensed with when paranoid self-destruction holds dominion over men's minds.

The Denunciation of Traitors

It is worth remarking that ideological terror, no matter in what part of the world or in what century, produces the same perverted forms of political discourse. Trotskyist trials, Cultural Revolution denunciations, Jacobin accusations and purifications—all are the inevitable result of the culture of terror, wherein the paranoid view is sovereign. The Jacobin obsession with traitors and conspirators against the Revolution has been sufficiently, and easily, documented. "All are suspects," writes Gerard Walter, a principle historian of the clubs, "or are susceptible of becoming such. That is one of the principle articles of Jacobin faith. . . . It is thus that the denunciation becomes more and more the principle preoccupation of the Society, the principle object of its meeting. The more the Revolution advances, the more its enemies develop their intrigues. One exterminates one, ten others come to take his place. One needs, then, more and more numerous, more and more vigilant denunciators. The result is continual abuse."[25]

In the provincial clubs, successful candidates were required to swear an oath of allegiance. At first, this was obvious and harmless: "the Nation, the Law, the King, and the Constitution." By early 1791, however, defense against an ever-present danger became foremost, and the avowal was changed, in conformity with the Paris club: a *serment de délation*, an oath of denunciation, was substituted, requiring all new members to "swear to defend with their fortune and their blood, every citizen who had the courage to devote himself to the denunciation of traitors to the Fatherland and conspirators against liberty."[26]

The basic assumption in a culture of denunciation is that those closest to one—neighbors, fellow club-members, brothers, fathers—are potential traitors. All ideological terrors end up eating their own children. It is not just a by-product of extermination gone out of control, it results from a fundamental mindset of the extreme paranoid position: there is an ever-present danger that we will be betrayed by those we have most trusted. The defense against the continuing anxiety that we are surrounded by conspirators is a constant review of the membership that results in purging those found wanting and certifying the purity of those who are allowed to remain. During the crucial years 1792–1794, these "purifications" were a common phenomenon in both the provincial and Paris Jacobin clubs.[27] This particular property of Tocqueville's "*virus of a new and unknown kind*" was always given new life wherever, in the next two hundred years, ideological terror came to power.

A Culture of Anxiety

A significant degree of anxiety is a characteristic of all human societies. Anxiety demands psychological defenses to contain it. Defenses against anxiety, therefore, are characteristic of all human societies. Beyond this, there are historical situations in which one can perceive a quantum leap in the anxiety level within society. These radical increases necessarily call for a heightening, possibly an exaggeration, of defensive maneuvers to restrain panic. Many, if not most times, these defensive maneuvers entail a regression to a more primitive mode of acting-out of social aggression. We should never be surprised to observe primordial aggressive behavior when a society is experiencing near panic. The September Massacres, the guillotine, the Terror were all primitive modes of defense against an almost unbearable anxiety.

It is the argument of this work that Modernity, by its very nature, produces such a quantum leap in disquiet. Only by erecting nonprimitive defenses against that angst can a stable democratic society be achieved. There is no way of "proving" the proposition, as we have no "scientific" barometer of social anxiety, but it is difficult to read the history of the French revolutions without observing that the period from 1789 to 1799 was one of almost unbelievable social stress. Underlying all this was paranoid panic: fear of things that did not exist or exaggerated dread of circumstances that were, rightly, of concern. In this section, I give only a few typical examples, as representative of a culture suffused with anxiety that was bordering on panic.

One small example typifies the pressure under which people were living. For the provincial Jacobin clubs, newspapers from the capital and letters from other clubs, or from the mother club itself in Paris, were of enormous importance. They were the very lifeline to the Revolution itself. Great impatience greeted any delay in their arrival. The club at Toulouse considered giving a 12-livre bonus to its postal agent if he would speed the delivery of these precious communications. When they failed to arrive on time, a calm response and explanation were not in the offing. Michael Kennedy, who is not given to exaggerated vocabulary, writes that: "Unexplained delays in the arrival of the courier led occasionally to outbreaks of hysteria." In November 1790, flooding of the Loire prevented, for several days, the delivery of communications from Paris to the southwest. At Montauban, the explanation was that counterrevolution had occurred; the Limoges club organized its young men to march on Paris. Similarly, at Pau in August 1791, when the delivery agent did not appear, the Jacobin club asked the municipal officials to put the National Guard on alert, and organized an eighteen-man emergency committee to maintain vigilance all through the night and "take whatever measures necessary to secure peace."[28] The point being that, under circumstances of unusual anxiety, rational explanations and advice of patience could not prevail.

In George Rudé's introduction to the English version of Lefebvre's book on *The Great Fear*, he lists the various occasions and circumstances of unusual dread during revolutionary times: the Great Fear of '89, revived again in the summer of '90 after the flight of the king to Varennes; the September Massacres; prison plots in Paris in '94 and '95. All of which examples lead him to conclude: "So, fear and rumour were potent springs of collective behaviour that marked the whole course of the French Revolution."[29]

Blanning, no psychological historian, in his book on the revolutionary wars, does not refrain from resorting to psychological categories to explain the dominant *mentalité* in the country, giving us insight into a culture of paranoia. He sets forth a brilliant description of the downward slope from paranoid anxiety, to theories of conspiracy, to the annihilation of "traitors," to the great Terror itself. It is of value to quote him at length:

> Spies and traitors were to be found everywhere—among the courtiers at the Tuileries, French ambassadors at foreign courts, among the refractory priests, among the émigrés' army of agents, among the speculators engaged in economic sabotage, and so on, and so forth. An early and ominous reaction, fueled by the fear and hatred these denunciations inspired, was the creation of a *comité de surveillance* on 25 November 1791.
>
> Equally ominous were the demands for an end to political pluralism and the growing popularity of the concept of political crime. In his passionate intervention of 14 January 1792 . . . Gaudet ended his speech with the demand: "Let us mark out a place in advance for traitors, and let that place be the scaffold." (*Bravo! Bravo!*

Enthusiastic applause.) . . . In the good old days of 1789, Gensonné [another Girondin, not a Jacobin radical] argued, it had been possible for men of good faith to join all matter of parties; but no longer—now there were only two parties: for the Revolution and against it, right and wrong.[30]

We know where that terrible dichotomy can lead us.

HUMAN SACRIFICE AS PARANOID REVENGE

In the ancient Polynesian kingdom of Hawaii, that flourished during our eighteenth century, the number of annual victims of ritual human sacrifice came close to 4,000. The mythological legitimation of this religious rite was that the gods demanded such a holocaust. In the days of Umi, that king was sacrificing at Waipo, when the voice of Kuahiro, his god, was heard from the clouds calling for more men. The king kept sacrificing, and the voice continued to call for more, till he had slain all his men except one, when, as he was a great favorite, he refused at first to give up. But the god being urgent, he sacrificed him also, and the priest and himself were the only two that remained of all his company. Upwards of eighty victims, they said, were offered at that time in obedience to the audible demands of the insatiate demon.

And what did the gods do with all these human victims who were slaughtered on request? They ate them, of course. One Hawaiian myth says that after the bodies had been placed on the altar, the disembodied tongue of the god descended from heaven. It "quivered downward to the altar, accompanied by thunder and lightning, and took away all the sacrifices."[31]

"*Les dieux ont soif.*"[32] "The gods are thirsty," declared Camille Desmoulins during the height of the Terror. He was guillotined with the Dantonists, April 6, 1794.

September 1792 witnessed prison massacres not only in Paris, but in provincial cities as well. "At Reims on September 3," Mathiez informs us, "at Meaux on the 4th, in the department of Orne on the 3rd and the 6th, at Lyons on the 9th, at Caen on the 7th, at Vitteaux on the 12th, officers, priests, and suspects of every kind met their death, even in the prisons. At the electoral assembly of Bouches-du-Rhône . . . the news of the massacres in Paris was enthusiastically applauded. Like the ancient gods, the new god 'patriotism' demanded human victims."[33]

Robespierre, December 3, 1792: "You ask for an exception to the penalty of death for the one man in whose case it would be justified. Yes, the death penalty in general is a crime, and for this reason: that, according to the indestructible laws of nature, it can be justified only in cases where it is necessary for the security of the person or the State. . . . Louis must die in order that *la patrie* may live."[34]

"There is about the stately ceremony of the royal execution in Whitehall," Lawrence Stone suggests concerning the execution of Charles I in 1649, "more than a hint of the ritual murder of the priest-king, in expiation for the sins of the tribe and to cleanse the land of the evils which had befallen it."[35]

Bertrand Barère, a foremost terrorist, member of the great Committee of Public Safety, with extraordinary luck, managed to live to be 85 years old, and exercised the indulgent luxury of a regretful looking-back, writing in his journal: "During the pomp of power I was pensive and melancholy. Every day I saw my friends, colleagues, fellow men, go to their political death. Love of fatherland alone sustained me and gave me strength. But I did not believe that human sacrifices were necessary in Paris at the feet of the statue of liberty as they had been in Carthage at the temple of Neptune."[36]

"Well then, citizens, it was reasonable to fear that the Revolution, like Saturn, successively devouring all its children, would finally end at despotism with all the calamities that accompany it." [Vergniaud, March 10, 1793][37]

Human sacrifice is one of the most ambiguous, most difficult to understand or to explain, forms of human ritual. No one, as far as I know, has really explicated for us the seeming total irrationality and complexity of the experience. Even in its most sublime manifestations, great questions remain: Granted that it was all-praise-to-his-divinity that Yahweh substituted a ram for the child Isaac, but why, in heaven's name, did Yahweh demand that particular form of obedience in the first place? And why was it righteous of Abraham to obey? And for what strange human salvation was it necessary for God to show his love for the world by giving his only begotten son to be crucified? And for what reason did Jesus, who had to know beforehand all that was to happen, cry out on the cross that he was forsaken and betrayed by God, his father? When the Christian missionaries were proselytizing in ancient Tahiti, a culture suffused with actual human sacrifice, one of them asked whether it was the father or the son who died on the cross, and whether the reason Europeans did not practice human sacrifice was because they had a god who had suffered that penalty.[38] Even today, we have no ready answer for that philosophical Tahitian.

The actual ritual of human sacrifice is capable of combining the most celebratory and most degraded of human actions in one complex religious ceremonial. Mathiez, with daring insight, presents the experiences of September '92 in Paris

as exactly such a circumstance: "The fever of patriotism, the approach of the
enemy, and the sound of the tocsin lulled men's consciences to sleep. While the
murderers gave themselves up to their horrible task, the women spent the nights
in the churches making garments for the volunteers and lint for the wounded.
. . . The lead out of coffins was melted down to make bullets. All wheel-wrights
were busy making gun-carriages and ammunition wagons. The enthusiasm was
magnificent. *The sublime and the vile were seen side by side.*"[39]

The terrible man-slaughtering logic within the *mentalité* of sacrifice is that
something—someone—has to die in order that others may live. In the terrifying
quote from Robespierre given above about the necessity of Louis's death, that
iron logic is apparent. Louis must die *"parce qu'il faut"* that *la patrie* live. *Parce qu'il
faut*—because it is necessary—so that—in order that. Human sacrifice has a
terrible instrumental rationality behind it; it is a means to an end. The means, in
itself, may be lamented, but the end it serves holds dominion over all action. *"Je
prononce à regret cette fatale vérité . . . mais Louis. . . ."*[40] ["I pronounce with regret that
fatal truth . . . but Louis. . . ."]

This exterminating logic was apparent over and over again during revolutionary years, justifying all manner of executions. During the trial of Danton, one of
the jurors, Souberbielle, confided: " 'This is not a trial but a [political] act. . . .
We are not jurors but *statesmen*. . . . The two [Danton and Robespierre] are
impossible and one must perish. . . . Do you want to kill Robespierre? No. Well
that alone means that you have just condemned Danton.' "[41] *Cette fatale vérité*:
Danton must die in order that Robespierre may live.

In September 1939, just before Hitler invaded Poland to begin the greatest
conquer-or-die war of all time, he gave orders that all the inmates of mental
hospitals should be exterminated.[42] For anyone with any acquaintance with
human sacrifices to assure victory in war, as were performed in some early societies,[43] this action of Hitler's had all the characteristics of these ancient sacrifices.
And, certainly, the Nazi mentality was not incapable of such regression. French
rhetoric at the time of the September Massacres gives perfect evidence of a
conscious awareness that the murders would assure success in the war. I have
quoted in a previous chapter the letter of the wife of Julien of Drôme celebrating
the executions at the prisons. She elaborates on what would be the benefit of
these actions: "The Austrians and Prussians might be at the gates of Paris, but I
should not take a step backwards. I should only cry the more confidently: 'Victory is ours.' "[44] And Fabre d'Eglantine—poet, playwright, friend of Danton—
was the author of a placard posted around Paris in that same September: "Once

more, citizens, to arms! May all France bristle with pikes, bayonets, cannons and daggers; so that everyone shall be a soldier; let us clear the ranks of these vile slaves of tyranny. In the towns let the blood of traitors be the first holocaust [*le premier holocaust*] to Liberty, so that in advancing to meet the common enemy, we leave nothing to disquiet us."[45]

The Nazi Holocaust of the Jews was replete with medical-surgical images of restoring health to society by excising the diseased members: contaminated, gangrenous, cancerous. Billaud-Varenne was one of the most murderous members of the great Committee of Public Safety;[46] his sacrificial logic anticipated by 150 years the paranoid ravings of the Nazis: "It is time to restore robust health to the body politic at the expense of its gangrenous members."[47]

And it made people feel better. It did its murderous-logic work. Vengeance was satisfied; order was restored; panic was downgraded to normal anxiety. In June of '93, the revolutionary tribunal sentenced twelve Breton conspirators to death by the guillotine. The police agent Dutard wrote an account of the executions that elaborated on the healing effects of these judicial murders:

> I must tell you that these executions produce the greatest effects politically, the most important of which is that they calm the resentment of the people at the ills which it is enduring. In them its vengeance is satisfied. The wife who has lost her husband, the father who has lost his son, the tradesman whose business has gone, the workman who pays such high prices for everything . . . perhaps consent to reconcile themselves to the ills which they endure only when they see men whom they believe to be their enemies more unfortunate than themselves.[48]

It must have been very difficult to abandon the use of such a killing-machine that could render so many benefits.

After Achilles finally succeeded in avenging the death of his dearest friend Patroclus, by the killing of Hector, the hero guilty of that crime, he prepared for his departed friend a magnificent epic funeral. On the pyre he took the lives of twelve Trojan youths captured for that purpose. The soul-ghost of Patroclus could now rest easy. It was only a myth—an epic tale; no Greek *polis* actually practiced human sacrifice in any form. Under certain circumstances of crazed rage, however, human sacrifice and vengeance go hand in hand. It took a most bloody revolution in France to make a reality out of that sanguinary mytho-poetic *mentalité*. The members of the William Tell Section of Paris had, probably, never even read the *Iliad*. They knew, however, what was required to avenge three dead martyrs, murdered because of their dedication to the Revolution. On November 12, 1793 the Section petitioned the Convention.

> The William Tell Section congratulates you. It will congratulate you still more if you maintain fear and terror as the great order of the day, that fear and terror which are the two most powerful levers of revolutionaries.
>
> Blood is necessary to punish so many liberticidal and nationicidal crimes; still more is necessary to prevent those that would follow.
>
> It is from this moment only that the soul of Pelletier, Marat, Chalier and so many other glorious martyrs of liberty begin to find appeasement.
>
> Representatives, the death of a handful of conspirators cannot sever all the threads of the most execrable plot ever conceived in the human heart; a hecatomb of traitors is necessary to bring health to all the wounds of the fatherland, butchered by unnatural children.[49]

One is not surprised to find *le peuple* calling for such bloody revenge, when the leaders of *le peuple* expressed their leadership in this area as well. In Robespierre's Louis-must-die speech that we kept returning to, he does not fail to announce that the regicide will satisfy the need for retribution. Immediately after pronouncing that "fatal truth," he asserts: "A people which is still struggling for its liberty after so much sacrifice and so many battles . . . a people among whom the crimes of tyranny are a subject of dispute, such a people must be avenged."[50] And in April '93, when the Gironde was still alive, Vergniaud delivered a speech to the Convention wherein he referred to the September Massacres and rebuked those who "insist on imputing to the entire people the odiousness of these scenes of blood." Applause from his allies interrupted at this point, but Marat, who was not one to let such accusation pass by, called out: "*Ce sont des vengeances nationales!*"[51]

The most spectacular vengeance of all was planned for the city of Lyons, which had revolted against the central Jacobin government and then had been overcome by national forces. The total plan of destruction was never carried out. The stated intent of the Convention, however, rivaled that of Rome toward its ancient enemy Carthage, which city was totally destroyed. October 12, 1793, the following decree was issued by the Convention. None of the delegates voting "yes," as far as we know, can be described as "psychotic," and yet one cannot imagine a more powerful example of Modernity Psychosis.

> 3. The city of Lyons shall be destroyed. Every habitation of the rich shall be demolished; there shall remain only the homes of the poor, the houses of patriots

who have been led astray or proscribed, the buildings employed in industry and the monuments devoted to humanity and public institutions.

4. The name of Lyons shall be effaced from the list of cities of the Republic. The collection of houses left standing shall henceforth bear the name of Ville-Affranchie—the Liberated City.

5. On the ruins of Lyons shall be raised a column attesting to posterity the crimes and punishments of the royalists of the city, with this inscription:

Lyons made war on Liberty

Lyons is no more

18th day of the first month of the Year Two of the French Republic, One and Indivisible.[52]

And Robespierre, whose paranoid fantasies were advancing toward paranoia itself as the Terror progressed, decided that Lyons must die so that he could live. "These monsters must be unmasked and exterminated, or I must perish."[53]

BLOOD, HEADS, CANNIBALISM

The theoretical first principle on which the argument of this section is based is that certain modes of acting out social aggression are, psychologically considered, more "primitive" than others. The quotation marks are there to indicate that I wish there were a better word—one that does not resonate with the argument about whether certain ancient societies were "primitive" or not—to express the desired meaning here. However, I know of no other and it will have to serve. If we take one particular evolution of social values, it may help illustrate the point being made. We can observe the progression in the West, from public executions for criminal offenses, wherein elements of ritual, and even festival, were apparent—to capital punishment performed in a nonpublic way—to (at least, in many countries today) the elimination of capital punishment altogether. Such an evolutionary development is psychologically, and morally, progressive. Any change in social values that would reinstate capital punishment where it has been abandoned or that restores public executions of criminals would be psychologically, and morally, regressive. It returns to a more "primitive" mode of social aggression.

A society, therefore, whose rhetoric and metaphorical usage is pervasively entwined with the causing of rivers of blood to flow and with the cannibalizing of one's enemies; a society in which the severing of heads from corpses and the erecting of these trophies on the ends of pikes for all to see and celebrate—such a society may, with reason, be designated "primitive" in its execution of social aggression, certainly in contrast to the fact that such society had embraced the Enlightenment with great enthusiasm, eliminated judicial torture, and enshrined the rights of man in both the law and the hearts of the people. Whether such rhetoric and head-hunting acting out should be considered regressive, or whether it was merely a continuation of a particular violence within a part of the French culture, I cannot speak to, but it is striking how contradictory these modes were with all the other movement toward an enlightened Modern world that the Revolution was undertaking. The persistence of—or regression to—these forms is another clear indication of the pervasive paranoid *mentalité* within the society, certainly during revolutionary years.

Blood

As in all sanguinary religious rituals, the blood that is shed is sacred and serves a healing function. Somehow, it restores order to a world temporarily disordered. It is indicative of the sacrificial nature of the victims slaughtered. The rhetoric leading up to the prison massacres in September emphasized the restorative quality of the bloodletting. The Luxembourg Section in Paris announced that "the prisons should be cleansed by the shedding of the blood of the inmates, before leaving Paris."[54] And Danton, by no means the most remorseless of the revolutionaries, told the Duke of Chartres (in later days, King Louis Philippe) that he had acted passively at the time of the September Massacres, even though he was the Minister of Justice, because "I intended that all the youth of Paris should arrive in Champagne covered with blood as a warrant of their fidelity. I intended to set a river of blood between them and the *émigrés*."[55]

And, if the blood of common prisoners could be so instrumental, how much more efficacious would be the blood, and the life, of the monarch himself. After the execution of Louis, one radical newspaper explicated the power of the sacrificial ritual: "The blood of Louis Capet, shed by the blade of the law on 21 January 1793, cleanses us of a stigma of 1300 years. . . . Liberty resembles that divinity of the ancients which one cannot make auspicious and favorable except by offering to it in sacrifice the life of a great culprit." At the scene of the guillotining itself: "A crowd of people ran up to the scaffold after the execution to dip their pikes and handkerchiefs in the blood of the former king. One zealot sprinkled blood on the crowd and shouted, 'Brothers, they tell us that the blood of Louis Capet will fall again on our heads; well, so be it, let it fall. . . . Republicans, the blood of a king brings happiness.' "[56] If not "primitive," "primordial," or "ancient," what other adjective could do justice to such behavior?

Headhunting

I have suggested, in a previous work, that the word "headhunting" would be more accurately rendered as "headpreserving." The body, or parts of it, of the cannibal victim are ingested and then expelled in the normal digestive manner. The head of the "headhunting" victim, or the skull that remains after the flesh decays, is preserved and, usually, hung up on the house of the victor. It is a trophy, a permanent symbol of power, prowess, domination, manliness, aggressive potency, the refusal to be a victim—and vengeance.[57] In revolutionary times, all the metaphors of taking heads—and all the actual heads on the ends of pikes—significantly resonated with all these ancient symbolic meanings.

The guillotine, of course, did its grisly work, most efficiently, by chopping off heads—in public. When the king was executed in January 1793, the executioner grabbed his severed head by the hair and raised it triumphally for the crowd to see, as a tremendous roar went up. This act was celebrated in a famous and popular print by Duplessis, which detailed the blood dripping from the severed neck and contained the inscription: *"qu'un sang impur abreuve nos sillons"*—"may an impure blood water our fields!" How much closer to the *mentalité* of human sacrifice can one come? But there was even more. In ancient days, we read that sometimes barbarian chiefs made drinking cups of the skulls of particular enemies so that they could taste, and retaste, their vengeance with great frequency. The revolutionary French, of course, were too civilized for that, but Sèvres demitasses were sold with a reproduction in gold paint of Duplessis's drawing on the side,[58] so one could remember Louis Capet when drinking one's coffee. In the days of democracy and mechanical reproduction, everyone can be a barbarian chief, provided he/she can afford sèvres china.

The heads on the ends of pikes did not have to wait for the great Terror; they were there almost from day one of the Revolution. After the capture of the Bastille, de Launay, the commander of the prison, was marched to the Hôtel de Ville, executed, and his head severed by a pocketknife and hoisted on the top of a pike. It was soon joined by that of de Flesselles, who was shot as he came out of the Hôtel. These two heads bobbing on pikes through the streets have the honor of being the first demonstration of to what dramatic lengths revolutionary justice could go. Nine days later, Bertier de Sauvigny and his son-in-law Foulon were lynched by the mob and treated to the same honor.[59] It was the display of these two latter heads that prompted Barnave to defend the vigilante justice with the celebrated phrase: "The blood which has just been spread, was it then so pure?"[60]

The next act took place three months later when the women of Paris brought the king, the queen, and their son ("the baker, the baker's wife, and the baker's boy") from Versailles, insisting that the king take up residence in Paris. When the crowd from the capital had approached the palace at Versailles, violence had erupted, two of the king's bodyguards were slaughtered, their heads cut off and erected onto pikes. "There was laughter, cheering and applause, and later in the day the trophies were taken back to the Palais-Royal [in Paris], where they were exhibited in the garden."[61]

At the time of the September Massacres, the Princesse de Lamballe, close friend and lady-in-waiting to the queen, had been arrested in August and confined at the prison of La Force. When the massacres began, she was interrogated, refused to swear an oath of hatred for the king and queen, and was hacked to pieces. Her head was severed from her corpse, placed on a pike, and carried to the Temple, where the royal family was being held prisoner after the overthrow of the monarchy in August. One crowd-member burst into the family's rooms and demanded that the queen go to the window and see her friend's head, "so that you may know how the people avenge themselves on tyrants." Declining to obey, the queen fainted.[62] The mob continued to parade the head of the Princesse through the streets.

It was totally predictable that the taking of heads should become a prime rhetorical metaphor for revolutionary "justice." Marat was a born terrorist. Already in May '91, he knew what a revolution was all about. In his most popular newspaper, L'ami du peuple, he proclaimed: "Eleven months ago, five hundred heads would have sufficed; today, fifty thousand would be necessary; perhaps five hundred thousand will fall before the end of the year."[63] Danton, however, was unlike Marat; he was no buveur de sang; in many ways, he was an average sensual man. But he was entrapped by Modernity Psychosis, condoning unnecessary slaughter, and urging on the very worst aspects of primitive violence. In the midst of the September Massacres, he announced in private that the "executions were necessary to appease the people of Paris . . . an indispensable sacrifice."[64]

Two days later, from the rostrum of the Convention, he urged the delegates to that national assembly to be nothing if not bloodthirsty: "Punishments remain to be meted out, both to internal enemies already imprisoned and to those you have yet to seize. The revolutionary tribunal must be divided into a large enough number of sections (*Several voices: It's done!*) that every day an aristocrat, a criminal, may pay for his crimes with his head. (Applause.)"[65] It was a killing frenzy that was destined to become worse before it was terminated. Nonpsychotic people, people who were not severely pathological, were caught up in it. Something—Tocqueville's *virus*—was terrifying them. They were desperately attempting to assure the fact that other people—not themselves—were to pay with their lives for this psychic fibrillation.

Cannibalism

Homer was one of the first, maybe even the first, to use cannibalism as a metaphor for the very extreme of hatred and vengeance. The almost-incredulous Zeus to his wife Hera:

> Dear lady, what can be all the great evils done to you by Priam and the sons of Priam, that you are thus furious forever to bring down the strong-founded city of Ilium? If you could walk through the gates and through the towering ramparts and eat Priam and the children of Priam raw, and the other Trojans, then, then only might you glut at last your anger. Do as you please then.[66]

When we perceive the primitive level of revolutionary violence, we are not surprised to find a very liberal use of cannibal rhetoric to express primeval rage. And one did not have to be a mediocre journalist like Camille Desmoulins, as quoted at the beginning of this section, in order to make the connection with that man-eating part of the mind. During the year of the Terror, the infamous Year II of the new calendar, a member of the *République* section in Paris exited the meeting of its general assembly, declaring: "The guillotine is hungry, it's ages since she had something to eat."[67] And Hébert, who certainly deserved the epithet *enragé*, announced that Marie-Antoinette should be "chopped up like meat for paté in revenge for all the bloodshed she had caused."[68]

These were, admittedly, crazed Parisian revolutionaries, operating in the midst of revolutionary frenzy, but in France, at the end of the eighteenth century, the *moyen* bourgeoisie in the provinces was capable of the same demented rhetoric—and, sometimes, almost equally mad action. After the Girondin deputies were expelled from the Convention in June '93, several of them fled Paris and went into hiding. A year later, the bodies of two of these erstwhile representatives were discovered in the south of France. The local Jacobin club issued a memorial on the event, indicating how much the traitors had deserved their fate and gruesome death: "their corpses hideous and disfigured, half eaten by worms, their scattered limbs the prey of devouring dogs and their bloody hearts the pasture for wild beasts."[69]

We preserve our fragile humanity, however, by implying that it is not we who eat; the dogs eat, the guillotine ingests. For the lifeless corpse, it matters not. In all this, it must be emphasized, it was only the cannibalism that remained a metaphor. The blood of the "enemies of the Revolution" flowed every day. The public decapitations were a quotidian experience. We are in the midst of a society and a culture suffering from a massive regressive experience. Such severe regression—and Nazism is another prime example—is always accompanied by a quantum acceleration of violence. The regressive mode of expressing and exercising aggression returns to an almost basic primitive level, going far beyond the other regressive phenomena in society. The Bosnian and Rwandan experiences of the last ten years are other examples of this exact ordeal. Anger, Sophocles insisted, was the last thing to grow old. Near-psychotic rage, we may say, is the inevitable accompaniment of intense social regression. Why this should be so, I cannot really say. We find it, nonetheless, over and over again. No one, no society, goes precipitously backward without the collaboration of primitive rage.

More Than a Hundred Thousand Scapegoats*

All circumstances of regressive paranoid behavior demand an inordinate number of scapegoats. The sins of the people, the difficulties and contradictions of the new revolutionary society, are laid on the heads of these chosen victims, who are then exterminated in the hope, or the conviction, that the world has been purified, that the paradoxes, contradictions, and impossibilities of ideological terror

---

*Donald Greer, the recognized authority on the number of victims of the Terror, gives a figure of 35,000 to 40,000 actually executed. Of these, 16,594 were pronounced guilty by a tribunal. The rest were put to death without trial, mostly as the aftermath of repressed rebellions against the central government: Nantes, Lyons, Toulon, etc.[70] In addition to these actual executions, Furet estimates the number of arrests (some people freed, some imprisoned) at close to a half-million.[71]

no longer exist. Scapegoating, witch-hunting, sacrifice, Holocaust, genocide. As history moved forward into the Modern world, as national states became larger and ever more efficient, as the technology of extermination became more and more prodigious, the number of victims accelerated from the thousands to the millions. The psychological motivation of terrorists remained the same, no matter how small or larger the number of sacrifices. In French revolutionary times, a fundamental cultural *mentalité* was the search for, and annihilation of, sacrificial victims who were responsible for the political, social, and psychological distress the nation was experiencing. Nobles, priests, counter-revolutionaries, federalists, the king, the queen, the king's brothers, *émigrés*, traitors of all kinds, Pitt, the Austrians, monopolizers, hoarders, Girondins, Dantonists, Enragés, and even for the local Jacobin club, the "impure" members. There was, seemingly, no end or limit to this *virus* that had become a plague.

A deliberate use of the word "regressive" occurred in the previous paragraph. I am agnostic on the question of whether people in a traditional cannibal or head-hunting society should be designated "paranoid" or not. Even if such designation is accurate, there would seem to be a profound difference between a society in which one is a head-hunter, one's parents are head-hunters, and one's children are destined be—and a society in which one becomes a head-hunter and a rhetorical cannibal when one's parents were not either of these things. Especially so, in a society that had experienced 100 years of Enlightenment, almost 300 years of the influence of a Catholic reform movement, and had joined in the powerful force of a European culture driving toward democracy and the Rights of Man. To become a *buveur de sang* [drinker of blood] in such a society could only be accomplished by retrogression to a profoundly paranoid position.

One reason that the current psychoanalytic theory of paranoia and paranoid behavior is so inadequate is that, even with all the critique of feminist theory, psychoanalysis, almost completely, still refuses to look at the psychopathology of the preoedipal situation. Theoretically fixated on problems of the Oedipus complex, it remains incapable of confronting and understanding paranoia and paranoid conduct. Paranoia remains a Medusa-head that paralyzes and destroys the beholder. Melanie Klein, who has given us the designation "paranoid position," feared not to confront this threatening irrationality, but elements of her theoretical structure (that a three-month-old child already has an Oedipus complex, as well as an overwhelming desire to go in and dismember the mother's body) seem so beyond reality that we find it hard to use her work to construct the adequate theoretical understanding we long for.

Regression to the paranoid position, then, would imply a movement backward to the preoedipal world of anality and orality. Head-hunting* and metaphorical cannibalism are appropriate to that circumstance. Once the regressive
juggernaut is set in motion, there seems to be nothing stopping its retrograde
journey. Only actual cannibalism seems to remain taboo, though the nonpsychotic Germans came very close in excavating the gold out of the teeth of their
scapegoats and in the construction of lampshades made of the skins of their
victims.

Tocqueville's *virus* was Modernity Psychosis—ideological terror. One of its
fundamental symptoms was massive psychological regression in regard to the
acting out of human destructive capabilities. Some people have read the Nazi-
Holocaust experience as demonstrating how thin is the layer of civilization covering and controlling primitive aggressive impulses. One might read this history
from exactly the opposite point of view. The layer of civilization, the demand
for the repression and/or sublimation of primitive aggression, is so powerful in
the Modern world that only a massive onslaught on it can confront and destroy
its potency. Those intent on overthrowing the civilizing superego and regressing
to a previous state of social evolution need powerful forces on their side. Paranoid panic, the threat of almost total dissolution of the self and society, are the
most potent weapons to which such terrorists resort. Over and over again, they
cry out that society is in danger of collapse or destruction. And only the blood
of others, the heads of others, and vicarious cannibalism can save us.

French revolutionary history is so pervaded by the creation of scapegoats and
victims that no extensive data need to be presented here. A few apt illustrations
should suffice. What is so remarkable is that Tocqueville's *virus* had infected not
only those destined to construct the Jacobin Terror but also the decent, bourgeois Girondins as well. In December '91 and January '92, as the Gironde was
pushing the Assembly to declare war on Europe, Gaudet had argued that the
war would help unmask the traitors: "Let us designate the place for traitors
beforehand, and let it be the scaffold." And Brissot had previously cried out:
"We need spectacular treason cases; the people are ready!"[73] The resort to the
classic paranoid defense would lead us to believe some intense paranoid anxiety
was driving these respectable folk; all this before the king's flight to Varennes,
and after a peaceful election under a new revolutionary, democratic constitution
had brought these strange beasts—bourgeois terrorists—to political power.

At the end of July 1793, the revolutionary armies in the north suffered sig-

*On the question of head-hunting as a form of anal-aggression, see my book on cannibalism,
Chapter 3.[72]

nificant defeats: Mainz and then Valenciennes were surrendered to the Austrians. The road to Paris was almost open to the enemy. In August, General Custine, who, unfortunately for him, was noble-born, had served the Revolution admirably before this, but was brought to trial on charges of treason in August. Robespierre became impatient at the slow speed of the tribunal. Mathiez explains what happened, and why.

> The public was obviously favourable to [Custine], and the jury wavered. The Jacobins became agitated. "It must not be," said Robespierre at the club on August 25, "that a tribunal established to help the Revolution should hold it back by its criminal delays; it ought to be always equal to the offence." Custine was sentenced two days later and died bravely on August 28. He was guilty of nothing but insubordination to the orders of Bouchette, incautious language, and defective organization in the field. *He was the scapegoat for the capitulation of Mainz and Valenciennes.*[74]

Patrice Higonnet has detailed the persecution of nobles—primarily because they were nobles—during revolutionary years, most especially at the time of the Terror. What he demonstrates, and emphasizes theoretically, was that nobles had become an important, particular category of scapegoat. What is being argued in this chapter is that scapegoating, with lethal consequences, pervaded the whole of revolutionary culture. What Higonnet emphasized is how easily appropriate it was for the nobility to play that role: "Finally, nobles were convicted simply because they were nobles, sometimes in whole batches, as happened on 29 germinal an II, when six noblewomen, one with her husband, and ten men, two of them with their sons, were lumped together in a single fournée: it was and is quite obvious that they were really killed as nobles and that the three non-nobles who accompanied them to the scaffold were there for variety's sake."[75]

In his analysis of why all this occurred, Higonnet emphasizes the structure: revolutionary change—anxiety—defense against that anxiety by resort to scapegoating and human sacrifice. He pays particular attention to the angst on the part of the newly empowered bourgeois class. I would argue that all classes were in a near-panic state. His analogy with the Nazi Holocaust of the Jews is striking. Both of these circumstances can be read as defensive panic reactions to the demands and new freedoms of Modernity:

> Bourgeois detested nobles not only because nobles were a marginal and traditional category, as were Jews, but because their own situation in the new class structure, which they did not fully understand, created within them an unprecedented anxi-

ety that was real but which they could not fully articulate. The persecution of Jews in the 1930s and of nobles in the 1790s came at moments when the fears and hatreds that characterized social life at the time were apprehended but not understood.[76]

When we see a culture diseased by the *virus* of Modernity Psychosis creating a killing-field out of an Enlightenment society, it is essential to ask: What quantum leap of anxiety has brought this about? Before beginning to address that question directly, however, in the next chapter, we look at even more indications that France was suffering from a pervasive culture of paranoia.

16

ENEMIES WITHOUT—TRAITORS WITHIN; PARANOID PURGING AND SELF-DESTRUCTION

Thus, the views of the radicals presupposed an *aristocratie* that was no less than the most ghoulish ogre of childhood fantasy. . . . The *aristocrate*, moreover, sought through secret plans to maintain his power and was ultimately willing to resort to the crudest villainies imaginable. While it is impossible for the historian to accept as fact this ubiquitous and horrible *aristocrate*, the existence of this spectre was unquestioned by the radicals. Theirs was a state of mind where paranoia and fanaticism ruled.

—Jack Censer, *Prelude to Power*, 58.

The [Jacobin] clubbists subscribed to what might be called "the devil theory of economics." Almost all believed that traitors and enemy agents wanted to provoke famine in order to destroy the nation from within. They repeatedly accused merchants, farmers, bakers, butchers, and millers of greedy profiteering.

—Michael Kennedy, *Jacobin Clubs . . . Middle Years*, 65.

[End of September '92] At the Jacobins, as in the Convention, the two parties were now ranged against each other, while between them floated the phantom of treachery to the nation.

—Albert Mathiez, *The French Revolution*, 233.

All that is valuable and virtuous in the world—the Nation, the Revolution, the Republic, Liberty, *le peuple, la patrie*—is threatened with destruction. Enemies surround us. Traitors secret themselves in our midst, ever-ready to strike. Only by exterminating the villainous traitors within and destroying the foreign enemies that surround us can our great virtuous Republic continue to live. And everyone is suspect; no one is to be completely trusted. Eliminate one traitor, and ten come to take his place. The process of purification is never-ending.

The paranoid worldview, under which democracy is impossible, is obsessed with the foreign threat (*l'étranger* in revolutionary parlance), the betrayers of *la patrie* within, and the intimate relationship between the two. When a democratic society, for whatever reason, begins the slide into a culture of paranoia, it is inevitable that these two threatening specters arise. Senator Joseph McCarthy was moving toward the toppling of American democracy by skillfully exploiting the panic-anxiety about the external Communist threat to conquer the world and the traitorous Communists in our midst who had intent to seize control of our own polity. For revolutionary France, the commitment to this paranoid *Weltanschauung* did not destroy an established democratic society; it made such establishment impossible.

The paranoid *mentalité* and agenda are so powerful because they resonate with two of the most profound and continuing anxieties within the psyche: destruction by the stranger and betrayal by those closest to us. Betrayal is the most threatening thing to a fragile psyche, a frangible sense of self. External enemies can be fought against and overcome, *provided* the citizens within the polity are united in one indivisible community. A traitor is a person who, having been a member of the commonwealth, breaks that bond and joins forces with the enemy. "The idea of treason," Michael Walzer writes, "depends upon a theory of membership, for only the member of a community can be a traitor to it."[1] A point well understood by Saint-Just, who recognized that Louis could be executed only after he had been cast out of the commonwealth: "Louis XVI must be judged as a *foreign enemy*."[2]

Treason is, by far, the greatest political crime. Once defined as a traitor, an individual can expect nothing less than death. Ideological terror finds it extraordinarily easy, and seemingly necessary, to designate people as traitors. Once again, Saint-Just: "For, since the French people has manifested its will, all that is opposed to it is outside the sovereign; all that is outside the sovereign is the enemy. . . . but between the people and its enemies there is no longer anything in common but the sword."[3]

It was a reiterated device of paranoid rhetoric to link, intimately, the enemy without and the traitor within. It became almost impossible to talk of one without referring to the other. Robespierre's tirade, during the height of the Terror, was typical: "Social protection is due only to peaceful citizens; there are no citizens in the Republic but the republicans. The royalists, the conspirators are, in its eyes, only strangers or, rather, enemies. Is not the terrible war, which liberty sustains against tyranny, indivisible? Are not the enemies within the allies of those without?"[4] This paranoid culture had not been invented by the Jacobin terrorists. Already in November–December 1791, the Girondists, in the advocacy of the war-agenda, had struck the same repetitious, conspiratorial notes. After an extreme warmongering speech by Insard to the Assembly in November, several speakers supported the frenzied emotion by linking the *émigrés* to counter-revolutionaries at home. "While the enemies without were allowed to carry on their wicked work, it was argued, the enemies within would continue to flourish."[5]

All of this, of course, makes the annihilation of those suspected of treasonable behavior extraordinarily easy. Suspected—not proven—was sufficient during this reign of paranoid culture. The Gironde was brought down in the spring of '93 with the aid of the treason accusation. Danton and his allies were executed in April '94 under the same banner. Thousands would be butchered after similar miscarriages of justice. Robespierre—erstwhile moral genius—led this kind of paranoid *blitzkrieg*. In preparation for the overthrow of the Gironde, he delivered a speech to the Convention, in April '93, full of the clichés of paranoid accusation. "Brissot, Gaudet, Vergniaud, Gensonné, and other hypocritical agents of the same coalition" were involved in criminal and treasonable conspiracy. "A profoundly corrupt coalition. . . . links in a chain connecting all the hostile chancelleries of Europe."[6] What punishment did such betrayers of the Revolution deserve? Merely to deprive them of their seats in the Assembly would, obviously, be cowardly behavior. Only fratricide could serve.

Bronislaw Baczko has, with his usual penetrating insight, summed up this whole dehumanizing, pathetic drama:

A very swift overview allows the picking out of a repetitive theme—the *plot*—inseparable from another—the *hidden enemy*. The rumour is bolstered by a rich and compact symbolism, of occult and menacing forces, of the shadows where the wicked weave their machinations. The precise goal of the plot varies according to the case and circumstances. It is, however, striking that the great waves of popular rumours speak not only of a plot against the Nation, the Revolution, but point to a conspiracy menacing the vital substance of the People. The "enemies" are attacking its health, its life even, its women and its children. In this way, the rumour which accompanies a rise in popular violence has the direct result that the carrying out of this violence is viewed as a legitimate act of defence or of revenge against the "villains" who are plotting abominable crimes—if they have not already committed them.[7]

Robespierre and Saint-Just were masters of the paranoid rhetoric. And, like Hitler who came much after them, this expertise arose not from some conscious manipulation of the perceived fears of the masses but from cries within their own hearts. Their political power—short-lived though it was—maintained itself because they and *le peuple* shared the same nightmare. In December '93, Robespierre appeared before the Assembly to argue against the position of the "Indulgents" and to assert, in the name of the Committee of Public Safety, the necessity of the Terror. It is revealing to quote at length this paranoid raving:

Thanks to five years of treason and of tyranny, thanks to too much carelessness and credulity, thanks to some traits of vigour too much denied by a pusillanimous repentance, Austria, England, Russia, Prussia, Italy have had the time to establish in France a secret government, a rival of the French government itself. They also have their committees, their treasury, their agents; this government acquires the power that we take away from our own: they have a unity which, for a long time, we have lacked; policies which we believe are too powerful to serve for us; an uninterrupted spirit and the kind of agreement that we have not enough but always felt the necessity.

   Thus foreign courts have, for a long time, vomited onto France all the clever villains that they have in their pay. Their agents still invest our army; the very victory at Toulon is the proof of it; all the bravery of the soldiers, all the fidelity of the generals, all the heroism of the representatives of the people, were necessary in order to triumph over treason. They deliberate in our administrative committees, in our section assemblies; they insert themselves in our clubs; they have secreted themselves even as far as the sanctuary of the national representation; they direct, and will eternally direct, the counter-revolution on the same plan.

   They prowl around us; they capture our secrets by surprise; they flatter our passions; they search for a way to inspire our opinions; they turn our resolution against us. Are you weak? they praise your prudence. Are you prudent? they accuse you of weakness; they call your courage, temerity; your justice, cruelty. Treat them kindly, they conspire publicly; menace them, they conspire in the shadows, and under the mask of patriotism. Yesterday they assassinated the defenders of liberty; today they insert themselves at their funeral ceremonies, and demand for them divine honors, yet still seeking out the occasion to cut the throats of those equally deserving of honor. Is it necessary to rekindle the civil war? they preach all the follies of superstition. The civil war is close to being extinguished by the torrents of French blood? they recant and invoke their priesthood and their god in order to rekindle it.

✳   ✳   ✳   ✳   ✳

Yes, the perfidious emissaries who speak to us, who flatter us, they are the brothers, they are the accomplices of the ferocious henchmen who ravage our crops . . . who have massacred our brothers, cut the throats without pity of our prisoners, our wives, our children . . . and the representatives of the French people. What say I? the monsters who have committed these crimes are a thousand times less atrocious than those wretched villains who secretly rend our bowels and, yet, they breathe, they conspire—impunitively.[8]

The paranoid litany quickly became as formulaic as those repetitive parts of the great Homeric epics. All the homicidal orator had to do was to repeat the long line of clichés about treachery and then insert the name of the soon-to-be-executed victim in the appropriate place: Brissot, Condorcet, Hébert, Desmoulins, Danton. Saint-Just was capable of superb rhetoric, but in what follows—the report to the Convention on March 31, 1794, on the Dantonists, which report was followed within a week by the execution of Danton and his closest colleagues—we get nothing but the same old paranoid shibboleths, with only the target of the attack having been changed:

Do not, then, expect peace in the State until the last partisan of [the Duke of] Orleans, until the faction of the indulgents that protects the aristocracy, until the last friends of Dumouriez [meaning Danton] and those who have drenched themselves in treasons without being discovered until today, will be dead: all that constitute the conspiracy of l'étranger [the foreigner, the enemy, the stranger]. He has conspired without cease in the midst of us (for five years) corrupting orators in order to give us deadly counsel . . . overthrowing our colonies, bribing our generals and those in power, destroying our commerce, intercepting the movement of our foodstuffs, constituting each department, each district even, in a federalism with authority independent of the national representation.[9]

What reasonable person, interested in preserving his own life, would assert publicly that Danton was incapable of all these forms of treason?

THE CLICHÉS OF THE PARANOID POSITION

Over and over again, from the most brilliant of revolutionary orators and leaders to the ordinary outspoken sans-culotte, we hear the same paranoid banalities.

Égorger nos femmes

Some people are born terrorists. They carry into adult life strong sadistic and cruel impulses, the acting out of which is made possible by a hazardous time like the Revolution. Marat and Claude Javogues, who is the main biographical subject of Colin Lucas's book on the Terror, fit this description. Others, however, arrived at the terrorist-extreme paranoid position as a result of the increasing anxiety-panic caused by revolutionary events and the failure to resolve and stabilize the political position. "By the middle of the 1793," Lucas observes, "a man was in many ways predestined to become a terrorist because his political attitude at that time had emerged progressively from his reactions to such issues as the Flight to Varennes, the religious question, the fall and execution of the King, the September Massacres, the economic crisis, popular misery, military defeat, and the Fall of the Girondins." When a man who was not a born terrorist nevertheless arrives at a terrorist stance, he usually has recourse to the clichés of the paranoid position in order to justify his arrival in this strange land. "Brunon-Soviche's opinion on the execution of the King," Lucas goes on, "demonstrated the emergence of a future terrorist from a political preoccupation with the fragility of the new republic:"

> Citizens, you know my character; you know how much I am remote from blood and carnage. So then, I do not conceal from you that I would regard as an unhappy necessity the annihilation of some individual that the laws are not able to reach and whose refined perversity harms the Republic as much as an innumerable army. Know for sure, these scoundrels are only waiting our departure for the frontier in order to cut the throat of our women and our children [*égorger nos femmes et nos enfants*] or to reduce them to starvation.[10]

And lest we assume too readily that *égorger nos femmes et nos enfants* is merely a metaphor, the reality of which most people discount, it may be remembered that in the years 1916–1917 the United States was propelled into World War I in part because the Huns were spearing Belgian children on the points of their bayonets.

The Plot

The plot against the Republic, against the Revolution, was all over the land. No place was safe. One could never know where it could crop up tomorrow. Furet, in his analysis of the plot, does not use the paranoid vocabulary, but in his description of it as the perversion of the revolution, its "antiprinciple," he gives us an extraordinarily accurate picture of the use of projection in the paranoid worldview. What we have done, or wish to do, we insist that the others, the enemy, has done or wishes to do—even if in a negative way. "There was no need to name the perpetrators of the crime and to present precise facts about their plans, since it was impossible to determine the agents of the plot, who were hidden, and its aims, which were abstract. In short, the plot came to be seen as the only adversary of sufficient stature to warrant concern, since it was patterned on the Revolution itself. Like the Revolution, it was abstract, omnipresent and pregnant with new developments; but it was secret whereas the Revolution was public, perverse whereas the Revolution was beneficial, nefarious whereas the Revolution brought happiness to society. It was its negative, its reverse, its antiprinciple."[11]

Designating and Finding Those to Blame for Failures

A fundamental first principle of the paranoid position is that we are not to blame for failure. "They" are doing it to us: the enemy, the traitors, *l'étranger*: those suspected of traitorous inclinations must be kept under close surveillance. Most significant is the fact that this attitude, like so many other paranoid perceptions, did not originate with radical Jacobins and the Terror. Already by May of '92, after the first serious defeats in the war, the Brissotins, as the Girondists were now known, were looking for scapegoats to blame for the failure of their war program. One moderate Jacobin noted: "Everywhere you hear the cry that the king is betraying us, the generals are betraying us, that nobody is to be trusted; that the *Austrian Committee* has been caught in the act; that Paris will be taken in six weeks by the Austrians."[12] One doesn't remain passive in the face of such threatening panic; one acts; one reacts; one takes defensive actions and finds victims to sacrifice. The Brissotins placed all foreigners in Paris under surveillance. The Assembly passed a decree allowing the deportation of any refractory priest who was denounced by twenty citizens.[13] How all this would aid in defeating the Austrian army, no one bothered to ask.

Rounding up and arresting suspects (and, during the worst of the Terror, executing many of them) became a standard operation to assuage panic-anxiety. In August of '92, Doyle writes: "The paranoid atmosphere only grew worse when it was learned that the Prussians had invaded French territory; and news arriving on the twenty-sixth of the fall of Longwy, with scarcely any resistance, seemed to confirm that traitors were everywhere." Danton then ordered a search of all dwellings in Paris for people suspected of possible treason. Almost 3,000 victims were incarcerated, severely trying the capacity of the prisons.[14]

Suspects, Suspects, Suspects

Everywhere! The equation of suspicion with conviction is an elemental attribute of the paranoid *mentalité*. The conception that a person is innocent until proven guilty is not only humanly, morally, juridically progressive—it requires the capacity to advance beyond the paranoid position. The revolutionary obsession with suspects—and "obsession" is the accurate word—is another powerful indicator of how steeped it was in the paranoid culture. As the great Terror advanced, to be seriously suspected meant to be facing imminent death. On the 8th of Thermidor—the day before his overthrow—Robespierre delivered a two-hour speech to the Convention: a raving, self-justifying, accusatory discourse. To describe it as merely "paranoid" is to be generous; it was pushing at the very borders of paranoia itself. "A conspiracy against public liberty" existed, perpetuated by several unnamed deputies of the Convention; it penetrated even into the Committee of General Security and the great Committee of Public Safety itself. "These 'traitors' must be punished, their 'factions' crushed."[15] In the debate that followed the speech that considered whether it should be printed and distributed by the Convention, Couthon completely supported Robespierre. The deputy Panis challenged Robespierre and Couthon to name the deputies on Maximilien's list. He refused. "This was his ruin. All those who had anything to reproach themselves with felt themselves threatened."[16] Far better that Robespierre should die than that one should risk the consequences of one's name appearing on that list. On his part, it was a fatal mistake to threaten so many: a "mistake" consistent with the self-destructive impulse within the paranoid view.

So consistent, so limited, so banal are the clichés of the paranoid position that we find them reappearing over the years when society feels itself threatened in that identical manner. In the early 1950s, Senator Joseph McCarthy, a champion of the paranoid thrust who probably had never even heard of Robespierre, periodically announced that he held in his hands a list of "traitors" ensconced within the midst of the government itself. And, like the Incorruptible, he held back making the specific names public: a paranoid tease. He, too, illusioned by an indestructible sense of omnipotence, pushed his paranoid attacks too far and ended in self-decreed defeat. In our nonparanoid, stable democratic society, however, the vanquished warrior did not have the guillotine to face. The form of Robespierre's punishment had been decreed by Robespierre.

The threat of treason, and those suspected of treason, was so great that it allowed for the complete abandonment of any sense of rational justice or rights of the accused. Baczko elaborates on the Law of Suspects, September 17, 1793:

> It decreed, first, that "all suspected persons within the territory of the Republic" be placed in custody "immediately." The definition of "suspected persons" is notable for its lack of precision—to say that this vague, blurry language lent itself to several interpretations would be to overstate its rigor! Quite simply, it allowed the arresting authorities full power to decide who was a suspect. "Suspected persons" were all those "who, by their conduct, associations, talk, or writings have shown themselves partisans of tyranny or feudalism and enemies of liberty," all those . . . "former nobles, husbands, wives, fathers, mothers, sons or daughters, brothers or sisters, and agents of the émigrés, who have not steadily manifested their devotion to the Revolution."[17]

It was a net capable of ensnaring anyone. It did not languish unused.

L'ÉTRANGER

There is a concept in psychoanalytic developmental theory—based on direct observation of children—of "stranger anxiety" that occurs at around seven or eight months of age. Whereas, at five or six months, the child is at ease, being passed from one hand to another, and welcomes guests with a warm smile, suddenly—and, from personal observation, it is remarkable how suddenly—that whole view of the world changes, the child screams on leaving the mother's arms for another, even responding to incoming guests in an identical manner. I have observed it in my own grandchildren and have also heard from their mothers how, almost uncannily, that syndrome arrives on schedule. It seems that something in the nature of the child's attachment to the mother—and the security derived therefrom—has radically changed. Attachment and security seem to have become particularized: the mother has, most intensely, become a particular person. A generalization to people in general will no longer serve. The child has ceased to be content with a mother, or motherly person, but wants—most steadfastly—*its* mother. Others—strangers—are not only inadequate but threatening.

For some time I have felt, but had no way of establishing, that this period of stranger anxiety was intimately connected with subsequent adult fear of strangers, with prejudice of all kinds, most particularly racism and anti-Semitism. And, in most recent times, with fear and hatred of immigrants. Any adequate psychological theory of intolerance and prejudice, I feel, must begin with stranger anxiety: how it is dealt with, its progress through subsequent developmental stages.

In addition, I have felt that stranger anxiety, and its subsequent developmental history, plays a crucial role in determining how pervasive is the paranoid position in adult life and even sheds light on the occurrence of paranoia itself. Paranoid adults, almost inevitably, are deeply concerned with foreigners and strangers. Those suffering from paranoia are, most times, psychotically obsessed with these same threatening demons.

It was therefore startling to discover that during revolutionary times, *l'étranger* (the stranger, the foreigner, the enemy)—a vague ghost-like presence—in certain circumstances became the very essence of the evil threatening the Revolution. It was *l'étranger* who was conspiring against the Revolution; it was *l'étranger* who was manipulating the counterrevolutionaries within the country. The ghost-like, demon-like quality of this threatening presence arises from the fact that it is nameless and faceless. It is not as if revolutionary rhetoric had no specific, identifiable names for its enemies: Pitt, the Austrian Committee, the Prussians, Orléans, the émigré brothers of the king. All these had faces; only *l'étranger* existed like those in a dream who are alive and do things good or evil but who remain unrecognizable. *L'étranger* became one great objective correlative of the paranoid threat of disaster.

It is the height of irony that paranoid terrorists, who are capable of sending thousands to the guillotine, do not imagine that they are increasing the chances that they themselves will mount that awesome scaffold someday. They are completely adroit at hurling the clichés of paranoid rhetoric at their present enemies, seemingly unaware that it becomes a simple matter, later on, for someone to insert their names within the same simplistic organization of good and evil. Euripides says that when a citizen votes for war in the Assembly, he does not foresee his own death. So, Danton in November 1793, could not foresee that, having evoked the evil conspiracy of *l'étranger*, four months later he would become the object, not the subject, of the exact same accusatory mode. "Il faut que les Comités préparent un rapport sur ce qu'on appelle une conspiration de l'étranger. . . . Mais il veut que la terreur soit reportée à son vrai but, c'est à dire contre les aristocrates, contre les égoïstes, contre les conspirateurs, contre les traîtres amis de l'étranger."[18] ("The Committees must prepare a report on that which has been identified as a conspiracy of *l'étranger*. . . . But, it is desired that the terror be carried to its true end, that is to say, against the aristocrats, against the egoists, against the conspirators, against the traitorous friends of *l'étranger*.")[19]

On March 31, 1794, Saint-Just delivered to the Convention a report on Danton and the Dantonists: the indictment that quickly resulted in their execution. So pervasive was the role given to *l'étranger* in the spreading of their treachery that it reminds one of the former Christian use of the Devil in sermons directed at sin and sinners. *L'étranger* was close to being the Devil of revolutionary rhetoric:

> L'étranger favorisa ces diverses factions; il leur donna des armes dans la Vendée: avec elles il incendia les arsenaux, par elles il disloqua l'empire et le fit tendre au fédéralisme, pour réunir les débris sous le régime monarchique; par elles il soutint Dumouriez; par elles il a tout tenté pour vous détruire, pour renverser votre government, vous amollir et vous renouveler. L'étranger employa ces factions à tous les crimes par lesquels il prétendit à reveler le trône, ou à nous empêcher à constituer la Republique.[20]
>
> Les partis criminels, chargés par l'étranger d'attaquer la représentation nationale et de provoquer votre renouvellement. . . .[21]
>
> Citoyens, la conjuration d'Hébert étant devoileé ces jours derniers l'étranger s'efforça de verser le scandale sur tout ce que la liberté honore. . . .[22]
>
> . . . vous avez travaillé pour l'étranger qui jamais ne voulut autre chose que le renouvellement de la Convention, qui eût entraîné la perte de la Republique.[23]
>
> N'espérez donc la paix dans l'État que lorsque le dernier partisan de d'Orléans, que lorsque la faction des indulgents qui protège l'aristocratie, que lorsque les derniers amis de Dumouriez et ceux qui ont trempé dans les trahisons sans être découverts jusqu'aujourd'hui, seront morts; tout cela compose la conjuration de l'étranger.[24]

L'étranger encouraged the various factions; he gave arms to them in the Vendée: using them, he incinerated the arsenals, by means of them he dislocated the empire and held out a hand to federalism, in order to join together again the remains of the monarchical regime; with their help he sustained Demouriez; by means of them he has wholly attempted to destroy you, in order to overthrow your government, to weaken you, and to remove and replace you. *L'étranger* employed these factions for all the crimes in which he pretended to betray the throne, but actually intended to prevent you from establishing the Republic.

The criminal parties, charged by *l'étranger* to attack the national representation and to instigate your removal and replacement. . . .

Citizens, the conspiracy of Hébert having been unveiled in recent days, *l'étranger* makes every effort to pour scandal on all those who honor liberty. . . .

. . . you have worked for *l'étranger* who has not wanted anything else but the removal and replacement of the Convention, who has provoked the ruin of the Republic.

Do not, then, expect peace in the State until the last partisan of Orléans, until the faction of the indulgents that protects the aristocracy, until the last friends of Dumouriez and those who have drenched themselves in treasons without being discovered until today, shall be dead; all that constitutes the conspiracy of *l'étranger*.

It is hard to imagine that grown-up men listened to this drivel and felt justified by it in sending real people to a real death. They were drowning in a dream of destruction, where ordinary reality had been transcended. *L'étranger* was, perhaps, responsible for that as well.

That the rhetorical utilization of *l'étranger* resonates with the older Christian symbolism of the Devil is hinted at in the use it was put to in revolutionary ritual celebrations. Mona Ozouf writes: "As in the Festival of the Supreme Being, it is, from now on, on the allegorical figures of Atheism, Ambition, Egoism, Discord, and False Simplicity that one will read these words: 'Sole hope of *l'étranger*.'"[25] One can imagine, at another time, the attribution of the sins of ambition, egoism, and discord to the work of the Devil.*

Whether *l'étranger* should be translated "stranger," "foreigner," "enemy," or "foreign enemy" depends upon the context in which it was used. One particular use, for instance, was for foreigners, or noncitizens, resident in France. Today, Turkish nationals living in Germany are a comparable category. And as with the

---

*On the very day, after writing this sentence, I observed, at the Morgan Library in New York, a medieval illumination of the fourteenth century from Poitiers, illustrating the perennial topic of LUST. In the lower right-hand corner, a couple was in the process of beginning to go at it. On the left, an agitated devil was either urging them on or causing their sinful ardor or both.

noncitizen Metics who lived in ancient Athens, the status of these residential foreigners was subject to legislation. One particular decree, for instance, of August 26, 1792, permitted the election *"des étrangers à la Convention,"* but as the paranoid attitude accelerated under the Terror, this decree was abrogated on January 2, 1794, even retroactively, and resulted, among other things, in the exclusion of Tom Paine from the Convention, where he had served after being elected a deputy. After Thermidor, a certain persecutory stance continued toward resident foreigners. In these circumstances, crucial for the psychological point being made here, the word appears in the plural in a similar way to which we would use it: "the foreigners." The Ministry of Police, which had been created in 1796, was instructed to: *"faire exécuter les lois sur les étrangers."*[26] ("To enforce the laws concerning foreigners.")

Though one may observe a paranoid fear of foreigners in this usage, the resort to the singular, especially when the rhetorical purpose is to send someone to his death—*"Les partis criminels, chargés par l'étranger d'attaquer la représentation nationale"*— has a much more sinister dimension. "Foreigners" may be a threat to the Nation, but *l'étranger* is a dark, sinister, devil-like manipulator of the body politic. He deserves a special place in the political culture of paranoia.

And, like other mythical creations, he never died. When college campuses in America erupted against the war in Vietnam, in the late 1960s and early 1970s, it was unimaginable to some that students at Berkeley, Wisconsin, and Harvard could behave in such a manner from their own internal prompting. Someone was, obviously, manipulating them: "outside agitators" became the slogan to describe those dark, secret figures lurking around the edges of the campuses and infecting our students with hatred of America. *L'étranger* lived on.

PARANOID PURGING

The periodic political purge became a fundamental attribute and activity of ideological terrorism in the twentieth century. Purifying, cleansing, extirpating the unclean—and therefore evil—elements in the vanguard of the revolution. The medical analogy of the purge, which cleans the bowels of unwanted fecal matter, may or may not have resonated in the (unconscious) minds of these murderous Stalinists and their imitators, but we are certainly justified in wondering. The severely paranoid person is, many times, obsessively concerned with what goes into and out of the body. The periodic purging of the body politic represents one more fundamental aspect of the paranoid position exhibited by ideological terrorism. The very first time, in the modern world, when we can observe this happening with fatal frequency was during the Great Terror, within the Jacobin clubs, which were, at that time, the advanced instruments of the Revolution. It was another perversion of Modernity that the Revolution bequeathed to our own tragic century.

It became a regular occurrence for a Jacobin society to review the current status of each of its members and to purge those found unworthy. "Psychologically," Brinton writes, "[an] other sort of *épuration* [purification, purging] is more interesting. Sessions were held to determine the orthodoxy of the whole membership of a society, a process which often meant the stringing out of meetings for days."[27] During the Terror, everything of violence and paranoia became more and more primitive as time went on. Walter comments about the Paris Club; "*Lépurment* [the purifying, the refining] (it is the term that is used during these occasions) becomes in the last months of the society a veritable obsession."[28]

The self-interrogation at the clubs became more and more formalized. The society as a whole faced each member in an adversarial stance:

What did you do in 89?
What have you done since then until 93?
What was your fortune in 89?
What is it now?
If your fortune has grown, what means have you used?
What have you done for the revolution?
Have you signed any counter-revolutionary petition?
If you are an administrator, journalist or representative
of the people, have you used your pen or your advice
to serve liberty?[29]

Everyone was suspect, even in the heart of the vanguard of the Revolution—or possibly, most especially in the heart of the vanguard. Nothing was done moderately; any risk one took had to be of life itself. On December 30, 1790, the president of the Paris Club was asked to "pose to each Jacobin who presents himself to be purified, the following question: What have you done to be assured of being hung if the counterrevolution succeeds?"[30] They were intent on living out the most exaggerated fantasy of cataclysmic revolution.

Michael Carter gives us an extended description of the purification proceedings at the Paris Club on December 12, 1793: a pure culture of psychopathological politics. First, Coupé (of Oise) was expelled from the Club after being attacked by Fabre d'Eglatine. Then, Robespierre and Billaud-Varenne, also a member of the Committee of Public Safety, were certified amidst "very flattering applause." Casabianca was purged because he had voted against death for Louis, even though he had voted "Yes" as to his guilt. We cannot help but observe that Casabianca's vote against death had taken place almost eleven months previous to his expulsion, during which time his revolutionary credentials, as a deputy to the Convention, had been perfectly acceptable. Looking for more scapegoats, Eustache-Jean-Marie d'Aoust was excluded even though he was a Convention deputy, because he was "tainted with 'original sin,' that is, he had been a marquis."

The most explosive, hysterical debate concerned Anarchasis Cloots, who had been an active participant in the Revolution from its beginning. He was, however, a person of independent, if not idiosyncratic, mind. Cloots was, first, questioned about his relationship to certain bankers and defended his actions by insisting he used them only for private purposes. At this point, Maximilien himself stepped in and attacked him vehemently with all the fatal paranoid clichés. "Cloots, tu passes ta vie avec nos ennemies, avec les agents et les espions des puissances étrangers; comme eux, tu es un traître." ("Cloots, you spend your life with our enemies, with the agents and spies of foreign powers; like them, you are a traitor.") He had been a supporter of the party of Brissot and Dumouriez, promoted federalism, and tried to cause trouble for the Revolution by unnecessarily suppressing religious worship. "Je vous ai tracé l'historie de sa vie politique." ("I have portrayed for you the history of your political life.") And, turning to the Club itself, he commanded the fatal action: "Prononcez."[31] Arrested less than a month later, Cloots was executed with Hébert on the 24th of March, 1794.

This kind of sanguinary politics also allowed for—possibly even required— its seeming opposite: a quality of sentimentality, especially where children were concerned, leading to scenes that came remarkably close to political *kitsch*. Citizen Petit was questioned as to why he had refused to serve on the Revolutionary Tribunal and responded that he did not feel competent to accomplish such duties. "His twelve year old son then ran to the rostrum and declared to the assembly that his father was a good patriot and that he had been raised by him according to the purest principles of the revolution. His enthusiasm merited the applause of the members and an accolade from the chairman. His father was admitted."[32] Such was the level of political sophistication and maturity by which the revolutionary elite lived and died.

The exact same paranoid view prevailed during the Terror, in the civilian oversight of the generals. Purging and execution were the sentences for military incompetence. Houchard was the general of the Army of the North. In September '93, he and it won a crucial battle against English forces at Hondschotte. He failed, however, to follow up this victory and annihilate the enemy's forces; the Duke of York's army escaped intact. Houchard was subsequently accused of treason by one of the representatives of the Convention on mission to the north. "An established government," writes Palmer in an unnecessary apology for the Terror, "when it removes a general, can afford to admit that it made an error in appointing him. Revolutionary governments cannot so easily admit mistakes."[33] The problem was not that this was a revolutionary government, since, among other considerations, at least three revolutionary governments had preceded it. The difficulty was that this was a Jacobin dictatorship, soon to be an ideological terror, steeped in a culture of paranoid purging, betrayal, and panic-anxiety about everything and everyone. "Houchard was charged, therefore, not only with failure but with treason."[34] His traitorous guilt was affirmed by the leaders of the Revolution, members of the Committee of Public Safety: Barère, Bilaud, Robespierre, Saint-André. Brought before the Revolutionary Tribunal on November 15, he was guillotined the following day.[35]

What we see happening is that, as panic-anxiety increases as a result of the ambivalence about entering the Modern world, the culture regresses, not only to a premodern traditional society, but to an even more ancient social form: a kinship-system society. In such societies, social cohesion requires an almost unanimous agreement on values. Pluralism of beliefs is not only intolerable but actually not even to be imagined. The constant elimination, during the dictatorial and terrorist year II, of all political opposition; the insistent expelling of anyone, for even the slightest disagreement from the revolutionary vanguard—all this was an attempt to establish moral unanimity in a society simultaneously advancing toward, and in panic retreat from, Modernity. Needless to say, it was doomed to fail, the only question being how many would die before it gave up that fatal ambition. Baczko, once again, has seen this with great clarity: "*Exclusion* swiftly became the regulatory mechanism of the political game; the adversary was excluded in the very name of the fundamental unity of the Nation, of the People, or of the Republic. This principle is, moreover, appropriate to the functioning and preservation of traditional communities, where unity and solidarity tend to be confused with unanimity."[36]

That one could, even at the end of the eighteenth century, be a revolutionary without becoming severely paranoid, was demonstrated by Tom Paine, whose revolutionary credentials were unassailable. A great supporter of the Revolution from the beginning, an elected delegate to the Convention, even though a foreigner, Paine observed, in May '93, that the greatest danger to the Revolution was: "the spirit of denunciation that now prevails. . . . Calumny is a species of treachery that ought to be punished as well as any other kind of treachery. It is a private vice productive of public evils; because it is possible to initiate men into disaffection by continual calumny."[37] Paine was clearly capable of going beyond the paranoid position and knew what was necessary to create a stable democratic society. He almost paid with his life for this moral autonomy and his advanced psychological position. Arrested by the revolutionary government, he came within an inch of facing the guillotine.

MARTYRDOM AND SELF-DESTRUCTION

Martyrdom is the unidentical twin of human sacrifice; they mirror each other. Two things happen to create this twinship. First, when a person active in the cause of religious, political, or social reform becomes a victim of established power—is killed as a sacrifice to preserve the status quo—the movement of reform may establish this person as a sacred martyr to the cause. In the twentieth century, the public funeral of the deceased martyr becomes the typical moment of apotheosis. The revolutionary rhetoric under the Jacobin dictatorship and the Terror, for instance, made recurrent references to "la trinité des martyrs de la liberté:"[38] Marat, Chalier, Lepeletier. Their human sacrificial nature was implied under the many times unstated, but understood, notion that their blood would fertilize the Revolution.

More complicated, and more entwined with the paranoid position, is a second phenomenon that occurs: those most active in the reforming or revolutionary process announce that they are more than willing to die for the cause. In dramatic moments of grandiosity, they declare that they will never give up the struggle, never abandon their principles, never betray their ideals—even if it means death. The tone is such that it makes one wonder whether or not that death is longed for. What the future martyr accomplishes is to erect for himself a no-lose situation: either he wins the struggle for the new world, or he dies a glorious martyr's death: either outcome is a triumph. It is a complex symbolic form, making remarkable use of the transformed self-destructive impulse within the paranoid position. CONQUER OR DIE! become one of the great banners of a culture engaged in political struggle and steeped in a paranoid value system.

Robespierre at the Jacobins, June 21, 1791, the day after the king's flight to Varennes, as described by J.M. Thompson:

> He had come to think that there was a conspiracy afoot, not only against France but against himself—"One man of honesty and courage prepared to unmask their plots, one man who thinks so lightly of life that he fears neither poison nor the sword, and would be supremely happy if his death contributed to the freedom of the fatherland." Upon which (it is reported) Desmoulins cried, "We would all give our lives to save yours!"; and the whole audience of 800 rose, and took an oath to defend Robespierre's life.[39]

All this before the declaration of war, before the overthrow of the king, before the coup against the Gironde, way before the institution of the Terror. And, in a pamphlet written in the same month, the Incorruptible is already preparing martyrdom for himself. In this *Addresse de Maximilien Robespierre aux Francais*, he concludes by comparing himself to Socrates: "Did the Athenian philosopher cause more offence to the great people, the ecclesiastics, the sophists, and the political charlatans, than I have? Have not I too spoken ill of false gods, and tried to introduce into our modern Athens the worship of nature, justice and equality?" All the money, all the bayonets, however, are possessed by his enemies. He is a "simple, weak, isolated individual" with no support but his courage and the rightness of his cause.[40] Either way, he wins. Either he succeeds in destroying those evil enemies and erecting a virtuous society, or he will wear—eternally—a martyr's crown.

There is almost always some truth in the paranoid's perception. It was not a total distortion of reality for Robespierre to worry about assassination. It was, however, the rhetorical response to this threat that gives us insight into the paranoid narrative of self-destruction and martyrdom. In January '94, after the institution of the Terror, he declared: "Because I have exercised one twelfth part of the authority of the Committee of Public Safety, they call me a dictator! . . . The only dictatorship to which I plead guilty is that of Le Pelletier, and that of Marat. (*Applause*) . . . I am not yet a martyr for the cause of the Revolution. But my dictatorship is the same as theirs, Because I share with them the threat of assassination."[41] Because I am such a virtuous and courageous person, I have risked the destruction of my life. Could anyone claim a greater heroism? Grandi-

osity and self-destruction inexorably bound together: the perfect paranoid symptomology.

The self-destructive impulse toward martyrdom did not remain a purely rhetorical and inner-psychological manifestation. In the weeks before his fall, Robespierre was acting in a manner that can only be called suicidal. At one period of
the Revolution, an absolutely brilliant tactician, he had come to the point where
his actions force one to think that he was inviting the martyr's hemlock. George
Rudé describes his behavior at the time as "unbelievably foolish . . . by lending
credence to the suspicion that he was engaged in behind the scenes intrigues
with a cabal of his intimates, [he] played right into the hands of his opponents."[42] When a man who rose to dictatorial power in an incredibly complex
and treacherous political circumstance begins to act in an "unbelievably foolish"
manner, it is legitimate to suspect that some deep psychological conflict is being
played out. In the chapter that I intend to devote to Robespierre, I will return
to this question of the self-destructive impulse within the paranoid worldview.

And it was not only a question of the man Robespierre. The entire revolutionary *Weltanschauung* was vulnerable to suicidal action. The declaration of war
against Europe and the exaggerated and unnecessary attack on the Church have
already been touched upon. As others have demonstrated and been cited to
that effect, the anticlerical hysteria continued unabated after Thermidor, just so
Blanning observes the same irrational attitude toward war, even after the demise
of the Terror. "After Fructidor the revamped Directory fell prey to the same sort
of over-confidence which had taken their Brissotin predecessors down the slippery slope to perdition."[43]

Edgar Quinet, brilliant historian and critic of the Revolution, has observed
this self-destructive force in revolutionary culture and proposed that answering
"Why?" is one of our fundamental theoretical tasks. Arguing against the conten-
tion of Louis Blanc that the Terror of '93 and the British violent domination of
India were of the same order of aggressive political behavior, Quinet responds:
"The conduct of the English in India has been compared to the regime of 93.
Where is the analogy? The world is full of violence and war. Who can doubt it?
But that is not the question here. The English generals in India, did they kill
each other? That is what is necessary to establish in order to be able to maintain
the comparison. Do you not see, then, that one of the particular traits of the
French Revolution is that the revolutionaries were put to death by the revolu-
tionaries, the Jacobins by the Jacobins, the Montagnards by the Montagnards?

Why did that happen?"[44] Even Saturn, devouring his children, is a form of self-destruction; they were, after all, his own children.

THE ACCELERATION OF PRIMITIVE VIOLENCE

When I began writing these two chapters on the paranoid position and the Terror, I did not consciously intend to devote so much discussion to primitive violence. I did expect to talk about an exaggerated concern for enemies and plots, intense feelings of anxiety and panic, and the projection onto others of one's fears and aggressive impulses: those attitudes one usually associates with the concept "paranoid." I did not clearly see, however, when I started, how important the acting out of aggression in a primitive manner was to the increasing paranoid view of the world. I did have, among the many acronyms that organize my notes, one: HSPR = Human Sacrifice as Paranoid Revenge, which became a starting point for the revelation of how important such primitive rhetoric and actions were. What has now become clear—and pervasively supported by the history of the Terror—is that any serious regression into a significantly more paranoid state (whether on the part of an individual or a whole culture) will inevitably produce an augmentation of the most primitive forms of aggression. Intense anxiety-panic results in regression to a more primitive paranoid state; in such a condition, one tries to defend oneself against even further regression (the possible loss of the ego itself) by lashing out against almost everyone and everything. Moral heroes of the Enlightenment born, become berserker killers.

I am not interested, here, in Marat or Hébert or others of their ilk, who were born terrorists. In times of revolution, or warfare, or social unrest—when the normal constraints against social aggression are lifted—certain sadistically inclined members of society, who ordinarily would not become killers, have themselves a field day exercising the most extreme aggression under the banner of "the cause." The Nazi experience in Germany; the Cultural Revolution in Mao's China; the American catastrophe in Vietnam—all these provide thousands of examples. It is of interest, for instance, to determine how Marat got to the point of demanding half a million heads—and he was not talking metaphorically—but it is much more important, if we are ever to understand the contradictions and paradoxes of Modernity, to try to comprehend how Barère, Saint-Just, and Robespierre became *buveurs de sang*. I am not optimistic that I can go more than a small part of the way toward that comprehension. There is, nonetheless, no more important theoretical project. Its successful undertaking would bring us closer to fathoming Lenin and Mao and Pol Pot—and, therefore, Russia and China and Cambodia in the twentieth century. It would reveal to us the very nature of ideological terror.

Madame Roland, for instance. One cannot read the facts of her biography without taking pride in human possibilities. Daughter of the upper reaches of the *moyen* bourgeoisie, she began reading Plutarch at age eight, and then moved to the main authors of the Enlightenment, most particularly Rousseau, who had a profound influence on her view of the world. Filled with an acute sense of the injustices perpetrated by the social world of the *ancien régime*, once established in Paris, she became the very symbol of the *"vertus domestique et civiques."*[45] She was, probably, the most influential woman in the politics of the first two revolutions. Her profound influence on the Gironde faction arose not through the use of "feminine wiles" or seductive behavior but purely from the power of her intellect, freely exercised because of the central position occupied by her husband. The fall of the Girondins marked her for death. After a sham of a trial that lasted less than one day, having been accused of conspiracy against the unity of the Republic, she was executed that very day, November 8, 1793.[46]

It hardly reads like the biography of a terrorist. And yet, in the summer of '91, as the conflict with the refractory clergy and the émigré nobility accelerated, she wrote that "a civil war would be a great school of public virtue. Peace will set us back . . . we can be regenerated by blood alone." Norman Hampson, after quoting this, goes on to say: "The Girondin deputies in the Legislative Assembly seem on the whole to have shared her conviction that the division of French society was too deep for conciliation and that the society of the revolutionary cause demanded the violent destruction of its opponents."[47] All this from the virtuous leadership of the Gironde; we can imagine what we will get when the Montagnards come to dictatorial power.

Just a metaphor, some argue about such expletives. She was not really calling for real blood. And even if this contention is true, which is not proven, we may still ask: Why have recourse to such a metaphor? And the *virus* of left-wing terror lived on in parts of French culture for nearly two centuries. Jean Paul Sartre never publicly acknowledged, or condemned, the atrocities of the Stalinist terror. During the student rebellion in Paris in 1968, he wrote: "Bosses should be locked up . . . deputies lynched. . . . Three cheers for the people's war. . . . Three cheers for the extermination of the bourgeoisie."[48] If these, also, were only metaphors, they were metaphors urging people, who might not understand the metaphorical nature of such cheerleading, to spill real blood. That blood, however, would it have been so pure? And if only metaphors, they arise nevertheless from a psyche in good part enslaved by the dominion of the paranoid position.

Sensible of the Aristotelian categories of our emotional response to tragedy, it seems reasonable to assert that, contemplating the life trajectory of a Saint-Just or a Robespierre—from a person of great moral gift, even moral genius, to an ideological cannibal—fills us with terror. Betrand Berère, who took the journey from good, solid, virtuous, admirable, bourgeois, Enlightenment liberal to end up a member of the great Committee of Public Safety and a foremost apologist for every last atrocity of the Terror—ruminating on such a degraded odyssey can fill us with profound pathos. Our pity, however, does nothing to answer the crucial question of what was driving such a man to such a course? Why didn't he opt out, as so many others had, at some crucial point of the acceleration of the Terror? The perverse pilgrimage of Robespierre will necessitate a full chapter in this work. Only a brief comment on Barère is required here, since Leo Gershoy has given us such a comprehensive and sympathetic biography. His life takes on, for us, such great symbolic meaning, for there is no way in which he may be described as a born terrorist or as a person of strong sadistic impulses waiting for society to open up the possibility of expressing these under a banner of morality. He began exactly as that solid, virtuous, bourgeois liberal. And yet.

When Louis was tried in January '93, each deputy to the Convention had two votes to make: yes or no on the question of guilt; and for or against the death penalty as punishment. Some delegates did vote for guilty but not for death. The Girondins were pushing for a referendum to the country at large concerning the question of execution. Barère voted guilt and death and in explaining the reason for his vote, the great paranoid symbol of blood shines forth: "The law tells me that between tyrants and peoples there are struggles only to the death. . . . As a classical author said, the tree of liberty grows only when it is watered by the blood of all species of tyrants. The law says death and I am only its voice."[49]

Gershoy describes the crucial point of Barère's revolutionary life: the coup against the Gironde in June '93, and the establishment of the Jacobin dictatorship. We should be extremely careful not to resort to the usual, simplistic explanation of "cowardice" in such circumstance. Any rational coward would surely know that the time for his blood was destined to come. A true coward, concerned only for his self-preservation, would have left for England, or some other haven, or given some excuse to return home to Tarbes. Barère stayed on, became a leader of the terrorist regime, courageous enough to send many children of Saturn to their death.

> This dramatic finale shattered Barère's hopes. He had done all that could be done to save the Girondins short of sharing their fate and he had failed. Failure was a *fait accompli*; in a revolution, he had said again and again, one accepted results, one did not look back. He was no hero and he had decent respect for his own security. He chose to survive and serve. With eyes suffused with tears—so reported a former friend, Helen Williams—he set to work to prepare a report to the French people which would prove that the cause of liberty had prevailed on June 2. Though he still refused to sacrifice parliamentary immunity and persevered for several weeks more to have the arrested deputies reinstated, June 2 was not to be undone. Step by step he accepted the consequences and before the summer was over he was speaking the language of terror.[50]

For some people the *virus* of ideological terror was extraordinarily infectious. Is it possible that, despite all appearances to the contrary, deep down they shared that thirst for blood? And what was it that prompted some of the foremost historians of the Revolution, in a recent generation, to bring us remarkably complex apologies for the Terror and the guillotine? Barère was, by no means, sui generis: a unique example.

I have, in a previous work,[51] attempted to differentiate between normal warfare and massacre. Massacre goes beyond the accepted—and, therefore, "legitimate"—actions of a nation at war. It, many times, calls up a moral critique, even abhorrence, that ordinary warfare killing does not. It is a more primitive acting out of violence: the killing machine gone berserk. Three categories of people, ordinarily excluded from death by warfare, are the victims of massacre: women, children, captured prisoners. The ordinary warfare of the United States in Vietnam was not condemned by most Americans until several years had passed. The My Lai massacre, however, was immediately responded to as something abhorrent. The Israeli incursion into Lebanon was a valiant defense of the autonomy of a brave little country, supported by the vast majority of Israeli citizens, but the subsequent slaughter allowed in one of the camps was considered a massacre, and triggered street protests from almost one-fourth of the Israeli populace. In ancient and traditional societies, the one circumstance that seemed most likely to trigger a massacre was when a city held out for a long time against a siege by an invading force. When the walls were finally breached and the invaders poured in, their rage at having been hindered so long resulted in the probability that rapine, pillage, plunder, indiscriminate slaughter (i.e., massacre) would result.

French revolutionary history had its share of this particular form of massacre and of the temptation to perform it. As such, taken by itself, it cannot be attributed to revolutionary Terror, but we can see this "normal" human inclination for massacre combine with the cannibalism of the guillotine to produce, most especially in Lyons and the Vendée, the most horrendous results. Let the enlightened Bertrand Barère guide us into this hell. Less than a month before the fall of Robespierre, "after obtaining the passage of a decree ordering that the enemy garrisons of Condé, Valenciennes, Le Quesnoy, and Landrecies should be put to the sword if they did not surrender within twenty-four hours after being called upon to do so, Barère uttered an enthusiastic apology for the Terror, and gave warning against premature clemency. 'Compromise with them [the enemies at home] today . . . and they will attack you tomorrow and massacre you without pity. No, no, let our enemies perish! I have said it before; it is only the dead who never come back.' "[52] This followed a previous decision a month before, that was acted on only once, that no British or Hanoverian prisoners were to be taken—that is, slaughtered instead.[53]

Those who had the temerity and the arrogance to revolt against the revolutionary government were even worse than a city that held out against siege and refused to surrender. Any punishment meted out to them, after they were defeated, was more than deserved. We have already looked at some of the revenge against Lyons. In October and November 1793, three different revolutionary courts tried and executed the unsuccessful rebels. The most efficient, the *commission revolutionnaire*, also called *Parein*, after its president, tried as many as twenty prisoners each hour, used both the firing squad and the guillotine to execute an average of twenty-eight prisoners per day for two months.[54] Since this was an Enlightenment society, the superficial forms of justice by trial were maintained. What was really happening, however, does not escape the critical eye of R.R. Palmer: "It is only necessary to observe the combination of blood lust with the jargon of revolutionary idealism. It is necessary to realize that those men inflicted death with a holy glee."[55]

One defense that we erect today, as was said earlier, when reading some of this barbarian rhetoric, is to assert that they didn't mean it literally; it was only a metaphor; they were not actually supposed to do those things. Palmer, again, in a fascinating passage, in regard to Lyons, excuses the Committee of Public Safety in exactly this manner. Each of us can decide for him- or herself how acceptable are the phrases "They did not intend," or, "They were surprised."

> The Committee of Public Safety was caught in this predicament with respect to the slaughter at Lyons. Its members had stated their aims. They had used inflammatory language: the sword of law must wave; monsters must be exterminated; a nest of conspirators is not a city; republics are exacting. They had declared grandiosely without meaning it (as the wording of the decree showed): "Lyons shall be destroyed." They believed in the Terror in creating confidence by fear, and purity by excision. They did not intend to have two thousand people killed, or to have massacres theatrically staged to the taste of overheated playwrights, or to have a great city pillaged by unscrupulous intruders in the name of public duty. They were surprised when all this happened. Whether they should have been is another question.[56]

I think it is more accurate to judge the intentions of the Committee of Public Safety in October '93 by taking cognizance of its members' own actions from November '93 to July '94. In those months, it was certainly they who became *les massacreurs*.

The punishment meted out to failed rebels of the Vendée, it may be said without exaggeration, proceeded from the genocidal mentality. By strict definition it was not an intended genocide; there was no design to annihilate all people in the area. It was of such an horrendous order, however, that it seemed calculated to satisfy the most extreme forms of the lust to annihilate. "The slaughter of the Vendeans, along with the destruction of the Vendée," Furet writes, "was the greatest collective massacre in the revolutionary Terror."[57]

It was General Turreau who was the architect of this annihilation. He commanded twelve "infernal columns" of soldiers, each under its own commander, and instructed by the General in January '94: "You will employ every means to discover the rebels, everyone will be bayoneted; the villages, farms, woods, wastelands, scrub and generally all which can be burned, will be put to the torch." He was far from acting against the wishes of the central government. Two representatives, Garrau and Hentz, were sent out from Paris to oversee Turreau and "to coordinate the means of exterminating the Vendeans." In some communes as many as one-third of the population were exterminated.[58]

One typical action took place at Gonnard on January 23. "General Crouzat's column forced two hundred old people, along with mothers and children, to kneel in front of a large pit they had dug; they were then shot so as to tumble into their own graves."[59] One may assume that the perpetrators of the Nazi Holocaust and of the recent massacres in Bosnia and Rwanda had not read the history of the Vendée revenge. These were merely cases of independent invention. In all these circumstances, however, it was an identical expression of Modernity Psychosis: that great plague of the Modern world, wherein nonpsychotic people perform acts that can only most accurately be described as "psychotic." The great moral paradox of Modernity is that it produces nonpsychotic psychotic acts.

The true nature of the Terror—that it was, simply, a terror, with no means-ends rationality, with annihilation its sole purpose: a malignant end in itself—that nature is nakedly revealed by the circumstance that it kept on accelerating, despite victories in the civil and foreign wars, and came to its sanguinary climax when the Revolution was increasingly victorious and secure, the king dead, the Convention in control, the revolts in Lyons and the Vendée suppressed. June 10, 1994, saw the infamous law of Prairal, which destroyed all remaining semblances of justice in the trials before the revolutionary tribunal. Merely being accused became a death sentence. From that date until the fall of Robespierre in July, 1,515 citizens were beheaded in the place de la Révolution, whereas in the fifteen months previously, only a mere 1,124 had met the same fate.[60]

The most outrageous accusations against defendants were believed and became the basis for execution. Typical of the madness was the case of Osselin, a deputy to the Convention, who had been held in prison for over six months but was suddenly brought to trial and guillotined because of his participation in a plot to "break out of prison, murder the two Committees, tear their hearts out, roast and eat them!"[61] If one of the great manifestations of paranoia and paranoid thinking is the projecting onto one's enemies of one's own unacceptable, primitive aggressive inclinations—and then attempting to destroy those inclinations by exterminating that now contaminated enemy—this certainly is a textbook case. The cannibals were beheading their enemies because they were cannibals. Once again, it was nonpsychotic people who engineered and carried out this catastrophe.

Hampson quotes a statement made about Thermidor by Marc-Antoine Baudot, who had been a Montagnard delegate to the Convention: "Principles had nothing to do with it; it was a matter of killing," and then goes on to say that such analysis was applicable to the whole period from the execution of Danton onwards.[62] The killing machine, once in place and functional, can't stop. It feeds on itself. Once the restraints on acting-out the most primitive fantasies of aggression are lifted, near-psychotic violence accelerates. Paranoia feeds on paranoia. The descent into a moral abyss becomes precipitous. Since the French Revolution, Cambodia, for instance, provides one of the most horrendous examples. At some point, for some reason, people have had enough, and a form of civil order is restored, very likely not by the institution of a democratic polity. Having lived so close to borderline paranoia, some kind of "rational" authoritarian regime is necessary for even a minimum of social stability.

And always this killing mania is disguised under a moral banner, whose purpose is to disprove Baudet's statement and to insist that it *is* a matter of principles. The most bizarre rituals are instituted in the attempt to moralize the killings. On June 2, 1794, fifty-four persons were sent to the guillotine, clothed in red costumes of the "parricide" and with labels describing them as "Robespierre assassins." The ritual procession and beheading took four hours.[63]

Some people at the time, especially after the execution of Danton in April '94, knew that the machine was unstoppable. A contemporary poem commemorated Danton's death:

> Fifteen victims, one by one,
> Crossed the fatal Acheron:
> Last among them, proud Danton
> Hung back in the rear, alone,
> "You there, step up!" cried old Charon
> "What are you waiting for? Come on!"
> "I'm waiting," he said, "for friend Couthon,
> For Saint-Just, and for Robespierre."[64]

And Robespierre made sure it would happen. "He was suspicious by nature," Doyle ruminates, "and over the spring [1794] the stresses of government drove him to the verge of paranoia. Surrounded by rumors of plots, not to mention assassination attempts, yet completely sure of his own rectitude, he took contradiction for bad faith and independence for opportunism. In the end he seems to have concluded that hardly anybody in public life could be relied on, and by saying so openly he ensured that they could not. And by implying that those of whom he disapproved or with whom he disagreed deserved execution, he forced them into destroying him before he destroyed them."[65]

The severely paranoid political leader (Robespierre, Hitler), when he sees defeat coming for his omnipotent plans to transform society totally, becomes more and more committed to destroying as much of the evil in the world as possible before going down himself: a Samson maneuver. Hitler's famous inquiry: "Is Paris burning?" Even the decision to attempt a total genocide of the Jews was not taken until the first intimations of defeat in the war became apparent. It was as if the leaders of the Nazi regime had said to themselves: "If we are going to go down to defeat and death, at least we will have accomplished something toward making the world a purer place; we will have excised the Jewish cancer from society."

Robespierre was also engaged in total war: a war of Virtue against Evil, involving the creation of a *nouvel homme*, and the total moral transformation of society in one generation. It is every ideological terrorist's dream of omnipotence. His rage at this betrayal of his virtuous dreams was directed, first, at his enemies—those who, in his mind, opposed this total transformation (Danton, a perfect representative of this position)—and then at himself. Those in the enemy camp had betrayed him by not going along with the radical Terror. *Indulgents* they were, significantly, designated. It was said, at the time of his execution, that Danton could have declared: "I have the sweet consolation to believe that the man who goes to his death as the chief of the faction of the *Indulgents* will find favor in the eyes of posterity."[66] Robespierre's rage, having destroyed as many as he could, finally was directed at himself, bringing on his execution along with his faithful lieutenants, Saint-Just and Couthon.

What can clearly be observed is that *regression* into a more primitive paranoid state produces an explosion of primordial violence. The traditional, authoritarian, predemocratic society exhibited many basic symptoms of the paranoid position, both acting out and containing paranoid impulses. The significant institutional arrangements to accomplish this task were autocratic monarchy, authoritarian religion, and a regular exercise of military killing. Like all societies, they exhibited a significant amount of "legitimate" social aggression—"normal" violence. When we look at the French Terror or any of its twentieth-century descendents (Stalinism, Nazism), we observe a world radically different from "normal" or "legitimate" violence. We have entered a place of unstoppable, self-destructive, cannibalistic rage. No longer "normal" paranoid behavior, but regression to the most primitive position possible that still allows the perpetrators to act in the real world. From Robespierre we hear: "We must exterminate these miserable villains who are eternally conspiring against the rights of man." New laws were not required for this task: "Not at all, we must exterminate all our enemies with the law in our hands."[67]

What was it in emerging Modernity that produced these fatal regressions? What massive increase in anxiety-panic made drowning people grab the most primitive form of defense? What made them imagine that the extermination of others would save them? Save them from what?

17

THE GREAT PROMISE AND THE GREAT ANXIETY OF MODERNITY

In our days everything seems pregnant with its contrary. . . . At the same pace that mankind masters nature, man seems to have become enslaved to other men or to his own infamy. Even the pure light of science seems unable to shine but on the background of ignorance. All our invention and progress seem to result in endowing material forces with intellectual life, and stultifying life into a material force.[1]
— Karl Marx: "Speech at the Anniversary of the *People's Paper.*"

THE FRENZIED AMBIVALENCE ABOUT MODERNITY

For the thoughtful humanist, there can be no absolute acceptance, or absolute rejection, of Modernity. So paradoxical and contradictory has it been in the benefits and catastrophes it brings—from the greatest equality for women that has existed since the end of primitive society to Auschwitz and Hiroshima—that it seems to demand a permanent ambivalence in our judgment of it. E.M. Forster's "Two cheers for democracy"[2] can be rendered, with equal sagacity, as "Two cheers for Modernity." It requires a great deal of wisdom, a great deal of psychic maturity, and a conscious willingness to take certain risks with life, in order to live with any kind of peace in the modern world. In a similar way, no one should advocate living in a democratic society without being keenly aware that giving sovereignty to all people may be one of the riskiest social ventures one can undertake.

In order to live in a democratic society, in order to enjoy the great benefits of Modernity, one must be willing to endure a state of ambivalence in regard to which one can see no ending. Modernity is to be celebrated—and mistrusted—daily. It is inevitable that every person of moral sensibility both wants, and doesn't want, the arrival and the institutionalization of the Modern world. All of this is to lay a great psychological burden on *le peuple*. In an earlier work, I asserted that democracy is a miracle when one considers human psychological disabilities.[3] The same must be said of Modernity. The great moral progress that the Modern world brings makes incredible psychological demands on the average citizen. And when these demands are refused, when the Modern political and psychological agenda is forcibly rejected, such proscription is usually accompanied by an acceleration of primitive violence. Murderous religious fundamentalism, fascism, ideological terror of the left and the right—these are the great perversions of Modernity.

One significant attribute of the paranoid person is that he/she cannot tolerate ambivalence.[4] Everything must be settled one way or another, clearly, and dogmatically. Ambiguity is the great enemy. In order, therefore, to live in a Modern society, to enjoy a democratic polity, a culture and/or a person must go beyond the paranoid position. Failure to do so makes the attainment of these goals impossible. And it is not merely a question of the fact that, in the Modern world, some people can tolerate this ambiguity and some cannot. What will be argued in the section on splitting is that in many cases—possibly, even an enormous number of cases—the person who, on the surface level of action, accepts and furthers Modernity and the person who rejects it forcibly with primitive violence are one and the same person, with a psyche split between these binary opposites. The most radical hypothesis offered is that this description fits all leftist ideological terrorists: explains why people who are capable of offering a powerful moral critique of bourgeois society—and a prescription for its righteous transformation—end up annihilating thousands (during the French Terror), and, as the twentieth century progresses, millions (as in Stalinist Russia and Maoist China). What was terrifying the terrorists, to cite once again the question implied in Engels's letter, was that very Modernity-ethos that they were instituting with such precipitousness. One historian who has postulated this same enigmatic position is Simon Schama, who has declared that "Much of the anger firing revolutionary violence arose from hostility towards that modernization, rather than from impatience with the speed of its progress."[5] We are faced with a great paradox: the possibility that what was driving Robespierre into Modernity psychosis—was Robespierre.

It could be helpful to sum up those fundamental attributes of Modernity that inevitably must produce an acceleration in personal and social anxiety. For all people, not just those who are resistant to its message. Even those who become Modernity's greatest advocates cannot help but feel, even if totally unconsciously, that this new center may not hold. Voltaire, we remember, talked of a civil war in *every* soul.

Every one of the seven anxiety-generating attributes listed further on involve the giving up of a defense against paranoid panic that was operating, more or less successfully, in the traditional pre-Modern world. Kinship, for instance, the sense of belonging, the feeling that others will take care of one in times of crisis, is a great defense against the general anxiety of living in an uncertain world. To give up the intense bonding of a kinship system is to experience a quantum leap in anxiety and to risk a significant dissolution of the sense of self. We have invented complex notions to describe this situation where a person—or a culture—has left the secure base of the kinship system behind and has been unable to replace it with an equally supportive psychological ecology: Anomie; Alienation; the Age of Anxiety; Future Shock. All of these describe a liminal situation wherein we have driven ourselves into a separated-individuation world and have discovered that we are, for all intents and purposes, alone. Every one of the demands of Modernity catalogued as follows result in this very same liminality anxiety. The French revolutionary culture, whose overriding ambition was a progress into Modernity, experienced acutely the conflicts and anxieties concomitant with each of these great renunciations that Modernity demands.

I. *The Breakdown of the Kinship System.* Cities are the creators and carriers of Modernity. The city, unlike the countryside, is *the* place of anomie and alienation, for the simple reason that in the cities the kinship forms of social cohesion that operate in the countryside no longer abide. And when a "city ethos" invades a village, it begins to dissolve that cohesion. One illustrative example from the twentieth century: Marshall McLuhan refers to a UNESCO project to install running water in villages in India: " 'Soon the villages requested that the pipes be removed, for it seemed to them that the whole social life of the village had been impoverished, when it was no longer necessary for all to visit the communal well.' "[6] One of Max Weber's earliest works was a study of the resistance made by German peasants to the conversion of their economic situation from one in which patriarchal relations with their landlord were crucial, including some kind of assistance in times of crisis, to one with a purely rational, monetary basis. Theoretically, the move resulted in greater economic freedom. Psychologically, it was threatening because it removed all elements of kinship (i.e., familial) support.[7]

Modernity results in the most intense breakdown of kinship system psychological support that human beings have ever experienced. It cannot be unambivalently welcomed. Every movement hostile to Modernity offers, as one of its fundamental values, some form of restoration of the kinship system: *Das Volk* returned to its rightful place. Even left-wing ideological terror brings back intense kinship forms of social cohesion; the authoritarian state becomes mother, father, aunt, and uncle to all. Big Brother becomes the caricature of Stalinist despotism. And, after three hundred years of liberalism and its exaggerated emphasis on, and acclamation of, individualism, those thoughtful, critical people today who feel that our moral task is to go beyond Modernity, without rejecting or repressing its great achievements, understand that this metamorphosis can only be accomplished by a new, transforming sense of community: a democratic, nurturing society that leads, rather than is led by, its remarkably individuated citizens. Meanwhile, we wait, full of normal Modern anxiety.

2. The Speed of Change. Most people do not want to live lives radically different from their parents. Most people do not want their children to live lives radically different from their own. And it is not just a question of preference; it is deeply a question of anxiety. Continuity gives security; discontinuity brings anxiety; radical discontinuity results in panic. To continue to do what is familiar is a fundamental healthy defense against the general and universal angst of life. "Social mobility" is the theoretical phrase that describes the situation where there is generational discontinuity in the mode in which people live their lives. The Modern world places, at the very top of its agenda, the possibilities, and the promised great pleasures, of being upwardly mobile. Very few people pose the question of what great psychological disquiet this may give rise to. We may look again at what Lawrence Stone, who has addressed this consequence, writes about society at the very dawn of Modernity: "The upsetting of the hierarchy of status as a result of rapid social mobility was just one of many factors which generated unease, anxiety, anomie. Social mobility, personal insecurity, geographic migration, and ideological chaos were all part of the life experiences of early seventeenth-century English men. They were deeply unsettling."[8]

And what could cause more generational discontinuity, and its accompanying distress, than a revolution, especially one as violent and as radical as that which happened in France? It is remarkable that any individuals survived that earthquake with their sense of self intact. Even the Thermidorian reaction, which overthrew the Jacobin dictatorship, could not possibly restore prerevolutionary stability. In the period between Thermidor and Napoleon, Richard Cobb writes, "the recognition signals had been lost, without being replaced by others, so that people had to grope along a narrow ledge, uncertain of the direction in which they were going or of what they might meet around the corner."[9]

This level of uncertainty and anxiety was, obviously, unbearable and had to be lessened in one way or another, if chaos were not to ensue. The great problem, however, is that no Modernity culture (that includes democracy and the ideal of equality for all people) is possible without a significant degree of psychological tolerance for some uncertainty, some willingness to live without knowing what the next turn will bring. It is saddening, but understandable, if many cultures in the twentieth century have announced, in essence: "We cannot live that way. No unrestrained 'progress' for us. We will do something different."

3. *The Overthrow of Authoritarian Power.* The greatest triumph of the Revolution—the localization of sovereignty within the people as a whole: the fundamental characteristic of democratic society—produced, along with the overthrow of the authoritarian power of the church, the greatest possible anxiety. The most difficult task Modernity has laid on humankind is to learn to live without the primitive psychological security offered by those authoritarian powers. The sovereignty of the people, no matter how complexly developed, no matter how profoundly believed in, can never substitute for the sense of safety offered by huddling under the omnipotent power of the king. Democratic society is only possible when a people renounces the need for that kind of primitive omnipotence. "The reason why the French Revolution was," Clifford Geertz writes, "at least up to its time, the greatest incubator of extremist ideologies, 'progressive' and 'reactionary' alike, in human history was not that either personal or social disequilibrium was deeper and more pervasive than at many earlier times—though they were deep and pervasive enough—but because the central organizing principle of political life, the divine right of kings, was destroyed."[10]

Social and cultural evolution does not proceed in an orderly, meticulous, one-step-at-a-time, one-small-increment-following-another manner. In the rush toward psychological and political progress, societies can, and most often do, become overextended. They push out further and further before the structures that would support such extensions have been erected. Sometimes, they crash; sometimes, they retreat; sometimes, they are able to erect the supporting structures in time before the crash or retreat. The French Revolution and its eighty-year aftermath are a perfect example of exactly this kind of historical circumstance. Rushing headlong into the Enlightenment future, they destroyed the potency of the church, overthrew the king, unleashed the awesome power in the lower classes—all of this without having constructed new forms of social cohesion that would allow for such progress. First, they crashed into the Terror; then retreated into a pathetic Directory politics; retreated further into an artificially manufactured heroic age; and, when it collapsed, spent the next sixty to seventy years alternating between tragedy and farce, before finally putting into place structures that would support a democratic society.

Those periods in human history, when old forms of cohesion and security have been renounced and new forms not fully put in their place, are extraordinarily costly in human terms: anxiety and panic, and the defenses erected to contain these, rule the polity. "As revolutionaries cut themselves adrift from the moorings of patriarchal conceptions of authority," Lynn Hunt reasons, "they faced a dichotomous, highly charged set of feelings: on the one hand, there was the exhilaration of a new era; on the other a dark sense of foreboding about the future. A mythic present and charismatic language were fragile underpinnings for a new community whose boundaries were ill defined. The reverse side of the mythic present of national regeneration was an enormous collective anxiety about the solidity of the new consensus."[11]

That was the fundamental problem the Revolution failed to solve. The great trials and tribulations of this marvelous and terrible last century can be understood as being caused, in good part, by this same paradoxical, contradictory, ambiguous struggle for Modernity.

4. *"The Dread of Women."*[12] The statement that all human societies, with rare and very few exceptions, if any, have been male dominated may not have been true of kinship societies (tribal, nonliterate, "primitive" societies). What valid generalizations can be made about the position of women in this latter group can still not be given a satisfactory answer. Beyond kinship societies, however, after the evolution of the State and the breakdown and transformation of the kinship system, it seems incontrovertible that society and male domination have been contemporaneous. Again, allowing for the possible rare exceptions.

There is one stage of social evolution that has put equality for women and men on the moral agenda. At first, it was only a faint voice heard in a few isolated places. In the latter part of the last century, especially in the most advanced Modern societies, the demand for gender equality has become so strong that it seems accurate to say that, barring some social catastrophe that would result in a massive moral regression, the ordinary development of society will bring it about: that patriarchy will be thrown on the same scrap-heap of history as cannibalism and slavery.

Gender equality is a fundamental telos of Modernity, in the same way that democratic society has been and is. It came, with any kind of force, much later on the scene, but the remarkable thing is that the first intimations of it were there from the very beginning. And the French Revolutionary experience confirms this statement. As soon as the struggle for Modernity began, the struggle for equal rights for women made itself visible. Intimately related to this concurrence is the fact that any kind of radical anti-Modernism invariably turns out to be antifeminist: Note has been made previously of the repression of women that almost all radical religious fundamentalism undertakes. Fascism in Europe attempted to stop the movement toward gender equality or actually regressed to a pre-Modern position. Even among the intellectual elite of this country, I have noticed that any book that adopts a super-critical stance against Modernity, usually from a stated moral point of view, ends up expressing some form of antifeminist sentiment, usually in a subtle, often disguised way. No thoughtful person can totally embrace the movement to Modernity, but to reject it, almost totally, implies a very deep antipathy to equality between women and men. To turn the clock back on Modernity is to do the same for the feminist project.

The Revolution unleashed an energy toward feminism in three areas: first, revolutionary action on the streets by women—as early as October 1789, three months after Bastille, the women of Paris forced the king to move to the capital; second, participation, although on a limited basis, in the political activity of the Revolution; and third, theoretical statements by both men and women. Crucial to this point being developed in this chapter—that there was a profoundly split-off, anti-Modernism in Jacobinism and, eventually, in the Terror, even though it may seem on first observation that it was Jacobinism that was pushing the Modern agenda with such urgency—most significant is the fact that it was the Jacobin dictatorship that totally repressed any feminist political activity or discourse. And it did so less than five months after it had liquidated the Girondin faction.

The Gironde, which had its own share of Modernity-anxiety but never became an instrument of ideological terror, exhibited, on the contrary, a welcoming attitude toward feminist thought and action. Revolutionaries, but not terrorists, they could deal with the universal male dread of women. Ideological terror is as incompatible with women as real people as it is with democratic discourse. That says something of what the horrendous splitting that results in terror was about. Jacqueline Chaumié has elaborated for us the discrepant views of the Gironde and the Mountain:

> The anti-feminism of the Montagnards has made us believe that the Revolution was not favorable to the aspirations of women. But here also, it is necessary to distinguish between Montagnards and Girondins. . . . the most anti-feminist of the Montagnards is Robespierre, from whom we are able to cite numerous declarations on the incapacity of women for understanding political problems. . . . One must remark, on the other hand, that the women who circled the Montagnards were not distinguished by their political sense nor their love of the Republic, and certainly not by their intellectual merit. . . .
>
> If the Montagnards are anti-feminist, the Girondins, on the contrary, promoted the feminine agenda. Condorcet, in a number of writings, defended the rights of women. "One has violated the principle of equality of rights," he wrote in 1789, "in quietly depriving half the human race of the right to contribute to the making of the laws." Condorcet was not the only girondin feminist. Fauchet shared his ideas. Lanthenas, in June 1794, wanted to give to women the right to vote; he grated them a great place in his plan for education. Brissot was also very favorable to the equality of women; in the gatherings which were held in his house, his young wife, his sister-in-law, and above all, his mother-in-law, took an active part in the conversation and their revolutionary ardor set the tone. . . . Rouzet, in his projected constitution written in April 1793, even allowed some woman to be elected representatives of the people.[13]

Marie Olympe de Gouges, the most important feminist voice of the Revolution, forcefully and deliberately allied herself with the Gironde and in opposition to the Mountain. Her most significant text was the *Déclaration des Droits de la Femme et de la Citoyenne* (September 1791), in which she declared that the Revolution would not be complete until women had totally established their rights. She wrote pamphlets against Marat and Robespierre. After the overthrow of the Gironde in May–June 1793, she openly expressed her solidarity with it, was arrested July 20, condemned to death November 2, and guillotined November 3.[14]

Women had absolutely no right to vote and had almost no access to the majority of revolutionary organizations (clubs, sections, etc.). As a result, the more militant feminists organized themselves, in Paris and some thirty provinces, into clubs of women: *Citoyennes Républicaines Révolutionnaires.* The Jacobin dictatorship would have none of this. The clubs were interdicted and closed down October 30, 1793.[15] The *nouvel homme* could obviously not abide the *nouvelle femme.*

5. *"Inferior" People as Equals.* 6. *Repression of Day-to-Day Violence.* Both these attributes of Modernity are considered together because they prescribe how one is supposed to act in ordinary social congress, within the public space. *Égalité* is a fundamental ideal of Modernity, enshrined in several public declarations of rights. *All* people are equal—at least in theory. In premodern, traditional society, there were many different kinds of "inferior" people, along with women: Protestants, Jews, actors, poor people, or even anyone poorer, or of less status, than oneself. In such society, there was nothing inappropriate in treating such people as if they were what they were: inferior people, not fully human. Aristotle says that some people have a passion for inequality.[16] We may supplement that by declaring that almost all people have some degree of passion for inequality. But only in the Modern world does the notion of such inequality become illegitimate. That thrust toward an ethos of equality is never-ending in a healthy, developing Modern society. The latest manifestation of this drive in America has demanded that one treat black people, other people of color, homosexuals, and immigrants as equals—and, of great importance, women.

It is an error to underestimate the psychological strain it causes people to carry out this moral revolution. The politics of America, for the last twenty years, cannot be understood without acknowledging the psychological and political backlash engendered by the new cultural demands to regard women, black people, homosexuals, and poor people as within the same moral universe as one's family and friends. Not only does this conflict produce strain, and then anxiety, but, inevitably, aggression of a greater or lesser intensity, running all the way from racist and antifeminist jokes to the bombing of abortion clinics. Our present society can be understood as dancing on the cliff-edge of ambivalence, undecided whether to move forward by truly embracing the moral future of equality or to regress to a former state by putting certain people "back in their place." The demand for total equality, for all people, is one of the great generators of anxiety in the Modern world.

One almost humorous, noncatastrophic aspect of revolutionary history reflects this thrust toward equality in the public space. As almost all readers of this book know, but not all, the French language has both a formal and a familiar word for "you." And each pronoun requires a different verb form. Familiar: *tu as*. Formal: *vous avez*. The familiar is used among family, close friends, lovers. There is a verb meaning to use the familiar: *tutoyer*; and a noun indicating such usage: *tutoiement*. As part of the growing *mentalité* of equality, people decided that the formal *vous* should be dropped, and all citizens, and even women citizens (*citoyenes*), which meant in practice, all people, should be addressed with the familiar *tu*. Beginning as popular usage, it became a matter of decree from the great Committee of Public Safety. In response to a number of popular societies that declared, through their spokesman Nalbec, that using the *tutoiement* would permit: "less distinction, less enmities, more visible familiarities, and therefore equality," the Committee decreed its general usage on November 10, 1793.[17]

All this led to many different kinds of altercations, of greater or lesser violence, when, for instance a patron in a restaurant continued to address the waiter as *vous*. Among the clubs and the sections, when a person was brought up on charges of being antirevolutionary, the fact that he had refused to use the *tutoiement* could also be hurled against him. However, the future, as we know, belonged to bourgeois society, which cannot live without clear status distinctions. By the year III, such usage of the familiar had almost disappeared, and the traditional distinctions reinstated.[18] One was no longer to pretend to intimacy (equality) with the strangers one lived with.

Bourgeois society does demand a certain level of peaceful conduct on the street. We are so accustomed to the notion that elite members of society are not supposed to carry swords or give vent to violent encounters in public places that we do not realize that such has not always been the case. One reads the history of Italian city-states in the late medieval or early Modern period and discovers the existence of a significant number of "rumbles" in the city's public places, created not by gangs of juvenile delinquents, but many times by competing factions of the highest-status families.

Modernity decrees an end to such primitive acting out in public places. We can observe the conflict and ambivalence about renouncing this kind of individual aggression and vengeance in the nineteenth-century equivocation about the legality and moral legitimacy of dueling. Duels continued in most countries in Europe, even after they were declared illegal. They became grist for the novelist's mill, many times providing a dramatic climax for a narrative. It is only in the twentieth century that a man, in almost all countries, who engaged in a duel would be considered a damn fool, rather than a tainted hero.

French revolutionary history was so replete with all kinds of violence that, it seems, this particular form of aggression and its repression never became a real issue or problem. This inhibition of aggression, this renunciation of personal public violence, nevertheless, is another significant imperative that Modernity insists on without paying heed to the anxiety that such renunciation engenders. Revenge has been an elemental human problematic from the year one. It is remarkable how much of the West's greatest literature includes a fundamental story of revenge: the *Iliad*; the *Odyssey*; the *Oresteia*; the *Bacchae*; the *Nibelungelied*; *Hamlet*; *Moby Dick*. Ancient Hebrew culture attempted the suppression of this revenge-imperative when Yahweh declared: "Vengeance is mine," but the effect in the real world was minimal. It was only Modernity that succeeded in placing all punishment under the law, eliminating any legitimate recourse to private vengeance. And so was constructed another significant discontent with civilization.

7. *The Interregnum between the Overthrow of One Authority and the Erection of a New One.* The remarks of Raymond Aron, previously quoted, "that the *Ancien Régime* collapsed at one blow, almost without resistance, and that it took France nearly a century to find another régime acceptable to the majority of the nation,"[19] powerfully underlines the fact that Modern society does not go forward in a smooth, orderly way. It may overthrow one fundamental legitimate form of social cohesion before it is ready to put another in its place. These times of uncertainty, of disequilibrium, are by no means easy to live in. True, they are not as raucous or catastrophic as times of violent, out-of-control revolution; most good people die in their beds and not on the scaffold. They do, nevertheless, put a severe psychological strain on those thoughtful citizens who do have to endure this period of ambivalence, vacillation, and irresolution.

> Between the idea
> And the reality . . .
> Falls the Shadow
>
> Between the conception
> And the creation . . .
> Falls the Shadow
>
> . . . Between the potency
> And the existence . . .
> Falls the Shadow[20]

And that shadow, in Aron's terms, can endure for a hundred years.

Modernity, moreover, gives us no rest. It pushes forward—morally—whether we are prepared or not. Most of the time it seems as if we are not riding it, but it is riding us. I am not referring here to radical changes in technology or in the economic structure, which are powerfully disconcerting in themselves, but to that inevitable moral imperative toward full democracy and full equality that is an integral part of the Modern agenda.

In regard to the relationship of women and men, we are in such a period of interregnum, disequilibrium these days. In the most advanced Modern societies, the old, stable, "legitimate" forms of the sex-gender system—patriarchy and male domination—have been dethroned, but we are very far from having reached a situation where we are comfortable with true equality, where the cold war between women and men has ended in a lasting peace. Marriage has been the great victim. The feminist demand for equality, and the ambivalent male acceptance of this imperative, has destroyed the traditional patriarchal marriage, without however, being able to create as yet a new stable basis for matrimony. The divorce statistics tell the story.[21] And even those of both sexes who remain happily married are full of complaint about the refusal of the partner to accept full equality. She: "He refuses to do his share." He: "She is too demanding; she leaves me no space for myself." The shadow of an incomplete revolution falls on the most private place in our lives.

Modernity, however, drives on, seemingly regardless of our readiness, and nonreadiness, to move forward. And such periods of profound disequilibrium are full of anxiety and stress, not only because the center is not holding, but also because there is great uncertainty as to how it will all come out. One cannot be sure that the new regime "acceptable to the majority of the nation"—and compatible with the moral thrust of Modernity—will be born. In Europe, one result of the Modern insistence on full democratic equality was fascism in Spain, Italy, and Germany. Modernity gives birth to anti-Modernity and violent warfare between the two. Tocqueville, in his genius for social analysis, knew that. This insight tempered his optimism, to which he was inclined by his nature, and made him skeptical about what the future might bring. He knew that there was no going back. The old patriarchal monarchy could not be reconstituted. From that knowledge, he then proceeded to give insight, with almost incredible prescience, that one possible outcome of this momentous conflict could be that fascism that has ravaged the last century:

> But of the barriers that formerly held tyranny back, what remains with us today?
>   Religion having lost its sway over men's souls, the clearest line dividing good from ill has been obliterated; everything in the moral world seems doubtful and

uncertain; kings and nations go forward at random, and none can say where are the natural limits of despotism and the bounds of license.

But when once the prestige of royalty has vanished in the tumult of revolutions, and when kings, succeeding one another on the throne, have taken turns to display the weakness of *right* and the harshness of *fact*, no one any longer sees the sovereign as father of the state, but each man sees him as his master.

What strength can customs have . . . where nothing ancient remains which men are afraid to destroy, and where they dare to do anything new that can be conceived?

I know that there are many worthy persons nowadays who are not afraid of this alternative [the rule of one man] and who, tired of liberty, would like finally to rest far from its storms.

But such people have little knowledge of the haven to which they are steering. Preoccupied by memories, they judge the absolute power by what it was formerly and not by what it maybe nowadays.

If absolute power were to be established again among the democratic nations of Europe, I have no doubt it would take a new form and display features unknown to our fathers.

I find those very blind who think to rediscover the monarchy of Henry IV or Louis XIV. For my part, when I consider the state already reached by several European nations and that toward which all are tending, I am led to believe that there will soon be no room except for either democratic freedom or the tyranny of the Caesars.

But if it is true that there will soon be nothing intermediate between the sway of democracy and the yoke of a single man, should we not rather steer toward the former than voluntarily submit to the latter? And if we must finally reach a state of complete equality, is it not better to let ourselves be leveled down by freedom rather than by a despot?

I foresee that if the peaceful dominion of the majority is not established among us in good time, we shall sooner or later fall under the *unlimited* authority of a single man.[22]

All the question marks, all the either/or pronouncements, all the "ifs" indicate how uncertain the future felt at such a time of interregnum. Sometimes one wonders whether Modernity is not one continuous, unending time of uncertainty and disequilibrium. When one considers the psychological maturity required to live in such a paradoxical era, there should be no surprise that it brings out the very best—and the very worst—of which humanity is capable.

Hegel, too, understood that the Revolution was, essentially, an incompleted revolution, that it had created a paradoxical time that would require a massive human effort to resolve. "So at the end of the *Philosophy of History*," Joachim Ritter writes, "there stands left the unresolved status of all the political problems thrown up by the Revolution: 'Thus agitation and unrest are perpetuated.' The problem of political stabilization remains the 'nucleus . . . with which history is now occupied, and whose solution it has to work out in the future.' "[23] Ritter goes on to elaborate on Hegel's confrontation with this era of discontinuity and disequilibrium:

> For the revolutionary theory and its followers the present signifies the end of the old world and the liberation of man from what have become the "unreal" powers of religion and metaphysics. From the other side this identically recognized end of the historical tradition appears as the elimination of divinity from the world, as the loss of the true, the holy, and the beautiful, as the downfall of the humanness of man himself. *The revolutionary negation of the past and the restorative negation of the present are therefore identical in their presupposition of the historical discontinuity of tradition and future, and this discontinuity thus becomes for Hegel the decisive problem of the age; it goes unresolved in all the tensions and antagonisms of the period.*[24]

When we observe, on the front pages of our morning newspaper, in many parts of the world, the violence unleashed by the continuing failure to resolve "the tensions and antagonisms of the period," we cannot help but reflect on what great catastrophes—and yet what great gifts—the Modern world brings us. Almost simultaneously.

*   *   *

If all of these panic- and anxiety-producing aspects of Modernity were frightening only reactionary, counterrevolutionary, conservative, religious members of society—and we may add, good moral liberals like Madame de Staël and Benjamin Constant—it would be understandable and something of great importance, but it would not help us comprehend the great bringers of Modernity: the ideological terrorists themselves. A paradoxical explanation has been proposed in this chapter to explain a paradoxical circumstance: What was terrifying the terrorists was the very same Modernity they were promoting with such radical enthusiasm. It takes more than the average neurotic psychopathology to engender this kind of radical symptomology, which is why I will shortly be offering the hypothesis that people like Robespierre and Saint-Just—and Stalin and Mao—were suffering from a particular kind of psychological pathology, deeply involved with a pervasive paranoid view of the world. Not psychotic; capable of functioning in the real world of politics and armies. But more than just neurotic. Capable—and this is the crucial aspect—of a kind of radical splitting that is alien to most people. Capable, on the one hand, of pushing and celebrating the moral agenda of Modernity, including the concept of freedom and equality for all people. And yet capable, with the other self, of reacting to Modernity anxiety with Modernity psychosis: ordering human sacrifice in tremendous numbers, exterminating thousands and millions of innocent people.

A wildly irrational hypothesis? Is there a rational explanation for the great French Terror waiting to be discovered?

18

THE SPLITTING OF THE PSYCHE; THE SPLITTING OF THE WORLD; THE PROJECTION OF UNCONTAMINATED VIRTUE AND ABSOLUTE EVIL

I do not know of another event in history that contributed more to the well-being of succeeding generations or more entirely demoralized the generation that brought it about.[1]

—Tocqueville

It is, perhaps, easier to think about and understand the paradoxes, contradictions, ambivalences, seemingly unreconcilable desires in Modernity—as well as the anxiety, panic, psychic fibrillation, cultural despair—and, even further, the psychic and social defenses erected in response to all this—perhaps easier to understand by looking at a situation that reflects all these circumstances, but one not as catastrophic as the French Revolutions, 1789–1799.

. Religious fundamentalism, in the last twenty-five years, has become a powerful social and political force in many parts of the world. And, even among the most thoughtful people, nobody saw it coming. I came to social and political consciousness after the second World War. At that time, everyone knew that international peace was an issue of primary concern. Certain aware people felt that changes in race relations in America were on the social agenda: some actions, like sit-down strikes in restaurants in Chicago that refused to serve black people, had already begun. And even the great second wave of feminism, although inchoate, was intimated in a few isolated places. Attending a leftist seminar in

1946, we were instructed that we were not to use the words "Negress" or "Jewess" because they implied that the female members of these groups were second-class people. The phrase "male chauvinism," as a term or opprobrium, was already within use in this particular cohort.

Nobody, however, foresaw that the rise of religious fundamentalism would become of major political concern. Just the opposite was predicted. God was dead; the rise of science had made religion unnecessary; the Enlightenment made it possible to live without all that childish dependence on supernatural powers. *We* might have to struggle against the religious beliefs we inherited from our parents, but our children would be free from any such conflicts. An almost completely secular world, allowing for a few small pockets of religious belief, was in the offing. All of this grossly underestimated the great internal conflicts that Modernity could engender.

> I am exactly fifty years old. I have passed thirty of them [since 1789] in this eternally agitated time of fearing and hoping it would be done with. Now I am forced to see that it goes on without halt, indeed, in troubled hours one imagines that it grows worse and worse.[2]
>
> —Hegel to Creuzer, October 30, 1819:

By the 1970s, it was becoming apparent that the efflorescence of Islamic fundamentalism and political orthodoxy in Israel were not exceptional circumstances. In the spring of 1977, Daniel Bell delivered a prescient address at the London School of Economics entitled "The Return of the Sacred?" in which he predicted that one response to what he called "the exhaustion of Modernism . . . the tedium of the unrestrained self and the meaninglessness of monolithic political chants" would be a "Fundamentalist faith, evangelical and scourging, emphasizing sin and the turning away from the Whore of Babylon. In the United States, in recent years, the largest-growing voluntary associations have been the Fundamentalists churches."[3] We have seen it happen.

The case of twentieth-century Turkey is arrestingly illustrative. It began, in the early part of the century, as the great pride of the modernizing of Islamic society. It was to prove that Modernity and Islam could be reconciled in a progressive, stable society: veils were lifted from women, girls were sent to school, Western dress was adopted, and so on. For seventy-five years, or so, it worked well. And now, in the very month of this writing, January 1998, the highest court in Turkey has had to outlaw an Islamic fundamentalist party because it was judged to be a threat to the existent democratic polity. This is not to say that the majority of the Turkish people is ready to abandon Modernity, but the decision of the court expresses the great fear that the Modern polity may not hold, when threatened by religious fundamentalism. The impulse toward Modernity can be described as the greatest social force in this century. The impulse to reject Modernity may be the second greatest force.

The rejuvenation of religion in the last thirty years has taken three typical courses. First, there are those in the West, raised by secular or atheist parents, who have become religious practitioners and intend to raise their children in that manner. This is not an expression of fundamentalism, presents no threat to democracy, and may be considered as much a manifestation of Modernity as a rejection of it.

Second, there is the noncatastrophic fundamentalism of the kind exhibited in the United States. There is strong dissatisfaction with the most recent manifestations of Modernity, most particularly in the area of sexuality: divorce, abortion, free heterosexual expression, tolerance for homosexuality—and the invasion of these "immoral" ideas into the popular culture: movies and television. The vast majority of these citizens do not approve of bombing abortion clinics and work civilly within the boundaries of democratic discourse to allow prayer in the schools or outlaw abortion. Though deeply hostile, possibly even conflicted, about many aspects of the Modern world, such people can give us only a bare hint of what generated the French Terror.

Understanding the third form of twentieth-century fundamentalism, however, can give us great insight into the panic-anxiety France was experiencing as the traditional world was torn down overnight and no center that could hold had yet been put in its place. This particular form of fundamentalism is catastrophic for democracy, civil society, political freedom, and the equality and dignity of women. It proceeds out of a horror of Modernity. In some places, like Algeria and Afghanistan, it releases forms or primitive aggression that can only be compared with some of the worst butcheries in history. Massacre is its primary political instrument. No doubt, many of those committing the slaughter of women and small children in defenseless villages are born terrorists glad of the opportunity to exercise their sadistic bloodlust. But equally without doubt, there are among the leaders of these movements nonpsychotic, reasonably "sane" people giving the orders for these massacres, under the banner of a moral ideology. Ideological terrorists, exactly.

404 CITIZENS AND CANNIBALS

Later at the Jacobin Society, [Manuel, the *procureur* of the old Paris municipality] made an open avowal of what amounted to heresy, saying that the sight of the dead [massacred in the prisons in September] awakened an awful doubt in his mind: "Is it better to dream of liberty than to possess it?" (Sydenham, *Girondins*, 120)

This proximate-psychotic form of twentieth-century religious fundamentalism announces, in essence: "It is better not even to dream of liberty." My daughter tells me of two incidents in Israel that she had recently read about. Reform Judaism was the victim of each particular attack. In one, Orthodox fundamentalist Jews had drawn swastikas on a Reform temple. In the other, a kindergarten was being built, in which both boys and girls would be educated together, and it was fire-bombed by fundamentalist believers. "What is this?" she asked. Though I had never used the term before, I immediately responded: "It's modernity psychosis. People who are not crazy are being driven crazy by Modernity and are performing almost psychotic acts. They were willing to live for close to two thousand years as a righteous minority in a gentile world, but the notion that they, as a majority, have to share the world with a minority of Jews who are not Jews—this is intolerable." And forces them to act in a manner for which we have no adequate name: paranoid? severely paranoid? severely pathological? close to psychotic? Sometimes it seems that the just-plain vulgarity "crazy" says it best. "Crazy people"—psychiatrically undefined—can commit massacres in the Vendée and send thousands of their former allies to the guillotine. Tocqueville's *virus* gives crazy people enormous political power. And, as he mournfully says, "the same men are still with us . . . and they have progeny everywhere in the civilized world."[4]

Two kinds of religious fundamentalism are indicated here, both of which are engaged in a rejection of some of the values of the Modern world but with profoundly different levels of intensity: a nonmurderous kind (American organized fundamentalist churches, peaceful orthodox religionists in Israel, the Turkish Islamic fundamentalist party) and a murderous type (Algeria, Afghanistan, Egyptian Islamic terrorists, radical, violence-prone fundamentalists in Israel). That some people pass over from nonviolent to violent forms of action is clear: the person, of which type we have had several, who goes from barring the entrances to abortion clinics to actually bombing these enterprises. We would not be shocked, for instance, to read that, in Turkey, a violent terrorist group had split off from the main fundamentalist party and was proceeding to institute a reign of terror to protest the decision of the court. The trajectory goes from intense political activism to terror.

I want to hold up a very strange mirror to the idea expressed in this last sentence, in the hope it may help to answer one of the most difficult questions one could ask about the Revolution: What made Robespierre and Saint-Just and Barère into cannibalistic terrorists? They, too, this unconventional mirror reveals, traveled from intense political activism to the Terror. Mirror-like, however, to the left and not to the right. They were pushing the values of Modernity to its very extremity, just as the murderous fundamentalists are pushing their resistance to Modernity to the humanly extreme point. The advantage of this mirror conceit is that it allows one to offer an outrageous suggestion in the hope it may illuminate the answer to the problem raised by Engels's remark referred to several time before: What was it that was terrifying the terrorists? Could it be that it was the very same thing that is terrifying the murderous fundamentalists: the naked prospect of Modernity? Could it be that they were becoming increasingly terrified by the pushing of their own radical modern agenda? The fact that they were the authors of their own anxiety-panic may sound extraordinarily strange, but is it more difficult to believe than the fact that Robespierre ended up an executioner of mostly innocent people?

> Our aim will be to show that the structure of modern society affects man in two ways *simultaneously*: he becomes more independent, self-reliant, and critical, and he becomes more isolated, alone and afraid. The understanding of the whole problem of freedom depends on the very ability to see both sides of the process and not lose track of one side while following the other.[5] (Erich Fromm, *Escape from Freedom*)

If we take from Fromm's powerful insight and eliminate from it the abstract notion of "man," we can then ask of a man: Could a man be pushing himself and his society at breakneck speed, into a profoundly self-reliant, independent, free state and simultaneously become isolated, alone, and driven by anxiety-panic? And, if so, is it inconceivable that such a man would accelerate the primitive violence with which he is attempting to resolve this horrendous contradiction? Excruciatingly ambivalent about feeling the guilt that comes with annihilating others, he attempts to resolve that ambivalence by denying he has done it and therefore accelerates the killing machine. Somehow, more and more killing is supposed to assuage this personal and cultural despair. The murderous fundamentalist conceives that more and more massacre will clear his mind. He gives both an ideological (we are the truth) and a rational (only terror will make others see the validity of our program) explanation of his behavior. Similarly, the Great Terror was instituted by ideologically virtuous people, we are told, in order to win the war and save the Revolution from those who would destroy it.

Is such splitting of one person into two people conceivable? Let us look once again at the statement of Voltaire quoted at the very beginning of this book.

> [We] live in curious times amid astonishing contrasts; reason on the one hand, the most absurd fanaticism on the other . . . a civil war in every soul.[6]

We note that Voltaire does not declare the existence of a civil war in every country or in every culture, but in every soul. That is to say, a war rages within every member of society. On the one side, a propulsion toward Modernity: reason, enlightenment, freedom, tolerance. On the other, a force, equally as strong, of unreason, ignorance, authoritarianism, ideology. Granted this, the crucial question for each individual—and for society—is: How murderous does that war become? For some, it may be played out on the level of normal psychic ambivalence that a reasonably healthy person learns to live with in his/her life. For others, the ambivalence accelerates to an exterminating extreme, analogous to when a local violent incident gets magnified into a full-scale war. What is being suggested is that what drove the French Terror was an horrendous ambivalence about Modernity, wherein ideology could make one person into the greatest champion of the new world and a murderous fundamentalist—simultaneously. The contention being that such an analysis may accurately describe, as well, the twentieth-century ideological terrorists of the left: Lenin and Mao as foremost examples.

SPLITTING: THE REJECTION AND PROJECTION OF EVIL

That the worst terrorism was conducted by people who most accurately can be described as two persons within one psyche has been commented upon by other historians of the Terror. The great Michelet said of the Incorruptible: "Robespierre was two men. One loved the Good, one endlessly lauded the ideal of Balance; the other (just like the storm of the Revolution) was rent asunder by an inner violence that swept him right and left. He imposed on others an impossible middle ground on which he himself could not stand."[7] J.M. Thompson gives us what could be considered an elaboration of Michelet's insight. "Robespierre's detractors have been prodigal with the charge of hypocrisy. But a hypocrite is one who professes to be something which he knows he is not. . . . Robespierre can be represented as a hypocrite only by those who cannot or will not understand the real state of his mind. If anything is certain about him, it is that he was not so much anxiously trying to reconcile, as triumphantly certain he had succeeded in reconciling, apparent opposites—the belief in liberty with a policy of intimidation, love of the people with a suspicious distrust of individuals, dislike of the death penalty with wholesale executions, hatred of militarism with a national war, and a belief in an overruling Providence with a vindictive and merciless Inquisition into the conduct of his associates. His conscience may have been twisted, but it was all of one piece."[8] I would counter that what Thompson has shown us first is that, if it was, indeed, of one piece, it was a piece with two separate, distinct, and warring parts.

On the eighth of June 1794 was celebrated in Paris the festival of the Supreme Being. At the end of a long procession, which marched to the festival ground, came Robespierre dressed all in blue with a tricolor sash. The conscious or unconscious symbolism had as its purpose to associate the Incorruptible with this sacred Being. It was Robespierre's apotheosis. The guillotine had been dismantled for the day of celebration. Twenty citizens had been beheaded the day before; twenty-three would suffer the same penalty on the day following.[9] Robespierre's encomium to this new god of the Revolution was full of the division of the world into all-good and all-evil that had become typical of revolutionary paranoid, splitting rhetoric:

> He has certainly not created the priests in order to yoke us to the chariot of kings, and in order to give the world the example of baseness and meanness, of pride, of perfidy, avarice, debauch and lying. He has created men to help each other, to love each other mutually and to arrive at happiness through the route of virtue. It is he who has made maternal organs palpitate with tenderness and joy; it is he who bathes with delicious tears the eyes of a son pressed against the breast of his mother; it is he who has maintained the most imperious and tender passions before the sublime love of *la patrie*; it is he who has covered nature with charm and riches and majesty. All that which is good is his work, or he himself: the bad belongs to depraved men who oppress their fellow human beings, or those who allow them to be oppressed."[10]

Two days later the Convention passed the law of 22 prairial, "which announced the final, most murderous spasm of the Terror.[11]

Admittedly, even to establish unequivocally that Robespierre (and Saint-Just and even Barère) was supporting a severe psychopathology does not, in itself, explain French revolutionary culture and its creation and sustenance of the great Terror. It may, nevertheless, be profoundly indicative. That many hundreds of thousands shared Robespierre's Manichaean view of the world; that Maximilien was considered the foremost leader of the Revolution during the months of the Terror; that the people of Paris cheered the progress through the streets to the guillotine of Danton and his associates—of all this, there can be no question. One supporting example: "According to the *comité civil* of the Section du Fauborg du Nord, Joseph Morlot, a house-painter arrested on 5 Prairial, had two distinct natures: 'The one, when governed by his natural disposition, is gentle, honest, and kind; it presents a combination of all the social virtues which he practices discreetly in his everyday life. The other, awakened by momentary dangers, produces the worst possible evils presented in their most lurid form which he parades in the most indiscreet manner.' "[12]

Any analysis of the psychological conflicts in society must remain speculative. One can, however, support this particular speculation—that the culture was pervaded by intense paranoid anxiety that was defended against (only partly successfully) by a splitting of the world into radically evil and radically virtuous moieties, wherein the task of the virtuous was to exterminate the perpetrators of evil—such a proposition is sustained by attention paid to the rhetoric of the leaders of the Terror, wherein we find this Manichaean view repeated over and over again. And such speeches were roundly applauded and many times printed and circulated throughout the country. One cannot avoid the conclusion that, during the Terror, this binary rhetoric was exactly what a good percentage of *le peuple* wanted to hear and believed in.

Robespierre was a virtuoso of this bifurcating rhetoric: so passionate in the exaltation of virtue, so ardent in the condemnation of evil, that one listens to him at risk of believing and joining the crusade. " '[There are] two peoples in France, the mass of citizens, pure, simple, athirst for justice; this is the virtuous people which sheds its blood to found the Republic; the other people is this mob of ambitious and intriguing people, this chattering, artificial, charlatan people who appear everywhere, who persecute patriotism; . . . who abuse the education and the advantages the *ancien régime* gave them to lead public opinion astray; a people of scoundrels and foreigners who put themselves between the French people and their representatives to dupe the ones and slander the others.' "[13] And all of this is, of course, a prescription for action: " 'The Revolutionary Government owes to citizens protection; it owes the enemies of the people nothing but death.' "[14]

A few weeks before the decreeing of the infamous law of 22 prairial, which brought the most horrendous period of the Terror (June 1794), the Convention passed a decree stating that no English or Hanoverian prisoners should be taken. Those fighting against the Revolution were no longer human or, more accurately, were a form of debased humanity deserving extermination. Maximilien explicated the philosophy behind such an action: " 'That soldiers fighting for despots might give a hand to defeated soldiers to return to the hospital together, that is understandable; that a slave might deal with a slave, a tyrant with a tyrant, that is also conceivable, but a free man compromising with a tyrant or his satellite, courage with cowardice, virtue with crime, that is inconceivable, that is what's impossible.' "[15]

And, finally, there is the famous speech of February 1794, wherein Terror has become the greatest virtue:

> Il faut étouffer les ennemis intérieurs et extérieurs de la République, ou périr avec elle; or, dans cette situation, la première maxime de votre politique doit être qu'on conduit le peuple par la raison, et les ennemis du peuple par la terreur.
>
> Si le ressort du gouvernement populaire dans la paix est la vertu, le ressort du gouvernement populaire en révolution est à la fois la vertu et *la terreur*: la vertu, sans laquelle la terreur estfuneste; la terreur, sans laquelle la virtu est impuissante. La terreur n'est autre chose que la justice prompte, sévère, inflexible; elle est donc une émanation de la vertu; elle est moins un principe particulier qu'une conséquence du principe général de la démocratie appliqué aux plus pressants besoins de la patrie.
>
> . . . Le gouvernement de la révolution est les despotisme de la liberté contre la tyrannië.[16]
>
> (It is necessary to suppress the interior and exterior enemies of the Republic, or else to perish with her; now, in that circumstance, the primary rule of our politics must be that one leads the people by reason, and the enemies of the people by terror.[17]
>
> If the mainspring of popular government in a time of peace is virtue, its mainspring in a time of revolution is *virtue and terror* combined: virtue without which terror is fatal; terror without which virtue is impotent. Terror is nothing but swift, severe and inflexible justice; it is therefore an emanation of virtue; and it is not so much a principle itself as a consequence of the general principle of democracy when applied to the most urgent needs of *la patrie*.

. . . The government of the revolution is the despotism of liberty against tyranny.[18])

This Manichaean splitting of the world into those who are perfectly virtuous and those who are totally evil is a psychological mechanism of defense wherein, in typical paranoid fashion, one projects onto other people the unacceptable evil one unconsciously senses within oneself. The world so conceived becomes a perfect reflection of the radical split between good and evil, between eros and destruction, that this kind of pathological person carries within his/her psyche. Otto Kernberg, a foremost contemporary psychoanalytic theorist, has postulated that the characteristic mode of defense for neurotic people is repression, whereas the characteristic mode of defense for borderline people is splitting.[19] The hypothesis being developed here is that this drastic splitting of the world is characteristic of the psycho-social culture of radical Jacobinism and the great Terror and was, ultimately, one profound cause of that Terror.

Once the Manichaean defensive maneuver has been established, the intensity of the pathological conflict and the degree of the murderous inclinations of the actors will determine what action is taken against those unredeemable, unforgivable representatives of radical evil. One may annihilate them in the doomed-to-fail attempt to exterminate the evil within oneself. Once again, we can look at a situation of much less intensity and catastrophe in order to comprehend the psychological mechanism operating here. We know, in New York City, of many cases of small groups of young men who pay a nighttime visit to Greenwich Village for the purpose of beating up homosexual men they find on the street. It is no radical speculation to suggest that those toughs are obsessed with homosexuality, that their obsession originates in an intense conflict over their own homoerotic inclinations, and that in the attempt to beat down these impulses, they actually beat those whose public display they find so excruciatingly disturbing. Their wish is that these homoerotic impulses will be buried under a weight of repression, just as those they batter collapse under their blows. They are, in addition, also satisfying their homosexual desire by getting sexual satisfaction out of beating some other men. This makes of the activity a perfect representation of a psychological symptom. Freud has said that a symptom contains within it two essential elements: a repressing element that restrains an instinctual impulse and a substitutive satisfaction of that impulse, simultaneously.[20]

Some may find this mode of analysis wildly irrational, but can anything be more wildly irrational than what occurred in the Year II? Robespierre and Saint-

Just sent Danton to have his head cut off, first, by identifying him with absolute evil (*l'étranger*), and then by executing him for being that evil. No one, not even the gravest apologist for the Terror, has satisfactorily explained to us how the killing of Danton saved the Revolution or strengthened the war effort. And, then, from 22 Prairial to 9 Thermidor, the killing frenzy was uncontrollable. How rational was all that? One cannot explain such horrendous human excess with some reasonable, commonsense view of the psyche.

To sum up the argument being made here by returning to the question that has been haunting this book: How did it happen that Robespierre, a man of unquestionable moral genius, ended his life as a cannibalistic terrorist? Those primitive aggressive inclinations were there—in a serious problematic manner—from the very beginning. They were sealed off, however, by a massive maneuver of splitting, which left them pristine and untransformed and—for the moment—invisible. For most people, for the average psychopathological person suffering from a common variety of neurosis, eros and destruction are mixed within the psyche in an infinite variety of combinations. This kind of severe splitting does not occur. Robespierre and Saint-Just were not suffering from a common neurosis. Their psychopathology was much more severe. It was not, however, as has been argued here, psychotic. In current psychological parlance once calls it "borderline" or a "severe psychopathology." A subsequent chapter will treat the theory of the borderline personality and its relationship to ideological terror at length. For now, the point being made is that extreme splitting is a fundamental characteristic of the borderline personality.

It is of interest to note that, with all the new information being made available as a result of the fall of Communism, it is becoming more and more apparent that it may be accurate to state that all ideological terrorists—at least, those of the left—have exhibited this same severe psychopathology and the inevitable accompanying splitting. All of them have decreed massive executions or deaths under the banner of virtue: creating a new virtuous society and a new man. The latest revelations about Lenin, for instance, made it all but impossible to maintain the position some have held in the past: that Lenin was a virtuous person and that it was Stalin who instituted and maintained the terror; that if Lenin had lived, it would all have been radically different. And Mao, in the latter part of his life, exhibited behavior that it would be generous to describe as "severe psychopathology," rather than "psychotic." At one point Zhou Enlai had to resort literally to crawling on his hands and knees to the Chairman's feet to ask forgiveness, an action that Mao did not regard as inappropriate. Roderick

MacFarquhur, who has written a three-volume work on *The Origins of the Cultural Revolution* (Columbia University Press, Volume 3, 1997), is a judicious historian, not given to exaggeration, and yet he "compares Mao to Stalin and Hitler . . . finding him most like Hitler, minus the homicidal racism."[21]

The tremendous irony in all this, that which makes it so difficult to give an overall judgment on Robespierre (and, maybe, on many others as well) is that this extreme splitting also leaves the perception of virtue and the moral life almost totally uncontaminated by even the hint of evil. Again, whereas the average person, *l'homme moyen sensuel* [the ordinary sensual man], in his thoughts, feelings, and actions almost always demonstrates some complex mixture of virtue and vice, good and evil, eros and destruction, those who insist on this severe splitting not only represent evil in its blackest of black form, but they also perceive virtue and morality in an almost blinding white light, devoid of any shadow. So sharp a perception of what the moral, good life could be makes it almost painful that the real world is so inadequate to this vision. And a vision it is. For these visionaries insist on bringing a virtue to the world that it cannot support. We have the cliché about such people: "He sees the world totally in black and white, with no shades of gray." That usually is said to emphasize how unredeemably dark such a person perceives evil, but it should also signify that virtue and morality are apprehended in an almost surreal white light.

Robespierre's moral genius, which I keep attributing to him, resulted in part from the almost unearthly clarity with which, in the early years, he perceived in what manner a truly moral society should behave. The great temptation and corruption with such people is that they may become ideological terrorists; in Burckhardt's famous phrase, they evolve into the "terrible simplifiers."[22] They become terrorists, however, only if their radical moral perception is caused by the kind of extreme splitting that results from a severe psycho-pathology, for in that case, the other side of this terrible divide—the dark, destructive rage—is ever-ready to throw off repression, enter the world of action, spread devastation everywhere. I am arguing that the horrendous moral catastrophe of the Terror can be understood only by keeping this formulation in mind.

The distinction between the normal, morally mixed person and the murderous ideologue was perceived by Lamartine when he announced that Danton was a man, but Robespierre was an idea.[23] An even more tragically ironic comment comes from Mathiez that "Danton had too much contempt for human life to be bloodthirsty."[24] We may elaborate his irony and turn it onto Robespierre, who regarded life as so sacred, he could not refrain from taking it in bloody sacrifice, in order to create a moral order in society. And Louis Blanc provides his own metaphor for a psyche anesthetized by a catastrophic splitting. Robespierre he portrays as " 'That frozen embodiment of principle . . . [a] reflective but marble statue of justice,' whose feelings are all in his head: 'put your hand on his heart, and there is not a stir of life in it.' "[25] Put your hand, however, on the underside of the heart, the dark side, and you will find it aflame with the passions of destruction. How else could he have acted as he did?

None of this is to praise or excuse Danton. He is cited here primarily to contrast him to ideological terrorists. He, himself, was a wonderful mixture of virtue and corruption: a virtuoso of moral compromise. The bourgeois future of society, for good and for evil, was prefigured in this complex revolutionary. Hundreds of thousands of Dantons still live among us.

Assuming the validity of this analysis, an even larger question comes forward: What causes the virtuous part of the psychic divide to retreat and allows the destructive impulses larger and larger freedom until they dominate completely? Why is the paranoid-driven individual sometimes pushed to the very border of paranoia itself? No one answer can possible suffice. Modernity anxiety, repeatedly alluded to and discussed here, is certainly one factor. Another, to be looked at later, is the rage engendered by the feeling of betrayal of one's utopian ideals. Failure is certainly another: without resorting to the word "paranoia" itself, the evidence points toward the fact that, in the cases of Lyndon Johnson (failure to quickly win the war in Vietnam) and Richard Nixon (the Watergate catastrophe), failure, and impending defeat, drove both people into a deeper and deeper paranoid state.

One other significant consideration is the process of getting older. In the case of Mao, for instance, there seems to be no question that, although certain pathologies were indicated when he was younger, he became more and more paranoid as the years passed.[26] One such circumstance, of relevance for French revolutionary history, is that of Jean-Jacques Rousseau. Striking are the similarities of the psychologies of Rousseau and Robespierre: radical splitting of good and evil, blinding insights into the true nature of morality, obsession with one's enemies, self-destruction and martyrdom as final resolutions. Starobinski demonstrates that the pathological aspects of Rousseau's psyche became increasingly pronounced as he aged, to the point where he could be placed on the border of paranoia itself.[27] Starobinski's description of Rousseau's splitting is revelatory:

He not only relieves himself of responsibility, but shifts all possibility of error, implicit in any exercise of free will, onto the shoulders of others. He is incorruptibly pure because *they* are ineluctably wicked.[28]

Sin becomes more concrete, more serious, when it takes the form of an absolute evil of which Jean-Jacques is the innocent victim. In projecting his guilt onto others, he accuses them of crimes far blacker than any of his own. But he does so in order to grant himself, as the victim of injustice, absolute justification. He offers his neck to the sacrificial knife in order to acquire the purity of the victim.[29]

The pathology of Jean-Jacque's communication with others stems from his need to rely on absolutes, even if these absolutes are negative. . . . Rather than live in uncertainty among men, rather than accept the obligations of the human condition, in which the possibility of communication is always counterbalanced by the risk of obstruction and misunderstanding, Rousseau splits the ambivalence in two and makes the resulting terms into absolute, immutable opposites. Rather than confront the uncertainty of life and the dangers of active freedom, he prefers to appear before two tribunals whose judgement is known in advance, before judges who he can be sure will pronounce a loud and irrevocable Yes or No—judgements never encountered in the pure form in ordinary human experience.[30]

Maximilien did not, of course, learn this mode of perceiving the world from Jean-Jacques; he invented it for himself. There was one profound difference: Rousseau was only a scribbler of words destined to change the world. Robespierre held almost absolute power over the lives of multitudes. Before he offered "his neck to the sacrificial knife," he had the opportunity to decree the immolation of many thousands who were, in a deep irrational sense, surrogates for himself. Only a radical catastrophic splitting of the psyche could make such paradoxical behavior possible.

19

THE FLIGHT TO PERFECTION

UTOPIANISM AS A DEFENSE AGAINST MODERNITY-ANXIETY

THE PEOPLE ARE PERFECT

[April 24, 1794 in the Convention: Robespierre's proposal for a new Declaration of Rights] Article 30. Every institution is vicious which does not assume the corruptibility of public officials, and the goodness of the people.[1]

It is the people who are good, patient, generous; our revolution bears witness to this, as is shown both by the crimes of its enemies and its own innumerable heroic deeds in the recent past, which came naturally to it. The people ask only for peace, justice and the right to live. The rich and the powerful thirst after honours, wealth and sensual enjoyment. The interest and desire of the people is that of nature itself, of humanity; it is the general interest. The interest of the rich and powerful is that of ambition, pride, greed and the wildest fantasies of passions that are fatal to the happiness of society as a whole. The abuses that have ravaged society were always their doing. These men have always been the scourge of the people. Who made our glorious revolution? Was it the rich? Was it the people? Only the people could will it and achieve it. For the same reason the people alone can maintain it.

—Robespierre, December 1790[2]

For the political leaders involved with the kind of psychological splitting elaborated in the last chapter, there seems to exist an overriding compulsive need to create something in the moral and political world that is perfect, uncontaminated by even a hint of evil. For the culture of the revolutionary ideological terror, that unblemished object was manifest both in a present, actual existence: *le peuple*; and also in a future phenomenon that was the Revolution's job to create: *un nouveal homme*, who was not to be perfect but was destined to live and act like no other man ever previously seen on the earth.

Excruciating anxiety must be defended against, and the paranoid-future-borderline personality, who is not psychotic, has succeeded in good part in erecting defenses that, although pathological, prevent further regression into a near-psychotic state. The evidence is overwhelming pointing to the fact that revolutionary belief, rhetoric, and action were intent on creating a world split into pure good and pure evil as a defensive maneuver against this anxiety. I have dealt previously with the multiple paranoid constructions of all-bad objects: enemies, traitors, *l'étranger*, and so forth, and so on; here the purpose is to elaborate on the pure and the flawless. The two distortions of reality are, however, intimately related one to the other; each is the cause of the other. One cannot address one side of this symptomology without also paying attention to the other. "Constant projection of 'all bad' self and object images," Otto Kernberg elaborates, "perpetuates a world of dangerous, threatening objects, against which the 'all good' self images are used defensively, and megalomaniac ideal-self images are built up."[3] We recall that Robespierre announced: "*Je suis peuple, moi-même.*"[4]

One need not be an expert on paranoid-borderline personality, or even a psychoanalyst, to perceive this mode of splitting in revolutionary culture: it literally cries out to be noticed. Jack Censer observes:

> The radicals believed that the appeal of the *aristocratie* struck a resonant chord in the nature of man. All men were egotistical; all men wanted debauchery; all men wanted power; all men wanted money. . . .
>
> Consider the contrast between this human nature and that "nature" which endowed the *peuple* with "reason" and the knowledge of freedom. Obviously, these two concepts of nature are in conflict; yet the radicals believed both. . . . The radicals were not tortured by the apparent contradiction; they made no explicit attempt to resolve it. . . . perhaps they assumed that it required no explanation. In any case they accepted consciously or unwittingly the existence of two natures: one, a universal, prescriptive, harmonious nature, which spoke for freedom; and the second, the nature of man, which sought egotism and self-indulgence.[5]

The insistence on the existence of an all-perfect human nature is intimately related to another primitive mode of defense: a belief in omnipotence. Kernberg writes: "Primitive idealization . . . reflects the underlying omnipotence,"[6] and is reinforced by the creation of "fantastic ideals of power, greatness, and perfection."[7]

For those making a revolution and creating a never-seen-before new world, nonetheless, this fantastical notion of the people as perfect in virtue does not quite answer the requirements of omnipotence. If the people have been powerful enough to overthrow the Bastille, bring the king to Paris, and dethrone him; and if that same people is totally without corruption—how is it that the Revolution is still incomplete, still in trouble, and endangered? The answer lies in the fact that this same perfect people is innocent, not clever, seducible, and easily led astray by wily, conspiring, corrupt enemies of the Revolution. With this intellectual maneuver, the unblemished nature of le peuple is maintained, and the elimination of the corrupt, in order to establish the new world, continues. Over and over again: no perfect virtue without a perfect enemy. And Robespierre was a virtuoso of this kind of intellectual performance: "The people feels more vividly and sees better all that which pertains to the first principles of justice and humanity . . . and its good sense in that regard is often superior to the spirit of the clever people, but it has not the same skill in disentangling the detours of political cunning that they employ in order to fool and master it, and its natural benevolence disposes it to be the dupe of charlatan politicians. These latter know it well and profit by it."

At first, after the people rises up and demonstrates its power, despotism pays it homage and retreats. Not for long, however: "Soon [despotism] raises itself; it approaches the people with a caressing air; it substitutes ruse for force; one believes it converted, one has heard the word 'liberty' go out of its mouth: the people abandons itself to joy, to enthusiasm. . . . Soon whoever has some talents combined with vices belongs to the party of despotism; that party follows constantly a plan of intrigue and of seduction; it sets itself above all to corrupt public opinion; it raises up ancient prejudices, ancient habits which have still not been obliterated; it undertakes the depravity of those morals which are still not regenerated."

The enemies of liberty begin their domination of the representatives of the people. And soon, it is too late to recover freedom: "One looks to lead astray, to seduce, or to master the delegates of the people. . . . The people only recognizes the traitors when they have already done enough evil to be able to defy it impunitively."[8]

Perfectly virtuous, but childish, *le peuple* will lose its power to evil—unless. Unless a powerful leadership—not seducible, not naive, not innocent—asserts itself and shows the people the true road to victory. The radical leadership and the people must become one. Danton to the Convention, March 1793: " 'The Convention is a revolutionary body; this body must be *"peuple"* like the people itself. . . . Show yourselves terrible, show yourselves people, and you will save the people. . . . I insist on what is more than law: [*il faut que vous soyez peuple*] you must be people.' "[9]

This merger of people and leadership will have a magnificent effect: the delegates will resist the temptation to corruption and remain pure like the people; *le peuple* will give up its innocence and seducibility and make an alliance with virtuous power. It was all a fantasy. There were multitudes of people out there but no *peuple*. And if *le peuple* did exist, only a maker of myth could believe it would speak with one voice and that a virtuously pure one. No compromise with evil was to be allowed: to compromise with was to give in to evil. The only way to prevent *total* degeneration into corruption was to maintain something immaculate. The splitting of the world into the moieties of all good and all evil was the means by which this fantasy was kept alive.

The people being unblemished, democracy having been instituted and, therefore, the national representatives elected by the people as a whole, how does it happen that political life remains corrupt, that the struggle for a virtuous polity is, seemingly, unending? It is of great interest that the French-radical and the American answers to the question of the corruptibility of elected representatives were exactly opposite. In the famous *Federalist* #10, wherein Madison addresses the question of how a democratic society can overcome the natural tendency of factions to work only for their own interests and not for the good of the commonwealth as a whole, his first answer is that the elected representatives will behave more virtuously than the people as a body, and that political elites will tend to act more in the full interests of the commonwealth than the aggregated people. He does not venture a hypothesis as to why this should be so, and it is true that twice he uses the word "may" in elaborating their actions. The tyranny of the Athenian *demos*, which met in one huge assembly of all citizens and committed many immoral, self-destructive acts, was in his mind; Madison mistrusted the people, convened as a crowd, easily led astray.[10]

Since the people were perfect, French revolutionary radicalism had to discover the source of the misuse of political power in the representatives of the people and found within that elected body the source of corruption and despotism. "Let us pose at first this incontestable maxim," announces Robespierre, "*that the people is good, and that its delegates are corruptible; that it is in the virtue and the sovereignty of the people that one must look for a security against the vices and the despotism of government.*"[11] How he, as an elected deputy, and self-appointed *chef* of the people, has been able to free himself of this corruption, he never attempts to tell us.

In this same speech of April 10, 1793, two months before "*le peuple*" threw the Girondin delegates out of the Convention, Maximilien suggests an institutional means by which the despotism of the representatives may be overcome. Another fantastic flight: "The entire nation has the right to know the conduct of its mandatories. It would be necessary, if it were possible, that the assembly of delegates of the people deliberate in the presence of the entire people. An edifice vast and majestic, open to 12,000 spectators, would be the place of the deliberations of the legislature. Under the eyes of such a grand number of witnesses, neither corruption, nor intrigue, nor perfidy would dare to show itself; the general will [*la volonté générale*] only would be consulted, only the voice of reason and the public interest would be heard."[12] Some antimodernist regimes in the last quarter of this century have been more realistic and selective about assembling the "*nation entière*," convening 12,000 spectators, and even more, in stadiums for the sole purpose of witnessing the execution of convicted enemies of the regime.

And what happens when *le peuple* behaves in an obviously unvirtuous manner? Denial sets in. It is *not* the people doing this. At several times in '94, food riots occurred in Paris; stores were broken into; coffee and sugar were looted. Robespierre could not ignore the situation and offered an analysis. It was not *le peuple* who had committed these criminal acts: "the people can put up with hunger, but not with crime; *le peuple* is able to sacrifice everything except its virtues."[13] And Maximilien, the great martyr, could sacrifice everything except his illusions.

These illusions, of the unblemished and the totally unredeemable, however, had their cost. Those who are not pure, can be—should be—exterminated. Total evil deserves only one judicial sentence. Saint-Just is our guide into this manichaean hell:

There is no prosperity to hope for as long as the last enemy of liberty breathes. You have to punish not only traitors, but even those who are indifferent; you have to punish whoever is passive in the republic; and who does nothing for it. For, since the French people has manifested its will, all that is opposed to it is outside the sovereign; all that is outside the sovereign is the enemy.

If conspiracies had not disturbed this empire, if the country had not been a thousand times victim to indulgent laws, it would be nice to govern according to maxims of peace and natural justice. These maxims are accepted among the friends of liberty; but between people and its enemies there is no longer anything in common but the sword. It is necessary to govern with iron those who cannot be governed by justice. It is necessary to oppress tyrants.[14]

Ideological terror, intent, on the one hand, on creating a new perfect man and world, and, on the other hand, completely profligate in the use of instruments of extermination—ideological terror is erected on the foundation of this terrible human bifurcation of all perfect and all evil.

It is an inevitable human reaction to feel rage at having been betrayed by not having received, from caretakers and nurturers, the love one felt one deserved. And such fury may have two manifestations: the fantasy creation of a perfect love that will cure all pain; and the wild destruction that will revenge oneself on the betrayers.

There is no way of "proving" that this particular symptomatic construction was an important problematic within French culture. Two things, however, we do know for certain. First, it created the first political ideological terror in the history of the world. And second, the great intellectual and moral hero, and direct ancestor, of the radical revolution was Rousseau. Rousseau—one of the most contradictory, paradoxical, ambivalent people ever. Personally responsible for convincing many middle- and upper-class women to nurse their own children and not give them out to wet-nurses, he yet delivered all his own children to foundling homes, to be raised by strangers. His theoretical voice established many of the fantasy notions that were accepted as truth by those who followed him: that there was a pure and innocent state of nature that existed before society became corrupt; that elected representatives would be corrupt and that, therefore, only direct democracy (whatever that meant in a country of twenty million people) could preserve the integrity of the polity; that the "general will" was always virtuous and that the good of the commonwealth resulted from finding out what it was and not in creating it.

"It follows from what has been said above that the general will is always well-meaning and always tends towards the public good; but it does not follow that all decisions made by the people are equally sound. We will always will our own good, but we do not always see what it is. The people is never corrupted, but it is often misled, and only then does it seem to will what is bad [*Social Contract*, Book II, Chapter 3]."[15]

A certain fantasy mindset that continues in some quarters, even until today, was elaborated by Rousseau and taken up by the rhetoric of the radical Revolution: that human nature is essentially, and primarily, good and that all the evil in social life comes from society. How that society, which was created by essentially good people, managed to become the corrupter of the world, nobody bothered to explain. And, certainly, nobody could give any reasonable answer. Rousseau: " 'I found it in our social order, when being contrary in every way to indestructible nature, tyrannizes that nature and obliges it to insist constantly on its rights. I pursued this contradiction to draw out its consequences and saw that it alone explained all the vices of men and all the ills of society.' "[16] The great lie within Marxian socialism, especially in its twentieth-century manifestation, was that the evil in social life comes from capitalism, not from people. Eliminate capitalism and evil, like the state, will wither away. Capitalism was eliminated; people remained; evil was triumphant. Overstated to some degree because there was a certain ambivalence about this notion, as was true in the French Revolution as well: the new society also required the transformation of human nature, the creation of a new man. More of that later.

Robespierre, as we have seen, stands on the shoulders of Rousseau, and acknowledges that debt. In April of '89, he is elected a delegate to the Estates General, and celebrates the occasion by writing an essay: "Dédicace à J.-J. Rousseau," within which he reiterates the shibboleth of the perfect people:

> The people is always pure in its motives, it loves only the public good, since the public good is the interest of the people.[17]

And, as always, one cannot talk about pure virtuousness without confronting the question of where evil comes from. By an exercise in almost total illogic, the representatives of the people are the bringers of evil. Pride and arrogance are the causes of this circumstance. People, obviously, only become prideful, arrogant, and corrupt after they win elections. Robespierre in January '92:

> No one has given us a more accurate idea of the people than Rousseau, because no one has loved them more. "The people always wants the good, but it does not always see it." In order to complete the theory of the principles of government, it would suffice to add: the representatives of the people often see the good, but

they do not always want it. The people desires the good because the public good is its interest, because good laws are its safeguard: its representatives do not always desire it, because they wish to turn the authority that is confided in them to the profit of their pride and arrogance. Read what Rousseau has written of representative government, and judge if the people are able to sleep without risk.[18]

It would be wrong to imagine that the democratic, bourgeois world that succeeds to the revolutionary trial by fire is free from this fantasy of perfection. The people, naturally, have been dethroned, but the Nation inherits the mantle not only of the omnipotence of the king, as has been discussed, but also that of perfect virtuousness. "My country right or wrong," becomes the new dogma assuring us that perfection exists, and has power, somewhere in our political lives. In America, where, some thirty years ago, the unblemished virtue of the Nation was powerfully challenged, and a major war ended as a result of a democratic critique, the flag of the Nation became the objective correlative of the moral omnipotence of the polity. Burn it or bow before it were presented as our only alternatives, indications of how potently sacred, or negatively sacred, and certainly taboo, it was. Not surprisingly, Robespierre announced that the Nation and the people were one, that the Nation also was " 'neither corrupted by luxury, nor depraved by pride, nor carried away by ambition, nor troubled by those passions which are inimical to equality . . . generous, reasonable, magnanimous and moderate.' "[19]

What do we make, then, of the fact that, in the last two centuries, so many of the worst nightmares of history have been perpetuated under the legitimizing banner of the immaculate Nation: the millions destroyed in the conquering wars of Napoleon; the near genocide of peoples, and the full destruction of native cultures, under nineteenth-century imperialism; the suicidal havoc of World War I, which came close to destroying a whole generation of young people; the almost total annihilation of Enlightenment culture by *ein Reich* and *ein Volk*; the uncountable and unimaginable millions destroyed in the Stalinist project of, supposedly, making Russia strong; and, most recently, ethnic nationalism, which generates ethnic slaughter and ethnic massacre. Is there somehow a dark and tragic connection between this need for perfection and the slaughter of the multitudes? Is the insistence on perfect virtue the devil's work? Does the hallucination that one is acting under a banner of perfect virtue allow one to commit slaughters without number? Terrible questions.

THE CREATION OF A NEW MAN: REBIRTH

One may read the tragic history of the French revolutions as a failed rite of passage. Van Gennep, in his significant book *The Rites of Passage*, outlines three stages in rituals of transformation: (1) rites of separation; (2) rites of transition; and (3) rites of incorporation.[20] In the ceremonies for young boys that initiate them into the adult male world, for instance, we observe: (1) Separation from the social environment in which they have been living; in some cases, the men come to forcefully take away the boys from their mother's dominion, as the mothers weep for loss. (2) A situation of liminality, where there is no center of existence—many times frightening, like a dark cave or a mountainous wilderness. (3) A ritual of incorporation into the male adult world that implies no going back to the world of women. This sequence of rites of passage, Van Gennep demonstrates, can be observed not only in early societies but in the rituals of marriage or for the dead, as instances in almost all complex and modern societies.

At the end of the period of liminality, and just before the process of incorporation, in many cases there is a ritual the understanding of which may shed light on the deep psychological process that revolutions have to contend with: the death and rebirth of the initiate. Van Gennep cites the rebirth ceremony of the Ojibway: "A second hut is built; the child is attached to a board and during the entire ceremony behaves as if he had lost all personality . . . there is a general procession to the interior of the hut; the chiefs-magicians-priests kill all the participants and resurrect them one after the other. . . . During the course of the ceremony, the child receives a new name."[21] In several cases from kinship societies, not cited by Van Gennep, the initiate crawls through the spread legs of one of the men, in a deliberate evocation of birth. It is, most remarkably, a rebirth. The initiate dies to the mothers and is born again from the fathers. No longer the childish names—a new name, a new man—*un nouvel homme*. The baptism by water of a person who is no longer a child and the metaphorical "baptism by fire" resonate profoundly with these rituals of rebirth.

The argument is being made here that the revolutionary commitment to the creation of a new man resonates profoundly with these particular rites of passage: that the engendering of *un nouvel homme* was also a process of rebirth; that rebirth is only possible after the death of the old. One may read the revolutionary experience as a rite of passage in three stages. Separation: the overthrow of old values and the old authority. Transition-liminality: that condition of acute anxiety when it is not clear that a new center can be erected that will give the same stability and security as that which has been destroyed. Incorporation: a new ground of security and stability proved to be the hardest of all. The English, with the Glorious Revolution of 1688; and the Americans, with the presidency of Washington, succeeded in a reasonable time after the revolutionary overthrow. The French knew that rebirth was supposed to follow the killing of the old— that Louis must die that *la patrie* can be born again—but, somehow, it did not happen. Terror was the result—or the cause—of this failure of rebirth that would lead to incorporation.

Does the new man possess a different human nature? Is the task one of creating an entirely different human nature, or only that of radically transforming it? An old bromide of conservative citizens, who were resisting any fundamental change in social values, was that "You can't change human nature." People are selfish, have always been selfish, will always be so, and any attempt to alter that fact is doomed to failure. From one point of view and definition, the bald statement is correct: human nature is, by definition, incapable of change without the creation of a new species, which would no longer be *homo sapiens*. The real question is whether or not it is within human nature to be capable of transformation: Is a radical change in the value system within society possible? How adaptable, how capable of metamorphosis, is our nature?

A reading of history would support the concept that such radical changes in values are possible: the transition from a pagan to a Christian world; the Reformation in the sixteenth century; the passage that is the subject of this book, from an early Modern to a fully Modern stage of society. When contemplating the revolutionary rhetoric on the question of rebirth and a new man, however, especially from those who became terrorists, one is made uneasy. Are they really urging the same kind of transformation of values that occurred in the past, or is it some form of omnipotence fantasy at work? Is it more than a metaphor: an actual belief that a new human nature can be produced? It is one thing to invent a fantasied Utopia, in the manner of Plato and More; it is quite another to truly believe you can create such a new world on this planet—in one generation. When Billaud-Varenne, member of the murderous Committee of Public Safety, announces: " 'You will lose the younger generation by abandoning it to parents with prejudices and ignorance, who gave it the defective tint which they have themselves. Therefore, let the fatherland take hold of children who are born for it alone and let it begin by plunging them into Styx, like Achilles' ' "[22]—is this great symbol of death and rebirth only a metaphor for a long process of transformation that, in reality, will take generations and generations? Equally likely, it is a utopian-fantasy belief born of the anxiety that, in reality, no new world is possible in so short a time; that it will take more than one immersion in the river Styx. " 'Once public modesty is re-established in all hearts.' " was Billaud-Varenne's fond hope and belief, " 'from then on the citizens will learn to esteem each other as men and cherish each other as brothers.' "[23] What makes us so wary when observing of this kind of philosophical exercise is that we have now heard, for a hundred years, almost exactly the same kind of thing from too many empowered murderous ideological terrorists.

What is remarkable is that the notion of regeneration, and the word itself, was in the air during the first stages of the Revolution. Louis himself gave explanation of his decision to call the Estates-General; " 'The great enterprise I have undertaken for the *regeneration* of the Kingdom and the re-establishment of good order in all its parts.' "[24] And in Necker's apologia, *Sur l'administration de M. Necker par lui même*, 1791, he describes the meeting of the Estates as " 'the great enterprise that would ensure a *general regeneration.*' "[25] Mona Ozouf informs us that that word had a prominent place in the *cahiers de dolénces*, wherein was emphasized the "regeneration *of* the administration, *of* public order, *of* the state, *of* France." However, as the Revolution progressed, the "of" was dropped; regeneration became global: "Soon . . . this ballast was jettisoned, and people began to speak only of regeneration, a program without limits, at once physical, political, moral, and social, which aimed for nothing less than the creation of a 'new people.' "[26] The crucial words in her description being "without limits"—we are at the frontier of omnipotence fantasies.

It is very difficult to draw a fine line to separate the legitimate longing for moral transformation from the omnipotent belief in a new world. For one thing, this legitimate longing has produced some of the most moving writing and rhetoric the Modern world has known. Robespierre and Saint-Just do not begin their political and moral lives as terrorists. It is a mistake, and unfair to them and their circumstances, to imagine that their understanding of the need for moral transformation was confused, insincere, or hypocritical. They believed it and continued to believe it in their own, strange pathological way as the Terror spread its dominion over their lives. When reading their life-enhancing words, it is almost impossible to imagine the termination in terror. It is instructive to cite Rousseau, a moral giant and certainly no terrorist; we note the theme of (partial) death and rebirth:

> Anyone who dares to undertake the task of instituting a nation must feel himself capable of changing human nature, so to speak; of transforming each individual,

who by himself is a complete and solitary whole, into a part of a greater whole from which he, in a sense, receives his life and his being; of marring man's constitution in order to strengthen it; of substituting a partial and moral existence for the physical and independent existence that we have all received from nature. He must, in short, take away man's resources to give him others that are foreign to him and cannot be sued without the help of other men. The more completely these natural resources are annihilated, the greater and more durable are the required ones and the stronger and more perfect are the new institutions.[27]

Saint-Just, in turn, adopts as a first principle an optimistic view of human nature: that it is, in its foundation, just and virtuous. " 'I imagine if men were given laws in accordance with nature and their own hearts, they would no longer be unhappy and corrupt.' " The legislator's task, therefore, was " 'to transform men into what he wants them to be.' "[28] And what their own natures also desire.

And Tocqueville, who was a paragon of fairness, could understand how powerful was the revolutionary thrust toward moral transformation. In comparing its strength to a religion, although a "strange" one, he is offering a compliment, though he cannot quite understand how such a new religion exists and thrives:

> The French Revolution's approach to the problems of men's existence here on earth was exactly similar to that of the religious revolutions as regards the afterlife. It viewed the "citizen" from an abstract angle, that is to say as an entity independent of any particular social order, just as religions view the individual, without regard to nationality or the age he lives in. It did not aim merely at defining the rights of the French citizen, but sought also to determine the rights and duties of men in general towards each other and as members of the body politic.
>
> It was because the Revolution always harked back to universal, not particular, values and to what was the most "natural" form of government and the most "natural" social system that it had so wide an appeal and could be imitated in so many places simultaneously.
>
> No previous political upheaval, however violent, had aroused such passionate enthusiasm, for the ideal the French Revolution set before it was not merely a change in the French social system, but nothing short of a regeneration of the whole human race. It created an atmosphere of missionary fervor and, indeed, assumed all the aspects of a religious revival. . . . It would perhaps be truer to say it developed into a species of religion, if a singularly imperfect one, since it was without God, without a ritual or promise of future life. Nevertheless, this strange religion has, like Islam, overrun the whole world with its apostles, militants, and martyrs.[29]

Revolutionary religions and revolutionary France shared one crucial thing in common: the commitment to the moral transformation of the world.

In the midst of the Terror, February 1794, Robespierre delivered what was probably the most extraordinary speech of his career. Of such power was it, that Palmer describes it as "one of the most notable utterances in the history of democracy."[30] And there is no question that parts of it can stand with the most profound utterances of Pericles, Jefferson, or Lincoln.

> We wish an order of things where all low and crude passions are enchained by the laws, all beneficent and generous feelings awakened; where ambition is the desire to deserve glory and to be of use to one's country; where distinctions arise only from equality itself; where the citizen is subject to the magistrate, the magistrate to the people, the people to justice. . . .
>
> We wish to substitute in our country morality for egotism, probity for a mere sense of honor, principle for habit, duty for etiquette, the empire of reason for the tyranny of custom, contempt for vice for contempt for misfortune, pride for insolence, large-mindedness for vanity, the love of glory for the love of money, good men for good company, merit for intrigue, talent for conceit, truth for show, the charm of happiness for the tedium of pleasure, the grandeur of men for the triviality of grand society, a people magnanimous, powerful and happy for a people lovable, frivolous and wretched—that is to say, all the virtues and miracles of the Republic for all the vices and puerilities of the monarchy.
>
> We wish in a word to fulfill the course of nature, to accomplish the destiny of mankind, to make good the promises of philosophy, to absolve Providence from the long reign of tyranny and crime.[31]

After this extraordinary Ode to Virtue, Maximilien goes on to expound on the question of what kind of government could institute such a righteous program. "What is the nature of the government that is able to realize these wonders [prodiges]? Only a democratic or republican government: these two words are synonymous despite the abuse of vulgar language; because the aristocracy is no longer of the republic, but of the monarchy. Democracy is not a state where the people continually assemble, rule by themselves on all public affairs, still less is it where a hundred thousand fractions of the people, by some isolated, precipitous and contradictory measures, decide the destiny of the entire society; such government has never existed, and it could exist only to lead the people to despotism. Democracy is a state where the sovereign people, guided by the laws which are its work, make by themselves all that which it is able to make well, and by its delegates all that which it is not able to do itself."[32]

Democracy, in itself, is a virtuous state, most particularly because it implies equality among all men: "As the essence of the republic or of democracy is equality, it follows that the love of *la patrie* embraces necessarily the love of equality. . . . the French are the first people of the world who have established a true democracy, calling all men to equality and the fullness of the rights of citizens; and here, in my view, is the true reason that those under the league of tyrants opposing the Republic will be vanquished."

All virtue comes together under such a polity: "In the system of revolutionary France, that which is immoral is impolitique, that which is corrupt is counter-revolutionary. Weakness, vice, prejudice are the road to royalty." And finally, the kind of complex joining together of psychology and virtue that only Robespierre, the scion of Rousseau, could construct: "However, one can say, in a sense, that in order to love justice and equality, the people has no need of a great virtue; it suffices that it love itself."

The speech is not over, however. We do not live, unfortunately, in a time when such a virtuous program can be effectively instituted. "Here is the limit of all the development of our theory necessary if you have to govern the vessel of the Republic only in a calm. But the tempest roars, and the state of the revolution in which you find yourself imposes another task." A war rages between the forces of good and evil; at such a time, it will take more than virtue to ensure the triumph of virtue. "The two contrary geniuses that have been portrayed, disputing between themselves dominion over nature, battle in this great epoch of the history of humankind, in order to fix, without the possibility of regression, the destinies of the world, and France is the theatre of that redoubtable struggle. On the outside, all the tyrants surround us; within, all the friends of tyranny conspire against us."

What then is our other task? "*Étouffer* [to suppress? to stifle? to strangle?] *les ennemis intérieurs et extérieurs de la République*, or perish with it; now, in that situation, the first maxim of our politics ought to be that one leads the people by reason, and the enemies of the people by terror." And then follow the ominous words cited previously, wherein the mainspring of government in revolution is both "*vertu et la terreur*." It is clear, accordingly, what the enemies of the people are to expect: "It is necessary, however, that one or the other succumb. Indulgence for the royalists, some people cry out. Mercy for villains! No: pardon for innocence, pardon for the weak, mercy for the unfortunate, grace for humanity!"

The extraordinary power of the rhetoric sustains itself. "One of the most notable utterances in the history of democracy" becomes an Ode to Terror. Only a Robespierre, a genius of psychological splitting, could so brilliantly accomplish such a task.

EDUCATION FOR A NEW PEOPLE

The most enduring result of this whole configuration of the transformation of morals and values; one of the most important legacies bequeathed to us by the Enlightenment, and by the Revolution as its conflicted executor, was the conception that it was the obligation of the state to provide universal, free education to all citizens, at least to all male citizens. And this momentous idea partook in no way with feelings of omnipotence. The results of such educational system would, obviously, take generations to become apparent. Democracy and equality were impossible without it: if poor people were to be citizens with rights equal to the well-off; if giving the franchise to all people was not to prove a catastrophe—then, a system of universal education was essential. It comes as no surprise that no one understood this better than Robespierre.

Michel Le Peletier, a radical Jacobin, had drawn up a complex and complete plan of primary education before he was assassinated in January 1793. Robespierre made this project his own and in July presented it to the Convention in great detail. It was conceived, naturally, as part of the enterprise of creating a new world. "I assert that what has been said until now has not filled the idea that I have formed of a complete plan of education. I have dared to conceive of a much vaster idea; and considering how much the human species is degraded by the vice of our ancient social system, I am convinced of the necessity of conducting an entire regeneration and, if I may express myself thusly, in creating a new people."[33] Despite the real value and necessity of universal education, inevitably, a certain amount of miraculousness creeps in; a certain amount of exaggerated hope was inevitable: "Form such men, and you will see all crime disappear. Form such men, and the hideous aspect of misery will no longer affect our vision."

The new man will, inevitably and imperatively, be *social*. Le Peletier's plan provided for schooling from five to eleven for girls, and from five to twelve for boys. "At five years, *la patrie* receives the child from the hands of nature; at twelve, it renders it to society."

The mode of discipline resonates with ancient rituals of initiation and rebirth. No whipping or beating, but a hard antisensual existence will annihilate the soft babyhood and provide for the rebirth of a hardened, mature adult and citizen. Ironically, the description reads as much like the creation of a monk as it does of a revolutionary new man. "Each hour will be marked for sleeping, for eating, for work, exercise, relaxation; the whole regime of life will be invariably regulated; gradual and successive exams will be determined; . . . the exercises of gymnastics will be indicated; a salutary and uniform rule will be prescribed in total detail. . . . I desire that, for the ordinary needs of life, the children, deprived of all superfluity, will be restrained to an absolute necessity. Their beds will be hard, their nourishment healthy but frugal; their clothes adequate but coarse."

Isser Woloch, in conversation, persuasively asserts that the presentation of the Le Peletier plan to the Convention by Robespierre, and its passage into law, had no real administrative effect. The plan was too ambitious to ever be seriously instituted; the day after the decree approving it, the Convention suspended its application.[34] The whole symbolic action, Woloch contends, was a way of memorializing the assassinated martyr and nothing more. The serious attempt to establish, in reality, universal education was the Lakanal Law passed after the fall of Robespierre, in November 1794.[35]

Even though Le Peletier approval had no practical effect, still, Woloch has written: "The willingness to endorse this Spartan fantasy even momentarily may have been an ominous portrait of Jacobin mentality."[36] This accords with the point being made here. Though not important as *logos*, the whole experience is revelatory of *mythos*: the creation of *un nouvel homme* was imperative; that genesis required the drama of rebirth; rebirth must be preceded by the symbolic death of the old; the hard beds and the coarse clothes had deep symbolic meanings.

The bourgeois world, which was the actual successor to revolutionary upheaval, would have nothing to do with frugal nourishment and hard beds. Exactly the opposite. But, once born, Tocqueville's *virus* never disappeared from the earth, as he told us, and whenever ideological revolution and ideological terrorism gained a certain dominion over the world, the omnipotent myth of a new man, born out of fiery rebirth, rose like the phoenix. " 'Man will become immeasurably stronger, wiser and subtler,' " wrote Trotsky in *Literature and Revolution*, " 'his body will become more harmonized, his movements more rhythmic, his voice more musical. These forms of life will become dynamically dramatic. The average human type will rise to the heights of an Aristotle, a Goethe, or a Marx. And above this ridge, new peaks will rise.' "[37]

In this dream world, all fantasies were possible. Two things, however, were not only possible but inevitable: the omnipotent fantasy of a new man to be created with remarkable speed was doomed to failure; and second, multitudes would pay with their lives for this disappointment. In erecting a primitive form of the rite of passage, in which the final stage of rites of incorporation was unattainable because utopian, the Jacobin dictatorship had created another form of what Tocqueville called "the politics of the impossible."[38] This one may be designated: "the ritual of the impossible." The two "impossibles" were deeply connected to each other; each arose out of the unconscious commitment to a fantasy of omnipotence. Any obstruction (even one coming from reality) to the fulfillment of that kind of fantasy produces enormous rage. And rage must find a victim. Terror without victims is another impossible.

THE ANNIHILATION OF THE PRIVATE

[Fall 1793] "I want us to know each other," an unnamed Jacobin told his colleague, "as I know the five fingers of my hand. I want each member to be able to say, looking at his neighbors, there is an honest man, a good patriot, or there is an intriguer we must expel."[39]

Every ideological terror in history has moved in the direction of the annihilation of the private. No part of one's life should be secret and not subject to scrutiny. At its extreme extension, even one's private thoughts should become public in order to establish one's purity. Private loyalties, such as those to family or friends, must give way to the one fundamental loyalty to *vertu* and *la patrie*. Under the banner of virtue, the public good, the health of the commonwealth, this program is one of the most sinister manifestations of terror. It destroys individuality; it assures a continual supply of victims, provided by those who do not meet the test. There undoubtedly were examples of this form of oppression in the religious life previous to 1789. The French Revolution represents the first attempt to annihilate the private to serve a *political* purpose. Here, once again, we observe the tragic preview of the twentieth century that was provided by this autochthonous political terror.

On 25 Ventôse, in the Year II, the *Fontaine-de-Grenelle* section wrote the popular society of Auxerre that the "patriot had no privacy, he relates everything to the common good: his income, his pain, he shares everything with his brothers, and herein lies the source of the publicity character of fraternal, that is, republican government."

Publicity stemmed from the sans-culotte notion of social relations. . . . One
was secretive only if one had bad intentions; denunciation became a civic duty.
Publicity was indeed the *safeguard of the people*: this precept, put into action during
every period of crisis between 1792 and 1794 provided the sans-culottes with a
powerful revolutionary weapon.[40]

Since the moral standard of political virtue was at a utopian height, almost
no one could live up to it, most especially if even private thoughts, feelings, and
reservations were to be made public. The deeper one digs into a person, the
more sure it becomes that one will find something that is untrustworthy. No
one is exempt from this lack of perfection. One is reminded of all the "self
criticisms" in the revolutionary movements of this century. It is a psychological
tyranny of the most sinister kind: there is no space left wherein one can be
oneself.

The annihilation of the private served the cause of total agreement that has
been previously discussed as a foremost hindrance to the establishment of a
democratic polity, that which Sorel called, "The terrible postulate of unanimity."[41] Albert Soboul tells us: "The principle of publicity showed, in its extreme
consequences, the ardent desire for unanimity which animated the sans-culottes:
he related himself wholly to the mass movement; he could not conceive of isolat-
ing himself from it; conformity of sentiments, of mind and of votes struck him
as being not only desirable, but necessary." We are not surprised to discover that
such psychological regression to a more primitive mode of identity formation is
undertaken under the banner of the sacred. "Unity, therefore, was to be one of
the driving powers of their political activity, an almost mystical concept. . . .
Correspondence and fraternization were the means of achieving unity; the brotherly kiss was its symbol; the oath gave it a religious value."[42]

This attack on the private life, this vilification of individuality, has a profoundly anti-Modern aspect. Individualism is a fundamental attribute of Modernity: at its finest, a commitment to morally autonomous critique; at its most
degraded, an egoism that cares nothing for others and a license to throw off all
moral restraint. We observe this same antithesis to individualism in all regressive
anti-Modern movements. It is yet another indication of the paradoxical situation
wherein ideological terror, which superficially appears to be the vanguard of
extreme Modernity, has yet a deep anti-Modernism in its soul.

At its outermost limit, the Jacobin terror made it a sin not only to oppose
the revolutionary fervor but also to be neutral, to stay passively neither for nor

against. One was subject to civic penalty for being "uninvolved." On the first day of April 1793, the *Bondy* section issued an appeal to the "uninvolved." Since the response was tepid, ten days later came the *Last Appeal to the Uninvolved*. Now, negative consequences were indicated: "Those who missed three successive sessions of the general assembly [of the sections] would be declared a bad citizen: the names of the *Uninvolved* were to be sent to the sectional committee, which would refuse to honor their evidence for the issuing of the certificate of civism and passports. The uninvolved person was already considered an inferior citizen, and soon was to be suspect."[43] The next step after "suspect" was arrest; the last step after arrest was the guillotine. There was no place to hide; any form of dissent or neutrality was a lethal matter.

OPPRESSIVE UTOPIANISM—THE TYRANNY OF VIRTUE

There is a utopianism that, if allowed to live, can only give birth to tyranny. There is a pathological commitment to virtue that quickly becomes murderous and kills. These are the two foundation pillars of ideological terror. Whenever ideological terror achieves dominion over the polity, these two attributes assert themselves. The tyrannical and murderous implications in the politics of extreme virtue were observed by several people before, during, and after the great Terror.

[Emmanuel Sieyès] Not enough attention is paid to the fact that the prejudice which needs most careful handling is the one that is mingled with sincerity; that the most dangerous vested interest to arouse is the one to which sincerity lends the full force of the feeling that justice is on its side. We must deprive the enemies of the nation of this borrowed strength. We must enlighten them, and thereby condemn them to the *debilitating* consciousness of their insincerity.[44]

[Camille Desmoulins] Let us beware of connecting politics with moral regeneration—a thing at present impracticable. Moralism is fatal to freedom.[45]

[1793] Vergniaud, on May 10, rose to denounce the particular definition of virtue which was being used to denigrate him and his friends. He attacked what he called the "Spartan virtue of the Jacobins," which, he claimed, was leading them ever deeper into violence. "By chasing after an ideal perfection, a chimeric virtue," he said, "you are acting like beasts."[46]

[Montlosier in 1796] We insisted on believing that all decency was on our side.

We could never believe that others might be mistaken and that we might be mistaken ourselves.[47]

[Mona Ozouf on Germaine de Staël] Staël shows that the most frightening terror is not one led by ferocious men (whose ferocity can give way to fatigue or a change of mood) but rather the one led by pure consciences. Men of virtue and abnegation are the most dangerous of all. In their hands, the Terror is sustained by a double energy—the fearlessness of crime and the inflexibility of virtue.[48]

This ferocious and murderous virtue, with a close kinship with utopianism, has a particular relationship to Modernity. Utopianism seems to be a response to the anxiety-producing social situation in which traditional forms of social cohesion are breaking down, and there is intense concern whether or not new forms will succeed in holding society together. Utopianism—the flight to perfection—is a fantasy defense against that panic-anxiety. Without embarking on an extended discussion, it seems appropriate to consider that Plato's *Republic* was conceived at a time when there was a radical transformation of Athenian society in the direction of "proto-Modernism," especially in regard to the breakdown of kinship forms of social cohesion.[49] To notice, as well, that the early Modern period in Europe brings an efflorescence of utopias, of which More's is the most well-known. And finally, though deserving of a very complicated discussion, it still may be observed that Puritanism—that great transitional form from early Modernism to Modernity—has within it a certain capacity for totalitarian moralism. "The quintessential quality of a Puritan," Lawrence Stone observes, "was not the acceptance of any given body of doctrine, but a driving enthusiasm for moral improvements in every aspect of life, 'a holy violence in the performance of all duties,' as Richard Stibbs put it."[50]

"Holy violence" is a powerful, frightening description of the Jacobin Terror. The capacity for such paradoxical action is already prefigured in Rousseau: "Whoever refuses to obey the general will,'" he writes in *The Social Contract*, I, Chapter 5, " 'shall be constrained to do so by the whole body: which only means that he will be forced to be free.' "[51] Robespierre, of course, had no trouble adopting such a position. " 'Vice and virtue control the destiny of the earth: they are the two opposing spirits warring for it.' " And in the midst of the Terror, May 7, 1794, he made virtue "the order of the day" in the Convention. It was the one thing he was most proud of, reflecting later: " 'Of all the decrees which saved the Republic, the most sublime, the only one . . . which freed people from tyranny is the one that made probity and virtue the order of the day.' "[52] Such naiveté, from such a brilliant person, has sinister implications.

And then there was Saint-Just, whom Michelet called the "archangel of death."[53] Herein, Mathiez's description of the portentous speech of February 26, 1794:

> Saint-Just . . delivered a sensational speech containing the program of a fresh revolution. Hitherto the Terror had been regarded even by its most fervent authors as a transitory expedient which would disappear with the peace. Saint-Just represented it in a totally new light, as the necessary condition for the establishment of a democratic republic. He laid it down as a principle that the Republic could not be assured of survival unless it was provided with such civil institutions as should purify the morals of citizens and render them naturally virtuous. "A State in which such institutions are lacking," he said, "is but an illusory republic. . . ." Until the civil institutions of which he was shortly to outline the plan had been successfully created and had extirpated selfishness from the hearts of citizens, Saint-Just declared, the Terror must be maintained. . . . After an impassioned apology for the executions ordered by the Revolutionary Tribunal . . . [he] held the threat of the guillotine *in terrorem* over all those who spoke of indulgence, and indicated the chief of them by barely veiled allusions. . . . Every eye must have been fixed on Danton. . . . "There is one who has waxed fat on despoiling the people, and, glutted with their spoils, insults them and advances in triumph, drawn onward by the crime for which he thinks to excite our compassion, for we can no longer keep silence upon the impunity of those who are most guilty, who desire to destroy the scaffold because they are afraid of ascending it."[54]

Everyone expected that Danton's time had come, but Saint-Just changed direction and demanded, instead, a revolution in property. From then on, Danton lived on borrowed time: less than two months more would see the foreclosure.

There are several different kinds of utopias. Some are of a murderous variety. Was this sort of utopian exercise by Saint-Just merely an excuse for more and more executions? Or did he really believe in the possibility of a wholly new society tomorrow, and that Danton's presence was incompatible with that ideal? We will fail of an understanding of ideological terror unless we respond: "Both!"

Tocqueville, no surprise, emphasized the utopian dream that sustained the revolutionary project: "Thus alongside the traditional and confused, not to say chaotic, social system of the day there was gradually built up in men's minds an imaginary ideal society in which all was simple, uniform, coherent, equitable, and rational in the full sense of the term. It was this vision of the perfect State that fired the imagination of the masses and little by little estranged them from the here-and-now. Turning away from the real world around them, they indulged in dreams of a far better one and ended up by living, spiritually, in the ideal world thought up by the writers."[55] The great psychological problem of a dream world is that it is difficult, at times almost impossible, to isolate one particular aspect of fantasy and exclude all others. Once unconscious fantasy is given free play, dreams of destruction also throw off previous repression and become real possibilities. It is near impossible to indulge the dream of a perfect social world without having to deal with the vision of destroying all those who stand in the way of its becoming a reality. Far better to leave dreaming to "the lunatic, the lover and the poet"[56] and politics to those who are awake.

Kennedy's data support Tocqueville's observation about the ideal world. In September '92, the French forces turned back the threat of defeat by Austria with the victory at Valmy. The Convention decreed civic festivals to celebrate the victory. The Jacobin clubs responded with ritual and rhetoric. The grandiose vision was apparent: " 'Soon, it can no longer be doubted, the enemies of the human race and all the partisans of tyranny will be defeated.' " One speaker asserted that the French should not cease fighting, " 'until they have effaced from the globe all trace of its former servitude. Then we will enjoy the rights of man in peace. Then all peoples will adopt our laws. We will be as one family. . . . Citizens! That is the happy future that the Revolution prepares for us. And its end is not far away.' "[57] The whole future of humanity is dependent on what we do today.

AND IN THE END: THE EXTERMINATION OF SIN

If one is absolutely virtuous oneself, and if one is building an absolutely virtuous society, then those who oppose this project, or even those who do not see it in the same way, are not just mistaken but sinful. And sinful easily becomes identical with evil. And with evil, only two things are appropriate: expulsion and extermination. Norman Hampson, by bringing together the compulsion for unanimity and the threat of the death of virtue, provides us with an insightful summary to this chapter: "In the summer of 1789, the Assembly rejected the conception of politics as being about the balanced representation of necessarily divergent interests, for a belief in popular sovereignty and the construction of the ideal society. . . . The . . . view implied that any healthy society was a unanimous one. Politics was a matter of putting *vertu* on the statute book. The

French people formed an organic unit with a single general will. What was in accordance with that will was not merely in the interest of the people as a whole but morally incumbent upon each one of them. Once the general will was known, opposition to it was therefore illogical, unjustifiable and immoral."⁵⁸

As has been argued here, the insistence on unanimity is a premodern *mentalité*. Such insistence, after the march toward Modernity has begun, is no longer pre-modern but regressively anti-Modern. That anti-Modernity is a defense against the panic-anxiety of the Modern world. When people, who are suffering from a pathological psychic splitting and who are profoundly moral in one moiety of their minds, want to defend against Modernity anxiety, they resort to the fantasy of a *nouvel homme*, a new society—morally perfect. Utopianism becomes a fore-most defensive maneuver.

This is accomplished, however, only by an exaggerated emphasis on morality and immorality, on righteousness and sin, on virtue and vice. And all this has murderous implications. "A crime is met with punishment;" Arendt has told us in a different, but relevant, context, "a vice can only be exterminated."⁵⁹ An extreme, exaggerated, isolated moralization of politics is the prelude to terror.

20

REGRESSION TO THE
BORDERLINE CONDITION

ON THE PSYCHOLOGY OF IDEOLOGICAL TERROR

The psychoanalytic theory of the borderline personality was not in my mind when I began the writing of this book, unlike the theory of the paranoid process and paranoid personalities, about which I have previously written and concerning which I felt were important theoretical guideposts that would prove helpful in understanding the conflicts—and especially the failures—of the Revolution. It was not, in fact, until the writing of the chapter on splitting and projection and the recollection of Kernberg's statement that splitting was the characteristic form of defense in borderline personalities,[1] that I realized I could not proceed with this work without an acquaintance with the theory of the borderline personality.

What I discovered was that I had been moving not in a conscious deliberate way but as a result of observations made about revolutionary culture, rhetoric, and action—most especially the regression and degradation into Terror—moving toward that very theory. I had not carried a theory of the borderline condition into my analysis of revolutionary history and then looked for data that would establish that such borderline conditions were operating in the pathological places of French culture. What was happening was that I had been struck by certain cultural and psychological phenomena—not directly related to the paranoid mode of perception—that seemed of great importance for an understanding of the catastrophic outcomes of this great Revolution, but I was not yet aware of a psychological diagnosis that could bring these disparate observations into one theoretical framework.

First, it did seem clear that, no matter how horrendous, the actions under the Terror could not be described as "psychotic," nor should the actors be included under that attribution. Not psychotic, but certainly something more pathological than mere neurosis. Second, as elaborated in the preceding chapter, it seemed accurate that the bringers of the Terror were involved in a process of severe psychological splitting of the world into all-good and all-bad moieties: once again: *le peuple* as perfect. Third, along with this went an almost unbelievable kind of primitive aggression: "human sacrifice as paranoid revenge" was one category of the ideas by which my notes were organized. Cannibalism as a metaphor for the state into which the terrorists had fallen seemed an accurate and revelatory usage. All of this taken together had produced, in my mind, a summary formula: fantasies of omnipotence plus extreme paranoid perceptions plus extreme aggression equals Terror.

Without being consciously aware of it, I had arrived at a place in the very middle of the theory of borderline personality and process. That theoretical position has been importantly elaborated by Otto Kernberg, most especially in his book *Borderline Conditions and Pathological Narcissism*, in which is reprinted a foundational article of his, "Borderline Personality Organization"; and by Abend, Porder, and Willick, *Borderline Patients*, which is in good part a discussion of, and an argument with, Kernberg. Taken together, these works establish a theory of borderline phenomena, seven fundamental points of which have remarkable relevance for the French Terror and possibly for all ideological terror as well. The question that inevitably arises when coming face-to-face with such human experiences, including both the Nazi Holocaust and the Stalinist extermination frenzy, is: How could human beings do such a thing? Human beings who, unlike the serial murderers and berserkers of our newspaper headlines, are not suffering from a psychosis. It seems to me a reasonable hypothesis that what those human beings who could "do such things" were suffering from was not a psychotic breakdown but was precisely a severe regression into—and regression into is a very important aspect—the borderline position.

Not Psychotic

Both our authorities emphasize this fact: that the borderline condition is one between psychosis and neurosis. Abend et al.: "We are much more interested in exploring the idea, which has gradually emerged in recent years, that borderlines constitute a distinct class of pathological entities, of more or less stable configuration with characteristic mental phenomena peculiar to them alone."[2] And Kernberg: "The term 'borderline' should be reserved for those patients presenting a chronic characterological organization which is neither typically neurotic or typically psychotic. . . . although borderline patients have alterations in their relationships with reality and in their feelings of reality, their capacity to test reality is preserved, in contrast with patients with psychotic reactions."[3]

Severe Splitting

All human beings, to some degree or another, are involved with the use of splitting the world into good and evil as a defensive maneuver of the ego. Since ambivalence characterizes so many of the most important human relationships, a certain degree of psychological splitting is inevitable for everyone. With borderline personalities, however, we are not talking about a certain degree but a most severe degree of splitting that becomes the characteristic pathological defensive mode of such personalities. Kernberg describes splitting as the "essential defensive operation of the borderline personality organization which underlies all the others which follow. . . . Probably the best known manifestation of splitting is the division of external objects into 'all good' ones and 'all bad' ones."[4] He elaborates that, although the process of psychosis is also centrally involved with the splitting defense, there is a fundamental difference in the results that follow: "In the psychoses their main effect [of projection of intense aggressive inclinations] is regressive refusion of self and object images; in the case of the borderline personality organization what predominates is not refusion between self and object images, but an intensification and pathological fixation of the splitting processes."[5] It has seemed an easy task to demonstrate how steeped in a *mentalité* of all-good and all-bad images the Terror was; possibly, all ideological terrors manifest the same pathology.

Rousseau, who was certainly no ideological terrorist, represents, nevertheless, a remarkably illustrative case that can illuminate the theoretical points being made here. Like Robespierre, he began with an extraordinary moral vision for society, which had a powerful impact on the way people thought and acted: no one person's ideas had more influence on the course of the Revolutions than his. The tragic outcome, however, was that—again like Robespierre—he suffered a massive regression in his later life into a severe pathological state that could be designated near-psychotic or severely borderline. I am not equating Rousseau and Robespierre, but I do think that the psychological narrative of Rousseau's descent can shed significant light on Robespierre's tragedy. And with Rousseau, we possess two powerful instruments for understanding that we lack with Robespierre. First, he wrote extensively about his own feelings. Starting with his *Confessions*, one of the first of modern autobiographies, and continuing with later works, he opened his soul for all to see, in an almost masochistic manner, since much of what he revealed was by no means flattering to himself. He had, however, a passionate commitment to truth. With Robespierre, we get exactly the opposite. A more secretive, repressed individual is hard to imagine. All musing on what he was really feeling must remain speculative.

And second, with Rousseau we have the powerful psychological analysis of Starobinski, which brings us to the sense that we are really understanding the man. That analysis sheds light on both borderline and paranoid phenomena, since it seems clear that such were the conditions into which Rousseau had regressed. Nothing that may be said about Rousseau "proves" anything about Robespierre or Saint-Just, but it may, nevertheless, strengthen the possibilities of our understanding.

As for severe splitting, as one example, it is remarkable how passionately Rousseau became committed to this Manichaean division of the cosmos. "The pathology of Jean-Jacque's communication with others," Starobinski comments, "stems from his need to rely on absolutes, even if these absolutes are negative. He needs an immutable God and a 'congealed' evil. Once the hostility of others is established, Rousseau can then call upon that other fixed term in his scheme of things, the judgement of God, which will establish the opposite of human judgement: that Jean-Jacques is essentially innocent."[6]

The Projection of One's Own Aggression onto Others

Intimately related to the process of splitting, and possibly even an important cause of it, is the psychological need to expel from within oneself unacceptable feelings of hatred, anger, and destruction by projecting them onto others. It is not I who have these evil desires to exterminate them—it is they who want to exterminate me. In a reply to Robespierre, less than two months before the coup that destroyed the Gironde, the Girondin Guadet announced: "For a long time, and, citizens, you have been aware of it, their tactic has been to impute to others that which they have done themselves. They have ordered some pillaging in Paris, it is you, it is I who have provoked them; they have carried the people to excesses more criminal still, again it is you, again it is I; some brigands widely active in the sections of Paris subversively arrest some national authorities, once again, it is a maneuver of the Gironde faction!"[7]

This projection of primitive aggressive feeling onto others is enormously problematic and, oft time, has fatal consequences. Unlike the scapegoat in the Old Testament onto whom the sins of the people are laid before it is driven into the wilderness, the surrogates of one's evil do not disappear. They remain within the body politic, corrupting its existence. It becomes an act of virtue to exterminate them. "The main purpose of projection here is to externalize the all-bad aggressive self . . . and the main consequence of this need is the development of dangerous, retaliatory objects against which the patient has to defend himself." This maneuver, however, Kernberg writes, "is rather unsuccessful." Far from having eliminated evil, one has created a powerful, malignant enemy—intent on revenge. The pathological nature of this defensive operation is revealed because it threatens the psyche at its most vulnerable point: "The very intensity of the projective needs, plus the general ego weakness characterizing those patients, weakens ego boundaries in the particular area of the projection of aggression." The final result of this entire maneuver is the creation of a psychological need that resonates remarkably with what we have observed about the terrorists. "Their ongoing 'empathy' with the now threatening object maintains and increases the fear of their own projected aggression. . . . Therefore, they have to control the object in order to prevent it from attacking them under the influence of the (projected) aggressive impulses; they have to attack and control the object before (as they fear) they themselves are attacked and destroyed."[8] And thus, not only Louis, but also Danton and thousands of others must die so that the Revolution, and its makers, may live.

All of this projection, and the fear of one's own projected image, resonates profoundly with the theory of paranoid perception and process. The paranoid process also plays a significant role in two other fundamental attributes of the borderline personality: the grandiosity of primitive idealization and self-destruction, both of which are to be discussed presently. In the realm of theory, there seems to be an inclination to keep separate the theory of borderline personality and the paranoid process. Both Kernberg and Abend et al. briefly mention paranoid inclinations, but neither engage in any extended discussion.

I am suggesting that, for a full understanding of the psychology of ideological terror, it would be necessary to bring together, and elaborate on interconnections between, the two conditions. If, for instance, we wish to understand Robespierre and his descent into terrorism, it is important not only to stress his severe regression into a borderline state, but also to look at the significant degree of paranoid worldview that got worse and worse as time went on.

Primitive Idealization

"This refers," writes Kernberg, "to the tendency to see external objects as totally good, in order to make sure that they can protect one against the 'bad' objects, that they cannot be contaminated, spoiled, or destroyed by one's own aggression or by that projected onto other objects. Primitive idealization creates unrealistic, all-good and powerful images. . . . Idealization thus used reflects the underlying omnipotence, another borderline defense."[9] A perfect *peuple* implies that its true and virtuous leaders are even more perfect: the very essence of omnipotence itself.

Here, recourse is had, once again, to the life of Rousseau, and his descent into severe pathology, to illustrate the notion of "underlying omnipotence." If something in the world is perfect, and if I am of that something, then perfection also lies within me. It seems reasonable to suggest that resort to such fantasy takes place as a defense against the threat of total dissolution of the ego and the sense of identity. Starobinski: "Some passages tell us that Jean-Jacques feels he is living a nightmare from which he can never awaken, while others insist that he is the only man in a corrupt world who has been able to live in accordance with his ideal, as a 'man of nature.' He thus feels at times that his life stands outside all human norms, at other times that he is safeguarding the one essential norm, ignored by others."[10] Perfectly virtuous—perfectly potent—certainly significantly paranoid even if not yet borderline.

The defensive nature of the perfection process is observed by Kernberg: "Constant projection of 'all bad' self and object images perpetuates a world of dangerous, threatening objects, against which the 'all good' self images are used defensively, and megalomaniac ideal-self images are built up."[11]

Primitive (Oral) Aggression

The one thing that we ordinary people find most incomprehensible when contemplating the works of ideological terrorists is the incredible amount of human

destruction that they are accountable for: the literally millions of people exterminated by Stalin, Mao, and Hitler. We want either to cry out that they are psychotic or massively deny the implications of their actions, as Arendt did with
Eichmann, and designate that evil "banal."[12] And although in certain regards
there are significant differences between left-wing and right-wing terrorists, in
regard to the willingness—one may even say "compulsion"—to massacre millions, they seem to share an identical psychological position.

The theory of the borderline personality is singularly helpful in thinking
about how-could-human-beings-do-such-things? Primitive aggression, Kernberg
says, is characteristic of those in such a state: oral aggression—cannibalism. This
attribute, combined with that listed further on as a lack of a developed superego, absence of a mature moral sense—these two attributes together result in a
situation where anything is permitted, anything is possible. Once the killing
machine, under the banner of virtue, is operative, the numbers no longer matter.
That is what makes the French revolutionary Terror of world historical importance: the very first appearance of this particular model of a killing machine.
And one of the very first monuments to Robespierre anywhere was erected,
soon after the October revolution, close by the walls of the Kremlin: the tragic
prefiguration of the twentieth century.

Kernberg tells us: "Extremely severe aggressive and self-aggressive strivings . . .
are constantly related to borderline personality organization.[13] . . . Pregenital
aggression, especially oral aggression, plays a crucial role as part of this psychopathological constellation."[14]

The psychological maneuver undergone by these splitting, projecting, orally
aggressive people is complex. Kernberg's brief description, nevertheless, seems
remarkably revelatory of what is operative within the unconscious psyches of the
terrorists. The projection of one's own aggressive impulses onto others is a defensive operation; it preserves the superficial integrity of the ego and the sense
of self by saying in effect, "It is not me who carries these horrendous impulses,
but them." That anxiety, however, does not disappear after this defensive maneuver is undertaken. It centers on the object onto which the primitive aggression
has been projected. That object now becomes the occasion for fear; that object
now needs to be obsessively controlled; that object becomes an obvious candidate for extermination. "The anxiety which provoked the projection of the
[aggressive] impulse onto an object in the first place now becomes fear of that
object, accompanied by the need to control the object in order to prevent it
from attacking the self when under the influence of that [projected aggressive]
impulse."[15]

"Fantastical notions," some may be inclined to respond. And yet, Rousseau once again becomes exemplary. Guilty, in the latter part of his life, of pervasive projection of evil, near the end of the *Confessions* he declared that the "most reprehensible category of evil people" were those, "who denied his virtue," and therefore they " 'ought to be strangled.' "[16]

The terrorists, unlike Rousseau, held the power of life and death and, therefore, could do more than merely "unpack [their] heart[s] with words."[17] And Robespierre was not the worst of the pack. Collot d'Herbois, member of the great committee of Public Safety, already in September '93, Palmer tells us, "was emerging as the most insanely violent of the twelve. . . . There would have been more deaths if Collot d'Herbois had had his way. He advised . . . that suspects [note: not yet convicted people] be herded into mined houses, and that the mines then be exploded."[18] There is no way to accurately designate Collot as psychotic. That is what makes the theory of the borderline personality so important for our understanding of terror.

Self-Destruction

Many references have been made in this work to the self-destructive behavior of people who were enjoying the exercise of tremendous power: Robespierre, Napoleon, Hitler—even the example from ancient history of the Athenian expedition to Syracuse.[19] The connection was made between these suicidal impulses and the paranoid process; for a long time, I have felt there was an intimate connection between paranoid impulses and self-destructive behavior: that such behavior seemed to be an inevitable accompaniment of the paranoid view of the world. This particular psychological symptom, in addition, seems to be characteristic of the borderline position. Abend, et al.: "Several writers remark on the prominence of aggressive conflicts, often characterized as 'primitive,' with evidence of an unusual degree of self-destruction."[20] Kernberg, in his list of the basic attributes of borderline patients, cites and italicizes: *"Primitive Self-Destructiveness. . . .* Patients with severe self-destructiveness . . . are members of this group."[21]

These observations are purely descriptive. They do not tell us *why* borderline patients tend toward self-destruction. My commentary on the connection between such behavior and the paranoid process is equally only descriptive. Possibly theoretical insight into this particular question, deeper than description,

might result from bringing together the theory of the borderline and the paranoid.

Lack of a Developed Moral Sense

Returning, once again, to the haunting question of how nonpsychotic people
could do such horrendous things, it is of great interest that Kernberg asserts that
patients "without a well-integrated superego and with a remarkable absence of
the capacity to experience guilt are members of this group."[22] A statement important enough to call forth from him an almost exact repetition several pages
later: "Borderline patients frequently present deficiencies in the capacity for experiencing guilt feelings and feelings of concern for objects [other people]."[23] It
seems accurate to amend this last statement, in regard to ideological terrorists,
and assert that once they have descended into terror, they *always*, not frequently,
exhibit a pathological deficiency in feeling guilt or concern for other people. It
does not answer the deeper question of why they have grown to be adults with
these deficiencies, but it does help answer the question of why they were able to
do what they did.

In regard to this remarkable situation of not feeling guilt, it is of interest to
compare Shakespeare's *Macbeth* with the narrative of ideological terrorists being
developed here. Both the terrorist and Macbeth do not begin as borderline personalities but regress to that position (more of that at length later). At the
moment when Macbeth kills the king, Duncan, he is not psychotic but in a
borderline state, especially in regard to not feeling guilt and not even imagining
that he will do so. Shakespeare, then, presents us with an extraordinary narrative
of a man restored to a normal neurotic existence after the descent into a borderline hell. And the increasing capacity to experience guilt plays a crucial role in
that recovery. After murdering sleep; after raging about the scorpions in his
mind; after hallucinating the appearance of Banquo's ghost; after facing the horrible void of meaninglessness in the "Tomorrow and tomorrow" speech—
Macbeth recovers, one step at a time, the capacity to feel remorse for what he
has done, recognizes the evil in it—and thus, although still doomed to die, dies
a man, not as a caricature of one.

When an Enlightenment society descends into terror, most especially if this
descent proceeds under the banner of virtue and creating a new society, many
people who would not become terrorists on their own are swept along and do

things that, later in their lives, they can remember only as in a dream, not sure whether those things really happened or not. In his old age, Marc-Antoine Baudot, who had been a Montagnard and a Dantonist and survived, ruminated pathetically: "Who did our deeds? We know nothing about it."[24] A vaguely expressed guilt—but too late to save the life of anyone.

BORDERLINE SYMPTOMS AS DEFENSES

At one point, Starobinski raises an issue that, at first hearing, seems to be underlining a paradox but, with further reflection, is actually pointing toward a very important psychological phenomenon crucial for people in the borderline condition, which is an accurate description of Rousseau in the latter part of his life: What may appear to us as symptoms of a pathological condition are also a defense against an even more serious regression of the ego into a situation of dissolution:

> If attention is focused on selected symptoms, documents, and eyewitness accounts, no contemporary psychiatrist will have much doubt about the correct diagnosis: paranoid delusions [*délire sensitif de relation*] . . . The most insane passages of the *Dialogues* and the *Reveries* can be regarded either as signs of the disease or as defensive mechanisms whose purpose is to exorcise fear. Rousseau's flight into solitude, his bursts of lyrical imagination, his recourse to mechanical occupations, and his grandiose, pathetic pleas for sympathy may be either symptoms or spontaneously improvised forms of therapy. His reveries—those magical retreats from a hostile world that Rousseau creates for himself in response to his pathological suspicions—would not exist without his paranoia (which made him feel that it is "impossible to reach real people"). But his conversations with "creatures of his own devising" are moments of respite in which anxiety seems to end; persecution no longer affects or concerns him. Rousseau's pleasure in sham communication and simulated happiness, shared with companions created out of whole cloth by his fancy, represents the artificial respiration of a consciousness that would probably have died of asphyxiation if forced to live, besieged by his own obsessions, in the midst of a hostile world.[25]

Kernberg gives us the same theoretical insight that the symptoms of the pathology are themselves defenses. Powerful feelings of aggression and of eros, he writes, "are kept apart at first because they happen separately and because of the lack of capacity of the ego for integration of introjections not activated by similar valences, but then *gradually in response to anxiety, because of the ego's active use of this separation for defensive purposes.* This is actually the origin of splitting as a mechanism of defense."[26]

What, however, we may ask, is the ego defending itself from? From descent into an even worse pathological state. I have previously contended that almost all manifestations of the paranoid process are, simultaneously, defenses against regression into the psychotic state of paranoia itself.[27] In Kernberg's example of splitting, it may be answered that the ego, by projecting the concept of all-evil onto others, is defending itself against an almost total psychic dissolution that would result if the ego had to accept the fact that the devil is no longer "out there" but "in here." Such a perception is totally threatening; it must be avoided at all costs, even if the cost is the slaughter of innocent thousands. That defensive machinery, once established, is almost impossible to give up, just because the result of such renunciation is seen as total collapse. The killing machine has no logical place to stop.

MASSIVE REGRESSION INTO THE BORDERLINE CONDITION

Leon Balter is an American psychoanalyst who is almost alone within that group in addressing the task of using psychoanalytic theory to understand society, especially in its pathological manifestations.* He contributed one of the four cases used in the Abend et al. book. Balter's contention,[29] which makes great sense, is that Robespierre, Mao, and Hitler cannot accurately be described as "borderline" during the time of their rise to power. No borderline person, he argues, is capable of the kind of reality testing and organizational skill, coming close to genius in that regard, that were necessary to seize power in an enormously complex society.

The narrative that Balter offers is that the psychological state that produces ideological terror results from a massive regression into a borderline condition

---

*It is difficult to understand a certain intellectual phenomenon in our culture. Freud wrote, in 1930, that "in spite of all these difficulties, we may expect that one day someone will venture to embark upon a pathology of cultural communities."[28] After all the warfare, all the racism, all the ideological terrors, all the genocides, that have occurred since Freud wrote, it seems reasonable to assert: There can be no more important theoretical project. And yet, the American psychoanalytic community, since the decease of Erich Fromm and Karl Menninger, has been almost unanimous in avoiding that project. One wonders why.

by political leaders who were not yet in that circumstance in their accession to the highest political power. Abend et al. point toward this possibility in a passage where they discuss the etiology of the borderline personality. Arguing against Kernberg, whose position was that the origins of borderline phenomena lay in psychological conflicts in the preoedipal phase of development, they offer another possibility: "That certain profound traumas during the oedipal phase and later in development might be significant enough to cause a severe regression without the pre-existence of overwhelming preoedipal pathology. The clinical picture following such a regression might be severe enough to lead to a borderline disturbance."[30] Not to argue the etiological question of preoedipal vs. oedipal, the passage is cited here to reinforce Balter's notion of the borderline state resulting from a massive regression.

And, once again, Starobinski's analysis of Rousseau is of great help in thinking about this phenomenon. After the sentence in which he declares that Jean Jacques may be diagnosed as suffering from "paranoid delusions," he goes on to say: "But as soon as this diagnosis is put forward, some rather embarrassing questions arise. Taken as a whole, do Rousseau's life and work show evidence of the disease? Or was his mental disturbance a relatively late and episodic phenomenon?"[31] The "disease," however, Starobinski goes on to assert, was prefigured in earlier symptomatic manifestations: "It is clear that certain primary forms of behavior are the source of both Rousseau's speculative thought and his mental illness. Initially, however, these primary behaviors were not morbid in nature. Mental illness developed only when they became disruptive. What is mysterious about mental illness is not the initiation situation but *the extravagance of development.*"[32] This last italicized phrase is Starobinski's equivalent of what I am calling a massive regression into the borderline condition.

The parallel development of Robespierre is striking. One may equally ask of him: "Do Robespierre's life and work show evidence of this disease?" If by disease, we mean borderline or psychotic manifestations, the answer clearly is: not at first. Then, why later? How does one describe—and understand—the terrible descent from moral genius to cannibalistic terrorist? As far as the narrative is concerned, but not necessarily comprehension, one great no-turning-back place was the Louis-must-die-that-*la patrie*-may-live speech. Robespierre, the great defender of the absurdity and immorality of capital punishment, was now on a slippery slope, quickly descending into the coup against the Gironde, the execution of Danton, and the worst of the Terror. Was such a catastrophe inevitable? No easy answer presents itself. He was not, unlike Marat or Collot d'Herbois, a born terrorist. Terrorism, for him, was an achieved condition. A prodigious psychological regression was necessary in order to end up in that place.

It seems a fair estimate to assert that, even though in the latter part of his life, Rousseau had regressed to a borderline condition, one crucial fact distinguished him from Robespierre: he lacked the capacity—or the compulsive need—to become near-psychotically aggressive. Starobinski gives a fascinating description of Rousseau's terrifying fall:

> In imagining persecution in later life Rousseau invented no new facts; he merely allowed feelings that had always been present in his mind to become obsessions.
>
> . . . Expressions that belonged at first to the lexicon of love enter the lexicon of persecution. The *enlancé* (ensnared, entwined, embraced), used repeatedly in the *Dialogues* and *Rêveries* to characterize the situation of the victim, has an amorous meaning in the fifth book of *Emile*, where it is used to describe Sophie's tender solicitude: "Forgive her concern for the person she loves, her fear that he is never sufficiently embraced [*enlancé*]." . . . the unanimity that made the social compact so exalting an experience is turned against Rousseau in the inexplicable hostility of an entire generation. "The league is universal, irrevocable, without exception." The pronoun *on*, which in the *Social Contract* represented the general will, now stands for the anonymous memberes of the universal conspiracy against Rousseau.[33]

The borderline person becomes a degraded caricature of his former neurotic self.

Are certain kinds of neurotic people vulnerable to this mode of massive regression? And what symptomology might be significant in this neurotic earlier stage that would indicate this vulnerability? Reaching for the most extreme example, the case of Hitler may be illuminating. Balter insists that even Hitler—certainly no moral genius and probably to be accurately described as a born terrorist—even Hitler cannot be designated a borderline personality until late in his life. Borderlines are incapable of seizing and holding political power for such a length of time, Balter asserts. Incapable of the kind of organization and control that such exercise of power requires.

From the very beginning, however, Hitler did manifest a symptomology that seems to characterize all ideological terrorists, of both the right and the left: a severe paranoid view of the world that is not yet psychotic (suffering from paranoia itself) but is still more severe than the neurotic paranoid perceptions that many people deal with in their lives. The almost psychotic anti-Semitism was one particular manifestation. Again, we are describing a condition that is in between neurosis and psychosis. This one crucial pathological manifestation seems to be exhibited by all ideologies and all ideological terrorists: Hitler,

Stalin, Mao, Pol Pot, Robespierre. Severe paranoid behavior on the part of those in power may be the greatest cause of political and social catastrophe.

It seems reasonable to suggest that the degree of paranoid attitudes and actions is the great indicator of the degree to which the psyche is vulnerable to massive regression into the borderline condition. Again, this would point toward the intimate connection between borderline pathology and paranoid pathology of the nonpsychotic kind. It is significant that, of the seven fundamental attributes of the borderline condition discussed previously, four of them are equally descriptive of paranoid pathology: nonpsychotic, severe splitting, projection of aggression onto others, serious self-destructive impulses. A complex, convincing, accurate combination of the theory of borderline and paranoid pathologies will bring us powerfully close to understanding one of the greatest—if not the greatest—problematics within Modernity: How does it happen that a society suffused with the Enlightenment culminates, even for short while, in a political culture of Terror?

THE CAUSES OF THIS SEVERE REGRESSION

This section is, necessarily, speculative and incomplete. It may, nevertheless, be of value to discuss three possible causes, in the realms both of the psychological and the social, that could contribute to a massive regression to the borderline state. The theoretical erection of any inflexible boundary between the psychological and the social is an error. What we conceive of as the psyche, what we designate psychological needs or conflicts, cannot exist without the social, without society. If there is no social, there is no psyche. The opposite, however, is equally true. Everything that is social, every value considered legitimate within society, is dependent upon the psychological consent of individuals. I have observed many discussions attempting to determine the manner in which we should characterize Hitler's psychopathology: paranoid, severely paranoid, borderline, psychotic, borderline psychotic? All this was of interest. Of equal, or even greater, importance is the question of why the German people, at that particular time in their history, wanted a leader with such a psychopathology. Why they didn't just turn their backs on him as some kind of crazy crank instead of bestowing absolute power?

I wish to make it clear that any discussion here about the psychology, and the psychopathology, of ideological terrorists is not given for the purposes of a narrow, individual analysis. Such people, for a greater or lesser time, ruled society after working in a complex, effective manner to achieve that political power. At many points, the people gave its consent to their ule. It is not inaccurate to describe the dominant *Weltanschauung* in society as mature, neurotic, paranoid, or borderline. A society, like any individual, may demonstrate extensive neurotic conflicts. A society, like any individual, may be infatuated with feelings of omnipotence. A society may suffer from intense anxieties and take defensive measure to prevent panic. The study of the psychology of individual political leaders can help us understand the relative health or pathology within society. The analysis of the psychology of the social world aids us in understanding why certain intended leaders succeeded, and others did not. It was, for instance, the psychological health of American society that, ultimately, made it turn its back on Senator Joseph McCarthy in 1954, thereby preserving its democratic culture and polity. For a while, before that occurred, many of us felt the final outcome was in doubt. In essence, we did not know how mature or neurotic our society would prove to be.

I. *The Encounter with Omnipotence.* Leon Balter argues that a good number of cases, if not close to all cases, of the kind of massive regression to the borderline state that is under discussion here result from the circumstance that the subject under consideration has achieved a truly magical success, which results in the full efflorescence of feelings of omnipotence. To progress from being a moderately successful small-city lawyer to become the ruler of France is, perforce, to become carried away by fantasies of omnipotence that have been previously severely repressed. Considerations of reality-testing; knowledge of limits; acknowledgements of the existence of other people and of their needs; recognition of, and consent to, the imperatives of the superego—all this flies away, leaving only the dream of absolute power. To journey from being Monsieur Robespierre from Arras to being the worldly incarnation of the Supreme Being—all this is too much for the human psyche. Everything is now possible: a new man; a new society in one generation; an almost total transformation of human nature; absolute virtue instituted on earth; and absolute power to bring that about, by force if necessary.

To fulfill, in unconscious fantasy, all those illegitimate oedipal and preoedipal desires that one had to abandon and repress in order to grow up, is to conceive that all manner of the most primitive fantasies are now possible and legitimate. Including all manner of fantasies of aggression and destruction. In that primitive world, to become a head-hunter, or a cannibal, is no longer inconceivable. Saturn, it must be remembered, like the Revolution, did not merely destroy his children; he devoured them. Anything and everything is possible—for good or evil.

Balter's argument, on which I have elaborated to some degree, is that what happened to Robespierre—and Mao and Stalin—is that, having achieved the highest power, they succumbed to a fantasy world of omnipotence, a severely pathological world. Max Weber, who did not use such vocabulary or analysis, nevertheless, pointed toward a situation where magical success proves dangerous to the subject achieving it. "For monarchies," he writes, "it is dangerous to lose wars, since that makes it appear that their charisma [our 'omnipotence'] is no longer genuine. For republics, on the other hand, striking victories may be dangerous in that they put the victorious general in a favorable position of making charismatic [omnipotent] claims."[34] These charismatic claims can only become problematic for society, if the people—also carried away by magical victory that brings an encounter with omnipotence—render their consent. Any authoritarian destruction of a viable democracy—any terror—requires a charismatic leader and a people willing to regress into a pathological state.

Shakespeare's *Macbeth* is a remarkable illustration of the complex psychological process being elaborated here. Fighting for the king, Macbeth, the Thane of Glamis, has performed almost unbelievable heroic deeds. Meanwhile, the Thane of Cawdor has betrayed the king, been captured, and been deposed from his title and position. The king has named Macbeth to Cawdor's authority, but when we first see him, he knows nothing of all his. The first words he utters immediately bring us to a place where good and evil coexist: "So foul [the weather] and fair [his great victory] a day I have not see."[35] Immediately, he is confronted by the three sister-witches, who stand for, among other things, the unholy ambition within his psyche that knows no limit. They greet him as Thane of Glamis, his quotidian position. Then shock him with: Thane of Cawdor! And finally begin the process of overthrowing his mind: "All hail, Macbeth! that shalt be king hereafter."[36]

The tremendous magical victory in battle leads to unimagined success: the encounter with omnipotence; and then immediately to a place where anything and everything is possible. "That shalt be king"—even if it means a foul regicide. After the deed is done, and the kingship attained, Macbeth descends into a borderline and severely paranoid state, the nadir of which is reached when he orders the assassination of Banquo, not because the latter has done him harm, but because the sisters had announced that Banquo's progeny would be king and, by implication, that Macbeth's would not. A remarkable resonance with Saint-Just's and Robespierre's sending Danton to the guillotine, in good part because they felt he mocked their pretensions to omniscience and omnipotence: that they, like Macbeth, would have no progeny. The oridinary sensual man had no place in the Republic of Virtue.

Balter's argument is a powerful one, but it does not cover, I feel, all circumstances of similar severe regression. Balter agrees that not every charismatic leader is necessarily subject to this kind of psychic dissolution when faced with omnipotence possibilities. Such steadfastness, he asserts, is extraordinarily rare. Washington, it is agreed, was certainly such an exception, in his declination to ascend the throne. To be treated to the kind of acclamation, close to worship, that he received and not be carried away into the fantasyland of omnipotence was certainly exceptional. An opinion emphasized in Byron's "Ode to Napoleon," which is, in reality, an anti-ode: "All Evil Spirit as thou Art. . . . Thou homeless Homicide. . . . But thou forsooth must be king, // and don the purple vest, // As if that foolish robe could wring // Remembrance from thy breast."[37] One human being, however, was immune from this inevitable descent into grandiosity:

> Where may the wearied eye repose
> When gazing on the Great:
> Where neither guilty glory grows,
> Nor despicable state?
> Yes—one—the first—the last—the best—
> The Cincinnatus of the West,
> Whom envy dared not hate,
> Bequeath'd the name of Washington,
> To make men blush there was but one![38]

For Washington, there was an alternative that was not available to Cincinnatus, who could only withdraw from political life to a private existence, or to Napoleon, who lived in a society that had renounced democratic politics: Washington could become a citizen, and even the very first citizen, a status with its own *sublimated* glory. Primitive feelings of omnipotence could be given up because a more sublimated notion of power was now available. Thus, we see how, not only does it take grown-up men and women to make democracy, but also that a democratic polity establishes ways for men and women to grow up.

2. *The Failure of One's Paranoid Aspirations.* A person with strong paranoid tendencies, who enters the political realm to seek power, inevitably carries with him, and expresses, a grandiose ambition. This is true of ideologues on the right or the left and of mere civilizing pirates like Napoleon, who would conquer all of

Europe no matter how many deaths it took. Whether it is a Thousand-Year Reich or a totally new Communist world or a Republic of Virtue, an unrealistic and unattainable aspiration characterize all such paranoid purveyors of destruction.

Since the goal is, in reality, unattainable and since such people are not, at first, totally out of touch with reality-testing, at some point they begin to perceive that their grandiose ambitions are doomed to failure. This perception, conscious or unconscious, results in an intense feeling of betrayal and precipitates a further descent into a paranoid worldview and the borderline condition. On a lesser catastrophic level, but by no means unimportant, reference has already been made to the decline and fall of Lyndon Johnson and Richard Nixon after they perceived that the power of their wishes was not sufficient to order the world according to their liking. The Viet Cong would not go away; the war could not be won. Each president, in his own way, became more and more paranoid and self-destructive.

A healthy democratic society has the means to deal with such aberrations. A society living under the tyranny of an ideologue, or a group of ideologues, is doomed to suffer greatly as the tyrant descends further and further into pathology. That pathological state demands more and more victims; the acute sense of betrayal requires more and more revenge. An acceleration of executions is inevitable, until, for whatever reason, a halt is called for. Robespierre, tragically to tell, fits such description. It is appropriate to devote an entire chapter (22) in the attempt to support that assertion. For now, the comment may be made that what Robespierre, with his extraordinary moral insight, felt betrayed by was his own moral vision and promise. Recognizing, probably not consciously, that the project of a new man and a new society was merely a fantasy, he became enraged and exercised his revenge on mere mortals, who, somehow, were held responsible for the failure of the dream.

3. *Severe Modernity Anxiety.* Modernity anxiety, producing at its worst manifestation what I am calling "Modernity psychosis," has been discussed at length in Chapter 17. Here, it is only necessary to add that it appears to be a fundamental contributory to regression to the borderline condition. Modernity, pregnant with the possibility of great moral advance, also engenders an almost unbelievable psychological burden. Terror, then, presents itself as the pathological mode of resolving that anxiety-panic.

21

TERROR

A coup is not a revolution. The person anxious and willing to make a revolution is not necessarily the same person eager to engineer a coup. Many people, obviously, have been willing to attempt both types of uprising, but a great many (liberal) people have been ready to support a revolution but were in fierce opposition to a subsequent coup. Both the French and the Russian Revolutions presented the situation of a radical coup directed against the makers of a previous revolution: the Jacobins against the Gironde, Lenin against Kerensky. A revolution may or may not end in dictatorship; a coup necessarily must so terminate. All dictatorships follow a course of either rational or irrational terror. The political leader anxious and willing to engineer a coup is, almost invariably, susceptible to regression into irrational terror. The citizen sympathetic to revolution, but antipathetic to a coup, regards irrational terror as a catastrophe and is many times its victim.

A crucial distinction between these two modes of overthrow can be made by raising the question of what percentage of the citizenry favors the particular rebellion. Proof is impossible, but it seems most reasonable to assert that the *revolution* of '89 had the overwhelming support of the French people. By the time of the second *revolution* of '92 (the overthrow of the monarchy), undoubtedly a good amount of support had been lost, mostly as a result of the radical anticlericalism: the civil war in the Vendée commenced only seven months after the deposition of the King. Even so, it still makes sense to speculate that this second revolution held the support of a majority, or near majority, of the nation. The Jacobin coup of May–June '93, however, despite its possible majority support in Paris, was a minority affair: in addition to the Vendée, "federalist" revolts in Lyons, Bordeaux, and Caen were anti-Jacobin in essence. Not only did the radical Jacobins not enjoy the support of a majority, but the leaders of the coup understood that such was the case. Dictatorship, a police state, rational and/or irrational terror were inevitable. It was a question of adopting such practices or abandoning power, and that kind of renunciation was not what the coup had been made for.

The founding actions of the two great irrational terrors of the twentieth century were also not revolutions but coup d'états. In Russia, the rebellion of February 1917 (old-style calendar) was a revolution with the support of a majority of the nation. The Bolshevik revolt of October was a coup: it did not overthrow the Tsar, who had outlived his usefulness, but a provisional government headed in the direction of democracy.* Its minority status was quickly revealed, and it required the winning of a civil war to stay in power. And Hitler, who attained the Chancellorship by democratic process (the Nazi party vote, however, was less than 50 percent), then proceeded to destroy all the political opposition by violence and peaceful illegal means, in order to make sure he could not lose an election in the future. The democratic constitution was destroyed, in essence, by a coup subsequent to the election.

The Jacobin dictatorship had the honor of being the first modern irrational terror. A minority government, it was determined to annihilate all opposition: first, nobles *émigrés*, and counterrevolutionaries; then, good liberals like the Gironde; subsequently, radicals on the left, like Hébert and Roux; and finally, its closest former friends and allies: Desmoulins, Danton. Its example was not lost on the Bolsheviks. It gave inspiration to Lenin, who wrote: " 'The bourgeois historians see in Jacobinism a *downfall.* The proletarian historians regard Jacobinism as the general expression of an oppressed class in its struggle for liberation. The Jacobins gave France the best models of a democratic revolution. . . . It is natural for the bourgeoisie to hate Jacobinism. It is natural for the petty bourgeoisie to fear it. The class-conscious workers and toilers have faith in the transfer of power to the revolutionary oppressed class, for *that* is the essence of

---

*It was of great interest that, after I had decided that French revolutionary history was best described as two revolutions and a coup but not thought about Russia, we visited the former Soviet Union on a pleasure trip in 1996. The Intourist guides, obviously on instruction, were referring to the October rebellion, literally, as a coup, reserving the word "revolution" for the overthrow of the Tsar.

Jacobinism.' "[1] As early as 1903, when the Bolshevik-Menshevik split occurred, Lenin was citing the Jacobin precedent: " 'A Jacobin firmly committed to *organizing* a proletariat that has become conscious of its *class interest* is precisely what a *revolutionary social democrat* is.' "[2] Never mind the tens of thousands of hateful bourgeois beheaded on the guillotine, Lenin also was obviously not bothered by the fact that the Jacobin dictatorship destroyed the political power of the sans-culottes who had put it in power: he was perfectly ready to do the same thing—and did.

Any coup engineered by a minority party must result, once power has been seized, in a repressive political regime. How repressive, how violent, how full of irrational terror, may remain open questions. But repression, and the establishment of dictatorship are not in question, if the new regime is to stay in power more than a month. When the radical Jacobins decided to eliminate the Girondin political opposition by means of an insurrection, they were no longer free to choose democracy or tyranny. The only open question remaining was: What form of tyranny? How conscious Robespierre and Saint-Just were of the future restrictions on their actions can only remain a very speculative question. There is no uncertainty, it seems to me, that they were a minority party. Though all forms of massive denial are available to human beings, it is hard to imagine that the Jacobin leaders did not know where they stood in regard to mass support. "The law of 14 Frimaire (December 4, 1793)," Palmer writes, "definitely founded the revolutionary dictatorship. It was the constitution of the Reign of Terror. . . . The new organizing law was an instrument of Terror because the government which it strengthened was the creation of a minority, the triumphant leaders of the Mountain, itself a party among republicans, who in turn were only a party among the original revolutionists, who in turn did not include all the people in France. . . . The ruling group knew that in a free election it would not be supported."[3]

It is a question whether that ruling group ever truly believed in free elections; that is, majority rule. After the king was deposed in August '92 and the Republic proclaimed, the first order of political business was the election of delegates to the Convention, which body, in a myriad of forms, was to rule France until Napoleon's coup. In Paris, the *Assemblée électorale du department de Paris* met on September 2 to make the final selection of representatives. It consisted of electors chosen by primary assemblies. Robespierre proposed that this assembly exclude from membership and from further voting those previously elected citizens, " 'who had taken part in the proceedings of any unpatriotic (*incivique*) club, such as the *club monarchique*, the *club de la Sainte-Chapelle*, the *Feuillants* or their affliated societies, or any of those who signed the petition of 20,000 [Royalist petition against the aborted deposition of the king of June 20, 1792].' "[4] All these clubs, and the right to petition, had been legal at the time; *ex-post*, Robespierre was declaring them and the citizens who belonged to them, outside the polity. Anyone who is sure of electoral success by democratic means, or who is willing to risk failure in the greater interest of preserving a democratic polity, does not have to take such action. From the very beginning of the Republic, Robespierre was more than willing to subordinate democratic process to the seizure of power.

In regard to the question of who does or does not become a terrorist, I have found it helpful to offer a variation on the famous proverb about greatness. Some are born terrorists. Some achieve terrorism. And some have terrorism thrust upon them. The same for dictatorship. Some are born dictators: Marat and those to the left of him like Hébert were born terrorists and prospective dictators. From the very first indication that revolution is possible, they push toward terrorism as an instrument of revolutionary action. Neither circumstance nor rational calculation drives them toward terrorism. Robespierre and Saint-Just do not begin as terrorists; for them it becomes an achieved position. Something within them is constantly working its way toward that disposition, though they are also extraordinarily ambivalent, and how conscious they are of their situation and their motives is an almost unanswerable question. Untimately, they become terrorists after a long and complicated journey. Danton and Barère had terrorism thrust upon them. They would not have chosen it, but they do not repulse it, either, when it seems to become "necessary"—whatever that word may mean. The subtitle of Gershoy's wonderful book of Barère, *A Reluctant Terrorist*,[5] says it succinctly. They are the first to renounce terror when it appears politic to do so.

Dictatorship goes hand in hand with terror. It is not by chance that those who heralded the Dictatorship of the Proletariat soon become ideological terrorists. Marat, a genius of terrorism, had already announced, in 1774, that dictatorship would be necessary for a successful revolution: "Marat posed the idea of a dictatorship in his *Les Chaines de l'esclavage*, linking it to a distrust of the revolutionary spontaneity of the people. Masses of men and women are incapable of planning or of keeping a secret, thus giving their enemies time to stop them. For an uprising to succeed, therefore, it was essential to have a 'chef,' someone wise and courageous who would lead the masses against their oppressor."[6]

And, after the king had finally been disposed of, Marat insisted upon the pride of precedence. In the fall of '92, when there already were rumblings that

Robespierre intended to make himself a Cromwell: "'It is my duty in justice to declare that my colleagues, and particularly Robespierre and Danton, have consistently disapproved of the idea of either a triumvirate or a dictatorship. If any one is guilty of having disseminated these ideas among the public, it is I; for I believe I am the first political writer, perhaps the only one in France since the Revolution began, to propose a military tribune, a dictator, or a triumvirate, as the sole means of crushing traitors and conspirators'; and he went on to reiterate his belief in the need of 'a wise strong man' to punish the guilty, and to save the country."[7]

The necessity of dictatorship, the willingness to undertake such a démarche, is intimately related to the question of what percentage of the citizenry is supporting the rebellion. Marat was, obviously, ready to erect a dictatorship in a minority-supported revolution, in order to make it succeed, since its cause was just: no matter how many heads it took. Saint-Just and Robespierre were morally much more complex people: they had to convince themselves that they represented a majority of the nation, and that terror was required to control and defeat powerful, counterrevolutionary, *minority* factions. In October '93, Saint-Just argued that the Jacobin dictatorship was not a tyranny but a "free system."

> There is not government which can preserve the rights of citizens without a policy of severity, but the difference between a free system and a tyrannical regime is that in the former that policy is employed against the minority opposed to the general good, and against abuses or the negligence of authorities, while in the latter the severity of the State power is directed against the unfortunates delivered to the injustice and the impunity of powers.[8]

Dictatorship is necessary to all forms of minority rule, and all dictatorships make use of some form of terror. Irrational terror, however, is its own distinctive construct, and dictatorship does not imply the necessity of irrational terror; the Emperor Napoleon demonstrated that. What was unique and important about French revolutionary history was that it produced one of the first modern dictatorships (Cromwell had anticipated that), one of the first establishments of rational terror, and the very first example of irrational, self-destructive cannibalist terror.

RATIONAL AND IRRATIONAL TERROR

A fantasied, illustrative narrative of the past: Boris Yeltsin, in good health, perceives that he is destined to lose the next presidential election. Having decided that the country cannot do without him—or he do without the country—he engineers a coup, with the cooperation of some still-remaining military powers. Immediately, certain newspapers, which criticize this demise of democracy, are closed down. Those editors who attempt to re-open, or start up different journals, are jailed. Opposition parties are declared illegal, and jail awaits those who insist on continuing to function. In order to avoid future confrontations, five to ten thousand "unsympathetic" politicians, journalists, and capitalists are sent into exile. And the repression is effective. The country quiets down. No new gulag is erected; no artificially created famine destined to destroy millions is engineered; no extermination of the Jews or other ethnic minorities is decreed. True, there always remains a handful of "recalcitrants," and these are rounded up, incarcerated, and delivered over to the torturers, who never seem to leave us. These latter do their work secretly and quietly—only a few government officials really know what is occurring, and the majority of the ruling clique desires not to know anything about this small, hidden corner of the "regenerated nation."

Tyranny, yes. Terror, yes. But definitely what I am calling "rational" as opposed to "irrational" terror. Rational, because means-ends rational. The end is clearly and narrowly defined: Yeltsin and his clique to stay in power. In general, only enough force, only enough terror, to serve this end is called upon. Terror does not become an end in itself—it remains purely a means. No "new man," no "new society." Unlike Lenin, our fantasied Yeltsin has no desire to be a new Robespierre. There are a hundred other examples that he may imitate. It is Bonapartism all over again.

Irrational terror—murderous ideology—is a far different thing. Here, terror becomes an end in itself. The cannibal appetite cannot stop. Victims, over and over again, are constantly required. Far from being means-ends rational, such terror quickly exhibits deep self-destructive dimensions. Mao's "permanent revolution" means never-ending terror, never-ending annihilation. The Cultural Revolution re-energizes the terror machinery of the first revolution.

All tyrannies, even all modern tyrannies, are not alike. All terrors are not alike. A powerful insight in Arendt's book on totalitarianism is that all modern political tyrannies are not totalitarian states. Not even all fascist societies are of that order. Totalitarianism is a *particular* form of modern tyranny, and, in her view, only Nazi Germany and Stalinist Russia meet that criteria.[9] There is something horrifyingly unique about totalitarian states. The same claim is being made here for irrational terror, for ideological terrorism. I cannot address the question of what is the relationship between these two political pathologies. Was Mao's

China, for instance, an ideological terror but not a totalitarian state? Certainly, the Jacobin terror did not come even close to totalitarianism. Does this later require *late* Modernity, with all the complexities of mass communication? Questions beyond the scope of this work.

The almost total irrationality of the French Terror has been perceived by others, since its illogic was palpable. "For the government of the Terror, if originally directed against real enemies," Brinton writes, "was in the end almost wholly directed against imaginary ones. That, indeed, is what makes it a Terror instead of a mere government of national defense."[10] And Quinet, in the presentation by Furet, goes beyond description to analysis: the Terror was caused by, and fueled by, hatred. "Quinet thus criticized the Terror not so much for its violence as for its meaninglessness: it was an extermination process that operated in a vacuum and had no purpose other than to sacrifice individuals to the state. . . . The terrorist system as Quinet saw it had no higher logic; its purpose was not to grapple at close quarters with the old spiritual and moral world and attempt to displace it. It offered no collective purpose of civilization to justify the sacrifices it required but only hatred of individuals by other individuals."[11]

Up until very recently, many of the foremost establishment historians of the Revolution—especially in France—were apologists for the Terror. Proof that ideological terrorism continued to have its appeal in certain bourgeois, intellectual circles late into the twentieth century. The main argument of that apology was that the Terror was a necessity if the Republic and the Revolution were to be saved: saved from counterrevolutionaries within and foreign enemies without. This reasoning cannot hold because, as has been noted before, the great pathological quality in the Jacobin Terror is demonstrated by the fact that it continued to get worse and worse as the successes of the Republic and the Revolution became greater and greater. There was a significant acceleration of executions beginning in October 1793. The victories on the northern front, the most strategic of the war, took place on September 8 (Hondschoote) and October 16 (Wattingnies). Lyons, center of the most significant "federalist revolt," was recaptured on October 16. A great victory in the Vendée (Cholet) had occurred on the ninth. Furet correctly concludes that the Terror was not a defensive act against real threats to the Republic, but an offensive one against France itself: "The law of Prairal and the 'Great Terror' have lost any semblance of a connection with public safety."[12]

The heightened paranoid view that sees significant threats to existence everywhere provided essential fuel for the terrorist machine. Such a view never feels

secure; always perceives imminent danger; is always willing to struggle against
that threat by executing more and more people. " 'Under the constitutional regime,' " Robespierre announced, " 'it is more or less sufficient to protect individuals from the abuses of public power; under the revolutionary regime the same
public power is obliged to defend itself against all the factions which attack
it.' "[13]

Ideological terror also gives birth to another modern phenomenon: the police
state. There is nowhere to hide; the forces of repression are ever-vigilant, ever-
present. The police state becomes an essential instrument of totalitarian society.
The Jacobin dictatorship came nowhere close to this latter status, but it did
maintain a *mentalité* that was headed in that direction. A short time before the
acceleration of terror in October '93, Robespierre set down the essentials of
such a police state; it reads like a twentieth-century Orwellian nightmare: " 'To
purge the revolutionary committees, we must have a list of all members, with
their names, social position, and addresses. . . . In particular, we must know
about the President and Secretary of every committee. . . . Secondly, we must
make a revised list of counter-revolutionary agitation in each district, . . . and
take proceedings against them all. Thirdly, we must track down all deputies who
are at the head of the conspiracy, and get hold of them at all costs; all, without
exception, must be promptly punished. Finally, we must have a circumstantial
list of all prisoners, and decree that those who have given asylum to conspirators
or to outlaws shall suffer the same penalties as they do.' "[14] A license, obviously,
to execute anyone.

A fundamental aspect of a police state is that the courts lose all autonomy
and become purely instruments of repression. This was one of the first things
that happened under the great Terror. In October '93, political trials were limited to three days, in order to give defendants little chance of survival. The
verdicts delivered by the Tribunal had only two options: acquittal or guillotine.
At first, the judges deliberated in secret and rendered the decision by majority
vote. By March of '94, each judge was required to announce his decision.[15] The
courage to decide for acquittal, obviously, was at a minimum. The complete
degradation of the legal process was demonstrated in the paradigmatic symbolic
experience of the trial and execution of Danton.

THE TRIAL OF DANTON AND THE DANTONISTS

All the ideological terrorists, since they are ideologues as well as terrorists; since
they are manifestations of Modernity, even though its "rotten fruit," feel the

necessity of some hypocritical acknowledgement of liberalism; and because the political fiction they maintain is that the regime is merely carrying out the will of the whole people, all such terrorists feel the necessity of spectacular public trials of the traitors to the cause, soon to be executed. These legal fictions become a caricature of justice: simultaneously making obeisance to its principles and traducing it. One of the most extravagant spectacles of the Terror was the trial, in April 1794, of Danton and his cohorts. It represented the most incontrovertible truth that the Revolution had become Saturn devouring his own children.

Fourteen defendants, including Danton, were tried and found guilty in four days. Some of the fourteen were indicted for financial peculation; Danton and others for treasonable activity against the regime. No matter what, in most cases, there was no connection between those two forms of sinful behavior. The Terror had grown used to trying people in "batches." Many of those accused of financial misdoings were also supporters of Danton. That was enough to make up the batch.

The first day was taken up with financial matters. The second day belonged to Danton. He made a spectacular defense, so effective that the Committee of Public Safety gave an order—subsequently withdrawn—that the president of the Tribunal and the public prosecutor be arrested because they were "guilty of weakness."[16]

On the third day, the rest of the accused were examined. They reiterated Danton's insistence that the defendants be allowed to call witnesses! The prosecutor Fouquier, remarkably, retained an ounce of humanity and told Danton he had asked the Committee of Public Safety's permission that the accused call witnesses. So much for the autonomy of the legal system from political tyranny. Fourquier, in a quandary and powerfully ambivalent, wrote a letter to the Committee: " 'A terrible storm has been raging since the session began. The accused are frantically demanding the hearing of witnesses. . . . The accused are denouncing to the people what they say is the negation of their demand. In spite of the firmness of the president and the entire court, their repeated demands are disturbing the session and they are proclaiming that, short of a decree, [by the Assembly] they will not be quiet until their witnesses have been heard. We invite you to prescribe formally what our conduct should be concerning this request since judicial procedure gives us no motive for rejecting it.' "[17]

Saint-Just, responding disapprovingly to Fouquier's letter, went to the Convention and informed it that the prisoners "were in revolt against the court."[18]

He also announced the discovery of a plot to rescue the accused and assassinate the members of the Committee of Public Safety. The compliant Convention passed a decree that "prisoners who insulted the revolutionary tribunal's study be removed from the court and tried in their absence."[19] The exact wording being: "'any person accused of conspiracy who resisted or insulted national justice'" was to be placed "'*hors des débats.*'"[20] The following day, the fourth of the proceeding, when the remaining small-fry of the prisoners were examined, the decree of the Convention was read in court. "When the prisoners protested, they were immediately disbarred. Some of the jury were already convinced that Danton was 'an implacable enemy of the Republic'. Such of them as still hesitated were 'persuaded' by a secret document communicated to them, out of court, by the President and the Public Prosecutor."[21]

Danton, having been chosen as a human sacrifice, attempted to transform himself into a holy martyr to justice. When Fouquier put the question to the jury whether they had heard enough to render a verdict, Danton and Delacroix protested: "'We are going to be judged unheard! Let there be no deliberation! We have lived long enough and are ready to fall asleep on the bosom of glory! Let us be led to the scaffold.'" All but one of the fourteen were condemned to death.[22]

In such a nightmare did the hundred-year dream of a more just society collapse.

THE GREAT PUBLIC SUPPORT OF THE TERROR

What is remarkable about the French experience is how powerfully supported the machinery of terror was from below. It was, by no means, only a phenomenon decreed by the highest powers in the state and executed primarily by them, with the help of a repressive police bureaucracy. It is a question whether any other country in Europe, at that time, could have produced such a "democratically supported" terror, especially when one considers that, in good part, that support came from the *moyen* and *petite* bourgeoisie: the active members of the Jacobin clubs in both Paris and the provinces. It was one of the first manifestations of the great perversion that Modernity can bring: a mass society, democratically constituted, that allies itself on the side of antidemocratic repression. Fascism was destined to bring that particular form to its most formidable manifestation. In France, whatever it was that was driving Robespierre and Saint-Just into terror was also driving thousands of anonymous citizens, all over the nation. True, these latter were not a majority of the citizenry, but they were very far from being an insignificant minority. And they represented a fateful "popular support."

Michael Kennedy's description of the Jacobin world in early 1793, even before the anti-Girondin coup, gives evidence of what might have been expected when the full Terror was operative:

> La Vendée and the treachery of Dumouriez caused fear of treason to become obsessive. . . . Secret committees (variously styled *comités de surveillance, comités de sûreté publique,* and *comités centraux*) were founded by a host of clubs. The most elaborate security net was set up in the southeast. Its nerve center was the twelve-member central committee founded on February 12, 1793, by the society of Marseille. This committee met daily and corresponded with the central committees of at least thirty-three societies in the province.
>
> On March 21 the Convention ordered that all communes were to have an official surveillance committee to keep tabs on strangers. The societies hailed the passage of this law and were quick to demand its execution. . . . Title two of the law of March 21 included a requirement for which many clubs had been lobbying. Henceforth, every citizen over eighteen had to have a *certificat de civisme* showing his place of birth and profession, and attesting to his performance of civic duties. Quite often, the clubs were assigned the responsibility of investigating public officials and recommending to the surveillance committees whether they were worthy of receiving these certificates. . . .
>
> At Marseille rigorous surveillance soon ripened into outright terror. On March 14, a deputation from the central committee of the club presented to the municipality a plan for the disarmament of "suspects." Either at this meeting or a later one, the committees also called for the arrest of the "suspects" and the establishment of a revolutionary tribunal.[23]

Baczko describes the role of popular support after the passage of the infamous Law of Suspects in September '93, by which law almost anybody could be arrested, tried, and executed. "The task of establishing lists of suspects fell to the *comités de surveillance* created in each commune . . . which also had the right to arrest all 'suspects.' The committees, whose memberes were most often drawn from the radical political clubs, formed a very dense network covering the entire country. Since their mission was to gather denunciations and issue their own, the *comités de surveillance* formed the backbone of the Terror and were training grounds for a corps of terrorists."[24]

It is a thorough mistake to place the blame for the French Terror on the likes of Robespierre, Saint-Just, and their cohorts, alone. Whatever was sick in their souls found profound resonance in the psyches of multitudes of the politically most active citizens. The clubs did not, as Kennedy tells us, meekly follow the terrorist lead of the central state: the necessity of a *certificat de civisme* had been lobbied for by the clubs before it became law. Too many "respectable" citizens were willing and anxious to embark on a journey into terror. There was something profoundly pathological within the culture. And it was this pathology that, ultimately, made a stable democratic society impossible, that made of the Revolution one of the most tragic occurrences ever.

Kennedy's third volume reveals how pervasive this mass support for the Terror was, indicating that the percentage of *the total population* enrolled in the Jacobin clubs probably was a little less than 3 percent during the Terror.[25] Admittedly, attendance at meetings and enrollment figures were seriously discrepant. Think, however, what such a figure would mean for American politics if over six million people were members of political clubs dedicated to a revolutionary change in the values of society. Mass society, mass politics, mass culture were not invented in the twentieth century. There was, clearly, something remarkable in *ancien régime* culture that produced this incredible political efflorescence in a period of just a few years.

And the Terror that was instituted in Paris was not created in opposition to this mass politics, but with its support. The situation with the provincial clubs was an accurate reflection of the deadly contested politics in Paris. Clubs that can be described as "Girondin" and "Montagnard" are to be distinguished from September 1792 on. At first, the Girondin persuasion prevailed, but gradually more and more clubs supported the more radical position. This resulted, in good part, from a catastrophic political mistake of the Gironde. In the spring of '93, as a result of defeats in the war, the revolt in the Vendée, and the treason of General Dumouriez, a critical situation developed for the Revolution. The Convention, in order to strengthen central revolutionary control, decreed that eighty-two of its members should become *représentants en mission* to the provinces, with extraordinary political and police powers. They were the world's first commissars. The Gironde calculated that, if it made sure this group was heavily from the Mountain, its day-to-day prospects in the Convention would be strengthened with these deputies out of the capital. The tactic backfired. The primarily Jacobin *représentants* in the provinces increasingly radicalized the clubs, many times actually purging them of non-Montagnard members. As a result: "For the first

time," Kennedy observes, "the number of Montagnard clubs became a plural-
ity."[26] The stage was set for a thorough approval by a majority of the clubs of
Montagnard Terror.

The crucial circumstance was the May–June '93 coup against the Gironde. It
was one thing for Paris to purge the Convention and establish a Jacobin dictatorship. It was quite another thing to have the country approve. Failure to obtain
this approbation could quickly result in a national civil war. The so-called Federalist Revolt that sought to overthrow, by military force, the new Jacobin government—and that failed to become a full-blown civil war—was defeated by three
factors. It demonstrated any kind of serious power only in a limited part of the
nation. The central government responded with great urgency and efficiency in
putting down the rebel forces. And finally, the majority of the provincial Jacobin
clubs were in full support of the Paris coup.

Some ultraradical clubs had even anticipated that coup immediately after the
king was executed in January '93. In the Convention, the Gironde had suggested
an appeal to the people to determine if the king should be executed or not, after
having been convicted. The motion was defeated, but, after the death of the
king, those who had voted for this course of action became known, derisively by
the radical Jacobins, as "appellants." This attempt of the Gironde even had the
result of pushing some of the clubs leftward. "In societies where opinion on the
factions [Gironde and Montagnard] had been in uneasy equipoise, disgust at
what was regarded as a ploy to save the king's life tipped the balance toward
the Montagnards."[27] One of the most important clubs that experienced such a
conversion was that at Marseille. Almost immediately after the king's execution,
it sent out two circulars to its affiliated clubs demanding the recall of the "appellants." Outside of Province, there was a mixed reception to this proposal. The
Paris club itself did not announce support, but "in Marseille's own domain most
clubs adhered. Aix twice and Arles thrice demanded ouster of the 'unfaithful
representatives.' "[28] All of this, four months before the actual coup and purge of
the Convention.

Once the insurrection against the Girondin deputies had taken place, many
of the clubs had to be convinced by their own deputies of its legitimacy and
necessity. On the other hand, without any pressure, "scores of societies did praise
the 'brave Parisians' and 'Holy Mountain' for 'saving the fatherland again.' Givet
gloated over the 'regurgitation of the monsters' from the Convention. Sedan
questioned only whether they should be sent 'to Guiana or to eternity.' 'Extermi-

nate the hydra with 27 heads,' cried Lille. Arcis-sur-Aube marked down 37 deputies and ministers for death."[29]

The coup of May–June '93 was not the end of trouble for Girondin deputies. On October 3 order was issued for the trial of 41 Girondins and the arrest of 75 additional members who had put their names to a protest against the coup on June 6. Kennedy asserts that, to his knowledge, no Jacobin club objected to this October decree. "The only criticism was that the order had not gone far enough. Sedan, and sister clubs in the Ardennes, called for the trial of other deputies who had 'betrayed the trust of the people,' and anyone who tried to 'undermine confidence in the Committee of Public Safety.' When 21 Girondins were guillotined (October 31), there was jubilation, cosmetic or otherwise."[30]

Certain clubs even attempted to out-terror the terrorists. "Some societies urged the Mountain to 'finish the job.' Auch sought the death penalty for all deputies of the Right, and the deportation of their families. Blois, Périgueux, and Cahors howled for action against appellants and 'disgusting beings' of the Marsh [deputies of the Convention, sitting in the middle, and uncommitted to any particular faction]."[31]

When the infamous Law of Suspects was passed in September '93, some clubs not only supported it thoroughly but urged even more stringent measures: confiscation of property, forced removal of children from their families in order to send them to republican schools, strong preventative measures to keep suspects in their cities, preventing them from escaping to the countryside. The clubs became a primary instrument of public action under the Law. "In the Terror, the clubs were de facto courts of the first instance to which citizens brought allegations of wrongdoing. They spaded for evidence of uncivic behavior too, organizing house searches and opening mail, with or without legal sanction."[32]

Terror after the Terror

There was a strong tendency, during the whole period, for the provincial clubs to accept what happened in Paris as fait accompli. Sometimes they expressed serious objections, but almost always they ultimately went along with whatever political changes had taken place: the coup of May–June, the execution of Danton, and so on. After the 9th of Thermidor, there was overwhelming acceptance of the executions of Robespierre and Saint-Just. There was, however, a very powerful commitment, in some areas, to the notion that Robespierre's fall should not be the occasion for an end to the Terror. The Terror was to continue, notwithstanding the absence of the Incorruptible. There was, remarkably enough, more support in the provinces for a prolongation of the Terror after the fall of Robespierre than there was in the Convention itself. The central government, in several cases, had to resort to force in order to make the clubs conform to the new thermidorian political ideology.

The club at Marseille took the lead in attempting to keep the Thermidor experience from becoming a thermidorian reaction. Certain aspects of the Terror must be continued, announced a petition it drew up on August 22 that was distributed to clubs throughout the nation. Among other courses of action, it called for: "the rigorous execution of the September 1793 law of suspects, and the creation of revolutionary courts composed of 'just impartial Montagnards.' The Mountain was summoned to prove its existence. 'Thunder, strike, crush, and the Republic is saved!' "[33] In Provence, especially, a good number of clubs supported the Marseille position. Emboldened by this concurrence, in September the club issued three additional circulars, the third of which was a " 'Profession of Faith' in which the Marseillais pledged to die, if necessary, battling 'the evil coalition of nobles, aristocrats, and moderates.' "[34] In the same month, the club at Aurillac did not understand that the clichés of radical terrorism were a thing of the past and called for "a Revolutionary Government 'more terrible than before.' "[35]

After the fall of Robespierre, many of the deputies to the Convention who had been terrorists became ex-terrorists and remained in their seats in the Assembly. The central government had learned, during the Terror, how to control nonsubmissive clubs in the provinces. Now, its task was to use that technique to destroy whatever remnants of radical Jacobinism remained. The club at Grenoble had asserted its disagreement with the reactionary moves in Paris. In late October, "the *représentants* Gauthier and Cassaynès, arrived in Grenoble and bludgeoned the club into submission. A purification conducted on their orders . . . wrote finis to the dominance of the Montagnards."[36]

The repression in Marseille was even more violent and dramatic, reproducing the raucous live-or-die politics of Paris. The *représentants,* Augois and Serres, clashed with the club in their attempt to enforce the politics of the central government. Both sides resorted to an appeal to Paris: the Marseillais received support from the Paris Jacobins; the *représentants* succeeded in getting the Convention to decree that they should close the Marseille club.

When the decree arrived in Marseille . . . Auguis and Serres ordered the arrest of 35 clubmen. Rather than be taken alive when the soldiers surrounded his home, the club president leaped to his death from the roof. Another club leader, when apprehended, screamed defiantly: "I will always be a Montagnard; long live the Mountain and the Jacobins." At the news of the arrests, a riot broke out. The *représentants* used troops to quell it and made more arrests. The club was shut down for several days and "purified." After its reopening . . . it thanked the Convention for throttling "the criminals" who had led it astray. The emasculation of the Marseille club virtually ended resistance to the reaction in Provence.[37]

* * *

What seems to be called for is a profound study of the *ancien régime* that would help explain this extraordinary paradox of Modernity. On the one hand, the production in a few short years after the first revolution of an almost incredible efflorescence of political activism in the whole country. A situation in regard to which it is hard to find any parallel in history. Michael Kennedy asserts that: "In one monograph that I read about a small town in the Revolution, I recall the author said that *never before or since* had the population been so involved in politics."[38]

And yet, on the other hand, so much of that politics was a fantasy politics. Utopianism, creation of a totally new man and a totally new society, skipping a stage of social evolution, instituting the great ideal future of humanity *now*—all the shining banners of morality under which the "just" destruction of a myriad of citizens would become the reality. How these two contradictory, and seemingly opposite, *mentalités* could dominate a whole culture, even for such a short time—and in the twentieth century, for decades—no more important question remains to be satisfactorily answered.

EXALTED REGRESSION

All social regressions as a defense against increased anxiety are not, necessarily, as catastrophic as twentieth-century fascism and ideological terror. In a stable democratic society, such as ours, we may also observe this regression-as-defense phenomenon, for instance, in time of warfare. For a democratic society, lifting certain guarantees of personal freedom or violating individuals' rights are regressions into a predemocratic mode: paranoid anxiety prevails over democratic optimism. Lincoln suspends *Habeas Corpus.* Japanese American citizens are removed to civilized concentration camps.

One other, more damaging, mode of defense against accelerating anxiety is a kind of exaltation, attempting to demonstrate that, far from being fearful, we will now accomplish prodigies! "I will do such things," Lear cries out, defending against abysmal despair, "What they are yet, I know not; but they shall be // The terrors of the earth! You think I'll weep. // No, I'll not weep."[39]

Societies, in times of great crisis, may act in an identical manner. Such a complex, symptomatic form is, simultaneously, exalted and regressive. Circumstances such as that of a revolution or of the critical crisis of Modernity (1914–1939) are feverish: exaltation, actions without limits, panic-anxiety, fantasies of omnipotence, all matter of defensive maneuvers, follow one another with lightning speed. Christopher Lasch writes of Orwell:

> In 1940, George Orwell made the . . . point about fascism. That Western democracies, he observed, had come to think that "human beings desire nothing beyond ease, security, and avoidance of pain." Whatever else could be said about it, fascism was "psychologically far sounder than any hedonistic conception of life." Hitler knew that men and women wanted more than "comfort, safety, short working-hours, hygiene, birth-control." Whereas socialism, and even capitalism . . . have said to people, " 'I offer you a good time,' Hitler said to them, 'I offer you struggle, danger and death,' and as a result a whole nation flings itself at his feet."[40]

The great power in Tocqueville's metaphor of the Terror as a *virus* is that it points toward disease, pathology, fever. Such critical times are feverish. The fever is caused, in great part, by the tremendous conflict between the desires to regress precipitously and to charge forward into the heroic future. Just after the phrase "*virus* of a new and unknown kind," he writes: "there have been violent Revolutions in the world before; but the immoderate, violent, radical, desperate, bold, almost crazed and yet powerful and effective character of the Revolutionaries had no precedents, it seems to me, in the great social agitations of past centuries."[41] In such feverish times, Tocqueville notes, it only takes a few madmen to shake society: "When an entire nation undergoes a great political movement, it is impossible to hope that all its citizens will halt together or even at the same moment. The reasonable task for necessary or useful innovations always becomes transformed by a few into a disordered taste for novelty. After having accomplished the practicable, there is always a residue disposed to attempt the impossible. The sight of extraordinary events stirs up curiosities and monstrosities."[42] This enthusiasm, this exaltation, this recklessness also carries over into the area of aggression and destruction: "Revolutionaries of a hitherto unknown breed came on the scene: men who carried audacity to the point of sheer insanity; who balked at no innovation and, unchecked by any scruples, acted with an unprecedented ruthlessness."[43]

The forceful metaphor of disease does not escape the discerning intellect of Palmer, who sees precedents for it that antedated the Terror. "The Grand Terror was a psychological fever, like the Grand Fear that had gripped the peasants five years before. . . . The Terror was a disease that left a lasting disfigurement in France."[44]

People were swept away, given to enthusiasm, inebriated with an exalted view of what they might accomplish. It was easy, for some, to blame Rousseau for a *mentalité* that was very deep within the culture. Rousseau's " 'new style,' " ironically wrote Joseph Barnave, guillotined November 29, 1793, " 'made madmen of people who would have been merely fools.' "[45] In some cultures, people can become madmen from reading philosophical works; in other cultures, it takes more than that.

NAKED PANIC

If we do not perceive the panic-anxiety, the psychic fabrillation that lies behind this carnival of destruction, we will not succeed in understanding it. People were frightened half out of their minds. Their defense was to make *others* even more frightened than themselves. A transfer of inner terror to an external terror creates *the* Terror. Jean-Lambert Tallien, a man steeped in the Terror, who turned on Robespierre and managed to live until 1820, gave this analysis: " 'The system of terror assumes the exercise of arbitrary power within those who take it upon themselves to spread it'; thus, France was divided 'into two classes: *the one that frightens and the one that is frightened*, the persecutors and the persecuted.' "[46]

In this same speech, given a month after Thermidor, on August 29, 1794, Tallien elaborates on how terrifying was the Terror, totally consuming the culture. He "distinguished two ways of instilling fear in the governed, one directed towards actions, the other towards persons. In his analysis, the first inspires a contingent fear, the fear of punishment in the event of misconduct. [One may say *all* governments require such fear.] The second inspires essential, permanent, total fear—fear independent of particular actions, fear bearing no relation to guilt or innocence. This latter is terror. 'A habitual, generalized, trembling, an external trembling which affects the innermost physical forces, the disorientation of all the moral faculties, the disintegration of all ideas, the subversion of all the affections. It is a true disorganization of the soul . . . an extreme, total condition.' "[47]

Anybody could be taken away and executed at *any time*. That most totalitarian law of 22 Prairial, June '94, listed the characteristics of enemies of the people and prescribed death as the only penalty for being judged in that category: "Those who sought to reestablish monarchy, discredited the Convention, betrayed the Republic, communicated with the enemy, interfered with provisioning, sheltered conspirators, spoke ill of patriotism, corrupted officials, misled the people, gave out false news, outraged morality, depraved the public conscience, stole public property, abused public office, or worked against the liberty, unity and security of the state."[48]

Even before this monstrous law, the Terror had turned toward pure cannibalism: creating victims for the sake of having victims. The widows of prominent executed citizens were dragged out and dispatched: the wives of Hébert and Desmoulins. Officials of the *ancien régime* who had gone into retirement, and were guilty of no antirevolutionary action, were made to satisfy the need for numbers of heads.[49] Included in this category was Malesherbes, who, as a liberal director of the book trade between 1750 and 1763, had been responsible for the continuing publication of the *Encyclopédie,* after publication had been suspended by the censorship. He had made the fatal mistake of offering himself to Louis XVI as a defense counselor, in December '92. Sixteen months later: "Traduit devant le Tribunal revolutionnaire avec sa fille, sa petite-fille et le mari de celle-ci, il fut avec eux condamné à mort le 4 foréal an II (23 avril 1794); ils furent guillotinés le lendemain."[50] ("Brought before the Revolutionary Tribunal, with his daughter, his grand-daughter and the latter's husband, he was condemned to death, with them, the fourth of floréal, year II; they were guillotined the next day.") The rational intent, no doubt, was to make the Revolution that much safer by killing "sa fille, sa petite-fille et le mari de celle-ci," as well as the great traitor himself.

CLEANSING

As we know, some of the worst cannibalism of the late twentieth century has been practiced under the banner of "cleansing": ethnic cleansing to be more exact. The Nazis had already accomplished this on a grand scale. *Petits* and *moyens* tyrants have followed in their path. One has been struck by two things: the continuing human capacity for radical evil, and the powerful resonance of the metaphor. Why "cleansing?" Why does it speak so powerfully to the killers and give legitimacy to slaughter? And why, instead of rejecting it as a stupid or absurd word, do we, somehow, recognize its power, and feel the terror it inspires?

The triumvirate that perished on the 10th of thermidor knew how it felt to dream of a thoroughly "cleansed" society. A week before his death, Maximilien signed a note, along with Barère and Billaud, addressed to Herman, a sort of chief of internal affairs: " 'Perhaps we should purge the prisons at a single stroke and cleanse the soil of liberty of this refuse, these throw-outs of humanity.' "[51] This Nazi rhetoric could have been inspired, surprisingly enough, by a passage in Montesquieu published in 1745. According to Michelet, Robespierre knew it by heart and loved to repeat its "fâcheuses paroles" (lamentable words). Michelet comments that Montesquieu would have greatly regretted this passage, " 'if he had divined the usage that would be made of it.' " This startling passage announces: " 'Prosperity will find, perhaps, that one has not spilled enough blood and that all the enemies of liberty have not been proscribed.' "[52]

It is the dream of totality that is so terrifying. All the enemies, all the throw-outs of humanity! Leaving a pure world! Saint-Just to the Convention: " 'Destroy all the factions, so that there remains in the republic only the people and you.' "[53] In such a culture, a democratic society is impossible. Democracy is an inefficient, sloppy, exasperating political system: factions (parties) and competition are essential for its existence. Total purity is a dream—and an excuse for a killing regime.

Georges Couthon, the third member of the thermidorian triumvirate, was sent to Lyons, after its capture, to regenerate the city. He wrote to Saint-Just that the task would not be easy: the people were stupid and confused and had to be taught the alphabet again, from the beginning. "They should be given strong republican medicine: 'a purge; a vomit and an enema.' "[54]

The psychological origins of human evil are still, in a profound way, hidden from us. After writing six books attempting to pierce that veil, I still cannot say that I really understand it. The psychoanalytic discussion of evil is too much given to slogans and short-hand statements: anal-sadistic, oral aggression, identification with the aggressor. Couthon's "republican medicine" does point towards something of importance. Freud's wish that someday someone will give us a psychopathology of society[55] may come close to fulfillment when light is shone on the question of exactly what the "cleansing" of society is truly about: why does a purge, a vomit, and an enema—aggression committed against the body—serve the cause of virtue? That, somehow, shit equals evil, we know. Cleansing is undertaken to get rid of the garbage, the refuse, the shit of society—"these throw-outs of humanity." Purity is a condition of no shit. That confluence may be a pointer toward understanding: the road toward true comprehension has yet to be traveled.

THE BANALITY OF EVIL

Every evening between ten and eleven [Fouquier-Tinville, the executioner] crossed the Pont-neuf, accompanied by four *gendarmes,* from the concierge to the Tuilleries, to make his report to the governing committees. He submitted one list of persons tried today, another list of persons to be tried tomorrow, and sometimes a provisional programme of trials for ten days ahead. A few questions might be asked by the tired Committee men. A name might be added, or struck out. The new list was signed. Copies of it were made (there was always danger of mistakes here). Carts were ordered for tomorrow's procession to the scaffold. (Fourquier knew within one or two heads how many would be needed.) And so to bed.

—J.M. Thompson[56]

TOWARD A TOTALITARIAN SOCIETY

The French Terror never evolved into a totalitarian society. There was, obviously, not enough time to erect such a polity. Beyond that, however, it is doubtful whether any society at the end of the eighteenth century, no matter how efficient, no matter how pathological, had the capacity to create such a complex form. One essential condition was, obviously, lacking: the mass society of the twentieth century, with mass communication capabilities and a large, efficient bureaucracy.

Beyond that caveat, it is remarkable how many cultural and political values that would become necessary for a totalitarian state were endorsed at the time of the Terror, most particularly by the leaders of the Jacobin dictatorship. I have already elaborated, in Chapter 19, on the annihilation of the private, the prohibition against political inaction, and the totality of the plans for education. Here, we look at several other areas where the Terror insisted on dominating the totality of human existence: child-rearing, friendship, censorship, aesthetic attitudes, conscience. It is in the nature of irrational terror to become total terror.

Making People Virtuous

One characteristic of child-rearing in the early Modern period was that women of means did not nurse their own children. They either gave them out to a wet-nurse or brought such a nurse into the house.[57] One remarkable cultural and moral advance in the eighteenth century was the beginnings of strong encouragement of women to breast-feed their children. Rousseau was one important advocate of this revolution. And Beaumarchais dedicated all the profit from *The Marriage of Figaro* to a fund that would encourage young women to nurse their own infants.[58] For the totalitarian mind, however, this obviously virtuous advance was not a private matter but the direct concern of the State. In Robespierre's presentation to the Convention of the Le Peletier plan of national education, he felt it appropriate, and incumbent on himself, to add the voice of the most powerful politician in the State: "Thus, mothers, by their own concern, will be led to the most sweet of tasks, to that of breast-feeding their own infants."[59] And Saint-Just, always quick to separate the world into good and evil, announced: " 'Children belong to their mother until the age of five, if she has nursed them, and to the republic after that, until death. The mother who has not nursed her baby ceases to be a mother in the eyes of the fatherland.' "[60] Freedom says one may choose to nurse or not; the Terror says, if you choose wrongly, you are anathema to the fatherland. True, we know of no cases where mothers were prosecuted for not nursing; the mental construct, however, was there and expressed.

The ancient Greek republican *polis* was very much in the minds of French revolutionaries. What was deeply problematic for the future of democracy was that it was Sparta, much more than Athens, that fed the imagination. Friendship, which democratic people would consider a private affair, was, in the attitude of Saint-Just, a matter for public scrutiny. This very Spartan view of male bonding: " 'Every man twenty-five years old is obliged to declare in the temple who his friends are. This declaration must be renewed every year during the month of ventôse. If a man abandons his friends, he must explain his reasons before the people, in the temples. . . . If he refuses, he is banished.' "[61] Blum goes on to elaborate that, for Saint-Just, "friendship [was] an underlying impulsion toward virtue; friends were put side by side in combat; a Theban band, they wore mourning for each other. If one committed a crime, the other was banished."[62] There was no reality here. It was all pure fantasy. A totalitarian fantasy.

At some point in '93, Saint-Just had found the time to compose his political and moral testament: *Institutions républicaines*, from which the commandments of friendship, cited previously, have been taken. If the Jacobins had held power for even half as long as the Soviet tyranny, undoubtedly this work would have become a crucial part of the Bible of the regime, just as some works of Lenin and Stalin achieved that status under Russian communism. We are not surprised to find in it a clear prescription for censorship. "[A] key institution of the republic of virtue would be a class of 'censors' or 'magistrates to provide the example of morals.'"[63] It may be recalled that when Plato, who was the first to imagine a republic of virtue, prescribed what steps had to be taken, one of the very first was a censorship: a dictate as to what stories can, and cannot, be told. "'First . . . we must supervise the makers of tales; and if they make a fine tale, it must be approved, but if it's not, it must be rejected. We'll persuade nurses and mothers to tell the approved tales to their children and to shape their souls with tales more than their bodies with hands. Many of these they now tell must be thrown out.'"[64]

It was all logical. If the task of the State is to make people virtuous, it must pay great attention to what they can, or cannot, read. Saint-Just may, or may not, have known, but we know where that logic ends.

Possibly even more sinister was a certain attitude of mind. In the *Institutions*, Saint-Just declared that "'he who makes jokes while at the head of state tends toward tyranny.'"[65] We may see an exact opposite psychology: he who cannot make jokes—cannot see the irony, the ambiguity, the incongruity, the absurdity in the human condition, and respond with humor—is a most dangerous chief of society.

The Totality of Cultural Control

Ultimately, what the terrorists were heading for was a tyranny of virtue. Virtue—a moral conscience—becomes the instrument of absolutism. It is this extraordinary moral contradiction that has made it so hard for good, liberal people to judge accurately the French Terror. Robespierre was a virtuoso, if not the inventor, of this ambiguous form. "'The function of government is to direct the moral and physical forces of the nation.'"[66] "'There exists for all men but one morality, one single conscience.' "[67] This last, I have argued myself.[68] Whether that single conscience, however, also allows that one impose one's own morality on others by force is a separate question. Robespierre, who, like Rousseau, was willing to force men to be free,[69] did not perceive that there were *two* questions to be answered here. First, in what does a univeral morality and virtue consist? Second, knowing it, does one have the moral right to try to impose it by force from above?

Palmer sums up the ideal toward which the Jacobin Terror was driving:

> The new state . . . was not to be the liberal state that emerged in the nineteenth century. Jacobins were far from wishing to leave the individual to his own devices. Their democratic Republic was to be unitary, solid, total, with the individual fused into society and the citizen into the nation. National sovereignty was to check individual rights, the general will prevail over private wishes. In the interest of the people the state was to be interventionist, offering social services; it has to plan and guide the institutions of the country, using legislation to lift up the common man. It was to resemble more closely the states of the twentieth century than those of the nineteenth.[70]

One striking prevision of the twentieth century, with its dictates for Soviet Realism and its persecution of poets, was this decree, written by that "reluctant terrorist" Barère but signed by others as well, dated 27 floréal, An II [May 16, 1794]: " 'The Committee of Public Safety calls upon poets to celebrate the principal events of the French Revolution, to compose hymns and poems and republican dramas, to publish the heroic actions of the soldiers of liberty, the courage and devotion of republicans, and the victories won by French arms. It calls also upon citizens who cultivate letters to transmit to posterity the most noteworthy facts and great epochs in the regeneration of the French, to give to history that firm and severe character appropriate to the annals of a great people conquering the liberty attacked by all the tyrants of Europe.' "[71]

True, the language is polite and not dictatorial, "calls upon" and not "demands." With the terrorist mentality at work, however, had the Terror lasted another year or two, undoubtedly we would have heard of executions of those who did not respond adequately to this request of the Committee. Once a Modern totalitarian culture is in the making, it is remarkable how much all such cultures resemble each other, even though they may proceed from "the left" or from "the right."

THE PEOPLE'S REPUBLIC OF VIRTUE

Modernity, somehow, demands the sovereignty of the people. Ideological terror-ist regimes are tyrannies, and, therefore, illegitimate; but they always claim legiti-macy with the fiction that they are acting under the aegis of the people's sovereignty. To paraphrase Ozouf's contention that the notion of mythical unity in the nation was, "the rotten fruit of Rousseausim,"[72] we may say that the great myth of a people's republic is the rotten fruit of Modernity. As in so many other perversions of Modernity, the French Terror was the first regime to perform this ideological acrobatic trick, wherein the sovereignty of the people ends up de-stroying *le peuple*.

Living through the vastly conflicted and compromised attempt of the French nation to establish a stable democratic society (i.e., a legitimate Modernity), the genius of Tocqueville was able to perceive the nature of the portentous modern perversions of past and future People's Republics and the sinister manipulation of legitimacy they entail. "Until our day it had been thought that despotism was odious, whatever form it took. But now it has been discovered that there are legitimate tyrannies in this world and holy injustices, provided that it is all done in the people's name."[73]

The ideal of democracy and the creation of mass society allow the possibility of a situation that, superficially, one would have thought impossible, what Talmon calls "Totalitarian Democracy."[74] Tocqueville saw it with great clarity 150 years ago: "If democratic people substituted the absolute power of a major-ity for all the various powers that used excessively impede or hold back the upsurge of individual thought, the evil itself would only have changed its form. Men would by no means have found the way to live in independence; they would only have succeeded in the difficult task of giving slavery a new face."[75]

This powerful insight into future political pathology results from Tocque-ville's attempt to understand the French Terror. He recognized that it was new in the world—the very first manifestation of a certain historial confluence—but also that it was not unique: the future could see many such terrors. He could not truly put his finger on the *causes* of this particular historical catastrophe, but he intuitively felt that the circumstances would be repeated, and, therefore, future terrorists, and future terrors, were a distinct possibility.[76] We now know how right he was.

Mona Ozouf has succinctly summarized how the fiction of the sovereignty of the people can help perpetuate the greatest despotism. Of the Jacobin dictatorship: "Under this regime individuals were more radically powerless than under any other, because the constraints that bound them were supposed to emanate from themselves. Since the myth was that the people decided, opposition ceased to make sense. To have an opposition party, as in England, would according to Robespierre be proof that despotism had triumphed (since 'there is no opposition to patriotism'), that the majority was corrupt (since 'there is no opposition to the minority'). To admit that 'men equally devoted to the public good could be divided' was something . . . beyond the realm of possibility."[77]

And finally, this perfidious mythology becomes the ultimate excuse for human slaughter on a grand scale—the very essence of terror. "Collot d'Herbois," Palmer writes, "thus becomes a political fanatic. His mind is turned by the fundamental idea of the Revolution, the transfer of sovereignty from king to people. In the name of the people he pushes the meaning of sovereignty to its most hideous extreme: an absolute will; inhuman, unmoral, illimitable power. He has made himself a new God, the 'people,' from which he sees his enemies hopelessly estranged. His 'people' is omnipotent and wrathful. To glorify it he will blow up whole cities."[78]

We are forced to confront this strange, totally contradictory phenomenon. Collot is an ideological terrorist, not a murderer, or a sadistic killer, or a gangster, or a drinker of blood for the pure pleasure of it. He can commit the most horrible of crimes—the mass destruction of innocent people—but only under the banner of morality, virtue, the sovereignty of *le peuple*. The new biology today is attempting to understand the origins of human morality and immorality by the study of those animals, the great apes and monkeys, closest to the human species.[79] Though, apparently, there have been observed incidents of cannibalism among chimpanzees, still no one has insulted the great apes by finding them guilty of genocide and mass slaughter, and certainly not mass slaughter under the banner of virtue. That *virus*, that disease, has infected only humans. No claim is being made here to really understand this enormous contradiction. The only claim is that it is imperative that we look at it: raw, undisguised, without defense, without denial, without sentimentality, without apology. It is *the* great human tragic flaw.

22

ROBESPIERRE, VIRTUOUS; ROBESPIERRE, PARANOID; ROBESPIERRE, NARCISSIST; ROBESPIERRE, DICTATOR; ROBESPIERRE, GENIUS OF MORAL CRITIQUE; ROBESPIERRE, TERRORIST

This is the most terrible, most unbearable of stories. Though thoroughly suffused with pity and terror, it does not attain tragedy, for there is at its conclusion no redemption, no restoration of the moral order—no catharsis—that could reconcile us to life, despite all its inadequacies. It belongs to the world, not of Hamlet or Lear, but more to that of Herr K. "There is no god of healing in this story," cries Cassandra in Aeschylus' *Agamemmon,*[1] and it takes Aeschylus two more plays of the trilogy to bring us, ultimately, to the reconciliation that tragedy demands—and consoles us with. For Robespierre, all we can do—finally—is weep. The same for that greatest of all Revolutions that descended into terrorist catastrophe. First, for humankind itself, which is so ill-constructed that its greatest unhappiness comes from other humans. "Man is born free," begins Rousseau in Chapter I, "and is everywhere in chains."[2] The chains, we sometimes forget, are forged by other men.

And second, for Robespierre himself, who was—with everything—still part of humanity. It may seem senseless, at first, to pity one of the great exterminators of innocent people under the banner of morality. True understanding, however, may require exactly that. Even more, true understanding may require that we recognize that there is something of Robespierre in each of us, even though it never sees action in the real world.

This chapter is a summing up, a conclusion. In trying to say everything that should be said about Robespierre, we are also completing the discourse on the Terror. All great art, Aristotle tells us, has both a specific and a universal dimension. Robespierre was one unique person, but the universal meaning of his character, his pathology, and his life is that he, more than anyone else, was the symbolic objective correlative of the Great Terror. *Il était terreur, lui-même!*

In the attempt to compose a nearly complete picture, it may be advisable, in what follows, to repeat certain citations that have previously been given in the text. These repetitions are deliberate, not oversights. The reader's understanding is anticipated.

VIRTUOUS, NARCISSIST, PARANOID

These three psychological attributes are brought together here because there seems to be an intimate, complex relationship among them. Virtue, an undoubted human good, is subject to particular perverse manifestations. There is a narcissism of virtue: I shine because I excel most other human beings in integrity and honesty. This superiority gives me the right—the obligation—to judge harshly the mere mortals with whom I am forced to live. At its most complex stage of development, this perversion assumes a paranoid dimension, a grandiosity of moral critique: so far above the crowd do I soar, so far into the future extends my moral vision, that I inhabit a realm—like the heroes of old—midway between mortals and the gods.

I distinguish here between virtue and the more complex moral critique. Though others will surely differ, I use "virtue" in this particular context to mean those attributes of integrity, honesty, decency, concern for others that are exhibited on a day-to-day, personal level. Moral critique applies to the society at large, most particularly in its political aspects; moral critique means social critique.

These two attributes of righteousness do not, necessarily, march together, side by side, in the same person. I have known politicians who were intent that as much money as possible given for campaign purposes should slip into their private pockets, and yet these same people were early, courageous fighters against the war in Vietnam. Similarly, elected officials, great advocates of racial equality, who treated their staff workers horrendously, subjecting them to personal abuse. This discordance between the lack of private virtue and the existence of an honest moral critique of society, in regard to our present sitting President [1999], most especially in regard to his sexual peccadillos, has provided the text for hundreds of thousands of newspaper editorials, op-ed articles, and psychological analyses.

Robespierre exhibited no such splitting, in this regard. Personally, he was an individual of high virtue: the Incorruptible, himself. Socially, he was a genius of social critique. He did suffer, consequently, from *both* forms of perversion: the narcissism of virtue and the paranoid grandiosity of moral critique.

That he was personally virtuous everyone attests. Billaud-Varenne, member of the great Committee of Public Safety, who turned on Robespierre and Saint-Just in thermidor and managed to live until 1819, expressed himself in his "Mémoire Inedit," not published until 1910: " 'If someone asked me how he had succeeded in gaining so much ascendancy over public opinion, I would answer that it was by displaying the most austere virtues, the most absolute devotion, and the purest principles.' "[3] And the decidedly nonvirtuous Mirabeau was obviously struck by this amazing young man from the provinces: " 'That man will go far: he believes everything he says.' "[4]

What is so remarkable about Robespierre is that personal virtue that included a sincere sympathy for human suffering—one could even say, in a general sense, eros—was as important to him as the radical, aggressive critique of society. There was nothing hypocritical or deceitful in this stance; he felt it sincerely, no matter what else was going on, in his severely split psyche. And he never completely lost touch with it. In the very last raving, paranoid, self-destruction speech of the 8th of thermidor (to be looked at later in more detail), he still found room for this compassionate ideal view of human nature: " 'It exists, that generous ambition to found on the earth the first Republic of the world; that egoism of non-degraded men, which finds a heavenly pleasure in the calm of a pure conscience and in the enthralling spectacle of public happiness. You feel it, in this moment, burning in your hearts; I feel it in mine.' "[5]

How profoundly different from the nineteenth- and twentieth-century attack on bourgeois society, most especially from the Marxist camp. We cannot imagine Lenin or Stalin or Trotsky expressing any such sentiments—and for Marx, himself, they would obviously be bourgeois nonsense. From Robespierre, we learn to distrust and fear those who are overly virtuous. Such feeling reflects the title of a treatise by Joseph Trapp, published in 1739: *The Nature, Folly, Sin, and Danger of being Righteous Overmuch.*[6] In this century, however, we have faced the opposite catastrophe: ideological terror has come from those who despise personal virtue—and persons.

The perversion of personal virtue begins, harmlessly enough, in the criticism of the average sensual men who predominate in any human society. As early as May 18, 1789, having just recently been elected as a delegate to the Third Estate, he was already, in Henry James's memorable phrase, "bristling with discriminations."[7] Mirabeau was "nil"; Mounier full of "pretensions and [having] liaisons with ministers"; Target was one "in whom one has detected versatile principles"; and Malouet was "eaten up with artifice."[8] One might wonder where he would find anyone—beside himself—who could meet his high standards. Such virtuosos of virtue, come to power, cannot resist the temptation to *make* men virtuous. "'Let us beware,'" wrote Desmoulins, "'of connecting politics with moral regeneration—a thing at present impracticable. Moralism is fatal to freedom.'"[9]

In such people, moral criticism may give way to contempt, not only for particular people, but for humankind in general. Another form of splitting arises: love for people in the mass and the abstract, revulsion toward individual specimens. It was a symptomology that did not die with Robespierre. "Dostoevsky warned us repeatedly," Marshall Berman writes, "that the combination of love for 'humanity' with hatred for actual people was one of the fatal hazards of modern politics."[10]

Recognizing, then, the moral mediocrity, or even inadequacy, of most human beings, even after they have become citizens of a democratic Republic, what then is the solution? Are there only two choices: a bourgeois democracy with all the moral and personal sleaziness that Balzac and Stendahl so brilliantly, and angrily, chronicled for us, or the tyranny of an Incorruptible? Such is the terrible choice we all still have to make, if only in our minds: the visionary politics of the impossible, which truly is impossible and brings death; or the politics of the possible, that brings a society wonderful in many ways—and in others, manifesting attributes that make it a society almost impossible to love. Somehow we must create a third space, in between these two unacceptable alternatives. It is within that space that a moral politics becomes possible in an individualistic, bourgeois, capitalist world.

If Robespierre's life was a novel, written by a master of psychological analysis such as Stendahl or James, the great clue given us that things are not what they seem to be on the surface would be the intimation of a destructive narcissism. Here would be the great fault line. " 'I have never known jealousy except by hearsay. Never will a vile sentiment approach my heart.' "[11] And every narcissist needs a mirror. For Robespierre, the mirror in which he saw himself was the perfect people: " 'The first thing the legislator must know is that *le peuple* is good.' "[12] In the unblemished people, he saw himself. He assumed that, in him, *le peuple* would perceive its own perfection.

That narcissism may explain, in part, why Robespierre differed from most other radicals in his insistence on maintaining a belief in the beneficence of Providence or in the existence of the Supreme Being. When he intensely promoted the belief in the latter, it was definitely not because he felt the people needed it: that some form of religious belief was a social necessity. Robespierre, himself, was the foremost beliver. In the Paris Jacobin Club, March 1792, months before the overthrow of the king, when the Girondins were still members, Robespierre announced that Providence was keeping watch over the Revolution by taking the life of one of its most implacable enemies, the Emperor Leopold of Austria, who had just died. Gaudet, a Girondin, immediately attacked the regressiveness of such a notion, "denouncing it as an attempt to bring the people back under the slavery of superstition." As was his usual mode of operation, Robespierre did not retreat. He then presented an elaborate defense of the belief "that there was a Providence which presided over the destinies of nations and in particular guarded the Revolution, and the meeting ended in disorder."[13]

I am not equating religious belief with narcissism, but it certainly was unusual that such a position would exist in the mind of the most radical of radical Jacobins. If Providence was sustaining the Revolution, it certainly must be cherishing me.

One attribute of the narcissistic personality is that it cannot abide other forms of narcissistic expression that differ from its own. Robespierre and Saint-Just had antipathy to Hérault-Séchelles, one of the original twelve members of the Committee of Public Safety. "His noble birth, his wealth," Palmer tells us, "his elegant manners, his flippancy, his irony, his self-assurance and frank love of pleasure inspired in his two colleagues a chill hauteur, a stiff sense of middle-class disapproval. . . . Between two moralists and an esthete there could be little understanding."[14] In such a time, misunderstandings lead to death: Hérault-Séchelles was beheaded along with Danton, in April '94.

The narcissism and grandiosity of virtue, in their most corrupted form, lead to the perversion of one of humankind's most high-minded acts: the sacrifice of one's personal interest to the greater good of the whole. At its most extreme, this last means the willingness to risk one's life for a moral cause. Self-sacrifice, however, is a very ambiguous quality. The rhetoric throws an extremely wide net. The true feeling behind the rhetoric runs all the way from a manifestation of republican virtue, to narcissistic posturing, to paranoid self-destruction. In itself, the oratorical eloquence cannot tell us what is motivating the speaker. We need interpretation—always subject to error—for that. The American Revolution had its full share of such self-sacrifice rhetoric. "Live Free or Die," announced New Hampshire, and the concluding sentence of the *Declaration of Independence* strikes an eloquent, republican note: "And for the support of this Declaration . . . we mutually pledge to each other our lives, our fortunes and our sacred honor."

Robespierre, it may be said without exaggeration, was obsessed with self-sacrifice. Recognizing the complexity of his nature, it is a reasonable assumption that this obsession was composed of part republican virtue, part narcissistic posturing, and, eventually, a good portion of self-destruction. " 'The love of justice, of humanity, of liberty,' " he observed, " 'is a passion like any other. When it dominates one sacrifices everything.' "[15] Such calm, but passionate, analysis was not typical, however, especially when functioning within the frenzy of revolutionary times. At the Jacobin Club, on July 21, 1791, Robespierre played on all the paranoid clichés. He asserted the existence of a vast plot in the very heart of the Revolution and indicated the Assembly itself: "The National Assembly betrays the interest of the nation." The eight hundred spectators at the Club rendered him a delirious ovation. The demonstration went even further, as Camille Desmoulins reported:

> I was moved to tears . . . and then that excellent citizen, in the middle of his discourse, spoke of the certitude of paying with his head for the truths he had uttered, myself crying out: "We will all die with you." More than eight hundred people rose up all at once, and driven like myself by an involutionary movement, took an oath to rally around Robespierre.

The spectators then drew out their swords and surged toward Robespierre, proclaiming: "Liberty or death."[16]

This was mere prelude. As the Terror dominated the polity, the drive toward martyrdom accelerated. In May '94, in three different speeches, we can observe the progress from narcissistic grandiosity to the suicidal paranoid position. On the seventh of the month: " '*O ma patrie! . . . Je suis francais, je suis l'un de tes représentants . . . O peuple sublime!* receive the sacrifice of my entire being; happy is he who is born in the midst of you; more happy he who is able to die for your happiness.' "[17]

Two and one-half weeks later, he seems to have reached the point where only a martyr's death could resolve the conflict raging within him. On the 25th at the Jacobins: " 'I who do not in the least believe in the necessity for living, but only in virtue and in Providence, I find myself placed in the state where assassins wished to put me; I feel myself more detached than ever from human wickedness. Cowardly agents of tyranny, contemptible tools of the oppressors of the human race, come out of your dark hiding places, appear for what you are before the eyes of a people scandalized by your crimes! See us before your homicidal daggers, chests bared, not wishing to be surrounded by guards. Strike, we await your blows.' "[18] And he would not let go of it. The next day, he regaled the Club: " 'Let us rejoice and thank heaven that we have served our fatherland well enough to have been found worthy of tyranny's daggers.' "[19] Resolved on such a termination of his life, by the time the 8th of thermidor (July 26) rolled around, he had managed to place those daggers in the hands of his most intimate recent allies.

Lost in that mythical nightmare, life becomes unreal. People become unreal. Death has no reality. If one is so eager to die for the Revolution, should not Danton also be willing to do the same? Anything is possible and permissible. More than permissible: justified by a moral imperative.

The paranoid view of the world totally pervaded his psyche. No one was more intent in finding conspiracies and plots everywhere. As early as January 1790, Duquesnoy, a delegate to the Assembly, wrote: " 'M. de R, as usual, spoke of plots, conspiracies, etc. etc.' " Two months later, the newspaper *Mercure de France* announced that he had " 'once again enlarged on the plots and conspiracies of which he alone held the secret.' "[20] And Jerome Pétion, mayor of Paris and subsequently delegate to the Convention, said that Robespierre "saw everywhere conspiracies, treason, and plots; he never forgave an insult to his self-esteem . . . and always believed that he was being watched and persecuted."[21] Similar evidence causes Palmer to say that "In his account of foreign machinations there was a tone of almost psychopathic delusion."[22] The rhetoric of internal and external enemies was second nature to him:

Society affords protection only to peaceful citizens: *in the Republic there are no citizens other than Republicans.* Royalists and conspirators are, to her, strangers, or rather they are enemies. . . . Is not the enemy within the ally of the enemy without? The assassins that rend the country from within; the intriguers that buy the conscience of the people's mandatories; the traitors that sell it; the mercenary scribblers hired to discredit the people's cause, to kill republican virtue, to stoke the fires of civil discord and to prepare the way for political counter-revolution through the corruption of morals; are these people less guilty or less dangerous than the tyrants they serve?[23]

One could multiply these examples ten- or a hundred-fold, which would only prove how repetitious, how single-minded, how monotonous—as well as how deadly—the paranoid mentality is.

The paranoid seals himself off from reality, and the reality of other people, which maneuver enables him to maintain the most absurd views that never have to be tested. A certain Monsieur Hamel, an admirer of Robespierre, described him at the end as " 'retranché dans sa conscience comme dans une fortresse impéneaatrable.' "[24] [barricaded in his conscience as in an impenetrable fortress.]

His view of self-sacrifice for the good of the whole was much more primitive than the usual Live-Free-or-Die rhetoric of revolutions. There was a part of his mind that fully believed that "The blood of the martyrs is the seed of the Church"—and that he was a willing supplier of that blood. Long before he had become the Prince of Terror, in February '92, he was ruminating on a Samson death that would crush all the tyrants with one great act of destruction. It would be grossly unfair to him to suspect that he was not prepared for that oblation: " 'To what worthier end could one devote one's life? It is not enough to find death at the hands of tyrants; one must have deserved it. . . . If the first champions of liberty must be its martyrs they must carry tyranny itself to their tombs. The death of a great man must awaken the sleeping peoples and its price must be the welfare of the world.' "[25] One must be worthy! *One must have deserved it!* Incalculable is the evil that paranoid virtue has brought upon the world.

It all came to an end, terribly and pathetically, on the 8th of thermidor, the day before his fall. He knew that opposition to his reign was growing among the radicals themselves. He imagined that one more great speech would stem the tide of opposition by turning the Covention against his "enemies." The speech, itself, was rambling, out of control, suffused with all the paranoid maxims and cliché words about counterrevolutionaries: *fripons* [rogues], *scélérats* [scoundrels], *la violence des factions, l'empire des tyrants, tous les hommes corrompus* [all the corrupt men], *trahir le peuple* [to betray the people].

Then, he proceeded to force his own death. "Let us say, then, that a conspiracy against public liberty exists; that it owes its power to a criminal coalition that intrigues in the very bosom of the Convention; that that coalition has some accomplices in the Committee of General Security and in the sub-committees of the Committee in which they are dominant; that the enemies of the Republic have opposed that Committee to the Committee of Public Safety, thus constituting two distinct governments; that some members of the Committee of Public Safety have entered into this plot, that the coalition thus formed looks to destroy the patriots and *la patrie.*"

Since he refused to name the particular conspirators he had in mind, he made it inevitable that most people in the Convention would feel their lives would be more secure if he would be driven to the guillotine. No one was exempt: the conspiracy existed within the two great Committees and within the bosom of the Convention itself. He also made it unambiguously clear what course he was proposing: "What is the remedy for this evil? To punish the traitors, to remove and replace the sub-committees of the Committee of General Security, to purify that Committee itself, and to subordinate it to the Committee of Public Safety, to purge the Committee of Public Safety itself, to constitute the unity of government under the supreme authority of the National Convention . . . and to crush all the factions under the weight of the national authority, in order to raise up on their ruins the power of justice and of liberty."[26] After months of the Great Terror, everyone knew what he had in mind.

Defeated, not by his enemies, but by his own severe psychopathology, he went to the guillotine two days later.

DICTATOR

Starobinski succinctly makes the point I have been emphasizing concerning the psychological similarity between Rousseau and Robespierre; "Certainly not to see Rousseau as its theoretician (although Robespierre drew the essential part of his ideas from Rousseau), but because the Terror seems to me to be, on the political level, homologous with what unfolds on the mental level in the autobiographical writings of Rousseau."[27] There is one profoundly important area, however, where the disposition of Robespierre was *not* homologous with that of

Rousseau. Robespierre was willing to seize an authoritarian political power and use whatever means—honest or dishonest, legitimate or illegitimate, moral or immoral—that he felt necessary to destroy all political opposition. He was the heir of Louis XIV, but he was not a king. He was the first, with the possible exception of Cromwell, of that great scourge: the modern ideological dictator. His very short reign prefigured the much longer tyrannies of Mao and Stalin. Though he does not specifically refer to Robespierre, Tocqueville's prediction that the future holds the definite possibility of all power being concentrated in the hands of one man[28] must reflect (even if unconsciously) the course of Maximilien's rise to omnipotence. Michelet called him a "monarch." "The monarchy commenced at the death of Danton. . . . Suddenly, in six weeks, he seized the great central power. He had his police (Herman), the police of the Committee (Héron). He had the justice (Dumas), the great general tribunal, which judged for all departments. He had the Commune (Payan), the 48 Committees of the Sections. By means of the Commune, he had in his hand the revolutionary army (Henriot). And all this without title, without either writing or signature."[29]

In trying to elaborate on the psychopathology of Robespierre, I am, obviously, hoping to shed some light on all ideological terrorists. Not all virtuous, narcissistic, paranoid, politically motivated individuals are compelled to seize dictatorial power. The contrast with Rousseau is exemplary. What Robespierre, Lenin, Mao, and Pol Pot all shared was—in addition to other pathologies discussed here—a power-crazed ruthlessness that knew no limits. I have no capacity to explain why "Some do and some do not,"[30] but what seems apparent is that this quality of ruthless power is essential to the establishment of ideological terror, and, if really understood, would help explain how easily millions are brought to the slaughter. Once set on that course, killing as a means, and an end in itself, becomes as easy as getting up in the morning. Stalin is quoted as saying, "A single death is a tragedy, a million deaths is a statistic" (Bartlett's *Familiar Quotations*, 1968, 954b). It takes a certain kind of nonpsychotic psychopathology to turn dead men into a statistic. The great horror in this particular story is that Robespierre—erstwhile genius of moral critique—was capable of such catastrophic action.

In his pursuit of dictatorial power, which must include the elimination of all political opposition, he pursued the exact same policies that have become typical of all dictatorial gangsters, great and small. The crucial act was the coup against Gironde, in which duly elected delegates to the National Convention were forcibly removed from office and, many of them, subsequently guillotined. If the death of Danton sounded the beginning of the monarchy, the Girondin coup was the very beginning of the Jacobin dictatorship, of which Robespierre was the *chef*.

There is no question that he was the inspiration behind this act, treacherous to democracy. Four days before the start of the actual events, he gave a rabble-rousing speech at the Jacobins: " 'When the people is oppressed, when it has no recourse left but itself, he would be a coward indeed who should not call upon it to rise. It is when all laws are violated, it is when despotism is at its height [one would imagine he was calling for the overthrow of an authoritarian monarch], it is when good faith and decency are being trampled under foot, that the people ought to rise in insurrection. That moment has arrived.' "[31] "I urge the people to go into the Convention in insurrection against the corrupt deputies."[32] It is the blatant dishonesty of the rhetoric ("despotism is at its height") that alerts us to how corruptible was the Incorruptible, when it became a question of seizing power illegally. There was nothing he would not do.

After that elimination of political opposition, the dictatorship of the Committee of Public Safety, which was Robespierre's instrument, although the other members did exhibit a significant degree of autonomy from him—that dictatorship was erected step by step. In July '93, it was permitted to issue warrants of arrest; in August, secret service money, with no questions asked, was made available to it; by September, it chose the members of the other Committees. By October 10, the overseeing of ministers, generals, and public authorities became its responsibility; December saw the conduct of foreign policy committed to it. And finally, in April '94, twelve *commissions exécutives*, responsible only to the Committee, replaced a formerly independent *Conseil exécutif* of Ministers.[33] If not in the hands of one man, certainly all power was being concentrated within the bounds of a committee of twelve authoritarians.

The next essential step, as Trotsky understood so well in the circumstances of the Kronstadt sailors, was to repress any popular political activity that could threaten to become political opposition. Here, again, Maximilien was in the forefront of this repressive action. Rudé writes: "Already in September 1793, sectional meetings had been reduced to two each ten-day 'week' (*décade*); and after Hébert's fall in April, popular and 'fraternal' societies not under the direct control of the Jacobin Club were closed down, and the Paris Commune, so long seen as 'the citadel of liberty' in the struggle against Federalism, had its independence severely reduced. Robespierre either initiated such measures or gave them his active support."[34] If Barère was a reluctant terrorist, Robespierre was no reluctant dictator: he took to it as if destined for that position. We have not one piece of evidence, either from public speeches, private conversation, or diaries, that he expressed or demonstrated even the slightest hesitancy in traducing the democratic process.

And one last prefiguration of twentieth-century total societies, censorship of the arts in order to make them politically and morally acceptable, was very quickly assumed to be a function of the authorities. On August 29, 1793, the Committee of Public Safety forbade the continued performance of François de Neufchâteau's *Pamela*, demanded he submit the manuscript to them, and insisted on certain deletions before the play was performed again. In early September, at the Jacobins, a certain captain of the Dragoons asserted that he was appalled to hear reactionary statements at the theater; he had been arrested for breach of peace after protesting loudly. Responding, Maximilien called for stronger measures: the theater was shut and the playwright imprisoned. Even attitudes toward religion and the clergy were subject to censorship. In December '73, a decree drafted and signed by Robespierre demanded that the Opera not produce a play by Bourdon, *Le tombeau des imposteurs*, because of its anticlerical sentiments—" 'or any other of a similar tendency.' "[35]

Understanding this unrestrained commitment to tolerating no political opposition is crucial for the comprehension of ideological terror. Once an individual allows himself that particular stance, human life is downgraded to a thing. Taking it becomes no different than tearing down an old building that has become useless. If people have no right to loyal opposition, they are no longer people, and certainly not *le peuple*.

GENIUS OF MORAL CRITIQUE

He began political life as one of the greatest democratic voices of all time, equal in passion and understanding to anyone one might care to mention. The inspiration and confirmation of his own inclinations came, naturally, from Rousseau: "Those who would treat politics and morality separately will never understand anything about either one [*Emile*, I, IV]."[36] His vision of what the future democratic society had to be was extraordinary. He was more than a philosophical moralist, advocating equality and the rights of man: he knew what a modern, stable democratic policy must entail—and, even more remarkably, he understood what were the political (and moral) obstacles that would hinder such a consummation. "No one at the time of the Revolution," writes Alfred Cobban, "went as far as Robespierre in stating what were later to be recognized as the essential conditions of the democratic state. . . . Universal franchise, equality of rights regardless of race or religion, pay for public service to enable rich and poor alike to hold office, publicity for legislative debates, a national system of education, the use of taxation to smooth out economic inequalities, recognition of the economic responsibilities of society to the individual . . . religious liberty, local self-government—such were some of the principles for which he stood, and which are now taken for granted in democratic societies."[37]

So powerful was his perception, so penetrating the moral critique that he comprehended the moral mediocrity that could result, even after the establishment of a nonmonarchical society. A Republic, in itself, was not sufficient for him. In the fall of '92:

> Which of us would care to descend from the height of the eternal principles we have proclaimed to the actual government of the republic of Berne, Venice or Holland? . . . It is not enough, therefore, to have overturned the throne: our concern is to erect upon its remains holy equality and the inprescriptable Rights of Man. It is not the empty name, but the character of the citizens, that constitutes a republic. The soul of a republic is *vertu*—that is, the love of one's country, and a high-minded devotion which sinks all private interests in the interest of the whole community.[38]

Sharply, and painfully, he could perceive the great discrepancy between what society was supposed to be and what it is in reality. This mode of moral critique—the greatest gift of Western civilization that extends as far back as Plato and the prophet Amos—he felt within his very soul: "Man is born for happiness and for liberty, and everywhere he is enslaved and unhappy. Society has for its end the conservation of his rights and the perfection of his being, and everywhere society degrades and opposes him! The time has come to recall him to his true destiny; the progress of human reason has prepared this great revolution, and it is on you that it especially imposes the obligation to hasten it."[39]

He never forgot that, in Modern society, large numbers of people could go hungry, that all the talk of rights and equality was meaningless as long as some people did not have enough to eat. In certain democratic bourgeois societies like our own, even today we have not fully heard that moral imperative. His was not a socialist or communist vision: capitalism was not to be eliminated; commerce would have free play, but only *after* every citizen had enough to sustain himself. It was a prescription for capitalism with a human face. It was not until after the catastrophic descent into the nineteenth-century industrial hell, and the moral recovery by means of the welfare state in the twentieth century, that Western culture as a whole began to comprehend what Robespierre knew in December 1792:

> What is the first object of society? It is to maintain the imprescriptible rights of man. What is the first of these rights? That of existence.
>
> The first social law, then, is that which guarantees to all members of society the means to exist; all the others are subordinate to this one. . . .
>
> The food necessary for a man's existence is as sacred as life itself. All that is necessary for its preservation is the common property of the entire society. It is only the surplus that is individual property and can be left to the industry of merchants. All mercantile speculation that I make at the cost of my fellow human being is not commerce, it is brigandage, it is fratricide.[40]

It is this very principle upon which welfare-state capitalism exists: great riches are not prohibited; large differences in wealth and income are permitted, if not encouraged; but the metaphorical "safety net" is to be maintained in order to see that no citizen leads a life of total degradation. It may be asked: How many individuals at the end of the eighteenth century could see that far into the future?

The deep moral and psychological contradiction within Robespierre's psyche existed because he unconsciously knew, but would never express and was helpless before, one particular fact: the trouble in the world was not caused by monarchy, or aristocracy, or counterrevolutionaries, or selfish bourgeois republicans—the troubles of the world were caused by people, who were empowered over other people. And some people always sought such power. There was a way in which the substitution of a bourgeois world for an aristocratic world was, merely, the substitution of bourgeois masters for aristocratic masters. The continuity of hierarchy preserved the continuity of hierarchical arrogance:

> So many stupid merchants, so many bourgeois egotists maintain still for artisans the insolent disdain the nobles lavished on the bourgeoisie and the merchants themselves.[41]

He saw clearly, with tremendous insight, the tyrannical possibilities within bourgeois society, even though it would take a republican form. "Is it in order to fall again under the yoke of the aristocracy of riches that the people has smashed with you the yoke of feudal aristocracy?"[42]

How, then, does one create a society without yokes? His intelligence was too extraordinarily brilliant not to demand that he face that question. The true answer could easily drag one into pessimism. But pessimism was not allowed in his conscious mind. An unbearable conflict. Utopianism was the pathological resolution of that conflict: only the creation of a radically new man could put an end to disdain, hierarchy, and tyranny. And if that genesis was not possible—then let the whole house crash!

And there were no role models, either in the past or the present. At the beginning of the first Revolution, when constitutional monarchy seemed the answer, many looked to England as worthy of emulation. Four years later, in May '93, England had become, for Robespierre, the very objective correlative of hypocrisy and corruption. " 'Witness England, where the gold and power of the monarchy constantly weigh the scales to the same side, where even the opposition appears from time to time to canvas for representational reform only in order to defer it, in concert with the majority it seems to oppose; a monstrous form of government, whose public virtues are merely a scandalous show in which *the shadow of liberty annihilates liberty itself, the law consecrates despotism, the rights of the people are openly traded,* where corruption is uncurbed by shame.' "[43]

Having failed to create a new man, England had obviously moved from one form of iniquity to another. One can identify and sympathize with Robespierre's desire to create a man—and a society—impervious to corruption. The rage that he felt when it became obvious, even to him, that such a course was a fantasy—such rage, however, produced the greatest evil of all.

Limited vs. Universal Democracy

The history of democracy in the West from the late eighteenth to the late nineteenth century is the history of the movement from a limited democracy (financial requirements for voting or holding office) to a universal democracy (one man, one vote). That history in the twentieth century is about the inclusion of women and minority groups as citizens. The first French constitution, adopted by the National Assembly in September 1791, was of a definite limited-democracy type. One-third of all citizens were excluded from the electorate. To serve as an elector of deputies required an additional higher tax-paying basis.

And to be elected a deputy, one had to pay a tax equal to one silver marc—the *marc d'argent*. This latter provision could be met by fewer than twenty percent of the citizenry.[44] In April '91, Robespierre delivered a passionate speech against the *Décret Sur Le Marc D'Argent*. It is hard to imagine a more powerful discourse on the incompatibility of the political power of riches and true democracy: " 'All men *born* and *domiciled* in France are members of the body politic termed the French nation; that is to say, they are French citizens. They are so by the nature of things and by the first principle of the law of nations. The rights attaching to this title do not depend on the fortune that each man possesses, nor on the amount of tax for which he is assessed, because it is not taxes that makes us citizens.' "[45]

Such limitation on sovereignty is a direct violation of the Declaration of the Rights of Man previously decreed by the Convention:

> Is the nation sovereign when the greatest number of individuals that compose it are deprived of political rights which constitute the sovereignty? No; and nevertheless, you have just seen that these same decrees take them away from the greater part of the French. What will your declaration of rights be, then, if these decrees are able to subsist? A vain formula. What will the nation be? A slave; because liberty consists in obeying the law that one has given oneself, and servitude consists in being constrained to submit to a strange will. What will your constitution be? A true aristocratic one. Because aristocracy is the state where one portion of the citizens is sovereign and the rest are subjects. And what an aristocracy! The most insupportable of all; that of Riches.[46]

Robespierre sees the very purpose of law and society exactly opposite to that perceived by the new bourgeois world: "The laws, public authority, are they not established in order to protect the weak against injustice and oppression. It is, then, to wound all social principles to place the laws entirely between the hands of the rich."[47]

It is no wonder, then, that he became a near-god to the poor and the near-poor of France and especially of Paris. He was their voice in the largest political world. It would be a grave mistake to suggest that he took such a position only out of political strategy, to get the sans-culottes as his army. Had he been such a political schemer and opportunist, he never would have become a terrorist. Ideological terrorists are people who begin, as Mirabeau said of Maximilien, believing everything they say. They turn to terror, among other reasons, because they can no longer maintain belief in the utopian moral faith they have created.

The Penalty of Death

December 1789: " 'It were better that a hundred guilty men should be pardoned, than that one single innocent person should be punished.' "[48] I have dealt before with Robespierre's remarkable arguments against the death penalty and have suggested that no more profound reasons for abolishing it have been advanced, even in this century, which has seen the institutionalization of that life-enhancing notion. Here, it may be of value to present part of a speech in which the emphasis is upon the effect that such executions have on the moral ecology of the society as a whole. May 1791:

> Listen to the voice of justice and of reason; it cries out to us that human judgements are not always so certain that society is able to give death to a man condemned by other men who are subject to error. Even if you imagine the judicial order the most perfect, even if you find judges the most trustworthy and the most enlightened, you would still have to allow some place for error or for prejudice. . . .
>
> . . . If, in place of that powerful rigour, of that moderate calm which ought to characterise it, they put anger and vengeance; if they make human blood flow, blood that they ought to spare and have no right to spread; if they display to the eyes of the people cruel scenes of dead and tortured cadavers, then they alter in the hearts of citizens the ideas of justice and injustice, they cause to germinate in the bosom of society ferocious prejudices which then produce others in their turn.[49]

That *he* should become the very cause of the magnification of ferocious prejudices—that *he* should become the very thing he so passionately condemns at this moment—is certainly one of the cruelest ironies in all history.

The Abomination of War

In this regard, he stood almost alone. Not only did he differ from Brissot and the Girondins, who were impassioned to declare war in the early months of 1792, but even a majority of the Jacobin Club supported this suicidal démarche. On January 17, 1792, the Paris Club had informed its affiliated branches in the country that war was inevitable. At the end of February, a motion was entered to send another communication stating that " 'The majority of the society is in favour of war.' " Robespierre objected but lost the contest.[50]

Brissot irrationally imagined that war with Europe would serve and advance the Revolution. " 'War is actually a national benefit. . . . We need treachery on a grand scale; our salvation lies that way, for strong doses of poison remain in the body of France, and strong measures are necessary to expel them.' "[51] He fatuously imagined that war would put the king on the spot: he either had to support the conflict and the Revolution or reveal his hostility to the Revolution, in which case, " 'the people will be ready.' " Marie Antoinette knew better: " 'The fools! Don't they see they are serving our purposes?' "[52]

In his perception of the consequences of declaring war, Robespierre's moral and intellectual brilliance came together. Brissot had declared that the war would produce revolutionary uprisings all over Europe. Maximilien understood the wish-fulfillment dimension in such fantasy: " 'No one loves armed missionaries.' " Such a course was threatening to freedom in France: " 'To want to give liberty to others before conquering it ourselves is to assure our own enslavement and that of the whole world.' "[53]

For him, war was " 'the most dangerous course,' "[54] among other reasons because it would, inevitably, bring the generals to powers. When a king is weak like Louis XVI, " 'your real kings are your generals. . . . In troubled times . . . the army commanders become the arbiter of their country.' "[55]

We can only be amazed that he, who suffered so much from his own paranoid perceptions of the world, in the face of this mass war-hysteria and paranoia remained remarkably sane, carried away by neither grandiosity nor self-destruction. Like almost everything else about him that was psychologically mature, once he seized power, he abandoned the rational position, and, in this particular circumstance, became the foremost promoter of the war effort. It was Danton who had to face rumors that he was betraying the Revolution by trying to make peace with England.

Tolerance for Religion

It is extraordinary, and remarkably indicative of the unique individual we are concerned with, that in regard to the two fundamental, self-destructive "mistakes" of the Revolution—the declaration of war on Europe and the exaggerated attack on religion that could not help but produce a counterrevolutionary backlash—despite all the deep psychopathology being discussed here, he saw, with lightning clarity, the total inadvisability of both programs. In the fall of '93,

André Dumont was on mission to the Somme from the Committee of Public Safety and wrote back to it, with great pride, about his success in closing churches and burning images, including a famous "black Virgin" at Boulogne that had been destroyed to gleeful cries of: "*Vive la Montagne.*" The Committee responded with a letter, signed by Robespierre among others:

> It appears to us that during your recent activities you have shown too much violence towards the objects of Catholic worship. Part of France, especially in the south, is still fanatically religious. One must be on one's guard against giving the dishonest counter-revolutionists, who are trying to kindle civil war, any possible justification for their slanders against us. We must not afford them an opportunity for saying that we are violating liberty of worship, and attacking religion itself. It is right to punish seditious or unpatriotic priests; it is wrong to proscribe priests as such.[56]

His position on this issue had been carefully thought out. Unlike his response of grandiosity and utopian illusions in so many other areas, in regard to religious transformation he was keenly aware of how difficult a revolution is. A letter from the Paris Jacobin club to the Popular Societies throughout the nation, written and signed by Maximilien:

> Lay this lesson to heart: conscience cannot be dictated to (*on ne commande pas aux consciences*). Some people are superstitious in good faith, partly because, in the rapid transition from superstition to truth, only a few have thought out and seen through the superficial prejudices, while the rest hang bank, and need encouragement to join in the advance. If you intimidate them, you are only asking them to retreat. They are moral invalids, who must be encouraged, if they are not to be cured; a compulsory remedy will only turn them into fanatics.[57]

I have tried to elaborate on the great contradiction between the passionate moralist and the terrorist. Another attribute is exhibited here, in regard to antireligious fanaticism: an extraordinary intellectual clarity, a remarkable means-end rationality. " 'This man, who wishes to prevent the saying of mass is a greater fanatic than he who says it.' "[58] In the feverish condition of revolution, however, force was "necessary" to enforce rationality. A letter of December 10, 1793, from the Committee to its representative on mission at Lille, signed first by Robespierre, instructs him: "to arrest members of the *societé populaire* at Lille, who have been guilty of 'revolutionary exaggeration, especially in matters of public worship.' "[59] If Rousseau believed men could be forced to be free [*Social Contract,* I, Chapter 5], Robespierre hoped men could be commanded to be rational. The great disaster of utopian aspirations is that people are incapable of attaining them. Faced with this intractability, terror is one option.

TERRORIST

There should be no reason, at this point, for a lengthy argument and a weighty presentation of data to esablish that Robespierre was a terrorist. And, most important, an ideological terrorist. In this deliberately short section, only two fundamental attitudes will be addressed: first, the complete willingness to over-throw all liberal and enlightenment concepts and rules of justice; and second, the unambivalent use of judicial assassination, and subsequent execution, to elim-inate political opposition.

All judicial safeguards go out the window because those who are truly inno-cent have nothing to fear. March 31, 1794, on the arrest of Danton: "I say that whoever trembles at this moment is guilty; for innocence never has to dread public surveillance (*On applaudit.*)"[60] How many times have we heard from totali-tarian governments that only the guilty need worry about the lifting of judicial protections? This same tyrannical mentality led the Convention, at Robespierre's urging, to refuse to present arrested persons with written indictments because, as he put it, the evidence that would convict them " 'was public knowledge and in the hearts of outraged citizens.' "[61]

This severe moral regression to an almost pre–*ancien régime* society reached one catastrophic climax during the trial of the deposed Girondin delegates in Octo-ber '93. The accused, most especially Brissot, Vergniaud, and Gensonné, had the temerity in court to confront their accusers and defend themselves. For the Jacobin Club this was intolerable behavior and it demanded that the Convention pass a law that would eliminate the " 'formalities which stifle the conscience and hinder conviction [and would] give the jury the power to state that they had sufficient information.' " A deputy at the Convention made a proposal that Max-imilien considered too vague. The latter countered: " 'I propose to declare that after three days' discussion the president of the tribunal shall ask the jury if their conscience is sufficiently enlightened. If they answer in the negative, the trial shall go on till they declare that they are in a position to pronounce sentence.' " The decree was rushed to the Tribunal! At first, despite it being the sixth day of the trial, the jury indicated it was not yet prepared to issue a judgement. That evening, however, they made up their minds—we don't know under what pressure. All the Girondins on trial were condemned and guillotined to the cries from a huge crowd of: " 'Down with the traitors!' "[62] Such was the raw face of terror, and such the god-turned-devil who authored it.

Robespierre was on the road to this terrible place already in September '92, at the time of the Prison Massacres. He was willing, already at that time, that political opposition should be eliminated by a warfare that executes the losers:

> In his speech at the Commune on September 4, delivered some hours after the Massacre had begun, and subsequent to the announcement of this to the body of which he was a member, Robespierre went out of his way to denounce Brissot, if not by name, at least in unmistakeable terms, as a conspirator, and an agent of the Duke of Brunswick [that is, an obvious traitor]; upon which the Vigilance Committee issued warrants for the arrest of Roland, Brissot, and the other prominent Girondins. This could only mean one thing. Had not Danton, moved by the threat against a fellow-minister, secured the withdrawal of the warrant, the Girondin leaders would almost certainly have perished with the other prisoners. In short, a charge lies against Robespierre not merely of doing nothing to stop the massacres, not merely of condoning them as an execution of popular justice . . . but of trying to use them as a cloak for political assassination. Mme Roland had no doubt as to his guilt. "Robespierre and Marat," she wrote, . . . "are holding a sword over our heads."[63]

It is a first principle of political terror that there is no such thing as loyal opposition. All political disagreement is disloyal, criminal, traitorous. The just punishment for traitors is unarguable. There is little question that Robespierre fully embraced this catechism. An appropriate conclusion is to quote George Rudé, who is a paragon of fairness, unblinded by any ideology: "Even if Robespierre played an altogether secondary role in the great holocaust of June and July [1794], which, mainly on the orders of the Security Committee, sent many hundreds of victims to the guillotine, he played *the* leading part, throughout this period, as a watchdog of the Revolution in ferreting out its enemies and bringing them to justice."[64] "Justice" is an euphemism.

DANTON LAUGHED

Our greatest understanding of character, of personality, idiosyncrasy, passion fulfilled and passion denied—our greatest understanding of the whole person—

has come to us not through psychoanalysis nor general psychology but from literature: from the drama and the novel. Has any case history we have, even one from a genius like Freud, given us the confident sense that we know the subject as a complete person, the way we know Shakespeare's Hamlet or Stendahl's Julien Sorel? If I were a novelist and had undertaken the task of trying to get us to know Robespierre—the entire person—I would pay as much attention to two sentences as to the entire corpus of the public speeches.

" 'The word virtue made Danton laugh. . . . How could a man, to whom all idea of morality was foreign, be the defender of liberty?' "[65] Danton's laugh did something all the criticism and attack from so many quarters could not do: it *wounded* Robespierre in a vulnerable place. So much of Robespierre's character was the result of the erection of defenses against certain vulnerabilities that, most of the time, he appears almost invulnerable. But he was not so completely and successfully defended. An attack on his protestations of virtue—especially an attack by a revolutionary who had supported every action of the radical revolution from the very beginning, including the overthrow of the king, the coup against the Gironde, and the erection of the Terror—such an assault found the one place where Maximilien could be lacerated. And the gigantic rage engendered—he being who he was—was terrible in its consequences.

By itself, it certainly does not explain the worst of the Terror. But it does help explain Danton's death—an act that should have convinced anyone, except a person totally lost in a living nightmare, that France had gone mad. Danton's very existence was a reproach to Robespierre. The Incorruptible was not one to suffer reproach lightly or passively.

All of which might convince us that in the very deepest part of his psyche he himself had doubts about his own virtuousness. Hopefully, that was true. It would keep him, at least, from being a hypocritical devil-incarnate, which he certainly was not.

In his response to the compromised character of Danton, he exhibited not only rage but also contempt. That contempt was also brought forth by other *hommes moyen sensuels,* as in the case of Herault-Séchelles, previously cited. That feeling of detestation for Danton reflected a profound condemnation of the morally compromised bourgeois society that the Revolution had made possible. In regard to the future possibilities for society, Danton and Robespierre became exemplary. Danton represented the bourgeois future: Robespierre, an impossible utopian one. To kill Danton was a vain attempt to kill the hypocritical, egotistical, easily corrupted society that was to be. Palmer elaborates:

The great difficulty was the failure of the Mountaineers to agree. Danton would solve it be creating a vague and broad Republic, in which men of all kinds, good and bad, sound and tainted, might, after disposing of irreconcilable extremists, join together by not arguing over principles. The Republic after Thermidor, disfigured by cynicism, loose-living and peculation, would not have shocked him.

. . . To Robespierre it was unthinkable that after all the risks and suffering, all the struggle and the eager anticipation, all the dreadful decisions already made, the responsibilities bravely assumed . . . that all this should issue in a world no better than the old, a Republic in which vice, hypocrisy, irreligion, and egotism should be laughed at.[66]

Mona Ozouf is also keenly aware of the archtypical positions represented by these two monumental individuals. She reports that Danton insisted that some men "'are not born with revolutionary blood in their veins but should not therefore be treated as criminals.' . . . Should ardent patriots expel from their ranks 'those whose souls are less diligent in their pursuit of liberty but who cherish it no less than themselves?' Should this moderate element be treated as an enemy because 'it often condemns energy, which is generally believes to be misguided and dangerous?'" And, she concludes, the two great protagonists knew each other well: "Robespierre and Saint-Just were not mistaken in their choice of an enemy."[67]

For the future of humankind, it proved unfortunate that these were the only two alternatives. The nineteenth century proved that Danton was right: a morally compromised bourgeois society was the only culture of the possible. The twentieth century proved that Robespierre's utopianism was still a misfortune: forcing men to be "free" by creating the politics and the culture of the impossible—attempting to skip over the stage of bourgeois republicanism—could only lead to ideological terror. More than two hundred years after the deaths of both Maximilien and Danton, how morally transformable is that bourgeois democracy that the best of the Revolution has bequeathed to the world remains the great question.

BETRAYED BY ONE'S OWN IDEALS

One hypothesis that keeps recurring in my mind is that Robespierre, and all ideological terrorists, can be understood only by paying very close attention to rage. Rage, not anger, an all-comsuming frenzy that lashes out at everyone and anyone and ultimately injures oneself in acts of self-destruction. The postulate is that all ideological terrorists are susceptible to attacks of rage, either openly expressed in someone like Hitler or deeply repressed—but ultimately manifest—in someone like Robespierre.

Rage is almost always triggered by the sense of betrayal. The archtypical story of rage is Medea, betrayed by her husband, enraged beyond sanity, killing their children as a psychotic act of revenge. Who, or what, then, had betrayed Robespierre that he should become so enraged, seeking revenge by means of the deaths of innocent thousands? There is an extraordinary passage in the notebooks of Antoine Pierre Barnave, guillotined at Paris, November 29, 1793. It strongly suggests that a person may feel betrayed by his/her own ideal-utopian image of humanity and society and that this sense of perfidy could lead one to revenge oneself on that same faithless humanity. It resonates so powerfully with what we know, and feel, about Robespierre:

> People who have formed illusions abandon everything when these are dissipated; they have worked for a chimerical good which disappears. A real or possible good holds no charm for them. They fall into the contrary extreme, and seeing that humanity for which they destined the happiness and perfection of angels cannot rise to the value of their benefits, they wish upon it all kind of shame and evil.[68]

If, as has been postulated here, the original motivation for the creation of the fantasy of a place in the world that is blamelessly perfect has been a defensive response to the deficit of love and nurture from those who should have cherished one, then it is most appropriate that when this new utopian construction fails, all the primitive aggression from the original betrayal should reappear and manifest itself. The utopian world was a fantasy; it could not do the job it was supposed to do; it could not heal psychic injuries that were incapable of cure. It is no wonder that, when it all comes crashing down, one response should be betrayed Lear's great cry of despair and revenge: "Then kill, kill, kill, kill, kill, kill!"[69]

It is of interest to reflect on the fact that, more than 150 years after Barnave, Raymond Aron, a humanist French intellectual, trying to understand the second coming of the Jacobin Terror—both in its quotidian Bolshevik exercise and in the much more appalling manifestation: French bourgeois intellectuals supporting Stalinist exterminations—Aron echoes Barnave's powerful insight into betrayal: "He who protests against the fate meted out to mankind by a meaningless universe sometimes finds himself in sympathy with the revolutionaries, because indignation or hatred outweigh all other considerations, because, in the last resort, violence alone can appease his despair."[70]

☼   ☼   ☼

In conclusion, there can be no conclusion. I have gone as far into the heart of darkness as I am able. I am satisfied even if I have not come back with anything like a full understanding of the infinite extent of human destructiveness and evil, if there has been success in widening, and also sharpening, the inquiry, allowing someone else—at a later date—to start at least at a more advanced place. It will not let one go, however. One feels compelled to join with Mister Kurtz in giving voice to one's own cry of despair: "The horror! The Terror! The horror!" Suffused with powerful meaning and meaninglessness.

PART IV

SOCIAL EVOLUTION

23

WHY AND WHERE HAS GOD BEEN PUSHING US?

There is an extraordinary passage of Tocqueville's that is indicative of a strong inclination in his thought toward a theory of social evolution, even though he certainly would not have used such a phrase, nor did he attempt to erect a complex theory under that worldview. It is profitable, I feel, to begin this discourse on the theory of social evolution—with particular emphasis on the current stage of Modernity—with an exegesis of that remarkable statement:

> I cannot believe that God has for several centuries been pushing two or three hundred million men toward equality just to make them wind up under a Tiberion or Claudian despotism. Verily that wouldn't be worth the trouble. Why he is drawing us toward democracy, I do not know; but embarked on a vessel that I did not build, I am at least trying to use it to gain the nearest port.[1]

This present discourse consists, essentially, in an elaboration of what might be meant by four crucial words or phrases: *several centuries; equality/democracy; God; pushing.*

Before engaging on the latter project, it should be demonstrated that such an evolutionary view was not a unique or isolated phenomenon in Tocqueville's oeuvre. In the very introduction to *Democracy in America,* he emphasizes what he feels is the inexorable drive toward equality in the modern world: "The gradual process of equality is something fated. The main features of this progress are the following: it is universal and permanent; it is daily passing beyond human control, and every event and every man helps it along."[2] In his clear emphasis on the inevitability in the historical process, he takes a theoretical position remarkably similar to Marx's view of historical determinism. Tocqueville seems to be as convinced of the inescapable arrival of equality and democracy as Marx was of the end of capitalism and the advent of socialism.

Even further than this, his perception of the power in historical evolution allows him to see what the drive toward equality will accomplish almost a century later:

> I have shown how democracy destroys or modifies those various inequalities which are in origin social. But is that the end of the matter? May it not ultimately come to change the great inequality between man and woman which has up till now seemed based on the eternal foundation of nature?
>
> I think that the same social impetus which brings nearer to the same level father and son, master and servant and generally every inferior to every superior does raise the status of women and should make them more and more nearly equal to men.[3]

What, then, could it really mean to assert that God has been pushing us toward all this equality? And, if it is God and not something else, where had He been for the half million years of human history before the beginnings of early Modernity. Maybe, in reality, we are being pushed but not by God—by something else. Understanding what that "something else" might be is the crucial key to a full theory of social evolution.

SEVERAL CENTURIES

The last thirty years have witnessed the publication of a great number of intelligent, informative, perceptive books on the *ancien régime* and its conclusion in the first French Revolution: origins, causes, background, genesis of that Revolution. Why the revolution occurred. These works all share two characteristics: they deepen our understanding of eighteenth-century France, and they all point toward the inevitability, the fatal quality, the ineluctability of 1789. Discourses on the *causes* of the first Revolution prove remarkably uncontroversial. Exactly the opposite situation arises in response to any work that addresses the question of *causes* of the Great Terror: why 1789 degenerated into 1793. At present, no matter what position an author takes on that issue, it immediately provokes polemic. All of which would indicate that, to a large degree, we have a reasonably satisfactory understanding of why that first Revolution occurred but not of the determinates of the Terror. French society had been moving toward that first revolutionary denouement, in Tocqueville's terms, for "several centuries." Its occurrence was no mystery—it was the climax of a profound social movement. *Why* French society was moving, for one or two centuries, in that particular direction—this question elicits no generally agreed-upon answer. Why was God pushing society toward that particular moment? Observing that moment, nevertheless, gives a sense of an inevitability to the revolutionary climax.

There is no reason to repeat here all the evidence given in Chapters 2, 3, and 5 about the *ancien régime* antecedents of the first Revolution: the rise of public opinion; the revolt of the curés; all the democratic discourse; the increasing social power of the bourgeoisie and its foremost representatives, the lawyers; the amazing efflorescence of rational and secular thought. A myriad of observers, all the way from Chateaubriand to Tocqueville to Quinet to contemporary historians, have pronounced on the fated quality of the first Revolution. A few brief quotations from this galaxy of theorists may be helpful in reminding us of how powerful that drive of social evolution was.

Chateaubriand was one of the first observers to comment that "the revolution was accomplished before it occurred."[4] Tocqueville's genius for distinguishing historical continuity produced this comment on the Old Regime:

> Their starting point was the same in all cases; and this was the belief that what was wanted was to replace the complex of traditional customs governing the social order of the day by simple, elementary rules deriving from the exercise of the human reason and natural laws.
>
> . . . How was it that at this particular point of time it could root itself so firmly in the mind of the writers of the day? Why, instead of remaining in the past the purely intellectual concept of a few advanced thinkers, did it find a welcome among masses and acquire the driving force of a political passion to such effect that general and abstract theories of the nature of human society not only became topics of conversation among the leisure class but fired the imagination even of women and peasants? And why was it that men of letters, men without wealth, social eminence, responsibilities, or official status, became in practice the leading politicians of the age, since despite the fact that others held the reins of government, they alone spoke with accents of authority?[5]

A similar observation had provoked the baron de Bésenual, in the years before '89, to complain that dinner parties had become " 'miniature estates-general where women, transformed into legislators, spouted maxims of public law.' "[6]

Edgar Quinet, who did address the question of the failure of the Revolution—in regard to the lack of a previous religious revolution, as has been discussed—nevertheless, saw the advent of the revolutionary experience as a logical development of several centuries of social evolution. Furet comments on this position: "In this way, the society that began on August 4, 1789, was only the product of the centuries preceding, and the Revolution the sequel of the *Ancien Régime.*"[7]

Finally, two of our finest contemporary historians reiterate this developmental position. "The commitment to representative institutions, a political rather than a social principle," writes William Doyle, "was the product of a century of rising standards of education and public awareness."[8] And Keith Baker: " 'The decisive conceptual break with the past that lay at the heart of revolutionary political culture had already occurred before the actual meeting of the Estates General.' "[9]

What all this does is to solve one theoretical question by opening up an even larger one. If the Revolution was the product of several centuries of social evolution, what was the cause, then, of that amazing development? How far back do we have to go? Thirteenth-century France was already profoundly different from thirteenth-century England—and both a far different world from that which would become Germany and, certainly, Russia. Obviously, the task adumbrated cannot be undertaken here. Only a hint or two about its importance.

The evolutionary theory being elaborated in this section rests, in part, on the conception that society advances in *stages.* One could postulate an evolutionary theory in which social advance is continuous but in gradual increments. The theory of stages is a separate entity from a theory of development. Assuming stages as a first principle, the question immediately arises: What was the stage of society that preceded Modernity? The theoretical position elaborated by Parsons and Bellah,[10] which I accept, hypothesizes a stage of early Modernity, beginning in the early sixteenth century, essentially with the Protestant Reformation. The fundamental narrative of this work is that of the fateful attempt of French society—an attempt both succeeding brilliantly and failing miserably—to advance from a developing early Modern society to a fully Modern one, through the instrument of political revolution. Tocqueville's "several centuries" of being propelled by God is the metaphorical representation of this evolutionary history.

There is no question that France entered the early Modern stage at full speed:

a strong centralized monarchy and a rapidly expanding economy characterized that period. "From the time of Colbert on," Charles Tilly writes, "France never ceased its construction of the finest network of roads in Europe."[11] The *ancien régime*, with its full flowering of Enlightenment ideas and worldviews, with its empowerment of the middle classes, with its challenge, on so many levels, to an authoritarian *Weltanschauung*, represented the full, ripe maturity of early Modernity. It all made some sort of revolutionary experience inevitable: what sort remained to be answered.

In one regard, however, it may be argued that early Modern France did *not* accomplish one essential and appropriate task of early Modernity, when it so forcefully repressed the Protestant impulse and, along with it, those crucial values of self-government through self-discipline, antiauthoritarianism in religion, overthrow of the monarchy of the Papacy, and—ultimately as Reformation Protestantism was transformed into classic liberalism—viable democratic discourse, tolerance, secularism. This was precisely Quinet's argument about the failure of the Revolution: 1789 witnessed a society primed to make the revolutionary step from one developmental stage to the next but crippled by the failure to fully complete the work of the previous stage.[12] One support of this contention may be constructed from the fact that the leadership of even the first "bourgeois" Revolution began to institute its own "Protestant Reformation." Timothy Tackett, a foremost historian of religion and the Revolution, elaborates:

> To anyone, clergyman or layman, already obsessed by the Protestant "menace," the Civil Constitution of the Clergy might well be perceived as a Protestant document. The seizure of church property by the state, the suppression of religious vows, the elimination of all chapters: measures such as these were immediately compared to the actions of Henry VIII at the beginning of the English Reformation. The selection of parish clergymen by the laity seemed dangerously close to Calvinist practice. And the weakening of the bonds with the Papacy could be viewed only with apprehension. The patriots, including a substantial proportion of the French clergy, might insist that such actions marked a renewal of religion, a return to the primitive simplicity of the religion of Jesus and the early church fathers. But the argument itself was suspiciously evocative of sixteenth-century statements by Luther and Calvin. Indeed, the very idea of a simplified and purified religion, of the religious austerity apparently embraced by the Revolutionary leadership, might smack of Calvinism and clash with the aesthetic sensitivities of people who still identified themselves with the "baroque" expressions of the Counter-Reformation.[13]

To anticipate the concern of the next chapter about the difficulties, if not impossibilities, of skipping a stage in social evolution, this discussion of the necessity of certain Protestant values, but not necessarily Protestantism itself, for the fulfillment of the promise of early Modernity raises a crucially significant question. Is the attempt to institute a revolutionary new stage in social evolution, when the current stage has not reached full maturity, doomed to failure? Here, once again, it may be argued that the enormous importance of understanding the successes and failures of the French revolutionary experience is that this was the first time in the history of the world that such a skipping of a stage was attempted on such a large scale. The twentieth century took up such a phantasmagoric project on an even more catastrophic scale. We return to Soviet communism in the chapter following.

All of this discussion of the significance of the Protestant *Weltanschauung* may help us understand that Tocqueville's "several centuries" was, by no means, an exaggeration. The true history of the Revolution may be said to begin, without overstatement, with Luther and Calvin.

EQUALITY/DEMOCRACY

God has been pushing us toward a certain end: a telos. Equality and democracy. I decline to take up the valid argument, which fills many tomes, about the difference between these two conceptions. It is not important for this discussion how Tocqueville distinguished between the two, although that also has been addressed by others at length. What is of crucial importance is that they are both goods, in the Aristotelian sense. The drive toward equality and democracy is a *moral* drive; their achievement, a *moral* advance. Otherwise, it would be blasphemous to ascribe such a program to God. If society was being driven backward morally, it could only be the devil's work. If the projected course was arbitrary and erratic (forward, backward, sideways), then it would be appropriate to attribute the movement to an inadequate human nature. But a situation in which God is the engine of history—that could only be one of moral advance.

Tocqueville, himself, was most reluctant to state openly a moral position or one of moral progress, but there is no question that his whole work is suffused with Rousseau's notion that one should not talk about politics without, simultaneously, talking about morality.[14] At one point, in the latter portion of *Democracy in America*, he does what for him is the rare thing: he waxes indignant and expresses moral outrage: "There is one lot of people who can see nothing in equality, but the anarchical tendencies which it engenders. They are frightened of their own free will; they are afraid of themselves."[15] Tocqueville's genius consisted, in good part, in the brilliant elaboration of the new, and previously unseen, problems that the advance toward equality and democracy could bring. He was far from being utopian or naïve about what the new society would look like. He undoubtedly, had moments of great uncertainty and could not be sure that this momentous adventure would succeed, but he knew that, should the drive toward equality and democracy fail, it would be a terrible *moral* failure.

If the telos of early Modernity and Modernity itself is a resolution in a more morally constituted society than any seen before—certainly, than any after the breakdown of kinship society, and its transformation into State societies—this proposition forces us to consider the relationship of moral progress to social evolution. No more complex theoretical problem exists. Perceiving the interconnection between the French Revolutions and the drive for Modernity brings us to the very center of that question.

GOD

What is moral, the reader may ask at this point, with good reason. By what standard is one society more moral than another? Everyone who has thought about these questions has his/her own definition of morality. And none can be "proven" in the face of a different, or even opposite, contention. One's definition of morality is, in Aristotle's terms, a first principle; and first principles, he goes on to contend, cannot be argued about. They can be argued, but no resolution of radically different views can be accomplished by the use of reason or dialectic.[16] First principles are axiomatic: the start of thinking, not the result of the process.

My own definition of morality and immortality has three dimensions. Whatever moves in the direction of greater equality between people is moral; whatever moves toward greater inequality is immoral. Whatever tends toward an increase in freedom is moral; whatever tends toward an increase of domination or tyranny is immoral. That which enhances the attitude of nurturance in society (Rousseau's "pity and compassion"[17]) is moral—and its opposite.

Two examples. If a society abolishes slavery and does not put a new system of equal domination in its place, it has moved in the direction of greater morality: it has increased freedom and equality. Similarly, if a society like ours moves radically in the direction of greater equality between men and women, that course is a definite moral advance.

It is understood that there may be, and are, certain complex social circumstances where, for instance, an increase in equality for some is bought at the expense of a decrease in freedom for others. The argument today against affirmative action takes exactly that contradiction as its basis. The question, however, is what should society do, and not whether equality and freedom are good (moral) things in themselves. Society may be forced, in many circumstances, to choose or compromise between goods, but that does not cease to make them goods.

The first French Revolution, precisely in the areas of equality and freedom, burst upon Europe and permanently changed the world. Hegel, whose reputation among certain intellectuals, even today, is that of being conservative, if not reactionary, nevertheless celebrated Bastille Day every year of his life[18] and regarded that first Revolution as a "World-Historical" event—the world would never be the same again. A permanent change in the way of looking at political and moral realities had occurred. And, here again, his argument is based explicitly on the fundamental change in conceptions of freedom and equality. Ritter elaborates:

> The world-historical dimension of European history is the freedom of being human; that signifies, however, that *the Revolution itself must positively qualify as an epoch of European world history and its freedom of being human* insofar as it makes freedom the foundation upon which all legality is based. Hegel therefore calls it "in its substantial import . . . World-Historical" and speaks of it as a "world-historical turning point," as the "condition of the world," and as forming an "epoch of the world's history." . . . Whereas at the beginning of world history the citizens of ancient civil society had slaves and the unfree politically and legally alongside themselves, in the French Revolution, for the first time, political freedom taken as justice, and therewith man's capacity of selfhood, were raised to the principle and aim of society and the state. Through it man first becomes without restriction the subject of political order, "in virtue of his manhood alone, not because he is a Jew, Catholic, Protestant, German, Italian."[19]

What is being described is a radical (i.e., revolutionary) step of moral progress: an advance to a new stage of society. It is not surprising, therefore, that Hegel resorts to a comparison with a similar radical advance in freedom and equality in the past: the creation of the world of the *polis*—the very first time since the dissolution of the kinship society that a nonauthoritarian (nonmonar-chical) political system became possible. Ritter further elaborates:

> *Every present and future legal and political order must presuppose and proceed from the Revolution's universal principle of freedom.* Against this, all reservations concerning its formalism and abstractness lose their force. After the polis entered into history in the ancient world and therewith, human being as the principle of justice (*Recht*) (albeit in restriction to the citizen and in exclusion of the slave), all political and legal forms which did not correspond to it had to become inessential for political theory. Plato and Aristotle therefore grounded political philosophy upon the polis alone. Where justice had become the justice of man, there justice which is not justice of man can only be called "justice" in a homonymous sense. The same holds for the French Revolution. After it made freedom for all, as men, the principle of right (*Recht*), all institutions and positive laws which contradict it lose by the process of historical necessity, every legitimate claim to validity, and in Hegel's view, this is true objectively as well as historically. The freedom constitutive for European world history is raised to the principle of all political and legal order by the Revolution. It is no longer possible to retreat from this principle.[20]

The argument is formidable. The assertion of moral progress palpable. The emphasis on the Revolution, however, is entirely too narrow, unless it is being used in a metaphorical sense to represent the whole powerful development of equality of freedom. Certainly, the English Revolution, and the American, the whole advance of Enlightenment and liberal thought, and the development of parliamentary institutions have equal rights to these honors. Where Hegel uses the phrase "French Revolution," I would substitute Modernity.

What both Tocqueville and Hegel are asserting is that, in the Modern world, there is an inexorable drive toward a higher morality. Tocqueville's "several cen-turies" may indicate his intention to include early Modernity as well. Whether or not this is so, it is the definite intention of this present argument to state, categorically, that in Western culture, certainly since the Reformation and proba-bly since the twelfth century, something has been pushing us toward greater equality and greater freedom. And this impulse is so strong that it is not inappro-priate to call it a "drive"—to state that we are being driven. "Is it wise to suppose," wrote Tocqueville in the introduction to the French edition of *Democ-racy in America*, "that a movement of such duration can be suspended by the efforts of one generation? Does anyone suppose that democracy, which has de-stroyed feudalism and conquered kings will bend before the *bourgeois* and the wealthy?"[21] He is certainly describing something that is much more than an inclination or a possibility. He recognized that this drive could be denied, as the quotation from him previously given about the possibility of all power being concentrated in the hands of one man as a result of the failure of democracy, but it will require a great force to accomplish this denial and will necessitate the creation of "things our fathers never saw."[22]

One of the most cogent and persuasive essays of contemporary sociological theory on social evolution is Robert Bellah's essay on "Religious Evolution," written in 1964 when Bellah was a very close personal intellectual colleague of Talcott Parsons. At the present time, Bellah seems to object to my use of words like "driven," "inexorable," "inevitable," when talking of the struggle for Modernity. In that essay, however, in a tone much less passionate than Tocqueville's and certainly less animated than my own, he has given voice to a description of religious evolution, deeply embedded in and causative of social evolution, that delineates a definitive course of moral progress, with most emphasis being on freedom rather than equality. If humankind can take greater and greater responsibility for its own fate, that could certainly be described as an enlargement of freedom: "The historic religions discovered the self; the early Modern religion found a doctrinal basis on which to accept the self in all its empirical ambiguity; Modern religion is beginning to understand the laws of the self's own existence and so to help man take responsibility for his own fate."[23]

Bellah, like Tocqueville, is not unaware of the great ambiguities in Modernity: the fact that it produces new ways of not being virtuous, along with the clear moral advance:

> The search for adequate standards of action, which is at the same time a search for personal maturity and social relevance, is in itself the heart of the modern quest for salvation. . . . Yet the situation that has been characterized as one of the collapse of meaning and the failure of moral standards can also, and I would argue more fruitfully, be viewed as one offering unprecedented opportunities for creative innovation in every sphere of human action.[24]

In regard to a complex theory of social evolution, all these formidable quotations help establish—if one finds them acceptable—only one particular theoretical notion: that Modernity (and early Modernity) has within it a powerful moral thrust, which provides a significant part of the energy responsible for the evolutionary movement to the Modern stage. All of this says nothing, in itself, as to whether that same kind of energy has been operative in the past in other transitions—or, possibly, in every transition—from one stage of social evolution to another. It also cannot tell us whether that same, or a different, moral drive would be needed to go beyond the present stage. If not God, what then has been pushing us?

PUSHING

We are, consequently, in the very middle of the speculative question of the "engine of history"—what has caused the almost incredible journey of human society from simple hunting/gathering bands of thirty to fifty souls to the technological and bureaucratic wonders of the several-million-people societies of today? In many regards, the terms of this discussion have been set by Marxism, which up till now represents the most complex theory of social evolution every postulated. Not most accurate, but most complete. The Marxist theory (Historical Materialism) has done what a complex evolutionary theory would be required to do: outlined a progression through stages; defined, and partially described and analyzed, the stages themselves (Feudalism, Capitalism, Socialism); and attempted to answer the question of what is driving the whole process.

For Marxism, the engine of history is the assumed universal human desire for more and more economic goods. At one point, Engels stated that it was greed that was driving the whole process.[25] The desire for more and more goods produces technological change, which in turn creates radically new "modes of production," which in turn engender radically new "relations of production." These latter refer to the class relationships in society, most particularly the question of which class is dominant. The windmill equals feudalism equals the domination by an aristocratic feudal class. The steam engine equals capitalism equals the domination of the bourgeoisie.

Simple and elegant. In his description of Marxist theory, Schumpeter uses the metaphor of a propeller—that which propels. "Here, then, we have the propeller which is responsible first of all for economic and, in consequence of this, for any other social change, a propeller the action of which does not itself require any impetus external to it."[26] Like the God of old, it is a "prime mover." It is also important to note that the same energy is operating throughout all human history, that one explanation illuminates the transition from any previous stage to the next.

It is an explanation that, we may assume, Tocqueville, for one, would never have found acceptable, or he would never have called what is propelling us "God." And no one, not even the most brilliant Marxist, has been able to tell us convincingly why the movement from the windmill to the steam engine should bring us equality and democracy. Some people have hinted at the fact—it is not a developed theory—that there is an energy within our nature that is capable of driving us forward in an evolutionary direction. Kant, for one. "For the Revolution had proven indisputably," writes Ferenc Fehér of Kant, "that there is something in our phenomenal nature which rebels against despotism and shows affinity with freedom."[27] And he goes on to point out that Kant specifically used the phrase " '*the drive of freedom*,' " in his *Anthropologie* (*Werke*, 12:604).[28]

Kant's last published work, "The Contest of Facilities," (1798, 182) is translated by Steven B. Smith and goes even further toward the declaration that something in human nature itself is responsible for moral progress:

> The revolution which we have seen taking place in our own times in a nation of gifted people may succeed, or it may fail. It may be so filled with misery and atrocities that no right-thinking mind would ever decide to make the same experiment again at such a price, even if he could hope to carry it out successfully at the second attempt. But I maintain that this revolution has aroused the hearts and desires of all spectators who are not themselves caught up in it a *sympathy* which borders almost on enthusiasm, although the very utterance of this sympathy was fraught with danger. *It cannot therefore have been caused by anything other than a moral disposition within the human race.*[29]

In Bellah's profound essay on "Religious Evolution," two different, but probably related, global descriptions are given of evolutionary history. True, he is specifically discussing *religious* evolution and not stages in *social* development, but there is obviously an intensely close relationship between these two developmental tracks. For instance, the stages discussed—Primitive, Archaic, Historic, Early Modern, Modern—provide a productive starting point for an evolutionary social theory that takes the concept of progress-through-stages as a first principle. And such is my own intellectual orientation. At the beginning of the essay, Bellah's overall description of evolution is closely related to that of Parsons,[30] which states that increasing differentiation delineates the developmental process. No reference to a moral thrust is indicated: "What I mean by evolution, then, is nothing metaphysical but the simple generalization that more complex forms develop from less complex forms and that the properties and possibilities of more complex forms differ from those of less complex forms."[31]

At the end of the essay, after describing this amazing human odyssey, he clearly announces that he has made us witness to *moral* progress, though he does not use that particular word. I, of course, would argue that that which increases freedom is, without question, moral advance. "The schematic presentation of the stages of religious evolution just concluded is based on the proposition that at each stage the freedom of personality and society has increased relative to the environing conditions. Freedom has increased because at each successive stage the relation of man to the conditions of his existence has been conceived as more complex, more open and more subject to change and development."[32] Human beings have become freer and freer as society has evolved. I would suggest that one crucial "environing condition" that has been the essential restriction on human freedom has been the destructive, aggressive nature of the human psyche: those drives to dominate, degrade, and destroy other human beings. The process of increasing freedom has resulted from the critical capacity to repress, sublimate, and transform those drives. Human beings have freed themselves from the worst aspect of their own nature. Bellah's great contribution has been the insight into, and the elaboration of, the fact that the evolution of religion has been essential to that experience.

I find Bellah's theoretical analysis enormously persuasive. I would add, however, two additions or reservations that have a close connection one to the other. Between the "Primitive" and the "Archaic," which are Bellah's and Parsons's first two stages of human society, I descry a definite, most important, independent stage: the Early State, operating without written language and ruled by tyrannical monarchs. At the time of their first contact with European societies, such Early States were in existence in Polynesia, and both East and West Africa: Hawaii, Tahiti, Tonga, Buganda, Bunyoro, Dahomey, and so forth, and so on. Arguing that it seems impossible that human society should have evolved from Primitive (simple, kinship) societies to Archaic societies, such as ancient Egypt and Mesopotamia, in one (even if gigantic) evolutionary step, I have called that stage in between the Primitive and the Archaic "Complex Society." A previous work, *At the Dawn of Tyranny: The Origins of Individualism, Political Oppression, and the State*, is completely devoted to a description and theoretical elaboration of that stage.

Cognizance of this evolutionary event takes on importance for the discussion here about the relationship between evolutionary advance and moral progress. In no way can the movement from simple kinship societies to complex societies be described as a moral advance. In no way can we observe, in Bellah's terms, an increase of freedom in the society as a whole. True, the kings of such societies, and the small group of aristocrats who held political power, may be described as freer than everyone was under the constraints of kinship societies: thus, the conception of the origins of individualism. But that freedom was achieved only by the social oppression of vast numbers of common people within society, including the, literally, thousands sent to their deaths each year under the banner of ritual human sacrifice. If the political elite enjoyed freedom, it was of the nature described by Thucydides as a central Greek idea: "Freedom, or the rule over others."[33]

Primitive kinship societies have accurately been described as "egalitarian" societies: accurately, if "egalitarian" means specifically adult males.* There were no hierarchical classes, no degraded groups, no social tyranny. In Complex Society all that changed. The social world of the small group of the powerful and the mass of the powerless, as we know it, certainly up to Modernity, was born. And thus, the conception of the birth in this stage of political oppression and tyranny.

Certainly, no moral advance: a decrease, rather than an increase, in equality, freedom, and nurturance. And yet, I argue that this movement represents an evolutionary advance and made possible all the future developments of society. Bellah argues in discussion of this present chapter (1998), that what is missing in my evolutionary analysis is the conception of the continuing augmentation of social power—of the power of society—and, therefore as well, the growth of power of those dominant in society. Complex Society resulted in, and from, a quantum leap in social power. Certainly, the Kabaka of Buganda, who ruled a million people with the aid of a sophisticated and elaborate bureaucracy and was

---

*The exact situation of the gender relationships in kinship, tribal, "primitive" societies is one of the most unsettled theoretical problems. Put ten anthropologists/sociologists in a room to discuss the question, and you quickly get twelve opinions. The data seem to run all the way from Hopi society, wherein women enjoyed high status and equality in many areas, to certain South American tribal societies where women were degraded and gang-rape was an instrument of social control of the obstreperous. Elizabeth Marshall Thomas tells me, for instance, that she would describe the now nonexistent society of the Bushman of the Kalahari as a "patriarchal society"—most important social decisions were made by men, although there was definitely no degradation or putting-down of women. With it all, one thing seems certain: all Early States (Complex Societies) were patriarchal, in the usually accepted term: men ruled, with greater or lesser tyranny. A situation that remained essentially true, with some slight variations, through all stages in social evolution, until today, or maybe one should say optimistically, "until yesterday." No matter what negatives one may hold toward Modernity, one cannot ignore the fact that it is only Modernity, of all stages of evolution, since the breakdown and transformation of kinship society, that has set equality between women and men on the moral agenda.

capable of putting 30,000 to 50,000 soldiers in the field—such a monarch exercised a social power never seen or dreamed of in kinship societies. Even the capacity to sacrifice thousands was openly declared, in such societies, to be a praiseworthy manifestation of royal power.

Assuming the correctness of Bellah's critique, what it seems to be doing, in part, is substituting for Engels's greed for more and more goods, a greed for more and more power. It is a most reasonable assertion about the human psyche that such an insatiable drive exists. In the early Modern stage, Hobbes categorically and dogmatically, declared that such was the case, and of primary importance for human history: "So that in the first place, I put a generall inclination of all mankind, a perpetuall and restlesse desire for Power after power, that ceaseth only in Death [*Leviathan*, I, ii]." This "restlesse desire for Power after power" may be looked at from the viewpoint of society (social power) or of the psyche (psychological power, including most particularly, omnipotence). From the point of view of society, it seems rational to pursue more and more power: it allows one to conquer or dominate one's neighbors instead of suffering their domination. In a world of predators and pirates, only power can bring social tranquillity.

From the psychological viewpoint, however, the pursuit of power is one of the most contradictory and paradoxical of human activities. Even when manifest in sociological circumstances, where we are supposed to expect rationality, we many times get its opposite. Two of the societies in history most "restlesse" in their pursuit—ancient Athens and Nazi Germany—concluded their lust for power with acts of clear self-destruction. Hitler went to Russia (like Napoleon before him); Athens went to Syracuse. We cannot understand the pursuit of social power as a rational, expected exercised without understanding the tremendous psychic conflicts that surround this ambition.

To return to the development from kinship to Early State societies, by what standard do I designate it an "evolutionary advance?" We are back to the questions of whether there has been such a thing as the "engine of history"—and if so, what it might be?

THE PSYCHE AS ENGINE

If the evolutionary movement from kinship to complex societies indicates that the moral thrust—Kant's "drive of freedom"—cannot be *the* engine of history, it does not necessarily follow that it cannot be *an* engine. Possibly, each evolutionary stage, each task of transition to the next stage has its own unique configuration, requiring its own individual source of energy. If so, the moral drive could be of great importance in the progress of certain stages (Pagan to Christian society; early Modernity to Modernity), and of much less, or no, importance in other circumstances.

There is another possibility, one that is implicit in the work of Parsons and Bellah and one that I find most convincing: At some point in social evolution, the moral drive "kicks in," and from that time forward, it is of great—even primary—importance. Parsons's conception of ancient Israel and ancient Greece as "seed-bed societies"[34] leads us in that direction. Those societies represent a springboard from which all future history, at least in the West, develops. And the importance of moral transformation is crucial to seeing those societies in this light. By "moral transformation" I do not mean a mutation in human nature, but a metamorphosis into human beings more committed to freedom, equality, and nurturing than those living in the previous stage of society. Just as Hegel asserted that the French Revolution signified that, in the future, one could not talk of freedom without talking of a universal principle of freedom, so Parsons's conception seems to me to be saying that, after Israel and Greece, no social evolution that was truly evolutionary and not just some kind of change lacking meaning—no evolution could take place without an extension of freedom and equality.

It may be argued that the evolution from Complex to Archaic societies subsumed a moral dimension: that the Pharaoh of Egypt was a much more caring and nurturing monarch that the *buveur de sange* Kabaka of Buganda. With limited knowledge, I remain agnostic on this question. There seems no question, however, that after Israel and Greece, the "drive of freedom" becomes essential to social development. From Paganism to Early Christianity; from Early Christianity to Late Medieval Society (eleventh to fifteenth centuries); from Late Medieval to early Modern; and from early Modern to Modernity—all these developments can be read as revealing a greater and greater commitment to the morality of equality and freedom. All of which does not necessarily indicate that such a drive was the *only* thing propelling society forward, but merely that it was essential to that movement.

When the moral drive becomes an essential part of the energy propelling society from one particular stage to another, then the failure to accomplish that next task of morality announces the failure to attain the subsequent developmental stage. The struggle for Modernity is the struggle to establish a stable democratic society; that is, a substantial increase in freedom and equality. If that fails, some kind of perversion of Modernity, more or less catastrophic, will be instituted. Dictatorship, religious fundamentalism, terror. The Revolutionary Great Terror was the consequence of the denial of the democratic imperative. What all ideological terrorists are doing is forcibly *refusing* to institute a moral advance. That refusal ultimately contributes to the horrendous destruction of human life. With every guillotining they are, simultaneously, attempting to annihilate the moral imperative, in spite of the fact that their rhetoric announces that *they* are the representatives of the morality of the future. It is one of the most vicious psychological traps ever invented.

The conception that the moral drive "kicks in" at a certain point in evolutionary history leads me to look at another developmental history where the same kind of remarkable entry takes place: that of the human psyche from infancy to adulthood. And to make the most speculative inference of all. There is a remarkable agreement among those psychologists who have addressed the question of the psychology of the moral sense (Piaget, Kohlberg, Freud, among the foremost),[35] which is that there is a developmental course from childhood on, which needs to be described and analyzed. No five-year-old has the moral sense of a fifteen-year-old adolescent. No adolescent the moral sense of a mature adult. The criticism of Bellah et al., in *Habits of the Heart*, of radical individualism in our present culture may be read as an assertion that, instead of the morally responsible individualism that we would look for in a mature adult *Weltanschaaung*, we are getting instead a narcissistic, *adolescent* individualism, full of intense energy but locked in a solipsistic psyche.

These three theorists of morality elaborate not only a conception of moral evolution, but also one that proceeds in *stages*. Jürgen Habermas has used Kohlberg's theory of moral stages (preconventional, conventional, and postconventional) to extrapolate onto a thesis of social evolution, with societies corresponding to these specific psychological states.[36] Piaget has asserted that even stages in cognitive development can find correspondence at different stages of social development. "Piaget," Flavell writes, "will take a concept from a given scientific field—for example, the concept of *force* in physics—and analyze how its scientific meaning has changed from Greek or pre-Greek times to the present. He then attempts to show crucial parallels between historical and ontogenetic evolution of this concept; for example, in both evolutions there is a progressive shedding of egocentric adherences, rooted in personal experience of bodily effort, in favor of an objective conception which is independent of self. . . . the general strategy is to apply the constructs of his developmental theory (progressive equilibration, egocentrism, decentration, and reversibility) to the historical process, the latter construed as an evolution *across* a number of adult minds at least partially analyzable in the same terms as the evolution *within* a simple, immature one. There is a strong 'Ontogeny recapitulates history' strain in Piaget's thinking."[37] This same extrapolation—in both directions—from psychic to social evolution, and from social to psychic evolution, can be made for the development of the moral faculty, as well as for the cognitive.

Freud left us no complex theory of moral evolution, but he did assert, in the theory of the superego as the moral organ in the psyche, that the full possibility of a rigorous morality does not appear until the child is four or five years old. It is only then that the superego arrives on the scene. He was definitely postulating a pre-superego and a post-superego stage and, therefore, a stage antecedent to an internalized moral possibility and one following the advent of this capacity.[38]

Turning, once again, to Bellah's essay on "Religious Evolution," we may note a remarkable correspondence with Freud's pre- and post-superego narrative. Though it certainly is not accurate to describe Primitive and Archaic religions as nonmoral or premoral, just as it is not correct to assert that the four-year-old child has absolutely no moral sense, still it seems that something revolutionary happens in the movement from Archaic to Historic religion: a quantum leap in the breadth and depth of the moral dimension. When reading about Historic religion, we feel at home, as if we are reading our own history. For Primitive and Archaic religions, on the contrary, it takes a complex act of imagination to enter the thought and emotional processes of people in these stages. It seems worth consideration that the evolution from Archaic to Historic religion is homologous with the psychic development from a pre- to a post-superego stage.

"The criterion that distinguishes the historic religions from the archaic," Bellah writes, "is that historic religions are all in some sense transcendental. . . . an entirely different realm of universal reality, having for religious man the highest value, is proclaimed. . . . [T]he religious goal of salvation is for the first time the central religious preoccupation."[39] Though he does not emphasize the fact, it seems that Bellah is pointing in the direction of asserting that, at this stage, *guilt* and *sin* and *redemption* from the same become essential attributes of religious life. In Freudian terms, the pre-superego child is disciplined essentially by shame; after the superego has internalized the values of the parents, guilt at transgressing any of those values becomes central to the moral (and immoral) life. Bellah describes this revolutionary development: "Primitive man can only accept the world in its manifold givenness. Archaic man can through sacrifice fulfill his religious obligations and attain peace with the gods. But the historic religions promise man for the first time that he can understand the fundamental structure of reality and through salvation participate actively in it."[40]

The promise is that human beings can become *adult* and take responsibility for their own lives: cease to be children wholly dependent on superior powers. And for Freud, the superego, born after the outrageous adult fantasies of the Oedipus complex (kill the father/mother; sexually conquer the mother/father) is the first intimation of adult life. And we now know that adolescents, conflictedly embarking on a grown-up life, psychologically return to the intensity of oedipal feelings, after the quiescence of the latency period. A mature superego provides the gateway to an adult moral existence.

This particular homologous evolutionary track of society and the psyche, though powerful in its implications, is only one among many that I observe. Early systems of sacred symbols and actions are predominantly magical and become less and less magical as they develop. Society and culture evolve in the direction of Weber's "legal-rational," gradually liberating themselves from paleological ways of thought, because the development of the ego and the cognitive function of the psyche lie precisely in that direction. The animistic, magical, participatory, and paleological modes of cognition that are typical of early forms of human society are exhibited by *all* children in our society.[41] What was a cognitive stage in the development of culture becomes, in our society, only a stage of psychic development through which all children go. If the development of the forms of social cohesion within society has been from kinship forms to nonkinship forms,[42] this cannot be unrelated to the fact that the human psyche in its early stages cannot imagine a world that is not family-centered. Only with the development of the ego and its drives for separation and individuation does a nonkinship form of society become possible and, for the ego, desirable.[43] The earliest form of institutionalized aggression—cannibalism—is satisfied in the mouth, because the mouth is the original source of intense sensation, both aggressive and libidinal, for the human psyche. And a last example, E.R. Dodds demonstrates that an early archaic form of civilization develops from "shame culture" to "guilt culture."[44] The parallel psychic fact that shame is an early form of social control of children and that guilt develops only after considerable time must give us a working hypothesis as to why culture takes the same developmental direction.

Piling more examples on these examples will not convince anyone who finds this mode of thought alien. It would, therefore, seem appropriate here to state my own view of social evolution categorically. *The development of the psyche is the paradigm for the evolution of culture and society.* The psyche, in its development from infancy to a fully mature adulthood, follows a particular track. Society, in its evolution from simple kinship societies to fully mature Modern society (and, most hopefully in the future, even beyond this), follows a developmental track that is parallel to the psychic and, in a very complex way, dictated by that psychic path. Put succinctly, if there were no stage in psychic development when the desire and the need for freedom and equality became imperative, there would be no Enlightenment, no liberalism, no democratic society, no Modernity. Returning to Tocqueville's great metaphorical statement, what has been pushing us for several centuries is the drive of the human psyche to fulfill its own destiny.

People have objected to this psychological evolutionary view by criticizing it for something it does not say. Nothing in this theoretical stance asserts that people in kinship societies are infants, or that those in Archaic societies are children, or that adults exist only in advanced Western societies. It seems needless to say, but there are adults and children in all societies. Piaget's cognitive developmental approach, however, provides a paradigm for moral and reality-perceiving developmental tracks. When he postulates, as given previously, that certain views of the nature of force and motion as expressed by pre-Socratic philosophy correspond exactly to the perceptions of children in Modern society, he is not saying that Thales and Anaximander are children. He is saying, nevertheless, that in regard to certain views of force and motion, their thought is homologous with the spontaneous, uneducated expressions of children in Modern society.

Similarly, for myself, there is an analogous circumstance with the question of magical practices within the structure of religious systems of symbols and actions. Piaget elaborates on the fact that children spontaneously—without being taught—use magical practices to act on the world. When his daughter was sixteen months old, he had taught her to turn a matchbox over, insert her finger, and draw out a chain contained within. When Piaget closed the opening of the matchbox, so that it was too small to allow the chain to be pulled out, the child tried the usual procedure unsuccessfully and then: "looks at the slit with great attention, then several times in succession, she opens and shuts her mouth, at first slightly, then wider and wider!"[45] A perfect example of what Frazer calls "imitative magic,"[46] exactly similar to the action when people in early religious systems sprinkled water on the fields in order to make the rain come.

In the normal course of things in Modern society, as people grow up, as the psyche develops, they believe less and less in magical efficacy and more and more in reality-tested, or common sense, means. It is a continuing struggle and no one ever completely gives up resort to magic. Even our political life is plagued by delusions of omnipotence. Despite all of that, the rational ideal remains: in almost all cases, millions of dollars are made by hard work, not by fantasizing.

When we observe the history of religious evolution, we discover a remarkably analogous situation. The earliest systems of religious symbols and action are the ones most suffused with a magical *Weltanschauung*. It is not inaccurate, I feel, to read Bellah's description of religious evolution from stage to stage as one involving a significant abandonment of magical belief and practice as one stage replaces the previous one. Not only does each stage represent an increase in freedom in "the relation of man to the conditions of his existence,"[47] but each stage creates a system of religious symbols and action *less magical* than the one preceding. Why should this have been so? In my view, because this is exactly the developmental track the psyche will embark upon when freed to do so. Essentially, that is what is meant by the development of the psyche as paradigm for culture and society.

The phrase "when freed to do so" is theoretically of enormous importance. What is being elaborated here is not a theory of psychological reductionism, wherein sociology—the existence of society—is of no importance. It is crucially important to differentiate between the *track* and the *schedule*, by which the train does—or does not—go. The track is dictated by the stages in psychic development. The schedule—that is, the timing and intensity of movement, or the actual fact of no movement—is a far more complicated phenomenon, involving all the complexity of interaction between psychic needs and sociological values and institutions. I have elaborated, for instance, in the book on the origins of the State, that whenever a kinship society begins the process of social and political evolution it inevitably evolves into an early State under an authoritarian monarch, sharing certain important cultural values with other societies in a similar stage of development.[48] Data to support this contention were drawn from geographically widely separated societies that could not have influenced each other: ancient Hawaii and ancient Buganda in Africa, as examples. The evolutionary track, then, goes from Kinship Society to Early States to Complex Society. And that track allows for only slight variation.

The schedule, however, turns out to be a very different story. Right next door to complex kingdoms like Buganda existed many societies still in a traditional kinship stage, with no governors and no monarch. Traditional Africa, in the nineteenth century, presented the picture of hundreds of societies in the kinship, tribal stage, as well as a handful of societies that were still hunters and gatherers, along with the several dozen kingdoms (early states and Complex Societies with no written language). Why the Buganda had undertaken the elaborate journey from kinship to monarchical society, and the Nuer and Dinka remained content with a kinship society—that is a very different question than the one that asks what track the Dinka and Nuer would follow if they began the process of evolving out of tribal society. To use, once again, the very nonpoetic metaphor: the Buganda kinship society, before it began the evolutionary journey to statehood, and the Nuer faced the same possible track. The Nuer, however, never left the station.

I could discover no answer to this latter question. In part, because there seemed to be no data to indicate what would begin such a social evolution. But, also, in part because the schedule is a much more difficult thing to comprehend than the track. Sociology is a much more complex theoretical exercise than is psychology. The developmental path of the psyche is more readily understood than the answers to the great historical-sociological questions such as: Why, coming out of the same late-Medieval matrix, England succeeded in creating a stable democratic society—after two revolutions—and began the development of industrial capitalism, and France lagged so far behind in this evolutionary development to the Modern stage?

The movement from early Modernity to full Modernity inevitably involves a track that includes everything we subsume under the rubrics "Enlightenment" and "liberalism." That's a necessity of the track. But to understand the schedule, we have to comprehend why England and France and Spain and Germany all encountered Enlightenment and liberalism in radically different ways. A far more complex problem. Modernity was the telos of development for all four societies. History dictated four very different journeys to this end.

If Enlightenment, liberalism, democracy—and Modernity—are integral parts of the telos of psychic development, the logical question at this point obviously is: Why did it take so long? Just as I have previously asked, half ironically, if God has been pushing us for several centuries toward equality, where was He for the first 500,000 years of human existence, just so it is legitimate and important to inquire: If the drive toward Enlightenment and democracy is an imperative of the human psyche, where was it for the first 500,000 years of human existence?

What is needed to make this theory of social evolution more complete is a theory of *repression*. Human drives, inclinations, needs, desires can be repressed, both within the psyche and within society. In my work on the origins of the State, I attempted to establish that the psychic energy behind the movement to the stage of Early States was the universal human drives toward separation, individuation, and autonomy—that these human inclinations are repressed in kinship (primitive) societies, and that this repression is what keeps these societies in the kinship stage and prevents them evolving into Early States. Only when this repression of individualism was lifted was an evolutionary movement possible.

Every human society has a unique and particular evolutionary potential. Only by repressing that particular potential can the society stay in its current stage. This repressive situation can last for thousands and thousands of years. Nothing in the nature of any particular kinship society says that it must evolve into an Early State. When such a society, for whatever reason, lifts that repression of the drives toward individuation and takes the next step in social evolution, it does not have several options as to what kind of society it will become, even though it did previously have the option of not entering the evolutionary path.

Another way of putting this is that every society has an evolutionary agenda, which it may repress or embark upon. That agenda is determined by the distinct evolutionary stage the society finds itself in. And, naturally, not every evolutionary or moral advance is on the agenda of even very complex societies. The end of slavery, for instance, was not on the moral agenda of ancient Greek societies, even though they brought us the first stable democratic societies ever known. Two of the greatest moral geniuses of all time, Plato and Aristotle, expressed no reservations or ambivalence about slavery. The amount of ambivalence about the institution expressed by others in society was insignificant. When that ancient society (Greece plus Rome) took an evolutionary step into Early Christianity, the end of slavery was in no way considered. In the European West, however, in the eighteenth and nineteenth centuries, the demise of slavery became an essential element in the moral evolutionary agenda. Society could not truly enter the Modern world without putting an end to that institution.

It may be argued that, even though totally unexpressed, there was something deep within the psyches of Plato and Aristotle that knew that slavery was wrong: that there had to be. Because of the stage of society in which they lived, however, this particular moral insight into freedom and equality was so deeply and successfully repressed that it found no expression. The human capacity for repression is formidable. The history of social evolution is the history of the war between the drives toward development and the tremendous power of repression.

Once an evolutionary and moral advance, such as the end of slavery or the institution of democratic society, is permanently established on the social agenda, it may only be resisted, only be denied, only be repressed by means of tremendous force. The force of resistance to moral advance may unleash intensities of violence never seen before. To understand why this should be so, it is necessary to distinguish between *normal* and *critical* repression. In ancient Greek society the human impulse toward equality, which could declare that it was immoral for one human being to own another, was under normal repression. It was buried so deep within the psyche, it had so little possibility of actuality, that it had absolutely no social significance. When, however, as a result of social evolution, the end of slavery becomes a critical item on the social agenda, as in the eighteenth and nineteenth centuries, everything changes. Even the slave owners begin to exhibit an ambivalence about the legitimacy of the institution. In the first half of the nineteenth century, in the American South, a tremendous ambivalence— conscious, preconscious, and unconscious—about slavery was in evidence.[49]

In such circumstances, normal repression can no longer hold the situation and prevent the moral advance. Critical repression becomes necessary for that. Society becomes grievously bifurcated: on the one hand, those pushing into the moral future; on the other, those resisting that advance, and even finding it necessary to repress the impulse toward equality within themselves. These latter have two enemies: the external abolitionist and the internal one that knows that the abolitionist is right. Fighting on two fronts requires total mobilization: a quantum leap in psychic aggression is unleashed; people do things such people never did before; and we see a new form of power that displays "features unknown to our fathers."[50]

That is the brilliance of Tocqueville's prediction for the future. The days of Henry IV or Louis XIV are over. The normal repression of liberty and freedom necessary to maintain a nontyrannical authoritarian monarch will no longer hold society stable. It is not just a question for the monarch of staying put but of resisting a social advance. Once democracy comes to dominate the political agenda, there will be only two possibilities left. Either it will triumph, or it will be repressed by a previously unseen power.[51] Critical repression, as opposed to normal repression, will bring social catastrophe. Fascism and ideological terror of the left become the great repressors of the drive toward democracy and the greatest slaughterers of people the world has ever seen.

And what may happen when a genius of a political leader is so capable of psychic splitting that he incorporates both aspects of this intense ambivalence; the complete representative of the moral future, and the total suppressor of the new freedom—simultaneously? Terror is what happens.

The Manichaean nature of our psyche makes the course of human and social evolution so complex, so difficult to describe, almost impossible to believe in. We start our journey in this world living in small kinship groups, eating our enemies or else decorating our huts with their heads, infanticiding our children, conducting limited but still lethal warfare on a yearly basis, severely repressing the impulses toward individuation and autonomy. We end up, most recently, in the world of Jefferson, Condorcet, and Tom Paine, with people ready to die in order to institute the Rights of Man and democratic citizenship. And then comes the possibilities and realities of psychic and social regression that are, in some ways, worse than all the cannibalism of our ancestors. Sometimes it seems easiest to comprehend all this by the impossible assertion that we are two species, not one. Or possibly, one species with two natures.

Two opposite powerful drives rule our lives. Aggression: the impulse to dominate, degrade, and destroy other people. And divine Eros that extends the boundaries of community and love ever and ever wider. The greatest weapon Eros possesses against the dominion of aggression is the powerful potential for sublimation. Cannibalism gives way to head-hunting; cannibalism and head-hunting are sublimated into human sacrifice; human sacrifice yields to animal sacrifice; animal sacrifice is abandoned for prayer. Every movement of human society that is truly evolutionary, that proceeds from one distinct stage to another, involves a fundamental sublimation of a previous form of the acting-out of aggression. One of the greatest gifts of capitalism, Joseph Schumpeter has said, is that it is the first form of society where a man can prove he is a man without killing someone.[52] Under capitalism, however, we continue killing people—needlessly. This does not signify, as some like to argue, that the whole process has been meaningless. It indicates only that we have, in no way, come to the end of sublimation. Modernity, with all its faults, is a moral miracle. It may even make further miraculous transformations possible. Our present moral task is to fulfill the promise of Modernity by surpassing it.

24

THE POLITICS OF THE IMPOSSIBLE

Skipping a Developmental Stage

Ideological terrorism is the great black gift of Modernity. Concomitant with the imperative to create a *nouvel homme* in one generation is the fantastical idea that it is possible to skip over a stage in social evolution: that one can go from "feudalism" to "socialism" without bothering with bourgeois capitalism; that it is possible to advance from a morally compromised *ancien régime* to a Republic of Virtue in ten years. One of the important uses to which a theory of social evolution can be put is to reveal what the authentic stages of development are and, therefore, to illuminate the doomed-to-fail attempts to break the iron-bound trajectory of the evolution of society.

Marx, one of our first great evolutionary theorists, understood full well the boundaries that circumscribe freedom: "'Men make their own history, but not of their own free will; not under circumstances they themselves have chosen but under the given and inherited circumstances with which they are directly confronted. The tradition of dead generations weighs like a nightmare on the minds of the living.'"[1] The stages of social evolution are dictated by something other than people's utopian wish fulfillments. And there is no skipping a stage, no matter how powerful the wish to do so may be, no matter how morally compromised and inadequate the next legitimate stage may seem to be, when held up to the highest moral standard. This severe limitation to our freedom to choose is not welcome news, but the failure to accept it by people who are politically empowered can only bring catastrophe. The attempt to go from A to C, without experiencing B, will never result in C. The result can only be some kind of unstable perverted form of ABC. The great theoretical irony is that the notion, and the attempt to put into practice such conception, that a stage in evolution could be bypassed is itself the result of social evolution. Only with the arrival of the possibility of Modernity did people begin to believe, or act upon, the idea that a Republic of Virtue could be created by a far-less-than-virtuous people.

There were, surely, antecedents in the Early Modern period to the utopian catastrophe of the French Terror. Savonarola in Florence, for instance. Two things about the French Terror, however: first, it was truly the role model, whether consciously stated or not, for all the left-wing ideological terrorisms of the twentieth century. And second, Savonarola's short-lived reign of terror operated *primarly* in the areas of religion and culture. The French Terror was *overwhelmingly* a political phenomenon. It truly invented, to use Tocqueville's powerful image, the politics of the impossible:

> *The Convention which did so much harm to contemporaries by its furty, has done everlasting harm by its example. It created the politics of the impossible, turned madness into a theory, and blind audacity into a cult.*[2]

Robespierre's terror lasted for only about a year. The Bolshevik tragic experiment, with decreasing terror, went on for seventy years. The terrifying ambiguity in Tocqueville's observation is that the politics of the impossible, though impossible, is still possible. And once that possible-impossibility was powerful enough to infect the political life of Modern nation-states with huge populations, the victims were to be numbered in the tens of millions.

As soon as this great modern moral parardox entered the world—that our vision of a just society extends much further than society is willing to go at that particular point of time—certain characteristic ways of responding to this paradoxical situation become formalized and are repeated over and over again in different societal circumstances. Dostoevsky wrote *Crime and Punishment* more than fifty years before Lenin's coup d'etat against the Kerenski government. His Porfiry Petrovich enlightens us:

> I am not wrong. I'll show you their pamphlets. Everything with them is "the influence of environment," it follows that, if society is normally organized, all crime will cease at once, since there will be nothing to protest against and all men

will become righteous in one instant. Human nature is not taken into account, it is excluded, it's not supposed to exist! They don't recognize that humanity, developing by a historical living process, will become at last a normal society, but they believe that a social system that has come out of some mathematical brain is going to organise all humanity at once and make it just and sinless in an instant, quicker than any living process! That's why they instinctively dislike history, "nothing but ugliness and stupidity in it," and they explain it all as stupidity! That's why they so dislike the *living* process of life; they don't want a living soul! The living soul demands life, the soul won't obey the rules of mechanics, the soul is an object of suspicion, the soul is retrograde! But what they want though it smells of death and can be made of indian rubber, at least is not alive, has not will, is servile and won't revolt! And it comes in the end to their reducing everything to the building of walls and the planning of rooms and passages in a phalanstery! The phalanstery is ready, indeed, but your human nature is not ready for the phalanstery—it wants life, it hasn't completed its vital process, it's too soon for the graveyard! You can't skip over human nature by logic.[3]

We may be reminded that Quinet asserted that Robespierre had attempted to put philosophy in the place of religion.[4] What Porfidy Petrovitch understands is that "they" are not just talking—"they" want political power. "They" are not just mistaken—"they" are as dangerous human animals as ever existed.

It is the ice-cold abstraction that is most terrifying. In contrast to Marx, who exhibited a passion in everything he wrote, these soul-murderers hide behind an impenetrable wall of frigid, ultimate morality. We have learned to recognize the symptoms: a rhetoric replete with love for humanity in the abstract; a tactical stance that allows for any means (dishonesty, judicial murder, betrayal) to the supposed moral end. Quinet's unique and penetrating analysis of the revolutionary conclusion in terror is that a fragile, desiccated, barren *"philosophie"* can never replace the life-enhancing aspects of religious beliefs: can never engender the consent of the governed. *Philosophie*, nevertheless, is easily committed to skipping an evolutionary stage, to forcing a stage of human society that cannot be supported. The logical social development, in his view, runs: Catholicism→Reformation Modern liberty. France had refused the second stage. The terrorists, intent on the third stage without having traveserved the second, were doomed to fail. "The French," Furet tells us of Quinet, "who had refused the Reformation of the sixteenth century, and who had uprooted it by the persecution of the seventeenth, lacked the system of beliefs across which modern liberty is conceivable. They have had at their disposition only a system of ideas, formed by 'philosophy.'"[5]

If the creators of the Terror had truly studied their Rousseau, they might have paused in their attempts to create a new man and a new society overnight. Jean-Jacques was keenly aware—at least as far as Russia was concerned—of the impossibility of ignoring the logic of development. He wrote what should have been a clear warning to the radical Jacobins; they listened with as much care as Stalin listened to the clang of the guillotine. Great words of caution from Rousseau: "The Russians will never be truly civilized, because the attempt to civilize them was made prematurely. Peter the Great had a genius for imitation; he did not have true genius, which is creative and makes everything from nothing. He did some good things, but most of his efforts were misguided. He saw that his subjects were barbarous, but he did not see that they were not ripe for civilization; he tried to civilize them when they should only have been trained. He first tried to turn them into Germans or Englishmen when he should have begun by turning them into Russians. By persuading them that they were something they were not, he prevented them from ever becoming what they could have been."[6] The modernist Peter, at the dawn of Modernity, already infected with Tocqueville's *virus*. Authoritarian forcing—progress dictated from above—cannot work in the Modern world.

THE FRENCH TERROR AS A RESULTANT OF THE ATTEMPT TO PASS OVER A STAGE OF EVOLUTION

Several writers have observed the social discontinuity inherent in the radical Jacobin program. The institition of the kind of radically virtuous democracy that Jacobin rhetoric advocated as the *present* task of the Revolution was premature: a utopian fantasy. Not surprisingly, Tocqueville: "The democratic revolution [in France] has taken place in the body of society without those changes in laws, ideas, customs, and mores which are needed to make the revolution profitable. Hence we have our democracy without those elements which might have mitigated its vices and brought out its natural good points."[7] Albert Soboul, who is much more sympathetic to, and much more forgiving of, Robespierre than this writer, nevertheless, does indicate the impossibility of achieving what the present state of society will not allow. "We observe here how profound an antagonism may exist between the aspirations of a social group or an individual and the objective state of the historic necessities. Neither Robespierre nor Saint-Just had the least suspicion that their action might depend on something other than their will and energy. They had faith in the beneficent influence of laws and institutions; but the most rigorous laws are incapable of turning aside the course of history. Robespierre's case measures the inability of a man, however great, to pass beyond the frontiers of his epoch."[8]

To understand terror, however, that cannot be the end of the discussion. The deeper question is: Why, when it becomes apparent to even mediocre intellects that the Republic of Virtue is a fantasy, do some brilliant intelligences blindly persist in forcing its coming, no matter what it takes; that is, no matter how many deaths? Can we just accept, at face value, the notion that Robespierre just didn't have "the least suspicion" that his actions "might depend on something other than" his will and energy? How could such a brilliant politician and psychologist be in such a state of denial about an obvious truth? It was not, as Soboul implies, a failure of intellect—it was a failure of moral sanity. There were other ways to go, at that point, than into a catastrophic terror.

In the early months of 1973, at a small private gathering, Senator Stuart Symington of Missouri told a group of us, in regard to his position on the war in Vietnam: "I wanted to win that war as much as anyone, but when I realized what we had to do to win that war [among other things, indiscriminately setting fire to women and children]—I couldn't do that!" The question that Soboul leaves unanswered is: Why didn't Robespierre, at some point, say that as much as he longed for the Republic of Virtue, when it came to what seemed to be required to achieve it, he just couldn't do that? Part of the answer is that he knew, deep in his heart, that the Republic was a fantasy, unobtainable. Another part of the answer is that he had other needs as well as that moral one, and terror had become a necessity for him. The politics of the impossible, if pursued with dog-like tenacity, must always end in terror.

One who saw with crystal clarity the truth of this last assertion was Germaine de Staël: " 'Everything that is done in accord with opinion is protected by it, but the moment one precedes or combats opinion it becomes necessary to resort to despotism. France in 1789 wanted a temperate monarchy. No terror was needed to establish one. The Republic was established fifty years before minds were ready for it. Recourse to Terror was the way it was done.' "[9] It would also be appropriate, at this point, to make reference again to Quinet's argument about the reasons for the failure of the Revolution. Unlike England, France attempted to make a political revolution without having previously made a religious revolution (i.e., Protestantism).[10] The attempt to skip a stage in evolution, in his view, was doomed to fail.

MARX: THE REVOLUTION OF THE POSSIBLE?

Even the cool, theoretical head of Marx could be turned by the seductive power of an ongoing proletariat uprising. After agreeing with Engels about the political absurdity of the French Terror; after arguing passionately, both before and after 1848, that those revolutions could only be of a bourgeois nature; after asserting, six months before the uprising of the Paris Commune that the task of French workingmen was to " 'calmly and resolutely improve the opportunities of Republican liberty, for the work of their own class organization,' "[11]—after all this commitment to a theory of social evolution that denied the possibility of skipping a stage, he nevertheless exalted the defeated Commune as an heroic experience that was " 'of world-historical significance.' "[12] When it became a question of a political uprising, engineered, in part, by his own followers, there was no reluctance to embrace the politics of the impossible.

The theory, as stated over the years, was ironbound. From an article in the year before the 1848 revolutions:

> If therefore the proletariat overthrows the political rule of the bourgeoisie, its victory will only be temporary, "only an element in service of the *bourgeois revolution itself*," as in the year 1794, as long as in the course of history, in its "movement," the material conditions have not yet been created which make necessary the abolution of the bourgeois mode of production and therefore also the definitive overthrow of the political rule of the bourgeoisie. The terror in France could thus by its mighty hammer-blows only serve to spirit away, as it were, the ruins of feudalism from French soil. The timidly considerate bourgeoisie would not have accomplished this task in decades. The bloody action of the people in this only prepared the way for it.[13]

Throughout his active political life, Marx was constantly challenged by radicals on his left, who, among other things, insisted on the advisability of proletarian uprisings *now:* Blanquists, Bakuninists, and so on. Up until the Commune of 1871, he resisted that siren song with a passionate intensity. At a meeting in London in September 1850, when the Communist League split into a Marx-Engels and Blanquist faction, he anathematized his opponents thusly: "While we tell the workers: 'You have to endure and go through 15, 20, 50 years of civil war in order to change the circumstances, in order to make yourselves fit for power'—instead of that, you say: 'We must come to power immediately, or otherwise we may just as well go to sleep.' In the same way as the word 'People' has been used by the Democrats as a mere phrase, so the word 'Proletariat' is being used now. . . . As far as enthusiasm is concerned, one doesn't need to have much of it in order to belong to a party that is believed to be about to come to power. I have always opposed the ephemeral notions of the proletariat. We devote ourselves to a party which is precisely far from achieving power. Would the proletariat have achieved power [in 1848], then it would have enacted not proletarian, but petty-bourgeois legislation. Our party can achieve power only if and when conditions permit it to realise its *own* views. Louis Blanc serves as the best example of what can be achieved when one attains power prematurely."[14]

And even more pointedly, in September 1870, just five days after the proclamation of the "bourgeois" Republic, he cautioned the French working class:

> The French working class moves, therefore, under circumstances of extreme difficulty. Any attempt at upsetting the new Government at the present crisis, when the enemy is almost knocking at the door of Paris, would be a desperate folly. The French workmen must perform their duties as citizens; but, at the same time, they must not allow themselves to be deluded by the national *souvenirs* of 1792, as the French peasants allowed themselves to be deluded by the national *souvenirs* of the First Empire. They have not to recapitulate the past, but to build up the future. Let them calmly and resolutely improve the opportunities of Republican liberty, for the work of their own class organization. It will give them fresh Herculean powers for the regeneration of France and our common task—the emancipation of labour. Upon their energies and wisdom hinges the fate of the Republic. . . .
>
>   Vive la Republique![15]

Six months later, a working-class uprising and taking of political power in Paris resulted in the proclamation of the Paris Commune. Two months after that, the Commune was destroyed in a war-like military action. The uprising in Paris had been engineered by activists adhering to several factions of the proletarian movement: Bakuninists, Marx-Engels (the International) factions, and others. Never mind that almost twenty-five years of cautionary advice based on an iron-logic evolutionary theory; never mind the 20,000 Communards killed on the barricades of what would have previously been labeled a "premature" uprising—now the revolutionary in Marx asserted its dominion over his soul. He praised " 'the elasticity, the historical initiative, the self-sacrificing spirit of these Parisians. . . . History has no comparable example of such greatness.' "[16]

After the disastrous massacre, he composed an Address of the General Council of the International entitled "The Civil War in France." Here again, no regrets, no second thoughts about untimely revolutionary activity. Nothing but praise and elegy: " 'Working, thinking, fighting, bleeding Paris, almost forgetful, in its incubation of a new society, of the cannibals at its gates—radiant in the enthusiasm of its historic initiative.' "[17] The Address closes with these heroic encomiums: " 'The Paris of the workers in its Commune will be commemorated for ever as the glorious herald of a new society. Its martyrs are enshrined in the great heart of the working class. Its destroyers have been pilloried by history, and not all the prayers of their priests and parsons will be able to set them free.' "[18]

What kind of polity would have resulted had the Commune not been destroyed and had survived? It was not politic to raise such an unsettling question, and Marx never did. He continued to regard it as " 'A new point of departure.' "[19] We may reflect that the chances were good, if not overwhelming, that such an outcome would have produced a second coming of the Great Terror. Bakunin was keenly aware that the Commune had destroyed Marx's theoretical consistency and pushed him toward Bakunin's camp: "Bakunin declared mockingly that although the Commune had overthrown all Marx's ideas, the latter had doffed his hat to it in violation of all logic and been compelled to accept its program and its aims as his own."[20]

The tremendous psychological power in the politics of the impossible had managed to take captive and seduce a formidable evolutionary mind. It was now a simple thing for some of the most significant terrorists of the next century to declare themselves his followers.

LENIN: THE SECOND COMING

It is exciting, and most productive, to review the history of the Russian Marxist revolutionary parties in the forty years before the Bolshevik Revolution, precisely because the question of whether a stage in social evolution could be skipped over, or not, was a fundamental—if not the fundamental—theoretical political question. All agreed that Russia was a "backward country," that it had not yet succeeded in becoming a bourgeois-capitalist society. Was it necessary that this latter stage become a reality before one could consider a proletarian-socialist revolution? What was the true task of a revolutionary Marxist party under such "backward" conditions? Would any attempt at proletarian revolution that occurred before the bourgeois world was established be premature? What was of interest, and determined the grounds of the debate, is that the Marxist theory almost everyone had in mind was definitely of the pre-Commune variety, illustrated by the quotations from Marx given previously. No proletarian revolution could be successful until the bourgeois society had been established and had fulfilled its historic mission. To argue, in Russia, that one could go from "feudalism" to socialism, was felt by everyone to be a denial of received Marxist theory. For the Mensheviks, Lenin's seizure of state power in 1917 was a betrayal of Marxism.[21]

In the latter half of the nineteenth century, certain revolutionary factions in Russia acted on the basis of a theory of Russian exceptionalism. The Russian peasantry had the potential of becoming a unique revolutionary force: unlike the situation in the rest of Europe. This fact, combined with the backwardness of the Russian bourgeoisie, indicated that Russia could avoid the capitalist stage and institute a revolutionary socialist society. The most important political faction acting on such a theoretical basis was that of the *Narodniks*, who were engaged in individual terrorism. At the end of the 1870s, Georgy Plekhanov broke with the *Narodniks*, went into exile, converted to a strict-constructionist Marxism, and founded in Switzerland a Russian Marxist group, "The Liberation of Labor." "Plekhanov and his associates . . . waged unceasing literary war against the *Narodniks*, applying to Russia the Marxist thesis that the revolution could come about only through the development of capitalism and as the achievement of the industrial proletariat."[22] "The Mensheviks were Plekhanov's disciples."[23]

The 1905 revolution, and its violent repression, raised the discussion of revolutionary tactics to an intense degree. From 1905 to 1917, Wolfe outlines the three distinct theoretical stances taken by Russian revolutionaries, all of whom called themselves "Marxist."

The Mensheviks

The Mensheviks adhered to the classic, strict-constructionist Marxist position: "The coming revolution," Wolfe elaborates, "was the bourgeois democratic revolution. It would abolish feudalism, clear the ground for the free growth of capitalism, establish a democratic republic, bring the bourgeoisie to power. Under the republic there would be open political life, freedom to propagate socialist ideas, to organize the working class politically and economically and develop in it the culture, experience, self-consciousness and power necessary to prepare at some future date, a second revolution, a socialist revolution. . . . The proletariat in its present condition in this backward land could not dream of taking power. . . . To be a revolutionary now meant to fight Tsarism, to support the bourgeoisie in its struggle for power, to encourage it and push it and exact from it the promise of a maximum of freedom for the working class."[24] There could be no skipping of a stage of social evolution.

The Permanent Revolution

Parvus and Trotsky were two revolutionaries who never established a faction or a party of their own, allied themselves at various times with one revolutionary faction or another, but were of extreme importance because they were the first to bring a complex theoretical argument that the proletarian revolution could follow almost immediately after the bourgeois-democratic one. Their argument instisted that, as Wolfe elaborates, "the Russian revolution was taking place 'too late' in history to be a bourgeois revolution: the proletariat was already on the scene as an independent force, so that the two revolutions the bourgeois democratic and the proletarian socialist, would tend to be 'combined' or telescoped into one."[25] Again, it was an argument from the view of Russian exceptionalism: the history of Western Europe could not guide Russian experience. Not only was the revolutionary proletariat already on the scene, but the Russian bourgeoisie was a particularly cowardly one. " 'The bourgeoisie,' " Trotsky asserted, " 'will never carry their fight from the banquet hall into the streets, where alone revolutions are fought and won.' "[26]

It was Parvus, in an introduction to a pamphlet by Trotsky, published in 1905 after that revolutionary experience, who first used the expression "permanent revolution" to describe the scenario where the proletariat commences to make the bourgeois revolution, does not then renounce power, but goes on to produce its own proletarian-socialist revolution.[27] Trotsky himself wrote: " 'Once the revolution is victorious, political power necessarily passes into the hands of the class that has played the leading role in the struggle, the working class.' "[28] Classical Marxism notwithstanding, at least in the Russian circumstance, the social stage of bourgeois society could be passed over. The politics of the impossible was, once again, possible.

Lenin

Between 1905 and his seizure of power in 1917, Lenin's published works exhibited a pronounced vacillation between the Menshevik and the Trotskyist positions. "In formulae," Wolfe writes, "Lenin sounded much like the Mensheviks; in spirit he was forever attracted to the Trotskyist pole. With the Mensheviks, Lenin held that the economic level of a country determined whether or not it was ripe for socialist revolution. . . . he asserted categorically that economically, politically, and culturally, Russia was ripe only for a bourgeois-democratic revolution. But with Trotsky and Parvus he held that the bourgeoisie was too weak and cowardly to be trusted to accomplish their own revolution, so that the leading role would fall to the proletariat."[29]

Lenin, after 1905:

> He who seeks to advance towards socialism by any other road, by-passing political democracy, inevitably arrives at conclusions both economically and politically inept and reactionary. . . . We Marxists should know that there is not, and cannot be, any other path to real freedom for the proletariat and the peasantry than the road of bourgeois freedom and bourgeois progress.[30]

And yet, the weak and cowardly Russian bourgeoisie could not be counted on to create a bourgeois-democratic society. There was an enormous temptation for the proletariat to forget Marx, seize power, and institute the future now. Around this particular question, Wolfe asserts, "the usually precise Lenin grows indefinite. His forecast changes from page to page and from article to article, becomes a restless spark leaping up and back between the fixed points of his dogmas and his will. It is no longer a formula but a series of rival hypotheses, competing *perhapses*."[31] Events would resolve the theoretical bind.

The Seizure of Power: The Coup of October 1917

Lenin and his Bolsheviks called it a revolution. In reality, it was only a coup. And a coup, to stay successful, demands terror. Lenin in 1917, before the coup of October: " 'The seizure of power is the point of the uprising. Its political task will be clarified after the seizure.' "[32]

Lenin was out of the country when the "bourgeois" revolution had taken place, and the Tsar overthrown, in February 1917. Lenin arrived by sealed train in April 1917, and immediately gave a speech full of the imperatives of proletarian uprising. The discourse was very poorly received and attacked from all sides. "Steklov, the editor of *Izvestiya* and soon to join the Bolsheviks, added that Lenin's speech consisted of 'abstract constructions' which he would soon abandon when he had acquainted himself with the Russian situation. . . . On the same evening [Lenin] re-read the thesis to a gathering of Bolshevik leaders and once more found himself completely isolated."[33]

The oration, with the title *On the Tasks of the Proletariat in the Present Revolution*, was published in *Pravda*, with this significant passage, indicating Lenin's full acceptance of the Parvus-Trotsky view of permanent revolution:

> The peculiarity of the current moment in Russia consists in the *transition* from the first step of the revolution, which gave power to the bourgeoisie as a result of insufficient consciousness and organisation of the proletariat, *to its second stage*, which should give power into the hands of the proletariat and poorest strata of the peasantry.[34]

In this world of political chaos and personal psychological omnipotence, obviously the consciousness of the proletariat could become fully mature in six or seven months. In the middle of September, Lenin wrote two secret letters to the party Central Committee, insisting that the time was "ripe for the Bolsheviks to seize power."[35] The time was, indeed, ripe for the second great coming of the politics of the impossible, the turning of madness into a theory,[36] the tragic and pathetic attempt to skip a stage in social evolution by means of brute force.

What Parvus-Trotsky—and then Lenin—had done was to create a theoretical trick, in which it appears that there is only one theoretical question, whereas, in reality, there were two distinct questions: What was the true circumstance concerning the timing of the two different revolutions? And second, what were the world-historical possibilities for *stages* of society? Marx had been primarily concerned with the evolution of the *stages of society*. Feudal *society* gives way to capitalist *society*, which is transformed into socialist *society* by revolution. Socialist society was impossible until capitalist society had been instituted, developed, and come to full maturity. No eight-month or two-year period could bring a transition from bourgeois society to socialist society.

Parvus-Trotsky-Lenin stopped talking about *society* and insisted on talking only about *revolution*. The only question, they would have us believe, is whether a socialist revolution could follow almost immediately on the heels of the bourgeois revolution. The question was not raised by them whether one could answer "Yes" to the "permanence of revolution" and still be alarmed about what that would mean for society. They refused to consider, what turned out to be the reality, that this second "revolution" would only be a coup.

The great irony—and the proof of their theoretical hypocrisy—was that they did not cite, as support for their position, the three historical circumstances (all French) where a radical revolution (not necessarily proletarian) followed almost immediately on a bourgeois one.

All three circumstances ended in disaster. 1793. 1848. 1871. The latter two insurrections never succeeded in keeping any political power for more than a few months, were mercilessly crushed, and created a myriad of martyrs but no proletarian society. The one historical event where radicals kept power for more than a year—and throughout the whole country, not just in Paris—was, of course, the Jacobin coup of May–June 1793. Ten months after the "bourgeois revolution" in France that deposed the king and established the Republic, the radical Jacobins, with Robespierre at their head, seized power by eliminating the most important Girondins from the Convention. The first example of permanent revolution had already been given by the Jacobins, for whom, as we have seen, Lenin had only praise. The result, of course, had been the first great example of political ideological terror. If Lenin was reluctant to use the example of the Jacobin coup, it might well have been because he did not want people thinking—and himself, refusing to think—about the possible, or even the inevitable, consequence of skipping a stage in society: radical terror.

The Mensheviks were the Girondins of the Russian revolutionary experience. Their theoretical conception presumed that the evolution of society could not be forced, that capitalism had to come to maturity before a legitimate socialist revolution was conceivable, that the true task of a revolutionary was to push for the next feasible transformation of society. Like the classical Marxist, they understood that only the revolution of the possible made any political or moral sense. And like the Gironde, they paid dearly for their wisdom.

FREEDOM AND THE RECOGNITION OF NECESSITY

It was not enough to overthrow the arch-terrorist (*à bas le tyran!*) or to put an end to the Terror (*vive la liberté!*).* It was also a question of what kind of society

---

*Cries in the Convention, 9 thermidor, An II.

would succeed to the Terror—and to the Revolution. Once the wild-eyed utopi-anism of the Republic of Virtue had been abandoned; once the chimera of *un nouvel homme* had been recognized for what it was; once the contempt for human life of Danton had replaced the impossible idealism of Robespierre—what then was the society of the possible to look like? Balzac, Stendahl, and Dickens have told us.

In the Balzacian bourgeois world—a world of money, status, and hierarchy, one in which, in good part, we still live—two things are missing that radical Jacobinism, with all its potential for catastrophe, had put on the social agenda: true equality for all people, and that pity and compassion that Rousseau had asserted was the rightful basis of morality.[37]

The execution of Robespierre was the signal announcing that radical equality had to go. Revolutionary familiarity was to be replaced by bourgeois distance. "Many clubs revised constitutions to rid them of 'Jacobin principles.' St-Servan added the phase 'eternal hatred of terrorists' to its oath. Gary took 'Montagnard' from the title. Toul changed its membership cards so that the image of the Mountain was replaced by Liberty. *Everywhere, members gradually reassumed Christian names and stopped using the familiar 'tu'.*"[38] Lynn Hunt describes how "fraternity" became a tabooed word:

> Progressively after the fall of Robespierre, "fraternity" dropped out of the revolu-tionary slogans to be replaced by liberty and equality standing alone. Official engravers no longer included fraternity in their repertoire of themes, and royalist engravers represented it in derisory contexts. An engraving of 1797, for example, shows a sans-culotte trampling on the constitution. The word *fraternity* is written on his dagger. Fraternity and fraternization were now cynically limited to the relations with the "sister republics," the satellites and dependents of the conquer-ing French nation. Under the consulate, prefects were expressly forbidden to use the word. This brief history suggests that the word had a political charge that was indissolubly linked with radical revolution.[39]

Liberty and equality (of a kind) were compatible with the coming bourgeois world. Fraternity, we have yet to see, after the passage of two hundred years. It was briefly resurrected—in rhetoric—with the second coming of Jacobinism when the appelation *comrade* became the vogue. That, too, passed away. The politics of the possible can only be accepted with a large element of sorrow.

Is there, then, no place for freedom in this iron logic of evolutionary stages?

Is our only option to remain passive passengers on the locomotive of history: merely consenting to, or dissenting from, the direction and the speed to which, and with which, it is carrying us?

Three considerations may ameliorate against this conclusion. First, all societies within a particular stage of evolution are not identical. All stable Modern societies (democratic, bourgeois, capitalist, nationalist, etc.) are not alike. France in 1910 was not the duplicate of England at the same time, and both differed significantly from America, though all three societies could be designated stable Modern commonwealths and shared the nine basic attributes of Modernity discussed in the first part of this work. These discrepancies within an evolutionary stage are determined by differences in culture: *Weltanschauungen, mentalités,* mores, the spirit of society. And culture is made by people, both consciously and unconsciously. The degree of integrity vs. dishonesty in politics, for instance, can differ profoundly from one Modern society to another. One may renounce the fantasy of a Republic of Virtue without becoming passive on the questions of what kind of nonutopian bourgeois society should succeed to the Terror. One may accept the inevitability of bourgeois society without being unaware that there are a multitude of variations on bourgeois society. The Menshevik program of action, under the Russian revolutionary experience, reflected exactly that consideration. The task of a proletarian revolutionary party, in the particular circumstance, was to work as hard for a bourgeois revolution as possible, in order that the society would be as conducive to the development of proletarian political consciousness as possible. Nothing in the nature of the theory of social evolution indicates that the degree of political oppression or freedom in bourgeois society must be identical in all. Freedom is expressed in the actions that influence *what kind* of Modern society the future brings.

The second consideration is that the conception of evolutionary stages should not preclude—should, in fact, insist upon—the notion that development within a stage is of the essence of history. Flamboyant Gothic is a far different thing from early classic Gothic, though they are both legitimately designated "Gothic." Late (postindustrial) capitalism is a far cry from nineteenth-century capitalism. We have not, however, entered a postcapitalist stage. The last forty years in America have witnessed extraordinary moral advances in several areas of cultural and political values without having burst the boundaries of Modernity. The notion that we live in a postmodern world is the latest manifestation of the triumph of the wish for omnipotence over reality. There have occurred in this country radical, almost revolutionary, changes in values concerning equality be-

tween white people and those of color (civil rights); the capacity of a democratic
society to put an end to a nonrational war declared by political elites (Vietnam);
an almost unbelievable advance in the demand for, and the reality of, gender
equality (the feminist revolution); and a quantum leap in tolerance for sexual
choice (nonmarital heterosexual congress, abortion, homosexual lifestyle).

All of this, however, has occurred within the boundaries of Modern society.
To go beyond Modernity will require facing up to the problems of consumerism,
population, the destruction of the environment, and the fiercely competitive,
non-nurturing nature of our social life. Almost all the moral advance indicated
previously proceeded under the banner of *egalité. Fraternité,* it seems, must still wait
until we advance beyond the frontier of Modernity.

The third consideration, in regard to the question of freedom and necessity,
is the fact that, as society evolves within a stage of development, it may reach a
critical point where the old values and energy are exhausted, and yet the time is
not ripe for a revolutionary transformation of values that would herald a new
stage of social evolution. Europe witnessed this kind of moral uncertainty and
semiparalysis in the period when the Reformation was on the agenda, but its
realization was not yet possible: between the execution of Hus in 1415 and the
triumph of Luther, a little more than a hundred years later.

Such times, when a civilization sets itself a new moral agenda that it refuses
to carry out—when it dances on the cliff edge of ambivalence, not knowing
whether to take the leap for freedom or retreat in panic flight—such times
produce a quantum increase in expectation, anxiety, ambivalence, and cultural
despair. Livy characterizes the period when the virtues of the Roman Republic
were exhausted but the new moral and cultural regime of a responsible emperorship had not yet been established: "With the gradual relaxation of discipline,
morals first gave way, as it were, then sank lower and lower, and finally began
the downward plunge which has brought us to the present time, when we can
endure neither our vices nor their cure."[40]

Some thoughtful people would attribute the present moral malaise that seems
to infect much of our present society to this same kind of circumstance. "Western civilisation," André Malraux wrote in 1949, "has begun to doubt its own
credentials."[41] And E.R. Dodds has attempted to shed light on the "failure of
nerve" in ancient Greek society in the fourth and third centuries B.C., by an
analogous interpretation of the "fear of freedom" in modern society:

> I have purposely been sparing in the use of modern parallels, for I know that such
> parallels mislead quite as often as they illuminate. But as a man cannot escape

from his own shadow, so no generation can pass judgement on the problems of history without reference, conscious or unconscious, to its own problems. And I will not pretend to hide from the reader that in writing these chapters . . . I have had our own situation constantly in mind. . . . We too have experienced a great age of rationalism, marked by scientific advances beyond anything that earlier times had thought possible, and confronting mankind with the prospect of a society more open than any it has ever known. And in the last forty years we have also experienced something else—the unmistakable symptoms of recoil from that prospect. . . . What is the meaning of this recoil? Is it the hesitation before the jump or the beginning of a panic flight? . . . A simple professor of Greek . . . can remind his readers that once before a civilised people rode to this jump—rode to it and refused it. And he can beg them to examine all the circumstances of that refusal.[42]

At such a super-critical time—and one may, legitimately, designate as such Russia in 1917 and France in 1789–1794—if there is no human freedom, the struggle for social and moral advance is lost, even if only temporarily. If true freedom is the recognition of necessity, it does not mean that there are no choices, but merely that the possibilities are limited. We are free—or not—to recognize, and pay homage to, what is necessary. Freedom resides in pushing for the next possible stage of society—in its most humane conceivable form. There are those, of course, feeling trapped within this super-critical time, who refuse to accept the limits of human nature and human history and insist that society skip over the necessary next stage. We know, too well, where that endeavor leads.

FREEDOM. NECESSITY. OMNIPOTENCE.

Modernity has been, and still is to a great degree, the realm of necessity. What kind of Modernity is indicative of the realm of freedom. There are all kinds of Modernity and modernists. Antimodernity modernists; revolutionary modernists; perverse modernities, including ideological terror; severely compromised modernities, sleazy, egotistical, rapacious modernities; great democracies with powerful economies, where too many people still live on the streets, and 20 percent live at or below the poverty line; and, to the contrary, Modern societies that do not permit their citizens such an existence. One's acceptance of the necessity of Modernity does not imply that there is no work to be done.

Acceptance, however, necessitates the giving up of omnipotence. The ideolog-

ical terrorist knows no distinction between necessity and freedom. His commitment to omnipotence has him convinced that anything that can be imagined can
be instituted. Thucydides observed that, in the world of politics, wishes had a
tendency to overpower reality. "Their judgement was based more upon blind
wishing than any sound previsions; for it is a habit of mankind to entrust to
careless hope what they long for, and to use sovereign reason to thrust aside
what they do not fancy."[43] The ideological terrorist reacts as if to give up omnipotence is to remain helpless. As if there is no realm of freedom once the illusion
of all-powerfulness is abandoned. Live free or die! Utopia or nothing!

Recognizing historical necessity, are we obliged, then, to give up all ideals, to
abandon all dreams of freedom? That would be to adopt the terrorist's worldview. There is a realm of legitimate idealization, crucial to any transformation
of the world. For example, only in an ideal sense can it be asserted that all men
are created equal, and yet that ideal has revolutionized the world. The great
brilliance of Martin Luther King's "I Have a Dream" speech is that it begins
with the eloquent utopian rhetoric of perfect equality but brings us quickly to
the task that needs to be, and can be done, now. The dream of the impossible
becomes the politics of the possible. Freedom and necessity are reconciled.

It was Michael Harrington, a person of radical but mature and sophisticated
politics, who gave the succinct answer to Tocqueville's piercing critique of the
calamitous Convention. He claimed that his political position situated him on
the left wing of the possible.[44] In the great struggle between paranoid omnipotence and depressive resignation, there is an enlightened, moral solution available.
The all-consuming tragedy of the radical French Revolution of '92 to '94 is that
it was incapable of finding that way.

The greatest enemy of freedom is not found among the nobles, the *émigrés*,
the traitors, the monopolizers, the *enragés*, the plots and conspiracies, the *indulgents*,
l'étranger. The greatest enemy of freedom is the profound human need of the
psychological defenses of the paranoid position and the resort to omnipotence.
Every human advance in freedom necessitates a further overcoming of the need
for those defenses. That is the true limiting necessity in the great struggle for
freedom. At this point, in the evolutionary advance of civilization, once we have
further overcome our dependence on these defenses, we will be free to move on
to the next moral stage: a society wherein the great benefits of bourgeois individualism do not hinder the creation of a true community. And Robespierre, in his
finest moments of moral sanity, understood that.

NOTES

Notes to Chapter 1

1. Cited in Rudé, *Eighteenth Century*, 138.

2. Nietzsche, *The Will to Power*, 1012. Cited in Mitzman, *The Iron Cage*, 176.

3. See Sagan, "The Politics of the Impossible," passim.

4. Robert Bellah, personal communication.

5. Tocqueville, *The Old Regime*, passim.

6. *King Lear*, Act I, scene I, line 92.

7. Engels, *Family, Private Property, and the State*, 164, "Naked greed has been the moving spirit of civilization from the first day of its existence to the present time; wealth, more wealth and wealth again."

8. Chartier, *Cultural Origins*, passim.

9. Tocqueville, *Democracy in America*, 312–315.

10. Cited in Furet: *Interpreting the French Revolution*, 163, from a letter of May 16, 1858.

11. Engels to Marx, September 4, 1870. Cited in Aveneri, *Marx*, 193.

12. Aristotle, *Politics*, III, Chapter IV, 15.

13. Daniel Bell, "Resolving the Contradictions of Modernity," 72. Italics added.

14. G.V. Taylor: "Types of Capitalism in Eighteenth-Century France" and "Non-Capitalist Wealth and the Origins of the French Revolution," passim.

15. Sewell, *Rhetoric of Bourgeois Revolution*, 39.

16. David Bell, *Lawyers and Citizens*, passim.

17. Aristotle, *Politics*, III, Chapter VII.

Notes to Chapter 2

1. Tocqueville, *Selected Letters*, 294.
2. Stern, *The Politics of Cultural Despair*, passim.
3. Stephens, *Principle Speeches*, Volume II, 259. Speech of August 13, 1793.
4. Tocqueville, *"The European Revolution,"* translator's introduction, 28.
5. Woolf, *Captain's Death Bed*, 91.
6. Hegel, "How Christianity Conquered Paganism." Cited in Avineri: *Hegel's Theory of the Modern State*, 16.
7. Baker, *Inventing the French Revolution*, 188.
8. Marx, Article of December 1848. Cited in Furet, *Marx and the French Revolution*, 47.
9. Woloch, *New Regime*, passim.
10. Mona Ozouf, in HCD, 815.
11. Sydenham, *First French Republic*, 223.
12. Tocqueville, *The European Revolution*, 116.
13. Bronislaw Baczko, in HCD, 663.
14. Tilly, *The Vendée*, 160.
15. Woloch, *New Regime*, 356.
16. Chartier, *Cultural Origins*, 70.
17. Baker, *Condorcet*, 55.
18. Ibid.
19. Keith Michael Baker, in HCD, 207.
20. Palmer, *Democratic Revolution*, Volume I, 488.
21. Ritter, *Hegel and the French Revolution*, 52. Italics in the original.
22. François Furet, in HCD, 1024.
23. Ibid., 1030.
24. Tocqueville, *Old Regime*, 139. Italics added.
25. Van Kley, *French Idea of Freedom*, 1.
26. Mathiez, *French Revolution*, 53.
27. Robespierre, *Textes Choisis*, Editor's Introduction, Volume I, 11.
28. *Dictionnaire Historique*, 175.
29. Tocqueville: *Old Regime*, 272.
30. Ibid.
31. Chaussinand-Nogaret, *French Nobility*, 141–142.
32. Doyle, *Origins*, 156.
33. Tocqueville, *Democracy in America*, xiii.
34. Ritter, *Hegel and the French Revolution*, 51. Italics added.
35. Sagan, *The Honey and the Hemlock*, passim.
36. Palmer, *Democratic Revolution*, Volume I, passim.

37. Mona Ozouf, in HCD, 674.

38. Van Kley, *French Idea of Freedom*, 3.

39. Robespierre, *Textes Choisis*, Volume I, 74. "Décret Sur Le Marc D'Argent."

40. Cited by Bernard Manin, in HCD, 836.

41. Cited in Fehér, *The Frozen Revolution*, 33.

42. Cited in Mona Ozouf, in HCD, 673.

43. Plato, *Laws*, Book V, 743a and Book V, 744e–745a.

44. Cited in Kolchin, *American Slavery*, 76.

45. Rudé, *Robespierre*, 133.

46. Robespierre, *Textes Chosis*, Volume I, 71. "Décret Sur Le Marc D'Argent.

47. Ibid., 67.

48. Robespierre, *Textes Chosis*, Volume I, cited in Editor's Introduction, 27, from "Adresse aux Français," July 1791. Italics in original.

49. Rudé, *Robespierre*, 140.

50. Sagan, *Freud, Women, and Morality*, Chapters III and IV.

51. Lefebvre, *Thermidorians*, 177.

Notes to Chapter 3

1. Van Kley, *French Idea of Freedom*, 1.

2. Berlin, *Crooked Timber*, 132.

3. William H. Sewell, Jr., in Lucas, *Modern Political Culture*, 108.

4. Tocqueville, *Old Regime*, 6.

5. François Furet, in *HCD*, 607.

6. Palmer, *Democratic Revolution*, Volume I, 517.

7. Furet and Richet, *French Revolution*, 258.

8. Thompson, *Robespierre*, 280. Italics added.

9. Van Kley, *French Idea of Freedom*, 2.

10. François Furet, in *HCD*, 107.

11. Ibid., 110.

12. Higonnet, *Class Ideology*, 67.

13. Maza, *Private Lives*, 255.

14. Woloch, *New Regime*, passim.

15. François Furet, in *HCD*, 112.

16. Van Kley, *French Idea of Freedom*, 2.

17. Tocqueville, *Old Regime*, 263.

18. Maza, *Private Lives*, 236.

19. Thompson, *Robespierre*, 80.

20. Furet and Richet, *French Revolution*, 110. Woloch: *New Regime*, 357.

21. Thompson, *Robespierre*, 95.

22. Woloch, *New Regime*, passim.

23. Cobban, *Modern France*, Volume I, 110.

24. Thompson, *Robespierre*, 98.

25. Rudé, *Robespierre*, 164.

26. Stephens, *Principle Speeches*, Volume II, 300.

27. Ibid.

28. Ibid., 304.

29. Thompson, *Robespierre*, 139.

30. Ibid., 299.

31. Rudé, *Robespierre*, 179. Speech of December 25, 1793.

32. Garrett, *Estates General*, 172.

33. Ibid., 201–205.

34. Van Kley, *French Idea of Freedom*, 2.

35. Baker, editor, *Old Regime*, 249.

36. Maza, *Private Lives*, 30.

37. Baker, *Inventing the French Revolution*, Chapter 8 and passim.

38. David Bell, *Lawyers*, 11.

39. Robert Bellah, personal communication.

40. Doyle, *Origins*, 105.

41. Van Kley, *French Idea of Freedom*, 2.

42. Rudé, *Robespierre*, 101.

43. Woloch, *New Regime*, 65.

44. Dict. Hist., 22–24.

45. Ibid.

46. Jordan, *Robespierre*, 52.

47. Dict. Hist., 24.

48. Shanti Marie Singham, in Van Kley, *French Idea of Freedom*, 135.

49. Dict. Hist., 24.

Notes to Chapter 4

1. Baker, *Old Regime*, 201.

2. Doyle, *Origins*, 154.

3. Doyle, *Oxford History*, 232.

4. Woloch, *New Regime*, 87.

5. Doyle, *Oxford History*.

6. HCD.

7. Ritter, *Hegel*, 47.

8. Daniel Bell, *Cultural Contradictions*, 29n.

9. Cobban, *Modern France*, Volume I, 225.

10. François Furet, in HCD, 712.

11. McManners, "Historiography," 651.

12. Cobban, *Aspects*, 22.

13. Furet, *Interpreting*. Doyle, *Origins*. Baker, *Inventing*. Lucas, *Rewriting*.

14. Furet, *Interpreting*, 163. Letter of 16 May 1858.

15. Gershoy, *Despotism to Revolution*, 276.

16. Thompson, *French Revolution*, 62.

17. Doyle, *Origins*, 177.

18. Ibid.

19. Lyons, *Directory*, 5.

20. Furet and Richet, *French Revolution*, 65.

21. Hampson, *Prelude*, 46.

22. Thompson, *French Revolution*, 219.

23. Sagan, *Honey and Hemlock*, passim.

24. Hampson, *Prelude*, 112.

25. Hampson, *Social History*, 86.

26. Palmer, *Democratic Revolution*, Volume II, 29.

27. Ibid.

28. Doyle, *Oxford History*, 157.

29. Ibid.

30. François Furet, in HCD, 8.

31. Hampson, *Social History*, 89.

32. François Furet, in HCD, 240.

33. Kennedy, *Jacobin Clubs: First Years*, 268.

34. Ibid., 302.

35. Doyle, *Oxford History*, 188.

36. Ibid., 144.

37. McManners, *French Revolution and the Church*, 63.

38. Kennedy, *Jacobin Clubs: Middle Years*, 245.

39. Kennedy, *Jacobin Clubs: First Years*, 285–288.

40. Ibid., 296.

41. Brinton, *Jacobins*, passim.

42. Kennedy, *Jacobin Clubs: First Years*, 295.

43. Kennedy, *Jacobin Clubs: Middle Years*, 13.

44. Doyle, *Oxford History*, 188.

45. Kennedy, *Jacobin Clubs: First Years*, 302.

46. Kennedy, *Jacobin Clubs: Middle Years*, 283.

47. Thompson, *French Revolution*, 310.

48. Woloch, *New Regime*, 87.

49. Slavin, *Insurrection*, passim.

50. Mathiez, *French Revolution*, 322.

51. Ibid.

52. Thompson, *French Revolution*, 409.

53. Palmer, *Twelve*, 33.

54. Soboul, "Robespierre and the Popular Movement," 63.

55. Hampson, *Robespierre*, 266.

Notes to Chapter 5

1. Daniel Bell, *Cultural Contradictions*, 14.

2. Aristotle, *Politics*, III, Chapter IV, 15.

3. Quoted in Pitkin, *Fortune Is a Woman*, 83.

4. Sydenham, *Girondins*, 181, quoting Sorel.

5. Mona Ozouf, in HCD, 724.

6. Sagan, *Honey and Hemlock*, 28, quoting Simon Hornblower.

7. François Furet, in HCD, 607.

8. Tocqueville, "European Revolution," 124.

9. Stephens, *Principle Speeches*, Volume II, 259.

10. J.K. Wright in Van Kley, ed., *French Idea of Freedom*, 207.

11. Ibid., 222–223.

12. Ibid., 223.

13. Doyle, *Origins*, 110–114.

14. Ibid.

15. Ibid.

16. Ibid., 144.

17. Ibid.

18. Ibid., 146.

19. Baker, *Old Regime*, 200.

20. Van Kley, ed., *French Idea of Freedom*, 229.

21. Sieyès, *Third Estate*, 10.

22. David D. Bien, in Van Kley, ed., *French Idea of Freedom*, 23.

23. Patrice Gueniffey, in HCD, 578.

24. Ibid.

25. Brinton, *Jacobins*, 20.

26. Tackett, *Priest and Parish*, 248–250.

27. McManners, *French Revolution and the Church*, 17.

28. Tackett, *Priest and Parish*, 254.

29. Ibid., 256.

30. Tackett, *Religion, Revolution, and Regional Culture*, 145.

31. Ibid.

32. Rudé, *Robespierre*, 101.

33. Ibid., 102.

34. Rudé, *Robespierre*, 106.

35. Cobban, "Political Ideas," 79.

36. Baker, *Old Regime*, 371, speech of February 5, 1794.

37. Bienvenu, ed., *Ninth of Thermidor*, 46, speech of February 5, 1794.

38. Tocqueville, *Old Regime*, 272.

39. Soboul, *Sans-Culottes* (Princeton), 86.

40. Jordan, *Maximilien Robespierre*, 156.

41. Robespierre, *Textes Choisis*, Volume II, 159, speech of July 13, 1793. Translation by this author.

42. Jordan, *Maximilien Robespierre*, 156.

43. Plato, *Republic*, VII, 540d–541a.

44. Robespierre, *Textes Choisis*, Volume II, 162–163, speech of July 13, 1793. Translation by this author.

45. Woloch, *New Regime*, 182.

46. Ibid., 234.

Notes to Chapter 6

1. Gallo, *Robespierre*, 173.

2. Thompson, *Robespierre*, 275.

3. Hampson, *Robespierre*, 132.

4. Sydenham, *Girondins*, 127.

5. Stephens, *Speeches*, Volume II, 175–176.

6. Ibid.

7. Mona Ozouf, in HCD, 351.

8. Chaumié, "Girondins," 22. Translation by this author.

9. Kennedy, *Jacobin Clubs . . . Middle Years*, 297.

10. Hampson, *Robespierre*, 130–133.

11. Kennedy, *Jacobin Clubs . . . Middle Years*, 302.

12. Hampson, *Robespierre*, 130–133.

13. Thompson, *Robespierre*, 287.

14. Hampson, *Robespierre*, 130–133.

15. Thompson, *Robespierre*, 287.

16. Mona Ozouf, in HCD, 354.

17. Elkins and McKetrick, *Federalism*, 753.

18. Sagan, *Honey and Hemlock*, 111–112.

19. Stephens, *Speeches*, Volume II, 172. Translation by this author.

20. Chaumié, "Girondins," 38. Translation by this author.

21. Ibid., 39–40.

22. Mona Ozouf, in HCD, 358.

23. Chaumié, "Girondins," 33ff. Translation by this author.

24. Ibid., 38.

25. Sydenham, *Girondins*, 147.

26. Mathiez, *French Revolution*, 212–213.

27. Sydenham, *Girondins*, 131.

28. Ibid., 153–154 and Doyle: *Oxford*, 227.

29. Thompson, *Robespierre*, 285.

30. Sydenham, *Girondins*, 132.

31. Thompson, *Robespierre*, 285.

32. Sydenham, *Girondins*, 173n.

33. Sagan, *Honey and Hemlock*, 337.

34. Ibid., 342.

35. Quoted in ibid., 343.

36. *Cambridge Ancient History*, Volume IX, quoted in ibid.

37. Sagan, *Honey and Hemlock*, 357.

38. Hamilton, *Federalist*, #9, in Jacob E. Coke, ed., 50–51. See also Hamilton, *Federalist*, #1, and Madison, *Federalist*, #10.

39. Mathiez, *French Revolution*, 241.

40. Mona Ozouf, in HCD, 250.

41. Ibid., 248.

42. Ibid., 249.

43. Doyle, *Oxford*, 112.

44. *Dict. Hist.*, 78.

45. Hampson, *Robespierre*, 144.

46. Sydenham, *Girondins*, 174. Italics added.

47. Rudé, *Robespierre*, 176.

48. Baker, *Old Regime*, 339. Italics in original.

49. Sydenham, *Girondins*, 27.

50. Kennedy, *Jacobin Clubs . . . Middle Years*, 355.

51. Jordan, *Robespierre*, 176.

52. Ibid., 182.

53. Edmond Leites, personal communication.

Notes to Chapter 7

1. Mathiez, *After Robespierre*, 174.

2. Ibid., 214.

3. Doyle, *Oxford*, 329–331.

4. Furet and Richet, *Revolution*, 288.

5. *Dict. Hist.*, 303.

6. Ibid., translation by this author.

7. Doyle, *Oxford*, 336.

8. Woloch, *Jacobins*, 310.

9. Elkins and McKitrick, *Federalism*, 491.

10. Ibid.

11. Ibid., 289.

12. Ibid.

13. Ibid., 701.

14. Sydenham, *Girondins*, 181, quoting George Sorel.

15. Blum, *Rousseau*, 111.

16. Arendt, *On Revolution*, 156.

17. Blum, *Rousseau*, 111.

18. Talmon, *Totalitarian Democracy*, 115.

19. Mona Ozouf, in *HCD*, 724.

20. Ibid.

21. Soboul, *Sans-Culottes* (Princeton), 145.

22. Ibid., 146.

23. Sydenham, *Girondins*, 181n.

24. Ibid., 182.

25. Mathiez, *Revolution*, 235.

26. Bronislaw Baczko, in *HCD*, 410.

27. Hunt, Lasky, and Hanson, "Failure," 237.

28. Sieyès, *Third Estate*, 158.

29. Quoted in Palmer, *Democratic Revolution*, Volume I, 226.

30. Baczko, *Ending the Terror*, 107. Italics in the original.

31. Tocqueville, *America*, 194.

32. Talmon, *Totalitarian Democracy*.

33. Baczko, *Ending the Terror*, 109.

34. Ibid., 108. Italics in the original.

35. Brinton, *Jacobins*, 94.

36. Ibid.

37. Hunt, Lasky, and Hanson, "Failure," 737.

38. Baczko, *Ending the Terror*, 109. Italics in the original, except where indicated.

39. Ibid., 254–256. Italics in the original.

40. Dodds, *The Irrational*, passim.

41. Elkins and McKitrick, *Federalism*, 701.

42. Aristotle, *Politics* (trans. Barker), V, Chapter II, 2.

43. Tocqueville, *Old Regime*, 281n.

44. Constant, *Écrits et Discours*, 119. Translation by this author.

45. Mathiez, *After Robespierre*, 237.

46. Brinton, *Jacobins*, 115.

47. Ibid., 91.

48. Mathiez, *Revolution*, 192.

Notes to Chapter 8

1. Palmer, *Twelve*, 17.

2. Weber, *Protestant Ethic*, passim.

3. Livy, Book I, Preface, #9. Quoted in Sagan: *Freud, Women*, 230.

4. Colin Jones, in Lucas, editor, *Rewriting*, 93.

5. Ibid., p. 109.

6. Stephens, *Speeches*, Volume I, 1. Translation by this author.

7. Tocqueville, *Old Regime*, 94.

8. Wright, *Modern Times*, 276.

9. Tocqueville, *Old Regime*, 95.

10. Albert Soboul, in Soboul, editor: *Girondins et Montagnards*, 12.

11. Kates, *Cercle Social*, 85.

12. Wood, *American Revolution*, 197.

13. David Bell, *Lawyers*, 6.

14. Patrick, *First French Republic*, 261.

15. Quoted by François Furet, in HCD, 277.

16. David Bell, *Lawyers*, passim.

17. Ibid., 63–65.

18. Ibid., 3–4.

19. Ibid., 138.

20. Patrick, *First French Republic*, 261.

21. Thompson, *Revolution*, 34.

22. Palmer, *Democratic Revolution*, Volume II, 130.

23. Censer, *Prelude*, p. 35.

24. Colin Jones, in Lucas, editor, *Rewriting*, 100.

25. Ibid.

26. Ibid., 99.

27. Soboul, *Sans-Culottes* (Princeton), 40 and 42. Italics added.

28. Soboul, *Sans-Culottes* (Oxford), 50.

29. Slavin, *Insurrection*, 88.

30. Baker, *Inventing*, passim.

31. Habermas, *Public Sphere*, passim.

32. David Bell, *Lawyers*, 194.

33. Ibid., 12.

34. Ibid., 11.

35. Ibid., 104. Italics added.

36. Ibid., 174.

37. Habermas, *Public Sphere*, quoted in ibid., 24.

38. Kates, *Cercle Social*, 93. Italics added.

39. Tilly, *Vendée*, 12 and 340.

40. Ibid., 20.

41. Doyle, *Origins*, 138.

42. Ibid., 156.

43. Sutherland, *France 1789–1815*, 40.

44. Doyle, *Oxford*, 174.

45. Bell, *Lawyers*, 63–64.

46. Quoted in Brinton, *Jacobins*, 155.

47. Quoted in Maza, *Private Lives*, 105.

48. Cobban, *Aspects*, 104.

49. Patrick, *First French Republic*, 273.

50. Sewell, *Bourgeois Revolution*, epigraph to the book.

51. Ibid., 187.

52. Higonnet, *Rights of Nobles*, 47. Translation by this author.

53. Brinton, *Jacobins*, 175–177.

54. Kennedy, *Jacobin Clubs . . . Middle Years*, 204.

55. Palmer, *Twelve*, 324.

56. Soboul, *Sans-Culottes* (Oxford), 244.

57. Palmer, *Twelve*, 324.

58. Higonnet, *Rights of Nobles*, 38.

59. Brinton, *Jacobins*, 183.

60. Ibid., 181.

61. *Dict. Hist.*, 77.

62. Chill, *Barnave*, 143.

63. Joseph Schumpeter, Class lecture, spring 1947.

64. Tocqueville, *America*, 194.

65. Pirenne, "Social History," passim.

66. Furet, *Interpreting*, 112–113.

67. Cheyney, *Dawn*, 329.

68. Walzer, *Saints*, passim.

69. Edmond Leites, personal communication.

70. Maza, *Private Lives*, 61–63.

71. Ibid.

72. Ibid.

73. Ibid.

74. Ibid.

75. Ibid.

76. Weber, *Protestant Ethic*, passim.

77. Tocqueville, *America*, 531–532.

78. Ibid., 533.

79. Tocqueville, *Old Regime*, 168.

80. Tocqueville, *Old Regime*, xii.

81. Chaussinand-Nogaret, *Nobility*, 39.

82. Quoted in Feher, *Frozen Revolution*, 45.

83. Hunt, *Urban Politics*, 122–123.

84. Patrick, *First French Republic*, 179.

85. Ibid.

86. Kennedy, *Jacobin Clubs . . . Middle Years*, 55.

87. Woloch, *Jacobin Legacy*, 189ff.

88. Quoted in ibid., 155.

89. Sewell, *Work*, 138.

90. Quoted in Groethuysen, *The Bourgeois*, 236.

91. Eugen Weber, *Peasants*, 331.

92. Hobsbawm, *Age of Revolution*, 85.

93. Soboul, *Sans-Culottes* (Oxford), 50.

94. Kennedy, *Jacobin Clubs . . . Early Years*, viii.

95. Ibid., 74.

96. Ibid., 82.

97. Brinton, *Jacobins*, 54.

98. Ibid., 60.

99. Kennedy, *Jacobin Clubs . . . Early Years*, 112.

100. Brinton, *Jacobins*, 61.

101. Sutherland, *France 1789–1815*, 194.

102. Brinton, *Jacobins*, 66.

103. Hobsbawm, *Age of Revolution*, 85.

104. Cobban, *Social Interpretation*, 61.

105. Patrick, *First French Republic*, 263.

106. Ibid.

107. Cobban, *Social Interpretation*, 65.

108. Higonnet, *Nobles*, 39.

109. Elkins and McKitrick, *Federalism*, 71.

110. Ibid., 72.

Notes to Chapter 9

1. Quoted in Toulmin, *Cosmopolis*. Epigraph to the book.

2. Sydenham, *Griondins*, 120.

3. Fromm, *Freedom*, 124.

4. Stern, *Cultural Despair*, 259.

5. Ibid.

6. Engels to Marx, 4 September 1870. Quoted in Avineri, *Marx*, 192.

7. Blum, *Rousseau*, 264.

8. Ibid.

9. Tocqueville, *Democracy*, 506 and 508.

10. Berman, *All That Is Solid*, 235.

11. Ibid., 345–346.

12. Herf, *Reactionary Modernism*, passim.

13. Bellah, *Habits of the Heart*, passim.

14. Sewell, "Violence", 543.

15. Sewell, *Work*, 91.

16. Ibid., 37.

17. Ibid., 62.

18. Ibid., 91.

19. Tocqueville, *Old Régime*, 96.

20. Durkheim, *Educational Thought*, 181.

21. François Furet, in HCD, 991–1002 and Furet: *La gauche*, passim.

22. Furet, *La gauche*, 56. Translation by this author.

23. Ibid., 57. Translation by this author.

24. François Furet, in HCD, 996.

25. Furet, *La gauche*, 20–21. Translation by this author.

26. Hale, *Renaissance*, 277.

27. Furet, *La gauche*, 22. Translation by this author.

28. Pirenne, "Stages," 512. Italics added.

29. Sewell, *Work*, 72.

30. Ibid., 72–73.
31. Stone, *English Revolution*, 112–113. Italics added.
32. Paine, *Rights of Man*, 250.
33. Sagan, *Tyranny*, passim.
34. Higonnet, *Nobles*, 216.

Notes to Chapter 10

1. Durkheim, *Elementary Forms*, passim.
2. Durkheim, *Moral Education*, passim.
3. Aron, *Opium*, 7.
4. Desan, *Sacred*; Kennedy, *Jacobin Clubs, Early Years and Middle Years*; McManners, *Revolution and the Church*; Tackett, *Priest and Parish* and *Religion, Revolution*.
5. Baker, *Condorcet*, 359.
6. Tocqueville, *Democracy in America*, 295.
7. McManners, *Revolution and the Church*, 42.
8. Groethuysen, *The Bourgeois*, 23.
9. Ibid., 32.
10. Kennedy, *Jacobin Clubs . . . Early Years*, 165.
11. McManners, *Revolution and the Church*, 38. Italics added.
12. Aulard, *Christianity*, 88.
13. Ibid., 118.
14. Tilly, *Vendée*, 232.
15. Ibid., 247.
16. Ibid., 241.
17. Ibid., 195.
18. Aulard, *Christianity*, 98.
19. Tocqueville, "The European Revolution," 110.
20. Lefebvre, *The Directory*, 281.
21. McManners, *Revolution and the Church*, 120.
22. Desan, *Sacred*, 12.
23. Ibid., 90.
24. Taylor, *Sources of the Self*, 313.
25. Marx, *The Jewish Question*, quoted in Furet, *Marx*, 18.
26. Quoted in Groethuysen, *The Bourgeois*, 235.
27. Ibid.
28. Doyle, *Origins*, 105.
29. Ibid., 156.
30. Palmer, *Democratic Revolutions*, Volume I, 518.

31. Quoted in Thompson, *Robespierre*, 429–430.

32. Durkehim, *Moral Education*, passim.

33. Mona Ozouf, in HCD, 26.

34. Aulard, *Christianity*, 146.

35. Greenfeld, *Nationalism*, 113.

36. Doyle, *Oxford*, 38.

37. Walzer, *Regicide*, 14.

38. Wood, *Radicalism*, 167.

39. Tocqueville, *Old Regime*, 119–120.

40. Tocqueville, *Democracy in America*, 235.

41. Hobsbawm, *Rebels*, 186.

42. Ibid., 121.

43. Marx's famous deprecation in *The Eighteenth Brumaire of Louis Napoleon*.

44. Sagan's *Dawn of Tyranny*, Chapter 13.

45. Lefebvre, *Great Fear*, 52.

46. Ibid., 54.

47. Ibid., 56.

48. Van Kley, *Damiens Affair*, 185.

49. Mornet, *Origines Intellectuelles*, 402. Translation by this author.

50. Greenfeld, *Nationalism*, 58.

51. Sewell, *Bourgeois Revolution*, 6.

52. Baker, *Old Regime*, 200.

53. Palmer, *Democratic Revolutions*, Volume I, 518.

54. Greenfeld, *Nationalism*, 10.

55. Baker, "Political Thought," 301.

56. Tocqueville, *Democracy in America*, 235.

57. Chaumié, "Les Girondins," 41. Translation by this author.

58. Jordan, *Robespierre*, 158.

59. Syedenham, *Girondins*, 181.

60. All quotes from Blanning, *Wars*, 107–108.

61. Quoted in Sagan, *Honey and Hemlock*, 199.

62. N.G.L. Hammond, quoted in ibid., 202.

63. Durkheim, *Moral Education*, 9–11. Italics added.

64. Quoted in Jordan, *Robespierre*, 160.

65. McManners, *French Revolution and the Church*, 13.

66. Starobinski, *Rousseau*, 112.

67. Tocqueville, *Old Regime*, 156. Italics added.

68. Tocqueville, *Democracy in America*, 94.

69. Quoted in Blum, *Rousseau*, 245.

70. Chaumié, "Les Girondins," 47. Translation by this author.

71. Ozouf, *Festivals*, 258.

72. Aulard, *Christianity*, 65.

73. Ozouf, *Festivals*, 260.

74. Ibid., 252.

75. Ibid., 259.

76. David Bell, "Lingua Popoli, Lingua Dei," 1405.

77. Greenfeld, *Nationalism*, 163.

78. Furet, *La Gauche et la révolution*, 60. Translation by this author.

79. Ibid., 61.

80. Notations written on the original manuscript.

81. Greenfeld, *Nationalism*, 11.

82. Ibid., 10.

83. Smith, *National Identity*, 80.

84. Ibid., 11.

85. Ibid., 80.

86. Personal communication, Prof. Andrew Katz.

Notes to Chapter 11

1. Daniel Bell, *End of Ideology*, 436.

2. Arendt, *On Revolution*, 54.

3. Tocqueville, *Old Régime*, 139.

4. Ibid., 272.

5. Furet, *Interpreting*, 111.

6. Hunt, *Politics, Culture, and Class*, 210.

7. Tilly, *Vendée*, 160.

8. Tocqueville, *Old Régime*, 75.

9. David Bell, *Lawyers*, 23.

10. Maza, *Private Lives*, 255.

11. Doyle, *Origins*, 105.

12. Ibid., 50–51.

13. Ibid., 51.

14. Ibid., 52.

15. Wood, *American Revolution*, 219.

16. Tocqueville, *Old Régime*, 19, italics added.

17. Weber, *Protestant Ethic*, passim.

18. Palmer, *Democratic Revolutions*, Volume II, 339.

19. Ibid.

20. Tilly, *Vendée*, 17.

21. Tocqueville, *Old Régime*, vii.

22. Ibid., xii.

23. Tackett, *Becoming a Revolutionary*, 292.

24. Ibid., 295.

25. Palmer, *Democratic Revolutions*, Volume I, 517.

26. Tocqueville, *Old Régime*, 267.

27. Ibid., 60.

28. Furet, *Interpreting*, 113.

29. Ibid.

30. Furet, *Interpreting*. Cobban: *The Social Interpretation*.

31. Doyle, *Origins*. Chartier: *Cultural Origins*.

32. Lucas, editor, *Rewriting the French Revolution*.

Notes to Chapter 12

1. First sentence of the *Communist Manifesto*.

2. *Dict. Hist.*, 725.

3. Lord Acton, *Lectures*, 17.

4. Tocqueville, *Recollections*, 75.

5. Quoted by Mona Ozouf, in HCD, 673.

6. Rudé, *Robespierre*, 152.

7. Robespierre, *Textes Choisis*, Volume II, 85. Translation by this author.

8. Rudé, *Robespierre*, 152.

9. Soboul, "Robespierre and the Popular Movement," 60.

10. Mathiez, *French Revolution*, 208–209.

11. *Dict. Hist.*, 681.

12. Ibid.

13. Mathiez, *French Revolution*, 367.

14. Ibid.

15. *Dict. Hist.*, 463.

16. Sutherland, *France 1789–1815*, 212.

17. Hampson, *Robespierre*, 26. Italics added.

18. Robespierre, *Textes Choisis*, Volume I, 73. Translation by this author.

19. Cobban, *Modern France*, Volume I, 137.

20. Mathiez, *French Revolution*, 316.

21. Ibid.

22. Kennedy, *Jacobin Clubs . . . Middle Years*, 61.

23. Soboul, *Sans-Culottes*, Oxford, 24.

24. Ibid.

25. Palmer, *Twelve*, 166.

26. Ibid., 164.

27. Ibid., 167.

28. Ibid., 170.

29. Report of the speech, and quotes from it, that follow are from Mathiez, *French Revolution*, 450–451.

30. Ibid., 450.

31. Ibid., 451.

32. Kennedy, *Jacobin Clubs . . . Middle Years*, 46.

33. Ibid., 58.

34. Ibid., 60.

35. Ibid.

36. Ibid., 61.

37. Garrett, *Estates General*, 172.

38. Editor's introduction to Robespierre, *Textes Choisis*, Volume II, 23. Translation by this author.

39. Tocqueville, *Recollections*, 12.

40. Ibid., 13.

41. Quoted by François Furet, in HCD, 189.

42. Editor's introduction to Robespierre: *Textes Choisis*, Volume I, 24. Translation by this author.

43. Stephens, *Principle Speeches*, Volume II, 171.

44. Ibid., Volume I, 377.

45. Woloch, *New Regime*, 155.

46. Tocqueville, *Recollections*, 12.

47. François Furet, in HCD, 189.

48. Woloch, *New Regime*, 234.

49. Jordan, *Robespierre*, 156.

50. Ibid.

51. Robespierre, *Textes Choisis*, Volume II, 163. Translation by this author.

52. Soboul, *Sans-Culottes*, Princeton, 86.

53. Chaumié, "Les Girondins," 40.

54. Ibid., 38. Translation by this author.

55. Woloch, *New Regime*, 182.

56. *Dict. Hist.*, 580.

57. See supporting quotations in Sagan, *Freud, Women*, 146.

58. Gershoy, *Despotism to Revolution*, 201.

59. Tocqueville, *Old Regime*, 172.

60. Woloch, *New Regime*, 255.
61. Kennedy, *Jacobin Clubs . . . Middle Years*, 91.
62. Robespierre, *Textes Choisis*, Volume II, 183. Translation by this author.
63. Lyons, *France under the Directory*, 95.
64. Gershoy, *Barère*, 228.
65. Ibid., 228–229 and Rudé *Robespierre*, 140.
66. Soboul, *Sans Culottes*, Oxford, 90.

Notes to Chapter 13

1. This narrative and particular quotes from Mathiez, *French Revolution*, 180–183.
2. Stephens, *Speeches*, Volume I, 345.
3. William Butler Yeats, "The Second Coming."
4. Durkehim, *Moral Education*, 54.
5. Ritter, *Hegel and the French Revolution*, 45.
6. Tocqueville, *America*, 193.
7. Censer, *Prelude to Power*, 1.
8. Palmer, *Democratic Revolutions*, Volume II, 111.
9. Burke, *Reflections*, 193.
10. Rudé, *Crowd*, 161.
11. Jordan, *Robespierre*, 94.
12. Tocqueville, *America*, 168.
13. Robespierre, *Textes Choisis*, Volume I, 145–146. Translation by this author. Italics added.
14. Tocqueville, *America*, 168.
15. Sydenham, *First French Republic*, 302.
16. Quoted in Furet, *La gauche*, 299. Translation by this author.
17. Patrice Gueniffy, in HCD, 224.
18. Ibid., 230.
19. Doyle, *Oxford History*, 185.
20. Ibid., 202. *Dict. Hist.*, 379.
21. Slavin, *Insurrection*, 6.
22. Personal communication. Marcelo Suarez-Orozco.
23. Palmer, *Twelve*, 70.
24. Sa'adah, *Liberal Politics*, 189.
25. François Furet, in HCD, 552.
26. Feher, *Frozen Revolution*, 79.
27. Sutherland, *France 1789–1815*, 357.
28. Palmer, *Twelve*, 70.
29. Emerson, "Things are in the saddle and ride men."

30. Feher, *Frozen Revolution*, 95.

31. Sydenham, *First French Republic*, 151.

32. Furet and Richet, *French Revolution*, 288.

33. Palmer, *Democratic Revolutions*, Volume II, 260.

34. François Furet, in HCD, 277.

35. Sydenham, *First French Republic*, 200.

36. Doyle, *Old European Order*, 356.

37. Tocqueville, "The European Revolution," 129.

38. Sydenham, *First French Republic*, 221.

39. François Furet, in HCD, 278.

40. Quoted by McManners, *Revolution and the Church*, 140.

41. Palmer, *Twelve*, 117.

42. Feher, *Frozen Revolution*, passim.

43. Arendt, *Totalitarianism*, passim.

44. Bauman, *Holocaust*, 77.

45. Personal Communication. Robert Bellah.

46. Bruun, *French Imperium*, 35.

47. Quoted in Wright, *France in Modern Times*, 95.

48. Sagan, *Honey and Hemlock*, 71–74.

Notes to Chapter 14

1. Van Kley, ed., *French Idea of Freedom*, 2.

2. Burke, *Reflections*, 193.

3. Jordan, *Robespierre*, 86.

4. Lord Acton, *Lectures*, 88.

5. Palmer, *Democratic Revolutions*, Volume I, 332.

6. Lefebvre, *Fear*, 47–49.

7. Ibid.

8. Ibid., 117.

9. Ibid., 84.

10. Knecht, *Renaissance France*, 524.

11. Hampson, *Social History*, 77.

12. Thompson, *Robespierre*, 77.

13. Kennedy, *Jacobin Clubs . . . Early Years*, 252.

14. Hampson, *Social History*, 72.

15. Doyle, *Oxford History*, 110.

16. Soboul, *Sans-culottes* (Princeton), 186.

17. Ibid., 102.

18. Quoted in Hampson, *Social History*, 97.

19. Doyle, *Origins*, 190.

20. Stevens, *Speeches*, Volume I, 469n. Translation this author.

21. Soboul, *Sans-culottes* (Princeton), 187.

22. Doyle, *Oxford History*, 154.

23. Hampson, *Prelude to Terror*, 195.

24. Jordan, *Robespierre*, 90.

25. Alan Forrest, in HCD, 418.

26. Ibid.

27. Kennedy, *Jacobin Clubs . . . Early Years*, 196.

28. Alan Forrest, in HCD, 419.

29. Ibid., 421.

30. Palmer, *Twelve*, 96.

31. Alan Forrest, in HCD, 423.

32. Mathiez, *After Robespierre*, 224.

33. Doyle, *Oxford History*, 244.

34. Ibid., 251.

35. Estimate by R. Cobb, cited in *Dict. Hist.*, 41.

36. Doyle, *Oxford History*, 258.

37. Ibid.

38. Ibid., 264.

39. Alan Forrest, in HCD, 422.

40. Sagan, *Honey and Hemlock*, 176–185.

41. Kennedy, *Jacobin Clubs . . . Early Years*, 189–192.

42. Alan Forrest, in HCD, 422–423.

43. Rudé, *Crowd*, 161.

Notes to Chapter 15

1. Starobinski, *Rousseau*, passim.

2. Both examples: personal communication Professor Andrew Katz. On Schlesinger: Paul Brace and Barbara Hinckley, *Follow the Leader*. New York: Basic Books, 1992, 101.

3. Sagan, *Honey and Hemlock*, passim.

4. Hofstadter, "Paranoid Style," passim.

5. Quoted in Furet, *Interpreting*, 129. Letter to Marx, September 4, 1870.

6. English translation: Lefebvre, *The Great Fear*.

7. Ibid., 52.

8. Ibid., 156.

9. Ibid., 133.

10. Ibid., 64.

11. Ibid., 161.

12. Ibid., 160.

13. Sutherland, *France 1789–1815*, 155.

14. Cobb, *Police*, 278.

15. Rudé, *Crowd*, 222.

16. Ibid.

17. Baczko, *Ending the Terror*, 22. Italics in original.

18. William H. Sewell, Jr., in Baker, editor, *Modern Political Culture*, Volume 4, 259.

19. Sagan, *Honey and Hemlock*, 28.

20. Talmon, *Totalitarian Democracy*, 121.

21. Blanning, *Wars*, 111.

22. Ibid., 99.

23. Ibid., 101.

24. Ibid., 104.

25. Walter, *Jacobins*, 323–324, translation by this author.

26. Kennedy, *Jacobin Clubs . . . Early Years*, 32.

27. Ibid., 33.

28. Ibid., 54.

29. Rudé, in Lefebvre, *Great Fear*, xiii.

30. Blanning, *Wars*, 111.

31. Sagan, *Tyranny*, 128.

32. This quote became the title of a book, published by Anatole France in 1912.

33. Mathiez, *French Revolution*, 184.

34. Rudé, *Robespierre*, 165.

35. Stone, *English Revolution*, 90.

36. Gershoy, *Barère*, 216.

37. Stephsn, *Speeches*, Volume I, 349. Translation by this author.

38. Sagan, *Tyranny*, 117.

39. Mathiez, *French Revolution*, 182. Italics added.

40. Robespierre, *Textes Choisis*, Volume II, 80.

41. Hampson, *Danton*, 172.

42. Arendt, *Totalitarianism*, 326.

43. Sagan, *Cannibalism*, 59.

44. Mathiez, *French Revolution*, 182.

45. Schama, *Citizens*, 630.

46. Palmer, *Twelve*, passim.

47. Blum, *Rousseau*, 183n.

48. Mathiez, *French Revolution*, 396.

49. Baker, editor, *Old Regime*, 339.

50. Waltzer, editor, *Regicide*, 138.

51. Stephens, *Speeches*, Volume I, 369. Translation by this author.

52. Palmer, *Twelve*, 156.

53. Ibid., 163.

54. Thompson, *Robespierre*, 271.

55. Mathiez, *French Revolution*, 183.

56. Hunt, *Family Romance*, 10.

57. Sagan, *Cannibalism*, Chapter 3.

58. Schama, *Citizens*, 673–674.

59. Ibid., 405.

60. *Dict. Hist.*, 78. Translation by this author.

61. Schama, *Citizens*, 467.

62. Ibid., 635.

63. Bronislaw Baczko in Baker, editor, *Political Culture*, Volume 4, 24.

64. Schama, *Citizens*, 633.

65. Baker, editor, *Old Regime*, 348.

66. Homer, *Iliad*, IV, 30–37. Richmond Lattimore translator.

67. Soboul, *Sans-Culottes* (Princeton), 160.

68. Hunt, *Family Romance*, 112.

69. Palmer, *Twelve*, 316.

70. *Dict. Hist.*, 1023.

71. François Furt, in HCD, 143.

72. Sagan, *Cannibalism*, Chapter 3.

73. Lefebvre, *French Revolution*, Volume I, 219.

74. Mathiez, *French Revolution*, 397. Italics added.

75. Higonnet, *Class Ideology*, 137.

76. Ibid., 216.

Notes to Chapter 16

1. Walzer, editor, *Regicide*, 62.

2. Quoted by Baczko in Baker, editor, *French Revolution . . . Modern Political Culture*, Volume 4, 27.

3. Ibid., 29.

4. Bienvenu, editor, *Thermidor*, 39.

5. Blanning, *Wars*, 101.

6. Sydenham, *Girondins*, 163.

7. Baczko, *Ending the Terror*, 22.

8. Robespierre, *Textes Choisis*, Volume III, 105 and 107. Translation by this author.

9. Stephens, *Principle Speeches*, Volume II, 512. Translation by this author.

10. Lucas, *Terror*, 335. Translation by this author of Brunon-Soviche's remarks.

11. Furet, *Interpreting*, 54.

12. Doyle, *Oxford History*, 184.

13. Ibid.

14. Ibid., 190.

15. Ibid., 279.

16. Mathiez, *French Revolution*, 505.

17. Bronislaw Baczko in Baker, editor, *French Revolution . . . Modern Political Culture*, Volume 4, 26.

18. Stevens, *Principle Speeches*, Volume II, 267. November 26, 1793.

19. In this translation, and those of endnotes 20, 21, 22, 23 and 24, I have been aided by Burton Ruffel, especially on the question of whether or not to translate *l'étranger* or leave it in French.

20. Stephens, *Principle Speeches*, Volume II, 515.

21. Ibid., 518.

22. Ibid., 529.

23. Ibid., 531.

24. Ibid., 512.

25. Ozouf, *L'École de la France*, 125. Translation by this author.

26. *Dict. Hist.*, 427.

27. Brinton, *Jacobins*, 207.

28. Walter, *Jacobins*, 326. Translation by this author.

29. Ibid., 330. Translation by this author.

30. Ibid., 333. Translation by this author.

31. Carter, "Jacobin Clubs," 124–126.

32. Ibid., 138n.

33. Palmer, *Twelve*, 94.

34. Ibid.

35. Ibid., 96.

36. Baczko, *Ending the Terror*, 109.

37. Thompson, *French Revolution*, 350.

38. *Dict. Hist.*, 723.

39. Thompson, *Robespierre*, 154.

40. Ibid., 177.

41. Ibid., 446.

42. Quoted by Blum, *Rousseau*, 270.

43. Blanning, *Wars*, 179.

44. Furet, *La gauche*, 272.

45. *Dict. Hist.*, 927.

46. Ibid., 929.

47. Hampson, *Social History*, 134.

48. Quoted by Fareed Zakaria in the *New York Times* Book Review Section, December 31, 1995, 9.

49. Gershoy, *Barère*, 145.

50. Ibid., 165.

51. Sagan, *Honey and Hemlock*, 235–244.

52. Mathiez, *French Revolution*, 501.

53. Norman Hampson, in Lucas, editor, *Rewriting*, 61.

54. Thompson, *French Revolution*, 410.

55. Palmer, *Twelve*, 171.

56. Ibid., 484.

57. François Furet, in *HCD*, 174.

58. Sutherland, *France 1789–1815*, 240.

59. Schama, *Citizens*, 791.

60. Doyle, *Oxford History*, 275.

61. Hampson, *Robespierre*, 263.

62. Ibid., 262.

63. Blum, *Rousseau*, 267.

64. Thompson, *Robespierre*, 476.

65. Doyle, *Oxford History*, 281.

66. *Dict. Hist.*, 567. Translation by this author.

67. Thompson, *Robespierre*, 146.

Notes to Chapter 17

1. Tucker, *Marx-Engels Reader*, 577–578.

2. Forster, *Two Cheers for Democracy*.

3. Sagan, *Honey and Hemlock*, passim.

4. Meisner, *Paranoid Process*, 12.

5. Schama, *Citizens*, xv.

6. Quoted in Lyons, "Politics and Patois," 281.

7. Mitzman, *Iron Cage*, 119–137.

8. Stone, *English Revolution*, 113.

9. Quoted in Higonnet, *Class, Ideology*, 245.

10. Geertz, *Interpretation of Cultures*, 219.

11. Hunt, *Politics, Culture, and Class*, 32.

12. Title of essay by Karen Horney. *International Journal of Psycho-analysis*, volume 13, 1932, 348–360.

13. Chaumié, "Les Girondins," 49–51. Translation by this author.

14. *Dict. Hist.*, 512.

15. Ibid., 441.

16. Aristotle, *Politics*, V, Chapter II, 6. Translation Barker.

17. *Dict. Hist.*, 1057. Translation by this author.

18. Ibid.

19. Aron, *Opium*, 7.

20. T. S. Eliot, "The Hollow Men." *Collected Poems*, 104.

21. Hackstaff, *Divorce Culture*, passim.

22. Tocqueville, *Democracy in America*, 312–315. Order of paragraphs rearranged. Italics in original.

23. Ritter, *Hegel and the French Revolution*, 45.

24. Ibid., 62. Italics in the original.

Notes to Chapter 18

1. Tocqueville, "European Revolution," 124.

2. Ritter, *Hegel and the French Revolution*, 43.

3. Daniel Bell, *Winding Passage*, 353 and 349.

4. Cited in Furet, *Interpreting*, 163. Letter of May 16, 1858.

5. Fromm, *Freedom*, 124. Italics added.

6. Quoted in Rudé, *Eighteenth Century*, 138.

7. Michelet, *French Revolution*, Volume 7, 167.

8. Thompson, *Robespierre*, 586.

9. Jordan, *Robespierre*, 199.

10. Stephens, *Speeches*, Volume II, 419. Translation by this author.

11. Jordan, *Robespierre*, 203.

12. Soboul, *Sans-Culottes* [Oxford], 160.

13. Blum, *Rousseau*, 249.

14. Jordan, *Robespierre*, 174.

15. Blum, *Rousseau*, 263.

16. Robespierre, *Textes Choisis*, Volume III, 118–119. Italics in original.

17. Translation by this author.

18. Translation by this author based on Rudé: *Robespierre*, 118. Rudé's italics.

19. Kernberg, *Borderline Conditions*, 79.

20. Freud, *Inhibitions, Symptoms, and Anxiety*, passim. Various editions.

21. From a review by Jonathan Mirsky, *New York Review of Books*, February 5, 1998, 31–33.

22. Quoted in Hughes, *Consciousness*, 405.

23. Hampson, *Danton*, 4.

24. Mathiez, *French Revolution*, 183.

25. Quoted in Thompson, *Robespierre*, 122n.

26. See note #21.

27. Starobinski, *Rousseau*, passim.

28. Ibid., 248.

29. Ibid., 250.

30. Ibid., 252.

Notes to Chapter 19

1. Thompson, *Robespierre*, 357.

2. Hampson, *Robespierre*, 60.

3. Kernberg, *Borderline Personality*, 674.

4. Talmon, *Totalitarian Democracy*, 302.

5. Censer, *Prelude to Power*, 53.

6. Kernberg, *Borderline Personality*, 668.

7. Ibid., 674.

8. Robespierre, *Textes Choisis*, Volume I, 141–142. Speech of January 2, 1792. Translation by this author.

9. Sa'adah, *Liberal Politics*, 157n.

10. Madison, *Federalist*, #10, edited Cooke, p. 62.

11. Robespierre, *Textes Choisis*, Volum II, 145. Translation by this author. Italics in the original.

12. Ibid., 150. Translation by this author.

13. Blum, *Rousseau*, 198.

14. Baker, *Old Regime*, 255.

15. Rousseau, *Social Contract*, translation Lowell Bair, 26.

16. Quoted from a letter in Starobinski, *Rousseau*, 22.

17. Robespierre, *Textes Choisis*, Volume I, editor's introduction, 16–17. Translation by this author.

18. Ibid., 141. Speech of January 2, 1792. Translation by this author.

19. Talmon, *Totalitarian Democracy*, 94.

20. Van Gennep, *Rites*, 11.

21. Ibid., 77.

22. Blum, *Rousseau*, 183.

23. Ibid.

24. Sièyes, *Third Estate*, 209n, editors note. Italics in original.

25. Ibid.

26. *HCD*, 781. Italics in original.

27. Rousseau, *Social Contract*, Book II, Chapter VIII, Bair translation, 36.

28. Hampson, *Social History*, 222.

29. Tocqueville, *Old Regime*, 12–13.

30. Palmer, *Twelve*, 275.

31. Ibid., 275–276.

32. This, and all following quotations from this speech, Robespierre, *Textes Choisis*, Volume III, 113–119. Translation by this author.

33. This, and following quotations from this speech, Robespierre, *Textes Choisis*, Volume II, 159–169. Translation by this author.

34. Woloch, *New Regime*, 179.

35. Ibid., 181 ff.

36. Ibid., 179.

37. Quoted in Daniel Bell, *Cultural Contradictions*, 165n.

38. Tocqueville, "The European Revolution," 116.

39. Jordan, *Robespierre*, 189.

40. Soboul, *Sans-Culottes* [Princeton], 136. Italics in the original.

41. Quoted in Sydenham, *Girondins*, 181.

42. Soboul, *Sans-Culottes*, [Princeton], 145.

43. Ibid., 146. Italics in the original.

44. Sièyes, *Third Estate*, 170. Italics in the original.

45. Quoted in Talmon, *Totalitarian Democracy*, 142.

46. Blum, *Rousseau*, 201.

47. Hampson, *Prelude to Terror*, 110.

48. Mona Ozouf in Baker, editor, *Modern Political Culture*, Volume 4, 16.

49. Sagan, *Honey and Hemlock*, 149–150.

50. Stone, *English Revolution*, 99.

51. Cited in Miller: *Rousseau*, 183.

52. Blum, *Rousseau*, 27.

53. Mathiez, *French Revolution*, 450.

54. Ibid.

55. Tocqueville, *Old Regime*, 146.

56. *Midsummer Night's Dream*, V, i, 7.

57. Kennedy, *Jacobin Clubs . . . Middle Years*, 138–140.

58. Hampson, *Prelude to Terror*, 187.

59. Arendt, *Totalitarianism*, 87.

Notes to Chapter 20

1. Kernberg, *Borderline Conditions*, 79.

2. Abend, et al., *Borderline Patients*, 24.

3. Kernberg, "Borderline Personality Organization," 643.

4. Ibid., 667.

5. Ibid., 665–666.

6. Starobinski, *Rousseau*, 252.

7. Stephens, *Speeches*, Volume I, 436. Translation by this author.

8. Kernberg, "Borderline Personality Organization," 669.

9. Ibid., 668.

10. Starobinski, *Rousseau*, 204.

11. Kernberg, "Borderline Personality Organization," 674.

12. Arendt, *Eichmann*, passim.

13. Kernberg, "Borderline Personality Organization," 666.

14. Ibid., 678.

15. Kernberg, *Borderline Conditions*, 56.

16. Blum, *Rousseau*, 130.

17. *Hamlet*, II, ii, line 613.

18. Palmer, *Twelve*, 68.

19. Sagan, *Honey and Hemlock*, 219–220.

20. Abend, et al., *Borderline Patients*, 21.

21. Kernberg, "Borderline Personality Organization," 657.

22. Ibid., 657.

23. Ibid., 674.

24. Higonnet, *Class Ideology*, 174.

25. Starobinski, *Rousseau*, 202.

26. Kernberg, "Structural Derivatives," 244. Italics in original.

27. Sagan, *Honey and Hemlock*, Chapter 2.

28. Freud, *Civilization*, 91.

29. Personal communication. Conversation, and argument, with Balter have played a significant role in the writing of this particular chapter. He has greatly increased my understanding of borderline phenomena. Differences in our understanding of the configuration, however, do exist. He would dissent from some of the conclusions presented here.

30. Abend et al., *Borderline Patients*, 215.

31. Starobinski, *Rousseau*, 201.

32. Ibid., 203. Italics added.

33. Ibid., 204–205.

34. Max Weber, *Social and Economic Organization*, 382.

35. *Macbeth*, I, ii, line 38.

36. Ibid., lines 48–50.

37. Byron, "Ode to Napoleon."

38. Ibid., last stanza.

Notes to Chapter 21

1. Rudé, *Robespierre*, 88. Italics in the original.
2. Furet, *Interpreting*, 85. Italics in the original.
3. Palmer, *Twelve*, 127.
4. Thompson, *Robespierre*, 266.
5. Gershoy, *Barère.*
6. Slavin, *Insurrection*, 203n.
7. Thompson, *Robespierre*, 284.
8. Talmon, *Totalitarian Democracy*, 112.
9. Arendt, *Totalitarianism*, passim.
10. Brinton, *Decade of Revolution*, 120.
11. François Furet, in HCD, 998–999.
12. Ibid., 143.
13. Mona Ozouf, in HCD, 723.
14. Thompson, *Robespierre*, 403.
15. François Furet, in HCD, 140.
16. Mathiez, *French Revolution*, 464.
17. Hampson, *Danton*, 170–171.
18. Ibid., 172.
19. Ibid.
20. Thompson, *Robespierre*, 473.
21. Ibid.
22. Mathiez, *French Revolution*, 465.
23. Kennedy, *Jacobin Clubs . . . Middle Years*, 168–169.
24. Bronislaw Bazko in Baker, editor, *Modern Political Culture*, Volume 4, 26.
25. Kennedy, *Jacobin Clubs . . . 1793–1795*, 98–99.
26. Ibid., 99.
27. Ibid., 11.
28. Ibid.
29. Ibid., 22.
30. Ibid., 69.
31. Ibid.
32. Ibid., 74.
33. Ibid., 243.
34. Ibid., 246.
35. Ibid., 253.
36. Ibid., 249.
37. Ibid., 246.

38. Letter to this author, November 23, 1998. Italics added.

39. *King Lear*, II, iv, 283–286.

40. Lasch, *True and Only Heaven*, 79.

41. Quoted in Furet, *Interpreting*, 163. Letter of May 16, 1858.

42. Quoted in Drescher, *Tocqueville and Modernization*, 200. Letter of January 5, 1843.

43. Tocqueville, *Old Regime*, 157.

44. Palmer, *Twelve*, 305–306.

45. Chill, *Barnave's Introduction*, 51.

46. Bronislaw Baczko in Baker, editor, *Modern Political Culture*, Volume 4, 31. Italics added by Baczko.

47. Keith Michael Baker, in ibid., xiii.

48. Palmer, *Twelve*, 365–366.

49. Ibid., 316.

50. *Dict. Hist.*, 704. Translation by this author.

51. Hampson, *Robespierre*, 264.

52. Furet, *La gauche*, editor's note, 294. Translation by this author.

53. Blum, *Rousseau*, 226.

54. Schama, *Citizens*, 780.

55. Freud, *Civilization*, 91.

56. Thompson, *French Revolution*, 493.

57. Stone, *Family, Sex, and Marriage*, passim.

58. Mary Jacobus in Melzer and Rabine, editors, *Rebel Daughters*, 56.

59. Robespierre, *Textes Choisis*, Vol. II, 184. Translation by this author.

60. Blum, *Rousseau*, 190.

61. Ibid., 191–192.

62. Ibid.

63. Ibid.

64. Plato, *Republic*, 377b. Translation by Alan Bloom.

65. Blum, *Rousseau*, 188.

66. Palmer, *Twelve*, 311.

67. Blum, *Rousseau*, 223.

68. Sagan, *Cultural Diversity and Moral Relativism*, passim.

69. Rousseau, *Social Contract*, I, Chapter 5. Quoted in Miller, *Rousseau*, 183.

70. Palmer, *Twelve*, 311.

71. Ibid., 318.

72. Mona Ozouf, in HCD, 729.

73. Tocqueville, *Democracy in America*, 396.

74. Talmon, *Totalitarian Democracy*.

75. Tocqueville, *Democracy in America*, 436.

76. Tocqueville's comment on the Terror as *virus*, quoted in Furet, *Interpreting*, 163.

77. Mona Ozouf, in HCD, 729.

78. Palmer, *Twelve*, 166.

79. Frans de Waal, *Good Natured: The Origins of Right and Wrong in Humans and Other Animals.* Cambridge, Mass.: Harvard University Press, 1996.

Notes to Chapter 22

1. Aeschylus, *Agamemnon*, line 1248. Translated by Richmond Lattimore. University of Chicago Press, various editions.

2. Rousseau, *Social Contract*, translated by Lowell Bair.

3. Bienvenu, *Ninth of Thermidor*, 317.

4. Gallo, *Robespierre*, 53.

5. Talmon, *Totalitarian Democracy*, 68. Translation this author.

6. Stone, *Family*, 159.

7. *The Wings of the Dove*. Scribners, the New York Edition. Reprinted by Augustus M. Kelley, Fairfield, N.J., 1976, Volume I, 107.

8. Gallo, *Robespierre*, 60.

9. Talmon, *Totalitarian Democracy*, 142.

10. Berman, *All That's Solid*, 304.

11. Blum, *Rousseau*, 155–159.

12. Ibid.

13. Cobban, *Aspects*, 176.

14. Palmer, *Twelve*, 116.

15. Jordan, *Robespierre*, 64.

16. Robespierre, *Textes Choisis*, Volume I, Editor's Introduction, 26. Translation this author.

17. Cobban, "Political Ideas," 70.

18. Blum, *Rousseau*, 248.

19. Ibid., 249.

20. Hampson, *Robespierre*, 64.

21. Mazlisch, *Revolutionary Ascetic*, 88.

22. Palmer, *Twelve*, 266.

23. Rudé, *Robespierre*, 166. Speech of December 25, 1793. Italics in original.

24. Cobban, "Political Ideas," 77.

25. Hampson, *Robespierre*, 104.

26. Robespierre, *Textes Choisis*, Volume III, 193. Translation this author.

27. Starobinski, *Rousseau*, Neuchâtel, 34. Translation by Blum: *Rousseau*, 218.

28. Tocqueville, *Democracy in America*, 314.

29. Michelet, "Preface of 1868," in Furet, *La gauche*, 293–294. Translation this author.

30. A refrain from the first volume, *Some Do Not*, of the tetralogy *Parade's End*, by Ford Madox Ford.

31. Mathiez, *French Revolution*, 322.

32. Robespierre, *Textes Choisis*, Volume II, Editor's Introduction, 38. Translation this author.

33. Thompson, *Robespierre*, 385.

34. Rudé, *Robespierre*, 120.

35. Thompson, *Robespierre*, 399.

36. Translated by Alan Bloom.

37. Cobban, "Political Ideas," 79.

38. Thompson, *Robespierre*, 280.

39. Robespierre, *Textes Choisis*, Volume I, 10. Translation this author.

40. Ibid., Volume II, 85. Translation this author.

41. Ibid., Volume I, 11. Translation this author.

42. Ibid., Volume I, 74. Translation this author.

43. Fehér, *Frozen Revolution*, 55.

44. Patrice Gueniffey, in HCD, 574.

45. Rudé, *Robespierre*, 101. Italics in original.

46. Robespierre, *Textes Choisis*, Volume I, 67. Translation this author.

47. Ibid., 71. Translation this author.

48. Thompson, *Robespierre*, 80.

49. Stephens, *Speeches*, Volume II, 302–303. Translation this author.

50. Thompson, *Robespierre*, 211.

51. Jordan, *Robespierre*, 84–85.

52. Ibid.

53. Palmer, *Democratic Revolution*, Volume II, 13.

54. Jordan, *Robespierre*, 85.

55. Ibid., 87.

56. Thompson, *Robespierre*, 406–407.

57. Ibid., 419.

58. Aulard, *Christianity*, 114.

59. Thompson, *Robespierre*, 419.

60. Stephens, *Speeches*, Volume II, 387. Translation by this author.

61. Mona Ozouf, in HCD, 723.

62. Mathiez, *French Revolution*, 399.

63. Thompson, *Robespierre*, 275.

64. Rudé, *Robespierre*, 117. Italics in original.

65. Doyle, *Oxford History*, 274.

66. Palmer, *Twelve*, 257.

67. Mona Ozouf, in HCD, 221–222.

68. Chill, *Barnave*, 135.

69. *King Lear*, Act IV, Sc. Vi, line 191.

70. Aron, *Opium*, 49.

Notes to Chapter 23

1. Tocqueville, "European Revolution," editor's introduction, 28.

2. Tocqueville, *Democracy in America*, xiii.

3. Ibid., 600.

4. Gershoy, *Despotism to Revolution*, 276.

5. Tocqueville, *Old Regime*, 139.

6. Maza, *Private Lives*, 55.

7. Furet, *Le gauche*, 54. Translation this author.

8. Doyle, *Origins*, 208.

9. Quoted by Timothy Tackett in Keith Baker, editor, *Modern Political Culture*, Volume 4, 42.

10. Parsons, *Evolution of Societies*. Bellah: "Religious Evolution."

11. Tilly, *Véndée*, 25.

12. Furet, *La gauche* and Furet in HCD, 991–1002.

13. Tackett, *Religion*, 218.

14. Rousseau, *Emile*, Book I, IV.

15. Tocqueville, *Democracy in America*, 701.

16. Aristotle, *Posterior Analytics*, Book I, Chapters 2 and 3.

17. Rousseau, *Emile*, translated Bloom, 222 and 235.

18. Ritter, *Hegel*, 47.

19. Ibid., 51. Italics in original.

20. Ibid., 52. Italics in original.

21. Drescher, *Dilemmas of Democracy*, 190.

22. Tocqueville, *Democracy in America*, 314.

23. Bellah, "Religious Evolution," 42.

24. Ibid., 43 and 44.

25. Engels, *Family, Private Property*, 164.

26. Schumpeter, *Capitalism, Socialism*, 12.

27. Fehér, in Fehér, editor, *Birth of Modernity*, 206.

28. Ibid., 216 n. Italics added.

29. Steven B. Smith, in ibid., 223. Italics added in last sentence.

30. Parsons, "Evolutionary Universals," passim.

31. Bellah, "Religious Evolution," 21.

32. Ibid., 44.

33. Thucydides, III, 45. Translated by Crawley.

34. Parsons, *Evolution of Societies*, passim.

35. Piaget, *Child's Conception*, Freud: *The Ego and the Id*. Kohlberg, *"From Is to Ought."*

36. McCarthy, *Jürgen Habermas*, 250–251.

37. Flavell, *Piaget*, 252. Italics in original.

38. Freud, *Ego and Id*, passim. For a full discussion, see Sagan, *Freud, Women*.

39. Bellah, "Religious Evolution," 32.

40. Ibid., 33–34.

41. Piaget, *Child's Conception*, passim.

42. Parsons, "Evolutionary Universals," 496.

43. Sagan, *Dawn of Tyranny*, passim.

44. Dodds, *Greeks and the Irrational*, Chapter II.

45. Piaget in Flavell, *Piaget*, 120.

46. Frazer, *Golden Bough*, passim.

47. Bellah, "Religious Evolution," 44.

48. Sagan, *Dawn of Tyranny*, passim.

49. Personal communication, Eugene Genovese.

50. Tocqueville, *Democracy in America*, 312.

51. Ibid., 315.

52. Joseph Schumpeter, Class lecture, Cambridge, Mass., Spring 1945.

Notes to Chapter 24

1. Marx, *The Eighteenth Brumaire of Louis Napoleon*, as quoted in Furet: *Marx*, 206.

2. Quoted in Palmer, *Democratic Revolution*, Volume II, 130. Italics added. Fragment from an unfinished volume on the Revolution, published by J.P. Meyer, ed., Oeuvres complètes, (Paris, 1951–), II, part 2, 255.

3. Dostoevsky, *Crime and Punishment*, 227–228.

4. François Furet, in HCD, 995.

5. Furet, *La gauche*, 57. Translation by this author.

6. Rousseau, *Social Contract*, 40. Book II, Chapter 8.

7. Tocqueville, *Democracy in America*, 13.

8. Soboul, "Robespierre and the Popular Movement," 67.

9. Quoted by Marcel Gauchet, in HCD, 1005.

10. François Furet, in HCD, 994.

11. Aveneri, *Marx*, 199.

12. Nicolaievsky and Maenchen-Helfen, *Karl Marx*, 336.

13. Furet, *Marx*, 39. Italics in the original.

14. Aveneri, *Marx*, 195. Italics in the original.

15. Ibid., 199.

16. Nicolaievsky and Maenchen-Helfen, *Karl Marx*, 330.

17. Ibid.

18. Mehring, *Marx*, 478.

19. Nicolaievsky and Maenchen-Helfen, *Karl Marx*, 336.

20. Mehring, *Marx*, 478.

21. This history, the details of which most historians agree upon, has been narrated by many people. I have used, in particular, E.H. Carr, *The Bolshevik Revolution*, and Bertram Wolfe, *Three Who Made a Revolution*.

22. Carr, *Bolshevik*, 4.

23. Ibid., 40.

24. Wolfe, *Three*, 289.

25. Ibid., 290.

26. Ibid., 282.

27. Ibid., 282n.

28. Ibid., 290.

29. Ibid., 291.

30. Carr, *Bolshevik*, 54.

31. Wolfe, *Three*, 295. Italics in the original.

32. Ibid., 296.

33. Carr, *Bolshevik*, 79.

34. Ibid., 80. Italics in the original.

35. Ibid., 93.

36. Tocqueville, quoted in Palmer, *Democratic Revolution*, Volume II, 130. Italics added. Fragment from an unfinished volume on the Revolution, published by J.P. Meyer, ed., Oeuvres complètes, (Paris, 1951–   ), II, part 2, 255.

37. Rousseau, *Emile*, 222.

38. Kennedy, *Jacobin Clubs . . . 1793–1795*, 271. Italics added.

39. Hunt, *Family Romance*, 13. Italics in the original.

40. Livy, *Annales*, Book I, Preface, section 9.

41. Quoted in Dodds, *Greeks and the Irrational*, 254.

42. Ibid., 253–254.

43. Thucydides, Book IV, section #108.

44. Personal communication, Professor Edmund Leites.

BIBLIOGRAPHY

Dictionaries of the Revolution

Dictionnaire historique de la révolution française. Albert Soboul. Presses Universitaires de France, Paris, 1989.
Abbreviated in the endnotes as: *Dict. Hist.*
A Critical Dictionary of the French Revolution. Edited by François Furet and Mona Ozouf. Translated by Arthur Goldhammer. Harvard University Press, Cambridge, Mass.: 1989.
Abbreviated in the endnotes as: HCD.

Other Works

Abend, Sander; Porder, Michael; and Willick, Martin. *Borderline Patients.* New York: International Universities Press, 1983.
Dahlburg-Acton, John Emerich [Lord Acton]. *Lectures on the French Revolution.* New York: AMS Press, 1969 [Reprint].
Andrews, Richard. "Social Structures, Political Elites and Ideology in Revolutionary Paris, 1792–1794." *Journal of Social History* 19, no. 1 (Autumn 1985): 71–112.
Arendt, Hannah. *The Origins of Totalitarianism.* New York: Harcourt Brace Jovanovich, 1973.

————. *Eichmann in Jerusalem.* New York: Penguin Books, 1977.

————. *On Revolution.* New York: Penguin Books, 1990 [1963].

Aristotle. *Politics.* Edited and translated by Ernest Barker. Oxford: Oxford University Press, 1958.

Aron, Raymond. *The Opium of the Intellectuals.* Translated by Terence Kilmartin. Lanham, Md.: University Press of America, 1985.

Aulard, A. *Christianity and the French Revolution.* Translated by Lady Frazer. New York: Howard Fertig, 1966.

Avineri, Shlomo. *The Social and Political Thought of Karl Marx.* Cambridge, Mass.: Cambridge University Press, 1971.

————. *Hegel's Theory of the Modern State.* Cambridge, Mass.: Cambridge University Press, 1972.

Baczko, Bronislaw. *Ending the Terror: The French Revolution after Robespierre.* Cambridge, Mass.: Cambridge University Press, 1994.

Baker, Keith Michael. *Condorcet: From Natural Philosophy to Social Mathematics.* Chicago: Chicago University Press, 1975.

————. "French Political Thought at the Accession of Louis XVI." *Journal of Modern History* 50 (June 1978): 279–303.

————, editor. *The French Revolution and the Creation of Modern Political Culture,* Volume I: *The Political Culture of the Old Regime.* New York: Pergamon Press, 1987.

————, editor. *The Old Regime and the French Revolution.* Chicago, University of Chicago Press, 1987.

————. *Inventing the French Revolution.* Cambridge, Mass.: Cambridge University Press, 1990.

————, editor. *The French Revolution and the Creation of Modern Political Culture,* Volume 4: *The Terror.* Tarrytown, N.Y.: Pergamon Press, 1994.

Bauman, Zygmunt. *Modernity and the Holocaust.* Ithaca, N.Y.: Cornell University Press, 1989.

Bell, Daniel. "The Return of the Sacred?" 1977. Reprinted in *The Winding Passage.* New Brunswick, N.J.: Transaction Publishers, 1991.

————. *The Cultural Contradictions of Capitalism.* New York: Basic Books, 1978.

————. *The End of Ideology.* New edition. Cambridge, Mass.: Harvard University Press, 1988.

————. "Resolving the Contradictions of Modernity and Modernism," Part Two. *Society* 27, no. 4 (May/June 1990): 68–75.

Bell, David. *Lawyers and Citizens.* Oxford: Oxford University Press, 1994.

————. "Lingua Populi, Lingua Dei: Language, Religion, and the Origins of French Revolutionary Nationalism." *American Historical Review* (December 1995): 1403–1437.

Bellah, Robert. "Religious Evolution." In *Beyond Belief*. Berkeley: University of California Press, 1991.

Bellah, Robert N., et al. *Habits of the Heart*. Berkeley: University of California Press, 1985.

Berlin, Isaiah. *The Cracked Timber of Humanity*. New York: Alfred A. Knopf, 1991.

Berman, Marshall. *All That Is Solid Melts into Air*. New York: Penguin Books, 1988.

Bienvenu, Richard, ed. *The Ninth of Thermidor: The Fall of Robespierre*. New York: Oxford University Press, 1968.

Blanning, T.C.W. *The Origins of French Revolutionary Wars*. New York: Longman, 1986.

Blum, Carol. *Rousseau and the Republic of Virtue*. Ithaca, N.Y.: Cornell University Press, 1986.

Brace, Paul, and Barbara Hinckley. *Follow the Leader*. New York: Basic Books, 1992.

Brinton, Crane. *A Decade of Revolution, 1789–1799*. New York: Harper and Brothers, 1934.

Brinton, Clarence Crane. *The Jacobins: An Essay in the New History*. New York: Russell and Russell, 1961 [1930, 1958].

Brunn, Geoffrey. *Europe and the French Imperium, 1799–1814*. New York: Harper and Brothers, 1938.

Burke, Edmond. *Reflections on the Revolution in France*, edited by J.G.A. Pocock. Indianapolis, Ind.: Hackett, 1987.

Carr, Edward Hallett. *The Bolshevik Revolution, 1917–1923*. New York: MacMillan, 1951.

Carter, Michael Phillip. "Prolegomena to a Study of Revolutionary Discourse: The Jacobins Club of Paris in the Year II." Ph.D. thesis. Stanford, Calif.: Stanford University, 1974.

Censer, Jack Richard. *Prelude to Power: The Parisian Radical Press 1789–1791*. Baltimore, Md.: Johns Hopkins Press, 1976.

Chartier, Roger. *The Cultural Origins of the French Revolution*. Durham, N.C.: Duke University Press, 1991.

Chaumié, Jacqueline. "Les Girondins." In *Girondins et Montagnards*, ed. Albert Soboul. Paris, 1980.

Chaussinand-Nogaret: *The French Nobility in the Eighteenth Century*. Cambridge, Mass.: Cambridge University Press, 1985.

Cheyney, Edward. *The Dawn of a New Era, 1250–1453*. New York: Harper and Brothers, 1936.

Chill, Emanuel. *Power, Property, and History: Barnave's Introduction to the French Revolution*. New York: Harper and Row, 1971.

Cobb, R.C. *The Police and the People: French Popular Protest, 1789–1820*. Oxford: Oxford University Press, 1970.

Cobban, Alfred. "The Political Ideas of Maximilien Robespierre during the Period of the Convention." *English Historical Review* (January, 1946): 45–80.

————. *The Social Interpretation of the French Revolution.* Cambridge, Mass.: Cambridge University Press, 1964.

————. *Aspects of the French Revolution.* New York: George Brazilier, 1968.

————. *A History of Modern France,* Volume I: 1715–1799. New York: Viking Penguin, 1990.

Condorcet, Antoine-Nicolas de. *Sketch for a Historical Picture of the Progress of the Human Mind.* Translated by June Barraclough. London: Weidenfeld and Nicolson, 1955.

Constant, Benjamin. *Écrits et discours politiques.* Ed. O. Pozzo di Borgo. Tome I. Paris: Chez Jean-Jaques Pauvert, 1964.

Daumard, Adeline. *Les bourgeois et la bourgeoisie: en France depuis 1815.* Paris: Flammarion, 1991.

Desan, Suzanne. *Reclaiming the Sacred.* Ithaca, N.Y.: Cornell University Press, 1990.

Dodds, E.R. *The Greeks and the Irrational.* Berkeley: University of California Press, 1951.

Dostoevsky, Fyodor. *Crime and Punishment.* Constance Garnet, translator. New York: The MacMillan Company, 1954.

Doyle, William. *Origins of the French Revolution.* Second Edition. Oxford: Oxford University Press, 1988.

————. *The Oxford History of the French Revolution.* Oxford: Oxford University Press, 1989.

————. *The Old European Order, 1660–1800.* Second Edition. Oxford: Oxford University Press, 1992.

Drescher, Seymour. *Dilemmas of Democracy: Tocqueville and Modernization.* Pittsburgh, Pa.: University of Pittsburgh Press, 1968.

Durkheim, Emile. *Moral Education.* Translated by Wilson and Schnurer. New York: The Free Press, 1978.

————. *The Evolution of Educational Thought.* Trans. Peter Cullins. Boston, Mass.: Routledge and Kegan Paul, 1977.

————. *The Elementary Forms of Religious Life.* Translated by Karen E. Fields. New York: The Free Press, 1995.

Eliot, T.S. *Collected Poems, 1909–1935.* New York: Harcourt, Brace and Company, 1936.

Elkins, Stanley, and McKitrick, Eric. *The Age of Federalism.* New York: Oxford University Press, 1993.

Engels, Frederick. *The Origins of the Family, Private Property, and the State.* Introduction by Evelyn Reed. New York: Pathfinder Press, 1972.

The Federalist. Jacob E. Cooke, ed. Middletown, Conn.: Wesleyan University Press, 1961.

Fehér, Ferenc. *The Frozen Revolution: An Essay on Jacobinism.* Cambridge, Mass.: Cambridge University Press, 1987.

————, Editor. *The French Revolution and the Birth of Modernity.* Berkeley: University of California Press, 1990.

Flavell, J.H. *The Developmental Psychology of Jean Piaget.* New York: D. Van Nostrand, 1963.

Forster, E.M. *Two Cheers for Democracy*. New York: Harcourt, Brace and Co., 1951.

Frazer, J.G. *The Golden Bough*. One volume abridged edition. New York: MacMillan, 1955.

Freud, Sigmund. *The Ego and the Id*. 1923. Volume 19 of *The Standard Edition of the Complete Psychological Writings of Sigmund Freud*. London: Hogarth Press, 1953–74.

————. *Civilization and Its Discontents*. Translated by James Strachey. New York: W.W. Norton, 1962.

Fromm, Erich. *Escape from Freedom*. New York: Avon Books, 1965.

Furet, François, and Richet, Denis. *The French Revolution*. New York: MacMillan, 1970.

Furet, François. *Interpreting the French Revolution*. Cambridge, Mass.: Cambridge University Press, 1981.

————. *La gauche et la révolution au milieu du XIXe siècle. Edgar Quinet et la question du Jacobinism 1865–1870* Paris: Hachett, 1986.

————. *Marx and the French Revolution*. Chicago: University of Chicago Press, 1988.

————. *Revolutionary France 1770–1880*. Cambridge, Mass.: Basil Blackwell, 1992.

Gallo, Max. *Robespierre the Incorruptible*. New York: Herder and Herder, 1971.

Garrett, Mitchell B. *The Estates General of 1789*. New York: D. Appleton-Century Company, 1935.

Geertz, Clifford. *The Interpretation of Cultures*. New York: Basic Books, 1973.

Gennep, Arnold Van. *The Rites of Passage*. Translated by Monika Vizedom and Gabrielle Caffee. Chicago: University of Chicago Press, 1960.

Gershoy, Leo. *From Despotism to Revolution, 1763–1789*. New York: Harper and Brothers, 1944.

————. *Bertrand Barère, A Reluctant Terroist*. Princeton, N.J.: Princeton University Press, 1962.

Greenfeld, Leah. *Nationalism: Five Roads to Modernity*. Cambridge, Mass.: Harvard University Press, 1992.

Groethuysen, Bernard. *The Bourgeois: Catholicism vs. Capitalism in Eighteenth-Century France*. New York: Holt, Rinehart and Winston, 1968.

Habermas, Jürgen. *The Structural Transformation of the Public Sphere: An Inquiry into a Category of Bourgeois Society*. Cambridge, Mass.: MIT Press, 1989.

Hackstaff, Karla. *Marriage in a Culture of Divorce*. Philadelphia, Pa.: Temple University Press, 1999.

Hale, J.R. *Renaissance Europe, 1480–1520*. London: Fontanal Collins, 1971.

Hampson, Norman. *The Life and Opinions of Maximilien Robespierre*. London: Duckworth, 1974.

————. *A Social History of the French Revolution*. Toronto: University of Toronto Press, 1966.

————. *Danton*. London: Duckworth, 1978.

————. *Prelude to Terror.* Oxford: Basil Blackwell, 1988.

————. *Saint-Just.* Oxford: Basil Blackwell, 1991.

Herf, Jeffrey. *Reactionary Modernism.* Cambridge, Mass.: Cambridge University Press, 1984.

Higonnet, Patrice. *Class, Ideology, and the Rights of Nobles during the French Revolution.* Oxford: Oxford University Press, 1981.

Hobsbawn, E.J. *Primitive Rebels.* New York: W.W. Norton, 1959.

————. *The Age of Revolution, 1789–1848.* New York: New American Library, 1962.

Hofstadter, Richard. "The Paranoid Style in American Politics." In *The Paranoid Style in American Politics and Other Essays.* New York: Alfred A. Knopf, 1966.

Homer. *The Iliad.* Translated by Richmond Lattimore. Chicago: Chicago University Press, various editions.

Hughes, H. Stuart. *Consciousness and Society.* New York: Vintage Books, 1977.

Hunt Lynn. *Revolution and Urban Politics in Provincial France: Troyes and Reims, 1786–1790.* Stanford, Calif.: Stanford University Press, 1978.

————. *Politics, Culture, and Class in the French Revolution.* Berkeley: University of California Press, 1984.

————. *The Family Romance of the French Revolution.* Berkeley: University of California Press, 1992.

Hunt, Lynn; Lansky, David; and Hanson, Paul. "The Failure of the Liberal Republic in France, 1795–1799: The Road to Brumaire." *Journal of Modern History* 51 (1979): 734–759.

Huppert, George. *Les bourgeois gentilhommes: An Essay on the Definition of Elites in Renaissance France.* Chicago: University of Chicago Press, 1977.

Jordan, David P. *The Revolutionary Career of Maximilien Robespierre.* Chicago: University of Chicago Press, 1985.

Kates, Gary. *The Cercle Social, the Girondins, and the French Revolution.* Princeton. N.J.: Princeton University Press, 1985.

Kennedy, Michael L. *The Jacobin Clubs in the French Revolution: The First Years.* Princeton, N.J.: Princeton University Press, 1982.

————. *The Jacobin Clubs in the French Revolution: The Middle Years.* Princeton, N.J.: Princeton University Press, 1988.

————. *The Jacobin Clubs in the French Revolution, 1793–1795.* New York: Berghahn Books, 1999.

Kernberg, Otto. "Structural Derivatives of Object Relation." *International Journal of Psycho-Analysis* 47 (1966): 226–253.

————. "Borderline Personality Organization." *Journal of the American Psychoanalytic Association* XV, no. 3 (July 1967): 641–685.

————. *Borderline Conditions and Pathological Narcissism.* Northvale, N.J.: Jason Aronson, 1985.

Van Kley, Dale. *The Damiens Affair: And the Unraveling of the* Ancien Régime *1750–1770*. Princeton, N.J.: Princeton University Press, 1984.

———, editor. *The French Idea of Freedom*. Stanford, Calif.: Stanford University Press, 1994.

Knecht, R.J. *The Rise and Fall of Renaissance France, 1483–1610*. London: Fontana Press, 1996.

Kholberg, Lawrence. "From Is to Ought," in T. Mishel, ed., *Cognitive Development and Epistemology*. New York: Basic Books, 1971.

Kolchin, Peter. *American Slavery, 1619–1877*. New York: Hill and Wang, 1993.

Lasch, Christopher. *The True and Only Heaven*. New York: W.W. Norton, 1991.

Lefebvre, Georges. *The French Revolution*, Volume I. Translated by Elizabeth Moss Evanson. New York: Columbia University Press, 1962.

———. *The Directory*. Translated by Robert Baldick, New York: Random House, 1964.

———. *The Thermidorians*. New York: Random House, 1964.

———. *The Great Fear of 1789*. New York: Schocken Books, 1973.

Livy. *Annales*, translated by B.O. Foster. Cambridge, Mass.: Harvard University Press, 1976.

Lucas, Colin, *The Structure of Terror*. Oxford: Oxford University Press, 1973.

———, editor. *The French Revolution and the Creation of Modern Political Culture*. Volume 2. *The Political Culture of the French Revolution*. New York: Pergamon Press, 1988.

———, editor. *Rewriting the French Revolution*. Oxford: Oxford University Press, 1991.

Lyons, Martyn. *France under the Directory*. Cambridge, Mass.: Cambridge University Press, 1975.

———. "Politics and Patois: The Linguistic Policy of the French Revolution." *Australian Journal of French Studies* XVIII, no. 3 (1981): 264–281.

Mathiez, Albert. *After Robespierre: The Thermidorian Reaction*. New York: Alfred A. Knopf, 1931.

———. *The French Revolution*. New York: Grosset and Dunlap, 1964.

Maza, Sarah. *Private Lives and Public Affairs: The Causes Célébres of Prerevolutionary France*. Berkeley: University of California Press, 1993.

Mazlisch, Bruce. *The Revolutionary Ascetic*. New York: Basic Books, 1976.

McCarthy, Thomas. *The Critical Theory of Jürgen Habermas*. Cambridge, Mass.: MIT Press, 1981.

McManners, John. "The Historiography of the French Revolution." In *New Cambridge Modern History*, Volume 8, Chapter XXII. Cambridge, Mass.: Cambridge University Press, 1965.

———. *The French Revolution and the Church*. London: S.P.C.K., 1969.

Mehring, Franz. *Karl Marx: The Story of His Life*. Translated by Edward Fitzgerald. New York: Covici, Friede Publishers, 1935.

Meissner, W.W. *The Paranoid Process.* New York: Jason Aronson, 1978.

Melzer, Sara E., and Rabine, Leslie W., editors. *Rebel Daughters: Women and the French Revolution.* Oxford: Oxford University Press, 1992.

Michelet, Jules. *History of the French Revolution,* Volume VII. Translated by Keith Botsford. Wynnewood, Pa.: Kolokol Press, 1973.

Mitzman, Arthur. *The Iron Cage: An Historical Interpretation of Max Weber.* New Brunswick, N.J.: Transaction Books, 1985.

Mornet, Daniel. *Les origines intellectuelles de la Revolution Français (1715–1787).* Paris, Librairie Armand Colin, 1947.

Musil, Robert. *The Man Without Qualities.* Translated by Eithne Wilkins and Ernst Kaiser. New York: G.P. Putnam's Sons, 1980.

Nicolaievsky, Boris and Maenchen-Helfen, Otto. *Karl Marx: Man and Fighter.* Translated by Gwenda David and Eric Mosbacher. Philadelphia, Pa.: J.B. Lippicott Company, 1936.

Ozouf, Mona. *L'École de la France.* Paris: Gallimard, 1984.

———. *Festivals and the French Revolution.* Translated by Alan Sheridan. Cambridge, Mass.: Harvard University Press, 1988.

Paine, Thomas. *Rights of Man.* New York: Willey Book Co., 1942.

Palmer, R.R. *The Age of Democratic Revolution.* Two Volumes. Princeton, N.J.: Princeton University Press, 1959.

———. *Twelve Who Ruled.* Princeton, N.J.: Princeton University Press, 1989 [1941].

Parsons, Talcott. "Evolutionary Universals in Society." In *Sociological Theory And Modern Society.* New York: Free Press, 1967.

———. *The Evolution of Societies.* Englewood Cliffs, N.J.: Prentice-Hall, 1977.

Patrick, Alison. *The Men of the First French Republic.* Baltimore, Md.: Johns Hopkins University Press, 1972.

Piaget, J. *The Child's Conception of the World.* London: Routledge and Kegan Paul, 1929.

Pirenne, Henri. "The Stages in the Social History of Capitalism." *American Historical Review* (April 1914): 494–515.

Pitkin, Hannah Fenichel. *Fortune Is a Woman.* Berkeley: University of California Press, 1984.

Plato: *The Republic.* Translated by Alan Bloom. New York: Basic Books, 1968.

Ritter, Joachim. *Hegel and the French Revolution.* Cambridge, Mass.: MIT Press, 1982.

Robespierre, M. *Textes Choisis.* Préface, Commentaires et Notes Explicatives par Jean Poperen. Three volumes. Paris: Éditions Sociales, 1956, 1957, 1958.

Rousseau, J.J. *The Social Contract.* Translated by Lowell Bair. New York: New American Library, 1974.

———. *Emile,* translated by Alan Bloom. New York: Basic Books, 1979.

Rudé, George. *The Crowd in the French Revolution.* Oxford: Oxford University Press, 1967.

Rudé, George. *Europe in the Eighteenth Century.* Cambridge, Mass.: Harvard University Press, 1972.

————. *Robespierre: Portrait of a Revolutionary Democrat.* London: Collins, 1975.

Sa'adah, Anne. *The Shaping of Liberal Politics in Revolutionary France.* Princeton, N.J.: Princeton University Press, 1990.

Sagan, Eli. "The Politics of the Impossible: Or, Whatever Happened to Evolutionary Theory?" *Social Research* 59, no. 4 (Winter 1992): 739–758.

————. *Cannibalism: Human Aggression and Cultural Form.* Englewood, N.J.: Fish Drum Press, 1993.

————. *Cultural Diversity and Moral Relativism.* Waltham, Mass.: *Brandeis University Women's Studies Program, 1993.*

————. *At the Dawn of Tyranny: The Origins of Individualism, Political Oppression and the State.* Englewood, N.J.: Fish Drum Press, 1993.

————. *The Honey and the Hemlock: Democracy and Paranoia in Ancient Athens and Modern America.* Princeton, N.J.: Princeton University Press, 1994.

————. *Freud, Women, and Morality: The Psychology of Good and Evil.* Englewood Cliffs, N.J.: Fish Drum Press, 1996.

Schama, Simon. *Citizens.* New York: Alfred A. Knopf, 1989.

Schumpeter, Joseph A. *Capitalism, Socialism, and Democracy.* New York: Harper and Brothers, 1947.

Sewell, William H. Jr. *Work and Revolution in France.* Cambridge, Mass.: Cambridge University Press, 1980.

————. "Collective Violence and Collective Loyalties in France: Why the French Revolution Made a Difference." *Politics and Society* 18, no. 4 (1990): 527–552.

————. *A Rhetoric of Bourgeois Revolution.* Durham, N.C.: Duke University Press, 1994.

Sieyès, Emmanuel Joseph. *What Is the Third Estate?,* edited by S.E. Finer. New York: Frederick A. Praeger, 1964.

Slavin, Morris. *The Making of an Insurrection: Parisian Sections and the Gironde.* Cambridge, Mass.: Harvard University Press, 1986.

Smith, Anthony D. *National Identity.* Reno: University of Nevada Press, 1991.

Soboul, Albert. "Robespierre and the Popular Movement of 1793–4." *Past and Present* (May 1954): 54–70.

————. *The Parisian Sans-Culottes and the French Revolution, 1793–4.* Translated by Gwynne Lewis. Oxford: Oxford University Press, 1964.

————. *The San-Culottes.* Translated by Rémy Inglis Hall, Princeton, N.J.: Princeton University Press, 1980.

————, editor. *Girondins et Montagnards.* Paris: NP, 1980.

Starobinski, Jean. *Jean-Jacques Rousseau.* Neuchâtel: Baconnière, 1978.

————. *Jean-Jacques Rousseau: Transparency and Obstruction.* Chicago: University of Chicago Press, 1988.

Stephens, H. Mores. *The Principle Speaks of the Statesmen and Orators of the French Revolution, 1789–1795.* Two volumes. Oxford: Oxford University Press, 1982.

Stern, Fritz. *The Politics of Cultural Despair.* Berkeley: University of California Press, 1961.

Stone, Lawrence. *The Family, Sex and Marriage, in England 1500–1800.* Abridged edition. New York: Harper and Row, 1979.

———. *The Causes of the English Revolution, 1529–1642.* New York: Harper and Row, 1993.

Sutherland, D.M.G. *France 1789–1815: Revolution and Counterrevolution.* New York: Oxford University Press, 1986.

Sydenham, M.J. *The Girondins.* London: University of London Press, 1961.

———. *The First French Republic, 1792–1804.* London: B.T. Batsford, 1974.

Tackett, Timothy. *Becoming a Revolutionary.* Princeton, N.J.: Princeton University Press, 1966.

———. *Priest and Parish in Eighteenth-Century France.* Princeton, N.J.: Princeton University Press, 1977.

———. *Religion, Revolution, and Regional Culture in Eighteenth-Century France.* Princeton, N.J.: Princeton University Press, 1986.

Talmon, J.L. *The Origins of Totalitarian Democracy.* Boulder, Colo.: Westview Encore Edition, 1985 [1952].

Taylor, Charles. *The Sources of the Self.* Cambridge, Mass.: Harvard University Press, 1989.

Taylor, G.V. "Types of Capitalism in Eighteenth-Century France." *English Historical Review* 79 (1964): 478–497.

———. "Non-Capitalist Wealth and the Origins of the French Revolution." *American Historical Review* 72 (1967): 469–496.

Thompson, J.M. *Robespierre.* Oxford: Oxford University Press, 1939, One volume edition.

———. *The French Revolution.* Oxford: Basil Blackwell, 1985.

Thucydides. *The Peloponnesian War.* Translated by R. Crawley. Various editions.

Tilly, Charles. *The Vendée.* Cambridge, Mass.: Harvard University Press, 1976.

Tocqueville, Alexis de. *Democracy in America.* Edited by J.P. Mayer. Garden City, N.J.: Anchor Books, 1969.

———. *"The European Revolution" and Correspondence with Gobineau.* Edited and translated by John Lukacs. Gloucester: Peter Smith, 1968.

———. *The Old Régime and the French Revolution.* New York: Anchor Books, 1955.

———. *Selected Letters on Politics and Society.* Edited by Roger Boesche. Berkeley: University of California Press, 1985.

———. *Recollections: The French Revolution of 1848.* Translated by George Laurence. New Brunswick, N.J.: Transaction Books, 1990.

Toulmin, Stephen, *Cosmopolis.* Chicago: University of Chicago Press, 1990.

Tucker, Robert C., editor. *The Marx-Engels Reader,* second edition. New York: W.W. Norton, 1972.

Waal, Frans de. *Good Natured: The Origins of Right and Wrong in Humans and Other Animals.* Cambridge, Mass.: Harvard University Press, 1996.

———. *The Protestant Ethic and the Spirit of Capitalism.* Translated by Talcott Parsons. New York: Charles Scribner's Sons, 1958.

Walter, Gérard. *Histoire des Jacobin.* Paris: Librarie Sumogy, 1946.

Walzer, Michael. *The Revolution of the Saints.* New York: Atheneum, 1969.

———, ed. and intro. *Regicide and Revolution.* London: Cambridge University Press, 1974.

Weber, Eugen. *Peasants into Frenchmen.* Stanford, Calif.: Stanford University Press, 1976.

Weber, Max. *The Theory of Social and Economic Organization.* Translated by A.M. Henderson and Talcott Parsons. New York: Oxford University Press, 1947.

Wolfe, Bertram D. *Three Who Made a Revolution.* New York: Dial Press, 1948.

Woolf, Virginia. "Mr. Bennet and Mrs. Brown." (1924) In *The Captain's Death Bed and Other Essays.* London, 1950.

Woloch, Isser. *Jacobin Legacy: The Democratic Movement under the Directory.* Princeton, N.J.: Princeton University Press, 1970.

———. *The New Regime.* New York: Norton, 1994.

Wood, Gordon S. *The Radicalism of the American Revolution.* New York: Alfred A. Knopf, 1992.

Wright, Gordon. *France in Modern Times.* New York: W.W. Norton, 1981.

INDEX

thoritarianism, 209; secular sacred, 9,
230–35; sovereignty of people, 237
*Nature, Folly, Sin, and Danger of being Righteous Over-
much, The* (Trapp), 485–86
Nazi Germany, 15–16, 299, 300, 352; cleansing,
475–76; democracy following, 304–5; Hitler's rise to power, 458; human sacrifice, 342,
343; ideological terror, 304; invasion of Russia, 335; paranoia and Jews, 330–31; power
and self-destruction, 525
Necker, Jacques, 59–60, 97, 102, 217, 312; desire for English-style government, 78; dismissal of, 312, 313; property and equality,
181; regeneration of kingdom, 425
Neufchateau, François de, 247–48
neutrality as a sin, 432–33
New Deal, 115
new man, 472; creation of, 423–29; education,
429–30; failure of idea of, 431
New Regime, The (Woloch), 53
Nietzsche, Friedrich, 1–2
Nixon, Richard, 328, 413, 456
nobility. *See* aristocracy

Oath to the Civil Constitution. *See* Civil Oath of
the Clergy
"Ode to Napoleon" (Byron), 455
"Ode to Virtue" (Robespierre), 427–29
Old Régime, The (Tocqueville), 248–49
oligarchy, 15
omnipotence, 238–39, 554; regression, 453–55;
underlying, 444
On the Tasks of the Proletariat in the Present Revolution
(Lenin), 548
opinion, freedom of, 59–62
opposition, conception of loyal democratic, 91–
94, 115, 128, 133, 149, 482
optimism and Protestantism, 196–99
ordering of the world, 10
Origins of the Cultural Revolution, The (MacFarquhar),
412
Orleans, Duke of, 74
Orwell, George, 473

"Qu'est–ce que le Tiers État" (Sieyès), 225–26
outcomes, six possible of attempt toward modernism, 13–16
Ozouf, Mona, 27, 425, 434; differences between
Jacobins and Girondins, 116; explanation of
fratricidal struggle, 114; Festival of Supreme
Being, 366; Marat, 125; myth of sovereignty
of people, 481–82; myth of united people,
141; stages in advance toward equality, 39

pacte de famine, 334–35
paganism, 26
Paine, Tom, 119, 203, 367, 370–71
Palmer, R.R., 32, 79, 248, 268, 288; appointment of generals, 370; beginning of Reign of
Terror, 459; bourgeoisie, 155, 160; Committee of Public Safety, 296; glee from executioners at Lyons, 378–79; possibilities for
democracy after 1795, 299; puritan bourgeois
virtues, 170; Robespierre and psychopathic
delusion, 489; Robespierre and Saint-Just and
Hérault-Séchelles, 487; Terror as a disease,
474; unitary public, 480
panic, 370, 405–6, 474–75
paranoia and being paranoid, 327–28
paranoid panic, 331–40; aggressive behavior,
333; blood, 346–47; cannibalism, 349–50;
culture of anxiety, 338–40; declaration of
war, 335–37; denunciation of traitors,
337–38; the Great Fear of 1789, 331–33;
headhunting, 347–49; human sacrifice as revenge, 340–45; ideological terrorism, 352;
pacte de famine, 334–35; "primitive" acting out,
345–46; scapegoat, 350–54; in September
1792, 333–34; sources of, 330
paranoid position, 327–54, 355–83; acceptance
of loyal opposition, 149; as all-or-nothing,
126–27, 386; blame of others, 361–62; borderline condition, 443–44, 452; clichés of,
360–63; "cutting of throats of women and
children," 360; those who disagree as traitors,
128; as enemy of freedom, 554; establishment
of stable democratic society, 77; failure of as-

ABOUT THE AUTHOR

Eli Sagan is the author of several books, most recently *The Honey and the Hemlock: Democracy and Paranoia in Ancient Athens and Modern America*; *Freud, Women, and Morality: The Psychology of Good and Evil*; and *At the Dawn of Tyranny: The Origins of Individualism, Political Oppression, and the State*. He lives in Englewood, New Jersey, with his wife, Frimi.